THE GREAT ART OF LIGHT AND SHADOW
Archaeology of the Cinema

'The dream of being able to project moving illuminated images on a wall or screen is almost as old, in the history of humanity, as the dream of flight.'

Laurent Mannoni

First published in French in 1995 and now translated into English, Laurent Mannoni's account is widely regarded by historians of the early moving picture as the best work yet published on the pre-cinema world, throwing light on a fascinating range of optical media from the twelfth century to the turn of the twentieth: a strange mixture of science, magic, art and deception.

Starting from the earliest uses of the camera obscura in astronomy and entertainment, *The Great Art of Light and Shadow* encompasses, among other devices, the 'invention' and early years of the magic lantern in the seventeenth century, the peepshows and perspective views of the eighteenth century, and the many weird and wonderful ninteenth-century attempts to recreate visions of real life in different ways and forms. Along the way these include the panorama and diorama, early photography, stereography and numerous optical toys and devices of varying shape and size. Finally there is an account of the attempts to fuse these effects together into a medium which would combine the realism of photography with the movement of the phenakistiscope and zoetrope.

Laurent Mannoni is former Curator of the equipment collections of the Cinémathèque Française and the Centre National de la Cinématographie.

Richard Crangle is a freelance researcher and writer, formerly Assistant Director of the Bill Douglas Centre for the History of Cinema and Popular Culture.

Exeter Studies in Film History
General Editors: Richard Maltby and Duncan Petrie

Exeter Studies in Film History is devoted to publishing the best new scholarship on the cultural, technical and aesthetic history of cinema. The aims of the series are to reconsider established orthodoxies and to revise our understanding of cinema's past by shedding light on neglected areas in film history.

Published by University of Exeter Press in association with the Bill Douglas Centre for the History of Cinema and Popular Culture, the series includes monographs and essay collections, translations of major works written in other languages, and reprinted editions of important texts in cinema history. The series editors are Richard Maltby, Associate Professor of Screen Studies, Flinders University, Australia, and Duncan Petrie, Director of the Bill Douglas Centre for the History of Cinema and Popular Culture, University of Exeter.

University of Exeter Press also publishes the celebrated five-volume series looking at the early years of English cinema, *The Beginning of the Cinema in England*, by John Barnes.

THE GREAT ART OF LIGHT AND SHADOW
Archaeology of the Cinema

Laurent Mannoni

Translated and edited by Richard Crangle

UNIVERSITY
of
EXETER
PRESS

First published in 2000 by
University of Exeter Press
Reed Hall, Streatham Drive
Exeter, Devon EX4 4QR
UK
www.ex.ac.uk/uep/

This book is supported by the French Ministry of Foreign Affairs,
as part of the Burgess Programme headed for the French Embassy
in London by the Institut Français du Royaume-Uni.

Ouvrage publié avec l'aide du Ministère Français de la Culture

British Library Cataloguing in Publication Data
A catalogue record for this book is available from the British Library

Paperback ISBN 0 85989 665 X
Hardback ISBN 0 85989 567 X

Typeset in 11/13pt Adobe Caslon by Kestrel Data, Exeter

Printed and bound in Great Britain by
Short Run Press Ltd, Exeter

Contents

Illustrations

TRANSLATOR'S NOTE

When, in 1995, I was shown Laurent Mannoni's new book *Le Grand Art de la Lumière et de l'Ombre*—seemingly one of the few copies of the book to have crept across the English Channel—I immediately recognized an essential text. Not only did it take a bold and encyclopaedic sweep through the history of the media which preceded the cinema (an area, as Mannoni himself notes, sadly lacking in reliable historical coverage), it did so with an engaging and lively tone and a storyteller's turn of phrase. Compared to the dry and theoretical works of film studies with which I was used to wrestling, *Le Grand Art* came as a refreshing change.

Later that year, appropriately in a bookshop in Lyon, I succeeded in tracking down my own copy of the French edition, and began to agree with others who had seen it that it would be a good idea if somebody were to translate it into English. It came as something of an extended surprise to find that person to be myself, and also to find an interested publisher in the University of Exeter Press. Some years later, the present volume is the result.

After such an extended process of translation, my first acknowledgement has to be to Simon Baker, Genevieve Davey, Anna Henderson, Rosemary Rooke, and others at University of Exeter Press for their patience, understanding, and continued support for the project. Richard Maltby was also, as ever, a continuing source of support and encouragement. Laurent Mannoni was kind enough to read the draft and help with many of the last-minute questions and Jane Olorenshaw copy-edited the book with a light but assured touch; any errors or misunderstandings remain, of course, my own.

John and Bill Barnes, Michael Bartley, Stephen Bottomore, Tom Gunning, Susan Hayward, Stephen Herbert, Peter Jewell, David Robinson, and Deac Rossell, along with numerous other members of the Magic Lantern Society, have provided invaluable encouragement and great or small acts of assistance along the way. On a more personal level, the way of the translation was smoothed greatly by the good company of good colleagues, among whom were Giacomo Barisone, Kate Bowles, Leo Enticknap, Mark Gant, David Kennedy, Christopher McCullough, Katharine Murphy, Kate Offord, Amy Sargeant, Rebecca Selman, Kate Tyler, and the students of the Exeter MA in the History of Cinema and Popular Culture in 1997–8.

And as in all things, my greatest source of support and sustenance has been Ester Roosmaa; this piece of work is for her.

R.C., Exeter, Spring 2000

Foreword

by David Robinson

The first French edition of *Le Grand Art de la Lumière et de l'Ombre* appeared in 1995. Five years on, it is necessary to revise the original foreword, in order to place this book in the context of the extraordinary and continuing corpus of work that Laurent Mannoni has accomplished in the interim.

It was already clear, at its first appearance, that *Le Grand Art* represented a revolution in the study of the origins and prehistory of moving pictures. There had been a few attempts before at a comprehensive history embracing the whole panorama from camera obscura and peepshow to the arrival of cinema in 1896. None however had come near the regour of Mannoni's insistence on primary sources for his history—texts, documents and above all the two hundred years of patent specifications which, in the field of pre-cinema, he is the first to have extensively and critically explored. The book set challenging new standards for every future scholar.

By chance *Le Grand Art* appeared within a few months of that other fundamental and very different resource, Hermann Hecht's *Pre-Cinema History*, a vast annotated bibliography that encapsulates Hecht's own life-time of reading and research. It seemed fortuitous that in some respects the books were complementary: while both attempt a global survey, Mannoni provides the French perspective on which Hecht, exemplary on his English and German sources, is weakest. Hecht is a reference tool; Mannoni a running narrative. It is the mark of the exceptional scholar that the text, for all its fine detail and digressions, is lucid, unpretentious, personal, witty, a pleasurable read.

The book now appears, in retrospect, as the nucleus of Laurent

Mannoni's overall later activity. His subsequent voluminous writings have extended individual aspects of the history. In particular his definitive studies of Demenÿ and Marey* have altered perceptions of those friends who in the end turned into sorry foes. In the case of the latter, his research and documentation has fundamentally altered even his own view of film history, by establishing definitively that Marey had made chronophotographic images on celluloid film as early as the summer of 1889.

Perhaps Mannoni's most remarkable achievement to date has been as the curator of the collections of apparatus of the Cinémathèque Française—a post which he undertook almost at the very moment when *Le Grand Art* came out. The collections were begun in the 1930s by the omnivorous gatherer Henri Langlois, founder of the Cinémathèque, and were notably augmented around 1960 by the acquisition of the Will Day collection. Begun in the first years of the 20th century by the English film pioneer Will Day, this incomparable hoard of documents and artefacts had previously been on loan for forty years to the Science Museum, South Kensington, but the British had never found the incentive or means to purchase what should have been a national treasure.

Mannoni found the collections in a deplorable state, partly in dusty disorder in the cellars of the Palais Chaillot, partly scattered in inadequate warehouses across Paris. Much of the Day collection was still in the boxes in which it arrived at the Cinémathèque in 1960; some boxes even appeared to have remained untouched since Day put his collection in store during the First World War. Unbelievable though it may now seem, single-handed Mannoni sorted, cleaned and arranged the restoration of the thousands of objects, and, no less single-handed, personally repainted the Musée Henri Langlois where the iceberg tip of the collection was displayed.

His efforts were rewarded with thrilling discoveries. For the first time the monumental importance of the Day collection could be assessed. Mannoni found, entirely forgotten among the dirt, the legendary first films of William Friese-Greene and a stack of over one hundred large original drawings by Marey. Day turned out to have acquired many of the most celebrated lantern slides from the Royal Polytechnic. Even Skladanowsky's 1895 camera, mislaid for 40 years in the Cinémathèque,

---

*Laurent Mannoni, with Marc de Ferrière and Paul Demenÿ, *Georges Demenÿ: Pionnier du Cinéma*. Douai: Editions Pagine, 1997.
Laurent Mannoni, *Étienne-Jules Marey: La Mémoire de L'Oeil*. Paris/Milan Cinémathèque Française/Mazotta, 1999.

came to light and could finally be restored to its rightful owners, the Berlin film museum. Not content with these stirring resurrections, Mannoni has gone on to double the already vast holdings of the Cinémathèque through purchase, gifts and the annexation of other public and private collections.

All this was dramatically threatened on the night of 23 July 1997 when fire swept the upper part of the Palais Chaillot. For 20 hours, an ever more dishevelled Mannoni toiled alongside the firefighters to save his precious charges—a scene, in itself historic, that was fortunately caught by the television news cameras. Since then the collections have been kept under ideal conditions in one of the towers of the new Bibliothèque Nationale.

Work with the collections has developed Mannoni's experiments in museology. His exhibitions 'L'Art Trompeur' (on pre-cinematic shows), and 'Jules-Etienne Marey, La Mémoire de l'Oeil' have been as innovative as his books. Rigorously scientific, lucid in exposition, refusing to patronize the public with facile 'interactive' seductions, but created out of knowledge and passion, they have been visibly more thrilling and attractive to large audiences than modish theme-park methods.

Few would dispute that Laurent Mannoni is the most important single creative personality in the history of the Cinémathèque Française since its formidable founder, Henri Langlois. The fascination is always to know what he will do next, what new vista of the still mysterious lanscape of pre-cinema he will illuminate for us. The passion, knowledge and humanity and the vision of cinema history that have impelled this astonishing achievement are already apparent in *Le Grand Art*, completed when its author was 27, but with a genesis that went back to his teenage years. It is no cold, dry, academic study, but a pulsing, vital chronicle. Mannoni's history has been made by living people, whom he variously admires, loves, pities and sometimes despises, according to their deserts. 'The cinematographic industry, as Demenÿ, the Lathams, and Armat and Jenkins were already aware, did not come into being without a number of acts of betrayal, dubious compromises, and knives in the back'. His uncompromising scholarship in no way excludes a communicated fascination with these human dramas. That larger cultural drama which is the central subject of this book could not be better summarized than in the author's own thrilling evocative image: 'It was as though an eye, whose lids had been lifting, slowly, across the centuries, now opened completely on the world.'

David Robinson

Author's Preface to the 1995 Edition

This book was born out of a meeting, more than ten years ago, with Lotte H. Eisner, the historian and co-director (with Henri Langlois) of the Paris Musée du Cinéma. In her apartment-cum-museum in Rue des Dames, Neuilly, on the outskirts of Paris, this great woman (now sadly departed) showed me a polychrome magic lantern, still shining with its red, blue, green and gold lacquer. This object, if truth be told, had been banished to the top of a cupboard, and Lotte did not seem to attach very great importance to it, preferring her 'Japanese' painting signed by Louise Brooks or her baroque cherubs in gilded wood. However, it was the lantern we discussed: where had this strange and luxurious projector come from? What could it have shown, before the arrival of 'cinema'?

She recommended several recent books to me. This was a depressing experience: not a word, or at best a few lines, on the 'prehistoric' past of the cinema. Even the most serious author, Jacques Deslandes, absolutely refused to travel back further than the nineteenth century. But the dream of being able to project moving illuminated images on a wall or screen is almost as old, in the history of humanity, as the dream of flight.

Most historians accord the realisation of this dream no more than a small note in the margin, and mention no more than a handful of daring technicians: Edison, the Lumière brothers . . . In truth the invention of the cinema was a 'long march' which lasted for several centuries. It was a story filled with crowds of highly ingenious pieces of equipment, infinitely varied images ranging from the popular to the poetic, and researchers who, although occasionally charlatans, were often scientists with a rigorous and very modern approach. Reading other books (such as those by Jurgis Baltrušaitis, Franz Paul Liesegang, and David Robinson), I discovered that the little-explored heyday of 'pre-cinema' displayed an inexhaustible artistic and technical richness. As for the nineteenth century, there was even more to say about that period.

But some minor authors, contradicting each other about important facts, kept muddying the waters of my understanding. I decided, therefore, to return systematically to the sources, even the most ancient ones, in search of the truth. Having taken this course, I was overwhelmed by a whirlwind of books, pamphlets, articles, patents, letters, forms, manuscripts, glass slides, and antique equipment.

One day deciphering the folio volume by the German Jesuit Kircher, the next poring over the archives of Georges Demenÿ, the disciple of Marey; rediscovering the entrancing beauty of the works of Christiaan Huygens, then plunging into the great commercial enterprises of 1895; through all such adventures I was struck above all by one great consistency. From the illuminated shows of the Italian della Porta in the sixteenth century, through to the cinematographic projections of the Lumière brothers in 1895, there was certainly plenty of technical difference, but there was one overriding godlike desire: to recreate life, to see a human alter ego, either hand-painted or chronophotographed, living and breathing on the screen.

AUTHOR'S ACKNOWLEDGEMENTS

I have been constantly encouraged in the course of my research by a small group of learned friends, collectors and historians. I offer them my warmest thanks. I also owe much gratitude to Michel Marie, who advised me on many points with tireless kindness and patience, and to David Robinson, whose wonderful collection required several visits and who always put up with me with enthusiasm and generosity.

Two impassioned researchers, Thierry Lefebvre and Jean-Jacques Meusy, responded to all my questions with great friendship. Maurice Gianati, whose documentation seems inexhaustible, supplied me with a great many priceless pieces of information. François Binétruy allowed me to make close examination of some extremely rare, sometimes unique, devices. Olivier Auboin-Vermorel allowed me the benefit of his fine collection of cameras and projectors. John Barnes, Jean A. Gili, Tom Gunning, Dominique Lebrun, and Jean-Loup Passek always proved warm and encouraging.

Marianne de Fleury and Dominique Païni, before they welcomed me onto their staff, generously opened the reserve collection of the

Archives de la Cinémathèque Française, a magical place where important discoveries are always to be made. Emmanuelle Toulet kindly welcomed the results of my first research, and gave me the opportunity to explore the collections of the Bibliothèque de l'Arsenal. Isabelle Champion, Jean-Pierre Jeancolas, Jean-Pierre Mattei, and Lausa Susini also brought their friendly support to this long undertaking.

I should also thank for their kind assistance: Michèle Aubert, Danielle Chaperon, Catherine and Marianne Fricheau, Renée Génot, Aïcha Kherroubi, Michèle Lagny, Sabine Lenk, Marion Leuba, Frédérique Lefebvre, Françoise Levie, Madeleine Malthête-Méliès, Laura Minici Zotti, Frédérique Moreau, Donata Pesenti Campagnoni, Marie Anne Pini, Isabelle Raynauld; Richard Abel, Jacques Aumont, William Barnes, Raymond Borde, Stephen Bottomore, Henri Bousquet, Patrick Brion, Alain Brunet, Carlos Bustamente, Jacques Champreux, Paolo Cherchi Usai, Lorenzo Codelli, Roland Cosandey, Guido Convents, Freddy Denaës, Jean-Pierre Deseuzes, Philippe Dubois, Tony Dugdale, Guy Fihman, Michel Frizot, André Gaudreault, Angel Gil-Sastre, David Henry, Stephen Herbert, Robert Laugier, Pierre Lherminier, André Milcot, Carlo Alberto Minici Zotti, Charles Musser, Lester Smith, Maurice Trarieux-Lumière, Gérard Turpin, Yuri Tsivian, Marc Vernet, and Thomas Weynants.

And also the following institutions: Archives de Paris, Archives du Film (Bois d'Arcy), Archives Nationales, Archives of the Barnes Museum of Cinematography (St Ives, Cornwall), Association Française de Recherche sur l'Histoire du Cinéma (Paris), Domitor, Association Premier Siècle du Cinéma, Bibliothèque de l'Arsenal, Bibliothèque Nationale, Bibliothèque de l'Image-Filmothèque, Bibliothèque Mazarine, Bibliothèque du CNAM, Cinémathèque Française—Musée du Cinéma (Paris), Cinémathèque Corse (Porto-Vecchio), Cineteca del Comune di Bologna, Conservatoire National des Arts et Métiers (Paris), Le Giornate del Cinema Muto (Pordenone), Institut de Recherches sur le Cinéma et l'Audiovisuel (Sorbonne Nouvelle, Paris III), Institut National de la Propriété Industrielle (Paris), Magic Lantern Society (London), Musée des Techniques (Paris), Musée Marey (Beaune), Museo Nazionale del Cinema (Turin), Museum of the Moving Image (London), Société Française de Photographie (Paris).

Introduction
by Tom Gunning

More than four centuries of moving images: Mannoni's discovery of cinema

Origins are slippery things, figuratively and literally, and the cinema is possibly the most slippery medium that has ever existed. In his memoirs, Sergei Eisenstein lamented that he had no better luck finding out about the origins of the creative process from his mentor and creative father, theatre director Vsevolod Meyerhold, than he did learning about where babies come from from his biological father. Origins are shrouded in a mixture of forbidding taboos and driving curiosity, and constitute a troubling concoction of claims to power and ownership (often spurious, always simplified): myths of inevitable progress; national pride; and simple misinformation. Faced with the snake-pit of claims and counter-claims, pure egotism and obfuscation that marks accounts of the origins of cinema one might just throw up one's hands and decide to detour around the entire issue. In fact, the famous Brighton Project of the International Federation of Film Archives (FIAF), which took place in 1978 and (at least in some myths of origins) inaugurated a new scholarly investigation of early cinema, specifically targeted the years 1900–06 as its area of investigation, skirting the period of invention and origin. The organizers of the project diplomatically decided that to investigate the invention of cinema would immediately ignite partisanship of the various 'inventors' and pit one national claim against another.

Luckily for film studies—and for cultural history generally—two scholars have recently approached the origins of cinema with not only peerless and patient research, but with a broad perspective, unwilling to become promoters of either a single hero or a particular nation. Most recently Deac Rossell's *Living Pictures: the Origins of the Movies* (Albany, N.Y.: State University of New York Press, 1998) provides the most reliable handbook of the interlocking attempts to devise motion pictures in the nineteenth century, giving long-overdue attention to the relatively ignored German tradition of Ottomar Anschütz, and a history of the perfection of celluloid as a base. Rossell offers a wonderful sense of the variety of approaches tried out by motion picture technicians and refreshingly refuses to privilege one tradition over another, avoiding especially the writing of history from the perspective of the techniques that later became dominant. Uniquely, Rossell demonstrates the visual qualities of vanished techniques of projection, such as those employing glass images or multiple lenses.

The other great contribution to the rewriting of the origins of cinema you now hold in your hands: Laurent Mannoni's *The Great Art of Light and Shadow*. Although Mannoni himself has since supplemented it with a detailed study of Georges Demenÿ and essays on some of the other figures he discusses herein, this is the work that I believe most thoroughly and imaginatively redefines the shape of early film history, rethinking the issues of origins and thereby defining a new field for research and investigation. This field should no longer be called (as it often was in the 1970s) simply 'proto-cinema,' because it extends through centuries and includes a complex culture of projected and technological images that was not simply waiting for cinema to appear and perfect it. Mannoni extends the profound insight of cinema historian Charles Musser that the history of film cannot be understood unless it is seen as part of a long tradition of 'screen practice', centuries of projected images. But essential as it may be, the screen itself is not necessarily the centre of all these devices. The centre lies, rather, as Mannoni dubs it after Kircher, in 'the great art of *light and shadow*' a tradition which, while it made way for the projected moving image that appeared at the end of the nineteenth century, included many great achievements other than the flicker images of the movies. In our dawning age of new movement media, we can see Mannoni's work as outlining a tradition not simply for cinema but for video, computer-generated images, virtual reality, and a host of new media that pursue the delights that Mannoni chronicles—virtual images made of light and shadow. Mannoni sets out here not a simple pedigree or genealogy for cinema, but a whole complex and neglected visual culture, one of whose forms became the movies in the twentieth century.

Studies such as Mannoni's and Rossell's immediately discredit the metaphor of biological paternity and the family romance of discovering the true father (or mother) for cinema—that poor shivering foundling abandoned on the doorstep of art and commerce sometime at the end of the nineteenth century. With Mannoni's work, we discard a method which traces offspring back to a single point of origin. He substitutes almost the inverse figure: the device we recognize as motion pictures, when traced backwards, fragments and multiplies, unravelling a skein of influences and practices that move back into centuries-thick layers of culture and history.

If the twin metaphors of biology and invention are deconstructed by such an approach (which, while not discrediting the contributions of Edison, Marey, Muybridge, Demenÿ, Lumière, Paul, etc., no longer isolates them from the energies of a broader cultural history), what about the perhaps more useful metaphor of archaeology which Mannoni uses in his subtitle, again recalling an earlier milestone, C.W. Ceram's classic work *Archaeology of the Cinema*? Mannoni is not investigating a long-vanished civilization whose languages and customs are foreign and difficult to reconstruct, the subject of speculation as much as reconstruction. Instead he is uncovering a continuity of practices which can be systematically reconstructed without uncovering a foot of dirt (although in this contemporary era, of course, oblivion takes many forms and certainly a lot of dust has accumulated!). What Mannoni uncovers and describes here is part of history, not pre-history, and it is the fundamentally historical nature of his work that makes it so valuable. An alternative to the myth of cinema's sudden invention at the end of the nineteenth century by certain men of genius has often been to de-historicize cinema entirely, to situate its origins in pre-history, with analogies to cinema found not only in traditional shadow plays, but buried within the depths of humanity's most archaic origins, locating cinema's ancestors in the attempt to capture motion in cave paintings, the succession of images in Egyptian tombs, or in the shadows cast on the walls of Plato's cave. While this primitive myth is important for the way cinema has been understood (more revealing for film theory than film history), and the phenomenology of shadow and light lies undeniably at the core of cinema, Mannoni quite rightly does not engage in this sort of ahistorical speculation. The great art of light and shadow as Mannoni describes it neither sprang suddenly from the head of Louis Lumière at the end of the nineteenth century, nor is it an eternal factor of human culture. Rather, Mannoni traces it to a particular period of scientific and technological discovery: the sixteenth- and seventeenth-century renaissance of science and technology in Europe.

The great importance of Mannoni's book lies, therefore, not only in providing the single best and most carefully detailed history of the origins of cinema, but in laying out a multi-century trajectory for the invention of and fascination with illuminated, moving or technological images. Mannoni does not simply tell the story of cinema's 'invention,' but rather describes the intersection of a scientific fascination with elements of visual perceptions—the science of optics—with a delight in the creation of illusions. Thus cinema's history begins in 'Natural Magic,' as typified by a figure such as Giovanni Battista della Porta (1540–1615), who showed how magical illusions could be created through 'natural' means, by a combination of mechanics and optics, the knowledge of lenses and mirrors and a creation of new relations between the perceiving eye and the power of light. The camera obscuras, anamorphic images, parabolic mirrors, and catoptrical theatres of 'Natural Magic' constitute a vital and interconnected realm of visual experiments and devices which finds its most versatile and powerful form in the magic lantern of the seventeenth century. These illusory devices deserve as much cultural investigation as the more respectable offspring of the science of optics, the telescope, microscope and the devices of perspective, have received.

What Mannoni displays is, once again, not a sudden invention, but a rich and varied culture obsessed with the nature of vision and its deformation, and new possibilities of representation through technical devices. From the beginning we find here a delight in illusion which has an entertainment aspect and was promptly exploited as such, inter-twined with a desire to demonstrate principles of the science of light and vision. In this fascination with optical devices we find perhaps the strongest cultural expression of the fundamental energy of the era of the Renaissance as it moved towards the Enlightenment. This is the impulse originally condemned by the churchmen of the Middle Ages as a sin, and increasingly liberated and fostered by the new discoveries of the Renaissance: *curiositas*. Visual curiosity drove both the magical amusement offered by this new culture of optical devices and the scientific research which underpinned and was demonstrated by it. In this era of cabinets of curiosities, the new optical devices perfectly embodied a brave new view of the world, a world rendered strange and vivid in its novelty.

Thus Mannoni reveals the key place of visual culture in the dawn of modern sciences. He carefully establishes the importance of Dutch humanist Christiaan Huygens for the perfection of what became known as the magic lantern. Like Musser, Mannoni questions the traditional attribution of this device to the Jesuit Athanasius Kircher, and shows that the magic lantern appeared among a number of visual devices

Huygens developed. Huygens' lack of interest in publicizing or claiming his invention does not prevent Mannoni from demonstrating not only his key role in its invention, but also Huygens' immediate interest in creating an illusion of motion through this projection device, designing a movable glass slide portraying an animated skeleton removing its skull. A fascination with the uncanny aspects of the power of these projected image devices (which were often referred to in their early phases as 'lanterns of fear') and the paradoxical 'animation' of inert images is evident from their origins.

But for Mannoni the great art of light and shadow never restricts itself to the devices and inventions played with by a small number of savants in their laboratories. Like the cinema, the art of projected images is a social practice, involving audiences and showmen. Along with his detailed discussion of the various innovators and inventors, Mannoni describes the fully developed culture of exhibition through which the magic lantern took Europe by storm. Savants and priests, mountebanks and showmen toured magic lantern shows around the world, extending even to China where the Jesuit Claudio Filippo Grimaldi presented an exhibition to the Emperor in Peking in 1671 or 1672 as a marvellous example of Western technology. In the eighteenth century the lantern passed from an entertainment of the elite to a pastime of the people, as travelling showmen wandered the highroads and showed their wonders in towns and villages. At the same time the lantern never lost its ties to science and enlightenment and was seized upon as a particularly modern and effective mode of instruction, dragooned even to teach history and science to the Dauphin on the eve of the French Revolution.

With the passion and attention to sensuous detail of a true collector, Mannoni describes the variety and offshoots of the lantern, the various optical boxes and peepshows, and evokes the beauties of the hand-painted glass slides and their transformation during the eighteenth century. Episodes of history, fairy tales, *diableries* and gags, scatological and even obscene images were projected, along with trick slides of the sort Huygens first envisioned, creating illusions of motion or mythological metamorphoses. The projection possibilities of the magic lantern were also combined with the magnification of the microscope to produce the 'solar microscopes' which could display the mysteries of the unseen world of tiny infusoria cavorting in a drop of water, or enlarge the intricate articulations of a flea's legs. More terrifying to many than the painted devils of the Jesuits, these monstrous creatures with unheard-of dimensions loomed before spectators, creating a new sense of scope and scale that visualized a world of science more fantastic than the fairy-tales of giants projected for children.

Nowhere is the great art of light and shadow's ambiguous relation with the world of the fantastic better demonstrated than in Mannoni's thorough discussion of the phantasmagoria of Philidor and Robertson. This form of magic lantern entertainment has become part of our language, a term describing an impossible—yet fully convincing— illusion. Beyond its use to describe any experience in which the senses seem to be stimulated to the point of hallucination, 'phantasmagoria' was used by Marx and others to describe the non-reality of modern culture under capitalism, in which the spell of the commodity enwraps the masses in a sort of illusory wonder, obscuring the actual conditions of production. The lantern entertainment at its most complex became a metaphor for the peculiarly modern experience of a loss of a sense of reality, a world in which appearances could be so completely controlled that the possibility of seeing through them to an underlying actuality seems to be in peril.

Mannoni not only provides the most complete account of the phantasmagoria in its various forms, but clearly situates it in the crisis point of the age of Enlightenment: the French Revolution and its aftermath. The phantasmagoria balanced itself on the cutting edge of the art of light and shadow, exploring the ambiguous realm between phantom and substance. By a variety of projection devices (moving the lantern to create effects of enlarging or shrinking of the image, projection of a wavering and uncanny image on billows of smoke, effects of transformation through mechanical slides or anamorphic lenses), the images themselves were endowed with a sense of protean energy. As insubstantial projections seemingly came to life, these ambiguous images could be presented as manifestations of spirits and ghosts. As Mannoni shows, the presentation of these images set the stage for the modern magic show. Phantasmagoria showmen would invoke the spirits of the dead, display images of recent victims of the guillotine or newly deceased celebrities like Benjamin Franklin, yet at the same time proclaim their allegiance to the regime of reason and announce that there was nothing produced in their shows that could not be scientifically explained.

The greatest phantasmagorical showman, Étienne-Gaspard Robertson, held his seances on the grounds of a ruined Capuchin monastery, on the very site of the old religion overturned by the Revolution, yet still haunting the consciousness of the public. The visual and psychological effects of the ruins combined with the special decor of skulls and Egyptian hieroglyphics to produce a receptive and possibly fearful attitude on the part of the viewers. As Freud has demonstrated, the experience of the uncanny derives from the lingering of an irrational belief, often even unconscious, after the conscious has dismissed the old belief as nonsense. As the magic lantern had embodied the marvels of the new science in the seventeenth century, so at the close of the eighteenth it acted out the contest between superstitions and reason, with a form of illusion which could invoke both simultaneously. The attraction of the phantasmagoria, which soon became a world-wide form of entertainment, literally enacted the new consciousness of modernity: torn between doubt and credulity, fascinated by the ways its senses could be entertained as its logic sought, not always successfully, for explanations.

In the nineteenth century this rich visual culture became industrialized and found a truly mass audience. The creation of a commercial visual culture was at least a century old before the cinema appeared and appropriated it. Throughout the nineteenth century new technologies of visual reproduction and new sources of light appeared and supplied improved means to shape and fix its shadows, ushering in a new era of visual illusions. These included entertainments of light and shadow that created not a simple image, but rather a total environment. Secularizing and rationalizing the fearsome spectacles of Robertson's phantasmagoria and its creepy setting, the panorama and diorama sought to create a situation in which the viewer would be totally immersed in the illusion. While the panorama and diorama developed partly from landscape and history paintings, they sought to transform the very nature of perspective-based easel painting since the Renaissance, the enframed image seen from a single view point, as if viewed through a window. The 360 degree space of the panorama engulfed the viewer, using perspective to turn space inside out, so that the viewer constituted the vanishing point of a mobile, rotating point of view. Light itself was essential to the illusion, with the specially designed panorama exhibition spaces using the new architecture of glass to illuminate the painting from unseen sources with the actual light of nature itself, changing with meteorological conditions. But light played a much stronger role in the panorama's offspring, Daguerre's diorama, which sacrificed the 360 degree space for a more careful technological control of light projected through semi-transparent canvases, which could transform from one view to another or more subtly create changing effects of light and shadow, compressing time, for instance, by moving through the cycles of the day and night.

Daguerre, as a painter of stage sets, understood the theatrical effects of new technological control over light and shadow, but was equally drawn to the problem pursued since the beginning of the century: of actually securing, fixing for ever, the shadows cast by nature. Extending the research of Niépce, Daguerre turned from the massive scale of the diorama to the miniature image of the daguerreotype, offering a means to capture an image created by light itself as it affected sensitive chemicals. Although the intimacy and small scale of the daguerreotype seem to set it apart from the 'great' art of light and shadow, the pursuit of a technologically caused image would eventually intersect with the magic lantern and open new realms of visual pleasure. A new realm of investigation of the nature of visual perceptions and the possibility of tricking the human eye would pave the way for this, as the savants once more take took centre stage.

The optical illusions which cluster around the old-fashioned term 'persistence of vision' were a subject of investigation in the eighteenth century, although some related effects had been remarked as early as the writings of Aristotle. But it was primarily in the nineteenth century that scientists such as d'Arcy, Roget, Brewster, Faraday, Plateau, Stampfer and Babbage made careful observations of the way the eye could be tricked into creating visual superimpositions, or even illusions of motion, by viewing rapidly changing images. The various devices, known as 'philosophical toys', designed to demonstrate and exploit these frailties of human vision occupy the centre of Mannoni's account: the thaumatrope, anorthoscope, phenakistiscope, stroboscope, etc. Perhaps even more than the original projecting devices of the seventeenth and eighteenth centuries, these toys combined the fascination of illusion with the demonstrations of science. But, picking up a cue from Jonathan Crary's brilliant discussion of optical devices in his work *The Techniques of the Observer*, we could point out an important difference. The projected images of the original magic lantern amazed viewers because in some sense they did not know whether to take them for substance or shadow, image or reality. Careful observation and familiarity with the projection techniques could dispel these illusions, revealing them as figures merely composed of light and shadow. But in the optical toys of the nineteenth century (and we could add here Crary's main example, the stereoscope), the illusion of motion was no longer based on credulity: the viewer actually *saw* the images superimposed or the succession of motions or the illusion of three-dimensionality. In other words, the senses themselves were fooled; even understanding the nature of the device could not dispel the illusions. As Crary shows, in the nineteenth century the subject of investigation became not simply optics in the sense of the properties of lenses and light, but rather the actual human sensorium, the nature of perception and its physical basis in the eye. These new optical toys continued the long tradition of visual fascination through a combination of magical-seeming illusions and scientific demonstrations, but now the scientific interest was rooted in a new investigation of the human body as a perceptual device itself.

Lanternists were quick to try to combine these new illusions of motion with projectors which could display them to larger audiences. Mannoni painstakingly details dozens of such devices, now unjustly forgotten, which reveal that audiences watched projections of motion for decades before the innovation of modern motion pictures. But these special effects of motion were basically a sideshow to the key role the magic lantern took on, in much of nineteenth-century Europe, as the mass medium of visual information. The lantern show was adapted to every possible task of entertainment and instruction, and adopted by a huge range of institutions and practices from travelling entertainments, to temperance lectures, to the promotion of the principles of both religion and science and the conveying of distant lands and current events to masses of people. As a mass medium, the magic lantern was in-dustrialized in both the manufacture of lanterns (for professional exhibition as well as home use) and of the slides themselves, including the adaptation of photography to mass reproduction via photographs printed on glass slides. The magic lantern was the first medium to contest the printed word as a primary mode of information and instruction.

Mannoni maintains the dual focus needed for a vivid account of this new visual culture, balancing the popular with the scientific, as the new visual culture increasingly understood itself as participating in the key myth of the nineteenth century: the inevitable advance of science, industry and 'civilization'. Thus, as the showmen were adapting the new observations about the visual illusion of motion, physiologists such as Étienne-Jules Marey, fully aware of the manner in which the human senses were unreliable, sought new technological means of observation, quicker and more permanent than simple visual observation. Cued by the photographs of animal and human motion of photographer Eadweard Muybridge, Marey and his assistant Georges Demenÿ saw the usefulness (as well as the limitations) that photography might offer as a means of analysing the body in motion. Two new factors have entered into the mix here: a further perfection of photography in terms of time and a new attitude towards the body.

Daguerre and Niépce were concerned about fixing the photographic image, overcoming the gradual darkening that all previous photographic experiments had found inevitably obscured the images they obtained. They were less concerned about capturing an instant of time, and their original exposures took many minutes. Throughout the nineteenth century, however, the focus in photography began to shift from the fixing of the image to fixing of an instant through shorter exposure times. By the second half of the century (and especially towards its end), instantaneous photography could claim not only to capture an instant, but to seize a fraction of a second in a manner no human eye was capable of. Thus Muybridge could freeze a horse in full gallop and display the positions of its hooves, or Marey could capture the beating of a bird's wings. Chronophotography exploited the possibility of instantaneous photography not only to seize instants of time, but to place these instants into a series, dissolving the continuous motion of the world into singular points, creating a series of images which could trace the successive positions of the human or animal body in motion.

A whole new world of observation was opened up, and the physical body and its behaviour became subject to a new regime of not only visualization, but discipline. Georges Demenÿ arrived at Marey's Station Physiologique with a strong interest in the body-building possibilities of certain forms of gymnastics, which could possibly be demonstrated and taught through chronophotography. Mannoni makes clear that this is not an isolated instance, but part of a broad scientific culture interested in the way chronophotography could deliver the smallest increment of time for analysis and observation. The frozen sequence of images constituted the major form of chronophotography for a host of European and American scientists and photographers.

But for Marey and most of these scientists, it was the frozen image, or rather the succession of frozen images (which could analyse motion in a manner human eyesight could not) that embodied the great scientific possibilities of chronophotography—not the illusion of motion. Chronophotography allowed the breakdown of motion into bits of information. The reconstitution of motion, the synthesis of these separate images into a continuous illusion, served only a secondary purpose, that of demonstrating that these separate images could be reassembled as stages of a continual motion, a sort of guarantee of the accuracy of the frozen images themselves. Marey, Muybridge and other chronophotographers did devise projectors that allowed such reassembly and illusion of motion, but they were less important than the cameras and the images they captured. Mannoni details the various supports Marey employed for his chronophotography, from glass to paper to celluloid.

But it was the Phonoscope, first devised by Demenÿ to aid the teaching of lip-reading to deaf children, which became one of the first forms of photographic motion pictures to gain commercial backing as a device of entertainment. Like Anschütz's Tachyscope, it consisted of a wheel of glass slides created by chronophotography which, when spun, would produce a moving image. This commercial undertaking infuriated Marey, who felt not only that his work was being exploited, but that scientific research was being contaminated by entertainment profits. As Mannoni shows, however, the display of motion pictures was by the end of the century proceeding on all fronts with different combinations of the devices that had been appearing throughout the nineteenth century. Émile Reynaud combined his Praxinoscope with a projection device and created the first animated films, using hand-painted images on long bands of celluloid which were being projected by his Théâtre Optique at the Musée Grevin by 1892. In 1894 Edison finally launched his Kinetoscope, supplying celluloid bands of motion photographs which could be viewed by a single viewer through a peep-show device, which received a brief but world-wide success. More importantly, Edison showed the world how simple the mechanics of displaying photographic motion pictures could be, especially with the use of flexible celluloid. Each of these devices embodied a different combination of the various practices of motion pictures that had been developing through the nineteenth century. Not only were there many researchers and entrepreneurs busy working on these new forms of entertainment—rather than the sudden *Eureka!* of the isolated genius —but also the rich visual culture of illusions that was now centuries-old supplied a vast array of practices and devices to draw from.

Once the fateful year of 1895 was reached, the possibility of commercial exhibition of photographic motion pictures arose in an environment already saturated with technical devices and, as Mannoni shows, a complex and highly competitive entertainment industry (born, as he says, in an atmosphere of treachery and stabs in the back) came into being. Mannoni threads his way through claims of priorities and refuses to pay homage to the established figures of the 'invention of cinema'. Thus the later commercial career of Demenÿ and his various devices plays as strong a role in his account of the coming of cinema as do the Lumière brothers or Edison, as well as a host of other figures, whether machinists like Henri Joly or Jules Carpentier, or entrepreneurs like George William de Bedts or Ludwig Stollwerck. Mannoni ends his account with the well-known achievements of the Lumières, but urges us to see them as only one link in a long chain of devices and practices, a centuries-long tradition of images made of light and shadow.

It is precisely this approach, one which understands origins in terms of a broad range of cultural practices and the *longue durée* of centuries of history, rather than a founding father or mythical culture hero, that makes this book so uniquely valuable. Besides the treasure trove of information and facts that Mannoni has so carefully snatched from oblivion and assembled, it is his basic lesson that endures: that cinema is only part of a broad visual culture that stands at the intersection of modern science and modern media. This intersection still defines our media of information and entertainment and allows us, I believe, to rethink what the nature of modernity and its roots really are.

PART ONE

The dreams of the eye

1

Dark Rooms and Magic Mirrors

The camera obscura, or how to capture the sun

In a room dimly lit by candles, a group of nobles, burghers, and common people take their places on some benches. The candles are blown out: all is blackness. Bright illuminated images, coloured and moving, flash onto a white sheet secured to the wall. A scene appears; the people murmur to each other, some recognizing the village, the town, and the horses which they recently left to come into this darkened room. They exclaim at the faithfulness of the image, at the movement of the little shadows, at the amazing perspective so coveted by painters. A dancing devil appears, sending terror through the room. A few wise souls, initiated into the mystery of the camera obscura, are amused by the fear which grips their credulous neighbours, who are already reaching for their purses to buy the indulgence of the magician.

A dark room, with an audience gazing at a white screen and awaiting the arrival of a moving illuminated image. If we imagine ourselves to be at any point between the thirteenth and seventeenth centuries, what a scene of anticipation this is! If we could film the changes in costumes, the increasing size of the room, the appearance of a large projector behind the audience, we would see in a few minutes—like a time-lapse film of a flower blooming—the progress of a long wait which lasted over half a millennium. The only devices our ancestors could use to entertain and frighten themselves with optical visions borrowed from everyday life or from the fantasies of the mind, at least until the arrival of the magic lantern in the seventeenth century, were a dark room ('camera obscura', in Latin) and some complicated tricks with mirrors.

The principle of the camera obscura is simple: if a small aperture is pierced in the wall or window shutter of a fully darkened room, the scene

3

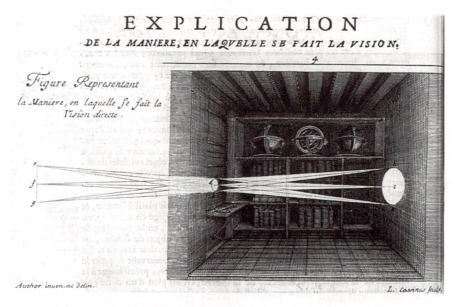

Fig. 1. Chérubin d'Orléans, *La Dioptrique Oculaire* (Paris, 1671).
Collection: Bibliothèque Nationale.

outside (or any other exterior object) will be projected into the interior of
the room, on the wall opposite to the aperture. A screen formed by a
piece of paper or a white sheet improves the image. If this screen is close
to the aperture, the image is reduced in size but very sharp; if further
away the image is larger, but also more blurred and less colourful. Either
way, it is projected upside down, since the light rays from the highest
and lowest points of the exterior scene, travelling in straight lines, cross
as they pass through the aperture. The result is a double inversion of the
image, both top to bottom and left to right. Leonardo da Vinci, in the
sixteenth century, and the astronomer Johannes Kepler in 1604, drew a
clear analogy between the human eye and the camera obscura. Our
crystalline lens takes the place of the aperture, while the retina which
lines the back wall of the eyeball is comparable to the screen mounted on
the wall opposite the aperture (see Fig. 1).

The phenomenon of projection of light rays has been known since
antiquity. The Greek philosopher Aristotle (384–322 BC), among
others, observed the passage of a beam of light through some kind of
opening. He did not specify if this experiment was conducted in a dark
room, and made no mention of the images which may have been visible.
Aristotle remarked only that the projection of the sun's rays through a

square, round or triangular aperture always produces a circular image. He could not explain this fact rationally. It was not until the seventeenth century that Francesco Maurolico, of Messina in Sicily, finally shed some light on this optical problem: compared to the size of the sun, the small aperture which Aristotle used was effectively a single point.[1] The light rays passing through that point took the form of a cone of light, with the aperture at its summit and the sun at its base. As they left the other side of the aperture the rays spread to form a second, smaller, cone of light. This problem greatly intrigued the scholars of the early middle ages, as manuscripts from that period demonstrate.

Without awaiting the theoretical explanation of the phenomenon, several thirteenth-century astronomers and opticians created the true camera obscura, which captured images from the exterior inside a darkened room. The English friar Roger Bacon (1214–94) recounted Aristotle's experiment, without crediting him, in his work *De Multiplicatione Specerium*[2] (*On the Multiplication of Species*) written in 1267, but he added one important element: the presence of a screen, a wall (*paries*) onto which the light rays were projected. Like his predecessors, Bacon noted that the opening through which the light rays passed did not need to be circular. This phenomenon was the basis of his theory, astonishing in its intuition, that light propagated by means of spherical waves. If the image projected through a square aperture was circular, it was simply because the light had resumed its natural spherical shape.

Roger Bacon is credited with an anonymous manuscript from the thirteenth century, found among the Latin holdings of the Bibliothèque Nationale in Paris, which contains the first known description of an eclipse viewed in the camera obscura:

> One day when the sun is in eclipse, would you desire to observe the whole eclipse, to know its starting point, its extent and duration, without damaging your eyes? Observe the passage of the sun's rays through any round hole, and watch with care the illuminated circle which the rays form on the surface onto which they fall . . .[3]

Even if this now seems obvious, this text does not state whether this marvellous experiment was conducted in a camera obscura. However, a contemporary and follower of Bacon, the English Franciscan monk John Pecham or Peckham (1228–91) of Canterbury, in a treatise on optics entitled *Perspectiva Communis*, did specify that the solar rays of the eclipse should be captured 'through any kind of aperture in a dark place'.

The camera obscura of the thirteenth century does not only appear to have been used for viewing eclipses. It allowed astronomers to avoid direct observation of the sun, which was dangerous for the eyes. The French scientist Guillaume de Saint-Cloud viewed an eclipse on 5 June 1285 without taking any optical precautions, and suffered a violent dazzling which lasted for several days. Wherever he looked, even with his eyelids closed, he saw a persistent bright disc. To observe the sun in safety, Saint-Cloud thereafter used the camera obscura, this time described quite explicitly:

> Make a hole in the roof or the window of a closed house, directed towards that part of the sky where the eclipse will appear, of about the same size as the tap hole in a wine barrel. As the light of the sun enters by this hole, place at a distance of about twenty or thirty feet from the hole a flat object, for example a board, and you will see that the light rays form a circular image on the board even if the hole is angular.[4]

The spectacle of everyday life

In Andrey Tarkovsky's 1966 film *Andrey Roublev*, set in fifteenth-century Russia, a character watches with surprise as an illuminated image forms on a blank wall in front of him. It represents a group of moving horsemen, but they are seen upside down. Tarkovsky then shows the closed shutters of the room: a small opening has allowed a shaft of light through to project the image onto the wall.

Although we know that scientists from the thirteenth century onwards observed the sun in a darkened room, we do not know if they sought at the same time to capture the outside world, whether that might be the road or countryside surrounding them, or the threatening horsemen bearing down upon them. 'What takes place in the street when the sun shines,[5] as the Italian Gerolamo Cardano would later describe it, did not appear on the screen of the camera obscura until the start of the sixteenth century.

The use of the camera obscura for viewing exterior objects, and not just for astronomical studies, appears to have been mentioned first in the writings of Leonardo da Vinci (1452–1519). Da Vinci did not, however, abandon Bacon's earlier use of it as a method of studying the sun without burning his eyes; he hoped to use the rays entering the aperture of the camera obscura to calculate the precise distance of the sun from the Earth. Without giving further details, he discussed 'illuminated objects' whose images 'penetrate through some small hole into a very dark habitation'. A sheet of white paper served as the screen:

> These images if they proceed from a place that is lit by the sun will actually seem painted upon this paper, which should be very thin and seen in reverse; and the said hole should be made in a very thin sheet of iron.[6]

To view the image by transparency from the reverse side of the screen was ingenious: in that way the true orientation of the image, laterally inverted at the aperture by the intersection of the light rays, was restored. But the scene or objects were still always projected upside down.

The first published graphical representation of projection of the sun through an aperture into a dark place is found in *De Radio Astronomico et Geometrico* ('On Astronomical and Geometrical Rays'), by the Dutch mathematician Reinerus Gemma-Frisius, published in 1545. On 24 January 1544 he observed a solar eclipse at Louvain from the safety of his camera obscura.

The principle and construction of the camera obscura did not change from the thirteenth century to the start of the sixteenth: the only variation was whether the aperture was formed in a wall or in a shutter. But between 1521 and 1550 an important modification was introduced: a biconvex lens (with both its surfaces rounded outwardly) was placed in the aperture, which greatly improved the quality of the image by concentrating the light rays. It was another Italian, Gerolamo Cardano, who disclosed this improvement in his book *De Subtilitate* ('On Subtleties'), printed at Nuremberg in 1550. From this time on, scenes in the street outside formed part of the repertoire of the camera obscura:

> If it pleases you to view what takes place in the street when the sun shines, place a disc of glass in the window and, the window being closed, you will see images projected through the opening onto the wall opposite; but the colours will be dull. Therefore place a very white sheet of paper at the place onto which the images are projected.[7]

The glass disc (*orbem e vitro*) might be assumed to be a biconvex lens. A French translation of *De Subtilitate* published in Paris in 1556 went so far as to use the description 'a round body made of glass' (*la rotondité faicte du verre*).

In the eighteenth and nineteenth centuries the camera obscura was deprived of a great portion of its history by the erroneous attribution of its invention to the sixteenth-century Italian scientist Giovanni Battista della Porta (1540–1615). In fact, della Porta merely published a description of it, in a four-part book entitled *Magiae Naturalis* ('Natural Magic'), printed in Naples in 1558. This mistaken paternity is found repeated in supposedly authoritative works, such as the *Leçons de Physique* of Abbé Nollet (1743) and the *Encyclopédie* of Diderot and d'Alembert (1753), among other sources.

Della Porta's book certainly enjoyed an immediate success. Republished several times, by the end of the seventeenth century it had been translated from its original Latin into Italian, English, German, and French. Hurriedly printed popular editions circulated in France at this period. This probably explains why the earlier works by Gemma-Frisius and Cardano came to be forgotten, particularly since della Porta carefully avoided referring to them.

Della Porta demonstrated quite an inclination for the marvellous. *Magiae Naturalis* is full of horrifying and repugnant recipes for 'creating a Mandragora', making a woman talk in her sleep, or transforming men into animals; we also learn the causes of the repulsion of an elephant when confronted with a sow, or the terror of the lion when it hears the crowing of a cockerel. It is hardly surprising that della Porta was accused of sorcery by Pope Paul V. He also indulged himself by issuing prophecies, some of which, by misfortune, came true.

Della Porta described the camera obscura in detail in the fourth book of the 1558 edition of *Magiae Naturalis,* which dealt with 'catoptric experiments' ('catoptrics' is the science of optical effects by reflection, especially at mirrors, as opposed to 'dioptrics', which deals with refraction effects, particularly through lenses). In the same account, without identifying it as such, della Porta noted the phenomenon of retinal persistence of vision. He advised the adjustment of the eyes to complete darkness—'you must stay a while, for the Images will not be seen presently'—before looking at the projected image:

> For when men walk in the Sun, if they come into the dark, that affection continues, that we can see nothing, or very scantly; because the affection made by the light, is still in our eyes; and when that is gone by degrees, we see clearly in dark places.[8]

A new edition of della Porta's text was published in Naples in 1589, this time in twenty sections rather than four. This edition presented a genuine innovation, in the idea of organizing a true optical show by means of the camera obscura.

How in a Chamber you may see Hunting, Battles of Enemies, and other delusions.

Now for a conclusion I will add that, than which nothing can be more pleasant for great men, and Scholars, and ingenious persons to behold; That in a dark Chamber by white sheets objected, one may see as clearly and perspicuously, as if they were before his eyes, Huntings, Banquets, Armies of Enemies, Plays, and all things else that one desireth. Let there be over against that Chamber, where you desire to represent these things, some spacious Plain, where the Sun can freely shine: Upon that you shall set Trees in Order, also Woods, Mountains, Rivers, and Animals, that are really so, or made by Art, of Wood, or some other matter. You must frame little children in them, as we use to bring them in when Comedies are Acted: and you must counterfeit Stags, Bores, Rhinocerets, Elephants, Lions, and what other creatures you please: Then by degrees they must appear, as coming out of their dens, upon the Plain: The Hunter he must come with his hunting Pole, Nets, Arrows, and other necessaries, that may represent hunting: Let there be Horns, Cornets, Trumpets sounded: those that are in the Chamber shall see Trees, Animals, Hunters Faces, and all the rest so plainly, that they cannot tell whether they be true or delusions. Swords drawn will glitter in at the hole, that they will make people almost afraid. I have often shewed this kind of Spectacle to my friends, who much admired it, and took pleasure to see such a deceit; and I could hardly by natural reasons, and reasons from the Opticks remove them from their opinion, when I had discovered the secret.[9]

Della Porta's show foreshadowed the magic lantern projections of the following century. But comparing them from a present-day viewpoint, the Italian's camera obscura appears almost superior to the lantern, whose hand-painted glass slides could not offer the complete illusion of this scenic device. Della Porta's images, projected into the room by the crystal lenses and the mirror used since 1558, showed real actors, who moved in front of scenery to the sound of accompanying music.

However, the camera obscura could offer nothing more than an ephemeral spectacle: at nightfall, its images vanished. Della Porta's productions must also have been very costly and difficult to assemble. The sun had to be out to illuminate the scene, and the scene had to remain within the field of view of the lens. The process was not perfect, but it did speed up research into more effective ways of obtaining illuminated moving images. Thanks to della Porta the camera obscura, suddenly diverted from its scientific vocation, became a 'théâtre optique', a method of illumination capable of projecting stories, enacted scenes and fantastic visions. It left the domain of science and astronomy to enter those of artifice, play-acting, the marvellous, and illusion.

After the appearance of *Magiae Naturalis*, the science of optics became one of the favourite recreations of the nobility and of scholars, and one of the most desirable accessories for acrobats and conjurers. For the 'commoners' of the sixteenth century who had not read della Porta, the sudden projection of a devil or wild animals onto the screen of the camera obscura would remain, for some time, a phenomenon which was inexplicable and therefore supernatural. A new resource was opened up for quacks and tricksters. Not long after the book's publication it was possible for an individual initiated into its mystery to profit from the more or less general ignorance of the world at large in optical matters, presenting shows of magic and sorcery whose sole 'device' was the camera obscura, and whose sole aim was to extort money from the gullible spectators.

The Belgian Jesuit François d'Aguillon (1566–1617) was one of the first to denounce this new form of quackery. In 1613, at Anvers, he published a magnificent folio volume dealing entirely with optics, perspective, and geometrical and stereographic projection: *Opticorum Libri VI* ('The Sixth Book of Optics'). D'Aguillon had attended one of these quack shows. The process of projection he described was the same as della Porta's, except that the image was presented upside down, without the use of a mirror. There was no music: the quack preferred complete silence, which was even more distressing, to accompany his trickery.

> The method by which certain tricksters attempt to take advantage of unknowing people: they pretend that they know Sorcery, while they know little of what that means; they boast of making the ghosts of the devil appear from Hell itself and show them to the spectators. They bring curious and interested persons, who wish to know everything on dark and secret subjects, into a dark room [*obscurum conclave*] where there is no light, excepting a narrow shaft which passes through a small piece of glass [the lens]. They then tell them in a severe tone to make no sound and remain calm. When all is complete silence and no person moves or utters a word, as if they were attending a religious service or a vision, they announce that the devil will shortly arrive. At the same moment, an assistant puts on a

devil mask, such that he resembles the images of demons which one is used to see, with a hideous and monstrous face and horns on the forehead, a tail, and a wolf's skin with claws at hands and feet. The assistant struts to and fro outside, as if he were sunk deep in thought, in a place in which his colours and shape may be reflected through the glass into the chamber. In order that these cunning inventions produce a greater effect, all must remain in silence as if a god were about to emerge from this device. Some persons begin to turn pale, while others, terrified of what is to come, begin to perspire. After this, they take a sheet of paper and hold it in front of the ray of light which has been allowed to enter the chamber. One may see on it the image of the imitation of the devil coming and going; the people watch this, trembling. The poor people and the inexperienced do not know that they are only watching the shadow of a trickster; they waste their money quite uselessly.[10]

The quack projectionist played upon the realism of the show, and his phantasmagorical apparitions produced their effect perfectly. Only the learned such as d'Aguillon or Nicéron remained calm. The Parisian Jean-François Nicéron (1613–46), a member of the monastic Order of Minimes, looked coldly on this witches' sabbath. Nicéron was an expert in optics and anamorphoses (distorted images which would reveal their 'secret' from particular viewpoints or by particular methods). He was famous in his lifetime for his transformation paintings which appeared in the galleries below the cloisters of the Paris monastery of the Minimes, in Place Royale. As one approached his 'optical wonders, the main subject disappeared, and one could only perceive a landscape'.[11] He was therefore well placed to denounce the spectacles of sorcery in the camera obscura:

This type of delightful Perspective has sometimes so deceived the eye that those who are in the chamber and who, after having parted with their purse, watch it completely in the hands of those who are counting and dividing their money in a wood or on a floor, believe that this representation takes place by magic . . . If there should be someone concealed behind the screen who plays the spirit, as they say, to speak like those who make the marionettes dance, the simpletons believe that it is the persons in the picture who are speaking, since they see them open their mouths and move their lips: and as soon as the window is opened, the whole scene disappears, just as one invokes the sabbath where one wishes the sorcerers to attend . . . Those who possess a place in the fields may have this sort of Perspective at little expense; and if one wishes to view the images, which appear reversed, the right way up, there are several methods for righting them, such as by means of convex lenses or by a mirror, and even to enlarge them to make them appear as in life, as I have seen done by Monsieur Le Brun, General of La Monnoye.[12]

The 'Perspectives' which Nicéron described presented a complete spectacle: a human image, in colour and moving, synchronized with the offstage voice of an actor. In spite of this technical achievement, the quacks and tumblers rapidly abandoned the camera obscura, because of the complexity of its productions and the intense light which was needed to illuminate the external subject. They soon found another agent for the spreading of superstition, the magic lantern. Meanwhile the principle of the camera obscura was taken up by some of the greatest scientists of the seventeenth century, such as René Descartes (1596–1650), whose *Dioptrique* ('Dioptrics'), published in 1637, contains a precise description of the camera obscura. After that the secret, of which della Porta had offered a glimpse, was completely unveiled. Rationalism imposed itself and the showmen's source of revenue dried up.

If scholars condemned the diabolical visions produced by the camera obscura when it was manipulated by unscrupulous 'directors', they approved and recommended without reservation the beauty and charm of its illuminated views when they represented, for example, exterior landscapes. The miraculous aspect was that the pictures moved. It was therefore necessary to capture 'some square, or busy street, or some beautiful building, or blossoming flower-bed, to have greater pleasure', according to the French Jesuit Jean Leurechon (1591–1670), for whom the camera obscura was 'one of the most beautiful experiments in Optics':

> Above all, there is pleasure in seeing the *movement* of birds, men and other animals, and the shaking of the plants in the wind . . . This beautiful painting, in addition to its being disposed in perspective, innocently represents that which the painter has never been able to place in his picture, namely *continuous movement* from place to place.[13]

Nicéron was equally struck by this 'continuous movement' (a phrase which might apply just as neatly to the whole progress of pre-cinematographic research): 'the outdoor objects convey not only their sizes, shapes and colours, but also their movements, which are always missing from the artists' paintings.'[14] The ideas of Leurechon and Nicéron curiously foreshadowed the nineteenth-century aesthetic controversy which set painting and photography against each other, photography being 'plagiarism of nature by optics' according to the French poet Alphonse de Lamartine (1790–1869), whose attacks on 'daguerreotypomania' also, indirectly, attacked the camera obscura. In Nicéron's time, some painters began to use the camera obscura to create their paintings with absolute precision: this amused Nicéron, who observed quite correctly that the artists were tracing 'a static picture taken from a moving one'.

The camera obscura, which gave a spectacle which was 'so delightful, and which suggested enchantment', which made 'little ghosts'[15] appear, remained a widely practised entertainment throughout the seventeenth century. Around 1630 a camera obscura opened to the public in Paris. It was situated at the Samaritaine, a fountain of huge dimensions constructed in 1603 on piles close to the second arch of the Pont-Neuf, on the Louvre bank of the Seine. Unfortunately it was demolished during the nineteenth century. From this position, the camera obscura captured a view of the Louvre, the sky and the birds, the Seine, and all the activity on the bridge: a glorious spectacle open to everyone.

Meanwhile, scientists had managed to multiply the spectacular powers of the camera obscura. In 1642 Mario Bettini, an Italian Jesuit, published the following instructions: if one pierced twelve holes through the wall or shutter and placed an armed warrior outside the chamber, a small army of twelve men, all following exactly the same movements, would appear projected onto the white sheet of the screen. To make the image appear the right way up, Bettini used a large powerful plano-convex (hemispherical) lens on a stand, placed in front of the aperture inside the chamber. The lens concentrated the incoming light rays towards another similar lens; between the two, the light rays crossed over again, and the image projected from the second lens appeared on the sheet (see Fig. 2).[16]

Technical improvements to the camera obscura

More refined applications of the camera obscura developed very quickly. Around 1611 the German astronomer Johannes Kepler (1571–1630) made a 'small portable tent' which could be put up anywhere, in the open countryside or in the street. Its lens turned 'like a windmill, which could view all the points of the horizon in turn'.[17] The images were captured on a sheet of paper laid flat inside the tent, and could be traced onto the

Fig. 2. Mario Bettini, *Apiaria Universae Philosophiae Mathematicae* (1642).
Collection: Bibliothèque Nationale.

sheet to form a drawn image of the scene. When the drawing was finished, 'one turns the tent slightly, one takes a new view of the landscape and one can again draw the whole horizon'. This highly practical system was repeated by the French optician Vincent Chevalier in 1823.[18] The great German writer Johann Wolfgang von Goethe (1749–1832) owned a camera obscura of this type, preserved today at the National Goethe Museum in Weimar, in which the canvas tent was replaced by four wooden panels mounted on four feet. One side of the chamber could be opened, to allow the user into the chamber to draw the landscapes captured by a lens located at the top of the device.

Nicéron, meanwhile, transformed the camera obscura into 'a form of portfolio'.[19] At the start of the eighteenth century, some craftsmen and opticians made camera obscuras in the shape of books, much sought by optical enthusiasts. One example preserved today in a private collection has the appearance of an enormous folio, bound completely in calfskin. On the gold-blocked spine, the title consists of the single word *Optique*. The 'book' is completely hollow, containing a mirror and three small sheets of wood decorated with hand-painted flowers and arabesques, which may be assembled together with the book cover to form a box. On the top is placed the mirror, which reflects all external landscapes and

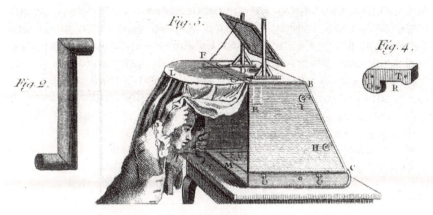

Fig. 3.   Camera obscura, after van s'Gravesande.
Collection: Bibliothèque Nationale.

views through a small aperture into the interior of the box.[20] The greatest refinement of this example is that it also functions as a *boîte d'optique* or peepshow box (see Chapter 4): with a biconvex lens placed on the flat portion of the binding it can be used to view engraved perspective views or *vues d'optique*.

The German Daniel Schwendter, in his book *Deliciae Physico-Mathematicae* ('Scientific and Mathematical Delights') printed at Nuremberg in 1636, gave a drawing of another type of camera obscura, known as the 'oeil artificiel' (artificial eye) in France and the 'scioptric ball' in Britain. A wooden ball was placed in the aperture of the camera obscura, so as to be pivotable within a fixed frame. The ball was pierced on opposite sides by a pair of holes, into which lenses were fitted. This ingenious system allowed exploration of the complete exterior landscape, since the 'eye' could be moved from left to right and top to bottom. In France, the Capuchin monk Chérubin d'Orléans (1613–97) described this method in 1671, adding a long tube of strong wood about a metre in length to the 'eye'. This tube would project onto a screen the 'eclipses and spots of the sun'.[21] Chérubin named his equipment the *Oculaire Dioptrique* ('Dioptric eyepiece').

In his book *Ars Magna Lucis et Umbrae* ('The Great Art of Light and Shadow') of 1646, the German Jesuit Athanasius Kircher also presented several quite complex new designs of camera obscura. Some of these methods using engraved mirrors will be described later. While this individual makes his appearance here quite discreetly—we will meet him again soon—in fact he played a major role, simultaneously genius, charlatan, and clown, in all the optical developments of the seventeenth century, even after the importance with which he credited himself has been reduced to its real dimensions. Kircher described one large camera obscura intended for landscape painters, which was located in the open air. Inside, he stretched a wall of papyrus. The painter had only to enter the chamber to be able to copy the whole exterior landscape onto the paper.[22] Kircher's camera obscura was, he claimed, portable, even though its dimensions would not have made mobility an easy proposition.

In the end, around 1670, it was the Bavarian mathematician Johann Christoph Sturm (1635–1703) who invented the simplest and most manageable camera obscura, which was very quickly adopted across the whole of Europe. He explained the construction of his 'portable camera obscura' (*camera obscura portatilis*) in *Collegium Experimentale Sive Curiosum* ('Gathering of the Experimental and Curious'), published at Nuremberg in 1676 (see Fig. 4). Sturm also used a 'wooden eye, which can turn and direct itself in all directions', and placed it at the front of a

Fig. 4. Two camera obscuras, after Johann Sturm. Illustrated in Martin Frobene Ledermuller, *Amusements Microscopiques* (1768). Collection: Bibliothèque Nationale.

box of strong paper, formed of two pieces arranged one inside the other 'in order to extend or shorten the length of the chamber according to need'. Daguerre's daguerreotype camera of 1839 would be constructed on nearly the same principle, as we shall see later. Sturm then placed an inclined mirror in the movable portion of the chamber:

> Above this mirror I place a thin transparent paper soaked in oil, and I also place above it another box so that the oiled paper is enclosed in darkness, when the observer places his head in the opening to view the objects which present themselves on the paper. This dioptric and catoptric machine is then placed in front of an open window, such that the face of the objective lens is directed towards the street. All objects in the street will be presented first to the objective lens, which throws them upwardly onto the oiled paper; which represents the best-known and most realistic paintings, in that one can recognize and perfectly distinguish the faces and clothes of the people passing more than a hundred feet away.[23]

These improvements brought a very distant possibility onto the horizon: if the objective lens could be improved, and the oiled paper could be replaced with a plate sensitized with a chemical agent, we might obtain a photograph. The dream of fixing the fleeting images of the camera obscura, other than by painting, would not become a reality until the start of the nineteenth century.

For the moment, the camera obscura of the seventeenth century could be found in all the great 'cabinets of curiosities' of the period. A fashion which lasted for many centuries, the cabinet of curiosities presented rarities of nature (precious stones, foetuses, stuffed animals), scientific and optical instruments, ancient coins, engravings of the great masters, in short anything and everything which could arouse 'curiosity', inside a room or a large piece of furniture. They were also, after a fashion, pre-cinematographic museums: as well as the camera obscura, they might contain lenses, prisms, anamorphoses, picture discs, and all types of 'mirrors of pleasure' or magic mirrors, whose projections rivalled those of the camera obscura.

Magic mirrors

From its birth, the camera obscura had a poor cousin of more complex character, which followed its own independent development, enlivened by occasional encounters with its parent, the mirror. By its nature, the magic mirror could never equal the realism and precision of the camera obscura. However it did have a certain mystery, and the human being has always been fascinated by the reflection of its own image, especially when that *alter ego* is deformed by subtle variations.

Magic mirrors, enchanted mirrors, mirrors of pleasure, deceptive mirrors, coloured mirrors, mirrors of sorcery, concave, convex, multi-faceted mirrors, catoptric theatres, and catoptric boxes: there was a huge range of strange methods of transforming real vision into 'aberration'. From the point of view of pre-cinematographic history, the methods mentioned here were the most important systems of projection, apparition, and animation using mirrors. For a discussion of other related media of the time, see Jurgis Baltrušaitis' remarkable book *Le Miroir* on the 'revelations and fallacies' of catoptrics.[24]

The thirteenth-century evangelist of the camera obscura, Roger Bacon, took up the subject of mirrors in his work *De Mirabili Potestate Artis et Naturae* ('On the Marvellous Power of Art and Nature'), written to clear himself of the accusation of sorcery which his superiors brought against him in front of Pope Nicholas III. Bacon, as a good Christian, did not deny the existence of magic, since the Church implicitly recognized and admitted the presence of demons. But he maintained that Art and Science combined gave results just as marvellous, when practised by learned minds, as the satanic forces manipulated by those who practised 'goety' (from the Greek *goeteia*, sorcery). His testimony proves that by the thirteenth century, the science of mirrors was quite well advanced. With 'special devices', wrote Bacon, one could take advantage of 'the common herd with wonders which in reality did not exist'. He suggested the possibilities of catoptrics, while remaining rather coy about the 'devices' to which he referred:

> One may construct devices and mirrors such that they produce a multiple appearance, and a man may resemble an army, such that one may make appear several suns or several moons . . . One can cause great terror in an enemy town by making multitudes of stars or men appear above it, such that its inhabitants scatter in terror. One may also construct devices in which bodies appear so that the largest appear small and vice versa, or those which are high appear low, or invisible objects are made manifest.[25]

In the footsteps of philosopher-scientists such as Euclid, Ptolemy, and Witelo (or Witek, of the thirteenth century) it was once again the Italian scientist della Porta who proved to be the most communicative and imaginative on the creation of apparitions using mirrors. His aim was to inspire fear in his visitors using deforming or coloured mirrors, or to catch them unawares with unexpected projections. Della Porta was also the author of *De Humana Physiognomonia* in 1586, a work which fore-shadowed the eighteenth-century work of the 'physiognomist' Johann Casper Lavater (1741–1801). This described mirrors which stretched or shortened faces, made men older or younger, twisted them and made them ugly, or gave them the heads of donkeys, the beaks of cranes, the snouts of pigs (the formulae for these effects appeared in *Magiae Naturalis* in 1558 and 1588), all of which were an inspiration to this seeker of morphological similarities between humans and animals.

Della Porta claimed that he succeeded in creating an 'image hanging in the air' with the aid of a mirror. In the centre of a darkened room, he set up an inclined mirror on the floor. An aperture was formed in the opposite wall, in the shape of a truncated pyramid with the narrower end pointing towards the mirror. In this pyramidal aperture an image painted on a slightly transparent paper sheet could be placed. The mirror caught the image (lit from behind by the sun or an artificial light source) and reflected it onto the ceiling or a wall. In this way

> the Picture placed without, which your eye cannot see through the hole, may seem to hang pendulous in the Air; which will cause admiration to behold.[26]

This system was repeated by Jean Leurechon in 1621, who also discussed distorting mirrors, 'which show on one side a death's head and on the other a beautiful face'. Nicéron, too, made transforming mirrors, with prismatic sections cut out, which presented secret images such as political or religious anagrams.

Unusual projections were (and still are) also created by Japanese and Chinese 'magic mirrors', which are apparently very ancient in their origins. These are mirrors of cast copper or bronze; on one of their two surfaces relief designs are engraved representing flowers, animals, monsters, or lettering. The other surface, which is highly polished and slightly convex, is formed of an alloy of tin. When this polished surface is presented to the sun, it reflects a large amount of light, and the designs which appear on the reverse, non-illuminated, surface can be seen projected onto a white sheet or screen. This phenomenon may be due to very slight convex, concave, and flattened areas in the polished surface caused by the engraving of the decorated reverse surface, although there is little convincing work in the west on these curious devices.

Enter Kircher

In the middle of the seventeenth century, just as the science of catoptric and dioptric magic appeared to be making no progress, it was set back on the road by Athanasius Kircher, a man of irrepressible imagination. He succeeded in combining the two techniques of projection: the camera obscura and mirrors. He created some quite elaborate optical systems and displays of illuminated images, which however always remained completely dependent on the presence of sunlight.

Kircher was born on 2 May 1602 in the village of Geisa, near Fulda in Germany. In 1620 he entered the Society of Jesus. At this time, Germany was torn by religious and political conflict: the Thirty Years War had begun in 1618. The young Jesuit had to flee to Münster, then to Heiligenstadt in Saxony, where he studied grammar, mathematics, Hebrew, and Syriac. One day he was asked to prepare a small entertainment in honour of the Archbishop Elector of Mainz; it was presumably on this occasion that Kircher's passion for optical illusion and scenic artifice revealed itself for the first time.

In 1631 the Swedish King Gustavus Adolphus invaded Franconia. Kircher took refuge in Avignon, at the Jesuit college, and installed a laboratory in the Tower of La Motte (which was demolished in the nineteenth century). Using assemblies of mirrors, he amused himself by capturing the rays of the sun and the moon. His second book, *Primitiae Gnomonicae Catoptricae* ('First Principles of Gnomonics and Catoptrics') dealing with experiments with mirrors, was published in Avignon in 1635. Three years later, Kircher gained the chair of mathematics at the College of Rome, then the centre of the Jesuit organization. In 1637 he travelled to Syracuse and attempted to repeat the experiment in which Archimedes claimed to have succeeded in using one or more mirrors to set fire to the Roman ships which were besieging the town. Kircher painstakingly recorded all his experiments, keeping in mind a future book dedicated to light and shadow.

'It is needless to state his name: his renown is known as far as the Antipodes.' This phrase, which accompanies the portrait of Kircher in a work by Giorgio di Sepi,[27] one of his pupils, was not an exaggeration. In this engraving Father Kircher, with white beard, bright eyes, and skull-cap on his head, looks out at the reader with a malicious air. Kircher was a great collector of 'curiosities'. His museum is now dispersed throughout the whole of Europe, but in his own day it was housed in the gallery of the College of Rome. The French noblewoman Sophie of Hanover met Kircher in Rome in November 1664 and noted: 'He is a strong good man. I have still not had the liberty to view his rarities, because it is necessary to ask the permission of the Pope.'[28] Kircher was also a prolific author: when he died in Rome, on 27 November 1680, he left forty-four books of his own composition, of which about twenty were folios, and some two thousand letters which are still unpublished today.

In 1644 he completed his book *Ars Magna Lucis et Umbrae*, a true monument in pre-cinema history. Kircher dedicated it to Archduke Ferdinand, the son of his protector Emperor Ferdinand III of Austria, who had granted him the privilege of publication at Vienna on 1 June 1644. Kircher's dedication is dated 1 November 1645. *Ars Magna* appeared in Rome in 1646, just after Innocent X had been named as the 234th Pope, although a few copies exist carrying the date 1645. With its 935 folio pages, thirty-six engraved plates, and over 500 drawings, Kircher's work is certainly one of the best optical compendia of the seventeenth century. All aspects of catoptrics and dioptrics are dealt with: light, shadow, illusions, colours, refraction, reflection, projection, distortion, mirrors, lenses, and so on. It also discusses astronomy: the sun, the stars, the moon, comets, and eclipses. Everything is explained in a learned tone, with greater or lesser degrees of success.

Like della Porta in 1558, Kircher dealt with 'natural magic': that is, the study of the numerous incomprehensible phenomena of nature. True 'black' and 'white' magic, like that of the 'Master Devil' and of Albertus Magnus, was vigorously condemned. Particularly in its second part, *Ars Magna* was also a scholarly compilation of the writings of Bacon, Cardano, della Porta, d'Aguillon, Bettini, and Schwendter. Kircher, whose imagination never seems to have stopped, accompanied this catalogue with some of his own inventions, for which he had to coin new names. A maelstrom of strange words sweeps the reader along: 'Sciagnomics' (the science of measuring shadow), 'Actinobilism' (the propagation of radiation), 'Echocamptics' (the propagation of echoes). 'Parastatic magic', presented in the tenth book, 'is nothing less than a closed science to those who know nothing of light and shadow.'[29] This secret science allowed illuminated images to be shown before a large number of spectators, using apparatus whose operation was often quite complex.

Among other achievements, Kircher claimed to have succeeded in making precious stones ('emeralds, pyrope, sapphires, amethysts') appear in the interior of a darkened room. After closing all the shutters, he opened a small rectangular hole through which the sun's rays entered. The rays passed through five crystal prisms arranged horizontally in a decorated wooden frame. The rays of the solar spectrum then passed through six lenses with surface facets, placed in a circle around a seventh lens of the same diameter. The facets dispersed the coloured rays from the prisms into a thousand splinters, forming bright multicoloured patches on the wall and floor of the room.[30]

Kircher also invented a *lucerna artificiosa* ('artificial light') which created one illusion which he could not have foreseen: some of the most serious historians have been deceived into believing (some still to this day) that this was the invention of the magic lantern. In fact, it was a sort of 'wine barrel'[31] topped by a chimney, with a handle on the side. Inside was a burning candle, whose light was reflected from a parabolic mirror and concentrated by a biconvex lens. In this way, Kircher says, one would obtain

a light so bright that in the night the letters of a book, even the smallest, can be seen as distinctly as if one used a telescope. Those

Fig. 5. Metamorphosis machine, illustrated in Athanasius Kircher, *Ars Magna Lucis et Umbrae* (1646). Collection: Bibliothèque Nationale.

who see this flame from a great distance can take it to be a large fire.[32]

Kircher's *lucerna artificiosa* was nothing more than a simple projecting lamp. *Ars Magna* also contained a description of the 'catoptric theatre' which Kircher had designed: this consisted of a large box whose interior was covered with mirrors, in the centre of which a scene or figure could be placed to be multiplied many times by the mirrors.[33] Nicéron mentioned the existence of such a theatre in Rome in 1638; perhaps he was referring to Kircher's device. Nicéron also said that Hesselin, a counsellor and chamberlain of Louis XIII of France, possessed an example of the catoptric theatre:

> Is it not to become rich at no cost, at least in appearance, to see by the combination of many mirrors placed in a box to that effect, to see, I say, medals, pistols, pearls and precious stones multiplied to infinity?[34]

Kircher also described himself as the inventor of a metamorphosis machine, inspired by della Porta's distorting mirrors, although his installation was much more elaborate (see Fig. 5). Kircher's 'catoptric transformations' took place in a quite vast room. The guest who was taken into it would only see a mirror inclined towards him, high on the wall, lit from the front by the sun's light entering through a window. As he approached, the visitor would see himself in the mirror, but on his shoulders would be the head of an animal. Eight different animal heads could be made to appear in succession. To do this, Kircher had constructed a large octagonal wheel, on the sides of which he painted eight different images representing the heads of animals resting on a human neck. The wheel was hidden in a casing, open only at its upper side, with a handle on the side to rotate the eight-faced wheel. Each image was reflected by the mirror, illuminated through the window of the room. The inclination of the mirror could be controlled by a cord. 'It is certain that the head will appear sometimes as a cow, as a goat, as a bear, etc. All these will appear as though natural, but on a human neck.'[35]

What Kircher aspired to more than anything, it appears, was to astonish his followers by the almost universal nature of his knowledge. However, he did not want to pass himself off as a sorcerer, and denounced the quacks who used optics to take advantage of the credulous. Kircher's aim in revealing all these illuminated and shadowy optical tricks was partly to enlighten the general public. For him, the methods of catoptrics were the domain of experimental science, and a practical way of teaching the laws of optics and light. The spectacular effects of mirrors made his object lessons on 'natural magic' all the more effective.

Kircher's 'new cryptology'

As well as his artificial light, multiplication of precious stones, catoptric theatre, and the octagonal wheel with its animal heads, Kircher gave performances based on projection, using concave mirrors onto which letters were engraved or biconvex lenses onto which he had painted images (see Fig. 6). He called his technique, which envisaged a secret language (or at least a language reserved for the use of the initiated), the 'new cryptology' or 'catoptric alphabet'. This consisted quite simply of an alphabet of inverted letters, which were reproduced at the end of his book. Outside a camera obscura, a mirror and a powerful biconvex lens were set up on a long shaft, with an image or inscription in inverted Roman, Greek or Hebrew characters painted or engraved on the mirror —*Pax vobis* ('Peace be with you'), in the illustrated example. The sun reflected off the mirror, whose painted or engraved image was transmitted, focussed by the lens, and projected onto a white sheet inside the camera obscura.[36]

This method was inspired by earlier work. In 1588 della Porta had given instructions for projecting letters with a mirror, and in 1621 the treatise *Steganographia* by Johannes Trithemius had appeared in Germany. This was a very comprehensive work, written in a deliberately obscure style, on secret, cryptographic, and magic writing. The German Daniel Schwendter, in 1638, also described a system of projecting shadows without a lens, which certainly provided Father Kircher with some inspiration:

> To project an inscription onto a wall by shadow, thanks to a mirror, with the sun: if I face the sun and wish to project a writing in front of me onto a place in shadow, for example the name of Paul V, I attach seven plane mirrors [corresponding to the seven letters of the name 'Paulus V'] next to each other on a plank, I cut out the letters from a thick paper like board, and I glue them one after the other onto the mirrors. And since I wish now that these letters will be represented on a wall in shadow, I place the plank with the mirrors facing the sun, such that the light will be reflected onto the chosen wall, and because the letters cover a part of the mirrors, that part is

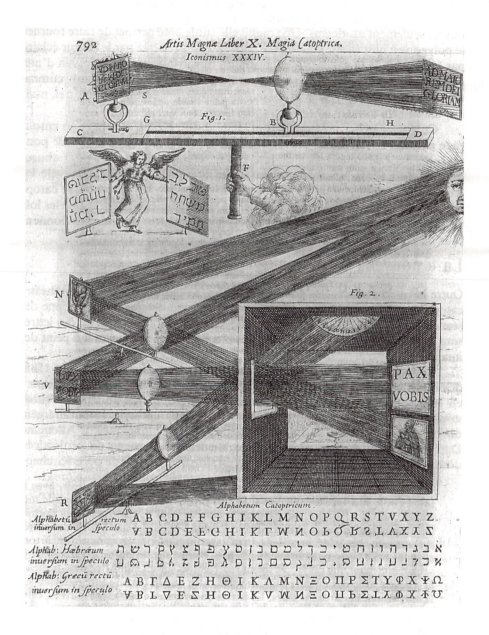

Fig. 6. Optical building for solar projection using engraved mirrors, illustrated
in Athanasius Kircher, *Ars Magna Lucis et Umbrae* (1646).
Collection: Bibliothèque Nationale.

not illuminated on the wall; but the letters appear in shadows and are recognizable in the middle of the light.[37]

Kircher therefore simply recycled the system which Schwendter had described, adding a set of lenses to the mirrors. This was a great improvement, as one of Kircher's pupils, the German Gaspar Schott, explained:

> Nowhere in literature have I seen the writings of the *Artificium Steganographicum* presented more subtly than in the *Ars Magna Lucis et Umbrae*, where Kircher sets out the new catoptric cryptology, by means of which, thanks to the catoptric art, that is to say with the aid of mirrors, two friends separated by a great distance may write to each other secretly and speak to each other, express the hidden thoughts of their souls as if they were present . . . This invention, certainly, was known at a certain time previously, in the time of Pope Paul V . . . However Father Kircher has developed and perfected this invention . . . And now, they are many who make use of the precepts of Kircher to show marvellous things to great applause and admiration from the spectators.[38]

Schott also disclosed, unfortunately without going into any amount of detail, that another Jesuit, Andreas Tacquet (1612–60), a Belgian mathematician born at Anvers, had achieved distant projection with Kircher's catoptric process, probably at Louvain about 1653–4. It is possible that Tacquet used another method described by Mario Bettini[39] in 1642 and repeated by Kircher in 1646. In this process an image was painted directly onto a large powerful biconvex lens, illuminated by the sun; perhaps Tacquet even painted his images onto plates of glass, to place them at the focus of this lens. Whatever the case, this provides a good example of public performance with illuminated images, before the appearance of the true magic lantern:

> The most excellent mathematician of Louvain, Andreas Tacquet, of our Society, presented the whole journey from China to Belgium of Father Martin Martini. And I myself saw in Rome these things realised by the same device. This invention is completely admirable and very worthy of the curiosity of kings and the greatest princes . . . We call this art Catoptric or Catoptrographic Magic.[40]

The science of illuminated projections as it stood at the middle of the seventeenth century was simultaneously highly ingenious, very complex, and extremely primitive. The human mind, following its natural inclination, sought to do better than these vague and fleeting images. It was in the course of the seventeenth century that the fundamentally important devices on which the development of the cinema would eventually rest were invented, replacing the older natural processes, which were limited by their very nature, with the mechanisms of science.

2

Light in the Darkness

The *lanterne vive*

The earlier stages of the ancestry of the cinematograph include the camera obscura, magic mirrors, and Kircher's 'cryptologic' projections. Mention of the name of Kircher, more wrongly than rightly, still tends to evoke the words 'magic lantern'. But before we come to that particular ancestor of our film projectors, we should pause in front of a simple light box, the modest pioneer of the great adventure which was to follow. This was the *lanterne vive* (literally 'bright lantern' or 'living lantern') of the Middle Ages.

The *lanterne vive* could only emit a coloured glow and did not allow true projection. A strip of translucent paper, on which were painted grotesque or devilish figures, was inserted into a cylinder of paper or decoratively pierced sheet metal. On top of the cylinder was placed a sort of propeller made of tin, which was free to rotate about an axis formed by an iron rod, and which secured the translucent drawing in place. A candle burned at the centre of the device. The heat given off by the candle caused the propeller to turn, rotating the painted strip so that the brightly coloured images travelled around the light at their centre. A viewer would see the pictures travelling round the cylinder, and projecting indistinct coloured images into the surroundings. If the cylinder was made of pierced metal, multi-coloured images could be made to dance on the surrounding walls. It was a rather limited effect, but did have a certain charm.

This small illuminated show remained very popular for a long time. In the sixteenth century, passers-by and children might stop, as night fell, in front of *lanternes vives* hanging like signs outside the shops of barbers, confectioners, and *oyers* (sellers of roast meats). The French poet

Mathurin Régnier (1573–1613), in one of his *Satires* written around 1608, wrote of an ancient Egyptian who

> . . . resembled the transparent *lanterne vive*
> Used by a baker to amuse the children,
> Where tied birds, she-monkeys, elephants,
> Dogs, cats, hares, foxes, and every strange beast,
> Run by, one after another . . .[1]

The moving bestiary of this *lanterne vive* seems to have quite captured Régnier's imagination. All the same, the images moved without true animation. The device's attraction arose from its light, the shimmering colours, and a mechanism which could appear supernatural to those who did not know its secret.

An older, and less common, design was described by Jean Prevost of Toulouse in 1584. His *lanterne*, without an adjective, showed 'by the light of a candle, horsemen and soldiers, coming and going'.[2] It was described in a small octavo book, *La Première Partie des Subtiles et Plaisantes Inventions* ('The First Book of Fine and Pleasing Inventions'), along with strange formulae for scaring the 'stupid commoners', such as placing a candle on the back of a tortoise and releasing it into a cemetery at night. The paper which surrounded Prevost's lantern was treated with nut oil to make it translucent. Using thick paper or card, he fashioned a type of wheel like 'that which turns the grinding stone of a mill'. The smoke and heat of the candle operated the wheel, which rotated a wooden platform on which a series of cut-out figures were placed. The figures cast simple shadows, rather than the traditional coloured images, onto the oiled paper as the wheel turned. Prevost tried, a little primitively, to recreate as much movement as possible by mixing warriors and animals:

> Arrange four men on horseback, each holding a lance at rest, except for the first who holds a type of trumpet to his mouth; and make sure that their front legs are raised, to represent a horse which is jumping . . . In the middle, place four helmeted harquebusiers with their swords at the ready. Lower down, arrange four pikemen, between whom, if you wish, a hound may be running after a hare, or some such fantasy. You should have this cut by a barber, since they are skilled in this lively art, and it is they who commonly keep these night lanterns against their window to amuse the passers-by, by contemplating the order of these men-at-arms . . . Then there will be the pleasure of viewing through the paper by the light of the

candle, the turns and rapid passages of these brave warriors, without their ever breaking ranks. But above all take care, as a very necessary precaution, that by some hindrance the movement does not stop: for fear that the fire will catch the fabric, at the risk of a military combustion: because it would be a great shame to lose such brave men so cheaply.[3]

In the eighteenth century, the *lanterne vive* was renamed to become, less poetically, the *lanterne tournante* ('rotary lantern'). It could be found in some cabinets of curiosities, such as that of Joseph Bonnier de la Mosson which was sold off in 1744.[4] In the nineteenth century it could be bought in markets, made by simple craftsmen; by 1884 it cost no more than 50 centimes. Even today, in some toyshops, modern versions of the old *lanterne vive* can still be found: its marvellous power is still effective, at least among children.

The family history of the magic lantern includes a few other 'lost children', which are difficult to name or illustrate with any certainty. These devices remain mysterious. Part of the problem lies in the poor interpretation of some old references, giving rise to many legends and confusions. For example, Henri Langlois, founder of the Cinémathèque Française, regretted never having tracked down for his Musée du Cinéma one of 'the multi-coloured magic lanterns described by Omar Khayyám, which brought joy to the markets of Persia in the eleventh century'.[5] He had no chance of finding such a thing: the Persian poet and mathematician Omar Khayyám, who lived in the eleventh and twelfth centuries, did not describe a magic lantern, but a shadow show enclosed in a box illuminated by the sun (a nineteenth-century English translation refers to a 'Magic Shadow-show/Play'd in a Box whose Candle is the Sun').[6] Langlois was probably confused by a poor French translation. Interesting as it is, the Khayyám reference is unclear: perhaps it refers to the traditional shadow show known as *ombres chinoises* ('Chinese shadows'), or perhaps to projection using the camera obscura. Shadow shows have not been covered in this account, since they appear to form part of a separate study.

A much more interesting lantern reference is found in an Italian manuscript preserved in the Bayerische Staatsbibliothek in Munich, dated to around 1420 and attributed to Giovanni da Fontana (1395–*c*.1455), a Venetian scholar of art and medicine. The work is entitled *Bellicorum Instrumentorum Liber cum Figuris Delineatis et Ficticiis Literis Conscriptus* ('Book of Instruments of Warfare with Drawings and Enciphered Descriptions') (see Fig. 7). Fontana describes all types of

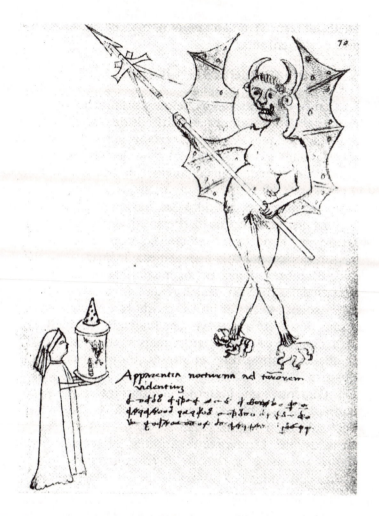

Fig. 7. Giovanni da Fontana, *Bellicorum instrumentorum liber cum figuris
delineatis et ficticiis literis conscriptus* (*c.* 1420).
Collection: Bayerische Staatsbibliothek.

equipment for warfare, including mechanical and hydraulic systems. One
page includes a drawing of a man in a cloak, holding in both hands a
large cylindrical lantern topped by a conical chimney pierced by small
holes. Inside the lantern is a rod-shaped object which may be a lamp,
and also the figure of a monstrous devil brandishing a spear, with two
wings on its back, horns on its beastly head, and claws on its feet. This
image appears again, by some miracle, on a much larger scale, in front of

the man holding the lantern. A caption explains the image: 'Nocturnal apparition for terrifying viewers.' However, the lantern shown does not have a lens tube, and the devil drawn inside the lantern is the right way up, as is its enlarged projected representation. It cannot therefore have functioned like a true magic lantern.

A second image shows a lantern with a long tube in the shape of a truncated pyramid, pointing upwards. The tube is attached to the front surface of the lantern, the rest of whose body is cylindrical. A wick is placed inside the lantern, and the body is open at the top. A note in the margin reads: 'The light of the night, which nobody in England is allowed to use, as a result of the bad use to which bandits have put it.'[7]

Fontana's text therefore describes two different lanterns. One, of conventional construction, resembles the *lanterne vive*. The other design could be a sort of hybrid lantern, simultaneously '*vive*' and 'magic'. It could perhaps have been used to project a bright image onto the type of mirror described by della Porta in 1558, to make an 'image hanging in the air' appear. We might imagine that because of the 'bad use' to which bandits applied the 'light of the night', Fontana was careful to word his description rather enigmatically, after the manner of Roger Bacon.

An anonymous text of the sixteenth century entitled *Le Journal d'un Bourgeois de Paris sous le Règne de François Ier* ('Diary of a Citizen of Paris in the Reign of François I') only makes the mystery deeper. This manuscript, preserved in the Bibliothèque Nationale, was not published until 1854.[8] It mentions a 'lantern by which one sees all things' which belonged to a priest named Cruche, a writer of farces who also performed in his dramas on a platform in Place Maubert. His lantern showed a pecking chicken underneath a salamander, 'which carried on it a thing which was enough to kill ten men'. This was a caricature of François I's love for the daughter of a courtier named Lecoq (hence the reference to the chicken, *coq* in French). The story ended badly for Father Cruche: a group of about ten gentlemen went to see 'the said comedy', violently beat up the showman, and were about to throw him into the Seine. Cruche managed to calm their anger by showing his priest's tonsure, which saved his life. Shortly afterwards, on 19 November 1515, François I forbade 'the performance of any comedy against the honour of the King and those who surround his person'.

Was Cruche's lantern 'magic' (a belief expressed by the photographer Frederic Dillaye in 1884) or '*vive*'? Or was it perhaps a type of *boîte d'optique* or peepshow, in which the pictures were lit from behind and viewed through an eyehole? Given an already imprecise description, it is safest to avoid drawing any definite conclusions.

The arrival of the magic lantern

A gap of some two centuries separates the invention of the 'light of the night' and that of the 'lantern of fear' or magic lantern. It is almost impossible to believe that it took two hundred years to add a group of lenses and a slide carrier to the lantern described by Fontana. However, there is no trace of the true magic lantern until 1659, perhaps 239 years after Fontana, seventy-one years after the second edition of della Porta's *Magiae Naturalis*, and thirteen years after the publication of Kircher's *Ars Magna Lucis et Umbrae*.

The 'magic' lantern (it was not christened as such until 1668) represents the longest-lasting, most inventive, and most artistic of the 'ancestors' which were eventually snuffed out by the birth of the cinema. For the whole length of its reign, which extended over three centuries, it presented artificial fixed and moving images to a public ever more filled with wonder, ever more demanding. It went round the world with prodigious speed. Scholars and craftsmen invented a thousand crude or ingenious ways to make its images move, to improve the 'illusion of movement', the driving force of pre-cinematographic research.

The principle of the magic lantern remained the same, with a few small variations, from the seventeenth century until the end of the nineteenth. It was an optical box made of wood, sheet metal, copper, or cardboard; it was cubic, spherical, or cylindrical in shape; and in a darkened room it projected images painted on a glass slide onto a white screen (fabric, a whitewashed wall, even white leather, in the eighteenth century). Its images covered every subject: diabolic, grotesque, erotic, scatological, religious, historical, scientific, political, and satirical. The image was generally 'fixed', but could also be 'animated' if the slide included a mechanism which allowed the subject to be moved. All that was necessary was to place the slide upside-down in the 'slide carrier', in front of light focussed from a candle or oil lamp, and immediately, as Goethe wrote in 1774,

> as soon as the little lamp appears, the figures shine on the whitened wall; and if love only shews us shadows which pass away, yet still we are happy, when, like children, we are transported with the splendid phantoms.[9]

Sometimes a silvered reflector was placed behind the flame or lamp, to concentrate the light towards the lens tube at the front of the lantern. A chimney on the roof of the box would clear the smoke from inside. The arrangement of the lenses in the tube varied from design to design, especially in the nineteenth century, but in general consisted of a powerful plano-convex lens, with its flat side facing the light source, which converged the light rays onto the painted slide, followed at the end of the lens tube by one (in the simpler designs) or two plano-convex lenses which enlarged the image and projected it the right way up.

Christiaan Huygens and Athanasius Kircher

Two great names are associated with the appearance of the magic lantern: the German Jesuit Athanasius Kircher, its pseudo-inventor, and the Dutch Protestant Christiaan Huygens, its true 'father'. Huygens, however, was loath to take personal responsibility for the dissemination of the lantern, and his exact role in this adventure has never been made sufficiently clear.

Christiaan Huygens was the first scholar in Europe known to have studied, designed, constructed, sold and distributed the magic lantern. He was also the first, it would appear, to use a moving slide. To understand why Huygens—a rationalist at heart, stern and rigid in character, sharp and demanding in intelligence—concerned himself with an instrument which might be imagined to be the preserve of whimsical souls in the spheres of entertainment or magic (Kircher was certainly one of these), we must go back to the time of Christiaan's father, Constantin Huygens.

Constantin Huygens, lord of Zuylichem, Zeelhem and Monniken-land, was born on 4 September 1596 at The Hague. On 6 April 1627, in Amsterdam, he married Susanna van Baerle, who gave him five children: Constantyn, Christiaan, Lodewijk, Philips, and Susanna. In his own time, Huygens the father was regarded as one of the best poets in the Netherlands, although his style was at times more than slightly tortuous. He was vastly learned, and corresponded with the greatest minds of Europe, such as René Descartes or the French philosopher and scholar Marin Mersenne (1588–1648).

In 1622 Constantin was in London. There he struck up a friendship with a compatriot, Cornelis Jacobsz Drebbel, who held a great fascination for him: Drebbel was an expert in black and white magic, dioptrics, and catoptrics. Born at Alkmaar in 1572, and first employed as an engraver and instrument maker at Haarlem, Drebbel then dedicated himself to the study of science and mathematics. He travelled, and was imprisoned in Prague for presenting magic shows. It was perhaps he who made appear before the Emperor Rodolphe II 'those who had held the

Roman Empire from Julius Caesar to Maurice; and that was done in a manner so alive and natural, that all those who were present at this spectacle believed that it could not have been created save with the aid of magic and necromancy'.[10] By the time Constantin Huygens met Drebbel, he had settled in London permanently.

Drebbel professed to be an alchemist, and claimed to have invented the barometer, discovered perpetual motion and perfected a design for an underwater boat. He had a laboratory, a *Wunderkammer* ('chamber of wonders') worthy of Doctor Faustus. In 1663 several parts of this great cabinet of curiosities survived at the house of Drebbel's son-in-law, one Doctor Keister.[11] Among the strange objects he collected was a mysterious optical device which captivated the young Constantin Huygens. To his father, Christiaan the Elder, who had reproached him for associating with a magician-alchemist, Constantin replied self-mockingly, on 17 March 1622:

> It made me smile that in your last, it pleased you to warn me against the magic of Drebbel, and to accuse him of being a sorcerer. But be assured that, finding nothing of the other nature in his work, there is no need of a bridle to hold me in check. Old De Gheyn will be pleased to hear that I shall bring the instrument of which he showed me the beautiful brown painting, which is certainly a masterwork of his sorcery.[12]

On 30 March 1622 Constantin described this strange device to his father a little more precisely:

> I have with me Drebbel's other instrument, which certainly makes admirable effects in painting by reflection in a dark room; it is not possible for me to describe the beauty in words; all painting is dead at this price, because here is life itself, or something more elevated, if the word is not misplaced. For the image, the outline and the movements come together naturally and in a most pleasing manner.[13]

This description is puzzling: it certainly has a suggestion of the magic lantern, although the word 'reflection' suggests the presence of a mirror. It was probably a catoptric camera obscura, a device which Drebbel had exhibited from 1608 onwards. Young Constantin returned home to his father at The Hague with his mind full of luminous visions. Drebbel died not long after, in 1634, but Constantin Huygens never forgot the lessons and projections of this great magician.

Christiaan Huygens, Constantin's second son, was born at The Hague on 14 April 1629. His father educated him in music, mathematics, and mechanics, and then sent him to the University of Leyden and Breda from 1646 to 1649. Constantin sung the praises of his genius of a son everywhere. Mersenne and Descartes paid attention to the first mathematical works by the young prodigy. After his stay in Breda, Christiaan returned to The Hague and lived with his father, brothers and sister. He published his first works on geometry in 1651 and 1654. Around this time, he also began to study dioptrics. He threw himself into reading the revered Descartes' *Discours de la Méthode*. Constantin too, no longer content with empirical lessons like those of Drebbel, began to study the elliptical and hyperbolic lenses suggested by Descartes. Christiaan, who was truly gripped by a passion for optics, worked in the attic of the house in The Hague, cutting lenses.

At the start of 1655 Christiaan employed a German workman named Caspar Kalthof (or Kaethoff, of Dordrecht), who had spent a long period in England. With Kalthof's help, in March 1655 Huygens constructed his first telescope, which was sent to the German pastor Colvius, with whom Huygens had already discussed work on dioptrics which he hoped to publish 'soon'. In September 1655, Christiaan and his brother Lodewijk travelled to Paris. Kircher had known the France of Louis XIII; Huygens, though, only dealt with the scientific circles and ministers of the reign (1643–1715) of the young Louis XIV. Some years later, on 4 June 1666, he even met the 'Sun King' in person, through the intermediaries of the King's Secretary of State Jean-Baptiste Colbert (1619–83); according to Huygens' own account Louis XIV told him 'strongly pleasing things'. It was while he was in Paris that Huygens came to know Kircher's *Ars Magna Lucis et Umbrae*.[14]

At the end of 1655, returning to The Hague, Christiaan and Lodewijk intensified their work on cutting and polishing lenses. With a telescope he had constructed, Christiaan observed the existence of a satellite (today known as Titan) around the planet Saturn. In following years, European scientists saluted successive discoveries by the Dutchman. In 1657, for example, taking up Galileo's work on the regularity of an oscillating pendulum, Huygens perfected the pendulum clock, which he gave the French name *horologe*. Huygens gave the world a machine which would measure the smallest intervals of time, thanks to the application of a regular escapement mechanism,[15] a mechanical process which would be employed once again in 1896 to drive the film through some types of cinematographic camera.

On 25 March 1658 Huygens released another thunderbolt onto the world of astronomy when he revealed that the 'arms' of Saturn, already observed by Galileo, were in fact a ring which surrounded the planet. As a result his fame spread considerably. Through discoveries such as these he came to rank alongside the great scholars of the seventeenth century: Galileo, Kepler, Descartes, and Newton, who in 1669 was still an adolescent. Next to Huygens, the work of Kircher appears quite insignificant, in the eyes of the seventeenth-century scholars just as much as for scientists of today. The unfortunate Kircher tried to cultivate the friendship of Descartes, who shied away from him, and the Protestant Huygens derided, or at least ignored, the Jesuit priest.

Christiaan Huygens' father Constantin was among the first to make fun of Kircher's works. In a letter to Descartes on 7 January 1643 Constantin warned him that Kircher's book *Magnes Sive de Arte Magnetica* ('The Magnet, or the Magnetic Art'), published in Rome in 1641, consisted 'more of posturing than of good material'. Descartes replied on 14 January, with cruel precision: 'The Jesuit [Kircher] has a great deal of boastfulness, he is more of a charlatan than a scholar.'[16] But it was only when *Ars Magna Lucis et Umbrae* was published in 1646 that Kircher's critics really went into action. The scientist Cavendish wrote:

> I have recently seen a book by the Jesuit Kircher on light and shadow. There are plenty of magnificent illustrations, which I suspect have not much substance behind them. Monsieur Gassendi [a French astronomer] does not recommend it. I therefore have no wish to purchase it, nor even to read it.[17]

Constantin Huygens took up the attack in a letter addressed to Mersenne, taking great delight in poking fun at the *Ars Magna*, the 'large volume by Kircherus', in which the 'miserable gnomonics so often repeated by those people [the Jesuits] occupies fully two-thirds of his book.' Constantin ended his letter with an incredible story, in itself worthy of a place in the pages of *Ars Magna*:

> You will know for something as strange as it is true, that serious people of age and position declare that they have seen taken prisoner at Anvers, during our recent wars, a man who has the ability to see through clothes; to show that it is not a piece of cunning, when the wife of his Gaoler went to see him with some other women, to console him in his distress, they were truly astonished to see him smile, and pressing him to say what had been the cause he replied coldly, *because there is one among you who is not wearing a shift*, which she had to admit. Consider the above and conclude that Kircherus

will not forget it in his second edition, because that could truly be titled *Ars Magna*.[18]

As for the young Christiaan Huygens—he was 17 years old in 1646—his opinion coincided with those of Descartes and his father, but with a little more restraint. From the catalogue of Christiaan's library, published after his death in 1695, we know that he kept several of Kircher's books close at hand; but neither of the two editions of *Ars Magna* was included in that magnificent collection.[19]

Huygens' moving slide

In 1659, already at the height of fame after his discovery of the rings of Saturn, Huygens drew ten macabre little pictures in one of his manuscripts, described as 'For representations by means of convex glasses in a lantern'.[20] The images represent a skeleton, sometimes enclosed in a circle, removing its skull from its shoulders and replacing it, and also moving its right arm. In the penultimate illustration the skeleton, with its own head on its shoulders, is shown juggling a second head in the air. The sequence of images is quite remarkable because of its clearly indicated desire for artificial recreation of motion: dotted lines show the required movement of the skeleton's arm. This is the earliest known representation of a moving slide for the magic lantern (see Fig. 8).

To make this moving slide, Huygens probably superimposed two sheets of glass: one fixed, representing the skeleton without the skull and perhaps without the right arm; and one movable, on which he painted the right arm and skull only. This type of slide remained in widespread use until the end of the nineteenth century. For example, around 1850 the London firm Newton & Co. was offering a moving slide featuring a remarkably detailed image of a skeleton; by pulling the movable glass the skeleton could be made to come apart completely, with bones going in all directions.

Huygens borrowed the idea for his slide from the painting *The Dance of Death* by the German Hans Holbein (1497–1543). In 1538 Holbein provided a magnificent set of illustrations for the book *Les Simulachres et Historiees Faces de la Mort* ('The Simulacra and Fabled Faces of Death'), printed at Lyon. These morbid engravings, sometimes terrifying and full of devilish movement, fascinated Huygens. In 1646 he made a large copy of Holbein's skeletons on the garden wall of his house in The Hague:

Fig. 8. Christiaan Huygens, animated magic lantern slide, drawn in 1659.
Collection: Bibliothèque Nationale.

> I have painted in our garden some figures as large as life, in charcoal
> mixed with oil and in white crayon, against the fencing which
> separates our garden from that of Count Maurits, they are the
> figures of Holbeen's *Dodendans* [*Todtentanz*, 'Dance of Death']
> which, having been as small as a finger, I have enlarged to the
> height just mentioned.[21]

In 1659, therefore, Huygens knew the secret of the lantern.
He probably used it to amuse his friends and family. But when had
he become a 'projectionist' or 'lanternist'? It is easy to put forward
hypotheses: very much ahead of his time in science and optics, he had
perhaps discovered the principle of the lantern by himself or with his
assistant Kalthof. Or perhaps he had set out to simplify Kircher's

'cryptological' processes. Or perhaps, inspired by his father Constantin's stories about Drebbel's catoptric camera obscura, he had the idea of constructing a device capable of creating even greater wonders, to re-create his father's wonderful memories.

Huygens knew how to bring movement to an image projected onto a screen: paradoxically, this first illuminated artificial recreation of life was a representation of death. This achievement of animated projection was certainly a considerable event. Shortly after 1659 the rumour was circulating in Rome that a 'Lantern' (not yet christened 'magic', and referred to respectfully with a capital 'L') existed at Huygens' house. One Father Guisony wrote a long missive to Huygens on 25 March 1660, including this important sentence:

> The good man Kirkher is doing a thousand tricks with the magnet in the gallery of the College of Rome here; if he had the invention of the Lantern, he would truly be terrifying the cardinals with ghosts.[22]

This seems to confirm that Kircher, in 1660 just as in 1646, was completely unaware of the invention of the magic lantern, whose invention has therefore been attributed to him inaccurately.

On 12 October 1660 Christiaan Huygens left The Hague for Paris, arriving there on 28 October. He was welcomed eagerly by the scientific community, and met Pierre Petit on 16 December. Petit (1598–1677) was a middle-ranking mathematician and scientist, who since 1642 had been adviser, engineer and surveyor to Louis XIV, shortly afterwards becoming the Intendant-General of Fortifications. Petit corresponded with Mersenne, Descartes, and the mathematician Blaise Pascal (1623–62). He welcomed Huygens with obsequious respect at his house located behind the Hospice des Quinze-Vingt in Paris, close to the site of the modern Gare de Vincennes. Petit proudly showed Huygens his cabinet of curiosities: 'very well-made' parabolic mirrors, Christiaan noted, as well as spectacle lenses ('too thin'), magnets, 'mirror lamps', clocks, and compasses. Among other encounters in Paris, on 20 February 1661 Huygens went to see a show of 'Italian marionettes' organized by M. de Guederville. In his diary he noted how they were animated, 'by stiff metal wires which are concealed by the feathers which they have on their heads'. On 17 March 1661 Balthazar de Monconys paid Huygens a visit. The names of Petit and de Monconys have a place in the history of projection and will reappear in our story.

Huygens had brought with him to Paris a long-distance telescope and two microscopes which he had made: perhaps he was also carrying a magic lantern, though there is no mention of it in his diary.[23] On 30 March 1661 he travelled to England, where on 3 May he went to see the London optician John Reeves, one of the great names of projection in Britain. It is perhaps not entirely surprising that shortly after Huygens' journey the magic lantern appeared in the hands of Petit, de Monconys, and Reeves, all of whom were his correspondents and friends, as if he had been sowing the seeds as he travelled around.

Huygens returned to The Hague on 27 May 1661 and set to work again: the editing of his book on dioptrics and light was proving especially difficult. Learned and revolutionary theories were taking shape, and as far as can be judged Huygens did not consider the magic lantern to be among his important works. The excitement which projection generated among his friends was of only passing interest to him. Probably it was the lantern's dual nature which bothered him: it was an interesting optical instrument, but the grotesque and devilish scenes which it projected made it less serious, less scientific; Huygens did not imagine that it could be used to represent scientific images, for example. For him, the device was suitable for putting in a cabinet of curiosities, alongside the marionettes, camera obscura, and anamorphoses. It was an instrument of entertainment for the 'pleasure of the evening', as it would be termed in the eighteenth century. Immersed in his research on the theory of the pulsations of light, Huygens had mentally classified the lantern as a pastime of secondary importance.

This was very different from the view of his father Constantin, for whom this optical box revealed marvels even more stunning than those Drebbel had shown him. He was enthusiastic about the lantern, and asked his son for an example of it in 1662. A ridiculous family quarrel began, resulting in an estrangement of several years—not between father and son, but between Christiaan and the lantern. Constantin asked his son to make a lantern for him in February or March 1662. Christiaan had to agree; he could not refuse his father. But, as he complained to his brother Lodewijk:

The Hague, 5 April 1662.
Here is another commission which my Father has given me, to arrange for him a lantern with two or three different pictures to be shown with it. I can make no reply to him except that I shall do what he wishes, and as quickly as is possible for me: but to you I confess that these commissions inconvenience me greatly, and that many others as well as my Father will ask me for similar things. You

would not believe the difficulty with which I occupy myself with such trifles, which already seem quite old to me, and in addition I am ashamed that people will know that they came from me. People are obliging enough to make it appear that they admire them, but afterwards they make fun of them and not without reason. For the future, if there is no other way, I beg of you to divert any similar chores away from me.[24]

Huygens' displeasure is quite clear. He was afraid that his lantern, or even worse he himself, would become a subject of ridicule, 'and not without reason'. Although he wrote that this 'trifle' was 'already quite old', he unfortunately neglected to specify that oldness. He seems to imply, with shame, that it was he who had invented the magic lantern: 'it comes from me.' But whether this refers to the concept of the device, or to actual examples constructed in the attic in The Hague, is unclear.

Although Huygens was reluctant to produce a lantern for his father, he seems to have responded differently to orders for purchase coming from abroad. The scholars of the seventeenth century often put their equipment on the market: a very lucrative activity, inaugurated by Galileo and adopted particularly by the scientists Chérubin d'Orléans, Robert Hooke, and Pierre Borel. In that same year, 1662, the Duke and Marshal of France Antoine de Grammont (1604–78), whom Huygens had probably met during his journey to Paris, asked him for a magic lantern, which appears to prove that the Dutchman was one of the few—possibly the only one—who possessed the secret of this device. On 12 April 1662 Christiaan wrote to Lodewijk that 'the glasses for the lantern and for the telescope for Monsieur le Mareschal de Grammont are already made and will soon be put into place.'[25] It therefore seems quite clear that one of the first magic lanterns constructed at The Hague arrived in France around 1662.

However, tension between Constantin and his son was increasing. Christiaan never delivered the promised lantern, since he had learned with horror of the true motive behind this request: Constantin wanted to show the magic lantern in Paris, before the Court at the Louvre. For Christiaan, a scientist of international reputation, who supplied Louis XIV with pendulum clocks, and who enjoyed the best of relations with the most serious minds of his time, this would have been a complete disgrace. The Huygens were scholars, not magicians like Drebbel and Kircher.

In order to obey his father while at the same time safeguarding his dignity, Christiaan planned to provide him with a lantern, but with one lens fewer than usual: that is to say a lantern which was completely unusable. He revealed this scheme to his brother Lodewijk on 19 April 1662:

> Since I have promised to send the lantern it must go, for I do not know how to invent a worthwhile excuse to avoid it. But when it arrives, if you consider it appropriate, you will easily make it incapable of use by removing one of the two glasses which are close to each other, so that there are still two remaining, since there are three in total. I will appear to be unaware of what is lacking, and by means of these explanations as much time will pass as is necessary. And all this is for the best: because it seems to me that ου πρεπει [it is not proper] for my Father to play with those marionettes at the Louvre, and that I am well aware that you would not be pleased to assist him there like cousin Micheli with the Seigneur d'Aumale.[26]

The first magic lanterns of the seventeenth century had a quite simple optical combination, but already it was essential to be familiar with it, and especially to have good lenses, without veins or air bubbles, pale in colour, and transparent. Huygens himself was a master of the art of casting lenses. The Netherlands was one of the leaders, along with Italy and Venice, in the manufacture of optical lenses, thanks to Huygens himself and the workshop of the Musschenbroeks of Leyden. For his lanterns, Huygens used one convex lens (forming a 'condenser' to concentrate the light onto the slide) and two biconvex objective lenses to transmit the projected image. Later in his career, around 1685, he worked on the phenomenon of chromatic aberration, which deformed projected images and surrounded them with a coloured fringe, but never succeeded in solving this problem.

Optical glass of this period was usually made of a mixture of sand, soda, borax, lime, and magnesia (magnesium oxide). The process of melting the mixture was delicate: the heat could form drops and streaks in the material, and cooling sometimes caused flecks and channels, making the lens practically useless. Polishing was done with sand, but Huygens, who readily revealed his methods to other scholars, such as the French Jesuit Claude-François Milliet Dechales, sometimes preferred 'other better materials, such as the spoltiglia which the mirror makers of Venice use, which they say is calcinated emery'. According to Huygens, several tens of hours of work were needed to obtain a good lens:

> After having rounded the glass in a highly concave bowl, and having made it of equal thickness throughout, I give it its first shape with

coarse sand without water, and then with sand which has been passed through a very fine sieve . . . I add some water, and with this sand I complete the smoothing of the glass, I use some eight or nine hours for each face of these large glasses.[27]

In the middle of the seventeenth century the complexity of lens manufacture remained the main obstacle to the spread of the lantern. Huygens could therefore deceive his father with complete peace of mind: Constantin was incapable of casting, cutting and polishing a new lens with the precise characteristics of the two others in the lantern's lens tube. However, Constantin could acquire the missing lens from elsewhere, for example from the Musschenbroeks. So Christiaan suffered a strange loss of memory: all of a sudden, he could no longer recall the optical combination of the lantern. In spite of all his knowledge, he wrote without humour to Lodewijk (who perhaps had taken his father's side, since Christiaan seems to have mistrusted him), he could not manage it. In short, the lantern he had promised his father could not be delivered. Huygens stalled, punning on the French verb *lanterner* (to keep someone waiting around) in his description to his brother:

> 17 August 1662.
> I still do not know when Monsieur Chieze will depart, sometimes Busero, sometimes Ketting *lanternes* him. It appears at least that he is doing what he can to hurry himself up. I had planned to *lanterne* him again on his departure, that is to say to put him in charge of the lantern which I have made for My Father; but he will be relieved of this, because in spite of all my work and knowledge I have not been able to manage it. I speak the truth, and the brother of Zeelhem can testify how my effort has been in vain, without being able to fit up the same as my first one which I made before, having removed the lenses a long time ago, I do not know how to find where they are at this time. Perhaps Signor Padre will no longer remember, but in case he does, let him know the above reasons, and what is more that I am close to making him a Telescope, microscope and all that he wants, except for the Lantern, whose invention must be counted *inter artes deperditas* [among the lost arts].[28]

The tone of this letter is too mischievous to allow its explanations to be taken at face value, and in any case they are hardly credible from a learned mind such as Huygens. 'Signor Padre' was well and truly fooled, and never did show the magic lantern at the Louvre. The Huygens honour was safe. For the next two years, at least on the evidence of his surviving correspondence, Huygens never once mentioned the magic lantern. On 3 May 1662, shortly before declaring formally to his father and brother that the secret of the device had disappeared from his memory, he wrote to Lodewijk with a curious remark on the magic lantern and retinal persistence:

> You will make of the Lantern as Heaven directs you: the most serious defect will be that of the length of the days, for as long as daylight lasts it is impossible to make these representations unless one places oneself inside a dark room; that arises from the impression which light makes on the eyes, which does not diminish for quite a long time afterwards.[29]

Perhaps to discourage his father and brother from their interest in the lantern, Huygens slightly exaggerated the strength of the phenomenon of the impressions of light on the eye. Almost word for word, his remark recalls della Porta's advice of 1558, concerning the duration of the dazzling caused by outside sunlight on entering the camera obscura.

In August 1662, then, Huygens abandoned the magic lantern in a corner of his cabinet of curiosities. He had removed the lenses, as he later admitted, presumably so that nobody would be able to use it without his permission. We do not know if he continued to sell it in other countries. The device, according to Huygens, now ranked *inter artes deperditas*. This assertion, probably intended for his father Constantin, was soon to be given the lie in no uncertain manner.

3

The 'Lantern of Fear' Tours the World

Around 1663, after a flurry of scientific exchanges between England, Holland, Italy, and France, the magic lantern finally escaped from Huygens' attic. The device, which a year earlier Huygens had dismissed as a 'lost art', in fact lost nothing but its secrecy. Its irresistible fascination allowed it to spread with great speed. It was immediately hawked around the entire world by scholars, travelling showpeople, craftsmen, Jesuits, opticians . . . This small scientific wonder spread just as quickly as the plague or cholera, and although some uncertainty still exists, it appears that Christiaan Huygens had been the unwitting first carrier of the germ. Its dazzling success was not unlike that of another box of optical tricks, named *Cinématographe*, some centuries later.

England: John Reeves

A 'lantern' was mentioned in London, in 1663, by the French traveller Balthazar de Monconys (1611–65), who was well acquainted with the small scientific world and the latest inventions of the day; he had met Drebbel's son-in-law, had admired Huygens since 1661 (the Dutchman had a very low opinion of de Monconys, because of his interest in alchemy), and in 1660 had made the acquaintance of 'father Kirker' (*sic*). On 15 May 1663 de Monconys was in London where, on the advice of Sir Kenelm Digby, he went to see 'Rives'—either John Reeves or his father Richard. 'I went to see him; but as the weather was dark and rainy, he put me off until another day,' wrote de Monconys. On 17 May he visited Westminster, and then

> On our return, after having dined we went again to Longueker [Long Acre], to the house of Mr. Rives, who makes Telescopes,

which he sells at six pounds sterling each. But he had none ready, and he put us off to another occasion, as much for that as to see the effect of a dark lantern [*lanterne sourde*], which had a complete hemisphere of crystal [the condenser lens] of about three inches in diameter, and which could throw for a long distance the representation of objects which he placed between the light and this crystal, by means of a sheet of glass on which these objects are painted, the strip or sheet he made slide in a frame in the square casing which extends outside the lantern, and which encloses the half-globe of crystal.[1]

Richard Reeves was the most famous English optician of his time. According to the scientist Robert Hooke, Reeves succeeded in cutting lenses with a focal length of 60 feet, and he constructed the first reflecting telescope (invented by James Gregory) around 1655. In September 1664 Richard Reeves killed his wife; he was released after only two months in prison, to continue the running of his London shop, situated in Long Acre, with his son John. It was not possible to let the best optician of the Royal Society rot in gaol.

The Reeveses became dealers in lanterns and also visited the homes of the rich to give private demonstrations of projection. For example, the great citizen and celebrated diarist Samuel Pepys, a high functionary in the Admiralty and Member of Parliament, invited one of the Reeveses to his home on 19 August 1666:

But by and by comes by agreement Mr. Reeves, and after him Mr. Spong; and all day with them, both before and after dinner till 10 a-clock at night, upon opticke enquiries—he bringing me a frame with closes on, to see how the rays of light do cut one another, and in a dark room with smoake, which is very pretty. He did also bring a lantern with pictures in glass to make strange things appear on a wall, very pretty.[2]

John Reeves had corresponded with Huygens since 1661. As already mentioned, it seems very possible that the Dutchman communicated the secret of the lantern to the English optician during his journey to London in April 1661.

Walgenstein, the 'curious Dane'

In 1664 the magic lantern appeared in the hands of a Dane, Thomas Rasmussen Walgenstein (1627–81). He appears to have been the first person to circulate the lantern from town to town around Europe, not by discussions between scholars but by playing the true role of the 'lanternist', the 'exhibitor of images'. According to contemporary accounts, Walgenstein was a very learned mathematician who seemed to take pleasure in astonishing his followers, somewhat after the manner of Kircher. Around 1659 he left Denmark for Italy. In Rome, on 2 September 1660, he astonished Balthazar de Monconys by showing him several bizarre formulae, such as one for 'printing all sorts of herbs on paper by smoking them over the flame of a lamp, then placing them between two sheets of paper, and passing a polishing tool over the top'.[3] Monconys referred to him as 'Walguestein [sic], the curious Dane'.

In 1660 Walgenstein, like Kircher at the same date, does not seem to have known of the invention of the true magic lantern; he certainly did not mention it to Monconys, who was always on the trail of new 'curiosities'. Yet four years later, the Dane not only possessed an example, but was organizing his own projection shows in Paris. We have a description of Walgenstein's lantern, thanks to Pierre Petit, who attended one of the Dane's Paris shows in amazement; Walgenstein allowed him to examine the strange box of optics, which Petit poetically christened the *lanterne de peur* ('lantern of fear'), since he found its effect so astonishing.

Filled with enthusiasm, Petit in turn dreamed of possessing a lantern for the cabinet of curiosities at his house in the Quinze-Vingt. He therefore ordered a 'lantern of fear' from a Parisian craftsman. It was not very difficult to construct, but the optical system in the sliding lens tube always remained the stumbling block. Petit therefore consulted Christiaan Huygens: he was aware that the Dutchman had known the combination of the lantern for some time.

> Paris, 28 November [1664]
> . . . I am engaged in setting one to work but he always makes mistakes concerning the work and the lenses. Convey to me if you please the size and proportion of the two lenses which you placed and which you judge it necessary to place in this lantern of fear. For I have not yet realized my own after the first attempts I have made. It appeared to me that the lantern of the Dane which I have seen had the lens marked A in the drawings adjacent to the hole of the lantern and at about two or three inches as at B a convex [lens] of seven or eight inches focus and at the end of the tube C another of about twelve inches which may be moved away from or towards B according to whether one wishes to present the pictures close or far away. But as one learns certain particularities from those who have

already created an object and which can reduce the enquiries or avoid the faults which one makes in the first attempts on a subject, I ask you to convey to me what was the construction of your lantern and all its dimensions.

I have already made a lamp stronger than any I have already seen which carries a concave mirror behind it and a convex lens in front in order to make the light greater. For the lantern, I would like to make it six inches square and nine in height. For the lenses, I believe them large enough at an inch and a half in diameter and from six to twelve inches in focus. If you have any particulars of the above I ask you to convey them to me and if there is any rule for the disposition and separation of the lenses ABC and likewise for their focus if one should wish to throw the images from forty to fifty feet rather than the length of a room, would you please indicate those to me also . . .
I am your servant always, Petit.[4]

So according to Petit, Walgenstein's lantern had three lenses: the first was convex and hemispherical and acted as a condenser; Petit describes the second as convex, but in his accompanying drawing (see Fig. 9) it appears biconvex. The third lens at the end of the sliding tube also appears to be biconvex. Petit wanted to project at a distance of between 12 and 16 metres from the lantern to the screen, and hinted that Walgenstein's lantern could not project beyond the 'length of a room'. From Petit's description, Walgenstein can also be credited with the first use of a reflector behind the lamp of a magic lantern. Huygens' reply to Petit was dry and evasive:

[The Hague, 11 December 1664]
Lantern, a long time ago the lenses were removed without my having known the size of them all, one was six inches, my lantern was not well adjusted. It was without a concave mirror. It was necessary to place the flame in the middle, between the centre and the mirror or slightly towards the centre.[5]

Huygens hastily sketched the layout of a lens tube to accompany his scanty explanation. Petit's letter clearly irritated him: while the Parisian was very courteous, Huygens' reply was almost rude. Mention of the lantern no doubt awakened some of Huygens' worst memories, such as the disputes with his father and the recent death of his workman Kalthof. Perhaps he was also offended to learn that the lantern was becoming the centre of an increasing interest.

As for Walgenstein, he continued to exhibit the lantern successfully.

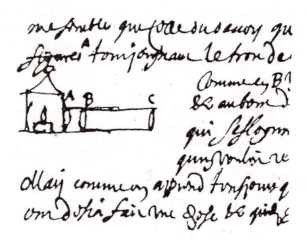

Fig. 9. The sketch of the optical tube drawn by Pierre Petit in his letter to
Huygens in 1664. Collection: David Robinson.

In 1665, a year after his Paris shows, he was in Lyon. This show
was another triumph: now it was the turn of the French Jesuit
Claude Dechales to go home in amazement. Some years later, in 1674,
Dechales published four enormous volumes in Latin, *Cursus seu Mundus
Mathematicus* ('The Course, or the Mathematical World'). In the second
volume, dedicated to dioptrics, he gave what was probably the first
scientific description published in France of the *laterna magica*:

> A learned Dane well versed in dioptrics, passing through Lyon in
> that year of 1665, showed among other things a lantern from which
> emerged a tube of about one foot in length, which was drawn out to
> a greater or lesser length, as the situation demanded. One could
> extend the tube to the length required, the tube being equipped with
> two convex lenses, which were unequal: that facing the interior
> being of a larger segment of a sphere and the other occupying the
> exterior part of the tube being smaller in relation to the larger
> sphere. In the interior of the lantern, a lamp fitted with a wick
> gave a bright light; behind the lamp was a concave mirror whose
> diameter was about two inches. All these things were arranged such
> that the light reflected by the mirror arrived at the first lens: the
> tube being adjusted and the lantern being lit, such that one could
> test the strength of the mirror, much light appeared and one saw a
> greater illumination on the wall than on the mirror . . . The image
> should not be larger than the lens, either the same size or smaller; it

was painted with strongly diluted transparent colours . . . One viewed the image on the wall, much larger in size, very clear in its colours, visible in the middle of a brightly illuminated circle . . . The wall on which the image appeared was at a distance of twenty feet [about 6.5 m].[6]

Dechales gave a sketch of Walgenstein's lantern: it resembled that drawn by Petit in 1664 (cylindrical body, long lens tube at the front, conical cap) but the optical system was not the same, with only two biconvex lenses. In both designs, the concave mirror formed a reflector for the flame of a small candle. Both Petit's and Dechales' sketches show a candle, but Dechales mentions a wick—this probably refers to a small bottle or container, filled with paraffin, wine spirit or olive oil.

Walgenstein's shows made enough of a noise to raise an echo from Kircher, in 1671, in the second edition of his *Ars Magna Lucis et Umbrae*. Kircher wrote:

> the Dane Thomas Walgenstein, a mathematician of great renown who took up my invention of the light of which we gave the description on p.767, brought it into a better form; then sold this device at great profit to various princes of Italy.[7]

After his travels in France and Italy, where he both showed and sold the lantern, Walgenstein returned to Denmark, taking his projection equipment with him. In Copenhagen in 1670 he gave a memorable lantern show to Frederick III (1609–70), King of Denmark and Norway since 1648:

> Magic lantern or miracle-worker: among these lanterns, which are presented by several inventors, those which the Danish optician Thomas Walgenstein has produced with great skill have easily taken the prize. With his lantern, he showed various things to the divine Frederick III of Copenhagen, among which must not be forgotten the figure of death, represented to the king some days before his demise. This figure inspired some horror among those surrounding the king, but the king alone, after reprimanding their cowardice, said that above all this spectacle did not appear terrible to him, but joyful, to such an extent that he could not see enough of it. He desired that it should be presented three times, at certain intervals.[8]

The metaphysical scenes of Walgenstein's lantern created a new and distressing sensation: *Memento Mori*. Having apparently predicted the death of Frederick III later in that same year, Walgenstein became a celebrity in Denmark until his own death in 1681. Ten years later, when the Danish naturalist Oligerus Jacobaeus published the catalogue of the museum of curiosities belonging to King Frederick IV (1671–1730), Walgenstein's lanterns took pride of place.

England: Robert Hooke

Leaving the phantasmagorias of Copenhagen, we return to Britain. On 17 August 1668 the scientific journal *Philosophical Transactions* published an article by the physicist Robert Hooke (1635–1703), a Fellow of the Royal Society. This gave, in rather circumspect terms, the secret of an invention which Hooke claimed as his own, consisting of the projection with convex lenses of transparent images painted on glass. The word 'lantern' did not appear in the article. In fact Hooke was proposing a hybrid system, inspired by both the traditional non-portable camera obscura and by Kircher's 1646 methods of placing painted mirrors and lenses outside the camera obscura.

Hooke claimed that 'his' invention was new. However it certainly predated the publication of the article by an unknown length of time, because the editor John Martyn remarked in conclusion:

> So far our Inventor; who has not contented himself with the bare speculation, but put the same in practice some years since, in the presence of several members of the R[oyal] *Society*, among whom the *Publisher* had the good fortune to see the successful performance of what is here delivered.[9]

'Some years' before 1668, therefore, Hooke had presented projected images in front of an audience. Along with the Reeveses, he could perhaps be regarded as one of the earliest English projectionists. A mathematician, physicist, engineer, and astronomer, and a brilliant mind, Hooke was also unfortunately a slightly disturbed character, as was his contemporary Isaac Newton. David Landes defines him perfectly:

> He was certainly inventive to the highest degree, but he liked to keep the secret of his inventions until he could exploit them to his own profit in a way which would satisfy him—all too often this came down to putting them in the drawer and then, when someone else proposed a similar system, Hooke would angrily claim his precedence.[10]

As if by coincidence, Hooke's worst enemy and principal rival, with whom he contested many inventions (including the spiral clock spring, among others), was none other than Christiaan Huygens. Perhaps, in 1668, Hooke had heard tell of the Dutchman's 'lanterns', for example through Richard Reeves, who also worked for him. He was certainly hurried into publishing 'his' invention, in an attempt to pull the rug out from under Huygens' feet. Hooke certainly deserves credit, but his claim is ambiguous, since even if this was a projection process with glass slides (or even objects or living animals), lenses and a white screen, it still lacked the box, the lantern itself which simplified everything and made the whole assembly easily portable.

Hooke revealed his method like this:

> This *Optical* Experiment, here to be described, is New, though easy and obvious; and hath not, that I know, been ever made by any other person this way. It produces Effects not only very delightful, but to such as know not the contrivance, very wonderful; so that Spectators, not well versed in *Opticks*, that should see the various Apparitions and Disappearances, the Motions, Changes, and Actions, that may this way be represented, would readily believe them to be super-natural and miraculous, and would as easily be affected with all those passions of Love, Fear, Reverence, Honour, and Astonishment, that are the natural consequences of such belief. And had the *Heathen* Priests of old been acquainted with it, their Oracles and Temples would have been much more famous for the Miracles of their Imaginary Deities. For by such an Art as this, what could they not have represented in their Temples? Apparitions of Angels, or Devils, Inscriptions and Oracles on Walls; the Prospect of Countryes, Cities, Houses, Navies, Armies; the Actions and Motions of Men, Beasts, Birds, &c., the vanishing of them in a cloud, and then appearing no more after the cloud is vanisht. And indeed almost any thing, that may be seen, may by this contrivance be very vividly and distinctly represented, in such a manner, that, unless to very curious and sagacious persons, the means how such Apparitions are made, shall not be discoverable.[11]

As in the construction of a simple camera obscura, Hooke pierced a hole in the wall. One could also use a window, so long as it was covered with cloth or a plank to leave an opening of only 'about a foot in diameter':

> Without this hole, or Casement open'd at a convenient distance, (that it may not be perceived by the Company in the room) place the Picture or Object, which you will represent, inverted, and by

means of Looking-glasses placed behind, if the picture be *transparent*, reflect the rayes of the Sun so, as that they may pass through it towards the place, where it is to be represented; and to the end that no rayes may pass besides it, let the Picture be encompass'd on every side with a board or cloth. If the Object be a *Statue*, or some living Creature, then it must be very much enlighten'd by casting the Sun-beams on it by Refraction, Reflexion, or both. Between this Object, and the Place where 'tis to be represented, there is to be placed a broad Convex-glass, ground of such a convexity, as that it may represent the Object distinct on the said place; which any one, that has an insight in the *Opticks*, may easily direct. The nearer it is placed to the object, the more is the Object magnified on the Wall, and the further off, the less; which diversity is effected by Glasses of several spheres. If the Object cannot be *inverted* (as 'tis pretty difficult to do with Living Animals, Candles &c.) then there must be *two* large Glasses of convenient Spheres, and they plac'd at their appropriated distances (which are very easily found by tryals) so as to make the representations *erect* as well as the Object.

These Objects, Reflecting and Refracting Glasses, and the whole Apparatus; as also the Persons employ'd to order, change and make use of them, must be placed without the said high window or Hole, so that they may not be perceived by the Spectators in the room; and the whole Operation will be easily perform'd.[12]

Hooke kept to himself the methods of preparing the objects, arranging the lenses, catching the rays of the sun, and 'making the representations of the Sky (by the help of other glasses) and of Clouds (by the help of Smoak)'. He added that if one wished to project at night, the transparent image would have to be illuminated 'by the help of torches, lamps, or other bright lights, plac'd about the Objects'.[13]

Hooke's account was simultaneously rather overwritten and more than a little secretive. Enigmatic as it was (for example, he did not specify whether he used a lens tube to mount the 'Glasses of several spheres'), this article clearly announced the possibilities offered by dioptric and catoptric projection: 'living' images, created by placing real animals between the lens and the light source; scenic tricks such as disappearance, transformation and substitution; and productions of a whole range of fantastic visions, with the appearance of the sky, clouds and demons, and of *movement* (the word appears twice) of humans and animals.

Much later, in 1692 (although the permission for publication dated from 1690), the Irishman William Molyneux (1656–98), a member since 1683 of the Dublin Philosophical Society (later the Royal Irish Academy), published a scientific description of the true 'Magick Lantern, sometimes called Lanterna Megalographica',[14] in *Dioptrica Nova, a Treatise of Dioptricks*. Molyneux's design offered a conceptual simplification of Hooke's system. His small lantern, which was made completely of tin-plate, was fitted with a strong hemispherical plano-convex lens and a second biconvex lens. The image projected was 'usually some Ludicrous or frightful Representation, the more to divert the Spectators'.[15] Molyneux added that the optical combination of the lantern had become 'so ordinary' that even the least able glass-grinder would be able to construct an example.

Italy: Eschinardi and Kircher

1668 was an important date in the history of 'pre-cinema' media: as well as Hooke's article in *Philosophical Transactions*, another scientific book devoted several pages to the magic lantern. Back at the College of Rome, the Italian mathematician Francesco Eschinardi (1623–1703), who had entered the Society of Jesus in 1637, had been initiated at an unknown date into the secret of the magic lantern. In 1666, he published *Centuria Problematum Opticorum* ('One Hundred Problems of Optics'), followed two years later by *Centuria Opticae Pars Altera* ('Another Part of the Hundred'). In the 1668 volume Eschinardi, less mysteriously than Hooke, clearly referred to a 'laterna, quam dicunt magicam' ('lantern, which they call magic').[16] In this account, the lantern was at last officially christened 'magic'. It changed its name several more times before the end of the seventeenth century, but it was the adjective 'magic' which stuck, much to the displeasure of some scientists of the time who preferred words such as 'megalographic' or 'thaumaturgic', which they considered altogether more serious.

Eschinardi described the optical systems of two different magic lanterns. The first had only a single convex lens, which must have given mediocre images; the highly convex single lens would certainly transmit more light, but the images would not appear so clearly. The other lantern, of more conventional construction, had two lenses like the design given by Dechales. Eschinardi's text was entirely theoretical: for him, the lantern was just one problem of optics and geometry among a hundred others. All the same, he noted that it was an 'admirable invention', although he said nothing about its origins or its creator. Eschinardi's account never mentions the name of Kircher, even though they both taught at the College of Rome.

In 1671 Kircher published the second edition of *Ars Magna Lucis et Umbrae*. This did not differ greatly from the first edition, but included three pages 'on the construction of the magic or thaumaturgic lamp'.[17] Making up for his late start, Kircher now threw himself into the mysteries of the magic lantern, unfortunately without throwing very much light on them at all.

Kircher claimed—with some success, since this legend was to last for centuries—that the invention of the principle of the magic lantern was his own. His cryptological process, featured in the 1646 edition, certainly described a projection device, but in an indirect and complicated manner. According to Kircher, Walgenstein had taken up the optical system he had described in 1646 and 'brought it into a better form'.[18] Walgenstein was therefore the first constructor of a true magic lantern, but he had taken the theoretical principle from Kircher; at least that was Kircher's opinion, remaining silent about the works of Eschinardi and his rival Huygens:

> There is no other difference which exists between this lantern and that which we described, than that the said Walgenstein showed with sufficient brightness and perfection several images in a dark room, to the great admiration of spectators. In our College we exhibit four of the newest things, to the great amazement of those watching. It is a thing most deserving of attention, since complete satirical scenes, theatrical tragedies, and similar things from life may be exhibited.
>
> The true Catoptric Artifice, which we described on p. 793 of Ars Magna Lucis et Umbrae, does not differ from this new Lantern, except that in this mobile Lantern, we reflect the rays of the sun from a mirror on which images of things are inscribed, by reflection into the interior of a building or onto the wall of a room, with all their colours of life, which are shown by the mobile Lantern. We have learned to represent such things without the rays of the sun, through a concave mirror and a diaphanous lens. . . . This new Lantern . . . is not without reason known as Magic or Thaumaturgic, since it can show such marvellous things in a darkened room and in the silence of a stormy night . . .[19]

Between 1660 (when Guisony wrote that he did not yet know of the lantern) and 1671 Kircher had therefore managed to simplify the 1646 projection system, thanks to the discovery of a 'mobile' and portable lantern which he credited to Walgenstein. He also implied, in the 1671 edition, that the cryptological method of 1646 left something to be desired; this hardly comes as a surprise.

Kircher went on to describe the operation of his magic lantern. It was constructed as a large wooden box (in the accompanying engraving, the box appears high enough for a man to stand up inside (see Fig. 10)), provided with 'a chimney, through which the Lamp may emit its smoke'.[20] The lamp, standing on a support or suspended by wires in the centre of the box, was aligned with an opening in the box wall, from which a long tube extended. 'A lenticular glass of the highest quality' was fixed at the inner end of the tube, while at the end outside the box would be placed 'a sheet of very well-made glass on which is painted anything you wish, in aqueous and transparent colours', supported on a type of slide carrier. The images projected could be 'joyous, sad, horrible, or frightening, and for those who were unaware of how they were produced would seem miraculous'.[21] They were painted on long 'parallelograms' mounted in wooden frames, with about eight different images on each

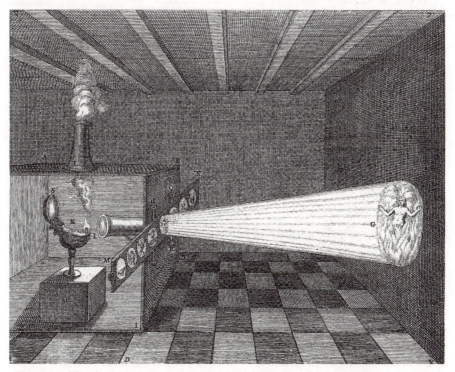

Fig. 10. The 'magic or thaumaturgic lamp' illustrated in Athanasius Kircher, *Ars Magna Lucis et Umbrae* (second edition, 1671).
Collection: Bibliothèque Nationale.

slide: a half-naked man surrounded by flames, a bird, a man holding a staff, a skeleton with scythe and hourglass, Christ on the cross, a man kneeling in prayer, and so on.

Kircher's text, and the two engravings which accompany it, pose a curious problem. The two lanterns illustrated could not have worked, since the slide is shown passing *in front of* the lens, which only consisted of a single element. Experiments have shown that it is impossible to achieve projection in this way. If parallel light rays are directed through the lens, a reproduction of the slide can be obtained (with some difficulty) on the screen, but not with any enlargement, and Kircher's description does mention a magnified image. On this point Kircher therefore made a mistake, by reversing the order of the slide and the lens. The engraver repeated the error, and made it worse: not only were the slides shown outside the lantern, but they were not inverted, so that both the slide image and projected image were shown right way up. In his text, Kircher does mention placing the slide upside down.

What is equally surprising is that such a well-informed scholar as Kircher should publish the description of such simplistic designs, equipped with only a single lens. Huygens, Walgenstein and Petit had for some time been using lanterns with two or three lenses, and their lanterns worked. In fact, Kircher's knowledge was so limited that he simply took Eschinardi's first design of 1668: the magic lantern described in *Centuria Opticae Pars Altera* had only a single convex lens. Eschinardi, though, placed the slide properly between the light source and the lens. Perhaps Kircher, who liked to mystify his followers, wanted to cover his tracks and lead future 'lanternists' in the wrong direction; perhaps he deliberately included the error in order to preserve the secret of the lantern. Either way, Kircher's lantern remains highly mysterious.

Germany: Johann Griendel and Johann Sturm

Having created enchantment in France, the Netherlands, England, Italy, and Denmark, the magic lantern also entered the 350 states which then constituted Germany, Kircher's homeland. German scholars, great lovers of curiosities, were to make some radical modernizations of the *Zauberlatern*. The state of Franconia seems to have been a particularly active centre of research and investigation. It was there that the most celebrated German projectionist of the time operated: Johann Franz Griendel, sometimes known as Gründel. Born in Lower Saxony, he studied mathematics, optics and military architecture, before establishing himself at Nuremberg between 1670 and 1677. There he opened a cabinet of optical curiosities, frequented by foreign visitors and the respectable classes. Griendel rapidly became expert in the techniques of dioptrics, in which role he was so much in demand that, from being a simple 'enthusiast', he transformed himself into an optical equipment manufacturer and dealer. His establishment could supply opera glasses and spectacles, *perspectives hollandaises* ('Dutch perspectives', paper theatres showing a scene or landscape with perspective effects), four-lens terrestrial telescopes and two-lens astronomical telescopes, binoculars, helioscopes (mirrors for observing the sun in a camera obscura), triangular glass prisms showing a rainbow effect, multi-faceted lenses, steel mirrors, anamorphoses, and the latest novelty, *Laternae Magicae oder Bilder-Laterne* ('magic lanterns or picture lanterns') of all sizes. Griendel was a master of the art of projection:

> At Griendel's one may see optical marvels: he offers views of Paradise, Hell, ghosts, the sky full of birds, village weddings, splendid palaces . . .[22]

Griendel offered the same visions to Charles Patin (1633–93, son of Guy Patin, a famous doctor), a French traveller who passed through Nuremberg between 1670 and 1673. Obliged to leave France after libelling a member of Louis XIV's family, Patin travelled around the main courts of Germany. In 1674 he published his travel letters, addressed to 'His Most Serene Highness' Antoine Ulrich, Duke of Brunswick and Lüneburg, in which he mentioned Griendel (whom he called 'Grundler') at some length. He gave some interesting biographical details: Griendel was a monk who reformed as a Lutheran, to Patin's apparent disapproval. This letter is certainly one of the best accounts of a magic lantern show in the seventeenth century:

> I shall only add one word concerning M. *Grundler*, a Monk, who (as he saies) had lately embrac'd the Reform'd Religion, according to the Doctrine of *Luther*. But to justifie to me the change of his opinion it would be requisite for him to have as much command over Men's Reason, as he has over their Eyes, to which he represents whatever he thinks fit, and in any manner whatever at his pleasure; for he is absolutely Master of the most abstruse Secrets in Opticks. This is that Art (My Lord) which is capable of fixing half the World in a Point, and which has found out means to extract visual Repercussions out of Chrystal, and to draw near the most remote Objects by certain Re-productions of *Species* and Correspondences of Prospects, which are extended in the most limited spaces from

the Distances as far as the Eye can reach. In short, 'tis that fallicious Art that deceives our Sight, and which with the Rule and Compass disorders all our Sences. But our Artist proceeds yet farther; for he can even remove Ghosts from their Stations at his pleasure, without any assistance from the Infernal Regions. Some mention has been already made to Your Most Serene Highness of that Spherical Looking-glass, which receives the several *Species* of remote Objects thro' a small Thread of light, and which rolling about in the dark, imprints 'em on it, and causes 'em to follow its Motion; so that real Phantoms and Ghosts are now no longer sensible of the other World. I know divers Persons of great courage who have chang'd pale at the sight of these Sports and of these Magical Artifices.

And with M. *Grundler*'s good leave, all the Esteem that I had of his profound Learning, was not able to free me from that Dread which seiz'd upon my Spirits on that occasion; insomuch that I was apt to believe that there never was in the World a greater Magitian than he. For it seem'd to me as if I had a sight of Paradise, of Hell and of wand'ring Spirits and Phantoms, so that altho' I know myself to be endu'd with some measure of Resoluteness, yet at that time I would willingly have given one half to save the other. All these Apparitions suddenly disappear'd and gave place to Shews of another Nature. For in a moment, I saw the Air fill'd with all sorts of Birds, almost after the same manner as they are usually painted round about *Orpheus*, and in the twinkling of an Eye, a Country-Wedding appear'd to my view, with so natural and lively a representation that I imagin'd myself to be one of the Guests at the Solemnity. Afterward the *Horizon* of my sight was taken up with a Palace so stately, that nothing like it can be produc'd, but in the Imagination; before which there were divers Personages running at the Ring. These Heroes seem'd to be the Gods that were ador'd by Antiquity, and among them 'twas pleasant to observe *Momus* mounted on a *Barbary*-Horse, and making Satyrical Reflections upon *Jupiter*, who had made a false step amidst so jolly a company. But let us put an end to these Visions and endeavour to divert Your Most Serene Highness with somewhat that is more solid.[23]

It is quite possible that Griendel, the remover of 'Ghosts from their Stations', was using mechanical slides: the images described were certainly full of life. The village wedding appeared 'so natural' that the spectator felt part of the scene, and in front of the splendid palace one could almost run at the ring oneself (a game of skill in which suspended rings were captured with a lance or sword from the back of a galloping horse).

Griendel left Nuremberg for Dresden in 1677. Around 1680 he was in Vienna, where he 'practised the art of dioptrics with fervour; at all times he gave the curious ones who asked him good information on the subject'.[24] He then returned to Nuremberg, where he published a folio volume on military architecture (*Fortificatiora Nova*, 1683) and a quarto volume on the minute bodies observed through the microscope (*Micrographia Nova*, 1687). Griendel died at the start of the eighteenth century, probably in Nuremberg. His wonderful projections had helped to disseminate the magic lantern through the whole of Germany, just as Huygens and Walgenstein had done in their own countries.

In 1676 the magic lantern began to emerge from its infancy when a German scientist devised uses for it other than simply frightening the crowds. Johann Christoph Sturm, already mentioned on the subject of the camera obscura, was Bavarian, and he too published his work in Nuremberg, in two parts dated 1676 and 1685. In the first volume, *Collegium Experimentale Sive Curiosum*, which covered all types of scientific and mathematical inventions, the magic lantern was placed just after the portable camera obscura. Sturm named it the 'dioptro-catoptric or megalographic lantern', because it represented on a large scale the very small images put into it. As Sturm put it, the lantern made 'an elephant out of a fly'.

Sturm published the first printed illustration of a non-moving slide for the magic lantern, showing the head of Bacchus, fat, smiling and crowned with bunches of grapes. This was presented as a design intended for reproduction on a slide. The slide would be inserted into a carrier located directly in the cylindrical body of the lantern. The lantern itself was mounted on a support foot with a widened base; it had a chimney with a conical cover including air passages, a lamp with a concave metal mirror, and a long narrow tin-plate optical tube which could slide for adjustment and which contained two convex lenses. Sturm's slides were circular, about 5 cm in diameter, and mounted in rectangular wooden frames:

> If now one lights the lamp and if one passes an image in front of the first lens, it will appear at a distance of twelve feet in the shadows in all its colours, so large that a wall of more than ten feet can receive it, and it will be enlarged still further if one moves back further from the wall.[25]

Sturm's lantern was very easy to manage: small, portable, and extremely simple compared to Kircher's installations of 1671. It was also very bright, because of its small size. As far as is known, only one lantern of this type survives today, very similar to Sturm's design: this can be admired in the collections of the ancient cabinet of curiosities which belonged to the Landgrave (Count) of Kassel, in Germany.

It was in 1685, in his second volume (entitled *Collegii Experimentalis Sive Curiosi*), that Sturm broke new ground by changing the original function of the lantern. Instead of being a diversion from everyday life, it could be put to use. Sturm devised a 'lantern clock' of which Huygens would probably not have been ashamed. This highly ingenious 'megalographic nocturnal lantern clock' would allow a person to see the time on waking up in the middle of the night, projected onto the wall of their room: a useful invention, long before the hands of clocks and watches were fluorescent. During the day, if a visitor wished to know the time, the owner of the lantern clock could immediately satisfy this demand by closing the shutters or curtains; once the room was darkened, the clock face would shine onto the wall and indicate the exact time. A surprise effect was guaranteed, and in fact this was the only purpose suggested, since in the daytime it would certainly be easier to carry a pocket watch.

To construct a device of this type, according to Sturm, the numbers of the hours had to be painted onto a circular transparent sheet of glass in the same arrangement as on a clock face. The image had to be inverted, with the number VI at the top, and the number XII at the bottom. On top of this sheet was placed a mica or glass disc, with a pointer or hand at the centre to indicate the time. The outer edge of the disc was cut to form forty-eight teeth, driven by a gear wheel of the same size with the same number of teeth. A metal shaft formed a drive connection between this wheel and the shaft of a small clock mechanism within the base or body of the lantern; as the disc turned, the hand turned around the numbers. If the smoke from the lantern disturbed its sleeping owner, the lantern could be hidden in a neighbouring room, with only its optical tube passing through a hole in the dividing wall.[26]

Sturm's lantern clock opened the way for all manner of possible improvements in the lantern. The method of projection was refined further, the light emerging from the optical tube became brighter, and the images more varied. The lantern ceased to be merely an object of curiosity: it came out of the *Wunderkammer* to be employed by scholars, teachers, even citizens who had forgotten their pocket watches. At last it became established, not only in scientific literature, but also in everyday life.

Germany: Johannes Zahn

In the year in which Sturm published his second volume another German scholar, Johannes Zahn (1641–1707, born at Carlstadt), a monk of the Premonstratensian order and Provost of the monastery of Niederzell, published a large folio volume at Würzburg entitled *Oculus Artificialis Teledioptricus sive Telescopium* ('The Teledioptric Artificial Eye, or Telescope'). This volume, along with Kircher's book, is one of the most beautiful books on catoptric and dioptric magic published in the seventeenth century. Its principal subject was the art of making telescopes, but there was also a great deal of information and many engravings on the camera obscura and magic lantern.

Even though *Oculus Artificialis Teledioptricus* was dated 1685, the chapters on 'mathematical dioptrics' and the 'mechanical practice' in which the operation of the 'magic catoptric-dioptric light or megalographic thaumaturge' was discussed were written in 1686. That is sufficient to prove Sturm's priority in making the first lantern clocks in 1685, but Zahn discussed this subject at length and added some interesting modifications. In one of these, he attached a small modified clock to a wall: it had no face and the conventional hands were replaced by much longer ones, delicately made from lime wood or reeds.[27] The clock mechanism was hidden within the wall (although it could also be hung from the wall), so that only the two long hands were visible. A magic lantern projected the image of the clock face with the figures for the hours, and the hands turned around this image to indicate the time, a simpler design than Sturm's.

In another variation, the clock hand was painted onto the wall, and a rotating image of the face was projected on top of it, driven by a clock mechanism inside the lantern. Or alternatively, the clock face could be painted onto the white wall, with the hand painted on a slide and moved by the clock mechanism. And finally, the clock hand could be fixed onto the first lens of the lantern's optical tube, which also projected the clock face from a painted slide. The lens tube itself rotated along with the hand, therefore needing a slightly more powerful drive mechanism to rotate the tin-plate or cardboard tube.

Lantern clocks of the seventeenth and eighteenth centuries are extremely rare today. In the few examples which have survived, the clock is located inside the body of the lantern, aligned with the optical tube. It is illuminated by a lamp and reflectors, with its image reflected to the focal point of the lenses (this 'megaloscopic' method was only used in the eighteenth century). In some cases the clock is mounted vertically in a recess at the rear of the lantern: the shaft of the clock mechanism rotates a small drive rod which moves the hands, which are located at the other end of the lantern in the slide carrier, just in front of the slide representing the clock face.[28]

The problem of projecting the time fascinated many generations of scholars until the nineteenth century. Between 1800 and 1850 lantern clocks began to be sold again. In London a manufacturer named Schmalcalder made some magnificent examples (one dating from 1810 is now in the British Museum) and several patents testify to a continuing interest.[29]

Zahn, building on Sturm's ideas, found still more ingenious uses for the lantern. He invented the 'artificial Anemoscope', a 'magic light' which projected the exact direction of the wind at any given moment onto the white wall of a darkened room. Its principle was similar to that of the lantern clock: the magic lantern was connected by a long metal rod to a weather vane mounted on the roof of the building. The vane and the rod reacted to the slightest breath of wind and caused a pair of gear wheels to move. A small blade, connected to these gears and positioned in front of the lamp of the lantern, indicated the direction of the wind via the projected light of the lantern. A slide positioned behind the blade showed on the screen the four points of the compass, and also the *Rosa Nautica* or compass card showing the thirty-two divisions indicating the wind direction.[30]

Zahn's volume contains a number of revelations: for the first time, the rectangular slide used since the appearance of the lantern was replaced by a glass disc, with images arranged around its circumference (see Fig. 11). The change from one image to the next could be made more easily, and given smoothness and speed of operation an illusion of movement could be achieved if the images consisted of a series of stages of a human, animal or mechanical movement. As illustrated in his book, Zahn's lantern disc carried six images, representing six successive phases of a movement: a man twirling a cane in his hand. Uninterrupted projection would give a slightly simplistic, but genuine, synthesis of movement. This appears to have been the first time that an attempt had been made to project a *continuous* animation on the screen; the moving slides used by Huygens had only consisted of a single animated image.

Kircher had already described, in 1671, an image disc on which were painted eight scenes of the Stations of the Cross. But, assuming that the eight views were different, this was not an attempt to analyse movement, and in any case Kircher's disc was viewed as a transparency and not designed for the magic lantern. Zahn took up the glass disc idea for his

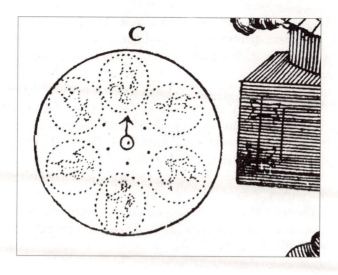

Fig. 11. Zahn's illustration of his glass disc.
Collection: Bibliothèque Nationale.

lantern, but also improved Kircher's process by designing an optical viewer mounted on a stand, in which specimens of plants, seeds and vegetables could be viewed, enlarged by a lens. In this design the transparent disc rotated about its centre, turned by a small key.[31]

One final application, a logical result of Zahn's intellectual path from lantern clock, to weather vane, to botanical image disc, was that projection would be well suited for the study of the sciences. We have already seen that Hooke, in 1668, had considered projecting living animals; Zahn showed 'on a white wall, to the astonishment of all spectators, an amazing quantity of assorted animals, snakes and other similar creatures'.[32] His method was to construct a long glass box with very thin walls, using sheets of transparent selenite (gypsum) secured together with strong glue. Between the glass sheets a space should be left, with an opening at the top through which small living animals could be inserted: snakes, worms, or insects with long transparent wings. The box could then be placed in the slide carrier of the lantern:

> The heat of the lamp and the brightness of the light will make the animals move. One sees their fangs, the long hairs on their legs, their horns, their shells . . . In the same way if one places various worms in clear water one can see on the wall astonishing great snakes.[33]

This produced a moving image, with a quite frenzied degree of animation. The more transparent or coloured the insects were, the more the spectacle was appreciated; if they were too opaque, they appeared only as moving shadows.

Zahn spoke of these living pictures as a scientific entertainment, stressing the amazement of spectators faced with the apparition of swarming insects and giant snakes. But he also saw this lantern as an excellent instrument for teaching: suddenly, in 1686, the magic lantern found a pedagogical vocation which neither Huygens nor Kircher had foreseen. Admittedly educational projection shows were still rare in the seventeenth century, and were still a long way removed from the great fashion for them at the end of the nineteenth century. But thanks to Zahn, scholars and teachers now knew that in the lantern they had an excellent method of capturing the attention of their pupils. With a lantern, the schoolmaster could become a magician, the class could be transformed into an entertaining and enriching show.

By the nineteenth century the tortures inflicted on insects and aquatic animals had become quite cruelly refined. Butterflies were crushed between two glass sheets, with a layer of Canadian balsam to preserve the insect. Some lanternists put acid into water containing tadpoles, to make them move more effectively:

> Then, without saying anything to the audience, you may drop a few drops of acid into the tank from a pipette. As if an alarm bell had sounded, the whole projection will be thrown into revolution and delirium. There will be dizzy charges in every direction, jumps, collisions, . . . I almost said shouts. In fact there will be shouts in the room, but they will be from the delighted spectators calling out and clapping their hands.[34]

Zahn's *Oculus Artificialis* ran to two editions, and Sturm also wrote other books which gave the magic lantern a place of honour.[35] These seminal works were widely read outside Germany: the international connections of all these researchers propelled the lantern around the world more forcefully than ever.

The lantern in France

The ways in which the magic lantern was received in different countries might be seen to offer general reflections of national attitudes. In France, the lantern was dedicated more to shows and entertainments than to the educational and scientific uses imagined in Germany. At the end of the seventeenth century, the lantern could be found in France only at the establishments of a few scattered opticians, while slides were pains-takingly painted by hand by individual artists, craftsmen, and miniature-painters. In 1692 there appears to have been only one address where a Parisian could acquire good-quality painted slides: at Rue Malaquais, in the monastery founded by Cardinal Mazarin in 1642, a Theatine monk (a member of a religious order founded in Italy in the sixteenth century) sold anamorphoses 'of an extraordinary beauty' and particularly 'pictures of all kinds for the *Lanterne Magique*'.[36] By this time the adjective *magique* had been definitively adopted in France, thanks to Antoine Furetière's *Dictionnaire Universel* of 1690:

> *Lanterne Magique*, a small optical machine which makes visible in the darkness on a white wall several ghosts and monsters so hideous, that those who do not know the secret believe that this is done by magic. It is comprised of a parabolic mirror which reflects the light of a candle, whose light exits via the small hole of a tube, at the mouth of which is a telescope lens and between the two of which slide several small glasses painted with divers extraordinary and horrific pictures, which are represented on the opposing wall, at a much greater size.[37]

The theologian Pierre Le Lorrain (1649–1721), Abbé of Vallemont, confirmed the popularity of the lantern in the 1690s: 'This machine has truly caused a commotion for some time.'[38] Le Lorrain's book of 1693, *La Physique Occulte ou Traité de la Baguette Divinatoire* ('Occult Science, or Treatise on the Divining Rod'), resembles those of della Porta and Kircher in its pretention to universal knowledge and attraction towards natural and supernatural magic. This text was put on the prohibited list around 1701 by the Papal Congregation of the Holy Office, which forbade the use of divining rods in criminal trials (Le Lorrain actually claimed that a divining rod allowed the discovery of the guilty person). The magic lantern found itself in the middle of this mess, cited as an example of 'occult science' along with other explanations concerning 'the most obscure phenomena of nature'.

Le Lorrain's lantern ('this is how what I have is made,' he announced) was constructed of tin-plate, with an illuminant consisting of a lamp ('whose wick which is of cotton must be very wide. One places on it olive oil or wine spirit') and an optical tube containing two lenses (see Fig. 12). The small images to be enlarged were 'painted with transparent colours

Fig. 12.   Pierre Le Lorrain, *La Physique Occulte ou Traité de la Baguette Divinatoire* (1693). Collection: Laurent Mannoni.

on glass or on pieces of talc [a translucent mineral] of about three inches in diameter'. This design could project over a distance of about six metres: 'One stretches a white sheet on the wall, on which the phantoms of the objects will appear painted in most beautiful colours, and at a gigantic and monstrous size.'[39]

Le Lorrain passed on some of the extravagant assumptions which had been put forward on the origins of the magic lantern. In truth he had no clear idea on the attribution of its invention, mentioning King Solomon of Israel, Roger Bacon, and (just as likely) the German scientist Daniel Schwendter, known as Swenterus. On the other hand, at least Le Lorrain never mentioned Kircher as the inventor. He also disputed the idea that it was through the magic lantern that the Biblical Witch of Endor had been able to make the dead prophet Samuel appear before King Saul.[40]

Huygens' last works

No text printed in the seventeenth century, as far as is known, makes any reference to Huygens' lanterns. It was not until the end of the nineteenth century, with the publication in the Netherlands of ten volumes of his correspondence, that the importance of this scientist and astronomer in the history of projection began to be understood. We have already seen that in 1664 Huygens wanted to hear no more of the magic lantern, because of his father's ambitions for it and the device's increasing popularization. It should also be said that many other concerns and more taxing subjects had taken over his mind.

In May 1666, returning to Paris, Huygens entered the newly founded Académie des Sciences. There he directed part of the scientific programme and continued his own research in a large apartment in the Royal Library in Rue Vivienne, lent to him by his contact Colbert, which had a laboratory and cabinet of curiosities. His famous *Traité sur la Lumière* ('Treatise on Light'), presented to the Académie in 1678 and published in 1690, did not contain a single line on the magic lantern: it was not relevant. In this publication Huygens revealed his theory of pulsations (the particles of a luminous body caused the luminous ether which filled the universe to vibrate; this ether was composed of tiny balls which by vibrating transmitted pulsations and created a spherical wave front) and discussed the strange double refraction of Iceland spar, a transparent crystalline substance.[41]

In 1672 a new Stadhouder (governor), William III of Orange, came to power in the Netherlands, and his anti-French policies eventually obliged Huygens to leave Paris, in August 1681. He never returned: as a good Protestant, he was offended by the revocation of the Edict of Nantes in 1685. On his return to The Hague, he returned to the attic of the family home on the Plein, where he had made his first lanterns. Apart from several visits to the family property at Hofwijck (a suburb of The Hague) and a journey to London from June until August 1689, Huygens never again left his work table.

He had recommenced the work on dioptrics whose foundations he had laid in 1666. This important work was not published until 1703, eight years after its author's death. *Dioptricam* ('Dioptrics')[42] dealt with the construction of telescopes and methods for observing solar eclipses. There was still not a word on the magic lantern, in the posthumous edition. However, in 1692, when the final version of this text was almost completed, Huygens considered adding some 'complements' to it, in the form of ideas, projects, and remarks which he planned to develop and include later in the final text. And in the first 'complement' of *La Dioptrique*, Huygens finally admitted the magic lantern as a subject worthy of further consideration. He noted simply, in the middle of some questions and notes on the telescopes of Newton and Molyneux, '*Et Laterna magica?*' ('And the magic Lantern?'). In a fourth complement in the same year, he made further reference to Molyneux's equipment and his book *Dioptrica Nova*: 'Unico folio explicat microscopia; dein Laternam magicam'[43] ('On one page he explains microscopes; then the magic Lantern').

In both these cases, Huygens wrote the word 'lantern' with a capital L: perhaps at last he had a little respect for it. In an appendix to the first complement in 1694, he even drew a sketch of the magic lantern, this time not forgetting the reflector ('*speculum cavum*') of his friend Pierre Petit. But by 1694 the lantern had long since been described in a number of scientific works, and other scientists were preparing to publish new technical details on the subject.[44] Huygens could have claimed the credit for making the first scientific publication on the projection device which he had known since 1659. But he had only seen the lantern as an object of entertainment and superstition; he fell behind more modern scholars, who immediately noticed the immense interest in this new optical invention, capable of fascinating, amusing, terrifying and teaching a whole roomful of people.

Huygens' last drawing of the magic lantern therefore dates from 1694. Unfortunately, he did not have time to insert the lantern into his work on dioptrics. Christiaan Huygens, who, whether he liked it or not, disseminated the first projection devices in Europe, and who can be considered as the inventor of the moving slide (that is, the projection of a moving illuminated image on a screen), died at The Hague on 8 July 1695. Among the celebrations of the centenary of the cinema in 1995, the tricentenary of the death of this first projectionist passed almost unremarked.

The lantern in China

The notion of the lantern going 'round the world' is not a mere figure of speech. An indication of the long journey taken by the magic lantern is given by the fact that, by the end of the seventeenth century, projection had even reached as far as China. It was an Italian Jesuit, Claudio Filippo Grimaldi (born at Coni, Piedmont, on 27 September 1638; died at Beijing on 8 November 1712), who introduced the Chinese to this 'great art of light and shadow'. This person should not be confused with Francesco Grimaldi, who discovered the phenomenon of the diffraction of light in 1665. Claudio Grimaldi entered the Noviciate on 13 January 1658; he was an expert in hydraulic machines, and above all in optics. On 15 April 1666, he left Italy for China.

In the preceding century, China had opened its doors to Portuguese merchants and Jesuit missionaries: Father Matteo Ricci had preached the good word there from 1582 onwards. By 1660 there were already 160 Jesuit churches across the Chinese empire. For the German philosopher and mathematician Gottfried Wilhelm Leibniz, in 1697, the Jesuit mission was 'the greatest business of our times, as much for the glory of God as for the general good of men and the increase of the sciences and arts, in our land as well as for the Chinese'.[45]

By 1669 Grimaldi had reached Canton; in 1671 he arrived in Beijing, in the role of an engineer and constructor. Since 1662, the emperor K'ang-Hi (1654–1722) had ruled the country with tolerance. Grimaldi received the name of *Min Ming-Ngo Tö-Sien*, and soon became close to the young Emperor, even accompanying him on his journeys to Tartary. Grimaldi left China in 1685 and visited Macao, Russia, Italy, France, Germany, and Persia. He then returned to Beijing, where he became Rector of the Jesuit College in 1700, and died there twelve years later, after an eventful life.[46]

As a correspondent of Leibniz, Grimaldi was up to date with all the latest developments in science and optics. Like many Jesuits, he was aware of the secret of the magic lantern, either from a book or by word of mouth. He knew that the Chinese were fascinated by all aspects of optics: certainly they already knew of the kaleidoscope, magic mirrors, and shadow shows. But apparently nobody in Beijing had ever seen the magic lantern, nor even the camera obscura: Grimaldi showed these two wonders to the Emperor, probably around 1671–2, when he first arrived in the capital.

Thanks to Jean-Baptiste du Halde (1674–1743), a French Jesuit and author of an immense and fascinating *Description de l'Empire de la Chine* ('Description of the Empire of China'), we know Grimaldi's precise role as a 'lanternist'. Du Halde first described the situation in China when the Jesuits arrived there:

> This naturally proud nation regards itself as the most scholarly in the world . . . It was disabused of this by the skill of the Missionaries who went to the Court . . . The late Emperor K'ang-Hi, whose favourite passion was to acquire some new knowledge every day, did not grow tired of seeing and hearing them. The Jesuits for their part saw how much the protection of this great Prince was necessary to them for the progress of the Gospel, overlooking nothing to excite the curiosity and satisfy the natural appetite which he had for the sciences.[47]

Du Halde continued: 'They first gave him the knowledge of Optics.' The standard objects of catoptric and dioptric magic, as found in Kircher, Sturm, or Zahn, were presented to the Emperor. First, a wooden cylinder fitted with a lens: a small portable camera obscura. The images entered the interior of the tube and 'as if portrayed in nature' appeared on a piece of polished glass or paper:

> The emperor, to whom this spectacle was new, took much pleasure in it. He desired that such a machine should be set up for him in his garden in Pekin [Beijing], with which, without being observed, he might watch all that passed in the neighbouring streets and squares.[48]

A Jesuit—presumably Father Grimaldi—pierced a hole in the wall of a 'large room closed on all sides and very dark', which looked over the gardens outside. A type of pyramidal window was constructed, with its apex, into which a 'glass eye' was screwed, pointing to the outside:

> It was there that the emperor came with his queens, to view the living images of all who passed through the square, and this view pleased him extremely; but most of all it charmed the Princesses who would never have been able to enjoy this spectacle in any other

way, the custom of China not permitting them to go outside the Palace.[49]

According to du Halde, Father Grimaldi demonstrated 'wonders of Optics' which astonished 'all the Great Ones of the Empire'. On the four walls of the garden of the building reserved for the Jesuits in Beijing, he painted four human figures. From the front, one would 'see nothing there but Mountains, forests, hunts and other things of that nature', but by standing in a certain position, 'one perceives the well-made and well-proportioned figure of a man'. The surprise of the Court can be imagined. K'ang-Hi came to admire this marvel, and 'considered these figures for a very long time; the great ones and the principal Mandarins who came there in a crowd, were just as surprised'. Then Grimaldi showed some anamorphoses, distorted drawings which were made to appear correctly by conical, cylindrical, or pyramidal mirrors. This also caused 'their surprise and their admiration'.[50]

If we can believe in all the wonders he presented, Grimaldi must have travelled to China with an impressive cabinet of curiosities: astronomical telescopes, spyglasses, and a tube like Nicéron's containing an eight-faceted prism, 'representing on these eight faces different scenes so lifelike that they took them for the objects themselves'. But Grimaldi kept the best of his optical surprises until last:

> Finally he showed him a Tube which contained a burning lamp, whose light exits via the small hole of a tube, at the mouth of which is a telescope lens and in which slide several small glasses painted with various pictures. These same pictures are represented on the wall opposite, smaller or of a prodigious size, according to whether the wall is close or far away. This spectacle during the night or in a very dark place, caused as much fear in those who did not know the art, as it did pleasure in those who had been instructed. It was this which caused it to be given the name of Magic Lantern.[51]

So, from Paris to Beijing, from The Hague to Rome, from Nuremberg to London, the magic lantern spread across the whole world. The coming 'Age of Enlightenment' of the eighteenth century would not only give it a warm welcome, but also adopt all sorts of other optical 'curiosities' which were just as enthralling as illuminated projection, and in one way or another represented equally important forerunners of the cinematograph show.

PART TWO

Triumphant Illusions

4

Magie Lumineuse in the Country and the City

It would be hard to find a more potent symbol for the century of the Enlightenment. For several decades, the whole population, from the humblest peasant to the greatest lord, had access to miracles of the arts and sciences emanating from the lamps of optical instruments. From the pedlar who set up his box on the village square, to Joseph Bonnier de la Mosson who turned his mansion on Rue Saint-Dominique in Paris into an extraordinary museum of curiosities, everyone, according to his or her degree of sophistication, could partake of illuminated visions enclosed in peepshow *boîtes d'optique* or projected by magic lanterns. Manufacturers were obliged to seek ever-increasing improvements in their methods, and optics was no longer the preserve of an elite group of scholars as it had been in the seventeenth century. The fashionability of experimental science, the enormous breach opened in the fortress of the sciences by Diderot's *Encyclopédie*, and the successful publication of books such as *Le Spectacle de la Nature* ('The Spectacle of Nature') by Abbé Pluche in 1732 or *Leçons de Physique* ('Lessons in Science') by Abbé Nollet in 1743, combined to develop the thirst for knowledge, the curiosity of the *voyeur* or observer, as never before.

Travelling showpeople

Projections and optical toys created a new trade: the pedlar or showman travelling with a magic lantern or peepshow. It was the trade of paupers, generating miserably low earnings. These travelling lanternists moved between towns and villages, with their show carried in a box strapped to their back, sometimes accompanied by a monkey or a *marmotte en vie*

Fig. 13.   Hand-tinted engraving showing a travelling 'Savoyard' lanternist family, *c*.1800. Collection: Laurent Mannoni.

('live marmoset') (see Fig. 13). They wandered the streets shouting their wares, waiting for a window or door to open or a citizen to wave them in:

> Trala, deri, traderi, dere; la, la, la, traderi tradere! Curiosity for the asking! Show the beautiful Magic Lantern in your home, it will cost you no more than fifty-five *sols* . . . You will see the Good Lord, Master Sun and Madame Moon, the stars, the King, the Queen, the *gendarme*, the hangman, the morning, the afternoon, the evening, the Seven Deadly Sins, the Elements.[1]

They would then go into the client's house, or take a booking for that evening or the next day, put up a white sheet, light the lantern or set up their peepshow, and the show would begin. Often a companion would produce a musical accompaniment with a hurdy-gurdy or barrel organ. Perhaps because of the poverty of their native regions, in France the inhabitants of Savoie ('Savoyards') and the Auvergne ('Auvergnats') dominated the field of travelling projection shows. In the eighteenth century young Savoyards were also known as chimney sweeps, wood-cutters, shoe cleaners, and errand boys. Their lantern or peepshow was these travellers' only treasure: their survival depended entirely on the quality of their show.

Thanks to these exhibitors of shadows and illuminated images, the lantern and other optical illusions were shown in every far-flung corner of Europe. The Savoyards and Auvergnats had no qualms about crossing frontiers. In 1782, a Dutch book recounted the adventures of 'Sneog the Savoyard' (also known as 'Goens of Savoy') with 'his new Dutch magic or comic lantern'.[2] It appears that the Low Countries were at the forefront of travelling shows: at the Amsterdam fair, from the start of the eighteenth century (and perhaps even earlier), could be seen Savoyards, 'jolly Walloons with cabinets of curiosities', and Dutchmen who called out *Lanterne magique! O soo mooi! Fraai curieus!* ('Magic lantern! Very beautiful, very curious!') while presenting 'the Optica of Gouda and Utrecht',[3] a peepshow. These showpeople enjoyed considerable popularity in the eighteenth century, if the large numbers of written accounts, engravings, paintings and figurines dedicated to them are any guide.

It is difficult to put a precise date to the birth of this new way of life. Walgenstein, in the seventeenth century, was one of the first travelling projectionists, but he was also a scientist and there is no evidence that he received payment for his shows. It was probably the Parisian engraver François Guérard, in *Les Cris de Paris* ('Cries of Paris') printed between 1700 and 1710, who represented a true travelling showman for the first time, accompanied by the text *'Voicy la Curiosita, la rareta à voir'* ('Curiosities, rarity to see').[4] The showman is carrying a tall rectangular box on his back, attached with straps, though whether this is a peepshow in which one could see illuminated views through a lens, or a box containing a magic lantern with its slides and lamp, remains a mystery.

Well after Guérard, the painter Christophe Huet drew a series of 'Cris de Paris' around 1753 for the famous porcelain factory of Meissen: a magic lantern showman; a showman with a marmoset; sellers of pastries, songs, fish, and vinegar; a lantern-carrier; a travelling cook; a prostitute;

and a beggar with his child. Huet's small, nightmarish, and strangely silent world of thirty-four drawings has been rediscovered in the archives of the Meissen factory, and the original figurines made from them can be seen in many museums and private collections. Comparison of the two is interesting: in his drawings Huet insisted on the deep poverty of these small earners, showing their clothes in tatters, yet on the graceful Meissen figurines these rags have disappeared.

Around 1775 another artist, Michel Poisson, drew seventy-two 'Cris de Paris d'après nature' ('Cries of Paris, from nature'). His lantern showman stands with his back turned to show clearly the large box he is carrying. His small lantern appears to be screwed onto a small box, on top of the large box. A simple white sheet hangs like old washing on a metal rod: this is the screen, while on one side of the box some wooden trestles are attached. The caption reads 'Ah! La Lanterne magique la pièce curieuse' ('Ah! The magic lantern, the curiosity play'). In 1742 the traveller drawn by Edmé Bouchardon was a woman, who must have had a well-developed back and shoulders, since she is shown carrying not only the heavy box which would contain the slides, the lamp, and paraffin or olive oil, as well as the lantern on top, but also a large barrel organ.

There are practically no surviving examples of the travelling lanternist's magic lanterns, although peepshow boxes are still relatively common. The only example currently known is in a private collection in Verona, and even in this case the design is not very old, dating from around 1840. It is a very simple lantern of soldered metal, unsophisticated in its construction, which slides into two tracks on top of a wooden box which opens at the side. The lantern and slides can be stored inside the box.

According to Marc-Mitouflet Thomin, author of a *Traité d'Optique Méchanique* ('Treatise on Mechanical Optics') in 1749, the equipment used by the travelling showpeople was of poor quality:

> The magic lantern with which they give shows from house to house in Paris is less well-made than that which I have just mentioned, and in addition does not have such a great effect; the circle of light is not so large, they only use two lenses, of which the first can have about three or four inches focus, and the second eight or nine inches; the first of these lenses is cast in a mould of the approximate size, and as a result it cannot be well adjusted. One does not see the reflecting mirror at the rear of this lantern, which causes a great reduction of light, and consequently makes the images less perceptible and more confused.[5]

It did not take very long for the optical showmen to begin to appear in literary texts. The reserve collection of the Bibliothèque Nationale in Paris contains an anonymous Italian play, *La Lanterne Magique ou le Mississippi du Diable* ('The Magic Lantern, or the Devil's Mississippi') printed in French at The Hague. This small seventy-page volume unfortunately does not carry a publication date: the title page is torn in half, and there is no other copy in Paris. If this text really dates from the seventeenth century (as attributed by the archivists of the Bibliothèque Nationale) it proves the existence of the Savoyard travelling lanternist at this early period, although as already noted illustrations of these show-people did not start to appear until the beginning of the eighteenth century.

This play is set in the Butter Market at the Amsterdam fair (not far from The Hague, where Huygens lived). In Scene III, Plutus and Fortune plan to 'upset the business of the humans':

> *Plutus*: The thing is possible . . . already an infernal scheme is suggesting itself to my mind . . . Yes, of course . . . Why not . . . There, I have it; behold a Scottish devil, who brings me here the Box of Illusions decorated with poisoned cloves. (A devil brings a box.) Here, Madame, inside it is enclosed a mystery, dreams, illusions, seductive charms and contagion; fraud and imposture, disorder, fright and despair; in a single word a small arsenal of my ways is enclosed within it.[6]

When the box opens, 'one sees emerge Dreams and Illusions, seductive charms and imposture, which make up a dance'. In the final climax in Scene V, a Harlequin 'disguised as the Savoyarts with their Magic Lantern' borrows Plutus' box and sets it down in the centre of the stage. The actors assemble around it, and Harlequin comments on the projected pictures (it is unclear whether these would actually have been projected on stage). As is so often the case in texts which feature magic lanterns, these images are ironic denunciations, in veiled and symbolic terms, of the vices of contemporary society:

> Hey, here is a bottle of the fountain of oblivion, from which people have a great need to drink to forget who they were . . . Hey, here are some letters of pardon, sent by those who wish to go bankrupt with honour . . . Hey, here is the innocent portrait of the trials of human affairs, in the shape of a woman, who turns the wheel of fortune in the woods of The Hague. Hey, here is the golden age, or the Devil's

doll in paper clothes. Hey, here is the conjuror's purse [*Gibecière de l'Algèbre*], or the art of spiriting away millions . . .[7]

In a later anonymous text, *La Lanterne Magique aux Champs-Élysées* ('The Magic Lantern in the Elysian Fields', with a double reference to the Champs-Élysées as a contemporary symbol of Paris life), the lantern showman projects the paintings of the 1775 Paris Salon de Peinture, before a gathering of the 'old masters' assembled above the clouds. Raphael, Rubens, Titian, Domenichino, Veronese, Van Dyck, and Poussin, among others, discuss the new paintings and mock their mediocre quality. Antoine Van Dyck arrives completely breathless:

> Well, Gentlemen, prepare yourselves. Behold the arrival of Mercury . . . I do not know what type of man he brings with him, with a box on his back.[8]

Mercury enters, and 'a Savoyard follows him with a Magic Lantern'. Rembrandt mutters scornfully to Teniers: 'Either I mistake myself, or it is a Magic Lantern!' Mercury explains: on visiting the 1775 Salon de Peinture, he found it 'so far from the rules, so baroque, so inexplicable', that he reproduced all the paintings on glass slides, to give his painter friends an idea of each composition:

> In less than half an hour, I copied for you, without missing a brushstroke, what seemed to me to be important at the Salon. Then, I took from in front of the Palais-Royal the scoundrel whom you see with his Magic Lantern, and dragged him here in a big black cloud, whipped up the horses, Boreus and Aquilon [the gods of the north and north-east winds] brought me here like a hurricane.[9]

Meanwhile, Mercury has pulled off Proserpine's bedsheet to serve as a screen, and the show can begin. More or less severe criticism is meted out to all the Salon painters in turn. The language of the Savoyard, mimicking his regional dialect in the French original text, is particularly interesting:

> *Mercury*: Hurry up then!
> *Savoyard*: Gawd, sir, I'm all in a spin, yer've brought me like a whirlwind. We must be at t'other end of Paris.
> *Mercury*: What, don't you recognize the *Champs-Élysées* [i.e. the Elysian Fields]?

Savoyard: That, the *Champs-Élysées* [i.e. the location in Paris]? What the devil's going on? I don't see the Coliseum!

But it seems that the poor Savoyard cannot deliver the required results:

Savoyard: (after setting up his Lantern and putting in a slide) For the start, yer'll see . . . Yer'll see the beautiful Armide and the brave Renaud. See how the beautiful Armide looks like wanting to kill herself? Oh the little madam! . . . Now here's number fourteen by the same artist. Yer'll see the . . . the . . . the . . . St . . . St . . .
Titian: Signor Mercury, spare us the indecent gibberish of this rascal, and have him show the slides without saying anything.
Mercury: I am at your service. I had thought that it would entertain you. The voices of these people are found very amusing up there. They imitate them sometimes at the Comédie Française with great success.[10]

As well as that little sneer at the actors of the Comédie Française, this account is worth noting for its criticism of 'those people', the Savoyards. Were their shows of such poor quality? Were their projections second-rate? It would presumably be sufficient that the common people enjoyed this pastime for it to become vulgar in the eyes of the great and good. Monsieur de Scévole, secretary to the king at Argenton in the province of Berry, preferred any stage play to a lantern show, even if performed by amateurs. In 1776 he encouraged the formation of travelling groups whose mission would be to 'stop in the small places which have nothing for a show except the magic lantern and some miserable puppets'.[11]

There were many other texts in which the magic lantern played a 'walk-on' role, as more than a mere stage prop: *La Lanterne Magique d'Amour* ('The Magic Lantern of Love'), a German comic opera of 1773 by Reichardt; *La Lanterne Magique*, a pantomime by Lazarri, at the fair of Saint-Germain; *La Soirée des Champs-Élysées* ('An evening on the *Champs-Élysées*'), a 'proverb-folly in one act' performed at the Montansier Theatre in Paris (with some Auvergnats on stage); or another *La Lanterne Magique*, a farce by Bernard-Valville shown at the Jeunes-Élèves Theatre and published in 1801.[12] This play met with some success: it tells the story of a poor family, 'who had nothing to survive on but the products of a magic lantern', and who were rescued by two newly wed couples. The newly-weds decide to adopt the small Auvergnat children, whose jobs are divided like this: 'Jerome is in charge of a magic lantern, Claudine carries in front of her a basket containing almanacs, Jacquinet has a marmoset, and Michelette a small hurdy-gurdy.'[13]

The Dauphin's magic lantern

According to Abbé Nollet, by 1783 the magic lantern had become

> one of those instruments which too great a fame has made
> ridiculous in the eyes of a good many people. It is taken around the
> streets, it entertains children and the common people; this proves,
> with the name it carries, that its effects are curious and surprising.[14]

In this light, the disdain which Queen Marie-Antoinette showed
towards the magic lantern is also significant. Around 1791, her son the
Dauphin (Crown Prince), then aged six, was showing very little interest
in his studies. 'Oh! Mother, if you knew how boring grammar is,'[15] the
child said to his mother, according to the account of a passionate
defender of the royal family, Jean-Philippe Gui le Gentil, Comte de
Paroy (1750–1824). 'I can understand that,' replied the queen, who liked
to find excuses for her son: he was 'so lively that he could not apply
himself. He remembers well what he hears but, if he has to concentrate
on a book, that disgusts him immediately. There must be another way of
teaching children.' She therefore turned to the Comte de Paroy, who
told this story in his *Mémoires*. Paroy was a curious character, whom we
shall meet again later in connection with the Phantasmagoria. He wrote:

> The queen said to me: What then do you think is the best method
> for my son?—It is quite simply the magic lantern.—Do you
> imagine, sir, that I am speaking seriously to you, replied the queen
> with dignity, and you are suggesting the ridiculous magic lantern to
> me?—Yes, madame, until now it has only been in the hands of
> ignorant Savoyards, who travel the streets with their marmosets.
> The subjects painted on glass are on the same level as their ex-
> planations, and the stranger they are, the more they please the
> children and make them laugh.[16]

An advocate of audio-visual teaching well ahead of his time, Paroy went
on to emphasize the 'fascinating' power of the magic lantern:

> Many children, gathered in a room, have their minds captured as a
> result of the darkness necessary for representation of the pictures
> which appear suddenly illuminated on a large disc which frames the
> picture like a medallion. Curiosity charges their imagination, which
> grasps eagerly the details of the object represented.[17]

Paroy pleaded the cause of the 'ridiculous' magic lantern so well that the queen changed her mind. The line this clever educational adviser took—a revealing fact in itself—was that he wished to 'enoble' the projection apparatus, which had been dishonoured by being dragged through the countryside on the backs of pedlars. Paroy also claimed to be the inventor of a process which allowed the manufacture of large numbers of slides at a modest price: he had succeeded, he wrote, in 'transferring the engraving of a print onto the glass':

> One may present in this way all the subjects of sacred and secular history, the holy mysteries and mythology, the objects of natural history and even of mathematics. One may add to this pamphlets explaining the subjects, with information about the works supplying more precise details. Colleges and houses of education will be happy to have one to occupy the children, in the evening recreations.[18]

This was a remarkable premonition of what, at the end of the nineteenth century, would turn into an enormous educational industry of popular lectures illustrated by lantern projection, with manufacturers supplying the state and its teachers (as well as the clergy) with mass-produced printed slides with the same explanatory pamphlets which Paroy had foreseen. The queen was completely convinced:

> It is perfect, I am very satisfied with your method and your reasons. It is absolutely necessary to put your ideas into practice and to begin with the Bible and the History of France, which I have a mind to teach to my son in this way.[19]

Marie-Antoinette therefore commanded Monsieur de la Porte to supply Paroy with funds for the construction of a magic lantern 'with good lenses'. The Count received a thousand crowns (each slide, he said, would cost one gold louis). But on 13 August 1792, after the Tuileries palace was ransacked, the Commune of Paris ordered the imprisonment of the royal family in the tower of the Temple. Young Louis XVII, the Dauphin, never did see the mysterious circular light. The magic lantern itself, which presumably was manufactured with some care, has not been found. Paroy kept the few slides he made for the Dauphin for many years, as precious relics salvaged from the 'revolutionary shipwreck': 'many subjects from the Bible, about sixty of them, as well as the History of France.'[20]

The travelling peepshow

The magic lantern and the peepshow box (known in France as the *boîte à vues d'optique*; in Germany as *Bilder-Guckkasten*; and in Italy as the *camera otticha* or *Il Mondo Nuovo*) were two quite distinct travelling 'curiosities'. The iconography of the eighteenth and nineteenth centuries cheerfully mixed the two devices under the generic term 'magic lantern', although they were quite different. The peepshow involved no projections, as in the magic lantern; the lantern could amaze one or two hundred people, while the peepshow could capture the attention of no more than ten or so of the curious at a time.

The peepshows which survive today in museums and private collections are of many different types (see Fig. 14). The most common consists of a pyramidal casing, truncated at the top and enclosed in a rectangular box which contains the optical components. An illuminated engraving, lying flat on the bottom of the box, is viewed through a biconvex lens (located facing the spectator) and a mirror inclined at 45 degrees (fastened inside the box, above the image and opposite the lens). The box may have several eyepieces, so that several people may enjoy the show:

> These types of *optique* are in the hands of the whole world. [They] represent naturally in appearance of depth all the views, landscapes, palaces and other architectural subjects which one places in the box, it suffices to place it in such a manner that the objects receive plenty of daylight; they are also most pleasant when they are illuminated with two or three lights.[21]

Some surviving examples are finished in decorative lacquer: these are delicate and truly magnificent objects, which would have been completely in place in elegant drawing rooms of the eighteenth century. The travelling showmen, though, generally ignored this simple design, which was reserved for the leisured classes, the curious, and the aristocrats. The Musée du Cinéma in Paris possesses one rare example of a pedlar's peepshow constructed following the design described above. The construction is less refined, the wood is not painted, but there are two eyepieces, and the two leather carrying straps for transporting the box have also survived.

More simple still, less expensive, and less bulky (and even less favoured by the pedlars) was the *machine optique diagonale*, known in Britain as the 'Zograscope'. A pedestal of turned wood—usually boxwood, sometimes mahogany—was screwed vertically into a baseplate, to

Fig. 14. Peepshow box in painted wood, with engravings enhanced in colour
and perforated to produce day-night effects (Germany, *c*.1730).
Collection: Cinémathèque Française, Musée du Cinéma
(photo S. Dabronski).

support a frame carrying a biconvex lens. A mirror, which could be
pivoted up or down as required, was also attached to this frame. An
engraving known as a *vue d'optique* was placed behind the device and the
mirror's angle of inclination adjusted so it could be viewed through
the lens. At the end of the eighteenth century, the painter Louis Léopold
Boilly painted Louise-Sébastienne Gély, the second wife of the French
revolutionary Danton (they married in 1793), together with a child
who was probably Antoine Danton, eldest child of the revolutionary
Tribune and his first wife, Gabrielle Charpentier. The woman is shown
positioning engravings behind the zograscope, while the child watches
the effects through the lens.

The effects young Danton would have seen with this device today
appear rather disappointing; the view seen through the mirror and lens
is nothing like as impressive as an original scene from nature. In its day
this type of optical recreation was appreciated for several reasons: the
mirror inverts the engraved image (which is usually printed in reverse)
and makes the descriptive caption legible; the lens gives an effect of

enlargement, of a scientific illusion; and the *vues* themselves are often fascinating. Some are printed and coloured in a hurry, others are small masterpieces of engraving and perspective. Monuments, gardens, and streets make up the majority of the subjects, but occasionally remarkable views of contemporary events can be found. One example is the 'Perspective View of the Shipwreck of Austrian Prisoners in the Baltic Sea, en route to Magdeburg', an engraving printed in the eighteenth century by Jacques Simon Chéreau of 257 Rue Saint-Jacques, Paris. The engraving is not very carefully executed, but the composition of the view is full of movement and expresses the details of the tragic event forcefully. The wind, in grey and blue, whips up a stormy green sea. Several boats are on the point of being swallowed up by the waves. Survivors try to cling to lumps of wood and barrels; some have reached the reefs and are praying and calling for help; a half-naked man is spitting out water. One can imagine the emotional impact of this print, at a time when the majority of people were illiterate and the image still took precedence over written text among the common people. The pedlar who showed such views of contemporary life, with a peepshow of greater or lesser effectiveness, and accompanied them with suitably harrowing commentaries, was sure of success. Even greater success might be achieved if the images were a little more risqué or gruesome. One Parisian publisher seems to have specialized in this genre between 1760 and 1781: Louis-Joseph Mondhare, of Rue Saint-Jacques, from whose house the police seized some prohibited engravings on 4 July 1768.[22] Among other scenes, Mondhare was the artist of a 'View Representing the Punishment of Voluntary Cuckolds as is Usually Practised in Venice':

> This view which denounces both complaisant husbands and their unfaithful wives, shows the voluntary or at least consenting cuckold, his head decorated with horns and bells, his hands tied, his torso stripped, paraded on his donkey and duly whipped by his wife. She does not escape from a just chastisement, for she is in her turn whipped by an officer of justice.[23]

Bawdy *vue d'optique* prints have today become very rare; they were certainly not very common among the publishers of the time, at least not officially. On the other hand, a large proportion of the enormous quantity of ordinary *vues d'optique* engraved in the eighteenth century appears to have survived. The Bibliothèque Nationale, for example, has a very rich collection. The main centres of production were Paris (Rue Saint-Jacques and its surroundings), Augsburg, London, and Bassano.

The phenomenal success of the zograscope in the eighteenth century appears quite astonishing today. Certainly, at the time, there were criticisms of the system of inclined mirrors, which after all only offered a transient illusion. On 20 December 1764, the philosopher Jean-Jacques Rousseau (1712–78) wrote to one of his admirers:

> It is actually an *optique* such as you describe which we have discussed. I do not like those which, remaining open, allow light in from all parts and present surrounding objects together with the image. You mentioned to me a method of so enclosing the image in the box with a kind of black frame that one may see nothing but the print. That, sir, is what I should desire, and if you can find some good lenses in Geneva, or if you know some good workman whom you would wish to order to make the box, I will be obliged to you to see that some care is given to this . . . I feel that in my condition, shut up for more than six months of every year, I have a great need of entertainment which would create a diversion from the wanderings of my head and prevent them from consuming me in my prison.[24]

Rousseau also asked his correspondent to supply him with a 'colour box' in order to 'illuminate plants and flowers in their natural colours and other prints and landscapes for an *optique*.' *Vues d'optique* were generally printed by line engraving on laid paper, and then enhanced in bright colours applied with a brush by the publisher or purchaser. In 1769, Edme-Gilles Guyot (1706–86), Director-General of Post in Paris and a great enthusiast for catoptric and dioptric magic, was offering for sale 'colours in tablets in the number of twenty, suited for these types of illumination': Prussian blue, gamboge (yellow), carmine, sea-green, bladder green (light green), indigo, saffron, bistre, gallstone (dirty yellow), 'Chinese' ink, Venetian lacquer (red), 'bitters' of beef or carp ('used to allow the colours to flow when the paper is greasy'), and alum (salt to soak the engravings).

Day and night peepshow effects

Travelling showpeople, driven by the need to earn their living, used peepshows which gave a show infinitely superior to the effects produced by the simple inclined-mirror zograscope. These fairground boxes were large (some could be over 2 m in height, mounted on legs), and did not contain a mirror. They usually took the form of a horizontal rectangular box, or sometimes a cube. The print was placed inside, opposite the lens, which was always fixed in the front wall of the box (there might be several lens openings). In some designs the rear of the box was open, with two vertical guide channels: one to receive a panel onto which the print was glued, the other to receive a second frame covered with transparent varnished paper, through which the image could be illuminated by natural or artificial light. An opening in the top of the box allowed light in to illuminate the front of the print, and could be covered with transparent paper tinted blue for night scenes, or reddened to give a natural shade to prints representing fires or illuminations. On the side of the box were cords which the showman could pull to lower or raise the frames. Some showmen used paraffin lamps or simple candles ('place there five or six rings filled with candles', Guyot directed) to illuminate the views, in which case there was also a chimney on top of the box.

Some glorious examples of travelling peepshows and cabinets of curiosities, dating from the eighteenth century, can be seen at the Museo Nazionale del Cinema in Turin. One private Italian collection contains a peepshow box in the shape of a church, decorated with beautiful statuettes, measuring 2 m in height by 1.4 m in depth, which was made at the end of the eighteenth century for a noble Venetian family. The Turin museum also has a rich iconography of paintings, engravings, and porcelain figures on this subject.[25] For example, a wonderful eighteenth-century painting by Giovanni Michele Graneri represents a showman standing next to his box. The box is rectangular, with two lenses (there may also be a third opening in the side), and topped by a large tower pierced by windows from which a small flag flies. The device, which resembles a church or a convent, rests on trestles. In front of it, two peasants are watching attentively at the level of the two lenses. The painter François Boucher (1703–70) also drew a peepshow showman, as a model for a figure group made by Étienne Falconet in Sèvres porcelain.

In all the engravings and paintings of peepshows, the crowd is shown pressing impatiently around the box. One fine engraving (see Fig. 15) published during the reign (1715–74) of Louis XV, shows a pedlar blocking the road with a huge peepshow box mounted on a handcart. A crowd is milling around the box, which has at least nine viewing holes. On top of the box, small figurines depict a battle scene, and the operating cords are clearly visible on the side of the box. The showman is close at hand, receiving some coins from a plainly-dressed young woman. A caption explains:

Fig. 15. Eighteenth-century French engraving showing a travelling
peepshow pedlar. Collection: Bibliothèque Nationale.

> Sellers of sweetmeats, curious Savoyards,
> Soldiers, people of every sex and age,
> To this ingenious contrivance,
> Come and give your patronage.
> Hurry to see without delay,
> What one will see in no other place,
> There they are showing the virginity,
> Of a chorus girl of the Opéra.[26]

In peepshow boxes which produced day and night effects, the image
was initially lit on its painted or engraved front surface, using natural
light (the showman would hold the roof of the box open) or artificial
light. If the roof was closed slowly, the image would become darkened
from the front, but remain illuminated from behind. The scene would

seem to pass from day into night, in a precursor of the magic lantern 'dissolving view' or cinematic 'fade' effect. The *vue d'optique* print could be pierced by tiny holes, carefully following the lines of its design, behind which small pieces of coloured transparent paper were glued. The windows of a house, for example, could be cut out and covered with coloured paper. For this type of 'illuminated *vue d'optique*', Guyot advised using 'very small cutters' of varying widths to pierce all the places in the print where one wished 'to make lights appear'. The print should not be at all transparent:

> One must cover it, on the reverse, with two good layers of black colour, made with the soot of smoke; having cut out the image, one attaches to the back and by its edges a single sheet of very thin oiled corrugated paper, which one has coloured on both sides with a very dilute saffron water.[27]

The 'miracle of vision' of this 'new world', to use its eighteenth-century Italian name *mondo nuovo*, can surprise the most blasé even today. In a 'Perspective View of the Interior of the Entertainment Hall in Verona in Italy', published in Paris between 1760 and 1775 by Jean-François Daumont of Rue Saint-Martin, the points of light indicate the location of candles, scattered throughout the room, along the rows of seats, in the private boxes, on the stage and the scenery. The drawing is meticulous, the depth of field astonishing, and the illumi- nation effect magical: it is quite possible to imagine oneself standing at the door of an eighteenth-century theatre or opera house. The same printer published another 'Vue d'Optique Representing the Church of All Saints at the University of Oxford', in which the initial view is of the street, which appears to extend in perspective to infinity, illuminated as though in full daylight. Then night gradually falls, all the windows light up, the church and the other buildings shine with hundreds of tiny points of light. Another example is the 'Perspective View of the Fireworks which were Fired over the Water, close to the Place de Louis XV, in Celebration of Peace, 22 June 1763', an engraving painted and printed in Paris by André Basset, whose shop at that time was at the corner of the Rue des Mathurins and Rue Saint-Jacques. The fireworks are pierced with small coloured holes, which when lit from behind transform the view into a flamboyant shower of light with a very beautiful effect.

In 1777 Jean known as Dauphiné, a showman at the Fair of Saint-Ovid in Place Louis XV, Paris, offered a peepshow with a mechanical system which he claimed would allow 'all the court and the royal hunting party, on a rolling stand mounted on four wheels' to pass in front of a fixed scenic background. Some showmen offered a very large selection of views. In 1750, the *Affiches de Paris* published the advertisement of a showman at the Fair of Saint-Germain:

> There is arrived from London an optical instrument, the most curious and most surprising which one could see of its type, constructed after the notes of the celebrated Mr. Newton, the English philosopher and mathematician. This device, which has been viewed with satisfaction by the King, represents faithfully in the full extent of reality views and perspectives of sea ports, royal houses, gardens, the castles of Fontainebleau, Trianon, Choisy, Chantilly, Sceaux, the entrance of the port of Marseille with the great Avenue, the view of the isle of Malta with the entrance to the great harbour, the Church of Saint Peter in Rome, a view of England, the castles of Antoncourt [Hampton Court], Kinsington, the house of Lord Cobsen, the Westminster Bridge on the Thames in London, and finally a ship on fire.[28]

This was a truly varied programme. The attribution of the 'optical instrument' to Isaac Newton was mainly to attract the curious, to give a serious scientific air to the entertainment. It was also said that the device had been invented by the Italian architect Leon-Battista Alberti around 1450. This type of attribution, repeated down the centuries, should be regarded with great caution—the example of the magic lantern and its pseudo-inventor Kircher is instructive in this respect.

More unusually, some showmen presented a 'perspective box', which gave another show of exceptional beauty. In a rectangular box, a series of scenes and figures cut from paper, each arranged at a distance of a few centimetres from the next, could be viewed through a conventional lens. The result was an illusion of perspective and depth. This box, also known as the *optique en forme théâtrale* ('*optique* theatre') or 'perpetual gallery', could be constructed in the form of a long vertical casing, which could be located in a corner of a cabinet of curiosities. At the top, the viewer would look horizontally through a hole at an inclined mirror, which reflected the image of the cut-out scenery arranged vertically along the height of the box in slider frames. The highest pieces of scenery formed a proscenium, through which the rest was viewed. To make the illusion more pleasant, a sheet of plain glass could be placed in each of the sliders, which produced a very beautiful effect by softening the images of cards progressively further away from the eye. The sliders and scenes could be changed quickly by means of small drawers in the casing. The

Museo Nazionale del Cinema has an example of such a box. Martin Engelbrecht (1684–1756), an engraver and seller of prints, made some good examples of this design, but without optics. Some still survive, formed as small half-open wooden boxes, in which the fragile paper scenes and figures are arranged for viewing in perspective.

Cabinets of curiosities

Because of their fragile construction, 'perspective boxes' tended to be mainly found in cabinets of curiosities. The eighteenth-century collector Grollier de Servière owned one example, of a particularly complicated design, which resembled Kircher's 'catoptric theatre':

> There was a cupboard . . . in which one could see in relief a castle and some gardens, which seemed to be multiplied by means of several mirrors which were all around and reflected the objects. One could open and close the doors of the cupboard in four different ways and each time one would find new objects, the second time, that is to say, after the castle, there were a great number of pieces of gold and silver. At the third, there were flowers, at the fourth, there was the representation of a meal in relief. All these different changes were made by closing the door of the cupboard, and by the single movement of the key in the lock.[29]

Grollier de Servière's cabinet also contained a magic lantern 'which showed extraordinary pictures', prisms, mirrors, anamorphoses and a strange phantasmagoria: 'at one end of this room, there is a door from which one sees a figure of Death emerge, the size of a human, which walks and disappears just as one commands.'[30]

Also in Paris, the cabinet of Joseph Bonnier de la Mosson (1702–44), 'bailiff and master of the hunt of la Varenne des Thuileries and former Colonel of the Regiment of the Dauphin', was considered the richest and most complete museum of curiosities. Bonnier de la Mosson's cabinet was in his private house, 58–60 Rue Saint-Dominique, demolished in 1861 to make way for the modern 244 Boulevard Saint-Germain. It extended through nine rooms, each covering a different subject: anatomy, chemistry, pharmacy, medicines, measurement and tools, natural history (two rooms), physics and machines, and a library including herbaria and prints. An eighteenth-century painting, signed Lajoue, shows room number eight, the part of the cabinet devoted to physics. The image is bathed in a strange, surreal light, and shows an astonishing decor: the painted ceiling is 10 or 15 m above the marble floor, which is decorated with geometric designs. The walls are covered with carved shelves, on which are arranged a magic lantern, prisms, magic mirrors, anamorphoses, lenses, concave and convex mirrors, telescopes, spyglasses, polyhedra, ivory sculptures and so on. The richly decorated central pillar contains a pendulum clock. In the distance, as if the room opens onto the outside at ground level, can be seen the foundations of a building under construction. All the objects in the cabinet were sold in 1744, after Bonnier de la Mosson's death. The catalogue was compiled by Edme-François Gersaint, an antique dealer whose famous shop sign was painted by Watteau. The magic lantern appeared as number 573:

> Magic lantern with casing of bronzed tin-plate, equipped with its lamp and reflective mirror, with a small box which contains twenty-nine frames, in which are enclosed well-painted glasses, and suitable for the performance of experiments.[31]

The most amazing item in Bonnier de la Mosson's cabinet was certainly his *Machine d'Optique*, whose mechanism and views were of an unprecedented standard. This was number 606 in the catalogue:

> It shows the various scene changes which take place during an Opera; these changes are operated by means of a button which one pulls towards oneself. At the opening of the Machine one sees a Forest, through which appears a Landscape with Hunters, Horses and other Animals. The first scene change gives the view of a cave filled with workers who are moving around. At the second change one sees a pleasant countryside, decorated with a wood in which Orpheus is attracting Animals by the sound of his Lyre; the Bacchantes who are coming to batter him to death appear in the distance. The third change shows a Palace of the richest kind, in which different persons appear. In the fourth change one sees a beautiful flower bed decorated with orange trees and fountains, having in the background a great garden formed by porticos of greenery, along which various persons are walking. Finally the fifth change, which forms the sixth and last view, shows an Ionic colonnade, which has been constructed at Rome for a public festival; in the background of this decoration are three porticos, through which one sees a flower garden ending in a country scene.[32]

This device was designed and constructed for Bonnier de la Mosson by Alexis Magny (1712–77), a great Parisian optician who worked for the

Duke of Chaulnes, among others. Magny lived at Saint-Germain-des-Près, 'at the Sign of King Childebert', and styled himself as 'engineer for timepieces, mathematical and physical instruments, also mechanics'. He was one of the best opticians of the time. He took as much care over the mechanism as over the external appearance of the apparatus, which according to Gersaint was entirely of polished wood:

> On the two sides of this Machine are brass arms to receive lights, in order to make possible the giving of shows at night, which can only give a more beautiful effect. This piece is all the more pleasant because its operation is very simple. It is only necessary, as has already been stated, to pull a button towards oneself when one wishes to make a change, and push it back to its original position to be in a state of readiness for another change. There is also another button next to the first which allows the lowering of a cloth to conceal the operation; the construction of its interior is infinitely satisfying in its simplicity and the ease of its components; its exterior has a very beautiful octagonal base made in varnished Dutch wood, measuring two feet in diameter by about four feet in height.[33]

Other great eighteenth-century Parisian cabinets were owned by the Duke of Chaulnes; by Louis XV at the Hôtel de Passy; and by the Académie des Sciences, which included a large and beautiful magic lantern which is shown in a 1698 engraving by Sébastien Leclerc. These glorious collections contained many other optical devices worthy of attention. The Polémoscope, for example, allowed one to observe without being seen. Abbé Nollet recommended this device (a sort of spyglass containing an inclined mirror, which allowed one to look at an angle) to discover the identity of the 'nuisance' knocking at one's front door.

Bonnier de la Mosson also owned a long catoptric box, divided horizontally into two chambers. In the upper part which one viewed through a transparent window, scenery formed a theatrical proscenium, behind which a mirror was inclined at about 40 degrees. The interior of the box was lit through the top by a simple opening. In the lower chamber, another inclined mirror was positioned opposite the upper one. An image such as a garden scene was drawn onto this mirror, with a hollowed winding track, along which a brass or ivory ball could descend and slide easily. This curious mirror was illuminated by a candle. A mechanism allowed the ball to be returned to the top of the inclined mirror, and then released along the track engraved in the lower mirror. To a viewer looking into the upper mirror, the ball would appear to be rising through various detours to come out at the top, from where it

Fig. 16. Johann Gütle's peepshow box (1794).
Collection: Bibliothèque Nationale.

would appear to fall down before beginning to climb again. There was also the 'incomprehensible telescope', the magic palace and pyramid, the box with three or four mirrors, and so on.

We should not leave the eighteenth-century peepshow without mentioning one more remarkable design, no example of which is known to survive today. This appeared in Germany at the end of the eighteenth century. Its inventor, Johann Konrad Gütle, was a scientist who was entranced by *Zaubermechanik* ('mechanical magic').

Gütle's device consisted of a rectangular box mounted on a base (see Fig. 16). A vertical picture was attached to the top of the box at its rear edge, showing 'a young Savoyard' in the process of projecting the illuminated disc of a magic lantern to a small audience of common people. But the projected disc was cut out of the picture, so that images painted on glass could appear in this opening, as if actually projected by the Savoyard's lantern. In fact no projection was involved: the painted discs were inserted behind the picture and turned to appear in the opening by a mechanical system. The discs were stored in the rectangular box, which formed a support for the picture. The images included: the head and shoulders of a woman, with a mask in her hand; a warship; a hunter blowing a horn; an elephant; the head of an old woman; a windmill; a stork; a conservatory; and a soldier. This very curious machine, which paid homage to the magic lantern and was not a true peepshow, was available in 1794 'fully painted and lacquered with its accessories, three Thalers twelve Groschen, or six Florins eighteen Crowns'.[34]

Clearly the peepshow, in all its different designs, whether enclosed in cabinets of curiosities or hawked around the festivals and fairgrounds, offered a very rich range of illusions, illuminated and otherwise, for the viewer of the seventeenth, eighteenth, and nineteenth centuries. However its spectacle could only be seen by a few people at a time. This prevented it ever achieving the same celebrity as the magic lantern; but the fashion for boxes with an eyepiece had begun, and was to find other moments of glory at the end of the nineteenth century in the shape of the Edison Kinetoscope.

The lanternist's revolution

It is perhaps not surprising that in eighteenth-century France, the ultimate refinement of the great cabinets of curiosities was contemporary with the first mutterings of revolution. An intellectual delight for the aristocrat, the optical instrument could also become a weapon in the hands of the people. At the start of the French Revolution and possibly even before, magic lantern pictures took a political turn which caused the nobility some dismay. The repertoire of the Savoyards became a vehicle for the claims of the people. Numerous anonymous pamphlets published from 1789 onwards portray travelling lantern showmen: the scenes they project are violent attacks on royalty, the commentary is ironic and insolent. These documents are very precious, not only for the history of the Revolution, but also for that of projection, providing evidence of the organization and patter of travelling lantern and peepshow showmen of this period. We have already seen some allegorical and fantastic texts; those published after 1789 were much more realistic.

For example, the small underground pamphlet *La Lanterne Magique de la France, Nouveau Spectacle de la Foire Saint-Germain* ('The Magic Lantern of France, New Show at the Fair of Saint-Germain'), printed in 1789, consists of a diatribe against Charles Alexandre de Calonne, who took over the finance ministry in 1783 after the dismissal of Jacques

Necker. The various expedient measures he introduced were not enough to fill in the abyss of the budget deficit, and his critics had a field day. He resigned in 1787, but remained in the mind of the people, two years later, as a prime example of a sleazy politician. The narrator of the pamphlet walks in the Fair of Saint-Germain and comes upon two travelling showmen haranguing the crowd. A footnote advises the reader 'that it is necessary to adopt a Savoyard accent':

> 'It's superb! It's magnificent! Ladies and gentlemen, roll up, roll up; we are starting in a moment, the room is already almost full; in all your life you have seen nothing so rare and curious! Roll up, roll up; it will cost you nothing, ladies and gentlemen, but the sum of two *sous*,' two great fellows were shouting with all their force and all their lungs, who from their wide shoulders and their fat faces, and their coarse homespun clothes, appeared to me to be industrious natives of Savoie.
>
> As these types of entertainment, however rude they may be, generally amuse me, because of the original tone which these good folk use to entertain the world, I was quite happy to partake of it once again . . . The room into which we entered was already filled with spectators; and we were scarcely in there before they began to show us the curiosities of the magic lantern.
>
> A small gentleman, with a sharp voice and very sunken eyes, who according to all appearances was the director of the show, immediately shouted: 'there, there, it's really him; it's the famous . . . the famous . . . the famous controller of finances who, greedy at any price for that which befits a great celebrity, began and ended . . . and ended with complete success, in robbing the gallant Frenchmen.'[35]

The friends of Calonne were then shown one by one ('How could he have had none, he was controller of finances?'), along with one of his mistresses, a group of journalists in the pocket of the king, a 'charming group of fat-bellied priests', some aristocrats, the unfortunate *canaille* ('bastard') who had to pay the taxes, and finally the last picture, 'a woman who was formerly in excellent health, but is today in a state of languour': France herself. The projection took place in a closed room, presumably a fairground booth.

Many of these revolutionary texts made use of a double meaning of the French word *lanterne*, which also referred to the scaffold on which enemies of the revolution met their deaths: the cry *'Les aristocrates à la lanterne!'* did not indicate that they were being taken to see a show. This usage appears to derive from the architectural term 'lantern' for a tower or similar structure; in any event the double meaning was played upon widely. For example, in 1790 the Vicomte de Mirabeau, brother of the Revolutionary orator Honoré de Mirabeau, published three or four issues of *La Lanterne Magique Nationale* ('The National Magic Lantern'), in much the same vein as the text just mentioned. Mirabeau set out a list of forty-five 'changes' of picture, in the three issues consulted (Pierre Larousse mentions a fourth issue, which has not been located). Mirabeau's *Lanterne* showed 'all the marvels of the Revolution': the heroes of the Bastille, the light troops of the Faubourg Saint-Antoine at Saint-Marcel, 'ladies of the nation and defrocked nuns', 'the *lanterne* of le Châtelet' (the scaffold), and, a great marvel in reality, 'the celebrated head-cutter'.[36]

Also in 1790, an anonymous pamphleteer promoted the travelling lantern, commandeered by the Revolution, in the avenging role (like its more sinister namesake) of 'Scourge of the aristocrats':

> Frenchmen, I've arrived from Switzerland, the land of liberty: I bring a rare and curious thing, which was given to me by a famous engineer. It is a magic lantern which represents the most faithful pictures of your revolution, from the moment when Calonne announced the deficit, right up to the point where we are now; to offer you this admirable optical machine as a gift, it's without doubt the best use I could put it to, it is only suitable for a people who have just captured their freedom.[37]

In the frontispiece of this pamphlet a man is shown operating a magic lantern, set on a base illustrated by the revolutionary 'phrygian cap' or 'cap of liberty'. The goddess of Truth is lifting the curtain which covers the machine. The showman has set up opposite the Paris Hôtel de Ville (Town Hall), in the Place de Grève. All the principal political events of the Revolution, from the dismissal of Calonne in 1787 to the Constitution of 1789, are to be passed in review. At this time Louis XVI is still in favour: the aristocrats are the only guilty ones, shown veiling 'the eyes of our august Monarch' with a wide blindfold. Before he begins, the showman sings ('to a Savoyard tune'):

> Hurry up to my Lantern,
> Proud and generous people,
> I bring with me from Berne,
> This very precious jewel.
> And hey and ho, and hey and ho, and hey and ho:
> See how they come.

The good Frenchman will enjoy me,
For Liberty will please him,
And the aristocrat will be sent (repeat),
Away beyond Mount Jura (repeat).

In my *optique* he will see,
How he breaks his chains,
Of his heroic bravery
The pictures here are shown.
And hey and ho . . .[38]

The twelfth and last picture represents the Constitution, appearing in the shape of a beautiful woman 'placed on a pedestal wide enough to demonstrate how durable is the basis of this constitution'.

There were also political engravings showing the magic lantern. In the print *Lanterne Magique Republicaine* ('The Republican Magic Lantern'), we see a travelling showman, a good *sans-culotte* (radical revolutionary) according to the caption, standing behind a huge smoking lantern which shows on the screen 'in the luminous disc, all that is happening in France'. Several images are arranged in the disc, under the title 'Virtue the Order of the Day': the guillotine ('punishment of traitors'), manufacture of saltpetre and weapons, '7,000 Spaniards surrendering their arms to the French', and so on. At the bottom of the screen, a 'young republican plays the refrain *Ça Ira* ['It will go', a revolutionary anthem] on the hurdy-gurdy'. Meanwhile 'Georges Dandin' (King George III of England) watches this scene with a look of horror, together with his Prime Minister William Pitt.

The political literary tradition of the magic lantern was picked up again under the Restoration, but the tone was less lyrical. In *La Lanterne Magique de la Rue Impériale* ('The Magic Lantern of the Imperial Way'), attributed to Antoine Caillot, the style is clearly rather sentimental:

> Behold, behold the triumphal entry of Louis XVIII into the city of Paris! What a beautiful day! What delights! What enthusiasm! The Monarch advances with a slow pace . . . His eyes are moistened with tears . . . As for me, Ladies and Gentlemen, it is impossible for me to continue; my voice is stifled with sobs: I close my Magic Lantern.[39]

Throughout the nineteenth century, French political pamphleteers and writers never lost sight of the lantern as a metaphor. Examples included *Lanterne Magique de la Restauration* ('The Magic Lantern of the Restoration'); *Lanterne Magique de l'Île d'Elbe* (1815, 'The Magic Lantern of the Isle of Elba'); *Lanterne Magique Républicaine* (1848, 'The Republican Magic Lantern'); *Lanterne Magique Illustrée de Fond en Comble* (1868, 'The Magic Lantern Illustrated from Top to Bottom', plagiarized from *La Lanterne* by Rochefort); and *L'Optique, Tableaux de Moeurs* (1824, 'The *Optique*, Moral Pictures'). There were numerous children's magazines, books and popular newspapers carrying similar titles. There was even one curiosity entitled *La Lanterne Magique*, a badly printed four-page poem from around 1830 in which a young girl travels with her magic lantern, which she loses at the same time as she loses her virtue.

The French Revolution increased the popularity of travelling show-men and projection with renewed force. The famous Étienne-Gaspard Robertson, for one, took advantage of this in opening his *Fantasmagorie* in 1798, as we shall see in Chapter 6. Jean-Pierre Claris de Florian (1755–94) devoted his 1792 fable *Le Singe qui Montre la Lanterne Magique* ('The Monkey who Shows the Magic Lantern'), which has become proverbial, to the travelling showman. In this story the absent lanternist is replaced by his monkey, who eloquently lectures an assembly of animals on the images which the machine would be showing if the monkey had not forgotten to light the lantern. The audience, seeing nothing, are naively astonished. But the monkey continues, unstoppable:

> Is there anything to compare?
> Gentlemen, behold the sun,
> Its rays and all its glory,
> Here now is the moon, and the story
> Of Adam, Eve, and the animals . . .
> Behold, Gentlemen, they are beautiful![40]

Exit the showman

In spite of its great popularity, the trade of the travelling showman began, little by little, to become less and less common. Numerous traces of it can still be found between 1820 and 1860. In 1839 the famous illustrator Paul Gavarni (real name Guillaume Chevalier, 1804–66) published two lithographs of a magic lantern showman and a fairground peepshow box, the latter captioned 'One must show man images, for reality troubles him'. In 1838 Frédéric Soulié wrote *La Lanterne Magique*, featuring a former soldier of the Empire who travels as a worthy showman. Paul Féval's 1863 novel *Les Habits Noirs* involved the lantern showman in the dark schemes of a band of criminals. But in reality there were fewer and fewer showmen. In 1885 Frédéric Dillaye wrote:

> Thirty years ago, one still heard the evening cry 'Magic Lantern' in the Paris streets . . . The toy sellers, by selling magic lanterns cheaply, have destroyed this industry of the streets.[41]

This is completely true: the industrialization of lantern manufacture, during the Second Empire (1852–70) of Napoléon III, undermined the trade of the travelling showmen in France. Dillaye dated the disappearance of this street cry to around 1850, which seems a little early. The lantern trade never really disappeared, at least not until the appearance of the cinema. Up until the end of the nineteenth century, many fairground showpeople ran very high-quality projection shows, using powerful lanterns with oxy-hydrogen burners. Yet the true travelling showmen, those who moved along the roads on foot with their poor lanterns on their backs, seem to have almost completely disappeared around the 1870s.

A few people in Brittany still remember the 'Termajis' or 'Termagics' who travelled the countryside at the end of the nineteenth century. It is difficult to tell whether these were true travelling showmen in the tradition of the eighteenth century, or fairground lanternists with all their cumbersome equipment. Pierre-Jakez Hélias mentions projections of science and current events by a 'Termajis', while in her novel Les Termagics Jeanne Nabert refers to the old entertainers as 'the first ones, [who] showed the magic lantern to the poor people of the towns'.[42] Whatever the case may be, thanks to these miserable and courageous travellers the magic lantern and other optical illusions knocked on the door of every house. In the eighteenth and nineteenth centuries, only a blind person would have been unaware of their charms and effects.

5

'Life and Motion'
The Eighteenth-Century Lantern Slide

The lanternists of the eighteenth century, whether they were travelling showpeople, opticians, scientists, or amateurs, displayed astonishing creativity. The slides in their magic lanterns captured both realist and mythical images; they also made mechanical slides which allowed them to obtain both instantaneous and continuous animation. Throughout the Enlightenment (a period known in French as the *siècle des Lumières*, the 'century of Light'), the technique of these transparent views improved incessantly, and the illusion of movement became more diverse. Numerous books appeared in German, English, and French, with the aim of placing the construction of lanterns and slides within the reach of everyone.

Painting on glass

Painting slides for the magic lantern is a difficult art. Projection enlarges every detail unforgivingly, so that tiny smudges become huge smears and a clumsy design displays all its distressing mediocrity. The transparency of colours is a problem: applying the paint too thickly, or with too much pigment, transforms the images into dark shadows. Today it is easy to recognize the very earliest eighteenth-century slides by their poorly controlled pigmentation.

From the start oil-based paints were ruled out, because of their opacity, and water-colours were generally preferred. A German, Christian Gottlieb Hertel of Halle, wrote in 1716:

> I used to paint with oil colours at the start, and thought them good, but with time the colours turn brown and become completely opaque and dark, also I have now chosen water-colours, because they remain much more stable and a lacquer varnish makes them bright and transparent. I can recommend this method.[1]

Hertel advised drawing the pictures one wished to show with the lantern onto paper first. He then placed 'a thin pure glass, French glass being the best' over the drawing and reproduced exactly, with 'a black or brown colour which one may remove with vinegar', the outline which he had traced on the paper. When this was done, he applied water-colours within the outline, gently and transparently, then covered the background with opaque black paint, so that the designs and colours would stand out more effectively. One could also, he added, inscribe a caption into this black background with a needle or brush. Finally, he covered everything with clear varnish to protect the pictures from humidity and heat. This very simple method was used right up until the end of the nineteenth century. The most difficult stage was the preparation of the water-colours. The projectionist was obliged to become a chemist, carefully manipulating such substances as 'dragon's blood' (a red resin), bitters of beef, or ground bladder. On this basis Hertel's recipes were beyond the reach of ordinary people: 'The *spiritu vini* must be *rectificatissimus* such that it does not leave any *phlegma*' ('the wine spirit must be of the finest quality such that it does not leave any residue'), he noted in his half-Latin jargon. To prevent his varnish—a mixture of sandarac (cypress resin), mastic, wine spirits, and lavender oil—from cracking, he added a little turpentine. He also mentioned that there were some slides whose images were baked in a fire, 'but they are expensive and do not equal in beauty those described above'.[2] Abbé Nollet, in 1770, confirmed the existence of this process:

> The glass strips which carry the most perfect and most solid objects are painted with transparent enamels, and baked afterwards; but it is quite unusual to find workers who know how to make these types of images.[3]

In 1735, the German Johann Bernhard Wiedeburg of Jena made up water-colours as described by Hertel, but used a slightly different recipe for treating the glass, before and after painting:

In order that the images adhere to the glass, the latter must be washed with tragacanth [astragalus gum] dissolved in white vinegar, and the colours themselves covered with a good varnish. One makes such a varnish with sandarac and grains of white mastic ground very finely, after which one places them in a jar and pours onto them rectified spirits of wine, lavender oil and Venetian turpentine. One closes the jar tightly and hangs it in the sun, or places it in very hot water until the mastic and the sandarac are completely melted.[4]

Another German author, C.L. Deneke of Altona, near Hamburg, gave very precise information in 1757. He took pure glass from France or Bohemia and had a glazier cut it into a disc, square or rectangle, slightly smaller than the condensing lens of the lantern. The glass was cleaned with ground chalk. Using a weight or some glue, he fastened the glass sheet onto the pictures which he had drawn previously on paper (an engraving could also be used):

Then with a fine pointed brush and some softly ground animal black, to which I have added some old linseed oil and painter's varnish, I retrace carefully and precisely the outline of the design onto the glass, and when it is done, I remove the glass and correct the drawing if there are some places where this is necessary. I leave it to dry and continue the work: for to begin it only to do a few pieces is not worth the effort.[5]

When the drawing on the glass was dry, Deneke 'brought the shadows' to it, that is to say that he drew in the black lines of folds in clothes and other features. Another wait followed. During this time, the painter would prepare his brushes. The colours were already prepared:

Berlin blue, the best indigo, yellow of sap or berries, gamboge, iris green, Florentine varnish, beautiful red pressed from real pernambouque [an exotic wood] boiled and prepared, brown of sap or nuts, distilled verdigris . . . These are the main colours from which, by mixing them with skill, one can obtain other colours.[6]

Once the 'shadows' were dry, Deneke took a little colour with a knife and mixed it with varnish (sandarac mixed with mastic and lavender oil), and then applied this mixture to the glass surface with a brush. When everything was dry, the background was covered with black oil paint. The 'shadows' could also be added to the pictures after colouring them: 'this method demands more effort and time than the first; but if one carries it out according to the art, the images have the appearance of a painting and the representation on the screen is more pleasant.' Finally, Deneke made frames of dry beech wood. If the glass was circular, he hollowed out holes in a board: 'I place in all six discs in a board; for square glasses, four, three, two or a single one, according to the size required for the story.' The pieces of glass were retained in their frame by a thin open ring, a method which was repeated in the nineteenth century.

To obtain pictures of any quality many hours, or indeed days, of work were necessary. Some slide painters specialized in grotesque or comic subject matter, in which case it was not essential for the work to be of the finest. But others, true artists, aimed to project very precise images onto the screen, to meet the expectations of delicate minds. It is quite clear that the 'great and good' of the eighteenth century were not impressed by mediocre slide painting. They scorned the generally trivial shows offered by the Savoyards, but did not ignore the magic lantern as a pastime: it might be slightly demeaning, but could be highly entertaining. Painters and professional miniaturists supplied these rich amateurs with magnificent slides, which an optician or a manservant trained in the operation of the lantern would present in front of a glittering audience.

If one anonymous contemporary account is to be believed, no less a person than Philippe d'Orléans, Regent of France between 1715 and 1723, included an erotic lantern show in the course of one of his habitual nights of debauchery. The pictures were not just any old bawdy scribbles, but some 'engravings of l'Arétin', presumably illustrating the famous *Ragionamenti* by the Italian writer Pietro Aretino (1492–1556). A commentary accompanied the images, which were perhaps copied from illustrations in a contemporary book. The Marquis Charles Auguste de La Fare, a mediocre poet but a debaucher of some distinction, took charge of the lantern:

> After the game we sat at table and Monsieur the Regent decided that he would get the ladies drunk, to find out their characters under the influence of wine. The party accepted, and we found ourselves all a little warm in the head. Monsieur the Regent, a little more distracted by the wine than the others, sang some songs which were more than cheerful, and accompanied them with gestures for the ladies which were still more expressive; everyone followed his example.
>
> La Fare offered to show us a magic lantern which he had made. The room was prepared, and he passed in front of us a series

of the engravings of l'Arétin, for which he had composed some
accompanying couplets. During the darkness necessary for this
show, everyone grabbed hold of a woman; I wanted to let my hands
stray onto one who was close to me, but in every direction in which
I tried to let them wander, I found there were already others
occupying the place . . .[7]

One of the guests at this memorable evening, Louis-François Armand
Vignerot du Plessis, Duke of Richelieu (1696–1788, great-nephew of the
Cardinal), was later the target of no less a lanternist than the great writer
Voltaire (François-Marie Arouet, 1694–1778). To brighten the evening
gatherings at the château of the Marquise du Châtelet at Cirey-sur-
Blaise, in the Haute-Marne region, Voltaire used a magic lantern which
presumably formed part of his friend the Marquise's wonderful collection
of scientific instruments. On 10 December 1738, Voltaire lit his lantern
and personally showed some slides (of his own design?) with a commentary 'in a Savoyard accent'. There could be few better 'masters of
ceremonies' than the brilliant Voltaire, but sadly nobody lucky enough to
hear it made a note of this priceless monologue.

Voltaire projected pictures caricaturing the Duke of Richelieu's
entourage. The Duke had been one of Voltaire's schoolmates during his
Jesuit education: Voltaire had always flattered him, lent him money, and
despaired at not being able to exert more influence over this person of
position. Using his lantern as an instrument of vengeance, Voltaire also
presented 'the story of the Abbé Desfontaines'. Pierre François Guyot,
known as Desfontaines (1685–1745) was one of his bitterest adversaries.
In 1738, the same year as the projection show at Cirey, the two men
were involved in a literary duel from which Voltaire, naturally, eventually
emerged victorious. Desfontaines started it in 1735, with his *Observations
sur les Esprits Modernes* ('Observations on the Modern Mind'); Voltaire
replied in 1738, with *Le Préservatif* ('The Preservative', or possibly 'The
Condom') in which he denounced the dubious morals of his rival,
a defrocked priest. Later the same year Desfontaines published *La
Voltairomanie* ('Voltairomania') in which he returned insult for insult.

The magic lantern show Voltaire gave on 10 December 1738 was
attended by Madame de Graffigny:

After supper, he gave us the magic lantern, with some remarks
which would make you die laughing. There was the circle of
Monsieur the Duke of Richelieu, the story of the Abbé
Desfontaines, and all kinds of tales always with the Savoyard accent.

> No, there was never anything so funny! But in the course of fiddling
> with the reservoir of his lantern, which was filled with wine spirits,
> he tipped it onto his hand, it caught fire, and there it was ablaze.
> Oh! Lord, we had to watch, since it was beautiful! But what was not
> well, was that it was burned: this slightly disrupted the entertain-
> ment which carried on again shortly afterwards.[8]

As this description suggests, adjustment of the lamp was not an easy
operation at this time. The flame would splutter, die away, or suddenly
brighten, the wick would go out or not give a sufficiently white light.
The lanternist had to keep a continuous watch to obtain a bright enough
disc on the screen. Voltaire, no doubt not very well practised, nearly lost
his precious hand, the hand which had just written *Les Lettres Philoso-
phiques* ('Philosophical Letters'), the reaction to which was the reason for
his retreat to the château at Cirey. In spite of this incident, it seems
likely that Voltaire continued to use the lantern to entertain his compan-
ions. Much later, on 31 December 1774, as a refugee in Ferney, he was
perhaps recalling one of these enjoyable evenings when he wrote to the
Marquise du Deffand:

> It seems to me that a retreat makes the passions more lively and
> more profound; the life of Paris disperses all one's ideas, one forgets
> everything, one is diverted only momentarily by everything in
> that great magic lantern, where all the pictures pass as rapidly as
> shadows; but in solitude one can pursue one's feelings relentlessly.[9]

Slides for all

A few examples of eighteenth-century slides still survive, having miraculously avoided accidental breakage, stupidity, and war. The author's own
collection includes four examples, of mediocre workmanship, but
probably highly representative of production at the time of Louis XV.
These slides (measuring about 5.5 cm by 24 cm, though of varying
lengths) are cut irregularly and crudely from thick glass, whose surface
undulates slightly and is scattered with small air bubbles. A paper strip
glued onto the right- or left-hand edge of each slide indicates the
subject, though unfortunately the text is often illegible. The caption of
one slide can just be made out as 'Mlle Friquette, M. Friquet', and the
slide shows four caricature figures, in costumes of the time of Louis XV:
a woman wearing a fine dress with ochre and red panniers, but with a
face featuring a very prominent nose, is sitting with a flower in her hand;

two well-dressed gentlemen, also with enormous noses, stand next to her. A manservant brings a second chair.

When the slide is examined with a magnifying glass, strong pigmentation is evident: water-colours, based on ground material, are bound to have this type of defect (by the nineteenth century dark and opaque colours were no longer used in lantern slides). The technique is still not very well mastered, but the influence of Hertel, Deneke, or Nollet is apparent, in that the outlines are traced in brown ink and the colours shadowed with care. However, the painter has left the background transparent. The colours are slightly cracked: the slides were not covered with a protective varnish, which explains the poor state of some of the colours. In spite of their commonplace surname ('Friquet' means 'tree sparrow'), the two grotesque figures are dressed as members of the upper classes, suggesting that this image is a caricature of the bourgeoisie.

Another of the slides is somewhat scatological, a genre much beloved of the eighteenth-century lanternist. A similar slide is reproduced in an engraving in Diderot and d'Alembert's *Encyclopédie* of 1751–76, showing a grotesque scene involving an enema. In this case the subject is just as crude: a woman, with her skirt lifted, extinguishes a candle placed behind her in place of a chamber pot. Next to her, a servant draws wine from a barrel while two drunkards dance, glasses in hand. The two other slides depict four giants in the middle of a quarrel, and a group of eight cavaliers.

Diabolical subjects were one of the commonest themes of lantern imagery over a long period, but curiously they have today become one of the rarest. Perhaps at some stage these slides were systematically destroyed; the same could apply to the erotic images of the eighteenth century, which are also difficult to find today. These two subjects were much in demand, however, from both the ordinary people and aristocratic libertines. A present-day Austrian collector has one eighteenth-century slide which might have satisfied the desires of the French Regent. This shows a group of elegant people ice-skating: one young woman has fallen over, with her legs in the air and her dress thrown up. In another slide, some monkeys wearing human clothes imitate scenes of everyday life, with a doctor-monkey wielding a traditional enema instrument.

Not all slides were so trivial. The Museo del Cinema in Turin has about twenty very well-preserved and very beautiful eighteenth-century slides measuring 5 x 20 cm. Most unusually, these were found with their original magic lantern, a roughly constructed wooden instrument about 30 cm in height which was discovered in the house of a noble family in

Verona. Eight of these slides show various expressions appearing on twenty-two different faces, painted with highly professional skill. Their captions are written on the framing paper: 'Laughter, weeping, sadness, desperation, anger, horror, pain, jealousy', and so on. Ten other slides show landscapes, rural views, and a hunting scene; three of these slides are animated. The Italian collector Laura Minici Zotti also owns eight slides from the end of the eighteenth century, probably made in Venice. One of these represents 'The visit of the Archbishop' in a long procession (35 x 9.5 cm). Another noted collector, David Robinson of London, has a wonderful set of eighteenth-century slides, whose subject is (once again) the *Dance of Death* by Holbein, but modified for satirical purposes, with some fat German burghers being driven by skeletons.

The Musée du Cinéma in Paris also has a slide showing a hunting scene, which appears full of movement: a huntsman blows on his horn, some dogs jump at a stag, and another stag bounds away into the distance and makes its escape (see Fig. 17). This prestigious collection, put together between 1910 and 1930 by the British cinema equipment dealer Will Day, is rich in other fine slides from the end of the eighteenth century: the Sun, Adam and Eve, Noah's Ark, Pluto, the spirit of Discord, Venus and Love, Venus scolded by Cupid. Another, older, slide (definitely from the reign of Louis XV), shows a romantic scene after the style of Fragonard.

The museum of the Paris Conservatoire National des Arts et Métiers (CNAM; 'National Academy of Arts and Crafts') owns a very precious collection, now in rather poor condition, which partly originated at the Collège de France. This includes some subjects which were reproduced as engravings in Abbé Nollet's 1770 book *L'Art des Expériences* ('The Art of Experiments'), such as a caricatured woman holding a monstrous baby in her arms. On the same slide, a hunchback plays a stringed instrument; on another, a grotesque figure grips a guitar in its hand. These two musicians appear almost identically in an English slide set of the 1820s, made by Watkins, which is now in the Musée du Cinéma. Certain images and subjects, whose meaning is now sometimes lost to us, appear again and again in lantern imagery. Also at the CNAM, a very beautiful slide of uniformly brown colouring shows a group of utterly hideous courtiers (one of them even has an elephant's trunk), in the middle of whom is a priest whose nose is half cut off. Standing back to observe the scene is a smiling peasant, who is not drawn as a caricature: a piece of vicious social criticism, to say the least.

The British collector John Jones has found a very interesting set of twelve eighteenth-century slides. The first six are numbered from one to

Fig. 17. Three eighteenth-century magic lantern slides. Collection: Cinémathèque Française, Musée du Cinéma.

seven (number six is missing) and represent a coronation procession at Westminster. The others, not numbered, show clowns, tumblers, a buffoon, jugglers, a pedlar of curiosities, in short, all the little world which circulates around the edges of a great festival such as a coronation. Jones has found an engraving in the British Museum, representing the coronation of William and Mary in 1689, from which his slides were copied with great precision. This does not definitely date these slides, since the painter could have recalled the event twenty or thirty years later; it does, however, provide proof that slide manufacturers sometimes took existing engravings as their sources.[10] Coronation commemoration slides were quite common in Britain. It was such a rare event, celebrated with so much pomp, that it was quite natural that projectionists should feed their lanterns on it plentifully. The Science Museum in London, the Bishop Ken Library at Longleat House, and the great British collector Lester Smith have several examples of this popular and ceremonious imagery.

In 1772 Benjamin Martin (1704–82), a British author of books popularizing science, mentioned a magic lantern show with views of a coronation in his book *The Young Gentleman and Lady's Philosophy*—this must refer to the coronation of George II in 1727 or George III in 1760. The text is presented in the form of a dialogue between a scholar, Cleonicus, and a young woman named Euphrosine:

> *Cleonicus*: However, I must entertain you with something of this Kind, and, because the Subjects shall not be low, I have procured an Artist, well skilled in this Miniature Painting, to draw on two or three Slips of Glass the whole PROCEEDING of the late CORONATION, which, when you observe the Motion on the Wall, you will certainly have a different Idea, than what you have hitherto entertained of these Subjects.—See, I put the Slips in, one after another, and will move them in a proper Manner, while you take a cursory View of them as they pass in the regal Procession.
> *Euphros.* This will be an elevated Subject, indeed:—Good Heavens! The Herb-Woman appears at a greater Advantage than when I saw her on the Plat-form at the Time. The Painter has certainly complimented her six Maids.—The Flowers lie as naturally on the Carpet as I then saw them:—A delightful Appearance, indeed; the various Orders and Degrees of Gentry and Nobility, with their proper Habits, Robes, and regal Investments, bring to my Mind so naturally the Thing itself, that I really judge this View, by Candle-light, much to exceed that by Day-light, if it may be so called when they returned from the Abbey.—The Canopies, under

which our Sovereigns walk, are very elegant and highly improved by the Painter's hand:—The King and his Royal Consort appear with all the Pomp of solemn Majesty.—Upon the whole, it is a most exquisite, grand and beautiful Scene . . .[11]

Finally, as far as 'fixed' slides are concerned (although some of them seem so full of life and movement that the term seems hardly accurate), there is one truly exceptional eighteenth-century set. An Italian collector has found fourteen magic lantern slides made around 1710 by the painter Giuseppe Maria Crespi (1665–1747) of Bologna. Crespi was fascinated, according to his son's account, by the projections of the camera obscura:

> He hollowed out a hole in his door. In front of it, on the opposite side of the street, was a white wall, exposed to the midday sun. When the peasants passed with cattle, he placed a lens into the hole and placed a white sheet opposite. He spent entire days there observing on the sheet all the objects which found themselves copied by means of this lens.[12]

Crespi came quite naturally to the magic lantern, which allowed him to project an imaginary world with ease. With a wonderfully skilful hand, he painted the different trades of Italy (similar to the 'Cries of Paris' mentioned in the previous chapter) on glass discs 6.5 cm in diameter, taking his ideas from existing engravings. In this way, *Le Mendiant au Rosaire* ('The Beggar with the Rosary') by the great French engraver Jacques Callot (*c.*1592–1635) was reproduced on glass, in magnificent transparent colours without too much uneven pigmentation. Crespi had discovered a good paint and, more importantly, he knew how to manage shadows and colours. He also left some parts completely transparent, giving a very beautiful effect when projected, and had learned to touch his finger lightly onto the paint so that his fingerprints would suggest the marks of an engraver's tool, a method which was to be widely used in the nineteenth century. *Le Ramoneur* ('The Chimney Sweep') and *Marchand d'Éventoirs* ('The Fan Seller'), engravings by Giuseppe Maria Mitelli, were reproduced in the same way, as well as *Vieille se Réchauffant à un Brasero* ('Old Woman Warming Herself at a Brazier') by Callot. Crespi also produced pictures from his own imagination, possibly derived from the images projected by his camera obscura. These include several beggars, a poor woman, a shepherd and his dog (the latter being in the process of defecating), and a layabout sitting on a chair, arms crossed with a happy expression.

Lantern slides painted by master painters were very rare, and at present this set is the only known surviving example. If only slides could be found signed by Watteau or Boucher! Who painted the slides after Aretino which the French Regent used? Who supplied the slides for the noble lantern of the Académie des Sciences, at the end of the seventeenth century—miniaturists, great masters, or simple craftsmen? A catalogue of the eighteenth-century slides still existing in private and public collections around the world is needed as a matter of urgency, to allow comparison of the quality, subjects, formats and methods used, and give an idea of the number of such hand-painted slides which have survived into our own times, as if by magic.

Moving slides

If only a few fixed slides from the eighteenth century survive, moving slides of this period, which were always much more fragile, are hardly represented at all in modern collections. Mechanized slides have had a very long history since Huygens showed the way around 1659. His *Dance of Death* was animated by the juxtaposition of two painted glass sheets which were presumably moved forward or back by pull tabs. This was a simple but delicate system, as befitted these earliest origins of pre-cinematography. Johannes Zahn recommended an ingenious method in 1686, though no contemporary examples survive, painting six successive stages of the same movement (the man twirling his cane) onto a glass disc (see Fig. 11).

In the eighteenth century good-quality animated views became much appreciated. They were described in the most serious scientific works, and their surprising effects attracted much praise. The lanternist was certain to please an audience with moving image effects such as substitutions, disappearances, sudden apparitions, and continuous movement: an aristocrat whose nose extended grotesquely, a courtier losing his wig, a windmill with turning sails, a young woman walking on the tightrope. The techniques of these effects were many and various, as we shall see. These illuminated images, like little moving playlets, were a naive but vital forerunner of the cinematograph show.

Very soon the Germans, particularly excited by the *Zauberlatern*, confirmed their technical superiority in the production of moving pictures. We have already seen that in 1676 Johann Christoph Sturm published an engraving showing a fixed slide of the head of Bacchus. Some twenty years later, German moving projections had achieved a great virtuosity. According to Christoff Weigel, who published a book[13] in 1698 on the artists and craftsmen of Nuremberg, the views which could be seen on the screens of that city included two goats fighting head-to-head, or a bear which stood upright and tried to grasp a Swiss man in its claws. This slide was made with a circular piece of glass fixed into a hole in a sheet of wood, and 'an area of field or earth' painted onto it, along with the unfortunate Swiss and the legs of the bear. This glass was fixed into the slide body. A second movable piece of glass was placed onto the first, painted with the body of the bear, and movable from top to bottom by a silk thread. Pulling the thread would move the body of the bear upwards, to make it stand up in front of the man; when it was released, the beast would fall back onto him.

Another view described by Weigel was highly educational: the mouth of Hell, from where emerged the three main vices of man (we do not know which), and into which they could return if desired. Hell, shown as the jaws of a monstrous animal, was painted on one side of a circular glass, which was encased in a grooved wooden frame. A second piece of glass showing the three vices could slide horizontally in the grooves. By pushing this piece of glass, the vices would appear to emerge from Hell or return into it. A third painted sheet could make an angel with a flaming sword appear and force the vices back into Hell. With this triple system, the projected scene could last for some time.

Some other examples described by Weigel included: Christ rising from the tomb and ascending to the heavens (the second glass plate was pulled towards the top); King Saul being shown the prophet Samuel by the Witch of Endor (Samuel was painted on the movable glass); an angel, or a genie, placing a crown of laurels on the head of the ruler of a country, or a hand emerging from the clouds with the name of the ruler; the beast of the Apocalypse rising from the sea and climbing the shore (here again, two glasses were juxtaposed: with the sea and shore painted on one and the beast on the other, so that the beast could be made to emerge slowly from the water by pushing the rectangular glass showing the sea).

Elsewhere in Germany, the Landgrave (Count) of the town of Kassel was a very early owner of a magic lantern, constructed on the principles described by Sturm. In 1709 a glass-cutter by the name of Temme or Themme began to assemble very elaborate slides there. A German traveller, Zacharias von Uffenbach (1683–1734), visited his workshop at the Gate of Zwirn on 19 November 1709:

> The glass-cutter Themme is a kind of very strange holy man, of
> extraordinary vanity. He showed us all sorts of spyglasses, enlarging

lenses, magic lanterns, lenses for viewing at a distance, of which he sang the praises quite insupportably, since they were very mediocre. He talked a lot about his magic lanterns and wished to show us what we had already seen, namely that his pictures moved and that they could fire gunshots. These pictures were quite attractive but when one discovered their great mystery they were of poor invention. In the coaches which moved forward, it was only the wheels which were engraved on the glass with a diamond; they were encased in tin and pulled by means of a thread wound around them. And in the same way the spinning wheel moved while Cupid span. To fire and launch bombs was even more simple but also much more engaging. Between the glass and the frame is a hole through which passes a paper disc. The drawing which represents the cannonball and the flame is hidden by this cover. When one wishes to launch the shot, one very quickly lifts the paper cover . . . Then the red colour gives the impression of fire, as if one had just suddenly fired. For ten Thalers I bought these painted views, twelve wooden boards in each of which there are four pictures, and then seven others which are movable.[14]

Von Uffenbach's scorn seems to have been only temporary, since he emerged from the shop with his arms filled with fixed and moving slides.

The first known engraving showing a moving slide was not published until 1713, in Jena, where the German Samuel Johannes Rhanaeus published a 'mathematical dissertation' entitled *Novum et Curiosum Laternae Augmentum* ('The New and Curious Improved Lantern'). Rhanaeus concerned himself first with retracing the still relatively recent history of the magic lantern, which he considered to be 'very noble and most worthy of presentation to the sight of Princes.'[15] He referred to the works of his German compatriots Sturm, Zahn, Schott, and Wolff, as well as the Irishman Molyneux. He also mentioned Kircher's *Ars Magna Lucis et Umbrae* (the second edition of 1671) but noted dryly that the magic lantern described there was 'imperfect'.

Rhanaeus described a number of moving slides, with a beautiful frontispiece illustration which he engraved himself. Following the designs of Christoff Weigel, he too described a view of Hell, with a mouth which took in or vomited out the three human vices. This terrifying image must have been highly successful. Rhanaeus also produced a quite complicated slide on a more reassuring subject, showing a woman bowing in front of a man. This had a moving piece of glass which descended and ascended along a groove, over the top of a fixed picture. A series of metal levers operated the glass, with a metal wire controlling the mechanism. This construction was very fragile indeed, which is one reason why few such slides have survived to the present day. To represent a windmill with its sails turning in the wind, Rhanaeus took a wooden or metal plate in which he had bored a central circular hole, into which he fixed a painted glass disc showing the mill without its sails. On a second movable glass disc he painted the sails. Movement was achieved by a complicated mechanism of three gear wheels. When this slide was slipped into the carrier of the lantern, the mill would appear in all its splendour on the screen, and the resulting moving painting (which no conventional painter could hope to rival) would appear miraculous to 'those who do not know its secret'. The mechanism for this slide was not easy to construct; in particular the gear wheels and toothed surround of the moving glass had to be cut very accurately.

Around 1736 the Dutchman Petrus van Musschenbroek (1692–1761) greatly simplified the mechanism of moving slides, including the well-known windmill. The Musschenbroeks had been established at Leyden since the start of the seventeenth century, and along with Huygens had made an unprecedented contribution to the business of scientific instrument manufacture. In Huygens' time, Samuel Joosten van Musschenbroek (1639–81) ran the workshop; he was succeeded by his brother, Johan Joosten van Musschenbroek (1660–1707) and then by the latter's son Jan (1687–1748). Petrus van Musschenbroek, after the death of his brother Jan, did not take over the family business, preferring to study philosophy and mathematics at Utrecht. Petrus very soon became interested in the magic lantern. His teacher was Willem Jacob Sturm van s'Gravesande (1688–1742), a Dutch scholar who described an improved magic lantern in one of his books in 1720. Jan van Musschenbroek had also worked for van s'Gravesande. It is possible that their uncle, Samuel Joosten van Musschenbroek, had very early knowledge of the lantern: after all, Leyden is not very far from Huygens' home at The Hague.

Whatever the case may be, during the 1730s Petrus van Musschenbroek was making moving slides for the magic lantern. Abbé Nollet, who visited the Netherlands in 1736, admired his work. In particular he remarked:

> A windmill with its sails turning . . . I found [these slides] well devised, in that the pictures had movements which seemed to bring them to life.[16]

Musschenbroek himself explained the operation of the windmill slide in his *Essai de Physique* published at Leyden in 1739. He had disposed of

Rhanaeus' gear system and substituted a cord mechanism, which Temme had already been using in 1709. Musschenbroek was a little mistaken about the history of moving slides, which he thought were very recent:

> We were content until now to paint pictures on small glasses, whose images appeared to be without action and without any movement: but recently we have learned how to make the images act, of which I shall give here the description of five methods, by the use of which one may make many other pictures, which will appear to be full of life . . . [One slide] shows a windmill, which, with the exception of its four sails, is painted on a piece of glass, which is secured firmly against the wood without the slightest movement. The four sails are shown on another circular glass, which is glued into a copper frame which may be rotated by means of a cord, which passes around the frame and a wheel; there is a handle with which one turns it. This is the method by which one may represent a turning windmill.[17]

This very practical method was adopted everywhere, and continued into the nineteenth century. Musschenbroek's other moving slides were all quite simple and ingenious. One projected the image of a man with a goblet in his hand. The figure was painted on the fixed glass, with the hand holding the goblet on another glass which could be moved freely over the first. The movable glass, framed in brass, was held by two 'tourniquets' which prevented it from coming away from the slide. A brass tab could be pushed and pulled to move the drinker's arm. 'It is in this way that the figure moves the goblet to his mouth, or moves it away again.'[18]

The next slide was quite unusual, in that it had to be moved vertically through the lantern's slide carrier (few lanterns had a vertical aperture), and it consisted of three juxtaposed pieces of glass. It showed a portrait of a man, wearing a wig and a hat. His comical bald head was painted on the fixed glass, the wig was painted 'on a piece of Muscovy glass attached to a brass rod', and the hat on a third piece of glass identical to the second. 'One can lift the hat and hide it in the cavity of the board [i.e. the wooden slide body]; one can do the same thing in respect of the wig, such that he appears only with a completely naked head.'[19] This highly comical scene showed what later was to become one of the favourite jokes of the practitioners of early cinema—for example in *La Course à la Perruque*, a Pathé film of 1906.

Van Musschenbroek's fourth slide (arranged horizontally, as normal) showed 'a small man who dances on the tightrope'. This had the same two-glass system: one fixed, showing the rope and the audience, the other movable, with the dancer who could be moved along by a brass rod. Finally, the very graceful fifth slide showed a young woman 'who appears to make a curtsey'. This was inspired by Rhanaeus' slide of the woman bowing before the man, but was simpler: half of the woman (the legs and feet) was painted on the fixed glass, but the rest of her could be lowered or raised as required by the second moving glass. This had to be done gently and without pushing too hard, or the young woman would appear to melt into herself. Nollet described almost the same images and mechanisms in 1770, in *L'Art des Expériences*: 'A man takes off his hat and puts it on again, a grotesque figure shakes its jaws, a blacksmith strikes on an anvil, and so on.'[20]

Petrus van Musschenbroek concluded his book by publishing a list of the assorted machines on sale at his brother Jan's premises in Leyden, including:

> A large magic lantern, very artistically worked, fitted with several magnifying lenses, a strong mirror and well-made pictures. Without the pictures, seventy-five Florins. With pictures, one hundred Florins. A wooden base for this lantern, fifteen Florins. Another magic lantern similar to the above, but much smaller, supplied with fifty small pictures, forty-five Florins. Various moving pictures for the above lanterns, such as a windmill, a young woman curtseying, etc., each three Florins and ten.[21]

The number of subjects illustrated was vast, although some did recur frequently. In 1769 Edme-Gilles Guyot drew up a list of the double-glass moving slides which he had seen most often:

> A woman who removes and puts on her mask. Two men sawing a stone. A carpenter planing. A bird which leaves its cage and perches on the hand of a woman. Two rams beating their heads together. A hunter firing at a hare which escapes to its burrow. Two men fighting with swords in their hands. A baker putting his bread in the oven. Two ships crossing the sea, etc.[22]

Guyot also noted that one 'could make changes with a single slide on which one painted five or six similar pictures, but in different positions, in order to be able to substitute one for another quickly'. This basic idea, as we have seen, had already been outlined by Zahn in 1686.

Moving maritime scenes were just as popular, as shown by accounts praising their beauty by the Englishman William Hooper[23] in 1774 and the German Johann Christian Wiegleb in 1779. According to Wiegleb, to represent a storm at sea using the magic lantern, two long glass sheets of about 30 cm in length should be painted and secured adjacent to each other in a wooden frame. They should slide vertically back and forth in the grooves of the frame:

> On one, paint the movements of the sea, from gentle waves through to the appalling tempest, with a calm sky, the start of the waves, clouds, and so on. On the other glass, paint ships of different types and sizes . . . If one moves the first glass gently in its groove, and begins to give it some movements as the storm commences, one will produce in this way the effects of the sea becoming gradually more and more rough and in the end producing a tempest . . . If at the same time one passes over it, very gently, the glass on which the ships are painted, it will appear that they are sailing in the middle of the sea . . .[24]

The Irish writer Jonathan Swift may have witnessed this type of projection, in London on 27 March 1713:

> I went afterwards to see a famous moving Picture, & I never saw any thing so pretty. You see a Sea ten miles wide, a Town on tothr end, & Ships sailing in the Sea, & discharging their Canon. You see a great Sky with Moon & Stars &c.[25]

Practically nothing else remains of the various simple or elaborate seventeenth- and eighteenth-century attempts to obtain 'moving pictures'. In the wonderful Museo del Cinema in Turin, among the slides accompanying the magic lantern found in Verona, are three moving slides of quite crude construction. As usual, the glasses are juxtaposed, but held in a simple paper frame rather than in wood. Two children see-saw on a beam, a woman throws a ball to her son, and a servant draws wine from a barrel. Each of them is operated by a roughly cut glass tab, which is a very rare feature. The CNAM in Paris has a slide similar to that described by Nollet: a grotesque figure which moves its jaw, as if about to speak (this design must have enjoyed some popularity, since it has also been found engraved on a lantern manufacturer's label from 1787). There is also a beautiful Cupid at a spinning wheel, an exact replica of the image described by Von Uffenbach in 1709, but its design appears to date from the start of the nineteenth century. The lantern image repertoire did not change much from one century to another. As a result some authors, collectors, and museum curators proudly present 'eighteenth-century' moving slides, but in fact the dating is almost always inaccurate. Authentic examples of slides from this period are extremely rare.

Technical evolution of the magic lantern

While slide mechanisms were being rapidly modernized, the technical evolution of the magic lantern proceeded just as quickly. At the start of the eighteenth century, the most common designs were based on the descriptions of Sturm and Zahn: small cylindrical lanterns, portable and light in weight. But everyone constructed their own lantern to their own design, and the examples described by European scientists display numerous variations.

For example, the lantern made by the German Johann Michael Conradi in 1710[26] was constructed entirely of tin-plate; it consisted of a vertical cylinder mounted on a base, with a conical chimney. It had a lamp with two wicks which could slide between a pair of rods welded to the base of the casing, so that the distance between the lamp flame and the condensing lens could be adjusted easily. In 1716, Hertel opted for a wooden lantern body, about 20 cm in length and height and 22 cm in width.[27] The chimney was pyramidal in shape, topped by a small roof, and the lens tube was of cardboard. The novelty of this lantern lay in the fact that it had two slide carriers, two slots formed parallel to each other in the lantern body. According to Hertel, this allowed a painted slide to be covered with another completely opaque one (if the opaque slide was then pulled out, the image of the first slide would appear instantly), but also the insertion of slides one after the other with perfect continuity. There was one problem: the focus would have to be adjusted each time the slide was changed.

The great Dutch scientist van s'Gravesande, intellectual mentor of the Musschenbroek brothers and professor at Leyden, described his own lantern in his 1721 book *Physices Elementa Mathematica*.[28] The body of the lantern was a smooth box, about 48 cm long by 36 cm wide, and about 20 cm in height. The chimney was very narrow and extended above the box by about 16 cm. A fine engraving accompanied van s'Gravesande's description, showing his lantern standing on a base and projecting a terrifying monster with two horns, a snout instead of a nose, and pointed teeth. With its face contorted and eyes closed, it has a displeased expression, as though the light from the lantern was shining right into its face.

Van s'Gravesande stated that he could place his lantern 9 m from the screen. It was fitted with a powerful lamp, with four wicks burning at the same time, and a powerful concave mirror 20 cm in diameter fixed behind the lamp. In front of the flame was a convex lens 12 cm in diameter. Two further lenses were located in the lens tube; between the two was a wooden ring which only allowed part of the light to pass through in order to avoid divergence of the light rays. Nollet later called this ring a 'diaphragm' (a term known to all photographers today, but one which had existed since 1690). Van s'Gravesande's lantern, with its various improvements, was very quickly adopted by a great majority of projectionists. The lantern described by the German Heinrich Johannes Bytemeister[29] in 1735 was entirely of wood, except for its sheet metal chimney. It was distinctive in having three successive lens tubes which slid within each other, 'like those of a telescope', as Christian Wolff, another German who took up the same design, observed. If the lamp was strong enough, this 'telescope' tube would allow projection over long distances.

All these lanterns were small, to ensure that their light would be well concentrated inside them. On the other hand, in 1743, an engraving from Nollet's *Leçons de Physique Expérimentale* showed a very large lantern mounted on a low table, cubic in shape and taller than the projectionist. It is likely, though, that the size of the lantern was exaggerated by the engraver, in order to make its operation comprehensible to readers. In 1770, in *L'Art des Expériences*, Nollet gave some more reasonable dimensions: between 35 and 40 cm in height, about the same in length, and 20 to 30 cm in width. It was necessary to place the lantern, said Nollet, about 4 m from the screen. It could be made

> equally well from tin-plate, sheets of brass or wood; but it is necessary that one side opens on hinges, to give access to adjust the mirror and the lamp; it is also necessary that in the centre of the roof it has a chimney, to allow the smoke to pass through, however such that the light does not escape at all into the room, and as soot will build up there it is advisable that it is attached on a collar, and that it may be lifted off for cleaning from time to time.[30]

Nollet took up s'Gravesande's principle of a four-wick lamp burning olive oil, without crediting it to the Dutch scholar. The mirror could be of white metal or 'mirror glass', rounded and curved by heating, or alternatively 'you may be satisfied by a copper reflector stamped by a tinsmith'. Nollet did not recommend the cardboard lens tube, which was much too fragile: 'It will be more solid, if you make it from two layers of shavings, covered in calfskin, or in basan [tanned sheepskin], in the manner of shagreen [rough untanned leather], or only in parchment.'[31] Scientific instruments of this time were often covered in hide with gilded decorations.

The German C.L. Deneke, in 1757, used a lantern of cubic shape, about 30 cm in height, length and width.[32] In this case the lens tube was of cardboard, but Deneke innovated by attaching a glass ball filled with water inside the lantern, between the lamp and the first lens, to magnify the light from the lamp, a single very wide wick. This method was probably borrowed from lace-makers, who used it to illuminate their work. The water-filled ball also prevented the flame's heat from damaging the paint of the slides. Much later, in 1897, the Lumière brothers (probably unaware of this precedent) filed a patent for an identical system, to prevent the film from catching fire when illuminated by the arc lamp of a cinematographic projector.[33]

Edme-Gilles Guyot, in 1769, differed from his contemporaries by making a lantern in traditional tin-plate, but with its lenses encased in

> a tube having the shape of an elongated square . . . I prefer to give it this shape, in order that the image on the sheet has the shape of a painting, which is preferable to the circular picture ordinarily given, which prevents one perceiving painted pictures in their entirety, before they are positioned in the centre.[34]

The illuminated disc, practically unchallenged for more than a century (although as we have seen, in 1663 Richard Reeves' lantern had been fitted with a 'square casing which extends outside the lantern'[35]), was therefore replaced by a square image. But this revolution came to nothing, and few lanterns were constructed in this way, although Wiegleb did adopt the square lens tube in 1779. The illuminated disc was not abandoned until the end of the nineteenth century, with the arrival of the rectangular format of the photographic slide. Without the latter, the first moving images of the *Cinématographe* would very probably have appeared on the screen in the circular frame dear to the hearts of the old lanternists.

Lenses

In the seventeenth and eighteenth centuries the success of a projection was closely tied to the quality of the lenses used. Since the days of Huygens, opticians had been able to supply better quality glass, paler in colour and more transparent, without too many air bubbles. Even so, projected images were surrounded by a blurred and coloured fringe which neither Huygens nor Newton were ever able to overcome. This phenomenon was known as 'chromatic aberration' or 'refrangent aberration'. A ray of light passing through a lens is decomposed into different colours, and therefore iridescent fringes are visible at the edge of the image. The defect can be reduced by using 'achromatic' glass, which diverts the rays.

It seems to have been the English optician John Dollond (1706–61) who succeeded in making the first true achromatic lens. There was endless controversy on this subject. The German mathematician Leonhard Euler (1707–83), who had worked on this problem, and Dollond wrote threatening letters full of algebra to each other; the English optician George Bass and the Swedish astronomer Klingenstierna also claimed the discovery; John Dollond and his son Peter were taken to court by Watkin, Bass, Jesse Ramsden, and Benjamin Martin, an enthusiastic user of the magic lantern.[36] The fact remains that on 8 June 1758 in London the members of the Royal Society were enraptured by an achromatic lens presented by John Dollond, capable of producing sharp well-illuminated images.

This miracle was achieved by the juxtaposition of two lenses. One was concave, made of 'flint glass' (white English crystal glass), and gave a strong dispersal of light; the other was convex or biconvex, made of 'crown glass' (slightly greenish glass), and gave a weak dispersal. The solution lay in bringing a convergent crown glass lens against the concave surface of a divergent flint glass lens. This revolutionary lens was not immediately adopted by lanternists: at first it was very expensive, because of the difficulty of obtaining flint glass. In addition, Dollond had taken out a patent, and his son Peter prosecuted anyone who dared to make achromatic combinations without his authorization. But at the end of the eighteenth century it was becoming more widespread, and the magic lantern used by Robertson for his phantasmagoria was definitely equipped with this indispensable lens.

The microscope lantern or 'solar microscope'

Around the middle of the eighteenth century another important invention caused a change in attitude towards the projected image. Until this point, apart from a few rare educational experiments, the magic lantern had remained a pastime which was more entertaining than serious or instructive. But quite suddenly, the lantern regained all its attraction in the eyes of scholars, thanks to an improvement which was too complicated to be picked up by the common Savoyards, who continued travelling the roads of Europe with their simple lanterns. Instead of simple hand-painted scenes, the lantern would project objects prepared for the microscope, using the sun as a light source (particularly strong illumination was needed to magnify tiny objects). For scientists, this improvement on the type of living insect shows put on by Zahn in 1686 was a real breakthrough: they could illustrate their classes in the physical and natural sciences, and their explanations became more easily comprehensible to a large audience. And in any case microscopic views, regardless of their scientific value, were just as amazing as moving slides: in the eighteenth century fleas were everywhere, but to see one 2 m tall was quite miraculous! What really stunned the uninitiated spectators were the unexpected details revealed by the gigantic magnification of an insect, for example a moth:

> If we compare the structure of a moth with that of an elephant, I believe that we shall be of the same opinion [as Boyle]. The size and strength of one can strike us with fear or admiration, but we shall be much more surprised if we examine closely the small parts of the other. The moth has more limbs than the elephant . . . it has eyes, a mouth and a trunk—just like the elephant—for taking in food, it has a stomach for digesting it and intestines to separate out the useless parts from it . . .[37]

The solar microscope was essentially a modified magic lantern, illuminated by the sun, not unlike Kircher's cryptological system of 1646 or the projection method described by Hooke in 1668. Its display was therefore entirely dependent on the weather and the seasons, and it could not be used in a traditional evening show. The rather complex operation of the new device, particularly its mirror (which had to follow the movement of the sun), its relatively high cost, the difficulty of preparing the slides, and the whims of the god Helios, all combined to make it unattractive to the Savoyard, who left this new invention to the scientists, professors, and curious aristocrats. For this reason the solar microscope never became as popular as its parent, the magic lantern.

The solar microscope consisted of two parts: an oblong mirror was mounted in a frame of wood or brass, connected by a double hinge to the second part, a board on which was fixed an iron or brass tube, sometimes covered in hide, which contained a convex lens. The microscope would be screwed onto the mouth of this tube. Some scientists, such as Baker and Smith, recommended the use of the microscope designed by the Englishman James Wilson at the end of the seventeenth century, because of its very practical slide carrier, a spiral spring which applied pressure to brass or ivory sheets to hold the slide in position.

The assembly had to be secured to the aperture of a camera obscura, with the microscope inside facing the screen, and the mirror outside to catch the sun's rays. The mirror could be adjusted to follow the movement of the sun, using a cord from inside or an assistant standing outside. The light rays were then directed through the aperture of the camera obscura, condensed by the lens, and arrived at the mouth of the tube at the focal point of the microscope which contained the prepared slide, for example a crushed louse. The image of the slide would appear magnified, up to 2 m high if desired, with all its tiniest details. Other subjects which could be projected included fish scales, the eye of a fly, herbs, and 'vinegar or flour paste eels' which appeared like small snakes, all of which were of scientific and also, in some sense, artistic interest: the more beautiful and curious an image appeared, the more it was applauded. The real triumph was achieved when tiny animals wriggled frantically in the burning light of the solar microscope, with an animation far more real than any mechanical slide. Benjamin Martin emphasized the pleasure generated by the intense movement of 'Living animals: they have really so much *Life and Motion*'.[38]

Through this kind of projection, the 'spectacle of nature' could be viewed by around a hundred people at a time. This was an important development, as Henry Baker observed:

> There are several other advantages which are enjoyed by no other Microscope, since the weakest eyes may make use of it without the least fatigue: a number of persons may observe the same object at the same time . . . whereas in the other Microscopes one is obliged to observe through an aperture one after another, and often to observe an object which is in neither the same light nor the same position.[39]

Baker had unconsciously revealed what would become the two competing directions of pre-cinematographic research: in one corner, individual viewing by one person at a time; in the other, popular projection to a mass audience.

The invention of the solar microscope, as usual, has been attributed to several different people. As we have already seen, the device had already been preconceived by Zahn, who projected insects enclosed in glass boxes, though without the aid of a microscope. In 1720, van s'Gravesande took up Kircher and Hooke's idea of a mirror and applied it to one of his magic lanterns, with the aim of obtaining a very bright illumination for painted lantern slides. An oiled paper sheet diffused the light, which otherwise was too strong. He also designed a remarkable device, which would be perfected by Léon Foucault in the nineteenth century: the 'Solsta' or 'Heliostat', a mechanism for automatically following the path of the sun and carrying a mirror, which would always direct the light rays into the optical tube.

Henry Baker attributed the invention of the solar microscope to the German anatomist Nathanael Lieberkühn (1711–56), who had demonstrated it to the Royal Society in the winter of 1739. However, according to Baker, Lieberkühn had not thought of using a mirror. The optical tube had to be placed directly in line with the sun, which was not easy to achieve. Baker stated that the 'Solar or Camera Obscura Microscope'[40] was perfected by the London optician John Cuff, who was one of the first people to commercialize it, and it is possible that it was he who added the mirror to catch the sun's rays. The scientist Robert Smith mentioned another great optician, George Adams, alongside Cuff.

One indication of the immense interest in 'the infinitely small' was the publication, in Nuremberg between 1764 and 1768, of three magnificent quarto volumes dedicated solely to *Amusements Microscopiques* by a German scientist, Martin Frobene Ledermuller (1719–69), 'Inspector of the Cabinet of Natural Curiosities of His Serene Highness Monseigneur the Margrave of Brandenburg-Coulmbac'. One of the hand-coloured engravings (Fig. 18) in these volumes shows John Cuff's solar microscope. The device was fixed into the exterior wall of a projection room, so that its light beam passed across the interior of a room and showed, on the opposite wall, the vastly magnified image of a microscopic preparation. Four empty chairs are shown against the back wall: 'You will position the seats of your spectators as you wish, for myself I have arranged them as you see for my own convenience.'[41]

Ledermuller also described a small camera obscura fitted with a solar microscope. The tube of Cuff's apparatus was connected to a small box, inside which an inclined mirror (as in Sturm's portable camera obscura) reflected the image onto a sheet of oil-coated transparent paper on top of the box. In this way, the projected view could be observed and traced easily on a small illuminated screen. Ledermuller also used the light of the sun to study the colours of the spectrum which Newton had described. For this purpose he removed the microscope from the

Fig. 18. Engraving published in Martin Frobene Ledermuller, *Amusements Microscopiques* (1768). Collection: Bibliothèque Nationale.

device: the strong light emerging from the tube (still fitted with its convex lens) passed through a prism to project into the room 'two magnificent rainbows, one high up on the wall, the other on the floor'.[42]

Among the enthusiastic advocates of the solar microscope it is worth mentioning the particular case of Jean-Paul Marat (1743–93), the household physician to the Comte d'Artois, and the future *Ami du Peuple* ('Friend of the People') during the French Revolution. Under the *Ancien Régime* Marat tried in vain to match the society successes of Nollet, Brisson, or the physicist Jacques Charles, to whom we shall return shortly. Marat used the solar microscope for his experiments on fire, the 'igneous fluid'. He presented a paper at the Académie des Sciences in 1779, which was published the same year: *Découvertes de M. Marat sur le Feu, l'Électricité et la Lumière* ('Discoveries of M. Marat on Fire, Electricity and Light').

The Académie nominated a commission to examine this work. Its report was very flattering, thanks to the Comte de Maillebois, a friend of Marat who was a member of the commission:

> The paper . . . covers more than 120 experiments, which all, or at least the greater part of them, have been achieved by a new, ingenious method, and which open a great field to new researches in Physics; this method is the solar microscope . . .[43]

For example, Marat presented the flame of a candle to the solar rays of the microscope:

> One saw immediately, around the wick, an elongated undulating cylinder, in which one can distinguish the image of the flame, which appears in the shape of a shuttle and of a reddish colour, and surrounding another image, less coloured, in the centre of which one saw shining a small dark black jet.[44]

On 18 April 1780, following these 'new, precise and interesting' experiments, Marat began a series of lectures at the Hôtel d'Alègre in Rue Saint-Honoré, Paris. In order to capture the strongest light of the sun, the showings took place at one o'clock in the afternoon. Marat gave a commentary on microscopic views projected by one of his friends, Abbé Filassier (at this period Marat frequently associated with the clergy and aristocracy).

The same year, Marat composed a second paper entitled *Découvertes de M. Marat sur la Lumière* ('Discoveries of M. Marat on Light'), again addressed to the Académie des Sciences. This time he went completely astray, claiming that Newton's ideas were wrong and the Académie had been working on false principles for forty years. On 10 May 1780, a second report by the Académie concluded politely that his theories were 'in general contrary to that which is known in Optics'. Marat, who in 1791 was to be the author of the pamphlet *Les Charlatans Modernes ou Lettres sur le Charlatanisme Académique* ('The Modern Charlatans, or Letters on Academic Charlatanism') took this decision badly. From that day on, like a 'fool who believed he could achieve fame by means of paradoxes' (in the severe words of Abbé Bertholon), he cursed the 'vain and mediocre' men of the Académie. Among the 'mediocre' ones were scientists such as Monge, Laplace, Lalande (an 'alley cat', Marat wrote), Condorcet (the 'literary rascal' who had dared to countersign the Académie report), Berthollet, and Lavoisier (a 'thief', author of 'scientific novels'), who would eventually mount the scaffold with the abuse of the embittered scholar ringing in his ears.

The 'Megascope'

Along with the invention of the achromatic lens and the solar microscope, a third very important improvement brought the magic lantern to its maturity: the invention of the Megascope, credited to Leonhard Euler. Euler had already addressed himself to the problem of chromatism, and he was also interested in projection. In 1727 he became a member of the Academy of Sciences of St Petersburg which Catherine I had recently founded. Between 1768 and 1772 he published his *Lettres à une Princesse d'Allemagne sur Quelques Sujets de Physique et de Philosophie* ('Letters to a German Princess on Different Subjects in Physics and Philosophy') for the Princess of Anhalt-Dessau, in which he explained his theories with great clarity. In this work, and in a paper published by the St Petersburg Academy, Euler not only described some improvements to the solar microscope, but also gave the first description of the Megascope. This name (from the Greek *mega*, 'large', and *skopeo*, 'I see') did not come directly from Euler's pen; he preferred to refer to the magic lantern or the improved camera obscura. The word 'Megascope' was not used until the 1780s, when Jacques Charles used this device to illustrate his lectures. Its invention was therefore attributed to him, in ignorance of Euler's innovative work.

The Megascope lantern could project a painting, a statue, a bas-relief scene, and all types of small opaque objects. Euler described the apparatus in a letter to his German princess dated 9 January 1762:

> I have found a way, and Your Highness will recall that I performed it in a machine of this type which I had the honour to present to her six years ago.[45]

A first example had therefore been constructed in 1756. Euler's Megascope consisted of a large wide box of wood and metal, in the rear of which was an opening. Engravings or paintings on paper, or a small platform large enough to support small opaque objects, could be placed inside. On the other side, opposite the opening, was a sliding optical tube containing a convex lens. The most difficult part of its operation was to light the object sufficiently: the image of the opaque object formed at the focus of the lens had to be very bright for projection onto a screen. Euler extended the sides of his lantern to accommodate two lamps with wide wicks, and two mirrors which reflected the light onto the opaque object.

Another German, Ulrich-Theodore Aepinus (1724–1802), admired this instrument at Euler's house in St Petersburg shortly before the mathematician's death in 1783. While Euler had compared his invention to a magic lantern or improved camera obscura, Aepinus preferred to describe it, most incorrectly, as a 'new Microscope':

> The Author maintains that he has never seen anything so beautiful as the pictures which this new Microscope produces, nothing which so much resembles the same object increased prodigiously in size, and which renders more perfectly the recesses and reliefs, which the old solar Microscope cannot achieve with transparent objects.[46]

Around the end of the eighteenth century there were also Megascopes with solar illumination. It is not known who had the idea of attaching a mirror to Euler's instrument. Perhaps he conceived this himself; sometimes the name of Jacques Charles is suggested, but there is no conclusive proof of this.

Jacques Charles (1746–1823) was one of the most brilliant professors of experimental physics of his day, along with Abbé Nollet and his pupil Jacques Mathurin Brisson, who taught at the Collège de France. Brisson could not compete with Charles, whose distinguished manner and attractive appearance made a female clientele suddenly keen on physics and science. Benjamin Franklin wrote of him: 'Nature refuses him nothing, it appears that she obeys him.' Indeed, when a storm broke over his splendid laboratory at Place des Victoires, Paris, Charles was capable of bringing down 'thousands of wonderful sparks of more than 12 feet in length'[47] with the aid of an electrical apparatus. After the brilliant success of a balloon ascent on 2 August 1783 (he had the idea of using hydrogen to inflate the balloon), Charles was awarded a chair at the Académie des Sciences and an apartment at the Louvre Palace. It was there that he successfully used the projection microscope and the megascope, illuminated by the sun and by paraffin.[48]

The scientific collection which Charles installed in the Louvre around 1785 was considered to be one of the finest in Europe. By 1792, it included more than 330 items. Charles made a gift of it to the nation in that year, and some magnificent pieces of equipment from this collection can still be admired at the Museum of the CNAM. Charles' projection microscope has been preserved: this is a huge metal lantern, 65 cm in height, fitted with a brass lens with the same spiral spring as James

Wilson's microscope. It operates with a powerful paraffin lamp. The collection of the CNAM also includes Charles' large magic lantern, which is also of very high quality, constructed completely of wood with a brass lens tube.

Charles succeeded where Marat had failed, in popularizing science through projection. A quarrel blew up between these two lanternists in 1783: Charles, who followed the theories of Newton, openly criticized Marat's ideas. Marat rushed round to the professor's house, their discussion became acrimonious, and Charles threw Marat out when he threatened him with his stick. Marat filed an official complaint and, around February or March 1783, provoked the physicist to a duel. In the end the swords were not drawn. Marat went to the local Prefect, Lenoir, to warn him of the duel. Not finding him in, he wrote to him:

> You know, Monsieur, of the outrage which I have received at the house of M. Charles. However unworthy it may appear to a man of honour, I came to make the sacrifice to you of my resentment. I will await further instructions from you . . . Your very humble and obedient servant, Marat.[49]

Some time later, after his violent demise in 1793, the ghost of Marat was resurrected by the magic lantern—a cruel twist of fate for this failed lanternist. Jacques Charles (whose young wife Julie was lovingly recreated by the poet Alphonse de Lamartine as 'Elvire' in his *Méditations Poétiques* of 1820) died in Paris in 1823. His body rests in the Père Lachaise cemetery under a very sober tombstone, shattered by frost, and only a few metres away from the magnificent tomb of Étienne-Gaspard Robertson.

Some eighteenth-century lantern manufacturers

The magic lantern could now throw fixed or moving images, microscopic images, or faithful reproductions of opaque objects, onto the screen. These improvements were highly profitable for the optical craftsmen, who offered their clients a whole range of mechanical slides and different designs of projectors, from the Savoyard's simple lantern to the powerful Megascope with reflecting mirrors.

During the reign (1774–92) of Louis XVI Paris had many optical workshops. After a considerable delay, the French optical industry had come to rival English and Dutch manufacturers in quality. Great French opticians such as Jacques and Pierre Lemaire, Claude Langlois, Claude

Paris, Claude Siméon Passemant, and Alexis Magny, produced work for the 'curious' nobility. In Paris the lantern was mainly available at the establishments of opticians of the second rank, for example Letellier, whose shop was at 'Quay des Augustins, opposite the Pont-Neuf', at the sign of the microscope. This mirror manufacturer and dealer also made 'telescopes, burning mirrors, magic lanterns, cylinders, cones, camera obscuras, all works of optics', as he claimed in a prospectus published around 1777.

Marc-Mitouflet Thomin, author of some good books on optics, had a shop in 1746 'between the Fontaine Saint-Benoît and the Collège du Plessis, in rue Saint-Jacques in Paris'. His stock included:

> triangular lenses, also called prisms, used by Painters to learn colours . . . Polished metal cylinder, with optical Cards by the best artist . . . Perspective illusion supplied with several pictures. Optical box, also known as camera obscura, for drawing without a teacher. Magic lanterns, with all types of grotesque objects painted on glass . . . And all sorts of curiosities depending on the Art of Catoptrics and Dioptrics.[50]

Another manufacturer who was particularly interested in the lantern was Laisne, 'optician of the Quay des Orfèvres at number thirty-five, where one finds all which concerns Optics Dioptrics Catadioptrics and Curious Perspective'. The print collection at the Bibliothèque Nationale has two of Laisne's brochures, dated 1786 and 1787, which were presumably given to each lantern purchaser.

Lanterns and peepshows could also be obtained at the Rue Saint-Jacques shop of Rabiqueau, in 1777, and from Bienvenu at 18 Rue de Rohan, in 1787. At that date L.V. Thiery, in his *Guide des Amateurs et des Étrangers Voyageurs à Paris* ('Guide for Amateurs and Foreigners Visiting Paris') advised visiting the scientific shop owned by the widow Bianchi, at 55 Rue de Richelieu; her husband Bianchi had been a scientific demonstrator in Rue Saint-Honoré. For a fee of 55 Louis, within six months from the date of the order, he would supply a complete scientific laboratory outfit: pneumatic pump, barometer, electrical machine, microscope, mirrors, and magic lantern.

London was even richer than Paris in opticians' shops and workshops. James Wilson, the inventor of the pocket cylinder microscope, offered lanterns for sale at the start of the eighteenth century from his shop 'At the Willow Tree'. A pupil of John Cuff, the optician Henry Shuttleworth of 23 Ludgate Street ('At the Sign of Isaac Newton') sold peepshows, camera obscuras and 'Magic Lanthorns'. George Adams, a specialist in microscopy, set up shop in London at the sign of 'Tycho-Brahe's Head' around 1735, and was a competitor of Cuff in commercialization of the solar microscope. Finally, in the same street, Benjamin Martin sold his own equipment and books popularizing science. It is possible that Martin was the maker of a very effective lantern, in black sheet metal, which is sometimes found in private collections and museums; it appears in an engraving in *The Young Gentleman and Lady's Philosophy* of 1772.

With the invention of achromatic lenses, the solar microscope and the megascope, some thought that the magic lantern had reached the limit of its possibilities. However, it was to be taken up once more, modified again, and changed completely by the 'Phantasmagoria', a show of animated devilish images which, in spite of its apparent novelty, was a reconnection with the sulphurous past of the first projections by the camera obscura and the 'lantern of fear'.

6

The Phantasmagoria

At the end of the eighteenth century scientists and magicians conceived a new type of illuminated show, to which they gave the French name *Fantasmagorie* or its English equivalent 'Phantasmagoria'. The term was derived from the Greek *phantasma*, 'ghost' (derived from *phantazo*, 'I make an illusion') and *agoreuo*, 'I speak'; an etymology which suggests a dialogue between the audience and the ghost called up by the magic lantern. An alternative derivation, indicating 'gathering of ghosts' (*phantasma/agora*) may also be possible.

The technique of the phantasmagoria depended on several constant principles. The spectators must never see the projection equipment, which was hidden behind the screen. When the lights in the room were extinguished, a ghost would appear on the screen, very small at first; it would increase in size rapidly and so appear to move towards the audience. This could also be done in the opposite direction, with the ghost moving away and appearing to grow smaller. The back-projection always had to be sharp: this was possible because of an improved lens tube of the magic lantern, which now included a diaphragm and a rack mechanism, allowing adjustment of the position of the lenses as the lantern was moved along rails or on wheels.

The pictures shown were animated and mobile, appearing to rush towards a terrified audience who were certainly not used to such an assault of images. In addition, the macabre show devised around this new type of projection heightened the impression of unease and fear in the spectators. Most of the time, the walls of the room were draped in black. A gloomy silence, interrupted only by the metaphysical pronouncements of a stern 'fantasmagore' master of ceremonies, or the lugubrious music of a 'glass harmonica', would seem like the prelude to a veritable witches' sabbath.

The phantasmagoria coincided with the popularity of the Gothic novel: the novels of Ann Radcliffe date from 1789–97; *The Monk* by M.G. Lewis from 1796; *Hymnen an die Nacht* ('Hymns to the Night') by Friedrich Novalis from 1800; and the devilries of Goethe's *Faust* were unleashed in 1808. This wave of fantasy broke over France a little later, but the fantasmagores themselves were well in tune with their times, presenting a new variation of old superstitions, and a strange perversion of the scientific rationalism of the Enlightenment which had contributed so much to the improvement of the lantern. But the phantasmagoria also foreshadowed the cinematograph show. At the end of the eighteenth century the crowds were pressing, in exchange for a few *livres* or *assignats* (the French currency of the time), to get in to lengthy shows of dazzling animated projections, in colour and with accompanying sound, which were infinitely superior in quality to any previous attempts.

Étienne-Gaspard Robert (1763–1837), known as Robertson, is generally accepted as having been the inventor of the phantasmagoria in 1798. He certainly presented himself as such, in his fascinating *Mémoires* published in 1831 and 1833. In reality, he did no more than borrow and exploit a method used by several others well before him, although he certainly did so with a great deal of skill. This truth, which Robertson tried to conceal, came to light around 1800 in the course of a trial to which we shall return shortly.

Phantasmagoria with a fixed lantern

The phantasmagoria was mentioned in several books of the 1780s. In 1784, for example, the magician and professor of physics Henri Decremps (1746–1826) published *La Magie Blanche Devoilée* ('White Magic Unveiled'), which included a description of an incredible show whose optical and acoustic effects greatly inspired future lanternists. Decremps' book, a wonderful rite-of-passage novel full of puzzles and surprises, recounts the journey of a young man named Hill to visit the Dutch magician Van Estin. Hill finds himself at the heart of an optical storm:

> In the middle of the shadows he saw a small ray of light shining, which did not last for more than an instant . . . A sulphurous and bituminous odour spread itself around him; the air rang with the most alarming noises . . . He distinguished some plaintive wailing voices, which suggested pain and despair: silence followed, but it was soon interrupted by a voice of thunder which rattled the windows, pronouncing the words:

You, madman, who only believe in white sorcery,
Tremble! Behold Hell with all its devilry.

Immediately he felt two or three earth tremors; he heard an underground noise similar to that of the sea. In the middle of the thunder and lightning, he saw appear three skeletons who, grinding their teeth, rattled their bones and creaked their arms, shaking lighted torches whose pale glow increased further the horror of this place. M. Hill, on the point of becoming ill, heard another voice which said: Be reassured, the trick is finished. In that moment the torches went out, the skeletons vanished and the windows opened.[1]

Decremps added: 'Those who wish to know [our methods] are invited to send us the last page of this little volume, and to add to it the sum of six *livres*, as much as a payment for our secret as for payment of the costs of writing and drawing.' He warned that it would be necessary to construct 'machines' and that 'our methods, however simple, are highly expensive . . . We believe it necessary to require this sum, to reduce the number of enquirers, in order that the secret will be revealed as little as possible.' In the copy of this rare book at the Bibliothèque Nationale, the last page is indeed missing.

But perhaps the 'secret' was revealed by Decremps himself, at the end of his text:

The veil which covers scientific recreations, and the astonishment which they have produced, sometimes, on certain minds, have caused to be seen as a species of Magic what has not been seen as a web of lies . . .

The dark catachresis becomes a debt,
By which are seen a thousand confused objects,
To the astonished Readers, a magnificent picture,
As if one showed it [with] the magic lantern.[2]

Decremps' book is a fundamental text: all this scene-setting was borrowed, almost identically, by the first fantasmagores. It is noticeable that this account contains no mention of images appearing to approach and recede from the spectator, the essential component which separated the phantasmagoria from the simple lantern show of diabolical scenes.

It is not known whether the 'ghost creator' (*Gespenstermacher*) Johann Schröpfer used moving back projection. Schröpfer organized shows of necromancy at Leipzig around 1774, in which the ghosts of the departed were called up using the 'nebulous lantern' which Edme-Gilles Guyot had been first to describe in 1769–70. This was used to project illuminated images, not onto the traditional textile screen, but onto a curtain of smoke. For this, Guyot used a type of brazier, with the beam of the lantern directed onto the smoke which emerged as a sheet through the top of the brazier casing: 'That which appears extraordinary, is that the smoke does not alter the shape which is represented there, and it appears as though one could grasp it with the hand.'[3] Guyot could also make 'a phantom on a pedestal' appear, thanks to a small magic lantern hidden inside a wooden chest. This projected its pictures onto an inclined mirror, which reflected the images onto the smoke screen given off by a simple stove located above the chest.

Guyot's nebulous system was quickly adopted in Germany, where it was described successively by Christlieb Benedikt Funk in 1783, Johann Samuel Halle in 1784, and Johann Georg Krünitz in 1794 (see Fig. 19). Funk stated that the most difficult part of the process was to produce and direct the smoke. If it spread throughout the room, 'not only would the eyes of the spectators not be able to stand more than five to eight minutes, but also the apparition would vanish just as quickly'.[4] Funk used moving slides in his lantern, for example a face whose eyes moved. The 1784 account by Halle is just as amazing as that by Decremps, published in the same year. Halle described a display of necromancy or phantasmagoria (described as '*Gaukelei*' by Krünitz) which allowed 'a calling together of the spirits of the dead or the Witch of Endor'. It is very possible that Halle had seen Schröpfer's show, since his description closely resembles what the '*Gespenstermacher*' of Leipzig was performing:

> The supposed magician leads the group of curious persons into a room whose floor is covered by a black cloth, and in which is situated an altar painted black with two torches and a death's head, or a funerary urn. The magician traces a circle in the sand around the table or altar, and asks the spectators not to step over the circle. He begins his conjuration by reading from a book and making smoke from a resinous substance for good spirits, and from foul-smelling substances for bad ones. In a single instant the lights are extinguished by themselves, with a sharp explosive noise. At that moment the spirit called appears hovering in the air above the altar and above the death's head, in such a way that it appears to want to fly up into the air or disappear underground. The magician passes his sword through the spirit several times, which at the same time emits a plaintive howling sound. The spirit, which appears to rise up from the death's head in a thin cloud, opens its mouth; the

Fig. 19.   Projection show using the 'nebulous lantern', illustrated on the title
page of Johann Samuel Halle, *Magie: oder die Zauberkräfte der Natur* (1784).
Collection: Bibliothèque Nationale.

spectators see the mouth of the skull open and hear the words
pronounced by the dead spirit, in a husky and terrible tone, when
the magician asks questions of it.

During all this ceremony, flashes of lightning cross the room . . .
and they hear a terrifying noise of a storm and rain beating. Shortly
afterwards the torches relight themselves, while the spirit
disappears, and its farewell perceptibly shakes the bodies of all
members of the audience . . . The magic performance comes to an
end, while each one seems to ask of his neighbour, with a livid
pallor on his face, what opinion he is inclined to draw from this
interview with the underworld.[5]

Halle then unveiled all the secrets of this prodigious infernal vision. On
the title page of his book, an engraving reproduced an exact view of the
scene. The device was the same as Guyot's, a lantern hidden in a large

rectangular box. However Halle added some precious information: as the projection had to be made obliquely, by means of a mirror, into the stream of smoke, the images would appear longer, like a kind of anamorphosis. In order that the 'optical spirit' should not seem ridiculously stretched, it was necessary to paint 'in miniature' on the slide. To accentuate the macabre nature of the scene, the wooden box concealing the lantern could be shaped as a coffin.

Two curious phenomena are noticeable in Halle's account: the sudden disappearance of the lights, and the shock which shook the bodies of the audience. Small explosive balls embedded in the candles, made of thin glass and filled with wine spirit, extinguished the flame at the moment they exploded. As for the shock, it was quite simply an electrical discharge passed through all the spectators. At the end of the show one of the magician's assistants sent current through wires hidden under the floor and connected to an electrical machine. The acoustic effects were created with a tin-plate tube. A second conspirator, hidden in an adjacent room, spoke in a sinister voice through this hollow tube, playing the role of the 'spokesman of Elysium', the kingdom of the dead.

All these tricks were later borrowed by Robertson (with the exception of electrocuting the audience), but these projections still lacked the crucial technical component of the phantasmagoria show: the image which advanced and grew, or retreated and diminished, and always remained sharp. Far from being a trivial detail, this innovation transformed the frame, perspective and scenic space of the projection. The traditional procession of images, used since Huygens' time, was abandoned: now animated figures crossed the screen in all directions, loomed up from the base of the screen, came towards the viewer at an astonishing speed, and then disappeared suddenly. The combination of the movable lantern and the moving slide were an essential step forward in the history of 'moving' projection.

Mobile back-projection

The invention of mobile back-projection, and therefore of the true phantasmagoria, is in all probability due not to Robertson, but to a very mysterious person lurking behind the pseudonym Paul Philidor. On Sunday 16 December 1792 the Paris daily *Les Affiches* carried this 'special advertisement' for the first time:

PHANTASMAGORIA, apparition of Ghosts and invocation of the Shades of famous Persons, such as Rosicrucians, the *Illuminés* of Berlin, the Theosophers and the Martinists. Those who wish to be witnesses of these invocations should have the goodness to present themselves to Paul Filidort (*sic*), Rue de Richelieu, Hôtel de Chartres, no. 31. He will perform these invocations twice per day, the first at half past five in the evening, the second at nine o'clock, at the start of the Show. The price of admission is 3 Livres. He advises Citizens that these operations have no dangerous influence on the organs, no unpleasant odour and that persons of all ages and sexes may view them without inconvenience.[6]

This event must be placed in its context: in 1792, following the capture of the Tuileries Palace, France had seen the Battle of Valmy and the Proclamation of the Republic; the people of Savoy—lantern showpeople included—had celebrated their reunification with France; and Louis Capet (the deposed Louis XVI) had been accused of 'a multitude of crimes' and his family incarcerated at the Temple.

The premises used by 'Filidort' were very close to the Bibliothèque Nationale and the Palais Royal, and not much further from the Couvent des Capucines in Place Vendôme, the future site of Robertson's phantasmagoria. The building where the shows took place, on the ground floor of 31 Rue de Richelieu (next to the Passage du Café de Foy and the Rue Villedo, notorious for its beautiful courtesans), still exists today, now numbered 40. It is an eighteenth-century building, built on the site of the house where Molière died, and between 1769 and 1793 was run as a lodging house known as the 'Hôtel de Chartres'.

A few days after this historic first Paris showing of the phantasmagoria, Philidor placed a second (much more discreet) advertisement, on 23 December 1792:

> Notice to Painters. A Painter is required capable of painting on glass, in miniature and in transparent colours. Enquire of the Porter at no. 31 Rue de Richelieu, opposite Rue Villedo.[7]

Perhaps Philidor had discovered that his slides were not painted well enough; perhaps he already wanted to replace his material; or perhaps he had broken some of his slides. A more likely explanation can be found in the following advertisement, published on Thursday 14 March 1793 (note the change of times):

> The PHANTASMAGORIA . . . Two showings per day, the first at six o'clock, the second at ten o'clock, at the start of the Show. *Nota*.

Persons who wish to avail themselves of individual showings, are requested to give notice the previous day: they may then request the apparition of any absent or deceased person of their acquaintance whom it pleases them to mention.[8]

This was why Philidor needed a skilled painter, experienced in miniatures. Each evening, a distressed lover or inconsolable widow would beg the necromancer to make the object of their distress reappear, through the phantasmagoria, an audio-visual dialogue between the dead and the living:

He offered to call up at will whatever person was asked of him, given a few days' advance warning. He obtained, perhaps by agreement, perhaps by trickery, a portrait of the person in question, had this image painted onto his object carrier, and then made it appear as large as life before the eyes of the parents or friends of the departed one.[9]

All Philidor had to do then was to collect the money from his gullible customer. Robertson also adopted this unscrupulous approach, some years later.

However, according to contemporary documents, Philidor had no desire to be mistaken for a true magician. He explained to the press, albeit in a somewhat abstract manner, that the phantasmagoria was merely the descendant of the *optique*:

Is it necessary to say that these prodigies are nothing more than effects of optics? They are the playthings of an artist skilled in benefiting from the contrast of light and shadow; the rays of a torch directed and concentrated onto a single object; the image, shape and movement of that object, calculated according to the rules of perspective, one part of the art of painting, there is the principle of these phenomena.[10]

This was not a particularly enlightening explanation. In Philidor's time, it is likely that spectators understood nothing of this illuminated dance of devils, and explanations like this would not have helped them. Philidor's aim, on the other hand, was quite clear. In the style of della Porta and Kircher, and the philosophical ideas of the Enlightenment and the Revolution, Philidor claimed to be debunking popular credulity towards sorcerers, prophets, visionaries, exorcists, and other charlatans (including priests, monks and popes), although at the same time he was somewhat ambiguously exploiting the public taste for the occult. Before beginning his show, Philidor would deliver this rationalist speech:

> I will bring before you all the illustrious dead, all those whose memory is dear to you and whose image is still present for you. I will not show you ghosts, because there are no such things; but I will produce before you enactments and images, which are imagined to be ghosts, in the dreams of the imagination or in the falsehoods of charlatans. I am neither priest nor magician; I do not wish to deceive you; but I will astonish you. It is not up to me to create illusions; I prefer to serve education.[11]

From some favourable articles published in the French and German press, it is possible to reconstruct Philidor's phantasmagoria show. It is perhaps six or eight o'clock in the evening; admission to the ground floor of 31 Rue de Richelieu costs 3 *livres*, payable in *écus* or even in *assignats*. Philidor 'introduces you into a room hung with black and covered with images of the dead, lit by a sepulchral lamp', where the walls are covered 'with solemn posters representing tombs, spectres, and ghosts'. The room is full: 'The Phantasmagoria draws a great throng', it 'meets with a prodigious success' and Philidor is making a lot of money.[12] A 'magic breath' extinguishes the lamp: total darkness falls and a heavy silence reigns. Dazzling lights flash from everywhere, accompanied by the howling of a violent wind:

> Rain, hail, and winds form simultaneously the overture and the symphony for the scene which will unfold. There rises, from the very floor, a white figure, which grows by degrees to human size. First you make it out indistinctly; a species of cloud still surrounds it: it becomes brighter, it disperses; the phantom becomes more and more visible, shining: you make out its features, you recognize it, it is Mirabeau: it is his living physiognomy, his own bearing, his hair bushy and carefully arranged . . . He walks, he wanders in the shadows, he approaches, he leans towards you: you shudder, he advances again: you go to touch him; he disappears, and you find yourself in the same shadows.[13]

This is achieved by a magic lantern with an adjustable-focus lens, hidden on the other side of the screen, moving gradually away so that the image appears larger and larger:

> A point of light pierces the distance of the dark night: it shines, it captures your eyes: soon it approaches, it grows at the same time and takes a shape which defines itself and becomes more distinct with each step it takes, until, arrived four or five feet away, this imperceptible point represents for you the shining ghost of Mirabeau.[14]

Philidor now moves his lantern, mounted on wheels or rails, back towards the screen. The projected image therefore 'imperceptibly moves away', becoming 'smaller to your eyes while keeping its shape and appearance', then 'gets lost and once again extinguishes itself in the shadow'.

'Twenty other phantoms follow and illuminate the shadowy residence in their turn.' They come out of the floor, appear to pass through the roof, descend from the ceiling, and burst out of the walls. Some are dressed not in white, the normal attire of ghosts, but in their official costume: thus Joseph II, the Emperor of Germany who had died in 1790, shows himself in 'the green uniform which he wore when he travelled in France'. But Philidor also called up the living: 'I have seen, I have recognized the impudent and villainous face of the priest Maury. He was speaking, you could believe you heard him lying' (Jean Siffrein Maury, 1746–1817, was a vehement ultra-royalist in the Assemblée Nationale). After a further procession of phantoms who 'moved, acted, gesticulated', one of the journalists present had the surprise of seeing his own image appear in front of him: 'I saw myself, coming and going, moving in front of me!'

Finally, the show comes to an end with a visit from a distinguished guest:

> The ingenious scientist ends this curious representation by making the Devil appear, that is to say the grotesque caricature imagined by frocked and mitred sycophants to frighten ladies and little boys; this spectre of fiery red, armed with claws, with horns on its head and showing a satyr's tail, changes astonishment into laughter and finishes by freeing the spectator from the spell.[15]

The French journalist who attended this astonishing evening published his account in *La Feuille Villageoise*, a small revolutionary magazine printed in Paris, on 28 February 1793. Perhaps, in his description of that last vision, he was being careful, in order to avoid political problems; or perhaps the 'fantasmagore' (the word first appeared in 1793) kept another, much more contentious, finale for some of his trusted friends. In any event, on 22 March 1793 a German journalist witnessed an extremely savage epilogue, whose audacity could have proved very costly for the lanternist of Rue de Richelieu:

> The most amusing thing there, is that he always ends his representations by calling up the Devil, and that he makes that distinguished gentleman appear sometimes with the face of Égalité ['Philippe Égalité', Duc d'Orléans, a supporter of the Revolution], sometimes with that of Robespierre, Marat, or Danton, but always with claws, horns and a long tail.[16]

For Marat, such a lover of projected images, to be treated in this way was indeed an indignity. If the German writer genuinely saw such images, Philidor must have been either a daring political operator or a reckless fool. In March 1793 the 'Friend of the People' Marat was still alive—Charlotte Corday did not pay her murderous visit to him until 13 July. The same applied to Robespierre and Danton, both alive and well, powerful and feared. Philippe Égalité did not mount the scaffold until 6 November. This period was the middle of the 'First Terror', following the formation of the Extraordinary Criminal Tribunal and the massacres of September 1792. As if by coincidence, Philidor vanished from France around April 1793. It seems that the Hôtel de Chartres changed owners and the fantasmagore was obliged to leave the premises. But it is quite likely that Philidor, worried or endangered by the German article, preferred to make himself scarce.

Who was Paul Philidor? He was certainly not the famous musician and chess player François André Danican, known as Philidor (1726–95), who was exiled to London at the start of the Revolution. According to *La Feuille Villageoise* in Paris and the *Journal des Luxus und der Moden* in Weimar, the fantasmagore was an Englishman; but in 1811 the scientist Breton mentioned a 'German named Philidor'. The mathematician Jérôme de Lalande, in 1802, clouded the issue further:

> In 1790, a Fleming named Philidor astounded the inhabitants of Vienna in Austria with a spectre. He came to Paris in 1792 and had a great following; his principal aim was to give illusions of the sect of the Illuminés ['Enlightened'].[17]

This sect was a secret society founded in 1776 by Adam Weishaupt, of Ingolstadt, which was officially dissolved in 1784. Philidor made an indirect reference to it in his advertisement of 16 December 1792.

Many theories are possible as to the true identity of the fantasmagore: 'Philidor' was an all-purpose name. During the Revolution, the pseudonym Philidor was used by a Frenchman named Joseph-Henri Flacon, who wrote plays which are completely forgotten today.[18] Another suggestion relates him to an American magician who practised his talents in Germany during the 1770s, under the name of Jacob Philadelphia. According to the German historian Hermann Hecht,[19] Philadelphia's real name was Jacob Meyer, and he used a magic lantern to project ghosts. An engraved portrait of 'Iacob Philadelphia, in raris rarissimus' ('Jacob Philadelphia, rarest of the rare'), in the collection of the Bibliothèque Nationale, gives the date and place of his birth: Philadelphia (hence his pseudonym), 14 August 1735. The man is wearing a wig, with a quite wide face, heavy chin and strong nose. It is possible, although there is as yet no conclusive proof, that Philadelphia and Philidor were the same person: the magician could have changed his surname while keeping the first syllable of his first pseudonym.

Robertson, the 'great man' of the phantasmagoria

Whoever he may have been, Philidor was completely overshadowed by an adversary of genius: Étienne-Gaspard Robertson, who opened his 'Fantasmagorie' in Paris in 1798. He achieved fortune and fame by exploiting a spectacle whose mystery remained intact for two years, before it was abruptly thrown away through his own mistake. While Philidor is still a somewhat enigmatic figure, in contrast the life of the scientist and aeronaut Étienne-Gaspard Robert, alias Robertson, is quite well known. He described all his adventures himself in the two volumes of his *Mémoires*. Robertson's life cannot be covered in more than general terms here; for more detailed information on the life of this pioneer, see his *Mémoires* and two other interesting sources.[20] The account which follows will be limited to new information on the phantasmagoria, drawn from the contemporary press and previously unpublished documents.

Robertson was the most celebrated and skilled projectionist of his time. Philidor has fallen into complete obscurity, but Robertson appears as an influential figure in all the encyclopaedias of the nineteenth century (he was also notable as an aeronaut). He stole everything from Philidor, but he did so with such a scientific approach, such an impassioned mastery, and in such a lasting manner (1798–1837, nearly forty years of projection), that he played a far more prominent role in pre-cinema history than his unfortunate predecessor.

Étienne-Gaspard Robert was born in Liège in Belgium on 15 June

1763; he died on 2 July 1837 at Batignolles, which at that time was not yet part of Paris. He was the son of Jean Robert, a merchant, and Élisabeth Balace, of Liège. After studying the humanities with the Oratorian order, he was destined for the priesthood and took the first steps into that career. But very soon 'Abbé Robert', as he styled himself, found other vocations: painting (in 1787 he exhibited *Apollo Killing the Serpent Python*, now in a private collection, a quite mediocre canvas which nonetheless suggested the phantasmagorical visions to come), and physical science. He made friends with the scholars Villette and Henkart, and published his first scientific article, on electrical experiments, in 1789. On the advice of Villette, Robert left his home town for Paris. He arrived there on 21 August 1791, for the *Salon de Peinture* at which Jacques-Louis David triumphed with his *Serment du Jeu de Paume* ('The Tennis Court Oath'). He attended the courses of Brisson and Charles, and no doubt also discovered the power which projection could exert over the masses. In 1792, after serving as private tutor to the son of Bénézech, future minister of the Directoire government, he took up the same position in the household of Chevalier, the former governor of the French West Indies. At this time, certainly, he must have discovered Philidor's phantasmagoria, but he never mentioned a word of it.

After a period back in Liège (at the time still annexed by France), where he tried to attract the attention of the scientific world by recreating one of Archimedes' mirrors which had never actually worked in the first place, Robert returned to Paris in 1796. On 21 October 1797 he accepted the post of teacher of physics and chemistry at the Central School of his home *département* of l'Ourthe, but after several months of negotiations (evidently he did not want to leave Paris) Robert finally turned this offer down on 10 April 1798. He threw himself into the phantasmagoria show, believing himself to have a vocation of 'physicist-philosopher':

> The *Bureau Central* has authorized me to give a class in Phantasmagoria, a science which deals with all the physical methods which have been misused in all ages and by all peoples to create belief in the resurrection and apparition of the dead. The Government protects this establishment: it has recognized the need to encourage the physicist-philosopher, whose works and morality tend to destroy the enchanted world which only owes its existence to the wand of fanaticism. This class, to which no more than fifty persons may be admitted at a time, must not last longer than two months,

but being greatly popular, I anticipate that they will keep me in Paris for longer than I wish.[21]

Robert had certainly seen and admired Philidor's show; he even borrowed its name (the spelling 'Phantasmagoria' in this reference is a Freudian slip; in January 1798, he changed it to 'Fantasmagoria'). However, two people claimed the honour of having given this idea to the priest-turned-physicist. One was the Comte de Paroy, whom we previously encountered as the enthusiast for the audio-visual magic lantern in the Dauphin's education. He met Robert, who was coming to the end of his engagement with the Chevalier family without much idea of where to go next. Paroy, rather curiously, claimed to have advised him:

> In your position, I would set up Philidor's magic lantern and create a small show for the children, more entertaining for them than the shadow show. Philidor died before he perfected his invention. I have often dreamed of it, and if you want to, we could turn ourselves to it.[22]

In his *Mémoires* Paroy added that, together with Abbé Robert, he made a projection device with an oil lamp and parabolic mirror, with 'a small trolley mechanism to allow it to make objects come closer, grow larger, shrink and disappear at will'.[23] All this is possible, but we should treat Paroy, who was fond of boasting about his own merits, with some caution.

The second person who awarded himself the credit was Baron Jean-Frédéric-Maximilien Waldeck (born Prague, 1766; died Paris, 1875). In 1863 the Baron, then nearly 100 years old, sent a 'Note on the phantasmagoria'[24] to the lantern enthusiast Abbé Moigno, in which he claimed with some self-conceit that in 1796 he had discovered the method for increasing the brightness of magic lantern images, by surrounding the pictures painted on the glass with black paint. He had projected the ghost of Louis XVI at the house of the scientist Béer. Among the spectators was Robert who, according to Waldeck, had desired to know his 'secret'. This was not much of a secret: black backgrounds had been used since the end of the seventeenth century. Waldeck had then helped Robert to put on his first show: 'I believe therefore, without vanity, that I may call myself the father of the phantasmagoria.'[25]

Robert, though, was quite intelligent enough to sort things out on his own. He probably worked out all Philidor's tricks without difficulty; in any case he knew the works of the German Wiegleb (who gave him the secret of the 'nebulous lantern') and those of della Porta, Kircher and Zahn. In his *Mémoires*, Robert declared that his first magic lantern attempts dated from 1784, in Liège, where he 'made the shadows limp along' in front of his friend Villette. Later, he mentioned the name of the scientist Béer, cited by Waldeck. Robert actually intended to give his first phantasmagoria shows in Béer's scientific laboratory in Rue de Clichy, but he eventually chose a place less tainted by 'ignorance and meanness', the Pavillon de l'Échiquier.

This 'Pavillon' still stands today, as 48 Rue de l'Échiquier. It is a small château, which in 1798 housed not only Robert, on the ground floor, but also the shows of the actor Thiemet and a 'Vauxhall' ballroom. The place did not enjoy a very good reputation, as a result of the mixed clientele attracted by the dances held there. On Wednesday 3 January 1798 Robert, who had restyled himself 'Robert-son' to give a little more scientific depth to his name, announced in the press that 'Citizen Robert-son will shortly open his Fantasmagoria, at number 28, Pavillon de l'Échiquier'. On 20 January, the programme was announced:

> FANTASMAGORIA at the Pavillon in the rue de l'Échiquier, by citizen E-G. Robert-son: apparitions of Spectres, Phantoms and Ghosts, such as they must have appeared or could appear in any time, in any place and among any people. Experiments with the new fluid known by the name of Galvanism, whose application gives temporary movement to bodies whose life has departed. An artist noted for his talents will play the Harmonica. One may subscribe for the first showing, which will take place on Tuesday 4 Pluviose [23 January 1798], at the Pavillon de l'Échiquier. Prices six *livres* and three *livres*.[26]

Robertson, who was one of the very earliest practitioners in France of Galvanism (experimentation with electricity, named after the Italian Luigi Galvani), had long been fascinated by electricity; he later became the friend and faithful supporter of the other great Italian pioneer Alessandro Volta (1745–1827). As for the 'harmonica', this was not the 'mouth organ' which is so widespread today, but an elaborate instrument consisting of about thirty glass cups mounted horizontally on a rotating axle, driven by a foot pedal. Pressing on the glasses with the fingers produced a very strange sound. Its invention is attributed to Benjamin Franklin, but the composer Gluck gave a concert in London around

1746 on twenty-six water-filled glasses, with orchestral accompaniment. The glass harmonica was forbidden in some towns, since the sound it emitted was supposed to be harmful to the health, being 'of such a weakening power on the nervous system of those hearing it, that it is impossible to bear its effect for more than a few minutes, without exposing oneself to going mad'.[27] That depended, of course, on the manner in which it was played: Mozart, no less, composed a very beautiful *Adagio for Glas-Harmonika* in 1791.

Robertson's first phantasmagoria show took place on Tuesday 23 January 1798, at six o'clock in the evening. This first attempt succeeded beyond all expectation: the audience crowded into the small room at the Pavillon de l'Échiquier, which contained no more than sixty seats. That evening there was such a crowd that Robertson was obliged to leave out 'three main ... riments of his Fantasmagoria'[28] (we do not know which these were). He quickly realized that the room was much too small, but at the same time knew that his fortune was made.

From the start Robertson's stated intention, like Philidor before him, was to expose by demonstration the 'absurd tales with which our child-hood was deluded: we wish to speak of the terror inspired by the ghosts, spells and occult plots of magic'.[29] His patter was lifted almost word for word from Philidor's ('I am not a magician', etc.). As if afraid of his new image, Robertson, the priest converted to the works of the devil, insisted strenuously:

> Robertson is a scientist, engineer, painter, optician; he is all that he has to be to work the greatest effects on the imagination through the senses, except that which he does not wish to be, magician, necromancer, in a century where all those tricks have vanished before the reason of man.[30]

Unfortunately, after the opening of the phantasmagoria, Robertson was effectively excluded from the circle of true scientists which he had frequented. His attempts to make his show resemble a class in scientific experiment, or a philosophical denunciation of 'the empire of prejudice', were completely in vain. Parisians went to the Pavillon de l'Échiquier to be entertained, to experience thrills, not to be instructed. Robertson was obliged to introduce spectacular theatrical effects, which by attracting the crowds gave their creator a very ambiguous reputation. The scientist Robert, in becoming the fantasmagore Robertson, passed from science to spectacle, and from here on his scientific contemporaries considered him a semi-charlatan, a type of Savoyard, or even worse, one of the 'amusing scientists' who entertained the Parisian crowds on Boulevard du Temple or at the Palais Royal.

Robertson never gave up his claim to be a scientist, even though the phantasmagoria made him rich and fashionable. He varied his projections, and perfected his macabre *mise en scène*. Journalists, as in the time of Philidor, emerged from the Pavillon de l'Échiquier filled with enthusiasm. On 28 March 1798, François Martin Poultier-Delmotte (1758–1826) gave an account of what he had seen for *L'Ami des Lois*:

> In a brightly lit chamber, at number 18, Pavillon de l'Échiquier, I found myself with about sixty persons on 4 Germinal [24 March 1798]. At precisely seven o'clock, a pale, dry man entered the chamber where we were; after extinguishing the candles, he said: Citizens and gentlemen, I am not one of those adventurers, those impudent charlatans who promise more than they have: I have stated, in the *Journal de Paris* [on the same date, 4 Germinal Year VI, Robertson had promised to evoke spectres, phantoms, ghosts and the Bleeding Nun], that I will resuscitate the dead, so I shall resuscitate them. Those of the company who wish for the appearance of persons who were dear to them, and whose life has been cut short by illness or otherwise, have only to say so; I shall obey their command.[31]

At the end of his account, Poultier-Delmotte stated that an old Chouan (a counter-revolutionary) had called for Louis XVI. Robertson had replied 'I had a formula for that, before 18 Fructidor [the *coup d'état* which took place on 4 September 1797], but I have lost it since that time'. A few days after the article appeared, Robertson was raided by the police. In March 1798, the Directoire regime was in power and a state of war existed, the French had just seized Berne, and a Republic had been proclaimed in Rome; it was therefore not a good time to be resuscitating royalty. In his *Mémoires*, Robertson refuted Poultier-Delmotte's fantastic account of his show. However, as a result of this article, various improbable conjuring tricks were attributed to him, such as the immediate presentation (not after a request the previous day) of William Tell to a Swiss enquirer, or a deceased girl to one who wished to see her again.

In subsequent issues of *L'Ami des Lois* and *Le Journal de Paris* there were a number of references to the magic lantern. The editors of these journals had presumably worked out the secret which Robertson had tried to conceal: it was once again the good old magic lantern which created these beautiful apparitions. The journalists' comments were always enigmatic. It would not do to alienate Robertson, a good client who published advertisements every week. But on 16 July 1798, some months after the opening at the Pavillon de l'Échiquier, Conselin, an optician and teacher of science of 179 Rue Fromentin, advertised magic lanterns equipped with 'concave mirrors for the phantasmagoria'.[32] This was a serious blow for Robertson, who had no desire to be imitated: having stolen everything from Philidor, he refused to be subjected to the same treatment.

As we shall see, thefts of equipment and plagiarisms soon became so aggressive that, in order to preserve his secrets and be able to lay legal claim to the phantasmagoria and prosecute counterfeiters, Robertson had only one option, which was fraught with uncertainty. This was to take out a patent, introduced in France by the law of 7 January 1791.

The patent for the 'Fantascope'

The security which a patent provides has always been rather approximate. Balzac expresses this very well:

> A man spends ten years of his life in search of an industrial secret, a machine, any kind of discovery, he takes out a patent, he believes himself to be master of his contraption; he is followed by a competitor who, unless he has foreseen everything, improves his invention by a single screw, and removes it from his hands completely.[33]

Nonetheless, on 26 January 1799 (we are jumping ahead slightly, because this document gives a precise description of Robertson's equipment), Étienne-Gaspard Robert, 'professor of physics resident in Paris, number 24, Rue de Provence', deposited a sealed envelope at the Secretariat of the Département de la Seine. The envelope contained a descriptive note and a request to the Minister of the Interior for a five-year patent for 'an apparatus which is the improvement of the magic lantern of Kircher, to which the author gives the name of Fantascope, and for the methods necessary to transfer onto glass the impression of a line engraving'. It is noticeable that Robertson chose to refer to Kircher, rather than to Philidor.

He had to hand over 350 Francs to pay for this patent, which was awarded to him on 17 March, with certain reservations: a little unwisely, Robertson had stated that his application was based on an 'improvement'. At the time a simple improvement was not considered to be an invention. Finally the Bureau Consultatif des Arts, which also had to

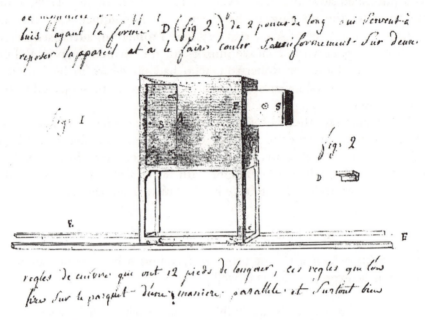

Fig. 20. Diagram from Robertson's patent of 1799.
Collection: INPI, Paris.

rule on the patent for Fulton's Panorama around the same time, returned a favourable opinion.

Robertson's patent, a document of fifty-two pages, is very interesting (see Fig. 20). It gives a careful description of the Fantascope, the magic lantern used to project the phantasmagoria. This device could also function as a Megascope. It was made of walnut wood, measuring about 1.6 m high by 95 cm long and 80 cm wide, and mounted on a stand formed by four legs which slid along two parallel brass rails, about 3.8 m long, fixed to the floor. Attached to the front surface of the Fantascope, in an opening about 20 cm square, was the lens tube, the essential component for the phantasmagoria process. The tube was square in cross-section (following Guyot's advice from 1770), and 38 cm in length. One of the great novelties, certainly the product of Robertson's inventive mind, was that the lens could very easily be replaced by another of different focal length. The lenses themselves were enclosed in casings which could slide easily in recesses in the tube. There were three lenses altogether, but the one in the middle was movable forwards and back by a rack mechanism operated by a simple button. In this way the lens could be gradually adjusted as the lantern moved on its rails, and lenses of different focal length would allow projection of objects or slides of different sizes. A brass plate at the end of the tube formed a diaphragm to adjust the intensity of the light.

If the lantern was set up as a Megascope, an opaque object (a skull, an engraving, a mask, or a mechanical scene made of metal or cardboard) was placed inside the body of the lantern, opposite the lens tube. A powerful four-wick oil lamp, with a single reservoir of 'very pure' oil and a reflector (which Robertson called a 'German mirror') strongly lit the object, whose image was projected through the lenses. When the device was used as a magic lantern, it was necessary to change the lenses to a focal length different from that of the Megascope; it was also necessary to soften the light output of the lamp with a piece of frosted glass. This excellent projector, which was a genuine credit to Robertson, was hidden behind the screen so that the spectator was not distracted 'by the preparations and manoeuvring'. Indeed, spectators must often have been absolutely unaware that it was a magic lantern producing such animated and mobile images on the screen. The screen itself was also constructed with painstaking attention to detail:

> I have acquired a sheet of three *aunes* [about 3.5 m] in width, such that it does not require a seam, and to render it translucent I have melted very white pure wax into which I have immersed it while it was boiling; I nailed it immediately into the opening formed in the wall and, passing a well-lit burner over it gradually, I spread the wax which gave my sheet the diaphanous quality I have sought for so long.[34]

According to some nineteenth-century authors, Robertson's Fantascope was constructed by the optician Molteni (of Italian origin, from his real name Moltono) who had founded a shop in Paris in 1782. His first workshops seem to have been situated on Rue Saint-Apolline, but he soon moved to Rue du Coq-Saint-Honoré, at number 11. On 2 April 1817 a company was founded by Pierre François Antoine Molteni and Joseph Duroni, for 'the optical trade and the handling of all types of merchandise'.[35] Certainly the Moltenis, father and son, produced excellent Fantascopes throughout the whole nineteenth century, in wood and metal, with one, two or three lanterns mounted side by side. After Robertson's death, the curtain from the Fantasmagoria was purchased by François Molteni.

Robertson's original Fantascope has disappeared, at least for the time being. But since the show survived for a long time, and since Robertson certainly owned a number of these devices, it is possible that one day a contemporary example will turn up. In 1924, a Fantascope was displayed at the Galliera Museum for an exhibition of 'Art in the French Cinema'. This device, loaned by the Collège de France, disappeared after 1927, the year when the film *L'Histoire du Cinéma vue par le Cinéma* ('Cinema History Seen by the Cinema'), was made by Raoul Grimoin-Sanson and Louis Forest. In this film (fortunately restored by the CNC Archive at Bois d'Arcy) this enormous machine, which must have been about 1.8 m in height, is seen moving about with its long legs mounted on wheels. Only a few frames remain to allow us to admire this design. This lantern probably did not originate in one of Robertson's shows: the lens tube does not correspond to the patent, consisting instead of several cylindrical tubes sliding telescopically within each other, operated by a handle. On the other hand, its body shape (a large cubic box, with a door in the side) does closely resemble Robertson's Megascope of 1799.[36]

In recent years the Belgian collector Thomas Weynants has found a very complete example of a French Fantascope, probably made by Lerebours of Paris (see Fig. 21).[37] This example is accompanied by several interchangeable lens tubes (one tube for the phantasmagoria with a 'cat's eye' diaphragm, one tube for the Megascope, and two tubes

Fig. 21. Fantascope-Megascope, probably made by Lerebours of Paris in the 1840s. Collection: Thomas Weynants.

with rotating shutters for 'dissolving view' effects), and also a fragile mechanical puppet representing a skeleton emerging from its tomb. The skeleton, moved by a handle, turns its head and moves its mouth. It was projected by the Megascope; it had to be placed upside down in the body of the lantern and powerfully lit. Projection of this sinister presence (which perhaps originated in the Molteni workshops) onto a screen gives an amazing impression of relief and realism.

The deluxe Lerebours Fantascope was an improved version of Robertson's lantern. This example must date from the 1840s, since it allows dissolving projection, a process which was not perfected until around 1839. From the start of the nineteenth century until the Second Empire, Parisian opticians such as Molteni, Lerebours, Chevalier, and Duboscq offered more or less complicated versions of the Fantascope in their catalogues. The Weynants example also has an eccentric chain drive system connected to both the wheels and the lenses, giving a gradual lens adjustment to remain in focus as the lantern moves forwards or back. This great improvement did not appear in the Fantascope 'lost' from the Collège de France.

The phantasmagoria at the Couvent des Capucines

On 23 December 1798, Citizen 'Robert-son' advertised the relocation of his phantasmagoria in the Paris press. Since the Pavillon de l'Échiquier was too small, Robertson set himself up (after a projection tour to Bordeaux), in a location which was much larger, more romantic, and as gloomy as could be wished. This was the Couvent des Capucines, a convent founded by Louis XIV in 1688, whose forty-two nuns had been driven out by the Revolution in 1790.

The convent and church of the Capucines, of which absolutely nothing remains today, occupied a large area bordered by the present-day Rue des Capucines and Rue Danielle-Casanova, close to the Place Vendôme. The Rue Napoléon (today named Rue de la Paix) was built through the site of the church in 1806, and the remainder of the area was sold off in thirty-six lots. In Robertson's time the entrance of the 'convent of the former Capucines' was in Rue Neuve-des-Petits-Champs (now Rue Danielle-Casanova). In the church demolished in 1806 rested the body of Louise de Lorraine, Queen of France and founder of the convent; also to be seen were the tombs of the Marquis de Louvois (1638–91) and the Marquise de la Pompadour (1721–64). The crypt where this high society rested was used as a cesspool during the Revolution.

Some writers have stated that Robertson installed his new show in the church of the Capucines. This is impossible. Its vaults were too high, and the engraving published as the frontispiece of Robertson's *Mémoires* shows the hall of the Capucines with a ceiling of the conventional type. Robertson gave his phantoms shelter behind the church, in the large rectangular two-storey cloisters. A long corridor led to the courtyard of Charon, where Robertson was installed in a number of halls and smaller rooms on the ground floor. To display the phantasmagoria to best effect, what was required was a large room for the audience (Robertson gave the measurements: about 20 m long, 7 m wide, with a dais in front of the screen concealed by a curtain), and another room on the other side of the screen long enough (about 8 m) for the operation of the mobile Fantascope on its rails. Further rooms were needed for preparing the tools and equipment.

The location Robertson had chosen was funereal, ideal for the phantasmagoria, but it was even less well-frequented than the Pavillon de l'Échiquier. On 30 September 1800, the prefect of police decided to install lanterns (not the magic kind) in the garden and courtyard of the cloisters, in order to 'prevent disturbances'. On 7 October of that year Aubert, the architect of the authority with responsibility for national properties, produced an eleven-page report on the convent, which tells us that the attics above Robertson's phantasmagoria were 'locations used as hiding places for prostitutes and other criminals'. Aubert advised the closure of the staircase leading to the attics, installation of a lantern, and closure of the carriage entrance of the courtyard of Charon once Robertson's show had finished. According to Aubert, the phantoms retired to bed at about ten o'clock:

> One notices that all Robertson's areas, up to the door of the phantasmagoria, are only lit on the days of his shows and that all the lights are out when they finish by ten o'clock in the evening at the latest.[38]

A self-contained little world lived in these enormous cloisters and their surroundings: some laundrywomen, opposite Robertson's location; the aeronaut and occasional fantasmagore Jacques Garnerin (1769–1823), one of Robertson's worst enemies, sublet a lodge built in the garden; there was the workshop of the Bureau of Printing, where *assignat* banknotes were printed; and a number of other small tenants, such as the porter Chouet or Mme Vacher-Lacour. Later, the painter Girodet set up his studio there. But the liveliest area was the garden which surrounded the cloisters, which had an area of more than 3 hectares. This was a popular place for walking in Robertson's time: passers-by could admire the fruit trees, the tombstones (the nuns were buried in this previously peaceful place), two panoramas, and some shops. In 1800 there was even a dancing hall, in a shed set against the wall of the Rue d'Antin; in 1804 Franconi's Circus appeared there; and the year after that the Théâtre des Jeunes Comédiens ('Theatre of the Young Actors'). The 'Enclosure of the Capucines', under the regime of the Directoire, became the meeting place of idlers, wanderers, prostitutes, and those in search of entertainment or a pleasant rendezvous. It was a cruel irony: under the *Ancien Régime* the convent had been noted for the austerity and extreme severity of its rite.

Robertson's first show in the cloister of the Capucines appears to have taken place on 3 January 1799, at 7.30 in the evening. On 8 January, the fantasmagore promised the usual appearances of spectres, phantoms and ghosts,

> offered by the same methods which must have been employed by the Witch [of Endor] when she invoked the spirit of Samuel, the three witches when they appeared to Macbeth, the priests of Memphis [in ancient Egypt] in the mysteries of their initiation.[39]

The thrill-seeking spectator was therefore invited to go to Rue Neuve-des-Petits-Champs. Once past the high wall which surrounded the close of the Capucines, which was falling dangerously into ruins, he or she had to find the way on this winter evening through a garden half plunged into darkness, and to avoid walking over the tombstones. Finally he or she would find the cloister and pass through a long corridor, decorated by Robertson with fantastic paintings, before entering a magnificent scientific exhibition where one could admire all sorts of curiosities inspired by Nicéron, Bettini, or Kircher. These included an anamorphosis entitled 'Monster found in the heart of a beautiful woman' (this monster, when deciphered by the anamorphic mirror, represented Love); an 'English caricature representing the heads of two noted doctors; if you pull the cord the faces change into asses' heads'; a cylindrical mirror which stretched the viewer's figure; a Polemoscope like Abbé Nollet's, which allowed one to see what was happening outside; a 'head representing sensual pleasure, placed in the centre of a crown of roses' (when viewed through an eyeglass 'the object is metamorphosed and creates only one idea, that the most beautiful rose will wither'); a magic mirror which answered more than two hundred questions; a peepshow offering twelve views of the mysteries of initiation (Robertson offered this box as a lottery prize on 4 June 1799); a painting showing three portraits at the same time (Franklin, Voltaire, and Rousseau); another larger peepshow with views of Egypt, Greece, and the tomb of Rousseau at Ermenonville (painted by Robertson); an 'optical panorama' representing the harbour of Naples;[40] and so on.

In 1800 Robertson opened a new room, next to the scientific exhibition. This was the 'Gallery of the Invisible Woman', where one could ask questions in front of a glass chest suspended in the air:

> One hears there the voice of an invisible young person answering all the questions, sighing, blowing on the hand which one offers her, and describing objects which are shown to her.[41]

An assistant was hidden in the neighbouring room, speaking through a hollow tin-plate tube, a method previously used by the fantasmagores of the 1780s. Robertson was not the only one to offer this acoustic illusion in Paris. The contemporary press was full of furious letters and vengeful slanderous advertisements, exchanged between the journalists, Robertson, and Laurent, a mediocre scientist who exhibited 'The Invisible Woman' in 'a pit' on the third floor of the cloister of Saint-Germain-l'Auxerrois. Around March 1800, a small book was published which humorously revealed the secret of the two scientists, who were referred to as 'gossips'. The author, writing under the pseudonym 'Ingannato' (meaning 'Deceived'), also described 'the invisible girl' exhibited at the Gardens of Paphos.[42] Robertson employed the acoustic talents of citizen Fitz-James, a ventriloquist, who could 'throw his voice to the end of a gallery, make it heard at five or six places at the same time, and produce illusions in all parts of the room'.[43]

After admiring all these curiosities, the spectator finally came to the object of desire: the hall of the phantasmagoria, protected by an 'ancient' door covered in hieroglyphics, which seemed to open onto the mysteries of Isis. As usual, the hall was dimly lit by a lamp hanging from the ceiling. 'A profound calm, an absolute silence, a sudden sense of isolation' overtook the audience. When everyone had taken their places on the wooden benches, Robertson would appear, with a grave and theatrical manner, his thin face framed by sideburns:

> That which will occur shortly before your eyes, Gentlemen, is not a frivolous spectacle; it is created for the thinking man, for the

philosopher who likes to lose himself for a moment, with Sterne, among the tombs.[44]

It was a pompous speech, tainted with hackneyed philosophy, but it pleased the audience, which would include women in spite of Robertson's address to the 'Gentlemen'. Like his predecessors, Robertson took great care to indicate in the press that the effects of the phantasmagoria 'are only due to fortunate combinations of optics', and that women 'need have no more fear of being terrified, than one may fear the sometimes disturbing effects of the light of the moon'.

The aim of the show was always stated as the destruction of 'absurd beliefs, the childish terrors which dishonour the intelligence of man'. However, with habitual ambiguity, Robertson kept the actual method of producing the phantoms and spectres which he created before the assembled crowd very much to himself. The aim of the phantasmagoria was therefore rather dubious: it sought more to create fear than to dispel the occult source of fear, and by showing the mysteries of ancient Egypt it was certain to disturb the most rational of its spectators (some of whom may perhaps have been freemasons). Whatever the case, the press was unanimous that the phantasmagoria was worth going out of one's way for:

> Here are the approximate details of a showing. In a scientific laboratory, where one finds every moment something to grasp the eyes and imagination, citizen Robertson carries out his experiments in galvanism, after which the Ventriloquist performs the most agreeable scenes; then the harmonica [this must be the 'Glas-Harmonika', to which Robertson sometimes added drums], by its gloomy tones, seems to lead to the opening of a great hall, illuminated by a pale trembling glow, which soon disappears and leaves the spectator in a deep dark night. Storms, the harmonica, the funeral bell which calls the shades from their tombs, everything inspires a religious silence: the phantoms appear in the distance, they grow larger and come closer before your eyes and disappear with the speed of light. Robespierre comes out of his tomb, begins to stand, a thunderbolt falls and reduces the monster and his tomb to dust. Beloved shades appear to lighten the picture: Voltaire, Lavoisier, J.J. Rousseau appear in turn, and Diogenes, his lantern in his hand, searches for a man and to find him goes up and down the rows, rudely causing fright to the ladies, which entertains everyone.[45]

Whether or not these projected images genuinely caused fear must have depended very much on the sensitivity of the spectator. At the start, at least, the phantasmagoria made a great impression, even on men who one might have expected to be more materialist. The famous gourmet Grimod de la Reynière visited the hall of the Capucines in March 1799, and declared:

> It is certain that the illusion is complete. The total darkness of the place, the choice of images, the astonishing magic of their truly terrifying growth, the conjuring which accompanies them, everything combines to strike your imagination, and to seize exclusively all your observational senses. Reason has told you well that these are mere phantoms, catoptric tricks devised with artistry, carried out with skill, presented with intelligence, your weakened brain can only believe what it is made to see, and we believe ourselves to be transported into another world and into other centuries.[46]

As for the cause of all these effects, Grimod de la Reynière could not explain it. The rumour was, he wrote, that 'the phantasmagoria is nothing other than a magic lantern turned back to front'. But there was one objection: he had seen a three-dimensional object pass across the room (perhaps Diogenes and his lantern), a quite tangible object, and when one of the spectators had struck at it with his cane he found something more solid than air. Robertson employed assistants to walk among the rows of spectators in the darkness, with papier-mâché masks lit from inside (a surviving example can be seen at the CNAM in Paris). On that particular day, the luminous ghost must have run off wailing.

It is possible to establish a list of Robertson's projected subjects from his advertisements in the press. As well as the unending procession of spectres and phantoms, the Fantascope projected the *Witch of Endor*, the *Three Witches of Macbeth* (these two scenes had been suggested to Robertson by a friend, M. de Sallabéry, who also advised him to adapt Holbein's *Dance of Death* for the screen, as Huygens had done); the *Sybill of Memphis*; the ghosts of Cagliostro, Voltaire, Rousseau, Condorcet, Lavoisier, Beaumarchais, Franklin, and Marmontel; the *Ghost of the Plenipotentiary Claude Roberjot* (shown on 11 May 1799—on 28 April the ministers Bonnier, Debry and Roberjot, the Directoire's peace negotiators at the Congress of Rastatt, had been assassinated—as we have seen, Robertson sometimes kept up with current affairs); the *Prophet Daniel*; the ghost of Héloïse; *Nymph Egeria and the Peacemaker*; *18 Brumaire and Napoléon Bonaparte*; Belshazzar's Feast; *Mohammed and his Pigeon*; *Mohammed Overcoming the Angel of Death* (shown on 15 September 1800); and *Young Burying his Daughter* (11 May 1802). This last scene, among others, was described by Robertson in his *Mémoires*. What is noticeable from that account is the length of these projected scenes: it is a little like reading a film scenario, with precise directions for *mise en scène*:

> *Young Burying his Daughter* [after *Night Thoughts on Life, Death, and Immortality* by Edward Young, published in 1742]. Sounds of a belfry; view of a cemetery illuminated by the moon. Young carrying the inanimate body of his daughter. He enters an underground passage where we discover a series of rich tombs. Young strikes on the first; a skeleton appears, he flees. He returns, works with a pickaxe: a second apparition and renewed terror. He beats on the third tomb; a ghost arises and asks him: What do you want of me? A tomb for my daughter, replies Young. The ghost recognizes him and gives up the place to him. Young places his daughter there. The cover is barely closed when we see the soul rising towards heaven; Young prostrates himself and remains in ecstasy.[47]

Of course all this was portrayed not on film, but on a series of glass slides or engravings projected with the Fantascope-Megascope. However these projected images were in colour and accompanied with sound, and their duration was certainly greater than that of the first cinematographic subjects. It is truly regrettable that the slides representing Robertson's repertoire have yet not been found.

Other small dramas of the same genre delighted the public between 1799 and the 1830s: the *Death of Lord Littleton*; *The Dream or the Nightmare* (projected in 1802); *Charon and his Boat*; *Birth of Country Love*; *Story of a Love*; *The Temptation of Saint Antony*; *The Dance of the Fairies*; *David Armed Against the Giant Goliath*; *Persephone and Pluto on their Throne*; *The Head of the Medusa* (see Fig. 22); and so on. The apparition of *The Bleeding Nun* needed two magic lanterns. One static lantern projected the scenery (a cloister) and the other, which was movable, represented the 'nun covered with blood' who 'arrived slowly and seemed to search for the object of her desire', with a dagger in her hand; 'she comes so close to the spectators that it often happens that one sees them move to allow her passage.' The use of two lanterns was an original technique. It is possible that Robertson may have used it to create dissolving views by means of shutters, with one image disappearing slowly, to be gradually replaced by another (this procedure did not appear publicly until 1839, in Britain). One further 'scenario', *The*

Fig. 22. *The Head of Medusa*, an animated slide for the Phantasmagoria,
c.1800. The eyes and tongue of the image are movable.
Collection: Laurent Mannoni.

Preparation for the Sabbath, should be mentioned since it is so full of
movement:

> A clock strikes midnight: a witch, her nose in a book, lifts her
> arm three times. The moon descends, places itself in front of her,
> and takes on the colour of blood; the witch strikes it with her wand
> and cuts it into two. She starts again to lift her left hand; at the
> third time, cats, bats, and death's heads fly about with will o'
> the wisps. In the centre of a magic circle one reads the words:
> *Départ pour le Sabbat* ['Beginning of the Sabbath']. A woman
> arrives astride a broom, and many figures follow her. Two monks
> appear with a cross, then a hermit, to exorcise, and everything melts
> away.[48]

Robertson's rivals and imitators

The hall of the Capucines was never empty: the phantasmagoria exerted an irresistible attraction for Parisians, provincial visitors, and foreigners. Madame Tallien, Joséphine Bonaparte, and Bonaparte's associate Paul Barras all came to 'pay tribute' to Robertson. Robertson himself was becoming rich and famous, and was also enjoying a happy domestic life: his mistress, Eulalie Caron, gave birth to a child on 27 September 1799. The former 'Abbé Robert' had adopted philosophical ideas and a lifestyle a long way removed from religion. Robertson had an unbeatable success on his hands, but the inevitable jealousy of his 'scientist-entertainer' colleagues and other showpeople was to spoil his happiness. It was not long before he was being copied. Robertson had already had to compete with his rivals in the business of the invisible woman. But for the phantasmagoria, the financial stakes were much higher and the competition much more fierce.

In 1798, Robertson had employed two assistants at the Pavillon de l'Échiquier: Martin Aubée (sometimes spelled Aubé) and his son Albert. They were paid as carpenter and designer, at a rate of 2 Francs per day. Robertson had complete confidence in them, but:

> during a journey which he made to his home province, the Citizens Aubée sought to learn his methods and appropriate the fruit of his discoveries; on his return he found the greatest disorder among his instruments, several of which were missing; in fact, the citizens Aubée had snatched them from the premises, which they had just left.[49]

When Robertson set himself up at the cloister of the Capucines, Martin and Albert Aubée, employed by the bailiff Léonard André Clisorius, opened a show named the 'Fantasmaparastasie' at the Pavillon de l'Échiquier. On 11 January 1799, without mentioning any names, Robertson issued a threat in the press against 'the individual who having no other talent than listening at the doors of the artist to steal from him the fruits of his labours, still dares to steal from him his name, to divert the public from the true location of his shows'.[50] In the same month, January 1799, an unknown individual stole some instruments necessary for his projections. Furthermore, on 15 February, 'a person mischievously broke into and robbed from the yellow room a curious object abandoned to public knowledge'.[51]

So it was in this atmosphere, alarmed by these two events and this unexpected competition, that Robertson hastily filed his patent on 26

January 1799. On 3 February, he announced forcefully that the Aubées had abused his confidence, that they were nothing more than scoundrels, and that he intended to 'appear before the magistrates responsible for overseeing the laws on the morals and ownership of the sciences and arts'.[52] But the affair dragged on, and his rivals profited. On 20 March 1799, one of them opened a 'Phantasmagoria' at the Palais Royal, which a month later became the 'Fantomagie'. This new counterfeiter projected 'Spirits, Sylphs, Gnomes, and other fantastic Beings'.[53] The most irritating aspect for Robertson was that the 'Fantomagie' was stated clearly in the press to be inspired by the methods of Philidor. By 1 November 1799, the Pavillon de l'Échiquier was offering 'experiments in physico-magico-philidorism'. It must have profoundly displeased Robertson for the true inventor of the phantasmagoria in France to be brought back to life in this way, through the magic lantern.

Perhaps the Aubées and their patron Clisorius were lurking behind these two shows at the Palais Royal (then called the Palais-Égalité) and the Pavillon de l'Échiquier. It was certainly they, on 11 March 1800, who presented the

> FANTASMA-PARASTASIE, or apparition of phantoms and evocation of ghosts, such as they appear to the enlightened . . . Among other apparitions, one will note the admirable appearance of cit. Gevaudan, in the *Delirium*, at the moment when he believes he sees the ghost of Clarisse; the tomb of Croesus and the black cat of the sabbath; the metamorphosis, a figure which changes its head several times, in the full view of the spectators. One will hear the finger Harmonica. The spectacle will end with charming fireworks, gases of different colours . . .[54]

This show took place on Rue du Bouloy, in the great Hôtel des Fermes, which extended as far as the Rue de Grenelle (the building was demolished in 1889). As if by coincidence, this was not very far from the Couvent des Capucines. The First Arrondissement (the district of central Paris around the Louvre palace) appears to have been the very centre of the phantasmagoria during the period of the Revolution and the Directoire.

According to contemporary accounts, the Aubée–Clisorius Fantasma-parastasie was a 'miserable' show, quite mediocre compared to that of Robertson:

It is not that Robertson might have had any great reason to fear the Fantasmaparastasie of Aubé, Clisorius and company. All those who have seen it maintain that this miserable spectacle, clumsily executed by a man who is no scientist, could not offer any troubling competition for the inventor. But . . . this clumsy performance could only damage an art in which the performance provides all the attraction.[55]

This is possible, but the programme of the Rue du Bouloy show was also very seductive: 'The walking Skeleton, the fertile Egg from which will emerge several persons, such as Love, Jealousy, Filidor who will be crowned by the grateful fairy, the Tomb of Croesus', and so on. These images, listed in the Fantasmaparastasie programme for 21 March 1800, had never been presented by Robertson—especially the coronation of Philidor!

On 27 March 1800, the Fantasmaparastasie on Rue du Bouloy closed its doors. Robertson had succeeded in the first phase of his counter-offensive: at his request, the *Tribunal de Paix* (local court) had applied seals to the equipment used by the Aubées and Clisorius, who was on a journey to Switzerland at the time. On 14 April the police commissioner for the Division of La Halle-aux-Blés certified the counterfeiting ('a perfect imitation') and, according to the law of 7 January 1791 which protected patent rights, the *Tribunal de Paix* ordered confiscation of the equipment to Robertson's advantage. Clisorius, Martin and Albert Aubée were sentenced in their absence to 200 Francs in damages, and ordered not to re-offend.[56]

Robertson believed that he had been vindicated. Unfortunately for him, Clisorius and the Aubées retained an excellent lawyer, Jacques Delahaye, and obtained an annulment of this judgement. The trial started again on 24 May, and all Paris discovered with astonishment that Robertson was not the inventor of the methods upon which the originality of his show was based:

> The affair of the Phantasmagoria yesterday drew a numerous crowd to the *Tribunal de Paix* of the Division of La Halle-aux-Blés. Citizen Delahaye, defending citizen Aubé, the collaborator of Clisorius, established that Robertson was not the author of the discovery for which he had obtained a patent . . . Philidor had put on the same spectacle in Paris in 1793, before Robertson dreamed of being a scientist. He demonstrated in his plea for the defence the talent of an orator and of a skilled legal mind, together with that of a trained scientist. Citizen Becquet-Beaupré, defending Clisorius,

discussed in a very pleasing way the improvements which Robertson boasted of having made to the trivial instrument known by the name of the Magic Lantern: he found them all drawn in Kircher and in the scientific recreations of Guyot.[57]

So the phantasmagoria was nothing more than an improved magic lantern show. The necromancer of the Couvent des Capucines lost all his status in the eyes of the public. For him, the trial was beginning to turn into a nightmare. Little by little Robertson became the accused: it was he who had stolen from Philidor, and he could not pretend to the title of inventor. He waited anxiously for the arguments of his own lawyer Lebon. During that time, the phantasmagoria at the Capucines remained open. The establishment of Aubée and Clisorius stayed closed; as a journalist from the *Courrier des Spectacles* remarked ironically:

> One might place on the door of the Fantasmaparastasie the inscription which may still be read on the cemetery of Saint-Sulpice: *Has ultra metas, requiescunt, beatam spem expectantes* [Beyond this limit, they—the ghosts—rest, waiting with blessed hope].[58]

This prophecy did not come to pass. On 14 June 1800 Lebon defended Robertson's position, but in vain. Clisorius declared the sealing of his equipment 'tortious and vexatious'. The report of the Tribunal was definitive:

> Robert not being the inventor of the phantasmagoria which existed before him as one may see in the printed works of Kircher, Nollet, Guyot, Philidor and other scientists, he must be stripped of his patent.[59]

An interlocutory judgement was given which ordered the appointment of experts to examine the instruments and machines of Aubée–Clisorius and Robertson, in order to determine whether or not there had been any counterfeiting. Two scientists were named shortly afterwards: Pierre Jamin, chosen by Clisorius, and Jean François Richer, nominated by Robertson.

The report of the two experts (reproduced as Appendix B), is remarkable in several ways. Over thirty-one pages, they described their successive visits (commencing on 17 July when the seals were removed from the Fantasmaparastasie) to the establishments of Clisorius and Aubée at the Hôtel des Fermes, and of Robertson at the Couvent des Capucines. For the first time, scientists entered the most secret place of the cloister, the room where Robertson's projection apparatus was located. Until then, at both the Pavillon de l'Échiquier and the Capucines, the fantasmagore had never shown his machinery to his friends or to the curious who wanted to know 'how it worked'. Much later, the magician and film-maker Georges Méliès would adopt much the same approach: in his own expression, he did not like people to 'knock the tricks' of the cinematograph and of conjuring. To let the public behind the scenes, to show them the mechanisms of dream and illusion, would reduce the pleasures of the eye and the mind to nothing.

In their official report to the *Tribunal de Paix*, Richer and Jamin noted the dispositions of the equipment, objects and rooms of both Robertson and Clisorius: 'It appeared to us that for the operations of the phantas-magoria and the Phantasmaparastasie, three rooms are required adjacent to one another.'[60] In the first room, where the audience would sit, a lamp was suspended from the ceiling by three chains. It was easily extinguished, since the wick was connected to a brass wire which passed to the other side of the screen: the projectionist only had to pull on the wire to lower the wick, making the room dark. Clisorius commented, in all seriousness, that he had not copied Robertson, since his own lamp was extinguished by means of a cord. While the lamp was lit, the screen was hidden from the eyes of the spectators by a curtain which was raised once the room had been plunged into darkness. In Robertson's arrangement, the curtain showed a picture of a tomb; for Clisorius, there was a slight variation in that the tomb was supported by caryatids (pillars carved as female figures).

A small door formed in the wall which supported the screen led into the second room, to which neither Robertson nor Clisorius admitted anyone. The visit to this part of Robertson's establishment took place on 25 July 1800, and went very badly for him. Furious at being obliged to open the doors of his 'projection booth', as we would call it today, Robertson showed the two experts a brand new lantern-megascope which did not correspond to the illustrations in his patent, which he had also been obliged to present to Jamin and Richer. This megascope was smaller (75 cm in height without its legs, 66 cm long and 50 cm wide) and it appeared very similar to that used by Clisorius. Possibly Robertson hoped to create the belief that his rival had copied him slavishly. Jamin and Richer walked round the device, and immediately spotted the deceit:

> they observed that the said apparatus had been made after the event, as indeed appears from what follows. That the legs of the table which supports the said box, the sides of the said table,

and the box itself are new, that the interior if it had been used would be blackened by the smoke of the oil lamps . . . that the wheels are not impregnated with oil . . . that the box which had been used for the four years in which Citizen Robertson has performed the Phantasmagoric should display some traces of handling . . . they maintain that this machine is cleverly copied from that of Citizen Clisorius.[61]

Somewhat embarrassed, Robertson refused to answer questions and signed the report without further objection. It included the following sentence:

the machine which Citizen Robert presented . . . is incapable of producing the effects which he produces daily before the public with his other machine which he has concealed from our view.[62]

Clisorius, for his part, lied just as shamelessly. In order to distance himself from Robertson's patent, he pretended that his megascope did not need rails to move forwards and backwards. The two experts, with some irony, therefore asked to see a projection. Clisorius performed it, pushing his megascope on wheels towards the screen, but the result was disastrous: 'it operates imperfectly and with a rocking motion because of the unevenness of the floor.' Robertson also agreed to project an image for the experts:

Robertson drew a figure which he then cut out, he . . . suspended it in the interior of the box in an upside-down position, the figure was portrayed on the transparent sheet [the screen] in an upright position . . . Then the figure increased or diminished in proportion on the transparent sheet according to whether the said box was moved backwards or forwards on its frame.[63]

The experts then passed into the third room. There they found, embedded in the wall, a square lens tube directed towards the screen. This was a second megascope, used for objects (or actors) too large or too heavy to be placed in the movable lantern. In this third room, Jamin and Richer noted the presence of two four-burner oil lamps mounted on stands. To demonstrate the power of his megascope, Robertson presented his face to the light of the lamps; immediately his image was projected onto the screen. In a corner, the experts also noted 'a table of tin-plate used to imitate thunder and a roll of cardboard used to imitate hail'.

On 2 August 1800, after fifteen days of enquiries, comings and goings between the Capucines and the Rue du Bouloy, of technical discussions and subtle objections, Jamin and Richer submitted their report. It damned both Robertson and Clisorius, and made it clear that one had copied the other. But who had copied whom? In spite of the evidence—Clisorius was well and truly a crude plagiarist—the two experts did not pronounce a conclusion. They had not appreciated the lies of Clisorius or the bad faith of Robertson, who had hidden his megascope. There had been a clear attempt to deceive the Tribunal. Robertson's slightly naive ruse was to backfire on him.

The conclusion of the report, cruel in its precision, is important: Jamin and Richer, the official scientists, established the true nature of all these phantasmagoria spectacles. They were not intended to 'destroy prejudices' or 'combat ignorance', but to earn money through provoking fear or astonishment:

> A dispute has arisen between two operators of optical illusions concerning the instruments and methods which they use to produce these illusions of pure charlatanism. We apply this name to effects which, without advancing by a single step or making any progress in the pursuit of the sciences, serve only to capture the admiration and above all the money of the public, to whom they are careful not to explain the causes.[64]

That is clear enough, and it confirms the scornful opinion of almost all true scholars towards Robertson, a 'charlatan', a Savoyard who believed he was progressing the science of optics by putting on a magic lantern show, as he was described by one contemporary, Dupuis-Delcourt. It was a severe, but correct, judgement. Only today can it be seen that, though Robertson did nothing to further optics or physical science, at least he was one of the greatest precursors of the cinematograph show.

The spread of projection

The *Tribunal de Paix* of La Halle-aux-Blés gave its judgement on 26 September 1800. The seals were removed from the Fantasmaparastasie and, for having prevented Clisorius' show since 27 March, Robertson was ordered to pay him 20,000 Francs in damages.[65] But the trial was not yet over. Lebon, Robertson's lawyer, demanded that Jamin and Richer's report should be annulled, since they had dared to insult both parties by calling them 'operators' and 'charlatans'. After yet more reports, pleas, and contradictory judgements, Robertson was finally ordered to pay Clisorius 2,072 Francs. The judge tried to calculate the total losses on the basis of some precious documents which have not survived, namely Robertson's and Clisorius' account books. He cited several revealing figures, which prove that the Clisorius Fantasmaparastasie was not greatly appreciated by the public: the hall had operated for a month and a half, during which period its director had banked 95 Francs in takings, of which 9.50 Francs went in tax to support the poor. Clisorius declared that his rent at Rue du Bouloy cost him 1,800 Francs per year; this means that his show, had it continued, would probably have made a loss. In comparison, Robertson reckoned his takings at 250 Francs per month, almost three times those of Clisorius; he paid 25 Francs to the poor. The amount of rent he was paying for the Capucines is not known.

Finally, on 12 July 1803 (after three years of litigation), the amount Robertson had to pay Clisorius was reduced to 871 Francs.[66] For Robertson, who had become considerably richer through the phantasmagoria and his aeronautical exploits, this was not a serious loss. But he had lost his case, and his projection techniques, revealed during the trial, were now largely in disrepute, as he acknowledged in his *Mémoires*:

> From that moment, the phantasmagoria became a very common object executed by fantasmagores of all classes, Paris resembled the Elysian Fields for the large number of ghosts living there . . . The fantasmagores mainly gathered on the river banks, and there was hardly a quay which did not offer you a little phantom at the end of a dark black corridor, or the top of a tortuous staircase. The ghost machines also became a commercial item then in Paris and London; the Dumortiez brothers [Robertson mis-spelled the name: this refers to the brothers Dumotiez, Parisian opticians who in 1806 operated at 31 Rue Copeau and 2 Rue du Jardinet] and the English opticians dispatched several thousand throughout Europe. The smallest amateur scientist, in every land, had his phantasmagoria. I have found these trolley boxes, made in Paris, in deepest Russia, at Odessa, and from the borders of Siberia to the far end of Spain, even in Ceuta.[67]

The credit for the dispersal of the fashion for mobile animated projection is entirely Robertson's—albeit against his wishes. Numerous new halls opened in Paris shortly after the trial, including one run by Rouy Charles, set up on 26 October 1800 at the Palais Royal, then on 2 December at Place du Caroussel, in the Maison de Longueville. This fantasmagore, who had no connection to the scientist Jacques Charles, claimed to have been inspired by the methods of Philidor. On 1 January 1802, the Hôtel des Fermes in Rue du Bouloy was once again occupied by an 'improved Fantasmaparastasie', operated by Martin and the conjuror Olivier (possibly employed by Clisorius).

In 1806 one Le Breton, author in 1811 of a book of popular science in which he proclaimed Philidor's priority over Robertson, opened the 'Psychagogie, or evocation of ghosts and the phantasmagoria' in the Abbey of Saint-Germain on Rue Bonaparte. In 1831, he set himself up on the *grands boulevards* in an open-air shed, shown in a watercolour by Opitz in the collection of the Musée Carnavalet. This establishment appears as a neo-gothic structure, with a large banner painted with images of ghosts and Death, and a platform on which a barker is playing the violin. There was also the scientist-ventriloquist Louis Comte (1788–1859) who offered scientific entertainment shows, with a 'historical animated phantasmagoria', from June 1809. Very much in fashion after the Restoration of the monarchy in 1814, he and his ghosts were resident in the Hôtel des Fermes in Rue du Bouloy, an extremely popular location among lanternists. In 1803, Robertson took his own phantasmagoria abroad for a tour of many European cities. This wave of projections very soon swept into the United States: the first 'Phantasmagory' show was given in New York in May 1803[68] and in 1825 Eugène Robertson, the son of Étienne-Gaspard, represented his father with dignity in the same city.

In Britain, the particular case of Philipstahl is worth closer examination.[69] In 1801, he opened a very typical 'Phantasmagoria' show at the Lyceum Theatre in London, with progressive appearances of ghosts, famous people, and so on. There is one curious element: Philipstahl, whose surname shared a first syllable with Philidor and Philadelphia, also had the same first name (Paul) as the lanternist of Rue de Richelieu, whose work in 1792–3 was of such importance, as we have seen. If Philidor-Philadelphia-Philipstahl was a single fantasmagore, why did he not proclaim his indignation when Robertson stole all his methods? On 26 January 1802, Paul de Philipstahl filed a deliberately vague patent[70] in Britain, in which he explained that 'after diligent research, with inconceivable problems and expenses' he had achieved the production of phantom apparitions. His apparatus, he wrote, was equipped with two concave reflectors and 'several lenses'; there was no further description of the equipment. But Philipstahl was wrong to be so secretive. By 1802, the phantasmagoria was in the public domain: the lawsuit Robertson brought against Clisorius had revealed the whole process of the spectacle to astounded Parisians. Much to Philipstahl's displeasure an English journalist, William Nicholson, who had attended a show at the

Fig. 23.　Two British playbills for Phantasmagoria shows in the 1800s.
Collection: Cinémathèque Française, Musée du Cinéma.

Lyceum Theatre, had no hesitation in revealing the most important technical element: a 'magic lanthorn' was hidden behind the screen.[71] Also in 1802, a Neopolitan named Gulielmus Frederico exhibited 'The Phantasmagoria' throughout England. On 10 May 1802, he presented his 'Spectrology' with the glass harmonica at Kingston-upon-Hull in Yorkshire. This competitor was perhaps the reason why Philipstahl filed his patent, in an attempt to safeguard his interests.

The rapid spread of the phantasmagoria can be compared with the 'world tour' of the magic lantern at the end of the seventeenth century. An interesting parallel can also be drawn between Robertson's presentation of the phantasmagoria to Tsar Alexander I in 1804 (*Le Moniteur Universel* in Paris even announced, on 3 September 1805, that the Academy of Sciences in St Petersburg had acquired Robertson's scientific laboratory: the Tsar had truly succumbed to the scientist's illusions!), and the demonstration of the Cinématographe Lumière before Nicholas II in 1897 by the French operator Félix Mesguich.

The years 1798–1800 were the most exciting of Robertson's life. We leave his story at the start of the nineteenth century, which was to be so rich in technical inventions. Robertson died on 2 July 1837, at Les Batignolles, without renouncing his philosophical convictions; his tomb at Père Lachaise is decorated with impressive phantasmagorical motifs. One bas-relief, sculpted by Moelkent and Hardouin, shows a magic lantern show, in which terrified spectators recoil before a monster which has just appeared before their eyes. Robertson was an incomplete priest, a lapsed scientist, and a reed in the political wind (his shows flattered every change of regime), but he captured the attention of thousands with his animated projected images. He did not invent the phantasmagoria, but he knew how to draw every possibility out of a method of projection which was 'in the spirit of the age', as would later be said on the arrival of cinema. It was only the likes of Robertson and Méliès who were able to open up the fields of artistic creation to simple mechanical inventions.

7

From Panorama to Daguerreotype

The panorama was invented at approximately the same time as the phantasmagoria; it was far more learned, more academic, and less inventive than the projected phantoms, and it involved no projection. Nonetheless the panorama holds just as honourable a place in the 'family album' of recreational uses of images and light. The spectator was admitted to a raised platform, in the centre and about halfway up the height of a cylindrical room with a conical roof, to view a large painted canvas stretched around the circular wall. This 'panoramic' view represented a landscape or a battle scene, a monument, or some similar subject. It was carefully created, with perspective, 'depth of field', and chiaroscuro effects. The canvas (which was effectively endless, since its two ends met and joined the picture continuously) was lit at an angle from above, through a glazed opening formed in the roof of the building.

Whereas the screen of the phantasmagoria was populated by many moving images, in the panorama there was no attempt at animation. The canvas was lit only by the shimmering of natural light. But it offered an immense 'point of view' which gave its audience the impression of being at the heart of an imposing representation. It hinted at the dream of a complete spectacle, of 'total cinema', which some cinematograph pioneers attempted to realize at the start of the twentieth century; a dream finally realized in the 1980s and 1990s by large-scale projection systems such as *Imax*, *Omnimax*, and the 360-degree cinema.

Today it is hard to imagine the power of attraction exerted by monumental circular paintings. These gigantic peepshows enjoyed prodigious success throughout the nineteenth century, and into the 1900s, when they were superseded by the cinematograph only after a fierce struggle. The account in this chapter will be limited to a rapid exploration of the birth of this new spectacle; the best starting-point in English for a wider study of this subject is the 1988 book *Panoramania!*[1] which accompanied an exhibition at the Barbican Art Gallery in London.

Inventors and evangelists of the panorama

Robert Barker (1739–1806), an Irish painter, is generally considered to have been the inventor of the panorama. On 17 June 1787, he was granted a patent by King George III for

> an entire new contrivance or apparatus, which I call *La Nature à Coup d'Oeil*, for the purpose of displaying views of Nature at large by Oil Painting, Fresco, Water Colours, Crayons, or any other mode of painting or drawing.[2]

In his patent Barker outlined the basic principles of the panorama, which were adopted more or less universally: a circular room, inside which was an enclosure which kept the spectator at some distance from the canvas. The lighting came from above, through a glazed roof or simple opening. Entry to the enclosure had to be made from underground, in order not to distract the audience's attention. As in Robertson's phantasmagoria, this also allowed the spectator to be deprived of light, passing through gloomy corridors before arriving in front of the brightly illuminated circular painting, a surprise effect which accounted for a large part of the panorama's success. Barker also included ventilators to allow a natural circulation of air in the building. The most difficult part was the composition of the panoramic view with the correct perspective:

> By the Invention . . . is intended, by drawing and painting and a proper disposition of the whole, to perfect an entire view of any country or situation as it appears to an observer turning quite round; to produce which effect the painter or drawer must fix his station, and delineate correctly and connectedly every object which presents itself to his view as he turns round, concluding his drawing by a connection with where he started.[3]

Barker exhibited his first panorama in Edinburgh in 1787, showing a view of that city painted in tempera colour on a canvas stretched in a semicircle. But it was in 1792 that he achieved his true triumph in London, with a panorama built in Leicester Square, where one could see 'a view at a glance of the Cities of London and Westminster'.[4] The subject was changed from time to time: the following year one could see 'a view of the Grand Fleet moored at Spithead'.[5] According to a German journalist of the time:

> The painting has a surface of more than 1,000 square feet and is attached on the inner surface of a circular building which is 90 feet in diameter. The spectator is placed in the centre of the painted sea, on the upper deck of a frigate. This maritime landscape is particularly delightful. The illusion is so strong that the spectators believe themselves to be truly between the harbour and the island, in the open sea; they even say that some ladies have suffered from seasickness.[6]

From 1792 until 1798 Barker presented, at the same London venue, views of *London from the Albion Mills, Southwark*; *The Fleet Moored at Spithead*; *The Battle of the Nile*; *Bathing at Brighthelmstone* [Brighton]; and *The Environs of Windsor*. He then exported his invention to Germany, sometimes under a different name such as the Nausorama. In June 1800 the Nausorama was set up in the market place in Hamburg, where the painting of the fleet at Spithead was displayed once again, in a semi-circle 6.5 m in height and about 15 m in length.[7]

In Germany the invention of the panorama was attributed to Professor Breysig, who had had the same idea as Barker around 1790 without being aware of Barker's patent. Breysig travelled to Italy in 1791 to make sketches for his first panoramic painting, representing the ruins of Rome. In 1794 he became the scene painter of the theatre in Leipzig and mentioned his idea to one Kreuchauf, who pointed out to him that Barker had beaten him to the idea, by some time, in Edinburgh and London. Shortly afterwards, in Berlin, Breysig met the painter Tielker, who told him of his intention to build a panorama like Barker's in that city. Breysig formed a partnership with Tielker and a third plagiarist, Kaaz, a specialist in landscapes. The years passed; Tielker concerned himself with building the rotunda, while Breysig and Kaaz painted the immense canvas, based on the sketches made in Rome in 1791. Finally, in June 1800, the Berlin panorama was ready to open its doors. But by that date, there were already panoramas in Leipzig and Hamburg.

The panorama in Paris

In France, the American Robert Fulton (1765–1815), inventor of a steam-driven boat, was behind the rapid spread of the panorama. He had seen and admired Barker's rotunda in London (Fulton had lived in

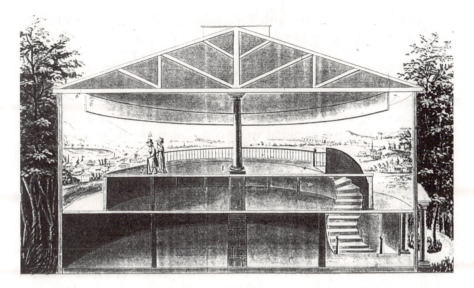

Fig. 24.   Cross-sectional diagram from Fulton's patent for his panorama
design, 1799. Collection: INPI, Paris.

England for many years, and had gained a civil engineering qualification there in 1795). At the end of 1796 he went to France, staying with
his friend the American diplomat and poet Joel Barlow. On 25 February
1799 Robert Fulton, 'engineer of the United States of America', resident
at 970 Rue de Vaugirard in Paris, applied to the Ministry of the Interior
for a ten-year patent of importation to

> establish, paint, exhibit and display exclusively, over the whole
> extent of the Republic, the circular paintings known as Panorama,
> of which he claims to be the inventor.[8]

Fulton was not content simply to describe what he had seen at Barker's
establishment in London, but set out to improve the invention. The
building he designed measured 19.3 m in diameter by 6.4 m in height
(see Fig. 24). The circular panoramic paintings could be changed at any
time, and up to eight times in succession. Fulton imagined constructing
a small cabin adjacent to the rotunda, in which eight other canvases
would be rolled onto long vertical cylinders. On the action of a handle,
the pictures would slide one after another along an iron frame around the
rotunda:

In this manner one may withdraw a painting and draw another into its place with great ease, and this work may be brought to such perfection that one may change the paintings of the panorama while the enclosure is full of spectators and they may in this way travel to one after another of the capitals of Europe without moving.[9]

A second logical improvement was to allow the panorama to be used at night. All that was required was to illuminate the paintings with oil lamps. But as the pictures were painted in oils with a glossy varnish, the light had to be quite subdued and distant: lamps with reflectors were therefore placed some way off, under the timbers of the roof and under the central pillar which supported the spectators. All this was well conceived, but there might be doubts about the smooth operation of the handle and cylinder mechanism. It seems hard to believe that it would be possible, every day, to manoeuvre the eight paintings and rewind them properly, without their becoming stuck on their rails. As for the illumination, in order for it to be even, there would have to be a great number of oil lamps scattered from top to bottom of the building. This dangerous assembly would have to be looked after very carefully.

However, the executive of the Directoire regime was not concerned with determining whether it would work or not. It did not guarantee the success of such an invention—later patents were issued 'SGDG', *Sans Garantie de Gouvernement* ('Without the Guarantee of the Government'). And in any case, Fulton had no chance of proving that his eight-fold panorama could work, unless he could construct it first. He was granted his ten-year patent on 26 April 1799. However, he never managed to raise enough capital to build his rotunda, and on 8 December 1799 he sold all rights to his patent to James Thayer and his wife Henriette Beck.

James Thayer formed a partnership with a painter, Pierre Prévost (1766–1823), whose style was highly classical, even academic. The circular paintings he created for Thayer were in some cases between 100 and 120 m in length, and exhibited an obsessive level of precision which caused the painter Jacques-Louis David to remark, while visiting Prévost's studio with his pupils: 'Gentlemen, this is where one must come to make studies from nature!' Thayer secured the services of this excellent painter for what proved to be a fruitful partnership: in all, Prévost created about eighteen panoramic canvases, sometimes in collaboration with other artists. It appears that some of the capital to finance the construction of two rotundas was put up by Jois Walker, a strap manufacturer of Rue des Colonnes, Paris. In June 1799, even before acquiring Fulton's patent rights, Thayer and Walker constructed their first panorama in the 'Gardens of Apollo' at the convent of the Capucines, opposite a fireworks shop and very close to Robertson's phantasmagoria. A second rotunda was opened a year later.

Robertson was hardly pleased by the arrival of this unexpected neighbour, for two reasons: first, the rotunda was located in front of the entrance to the phantasmagoria, creating a risk that his clientele might prefer Prévost's paintings. The panorama was Art, whereas Robertson's show remained an attraction of dubious taste, as we have seen. Secondly, Robertson claimed that Walker, a former friend, had stolen the idea of building a panorama in the garden of the Capucines from him. In his *Mémoires*, Robertson wrote that he had even chosen the subject for his first circular painting, which was to be created by the painter Denis Fontaine: a view of Paris from the Château of the Tuileries. He had already negotiated the rental of part of the Gardens of Apollo,

> when two Englishmen, one of whom was M. Robert Fulton [and the other probably Thayer], stopped my work by showing me the application they had made for a patent for the same object . . . I had devoted eight months to preparing my plans; this project became quite fruitless.[10]

The panorama in the garden of the Capucines opened in September 1799, presenting the view supposedly planned by Robertson some time beforehand—although we should probably not believe everything Robertson claimed, fond as he was of playing the martyr.

> The Panorama, or continuous painting, representing a superb view of Paris and its surroundings taken from high on the Palais des Tuileries, is open every day at the new rotunda, situated in the garden of the Capucines known as Apollo, from eight o'clock in the morning until eight o'clock in the evening. Price of admission 1 Franc 50 per person.[11]

There was no mention of successive paintings or artificial light: the devices imagined by Fulton remained on the drawing-board. Nonetheless, the public flocked in and the press was full of praise:

> I admit that I was agreeably surprised by the view which struck me on entering the Panorama . . . I believed myself genuinely transported up in the air, on the platform of the central pavilion of the Tuileries, and Paris and its surroundings spread themselves before my astonished gaze; when after a whole hour I emerged from

the Panorama, seeing nature again I had difficulty in distinguishing it from the painting which I had left.[12]

In the second rotunda, constructed shortly afterwards around September 1800, 'the view of Toulon and its surroundings, taken at the moment when the English were forced to abandon it in 1793', a painting by Pierre Prévost and Constant Bourgeois, could be admired.

All Paris wanted to see the Capucines panoramas, and Thayer cashed in by opening new rotundas more or less everywhere. On 9 July 1801, the 'Panorama de Lyon' was launched on Boulevard Montmartre in Paris: 'What a pleasant surprise to travel without leaving Paris!' Next to this rotunda, which was 14 m in diameter and constructed on the gardens of the former Hôtel de Montmorency-Luxembourg, a second panorama connected with the Théâtre des Variétés was constructed. In 1808 a lane separating the two rotundas was christened the 'Passage des Panoramas'. Although this delightful place still exists today, the two rotundas were unfortunately destroyed in 1831. Between 1815 and 1830 Robertson operated his new scientific exhibition and phantasmagoria at 12 Boulevard Montmartre, next door to the present-day Musée Grévin; he abandoned the Capucines when the demolition contractors moved in.

During 1806 the Empire had decided to sell off the huge grounds of the convent, divided into thirty-six plots. On 6 June 1807, James Thayer and Pierre Prévost acquired two plots at the side of the Rue Neuve-Saint-Augustin (the present-day Rue Daunou). The cost was high, at 91,100 Francs, which the two men paid grudgingly; in 1812 the bailiffs were still sending them furious demands for payment.[13] All of Thayer and Prévost's property transactions seem quite unbelievable: it is not at all clear how they raised the money to buy the land and erect the rotundas at Rue Montmartre and Boulevard des Capucines. They even raised further funds to open a new rotunda located on the uncertain site at Rue Neuve-Saint-Augustin. This building (about 32 m in diameter inside, and 16 m high) was opened in 1808, with an entrance on Boulevard des Capucines from which a 15 m corridor gave access to the hall. It was christened the 'Imperial Panorama' and presented a picture of the Congress of Tilsit, where Napoléon Bonaparte and Tsar Alexander I of Russia reached a peace agreement in 1807. It was said that the Emperor himself came to see this in 1810.

In a letter of 7 February 1809 addressed to the Minister of the Interior, Thayer asked for an extension of five years for the patent he had purchased from Fulton. He gave a sycophantic outline of his future projects, which could only please the Empire:

> For a long time I have had the intention of placing before the eyes
> of the inhabitants of Paris, by the sole method which can rival the
> appearance of nature in colour and precision, the battles and other
> memorable events which have taken place since the accession of the
> hero who is charged with our glory and well-being.[14]

Unsurprisingly Thayer obtained his extension, and so kept the exclusive
rights to his show until 27 April 1814. On 15 April 1816, Pierre Prévost
filed a patent for the art of painting panoramas. By that time the
monarchy had been restored, and James Thayer was seen in a very poor
light by those in power, since he had displayed such bad taste as to
glorify the former Empire. As a result Prévost clearly kept his distance
from his former partner:

> I have had the honour to humbly represent to His Majesty that
> when the first idea of the panorama, a patent of importation in
> which I had no involvement, was awarded to a foreigner who had
> given a sum of money to another speculator who had discovered the
> secret of recreating it; neither of these cultivated the fine arts;
> whereas I, I dare to say, over the seventeen years in which I have
> occupied myself with it, have brought this genre of painting through
> a considerable step towards perfection, which everyone may judge by
> comparison of the first work which I performed in this genre with
> that representing the disembarkation of His Majesty Louis XVIII at
> Calais, which at the present time is exhibited to the public at the
> Boulevard des Capucines.[15]

Prévost's patent gave some technical advice on painting circular canvases,
for example on the way in which a landscape was chosen, by placing
oneself at a raised viewpoint which would be of about the same height as
the platform of the panorama. The most difficult part, he said, was to
paint the sky: 'With a poor sky a panorama can never create an illusion
. . . The entire effect depends on its execution.' Prévost even gave classes
in Paris on panoramic painting. A painting by Mathieu Cochereau, a
pupil and nephew of Prévost, now in the Musée des Beaux-Arts at
Chartres, shows one such class with the master standing in front of a
large rectangular canvas before an attentive audience.

Thayer and Prévost's patents did not, of course, prevent imitation. All
that was needed was to change the name of the attraction, or slightly vary
the design of the building. So there was the Cosmorama, which appeared
around 1808 and offered 'the view of the most remarkable monuments
and sites of the four corners of the World, every day from six o'clock in

the evening until eleven'[16] in a glazed gallery on the first floor of the Palais Royal. In 1810 the Panstereorama, 'opposite the Porte Maillot, at the large iron gate', could be visited every day: 'One sees there models of Paris, London, St Petersburg, Lyon, constructed in relief to the same scale'.[17] This may not have been a true panorama, but the idea was the same, offering spectators a 'sight', a hyper-realistic image, an 'all-embracing view'. In a similar vein was the Navalorama, a spectacle 'consisting of infinitely variable animated maritime paintings', established on 28 May 1838 by the painter Louis Gamain.

The most amazing spin-off of the panorama was the Géorama, constructed in 1827 at 7 Boulevard des Capucines. This was the brainchild of Charles-François-Paul Delanglard, who filed his patent on 25 March 1822:

> The Géorama is a machine by means of which one may embrace almost any single view on the whole surface of the earth: it consists of a hollow sphere of 40 feet [about 13 m] in diameter, at the centre of which the spectator is placed on a platform of about 10 feet [about 3 m] in diameter, from which he discovers all parts of the terrestrial globe which are painted in oils on the canvas-covered framework . . .[18]

The whole interior of the sphere into which the public were admitted was covered in painted canvas, except for the very top (which represented the North Pole), which was open to allow light to enter. The opposite pole was occupied by a stairwell which led up into the centre of the sphere. Very precise in its design, the Géorama had the external appearance of a huge ball supported on ten columns, resembling the design by Lequeu for the Temple de l'Égalité. A similar structure, known as 'Wyld's Monster Globe', was later erected in Leicester Square, London, in 1851.

By 1833 Paris also boasted the moving panorama of Mezzara, in Rue de Provence. This was possibly of a mobile or portable construction devised by Charles Ogé Barbaroux in 1828.[19] In 1829, a theatrical scene painter named Gué even designed a Hydrorama, a beautiful boat with exterior decorations resembling the facade of a high-class theatre. Inside, peepshows, a camera obscura and a small semicircular panorama presented a 'geographical and historical spectacle'.[20] We should also mention the Néorama, which the painter Jean-Pierre Alaux (1783–1858) opened on 10 October 1827, on Rue Saint-Fiacre in Paris. In 1827 he showed *The Basilica of St Peter in Rome*, and in 1829 *The Abbey of*

Westminster in London. A few years ago these two immense canvases were rediscovered in the stores of the Musée du Louvre in Paris. They were unrolled and displayed for several days at the Grand Palais; since it was not possible to hang them on the wall they had to be spread out on the floor.

Many panoramic canvases have disappeared, but a certain number do survive. Among these are the *Panorama of Thun* painted by Marquard Wocher of Basle in 1814, a canvas measuring 7.5 m by 38 m, exhibited at Thun in Switzerland. The Museum of Modern Art in New York displays the *Panoramic View of the Palace and Gardens of Versailles*, a panorama of 3.6 m by 50 m, created by John Vanderlyn in 1819. At Salzburg there is *The Panorama of Salzburg* by Michael Sattler, completed in 1829 (5.5 m by 26 m). The panoramic views created in France have practically all been lost, except for some from the end of the nineteenth century which have been preserved, one way or another, in various European museums.

In Paris, the Champs-Élysées was for a long time the centre of attention for lovers of the panorama. The first company formed to run a rotunda on the avenue was founded on 9 May 1838, by the artist Jean-Laurent Poéte. This building was located close to Rue Marbeuf, and measured 40 m in diameter by 15 m in height; its architect, Hittorf, had made a very precise study of panorama buildings. Destroyed in 1855, this panorama was rebuilt in 1860 close to Avenue Franklin-Roosevelt (then Rue d'Antin), and demolished once more in 1893. In 1885, one could still visit the 'Diorama Across the Ages', which is one of the very few rotundas in France still existing today (as the Théâtre Marigny). But mention of the word 'Diorama' makes it necessary to begin another complete history.

The 'Diorama' of Daguerre and Bouton

In 1822, just as the fashion for panoramas was beginning to wane slightly, two pupils of Pierre Prévost radically transformed Barker's invention: Louis Jacques Mandé Daguerre (1787–1851) and Charles Marie Bouton (1781–1853) opened the Diorama.

Daguerre had sound experience as a theatrical decorator behind him. His first master had been Degotty, the scene painter of the Paris Opéra, and he had then attended Pierre Prévost's classes and assisted him with some of his panoramas. It was there that he made the acquaintance of Bouton, his future partner. As Georges Potonniée has observed,[21] Daguerre was never more than ordinary as a painter of small easel canvases, but according to contemporary accounts his theatrical scenery was stunning. This worthy pupil of Prévost knew how to work with shadows, chiaroscuro, light, and perspective. From 1817 to 1822 he worked at the Ambigu-Comique theatre and the Opéra. In collaboration with the prodigy Pierre-Luc Cicéri, he created the scenery for *Aladdin or the Magical Lamp*, presented at the Opéra on 6 February 1822 with great success; for one scene Daguerre designed a moving sun illuminated with gas, a most daring technical innovation for its time.

Charles Bouton was also a painter who loved shadows and effects of depth. In 1812 he exhibited in Paris a *Philosophe en Méditation* ('Meditating Philosopher') which one critic praised for 'the light so well understood and distributed in such a true manner, the stone floor covered with dust and the marble floor slightly damp, finally the tombs are perfectly in perspective.'[22] Daguerre probably admired Bouton's romantic, post-phantasmagoric imagination, and also the scrupulous precision of his compositions. For the future inventor of the daguerreotype, the more closely painting approached reality, the greater its success. But opinions varied on this subject; as Alfred de Vigny remarked:

> If the first merit of art is nothing more than the exact painting of truth, the panorama would be superior to the *Descent from the Cross*.[23]

Daguerre and Bouton decided in 1822 to adapt the scenic methods of theatrical design to the old panorama, adding the special effects of the eighteenth-century peepshow, with lighting changes and gradual passage from day to night or vice versa. On 3 January 1822, Bouton (resident at 33 Rue des Martyrs) and Daguerre (of 9 Rue de la Tour, Faubourg du Temple), filed the founding documents of a company in their joint name

> to succeed in the establishment of a spectacle which is named the Diorama, to be situated on Boulevard Saint-Martin, whose opening shall take place during the coming April at the latest.[24]

Bouton, Daguerre et Compagnie was incorporated for a term of twenty-four years, with a capital of 250,000 Francs divided as 250 shares, 200 of which were divided equally between the two founders. The works envisaged for building the Diorama were costed at 150,000 Francs, but this amount might be exceeded.

The deed of foundation of the Diorama, preserved in the Archives de

Paris, shows that Bouton and Daguerre set out on a major financial undertaking (readers of Balzac will know what a huge sum 250,000 Francs represented at that period). A later document, dated 2 February 1829, gives a list of shareholders of the company 'for exploitation of the Diorama'. Among them were painters such as Jean-Marie Vernet, Daniel Saint, and Jacques Augustin Régnier (who could possibly have been related to August Louis Régnier, inventor in 1848 of a children's 'miniature diorama'); a counsellor at the revenue court, Pierre Blaise Bernard de Gascq; an architect, Pierre Magloire Chatelain, who had charge of building the Diorama; a former auctioneer; two landlords; and a member of the nobility, the Comte de Poutalès-Georgies. There were ten shareholders in all.

A plot of land was rented at 4 Rue Sanson, close to the Place de la République, on the current site of the south-west corner of the Vérines barracks. The architect Chatelain set about construction of a quite simple external facade of stone blocks and wooden panels. The building measured 52 m in length, 27 m in width and 16 m in height. The interior was quite astonishing. Entry was via a staircase into a dimly-lit room in the form of a rotunda, 12 m in diameter, which could seat 350 people. This lightweight auditorium could rotate about its axis, on a mechanism of a central bearing, rollers and a driving handle. In the wall of this rotunda an opening 7.5 m wide and 6.5 m high was formed; when the auditorium was rotated, this opening could come into position exactly in front of one of the dioramic paintings, set up at a distance of 13 m from the spectator. To give the illusion of being in a real theatre, the audience was separated from the painting by a proscenium, around which Daguerre could arrange fountains, live animals, or scenery. When the scene had been fully appreciated (the viewing time was about a quarter of an hour), the auditorium would rotate about its axis until its opening revealed a second painting with a second proscenium. The Diorama building consisted of three such rooms radiating from the circumference of the auditorium.

The Diorama's superiority over the panorama did not only lie in this pivoting auditorium. Bouton and Daguerre, reusing the methods they had already employed on the stages of the Ambigu and the Opéra, played with lighting effects with virtuoso skill. The canvases (made of percale or calico), measuring 22 m wide by 14 m high, were painted on both sides. On the front was painted a daytime landscape, which was illuminated by natural light falling from above through large glazed panels in the roof. On the other side of the canvas, details of the same landscape were picked out in paint to give a night effect—the moon, patches of darkness, lighted lanterns, and so on. If the glazed panels in the roof were masked, and other windows behind the canvas opened, the night effects would suddenly appear as a 'dissolve' from the daylight scene. This technique was not applied immediately: at the start, in 1822, they were content with shadow effects and simple lights. Sometimes Daguerre used coloured transparent screens, moved by cables and counterweights, which allowed the creation of effects like brilliant sunshine, moonlight, dense fog, and so on.

The Diorama opened on Thursday 11 July 1822. The price of admission was fixed at three Francs for the balcony, or two Francs for the stalls. The doors were open every day from ten in the morning until five in the evening; the entrance was at 4 Rue Sanson, close to Boulevard Saint-Martin. The first two paintings were *The Interior of the Cathedral of Canterbury* by Bouton and *The Valley of Saarnen in Switzerland* by Daguerre. The gamble paid off: the public, having abandoned phantasmagorias and panoramas, turned to this new illuminated attraction:

> The opening of the Diorama yesterday was quite outstanding. During the whole day, the most attractive company came there and did not cease to express their admiration for the two paintings offered for their curiosity. Among the pleasing comments which were inspired by the astonishment of the spectators, we noted this one, which covers them all: nature could not do it better.[25]

Among the first spectators in the months of July and August 1822 was the fascinated Honoré de Balzac:

> I have seen the Diorama . . . Daguerre and Bouton have astonished all of Paris; a thousand problems are resolved from the moment when, in front of a stretched canvas, one believes oneself to be in a church [and] a hundred feet away from everything. It is the marvel of the century, a 'conquest of man' which I was not expecting at all. This devil Daguerre has unleashed an invention which will give him a good portion of the money of these gay Parisians.[26]

The writers George Sand and Juste Olivier also went to admire the paintings at the Diorama. The public were enchanted by the changes of lighting, the passage of a cloud across the canvas, the sun going down slowly, and so on. However, as one critic commented: 'If the scene were to be animated with moving characters, I could not believe that I found myself in front of a painting.'[27] In spite of all the effects of light reflection and refraction, the canvas still remained static. It was a step back from the animation of the lantern slide, even if the artistic ambition of the Diorama surpassed that of any projected show.

It appears that Daguerre did try to animate his pictures, notably in 1823 in *The View of the Port of Brest*. Perhaps this effort to give more life to his pictures was inspired by the attempts of Augustin Haton, a Parisian who filed a patent on 21 March 1823 for a method of making dioramic views mobile. The process was quite simple, consisting of sliding an object on rails across the main painting, which stayed still. One could obtain surprising effects, claimed Haton, 'especially when all these movements are combined with the effects of light and its gradual changes'.[28]

Whether static or animated, the Diorama was very quickly popularized in the form of relatively inexpensive parlour toys. The bookseller and publisher Auguste Nicolas Nepveu (a resident of the Passage des Panoramas) seems to have been the first to think of this. He designed the 'Panorama de Salon' ('drawing-room panorama') in 1829, the 'Cyclorama' or 'Autorama Catoptrique' in 1833, and finally the 'Diorama de Salon' in 1835. The latter device had the external appearance of a Gothic church, or a Greek or Egyptian temple: it was fitted with an enlarging lens, two inclined mirrors, and coloured prints illuminated from above or behind. Later, in 1840, the opticians Wallet and Morgand designed a quite complex 'portable drawing-room diorama', no example of which is known to have survived. On the other hand, the 'Polyorama Panoptique', a small box of mahogany and deal covered with embossed paper, fitted with a lens in an adjustable bellows, with day and night views printed on thin paper, can still be found in antique shops. The Polyorama Panoptique was invented in 1849 by Pierre Henri Amand Lefort, a Parisian toy-maker.[29] There were many other variants of these miniature dioramas, sometimes found in the shape of a cylindrical cone (the 'picturesque telescope') or in the form of a proscenium screen with paper wound on rollers. They continued the tradition of the peepshow boxes and optical toys of the eighteenth century, and above all demonstrated the popular success of Daguerre and Bouton's invention.

Each year, Daguerre and Bouton undertook to create three new paintings. They received the sum of 9,000 Francs from their company for each canvas, and also 4,000 Francs per month to cover ground rent, the salaries of the assistant painters employed, the costs of materials, maintenance of the machinery, wages of the attendants, and so on. After their run in Paris, Bouton and Daguerre's paintings were exhibited in a second Diorama, opened in London in 1823. Georges Potonniée has investigated the origin of this building: according to archive documents, it appears to have been financed by a French company, Le Diorama à Londres, founded on 11 November 1822 by James Smith, an English printer living in Paris.

In 1829 Bouton was in London, and on 21 September 1830 he retired from the company which ran the Paris Diorama. Officially, 'his health did not permit him to give the necessary attention to the running of the Diorama'. We do not know if this explanation was genuine. Bouton had painted ten pictures for the establishment, and they had not met with the same success as those by Daguerre. Daguerre had become a specialist in the genre, with his 'dissolving view' canvases and lighting effects. Bouton's work had always been more academic, in the tradition of the panoramas of his master Prévost. Perhaps Bouton had been aware of his inferiority; perhaps also Daguerre preferred to be the king of his own castle. Bouton returned to London, where he remained for about a decade before returning to Paris to start a new diorama in 1843.

The company Bouton, Daguerre et Cie. was therefore wound up, to be reborn immediately under the corporate name Société Daguerre et Cie. Bouton was not replaced: Daguerre trained some pupils to assist him. In any case, after 1830 the popularity of the Diorama dropped substantially. The Revolution of that year caused a sudden disinterest among Parisians in a show protected by the previous government and already eight years old. Daguerre, however, returned to public favour in 1834, with the canvas *Messe de Minuit dans l'Église Saint-Étienne-du-Mont* ('Midnight Mass in the Church of Saint-Étienne-du-Mont'), executed with his leading pupil Sébron. Here the technique of dissolving was exploited very well:

> This church shown in full daylight passes through all the changes of light to arrive at the effect of a Midnight Mass. All is painted on the same canvas; only the light which illuminates the picture actually moves . . . The effect, in the painting, is the appearance of a number of figures sitting on chairs which were unoccupied in the daylight view.[30]

The Diorama continued, struggling along, until 1839. The adventure ended for Daguerre on 8 March of that year:

> The Diorama is finished! Yesterday, at one o'clock in the afternoon, fire consumed this magnificent establishment in a few minutes. M. Daguerre, who lived on the premises, suffered irreparable losses. It

is not known how the fire took hold. It seems likely that it was a lamp producing the light in the church of Sainte-Marie. A fireman and a neighbour were injured. Ten paintings were destroyed, only three were saved . . . The Diorama has existed for seventeen years. And so the superb paintings of the Valley of Goldau, an irreplaceable masterpiece, and the Temple of Solomon have vanished for ever.[31]

Fortunately the workshop where Daguerre was working on what would become the daguerreotype was spared. According to a later article, published in 1874, Daguerre begged the firemen to save all his manuscripts, phials and optical instruments:

> For God's sake, officer! Let the Diorama burn, I have sacrificed it; but I beseech you, make efforts to prevent the flames reaching the fifth floor of this house; you will do me, perhaps even the country, an immense service! For pity's sake, try not to let me be shipwrecked in my own harbour![32]

Daguerre was ruined. On 5 July 1839, Daguerre et Cie. was wound up. But the daguerreotype, whose chemical formulae had very nearly gone up in smoke in the conflagration of the Diorama, was to save Daguerre from his shipwreck.

Niépce and Daguerre

For more than twenty years, Nicéphore Niépce (1765–1833) had worked at the invention which was to allow Daguerre a fresh start: photography. The origins of photography and the cinema have more than one thing in common. In both cases, one or more researchers worked in isolation with astonishing passion and foresight, on attempts which came very close to finding the ideal and definitive solution. Then a 'newcomer' appeared in the inventor's laboratory, studied the problem, and found the technical or chemical detail which was needed for commercial exploitation of the process, to his permanent good fortune. The newcomer's role as 'developer' was considerable, but he suffered from the self-important need to claim the invention for himself alone. So Daguerre tried to play down the immense contribution made by Niépce, just as later the Lumière brothers displayed a somewhat ambiguous attitude towards their predecessors.

The history of the appearance of photography (which was first named *heliography*, 'sun-writing', by Niépce in May 1826; then called the *daguerreotype* by Daguerre in 1839; the word *photography* appeared in Paris later the same year), and the life of Joseph-Nicéphore Niépce have been well-documented, through the works of Isidore Niépce, Victor Fouque, Georges Potonniée and Paul Jay, among others. These historians have been able to retrace the genesis of the invention through Niépce's correspondence, mainly preserved at the museum of Chalon-sur-Saône, his home town, and at the Academy of Sciences in St Petersburg. It is not possible here to cover in detail the whole process of Niépce's discovery: it is a long story lasting from 1816 to 1833. However, it can be summarized with a few of its essential dates.

At the start of 1816, at his estate of Gras at Saint-Loup-de-Varennes, near Chalon-sur-Saône, Nicéphore Niépce began his researches on fixing the images which can be seen inside a camera obscura. He had been dreaming of this since 1793, but political events, and after 1807 the invention of the 'Pyréolophore', a radical design of boat with an internal combustion engine which he had devised with his brother Claude (1763–1828), had absorbed all his energies. However, the invention of lithography at the end of the eighteenth century inspired Niépce to improve this process for printing engravings, by adding the camera obscura and a little chemistry. The Niépce brothers were gifted inventors, but all their attempts to commercialize their machines failed. The sensitive Nicéphore was not a businessman, and financial problems beset him throughout his life.

In May 1816 Niépce fitted one of the lenses of his solar microscope to a tiny camera obscura which was about 4 cm square. Inside the box, opposite the lens, he had placed a sheet of sensitized paper, probably treated with silver chloride. He was putting into practice an idea suggested by two Englishmen, Thomas Wedgwood and Humphry Davy, who had published a seminal paper on silver nitrate in June 1802 which envisaged 'copying paintings upon glass' and 'making profiles'.[33] On 5 May 1816 Niépce obtained his first negative, which he described emotionally to his brother:

> I placed the apparatus in the room where I work, facing the aviary and the window panes which were wide open. I performed the experiment with the method which you know, My dear friend; and I saw on the white paper all of the aviary which can be perceived through the window, and a faint image of the window panes which were less brightly lit than the objects outside . . . What you anticipated has happened: the background of the picture is black,

and the objects are white, that is to say lighter than the background.[34]

Some days later, the old Euler solar microscope was cannibalized further for one of its remaining lenses, to be used for a new camera obscura which was slightly larger than the first. On 19 May 1816 Nicéphore was able to send his brother two negatives of different sizes, fixed with nitric acid. Nine days later, Claude received four more 'sharper and more correct' examples: Nicéphore was now making effective use of the diaphragm which had been developed for projection in the eighteenth century.

So, in the mid 1810s, a solitary researcher succeeded in fixing photographic negatives on sensitized paper. The process was certainly a long way from perfection, all the more so given Niépce's considerable ambitions (already, in 1816, he hoped to obtain a positive image in colour), but the principle of photography was well and truly established. With no guides, no 'prior art' to draw on, no great knowledge of chemistry, and no financial backing, Niépce made slow, difficult progress with his mediocre equipment. He wasted time, often took wrong turnings, and passed over improvements which would have been very useful to him; but finally and doggedly he made progress.

In April 1817 he abandoned silver chloride for phosphorus and other substances. On 21 April 1820, believing he had arrived at his goal, Nicéphore wrote to his brother that he felt 'initiated in the marvellous work of nature'. We do not know what products he was using to achieve this. Perhaps he was already using bitumen of Judea, which he had known of since 1817. If bitumen of Judea was dissolved in animal oil, the liquid obtained would react to light when applied in a thin layer on a supporting surface. Using this process, in 1822 Niépce obtained a good reproduction on glass of an engraved portrait of Pope Pius VII. On 19 July in that year, he also created a *point de vue* (this was how he referred to his landscape photographs, recalling the terminology of panoramic painters) which was admired by all his relatives. On 16 September 1824 he set up his little camera obscura in front of his house at Saint-Loup-de-Varennes and took an exposure which 'truly had something of magic', as he put it himself: 'The image of the objects is represented there with an astonishing clarity and faithfulness down to their smallest details and most delicate shadings.' A dream had finally been realized: the images of the ancient camera obscura were no longer ephemeral. 'You may,' Nicéphore wrote to his brother, 'from today regard as a demonstrated and incontestable fact the success of the application of my methods to *points de vue*'.[35]

However, 'heliography' always needed a very long exposure of several hours, depending on the subject and the process used. It was therefore impossible to make portraits or capture a moment of everyday life, but 'still life', landscapes, monuments, and engravings already offered a large range of subjects. There is no doubt that Niépce would have been able to improve his process rapidly if he had found financial support and quality equipment. But optical apparatus was expensive, and Niépce was always on the edge of bankruptcy. Nonetheless, at the end of 1825 he decided to acquire some lenses and a new camera obscura from the best optician in Paris, Vincent Chevalier of 69 Quai de l'Horloge. In June 1823 Chevalier had developed a 'universal camera obscura' with a prism, which was portable and very practical. One of Nicéphore's relatives, Colonel Laurent Niépce, was commissioned to acquire one. But he became a little too talkative in front of Chevalier, and revealed the results of Nicéphore's research.

In January 1826, through the mediation of Vincent Chevalier, the first contact between Niépce and Daguerre took place. The optician knew Daguerre well, since he had supplied him with lenses and camera obscuras for creating dioramic paintings. The creator of the Diorama claimed to have been studying the problem of fixing the images of the camera obscura for a long time, and became extremely interested when Chevalier mentioned Niépce to him. Daguerre immediately wrote to Niépce: 'For a very long time I have also been searching for the impossible . . .' Niépce had the impression that Daguerre wished to learn his process and, with good reason, reacted with suspicion. He replied evasively, but politely. A year passed, during which Niépce collaborated with the engraver Lemaître, who was excited by the discovery. In February 1827, Daguerre approached Niépce again and asked him quite openly for some proofs of his composition. Niépce was naturally evasive, but shortly afterwards Daguerre sent him a sepia *dessin-fumée* ('smoke-drawing') achieved, he claimed, by means of his own process. This smoky drawing had nothing in common with photography, but out of courtesy Niépce sent him in exchange a reproduction of an engraving made by heliography.

From that point on, little by little, Niépce accepted the idea of collaborating with Daguerre. The creator of the Diorama was famous, he had a personal fortune, a sparkling personality, fashionable and political contacts, and there was no doubt that he was a very intelligent person. The two men met in Paris on 1 September 1827. Daguerre admitted his inferiority and Niépce, flattered, declared himself very impressed by the effects of the Diorama. It was not until 14 December 1829 that a provisional deed of association was signed. Meanwhile, Niépce travelled to London, where his invention had attracted the interest of Francis Bauer; his brother Claude died at Kew on 5 February 1828. On 24 November 1829, Nicéphore produced his *Notice sur l'Héliographie* ('Treatise on Heliography'), in which he revealed all the secrets of 'reproducing spontaneously by the action of light, with shades of black and white colours, the images received in the camera obscura'.[36] He included a mention of the famous bitumen of Judea, but also a new and important product, iodine, with which he had experimented around 1828.

Daguerreotypomania

The story of the collaboration between Niépce and Daguerre does not show the latter in a very flattering light; not for the last time in this field, the 'director' took the credit for the work of an unsung 'assistant'. As Paul Jay has observed, Daguerre gossiped a lot, criticized at length, and used Niépce as a laboratory worker. He was too occupied with his Diorama to give the unfortunate Niépce any practical assistance. Daguerre's involvement was not completely negative; he had some good ideas, and he was very thorough. But the greater part of the work of the partnership lay on the shoulders of Niépce. Niépce never saw the universal triumph which his initial discovery launched, since he died at Chalon-sur-Saône on 5 July 1833.

Between 1835 and 1839 Daguerre took up work on one of the chemical products Niépce had already used, iodine, and perfected a very effective process. He took a sheet of silver-plated copper and rubbed it lightly with a powder of very fine pumice and olive oil, using small pieces of hydrophilic cotton. When the silver surface was well polished, he washed the plate in a solution of nitric acid and distilled water. Then he heated it slightly by passing it above the flame of a lamp, with the copper surface towards the flame, and washed it in a second bath of nitric acid. The plate could then receive its coating of silver iodide, applied as a vapour. The silvered surface would become as yellow as brass. Finally, the plate would be placed in the interior of the camera obscura, which was fitted with a suitable lens, and exposed. The exposure time varied between five and forty minutes, according to the light, weather conditions, and time of year. The plate was removed, with nothing visible on it. It then had to be placed over a container of mercury, which was heated until the mercury vapours caused the image to appear. The plate was then washed in a saturated solution of cooking salt or hyposulphite of soda in distilled water. In 1839 Daguerre completed all these operations in seventy-two minutes (including fifteen minutes' exposure time), to produce a photograph of the Tuileries.

The 'daguerreotype' was revealed to the public in 1839. Ruined by the fire at the Diorama, Daguerre sold 'his' invention to the French government through the mediation of the scientist and politician François Arago. On 13 June 1837 Daguerre had greatly modified the contract of association between himself and Niépce (whose son Isidore had inherited his interests), stipulating that the invention should thenceforward carry only his own name. On 15 June 1839 a draft law was presented to the Chamber of Deputies: King Louis-Philippe granted Daguerre an annual pension for life of 6,000 Francs, and Isidore Niépce one of 4,000 Francs. In exchange they conceded the process for fixing images in the camera obscura to the state. Daguerre also profited by selling the principle of the Diorama. The draft law was passed on 3 July, with the enthusiastic support of Arago, who gave Daguerre his full due and scandalously neglected Niépce's role. The law was finally adopted on 30 July by the Chamber of Peers, proposed by the physicist Louis-Joseph Gay-Lussac.

As with the later invention of the cinematograph projector, a number of researchers could claim to have discovered the true solution at about the same time; for example, the Englishman William Henry Fox Talbot, who obtained a photographic negative on paper in August 1835. Fox Talbot claimed priority of invention before the Royal Society on 31 January 1839. There was also the remarkable and talented Hippolyte Bayard, who exhibited some high quality 'direct positives' on paper in Paris on 21 June 1839.

'Daguerreotypomania' gripped the whole of Europe, and even the United States, from 1839. The silver iodide process on a silvered copper base gave wonderful results. The surviving pictures from between 1839 and 1850 (there are many in museums and private collections) are often of a strange, ghostly beauty. These 'mirrors which keep all impressions', as Jules Janin called them in 1839, displayed an amazing delicacy and detail. Even so, while Daguerre had succeeded in finding the ideal chemical solution (which was to be greatly modified over the coming years), it remains the case that the daguerreotype was nothing more than an improved version of Niépce's Heliography. *Improvement*, praiseworthy as it may be, cannot be compared with the essential process of *invention*.

In spite of the birth of photography, for the whole length of the nineteenth century many researchers continued their attempts at projected animation of hand-painted pictures, as in previous centuries. But others, more daringly, now dreamed of achieving 'moving' photographic images. In the end the 'Ancients' and 'Moderns' would meet up, when the lantern techniques developed by Huygens fused with those of the photographic camera. But the journey would be a long one.

PART THREE

'The Pencil of Nature'

8

The Pirouette of the Dancer

First principles, after Aristotle

When we go to the cinema today, twenty-four photographic images are projected in front of us every second by what is effectively the good old magic lantern, to which a film drive mechanism and shutter have been added. Each of these projected images is perceived by our own two camera obscuras, our eyes, whose retinas have light receptor cells formed by a multitude of rods and cones which contain a substance known as rhodopsin. The receptors of the retina are connected to nerve cells, then to the brain, by the fibres of the optic nerve. The process of perception of the filmed image therefore consists of three stages: optical, chemical, and cerebral.

The researchers of the nineteenth century spoke of the phenomenon of 'retinal persistence' or 'persistence of vision'. This does in fact exist, but it does not play a part in the viewing of a film. Two other phenomena allow us to see the thousands of different images which pass over the screen without interference: the 'phi effect', explained by Wertheimer in 1912, and 'visual masking', which frees us from retinal persistence.[1]

The scientific study of the perception of light and retinal persistence had its origin, during the 1820s and 1830s, in a series of experimental discs. These were the 'Faraday wheel', the 'Phenakistiscope' (from the Greek *phenax*, 'deceptive', and *skopeo*, 'I look at') of Joseph Plateau, and the 'stroboscopic disc' (from the Greek *strobos*, 'rotation') of Simon Stampfer. The latter two, invented at the end of 1832, gave the eye a perfect illusion of movement. Researchers in previous centuries had sometimes been able to obtain this (with moving slides, for example), but without such simplicity or precision, and without having studied the phenomena of the duration of light impressions on the eye in such depth. It had been known for a very long time that when the eyes are closed after looking at a bright object (a candle flame, for example), its image does not disappear immediately, but persists for an interval of time which varies according to the light intensity of the observed object. This experiment had fascinated scientists since antiquity, and a host of different explanations had been offered.

Aristotle had found that when he stared at the sun, he was then unable to clear its image from his eyes, although the bright red marks he noted in his vision did eventually fade away. He concluded from this, in his work *On Dreams*, that the organs retained the impressions which they received. For him, dreams were caused by these sensations, which returned with intensity to disturb the sleep of the human being.

The Roman poet Lucretius (*c.*99–55 BC), in *De Rerum Natura* ('On The Nature of Things'), offered a different theory, but one that was just as poetic. Objects observed by the eye threw '*simulacra*' off into space, which retained the shape and colour of the objects. These emanations penetrated the eyes, but some of them seeped through to reach the soul, and it was these that gave rise to dreams. The soul was in some way overwhelmed by these *simulacra* ('idols' or 'forms') which manifested themselves particularly during sleep. Lucretius also noted how often a dream, or a nightmare, could be animated: the *simulacra*, he wrote, were born and died rapidly, one after another, and gave the impression of changing their position:

> For the rest, it is not wonderful that idols
> Should move, and rhythmically toss their arms
> And other limbs; for in our sleep an image
> Seems at times to do this; because in truth
> When the first image vanishes, and then
> A second has been born in a different pose,
> That former seems now to have changed its gesture.
> We must of course conceive this to take place
> Quite rapidly . . .[2]

This was an early hint at what, much later, would become the first attempts at dissection and animation of movement, although by that time the issue was no longer intertwined with the perceptions of the soul during dreams.

In the sixteenth century Leonardo da Vinci also dwelt on the subject and made some useful observations:

Every body that moves rapidly seems to colour its path with the impression of its hue. The truth of this proposition is seen from experience; thus when the lightning moves among dark clouds the speed of its sinuous flight makes its whole course resemble a luminous snake. So in like manner if you wave a lighted brand its whole course will seem a ring of flame. This is because the organ of perception acts more rapidly than the judgement.[3]

Observations on the subject became more numerous in the seventeenth century; it can be found in the work of almost every author who studied the camera obscura or the magic lantern, as if the three subjects were inseparable. The Jesuit Dechales, for example, noted that a vibrating string appeared to occupy a continuous solid volume. He also noted that if one looks at an eclipse of the sun with the naked eye, one may retain a trace of the image for an entire month. The same misfortune had befallen Johannes Zahn who, after observing an eclipse, saw a yellow spot with black centre on every object he looked at for a period of about thirty days. This experiment (also attempted in 1285, as mentioned in Chapter 1, by Guillaume de Saint-Cloud), nearly blinded Isaac Newton. Around 1691, he studied the impressions of light by observing the image of the sun reflected in a mirror with his right eye; after a short interval he turned his eyes to a dark place and analysed all the sensations which he experienced. As a result of repeating this dangerous experiment, his retina was damaged, so that he could not look at an illuminated object without seeing a shining black spot. To ease the inflammation, he shut himself for three days in a darkened room, but the 'spectre' refused to leave for several months.

Eighteenth-century measurement of the impressions of light

It appears that it was not until 1740 that anyone attempted to measure the duration of the persistence of impressions of light on the eye. This is an important question for the history of the cinema, since the techniques of cinematographic photography and projection depend on a knowledge of this duration. The German Johannes Segner (1704–77) reported— following plenty of others, such as Father Honoré Fabri in 1667—that if a glowing coal was rotated rapidly in darkness, it would be seen as a continuous circle. If the coal turned slowly, the circumference would not be complete: the impression faded in relation to the speed of rotation. Therefore, if the coal was rotated quickly enough for the illuminated circle to be just complete, the duration of image retention would be equal to the duration of one rotation. Segner obtained a duration of approximately half a second; but to give a more precise average he adopted the value of six *tierces* (six sixtieths of a second), or about one-tenth of a second.[4]

The second serious attempt, more ambitious in its scope, took place in 1765. This was the work of Count Patrice d'Arcy (1725–79), an Irishman closely linked with French scientific circles. His *Mémoire sur la Durée de la Sensation de la Vue* ('Report on the Duration of the Persistence of Vision') was published in Paris by the Académie des Sciences. D'Arcy used Segner's method, but built an astonishing machine with the aim of obtaining more exact measurements. He attached iron rods of different lengths, according to the size of the illuminated circle he wished to obtain, to a large X-shaped wooden frame. At the end of one of the rods he attached a glowing coal. The frame and rods were moved by a mechanical gear mechanism and a weight, with a system of flywheels to control the speed of rotation. The machine was fitted with an audible striker to allow the number of rotations to be counted, and also allow measurement of the interval between each striking sound.

The experiment took place at night in a garden. D'Arcy set up the bizarre and cumbersome apparatus, which resembled some kind of noisy illuminated crucifix, on a platform 6 m high. To make the period of observation as long as possible, the machine was placed next to a pit: as the weight descended slowly down into this hole, the cross would rotate. In the darkness, the glowing coal formed a much better circle of fire. D'Arcy, whose eyesight was poor, preferred to control the machine himself while an observer, about 50 m away, noted the quality of the impressions and measured the length of each rotation. After numerous experiments, D'Arcy conveyed his results to the Académie des Sciences:

> On a quite calm night, but with a little moonlight, one finds that the coal gives the impression of a wheel of fire when there is an interval of thirty-six seconds between each blow of the hammer, and so the coal makes one revolution in a period of eight *tierces* . . . This effect is the result of the time during which the sensation of vision persists, it follows that this sensation lasts for eight *tierces*, or that when an object makes an impression of a certain strength upon the eye, that impression exists after it has disappeared during this interval of time; I say after it has disappeared, because that is the fact of the matter.[5]

This measurement of eight *tierces*, about one-seventh of a second, was later refuted by Joseph Plateau. All the same, the work of d'Arcy, which has been generally ignored or misrepresented in histories of the cinema, deserves to be brought back out of the darkness.

The Thaumatrope

Between d'Arcy's work and the start of the nineteenth century, few new developments were made in the study of the impressions of light. In London in January 1821 the *Quarterly Journal of Science* published a note signed with the initials 'J.M.' (probably John Murray, the *Journal*'s chief editor) and dated 1 December 1820.[6] The author wished to draw the attention of scientists to a curious phenomenon: if the wheel of a carriage was observed passing behind a fence or railing of vertical posts, the spokes of the wheel, seen through the gaps in the railings, appeared as a series of completely stationary curved lines, even if the wheel was moving rapidly. The same effect could be observed if the wheel was not turning, by the observer moving his or her head or running past while looking at the spokes. On 9 and 16 September 1824, the English mathematician Peter Mark Roget (1779–1869) gave a brilliant explanation of this phenomenon by attributing it to 'the duration of the impressions of light on the retina'.[7] A deeper study of this optical illusion might, he said, allow still more precise measurement of the duration of these impressions.

More serious research began again all over Europe. In Britain, in 1825, a small and very simple instrument was invented which easily illustrated and popularized the phenomenon of retinal persistence. This was the Thaumatrope, which arose, if the contemporary account of Charles Babbage can be believed, from a combination of the thoughts of the astronomer Sir John Herschel, the cleverness of Dr William Henry Fitton, and the commercial sense of Dr John Ayrton Paris.[8] Babbage recounted the convoluted birth of the thaumatrope in his autobiography:

> One day Herschel, sitting with me after dinner, amusing himself by spinning a pear upon the table, suddenly asked whether I could show him both sides of a shilling at the same moment. I took out of my pocket a shilling, and, holding it up before the looking-glass, pointed out my method. 'No,' said my friend, 'that won't do'; then, spinning my shilling on the table, he pointed out his method of seeing both sides at once. The next day I mentioned the anecdote to

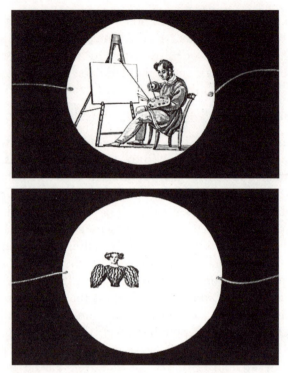

Fig. 25.   French Thaumatrope, *c*.1830, with hand-coloured engravings
printed on opposite sides of the disc. When the disc is turned, the image
of the young woman appears on the painter's canvas.
Collection: Laurent Mannoni.

the late Dr Fitton, who a few days after brought me a beautiful
illustration of the principle. It consisted of a round disc of card
suspended between two pieces of sewing-silk. These threads, being
held between the finger and thumb of each hand, were then made to
turn quickly, when the disc of card, of course, revolved also. Upon
one side of the disc of card was painted a bird; upon the other side,
an empty bird-cage. On turning the thread rapidly the bird appeared
to have got inside the cage. We soon made numerous applications,
as a rat on one side and a trap on the other, etc. It was shown to
Captain Kater, Dr Wollaston, and many of our friends, and was,
after the lapse of time, forgotten. Some months after, during dinner
at the Royal Society Club, Sir Joseph Banks being in the chair, I
heard Mr Barrow, then Secretary to the Admiralty, talking very
loudly about a wonderful invention of Dr Paris, the object of which
I could not quite understand. It was called the thaumatrope, and
was said to be sold at the Royal Institution, in Albemarle Street.

Suspecting that it had some connection with our unnamed toy, I went next morning and purchased for seven shillings and sixpence a thaumatrope, which I afterwards sent down to Slough to the late Lady Herschel. It was precisely the thing which her son and Dr Fitton had contributed to invent, which amused all their friends for a time and had been forgotten.[9]

The first description of the thaumatrope was given by David Brewster in the *Edinburgh Journal of Science* of January 1826. In France, its operation was revealed by Eugène Julia de Fontenelle, a friend of Robertson, later the same year.[10] In 1827, Paris published his three-volume *Philosophy in Sport Made Science in Earnest* in London, illustrated by George Cruickshank (who later created some impressive animated strips for the Zoetrope). An attractive drawing at the start of the third volume shows two children and an adult looking at a thaumatrope. The subjects Dr Paris described were very elaborate: Orpheus and Eurydice (after an illustration in the works of Virgil, published in Paris by Firmin Didot), Ovid's *Metamorphoses*, and various other mythological subjects.

Commercially published thaumatrope discs tended to use much simpler designs. Very soon, in both Britain and France, numerous printed sets were available, sold in small cardboard boxes. Some humorously illustrated plays on words: one British example shows a bald man on one of its surfaces, with the inscription 'Why does this man appear over head and ears in debt?' On the other surface appears a wig, with the words 'Because he has not paid for his wig'. If the two strings of this simple paper disc are twisted, the man is seen crowned with his wig, as the persistence of impressions synthesizes the two images.

The majority of thaumatropes were printed in outline and then coloured by hand, without captions. In a French example published around 1830 (see Fig. 25), a young romantic painter is pictured sitting in front of his easel. The canvas is blank, but on the other surface of the disc appears a delectable young woman. When the thaumatrope is turned, she appears in the middle of the canvas. Many similar amusing, poetic, or political subjects can be found. Thaumatropes from the years 1826–30 are rare; those which survive today generally date from the middle and end of the nineteenth century. The Musée du Cinéma in Paris has some beautiful examples, and the Bibliothèque Nationale has eighteen, in uncut sheets, which are certainly very early.

More precise measurements

The thaumatrope was amusing and interesting, and its popular success made several printers richer, but in scientific circles it was Roget's observations which attracted most attention. A Belgian student, Joseph Plateau, born in Brussels on 14 October 1801, chose as his principal subject of study the duration of the sensations which light produced on the eye. In 1822 Plateau was a student of philosophy and literature at the University of Liège. Orphaned at the age of fourteen, he had found a friend and teacher in Adolphe Quetelet (1796–1874), a scientist of the Belgian Académie Royale des Sciences. Guided by his mentor and his own enthusiasm, Plateau obtained his Candidate's degree in physical and mathematical sciences without difficulty, on 26 October 1824. In 1827 he became a teacher and published, in *Correspondance Mathématique et Physique* ('Mathematical and Scientific Letters') edited by Quetelet, a brilliant first study in which he challenged previous attempts to measure the duration of the impression of light:

> This impression, which lasts for some time after the disappearance of the object, does not itself disappear instantaneously; it is more probable that it decreases gradually to nothing; therefore, it is impossible for us to assign to it a precise duration: all that we are able to do is to assign approximately the length of time during which it retains a noticeable intensity.[11]

The system used by Segner and d'Arcy—rotating a luminous object quickly enough for the eye to perceive the image of a circle—formed the basis for all Plateau's first observations. He used a glowing coal, and also a number of discs each carrying a spot of a different colour.

In May 1829 Plateau defended his Doctoral thesis in mathematical and physical sciences, and was awarded his diploma on 3 June. His *Dissertation sur Quelques Propriétés des Impressions Produites par la Lumière sur l'Organe de la Vue*[12] ('Dissertation on Some Properties of the Impressions Produced by Light on the Eye') summarized his researches. He established:

(1) that any impression requires a discernible length of time for its formation, just as it does for its complete disappearance;
(2) that when an impression disappears, the rate of its decrease is slower as it gets closer to its end; and
(3) that the total duration of impressions, from the moment when they had acquired their full strength to that at which they were no longer

detectable, was roughly one-third of a second, or 0.34 seconds to be exact.

Plateau was even able to calculate different durations for impressions of different colours, for white (0.35 seconds), yellow (0.35), red (0.34) and blue (0.32).

To summarize a century of scientific research: in 1740, with an empirical method and no accurate measuring instruments, the German Segner obtained a duration of six *tierces*, or one-tenth of a second; using his bizarre machine with its glowing coal and striking hammer, d'Arcy claimed that the duration of the impressions was eight *tierces*, 0.133 seconds (about one-seventh of a second); and in 1829, Plateau fixed the duration at one-third of a second. In 1895, the Lumière brothers designed their Cinématographe to project each image for about one-fifteenth of a second, based on recent work by Augustin Charpentier:

> The duration of the persistence of the impressions of light on the retina varies with the illumination of the object; for an average illumination it is in the region of 2/45ths of a second, such that the visibility of the object, when the illumination is suddenly removed, is extended by 2/45ths of a second.[13]

The Plateau Anorthoscope

From 1827 onwards Plateau invented a series of disc devices intended to illustrate and experiment with the persistence of impressions of light. Two of these were produced commercially: the Anorthoscope (from the Greek *anortho*, 'I straighten', and *skopeo*, 'I look at'), devised in 1828 and put on sale at the start of 1836; and the Phenakistiscope, perfected in December 1832 and offered to the public the following year. The Anorthoscope's importance is undeniable: the development of the Phenakistiscope (one of the most important optical instruments in the pre-history of cinema) cannot seriously be imagined without considering this an essential stepping-stone between Roget's discoveries in 1824 and those of Plateau himself in 1832 on the analysis and synthesis of movement (see Fig. 26).

To construct this instrument, Plateau studied and developed Roget's theories, although his own research had already begun before he heard of Roget's report. On 20 November 1828, in a letter to Quetelet, he explained how he had discovered the principle of the Anorthoscope (although this name did not appear in Plateau's letters until the end of

Fig. 26.   The Anorthoscope and one of its image discs.
Collection: Cinémathèque Française, Musée du Cinéma
(photo S. Dabronski).

1835). He first rotated a toothed wheel, with regularly-spaced teeth, in a vertical plane; viewed from some distance, the image of a series of completely static teeth could be seen. The experiment gave the same result with two concentric discs, one turning behind the other. But if the two rotating wheels were not concentric, a number of static curved lines would appear. Struck by the analogy between Roget's work and his own research, Plateau resumed the study of his discs and achieved the following result: if two bright curves rotated in parallel at great speed about a common axis, the eye would discern the image of a third, static, curve. This 'spectrum' was the line of the points of apparent intersection of the two moving lines. If the moving lines were straight, and one was rotated at twice the speed of the other, the resulting image still took the form of a curve. 'I have constructed an instrument with which I can produce fixed images with ease, and I am delighted also to see curves drawing themselves in the air', Plateau wrote humorously in

November 1828.[14] On 12 March 1829, Plateau described the first design of Anorthoscope to Quetelet:

> The instrument which I have constructed for the production of fixed images is working perfectly; sometimes I amuse myself for whole days by producing curves of every sort . . . The instrument consists quite simply of two small pulleys of unequal diameter, moved by means of cords from another larger one with two grooves: I attach the moving curves to the axes of the small pulleys, whose diameters are such that one of their speeds is a multiple of the other, and I put it all into motion with the aid of a handle.[15]

Plateau very quickly grew tired of playing with curved lines. Around April or May 1829, he had the idea of replacing the geometric shapes with pictures of all types. The design of the Anorthoscope was thus complete, but Plateau did not present it at the Académie des Sciences in Brussels until 9 January 1836.[16]

In this final design of Anorthoscope, a curved anamorphic picture (for example a face or a galloping horse) was drawn on a disc of oiled paper which turned rapidly about its axis. In front of this, on the same axis but turning in the opposite direction and at a quarter of the speed, was a black-painted disc with four narrow slots arranged in the shape of a cross. From a position in front of the rotating instrument, on the same side as the black disc, the anamorphosis would be seen to transform into a perfectly steady and recognizable image. Somehow it was deciphered and made static, in spite of the rapid rotation of the two discs. The corrected image resulted from the successive intersections —the shuttering—of the slots with the different parts of the distorted picture, intersections which the persistence of vision made appear simultaneous. In this way Plateau managed to illustrate Roget's spoked wheel phenomenon, using equal measures of inventive science and artistic sensibility.

The definitive Anorthoscope was marketed in France during 1836 by a pair of Parisian fancy goods manufacturers, the brothers Amédée and Eugène Susse. The Susses also published the first edition of Daguerre's book *Historique et Description des Procédés du Daguerréotype* ('History and Description of the Methods of the Daguerreotype') in 1839; later editions were published by Giroux et Lerebours. Their shops at 31 Place de la Bourse and 7–8 Passage des Panoramas (a location much frequented by our inventors) dealt in miniature theatres and objects of entertaining science. They sold the Anorthoscope in a delightful wooden box covered in embossed paper. A large lithographed label on its cover showed a magician in front of five impatient children, pointing to a black circle in which was inscribed: 'THE ANORTHOSCOPE. Invented by Mr. Plateau. 1836. Paris, chez Susse, 31 Place de la Bourse.' This coloured label emphasized the attractive 'magic' side of the invention, and the instruction leaflet did not contain theoretical explanations, which the brothers Susse would presumably have considered rather uncommercial. This extremely rare document is worth reproducing:

> Instructions for use of the Anorthoscope. The effects of the Anorthoscope must be observed in the evening. 1. Screw the Instrument onto the board which forms its base, while taking care not to touch the cords. 2. Remove the nuts of the two copper pulleys. 3. Fix the black disc pierced with four slots onto the larger of them, using one of the nuts. 4. In the same way, attach one of the transparent discs [made of very thin paper] on which appear distorted pictures onto the smaller one. The coloured surface should be on the side facing the black disc. 5. Illuminate the transparent disc strongly from behind by means of an oil lamp whose flame is at the same height as the copper pulleys and at a small distance from the disc; if an oil lamp is not available for this purpose, one may illuminate the instrument with two candles placed close to the disc on either side of the pulley, with their flames at the same height as the latter. As far as possible there should be no other light in the room. 6. The person who wishes to observe the effects of the Anorthoscope sits several feet in front of the instrument, with his eyes at the level of the copper pulleys, and another person causes the discs to rotate by means of the handle.
>
> Soon the strange images, although turning at a great speed, will appear still and, as unrecognizable as they are, they will take on the appearance of perfectly regular pictures.[17]

The Anorthoscope is very rarely mentioned in histories of the cinema, perhaps because it is practically impossible to find today. One complete example, sold in France with Plateau's approval, survives in the collection of François Binétruy. Another example, of French or British manufacture, is preserved in the Paris Musée du Cinéma, with a complete set of discs. The device launched in 1836 by the brothers Susse does not seem to have sold very well, judging by the rarity of the object today and the absence of mentions of it in the contemporary press. Compared to the success of the Phenakistiscope, which had appeared in fancy goods stores three years previously, the Anorthoscope seems to have met an unenthusiastic public. The outfit sold in France was nevertheless very attractive: the instrument itself was made of varnished mahogany (assembled height 38 cm), with sixteen paper discs (19 cm in diameter; the shutter was slightly larger at 20.2 cm) of exceptional beauty. The curved anamorphoses printed onto them, in the surviving examples, were highly detailed and painted with great care, although some are in black and white. To the naked eye, they are practically indecipherable. The subjects of the discs, some of which recall Robertson's phantasmagorical images, comprised four images in black and white (a pair of dancers, a sorcerer and demons, two horsemen chasing a stag, and some leaves), and twelve in colour (flowers, devilish faces, some leaves, a demon, a fight between two men with staves, a woman with an umbrella, a circus horse, Cupid, the Ace of Spades and Jack of Diamonds, the Queen of Diamonds and King of Spades, and two pairs of embracing dancers).

Some amateur users were perhaps put off by the strangeness of the Anorthoscope's working principle. The discs turned but the image stayed still, whereas in the Phenakistiscope, as we shall see, everything moved: a vast difference in the eyes of contemporary users always in search of the illusion of movement. Around the middle of the nineteenth century, some scientific instrument makers such as Jules Duboscq (who will be discussed in more detail a little later) took up the invention and sold the Anorthoscope in a more deluxe version to schools and optical enthusiasts. At the very end of the nineteenth century, magic lantern manufacturers also offered mechanical slides in their catalogues, with a four-slot metal shutter disc, which could recreate the effects of Plateau's Anorthoscope on the screen. The subjects of these slides seem to have been purely geometrical.

To decipher anamorphoses or make straight lines curved by using a painted disc and a shutter, and to obtain still images from two rotating discs, already amounted to an unprecedented scientific achievement. To animate small figures representing the different phases of a movement over a period of time, using a different type of disc, would be a still more important advance. This breakthrough was achieved by Plateau and by Simon Stampfer, following a new discovery by Michael Faraday.

Faraday's Wheel

On 10 December 1830 Michael Faraday (1791–1867), then director of the laboratory of the Royal Institution in London, presented a paper which provoked much discussion in the scientific world. Once again, Roget's famous study formed the basis of Faraday's research. But curiously Faraday, who must have read the scientific journals, seems to have been completely unaware of the work of Plateau. Faraday's analyses included some theories already published by Plateau in 1829; the Belgian was rightly astonished by the false claim of newness in the observations presented by Faraday.[18] However, Faraday (who later voluntarily acknowledged Plateau's priority) had designed a new disc mechanism, known as 'Faraday's Wheel', which was to have a decisive influence on the invention of the Phenakistiscope.

The 'Faraday Wheel' was demonstrated during the paper at the Royal Institution on 10 December 1830.[19] It consisted of a pair of vertical wheels, with teeth around their circumferences, mounted on the same axis. On the side of the observer, the first wheel had sixteen deep regularly spaced cut-outs. The sixteen apertures in the second wheel were shorter, but arranged with the same regularity. The two discs were rotated by a handle, at the same speed but in opposite directions. A static toothed ring, with twice as many teeth as each of the moving wheels, would be seen to appear. If the wheels rotated at different speeds, the 'virtual' ring would appear to rotate slowly. Plateau had also used two toothed wheels, but had not noticed this 'stroboscopic' illusion which took place due to the persistence of vision. Stroboscopy is a method of observation which consists of making still or slowly moving pictures appear animated with a rapid periodic motion.

In 1831 Faraday invented two new discs and had the additional idea of using a mirror to observe them (this overcame the need to have two rotating discs). The first disc had forty-six apertures, spaced as follows over its entire surface: sixteen equally spaced teeth cut into the circumference of the disc; a ring of eighteen regular openings, arranged a little further in; and a ring of twelve regular openings very close to the centre of the disc. Sitting in front of a mirror, looking through the sixteen apertures, Faraday observed the effect produced by all these openings when the disc was rotated. The first series of teeth appeared still, the second row seemed to rotate in the same direction as the disc, and the third row in the opposite direction. Faraday's second 1831 disc was much more simple: its circumference was again cut with sixteen slots about 3–4 mm wide and 2 cm long. One of its two surfaces was entirely black. The slots of the rotating disc were observed with one eye in front of a mirror: once again, the perceived image of the sixteen slots appeared completely still.

Plateau's Phenakistiscope

In pursuit of his experiments on the persistence of the impressions of light, Faraday was content to decorate his discs with nothing more than greater or lesser quantities of teeth and apertures. Perhaps Plateau, who had recently imagined replacing the geometric patterns of his Anorthoscope with beautiful coloured drawings, dreamed of doing the same with Faraday's discs: as an optical recreation, observation of the Faraday Wheel was at first stunning, but soon very repetitive.

Plateau examined one of Faraday's wheels in Brussels in December 1832. If, he reasoned, a picture was drawn between each pair of slots around the circumference, and then the disc was rotated in front of a mirror, one would see these little pictures in perfect stillness, in spite of the rotation of the disc. This would at least be more entertaining than seeing the fixed image of a toothed wheel. Plateau probably made a first disc on which he drew the same repeated image (for example, a standing person) sixteen times on the sixteen teeth. The 'spectrum' of the immobile figure would appear in the mirror. Then, perhaps recalling the thaumatrope, he breathed life into the little stiff figure:

> If, in place of only having identical figures, we arrange it such that in following the series of figures, they pass gradually from one form or position to another, it is clear that each of the sectors, whose image in the mirror successively occupies the same place in relation to the eye, will carry a figure which differs slightly from that which preceded it; such that, if the speed is great enough for all these successive impressions to join up with each other and not so great that they become confused, one will believe that one sees each little figure gradually changing.[20]

So in December 1832 Plateau conceived the first disc which perfectly reconstructed an illusion of movement (see Fig. 27). He made a line drawing of a dancer (a subject already represented on two Anorthoscope discs) in sixteen different positions. Standing in front of a mirror, watching the reflected images through the slots of the rotating disc, one would see the little man in silk stockings, knee-breeches and puffed sleeves turn around, slightly lifting his arms and one leg.

> Each sector carries . . . a small dancer performing a pirouette; but by following the series of figures, one sees that the dancer turns further and further in the same direction to return to the position from which he started, although the ground on which he rests is perfectly

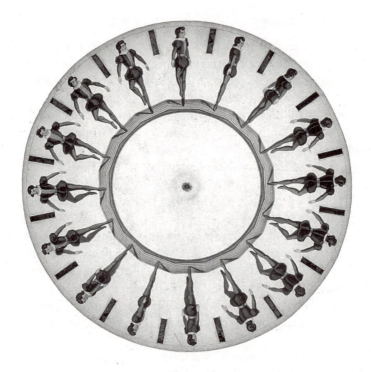

Fig. 27. Phenakistiscope disc designed by Joseph Plateau, printed by
Ackermann of London in July 1833.

identical in all the sectors. And so, when one subjects this disc to
the experiment in question, one sees with surprise, and the illusion
is complete, all these little dancers turning round, with the direction
of their pirouette depending on the speed and direction of the
rotation of the disc. The figures have only been drawn in outline;
but one feels that to produce the best possible illusion, they should
be shaded and coloured . . . I will not stress the variety of curious
illusions which one might produce with this new method; I leave
it up to the imagination of persons who wish to attempt these
experiments to draw the most interesting part of them.[21]

The illusion was easily explained: if several pictures, regularly separated
and differing gradually from each other in shape and position, are shown
successively to the eye at very close intervals, the successive impressions
which they produce in the brain (Plateau thought this took place on the
retina) become connected without merging. As a result one believes that
one sees a single object gradually changing shape and position. Plateau

described his discovery on 20 January 1833 in an article modestly titled 'Sur un Nouveau Genre d'Illusion d'Optique' ('On a New Type of Optical Illusion'). This was published shortly afterwards in Quetelet's *Correspondance Mathématique et Physique*, with an engraving showing the dancer on his disc. The word 'Phenakistiscope' was not mentioned, since Plateau had still not christened his invention.

Stampfer's 'Stroboscopic discs'

Before returning to the commercial exploitation of Plateau's discs, we should consider one curious point which occurs frequently in the history of the sciences: at the end of 1832, two researchers simultaneously invented the same device, without being aware of each other's work. While Plateau was developing the Phenakistiscope, an Austrian named Simon Stampfer (1792–1864) was doing precisely the same in Vienna. At the basis of Stampfer's research, once again, was Faraday's essential paper of 10 December 1830.

Stampfer was a teacher of land surveying and applied geometry at the Imperial and Royal Polytechnic Institute of Vienna. According to his account[22]—and there is no reason at all to doubt his good faith— he drew his first discs for breaking down and analysing movement around December 1832, exactly the same month as Plateau, and named them *stroboskopische Scheiben* ('stroboscopic discs'). This term survives in scientific parlance, whereas the name 'Phenakistiscope' applied to Plateau's discs in 1833 is no longer used outside histories of the cinema. Stampfer completed his first set of six discs by February 1833, and it was on sale throughout Germany shortly afterwards through the publishers Mathias Trentsensky and Vieweg. A second set of sixteen discs, 28.5 cm in diameter, came out in July 1833. In the first set of stroboscopic wheels, there were ten circular apertures, but in the second set Stampfer gave up this idiosyncrasy and adopted the narrow slots devised by Faraday and Plateau. The subjects Stampfer and his publishers offered were either fanciful (a pair of dancers, some cyclists, a Turkish juggler, a woman working a water pump, a carousel with horsemen, a man sawing wood or walking) or purely geometric (triangles, coloured balls, a toothed wheel, a wheel with spokes, and so on).

To protect their rights, in April 1833 Stampfer and Trentsensky filed an application for a two-year patent in Vienna. Plateau never did this: his paper of 20 January 1833 would serve as proof of the priority of his invention. To make a stroboscopic wheel, according to Stampfer's patent, it was necessary to:

draw these pictures onto discs made of cardboard or other suitable material, at the periphery of which, holes are made for looking through. When these discs are revolved quickly around their axis in front of a mirror, then the eye, when looking through the holes, will perceive the animated pictures in the mirror.[23]

According to J.C. Poggendorff,[24] Plateau soon learned of Stampfer's work from the account of a traveller returning from Germany, who had found stroboscopic discs everywhere. Plateau first thought that it was a crude imitation, but in 1836, after reading the leaflet which accompanied the second set of Stampfer's discs, he stated very honestly:

> My first publication [20 January 1833] was well before that of M. Stampfer. As for the time at which the first idea for this instrument came to me, the idea to which I also had been led by reading the paper by M. Faraday, it would be difficult for me to state it exactly; however . . . when I recall my attempts, the difficulties which I encountered in that first construction and the extreme care which I had to put into it, I believe that I was able to assemble the invention about one month previously, that is to say, like M. Stampfer, in the month of December 1832. And so my rights are clear, if priority is to be based on the date of publication; but I trust the assertion of M. Stampfer, the result of which is that we have been led, each of us separately, at about the same time, to the same invention.[25]

Stampfer can therefore be placed in the same rank as Plateau in the pre-cinematographic hall of fame. Around 1833 Stampfer had also imagined some technical variations to his discs: for instance, attaching a non-toothed painted disc and another disc with regular teeth to the same axis, making use of the mirror unnecessary. As we have seen Plateau had already used this system in 1829, to observe the spoked wheel phenomenon.

Stampfer also thought of drawing the various phases of a movement onto a long strip of paper, and observing them through the openings of a cylinder turning about its axis. In January 1834, the Englishman William George Horner (1786–1837) had the same idea, which he described under the name of 'The Daedaleum'.[26] But this invention was not marketed until 1867, under the name of the 'Zoetrope' or 'Zootrope'. There were numerous patents for this apparatus: the American Henry Watson Hallett (6 March 1867), his compatriot William Lincoln (23 April 1867), and the Englishman Charles W. May (May's French patent, dated 14 May 1867, was marketed by the Parisian manufacturers

Delacour and Bakes). Over a century later, the film director Francis Ford Coppola took this optical instrument as his emblem, when his American production company was founded as American Zoetrope.

Plateau himself also wished to modernize his Phenakistiscope, for example in 1849 by replacing the traditional drawings with photographic and stereoscopic images. However, the development of the first photographic phenakistiscope would not come about until much later, and it would be achieved by other researchers.

The Phenakistiscope craze

On 13 March 1834, the illustrator Paul Gavarni, together with the printer Aubert of the Galerie Véro-Dodat in Paris, published a delightful lithograph (see Fig. 28) entitled 'Le Phenakisticop' (*sic*). A young woman in a dress with puffed sleeves sits in front of a small mirror set upright on a table, holding a 'phenakisticop' in her gloved hands and observing the curious effects through the slots of the rotating disc. Behind her, a 'gallant' in a spotted waistcoat and frock coat is also looking at the mirror. The man holds two discs in his hand, presumably just taken from the cardboard box lying on the table. Plateau's invention seems to have arrived as a household instrument.

Plateau did not profit financially from the great European craze for his animated discs. It is quite likely that he never received any money for the sale of his invention; he never complained about this. Stampfer, on the other hand, knew how to exploit his first discs successfully, by forming a partnership with a printer, and it seems that his contemporary fame extended beyond the borders of Germany and Austria. At least some British and French phenakistiscopes carried Plateau's name on the box, so although he did not become rich, through this free publicity the Belgian scientist came to be just as well known as his Austrian counterpart.

Gavarni gave the discs a slightly incorrect name: 'Phenakisticop'. In 1833 complete chaos reigned so far as the exact name of the invention was concerned. Plateau had not given it a name by 20 January 1833; it was the first publishers of discs who devised the various names: 'Phenakistiscope', 'Phenakisticope', 'Phantasmascope', and 'Fantascope' (which of course recalled Robertson's magic lantern). After a number of false starts, the first of these terms eventually took hold, even though Plateau, in 1833 and 1849, preferred to use the second.

Plateau's Phenakistiscope was sold first in Britain. At the start of 1833 Plateau asked a friend, the Belgian painter Jean-Baptiste Madou (born

Fig. 28.   Paul Gavarni, lithograph entitled 'Le Phenakisticop' (1834).
Collection: Laurent Mannoni.

Brussels, 1796), to create a set of coloured discs. Madou achieved this
with some skill, and Plateau offered one or more examples to his mentor
Quetelet. Plateau also wanted to offer some to Faraday, whose work had
inspired this invention (in 1836, he also sent him an Anorthoscope). It
was Quetelet who presented the precious discs to Faraday, probably in
1833, while on a visit to London for the Congress of the British
Association. The discs certainly passed from hand to hand, inspiring
plenty of speculators, with the logical result that, from July 1833,
many different types of animated disc began to appear on the market
in London. Three very well-made sets were published by Rudolph
Ackermann, of 96 The Strand, with two different names: first, a set of
six discs of 24.5 cm in diameter called the 'Phantasmascope', including
the graceful pirouetting dancer (after Plateau's own drawing), a phantasmagorical subject (the green face of a monster, with its mouth open),
snakes which appeared to slither out of the disc (a small part of their
body was fixed at the circumference of the disc), a dancing monkey,

a running frog, and a very beautiful abstract design (coloured circles giving an effect of depth). For this first publication, directly inspired by Madou's paintings, Ackermann gave Plateau's name some prominence: the 'Phantasmascope' was 'designed by Professor Plateau, of Brussels'. Plateau himself noted, around 1833:

> I am unfamiliar with the manufacture of the Phenakisticope (*sic*); but in London, after my drawings and directions, a much more perfect instrument has been made, which bore the name of *Phantasmascope*, and which is now sold under the name of the Fantascope.[27]

In the same year Ackermann published a second set under the name 'Fantascope', created by one Thomas Talbot Bury, and finally, as proof of the success of the venture, launched a third set designed by Thomas Mann Baynes. Another London printer, S.W. Fores, tried to compete with Ackermann in 1833 with 'Fores' Moving Panorama, or Optical Illusions, giving life and activity to animated objects'.[28] Plateau's invention was also produced as the Fantascope in Belgium, by the printseller Dero-Becker in about December 1833.

In September 1833, Joseph Plateau was in Paris. He visited François Arago and the scientist Jacques Babinet. On 15 September he wrote to Quetelet, 'as you can see, the Fantascopes have gone very well, as they say in Brussels: they have been especially in favour at the establishments of Messrs. Chevreul, Babinet, and Villerme.'[29] Plateau had presumably acquired a complete set of the discs published by Ackermann; however in September 1833 excellent French 'Phenakisticopes' were available, manufactured by Alphonse Giroux from August of that year.

François-Simon-Alphonse Giroux (?–1848) is not an unknown: in 1839 he and his two sons painstakingly constructed the daguerreotype cameras officially endorsed by Daguerre himself. Under the Consulate regime (1799–1804) he had established a shop in Paris dealing in luxury goods, cabinet-making, fancy goods, and artist's colours, at 7 Rue du Coq-Saint-Honoré. His activities extended into shadow shows (he sold optical toys, portable theatres, and in 1825 published a collection of plays, *Le Petit Théâtre des Ombres Chinoises* ['The Little Chinese Shadow Theatre']) and kaleidoscopes (he took out a patent for this apparatus on 29 May 1818). His two sons, Alphonse-Gustave and François-Simon, took over his business in 1838.

On 29 May 1833, Giroux applied for a five-year patent of importation 'for an optical device which he calls the Phenakisticope'. This was not a patent for an invention, but a licence for the privilege of importing the apparatus invented by Plateau (whose name was not mentioned). Giroux also described the equipment which he hoped to offer Parisians:

> This instrument consists of a box containing a mirror and several discs of paper decorated in a circular fashion and representing different subjects; they are attached one after another to a handle of wood and copper by means of a screw and nut of the same metal, against a slightly larger sheet which is formed with rectangular holes all round. The two sheets fixed relative to each other are turned together in front of the mirror, and the eye, deceived by the speed and combination of coloured subjects, sees in the mirror which reflects them moving figures, such as jumpers, musicians, dancers, blacksmiths, balls passing through hoops, interlaced rings, and others.[30]

Giroux was granted his patent on 5 August 1833. He could then begin selling the discs, a month after Ackermann, although perhaps he did not wait for this authorization—it is noticeable that the patent was filed on 29 May 1833, which is very early in the marketing of the Phenakistiscope. The set which Giroux displayed in his shop on Rue Coq-Saint-Honoré was very luxurious, with its mirror, separate shutter disc, and twelve painted discs representing dancers, a leaping frog, a woodcutter, a windmill, and so on. Giroux soon met competition from other Parisian printers, who in 1833 were also publishing very attractive discs with subjects such as astronomy, phantasmagoria, guardian angels, and others.

The result of this intense marketing was that, in the years 1833–40, 'magic wheels' span rapidly before enchanted eyes in a great many homes: embracing couples twirled in an endless waltz, horses exhausted themselves leaping endlessly through hoops, gentlemen struggled not to fall off their fancy horses, snakes tried to escape from the discs, and shrewish wives never ceased battering their husbands. It was this type of little animated drama which—for the time being—offered the only satisfaction for the frenetic desire of the viewer for the illusion of movement.

9

The 'Vital Question' Resolved?

Projection of the Phenakistiscope

The Phenakistiscope offered such rich possibilities that, like the magic lantern, it very quickly became the most popular optical 'toy' of its day. It was manufactured throughout the nineteenth century, and even into the 1900s; twenty years after its invention the great French poet Charles Baudelaire was still singing its praises in *Le Monde Littéraire* of 17 April 1853. But alongside the production of conventional discs, a huge abundance of variations and often quite ingenious improvements began to appear. These modifications arose from two types of research: firstly, the projection of the Phenakistiscope's effects, and secondly the substitution of the traditional 'animated drawings' created by hand with a series of photographic pictures representing the different phases of a movement.

On 15 April 1843, ten years after the discoveries by Plateau and Stampfer, the London journal *The Mechanic's Magazine* published a drawing and letter dated 12 February 1843, signed by T.W. Naylor of Newcastle-upon-Tyne. Naylor claimed to have discovered a 'new principle capable of showing figures moving with all the appearance of life and reality':

> The figures will necessarily require to be drawn with the greatest degree of exactness, both with regard to position and similarity of form. The plan I adopt, and which I find a very good one, is to provide a few of those optical toys called 'Phenakisticopes' [*sic*] and place on one of them a glass circle previously obscured by grinding; then trace on the latter the outlines of the drawing, which must be afterwards painted in transparent colours mixed with oil-varnish,

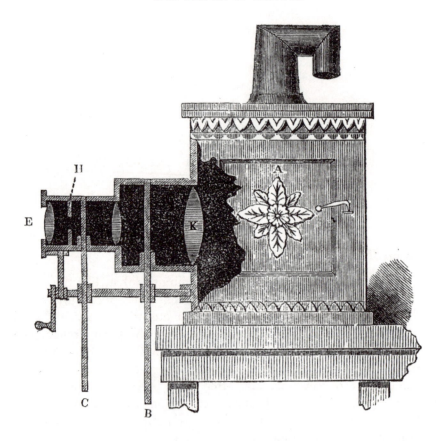

Fig. 29. T. W. Naylor's 'Phantasmagoria for the exhibition of moving figures'
illustrated in *The Mechanic's Magazine* (1843).
Collection: Bibliothèque Nationale.

which, from its refractive power, causes the dull surface of the glass
to resume its pristine transparency. The remaining portion of the
glass should be obscured with thick black paint.

The toys [Phenakistiscopes] mentioned above may be readily
had, I believe, at most respectable stationers. Some of those I have
seen bear the mark of Ackermann and Co., the eminent printsellers
of the Strand. The subjects (of my selection) consist of 1st: A fat
gentleman feeding, and a dog springing up to snatch his plum-
pudding. 2nd, Turn-out of a nest of serpents, which are gliding off
with great exactness. 3rd, A lady and gentleman waltzing. 4th,
Quadrille dancers. 5th, Indian juggler. 6th, A theatrical combat
between two bravos. 7th, A comic figure representing a man beating
the big-drum with all the characteristic antics. 8th, A bell-ringer.[1]

Naylor's apparatus (see Fig. 29) was very simple. The lens tube of a 'phantasmagoria' lantern was specially modified to receive the phenakistiscope: between the first two lens elements was placed a vertical glass disc (B) whose circumference carried a series of slightly differing drawings. A second disc (C) of silvered metal or opaque paper, pierced with small apertures, functioned as a shutter. It was mounted on the same axis as the first disc, and the whole assembly was operated by a metal rod turned by a handle. Finally came the last lens element (E). The results achieved must have been interesting, all the more so since the lantern was powerfully illuminated by the Drummond limelight (a block of calcium oxide brought to an incandescent state by a flame of combined oxygen and hydrogen), although the description published in *The Mechanic's Magazine* does not appear to have been followed up in Britain. However, according to David Robinson, the article was reprinted in a German journal, and it is very likely that this influenced an Austrian researcher, Franz von Uchatius, to whom the invention of the projection phenakistiscope has been wrongly attributed.

The lantern of Uchatius

Franz von Uchatius (1811–81) was the first military man to enter the pre-cinematographic hall of fame. His portrait shows him standing upright, sword in hand, in a uniform glistening with medals. His expression is gloomy and severe; his suicide on 4 June 1881 (not in 1864 as Jacques Deslandes has stated) remains unexplained. In 1853, when he published his first works on the projection of movement in a Viennese scientific journal, Uchatius was a captain of artillery in the Austrian army. He claimed to have begun his research in 1845, at the request of Field Marshal Ritter von Hauslab. As a good Austrian, Uchatius only referred to the discs of his compatriot Stampfer. What he aimed to do (like Naylor, whom he never mentioned) was to obtain 'an apparatus by means of which moving images can be represented on a wall, at the size which one desires, and with a clarity which Stampfer's disc does not obtain'.[2]

The mechanism of Uchatius' first apparatus, constructed in 1845, resembled Naylor's, consisting of a large wooden casing fitted with a chimney and a lens. Inside, a simple paraffin lamp illuminated the two vertical discs, one with slots and one on which the images were painted, which were moved by a single external handle. Uchatius explained:

As the discs are turned, the images appear on the wall one after another with brief interruptions which are imperceptible to the eye, in the way in which they appear on the retina with Stampfer's disc. The apparatus produces small, pretty moving images, but their size may not be greater than about six *pouces* [about 30 cm] in diameter: in fact, if one moves the screen further away, the images become less bright because of the slots. But an enlargement of the slots makes them too blurred. Although a moving image has already been obtained which may be viewed by a greater number of people at the same time, one would still wish to be able to produce this image on the wall at the desired size and thus to be able to show it in a large auditorium.[3]

In 1853, Uchatius developed a new version which 'satisfied all requirements'. To our eyes it seems more complicated, and its operation appears difficult or even dangerous. This time, the vertical disc carrying the images remained static in a wooden frame, fully enclosed in the body of the lantern. On the outside of the lantern body were fastened as many lenses as there were painted images, arranged in a circle and slightly angled towards the centre of the screen. It was the lamp, rather than the discs, which rotated. A drive handle rotated the lime block, which always remained upright, together with the small flame which brought it to incandescence; two rubber tubes delivering oxygen and hydrogen followed the same path. If one of the tubes should become detached, an explosion was more or less guaranteed. All the same, if Uchatius can be believed, the results were perfect:

> The illuminated images appear one after another on the wall, in the manner of dissolving views, but much more quickly and thus producing the complete effect of a moving image. The size of the image is not restricted by the slots, and clarity is not adversely affected since there is no movement of the painted images.[4]

Uchatius also mentioned that the disc he projected carried twelve images. Somewhat ambitiously, he was already planning a huge magic lantern with 100 images, measuring about 2 m in height.

Given that Uchatius did not invent the projection phenakistiscope —Naylor appears to have been the first to reveal its principle—what was the originality of this officer-lanternist's contribution? First, the successive illumination of each image constituted an ingenious novelty, in spite of the difficulty of the process. But also, Uchatius took the positive initiative of commercializing his lantern. As we have already seen, once an invention emerges from the secrecy of its laboratory, and especially if it is then put on the market, it immediately begins to generate new ideas.

Marketing began around 1853: 'Monsieur W. Prokesch, optician of Vienna, Laimgrube no. 46, constructs such apparatus with the greatest precision and also supplies images as requested.' The Viennese lanternist and magician Ludwig Döbler (1801–64) bought an example from Uchatius and gave phenakistiscope projection shows for about ten years, throughout Germany and Austria. The reputation of the Uchatius–Prokesch device lasted for many years: as late as 1892, the chrono-photographer and scientist Étienne-Jules Marey (who wished to project his successive photographs) wrote to his assistant Georges Demenÿ:

> Villa Maria, 24 January 1892.
> Received safely the stereoscopic camera. I note the mention of a lantern projection apparatus, with Drummond light, turning with multiple lenses. The constructor, W. Prokesh [*sic*] in Vienna.[5]

Uchatius appears to have been truly engaged by the question of animated images, while Naylor's interest was only passing. The Austrian organized small shows, as a drawing dated Vienna, 12 July 1854, indicates. In a bourgeois drawing-room, a couple are sitting in front of a screen formed by a white sheet nailed to the wall. Behind them stand two young officers, attentively watching an animated image appearing on the sheet, in which a pair of men fighting with sticks can be discerned. About 3 m from the screen, behind the enormous lantern set up on a table, where a double-disc Stampfer Stroboscope can also be seen, the operator (Uchatius in civilian clothes?) is turning the handle. Rubber tubes emerging from the apparatus are connected to a gas bottle. The scene is remarkable: the attention of this small audience is captured by the movement of the projected figures, by the regular and continuous animation which Uchatius' 'Bild-Maschine' seems to offer. Such a lantern, said its inventor, could offer great services for education, notably public classes in physical science. And once put on general sale, this improved magic lantern could be acquired by any father (assuming a certain degree of wealth) who wished to offer an almost unheard-of spectacle to his nearest and dearest.

The Duboscq projector

Among the readers of the Austrian journal which published Uchatius' studies was the Frenchman Louis Jules Duboscq (1817–86), one of the greatest manufacturing opticians of his day. Duboscq had joined the business of Jean-Baptiste François Soleil (1798–1878), a famous Parisian constructor of scientific and optical instruments, on 13 May 1834, as an optical technician. Soleil's shop, founded in 1819, was at 35 Rue de l'Odéon (then from 1852 in the courtyard of 21 Rue de l'Odéon); his workshops were at 30 Rue Monsieur-le-Prince. Soleil specialized in the manufacture of lenses and optical apparatus. His projection lanterns were used in public lectures to demonstrate, for example, the phenomena of polarization. Soleil retired in 1849 and divided his business into two parts: the workshop where instruments were constructed passed to Duboscq, who in the meantime had become his son-in-law, while the workshop where lenses and crystals were made remained with Henri Soleil, his son. The two inheritors continued to work hand in hand.[6]

With advice from his father-in-law, Duboscq greatly improved the scientific projection lantern. In 1850, he launched the Lanterne Photogénique ('Photogenic Lantern'), arguably the best projector of the nineteenth century. Standing proudly on four brass columns, illuminated by a very powerful arc lamp controlled automatically by an electrical regulator (the invention of Léon Foucault), the Lanterne Photogénique could use a whole series of accessories to demonstrate the phenomena of:

> reflection, refraction, dispersion, spectra, recomposition of light, spherical and refractive aberration, achromatism, rays of the spectrum, diffraction, interference, diffraction patterns, coloured rings, double refraction, polarization in all its forms and its thousand different appearances, coloured shadows, etc. Add to this the projection of machinery, geographical maps, geological or natural history charts, panoramic views, microscopic objects.[7]

However, in 1850, this very modern lantern could only recreate the illusion of movement with the traditional mechanical slides which had been used since the seventeenth and eighteenth centuries. For example, the 'Turk Playing a Drum' slide was operated by a very simple concealed mechanism: the arms of the Turk moved rapidly up and down, and if this movement was synchronized with a sound effect, 'the illusion was complete', to borrow Plateau's phrase. Many other mechanisms were used, but this type of animation remained somewhat limited compared to the effects of the Phenakistiscope. But in 1853, when Uchatius' article appeared, nobody in France had managed to project a stroboscopic disc.

The article must have fascinated Duboscq, who for several years had been working on stereoscopic animation, another sizeable problem to which we shall return later.

Duboscq's working notebook is preserved in the archives of the CNAM in Paris.[8] This invaluable source is a large folio volume in which the optician collected his drawings, copies, photographs, and assorted notes between 1850 and 1885. Reading through it, it is clear that Duboscq was always on the lookout for all the latest scientific novelties and technical developments. He cut out press articles relating to rival equipment: electric arc lanterns by W. Ladd of London, stereoscopes by Knight of London, solar microscopes by A. Abraham of Liverpool, heliostats by the Merz company of Munich, and so on. He carefully traced the engravings Uchatius published in 1853, and also drew various other designs of lantern, one of which worked on the same principle of the rotating light source, but in a different configuration. Duboscq's sketch includes the ring of thirteen lenses fixed in the lantern body, the handle, the curious rotating limelight lamp, and even the location for the painted disc (which must have carried thirteen images), with precision. This might be a sketch 'from life' of the Uchatius lantern sold by Prokesch, although it is impossible to be sure; no notes accompany the drawing.

Duboscq, in his turn, addressed the problem of projection of strobo-scopic discs, and succeeded with style and brilliance. The device he made around 1853–4 was very simple and well constructed. Today two differ-ent examples can be seen in Paris: the older one was donated to the museum of the CNAM in 1857 by Duboscq himself. It consists of a wooden frame fixed to the Lanterne Photogénique, which contains a shutter disc whose apertures are fitted with lenses and a glass disc onto which ten images are painted against a black background. These discs are mounted on the same axis and moved by a small handle. The other design, in the collection of the Musée du Cinéma, is certainly more recent. This is mounted on a brass stand; its painted discs carry twelve images and its shutter disc has four circular apertures each fitted with a convex lens. Two discs in the CNAM collection represent a close-up of a grotesque head with wide lips swallowing a tiny bull, and a circus rider jumping through a hoop from her horse. A disc at the Musée du Cinéma shows a man lying on his back, rotating a red and green ball on his feet. All the images are carefully executed, in very bright colours. Duboscq's machine appeared in his 1856 catalogue, alongside the ordinary Plateau phenakistiscope:

210. M. Plateau's Phenakistiscope, with a set of six pictures, supplied in a box: 30 Francs.
212. Phenakistiscope with transparent images for projection: 100 Francs.
213. Each picture for the projection phenakistiscope: 20 Francs.[9]

In 1869, and again around 1881, the British lanternist John Henry Pepper described a slightly different third version of the Duboscq apparatus in two of his books.[10] This seems to indicate that the device was on sale in Britain, a country closely involved in development of projection practice in the nineteenth century. But Pepper mentioned that the projecting phenakistiscope was 'an expensive instrument'. It is true that the painted discs cost 20 Francs each, and that the frame and shutter cost 100 Francs in 1856 and 260 Francs in 1885. In 1885 the Lanterne Photogénique, which was an essential extra, was priced at 250 Francs including its electrical regulator. A small set of six little paper stroboscopic discs cost 30 Francs in 1856. But at the time the spectacle of an illuminated image, animated with continuous movement (however limited it might be) offered such a joy to the eye and soul, that lanternists, wealthy optical collectors, and some professors certainly allowed themselves to be tempted by such a beautiful outfit.

In 1903—eight years after the appearance of the Cinématographe Lumière—Duboscq's business successor François-Philibert Pellin (the two engineers formed a partnership on 1 July 1885, founding a company in their joint names) was still offering the 'Large model Phenakistiscope with pictures for projection'.[11] This could mean one of two contradictory things: perhaps the device Duboscq had made since 1855 or 1856 never sold very well, and there was still remaining stock in 1903; or perhaps the invention was a successful product which had sold continuously since its launch. For the time being, it is difficult to shed light on that particular question.

The lantern of Gomez Santa Maria

Augustin Gomez Santa Maria is a completely forgotten figure, whose name does not appear in any history of the cinema, but he does deserve a few moments' attention. Spanish by birth, in 1868 he was practising as an architect in Paris. In that year he invented the 'Dinascope', a projection phenakistiscope of which two traces remain: a patent filed on 7 March 1868, and four glass slides preserved at the museum of the CNAM. His patent included the astonishingly self-important claim that the application to the magic lantern of the toy known under the name of the Phénisticope [*sic*] has not been possible to achieve up to this day, despite efforts and studies of all types made by eminently capable men.[12]

Gomez, of course, imagined he had achieved the perfect solution all by himself. His Dinascope consisted of a series of six fixed lenses mounted in a circle on a round wooden frame. A shutter disc called the 'movable diaphragm' was mounted on the same axis, with an opening of approximately twice the width of a lens. It was rotated by a small pulley mechanism. The inventor explained:

> As an accessory to this mechanism are supplied glasses on which are painted the figure or scene which is to be represented. If this is a single figure it must be represented in six different positions . . . in order to produce the complete illusion of general movement. Each of these images representing a different position must be placed at exactly the focus or centre of each of the six small glasses or lenses which must reflect its image precisely onto the screen.[13]

Gomez envisaged a smaller 'parlour' version of the instrument, which would include a music box. The Dinascope images which survive at the CNAM perhaps belonged to this model, since they are quite small (14 cm by 10 cm). These four square slides were donated to the Musée des Techniques in 1925 by Massiot, a magic lantern manufacturer and the successor of Alfred Molteni, who like Duboscq was one of the greatest nineteenth-century lantern projection specialists. Perhaps Gomez had given a small Dinascope to Molteni, or perhaps Molteni had tried to mass-produce them. The four slides show an 'acrobatic devil' (four round pictures of 2.5 cm diameter on a black background), 'Spanish dancers' (perhaps Gomez himself created this image from his homeland), 'M. Pointu with the bearded lady' (a character with a long pointed nose taking a beating from a fat bearded woman), and finally a 'dancing buffoon' (this slide consists of six pictures, like that described in the 1868 patent).

During the 1860s many other lanterns were designed for serial projection. These included the 'Lampadoscope' of the Parisian engineer Henri-Alexandre Lefèvre, in 1861, a spherical device with a series of glass slides around its periphery, which could be brought in front of the lantern lens one at a time. The projector invented in 1870 by Jean Marie Auguste Lacomme, a French doctor living in Middlesex, England, was also very typical of the over-active imagination of these researchers. His lantern projected a series of eighteen different glass slides, arranged around the circumference of a large vertical iron wheel which moved by means of an intermittent mechanical system. The assembly must have been fairly enormous.

The 'Wheel of Life'

The projection phenakistiscopes described above were heavy and expensive instruments, with sometimes complicated mechanisms. Another new improvement, though, offered all lanternists the chance of showing the effects of the stroboscopic disc, perhaps as an interlude between comic or scientific pictures. In August 1869, an American by the name of A. Brown[14] made a small wooden plate with a large circular hole in which he placed a glass disc, showing a jumping athlete in a series of eight hand-painted images. The disc was given an intermittent rotary movement by a toothed wheel with ten cut-outs, a type of Maltese Cross mechanism, stopped at intervals by a small metal pin. Brown placed this slide in the slide carrier of his magic lantern. The interruption between each pair of images was provided by a disc with two shutter sectors turning in front of the lantern lens, synchronized with the glass disc. The whole assembly was driven by a handle.

In the same year, on 6 March 1869 to be exact, Thomas Ross of Glasgow filed a patent for a new animated magic lantern slide, which he soon named the 'Wheel of Life' because of the frenzied animation it showed. It was not until a second patent, of 10 October 1871, that Ross described his invention more precisely.[15] The Wheel of Life consisted of two discs: one of thin metal pierced by a narrow slot, the other of transparent glass or mica with six images painted on it to represent different positions of a man jumping into the air (the same image as Brown's slide). The discs were placed adjacent to each other on the same axis, and a mechanism of gears and cords drove them in opposite directions. The magic lantern projected this assembly, and the whole phenakistiscope disc appeared on the screen with all its figures moving at the same time.

In 1871 Ross also envisaged drawing the picture of a chameleon on his transparent disc. The handle would turn a second disc, divided into segments of different colours, and an astonishing effect would result: the colours would gradually merge into one another, and the chameleon would appear to change colour. This slide, he imagined, would be greatly valued by lanternists.

The Ross Wheel of Life quickly became one of the most popular parts of a lantern show. This small phenakistiscope slide, which was extremely simple compared to the apparatus of Uchatius, Duboscq, or Gomez, was sold in Britain by the Pumphrey brothers of Birmingham, among others, and in France by Alfred Molteni.[16] In his notebook, Duboscq reproduced Ross's 'projection Phenakisticope' very exactly, with precise dimensions. One British design for a 'Wheel of Life' disc represented a bird in full flight: a symbol, perhaps, of the way in which animation was also now beginning to take off.

The 'Choreutoscope'

The lantern spectator was unlikely to be satisfied for long with the 'Wheel of Life', with its interminable dancers or frantically wriggling eels. There were plenty of criticisms to be made of the effect: the brightness of the projected image, for instance, was greatly reduced by the rapid passage of the shutter. Changing discs was also rather too delicate an operation.

Brown had sensed the direction to take in 1869 by using a ten-armed 'Maltese Cross', which gave the glass disc and its shutter a jerky inter-mittent movement. As a result, the images appeared one after another on the screen very rapidly, with the necessary shuttering to conceal the rotation of the painted disc. The intermittent movement of an image, and its shuttering during its motion phase, are the fundamental principles of the technique of cinematography, and the Maltese Cross mechanism is still used in present-day film projectors. It would be interesting to know whether Brown was really the first user of this technique in his animated slide of 1869.

Priority is sometimes attributed to J. Beale, a British engineer from Greenwich, London. This is quite possible, but Beale did not take out any patents on the subject. According to some accounts, he demon-strated an animated slide with a Maltese Cross movement at the Royal Polytechnic Institution, the 'temple of projection' in London throughout the nineteenth century. Some claim this took place in 1866, but there is no definitive proof of this. Great secrecy existed around some of the processes used at the Royal Polytechnic; the lanternist Thomas Hepworth recalled, in 1892, that an animated slide named the 'Astro-meteoroscope', invented by a Hungarian engineer by the name of S. Pichler and intended to demonstrate the phenomenon of persistence of vision, was shut away in a strong-box immediately after every use to prevent anyone examining its mechanism.[17] It is possible that Beale's

Choreutoscope would have been treated in a similar way at the very early period of its invention.

The Choreutoscope slide allowed the projection of a single image which gradually changed shape and moved gracefully, rather than several moving figures around the edge of a circle as in the Wheel of Life. This new animated slide was sold by all the principal lantern manufacturers in Britain, such as James Henry Steward of London. On 9 October 1884, the optician William Charles Hughes patented a new version, called the 'Giant Choreutoscope',[18] which was equally successful. In France, the Choreutoscope was made by Molteni, who sold it in his shop at 44 Rue du Château-d'Eau. By the end of the nineteenth century most, if not all, French and British lantern manufacturers offered different types of Choreutoscope in their catalogues.

The two commonest models of the time were the Choreutoscope Tournant ('Rotary Choreutoscope') developed by Molteni, and the Hughes 'Giant Choreutoscope'. The first of these was certainly the older and more interesting of the two. It consisted of a wooden frame covered with a metal plate pierced by a small round aperture. On the other side of the plate was a glass disc, on which were painted six different positions of the subject. This disc carried the Maltese Cross mechanism on its axle, with six slots corresponding to the six pictures. The shutter disc was made of very thin black card, cut into a semi-circle. A small wheel with a pin was placed between the Maltese Cross and the shutter. When the handle was turned, rotating the wheel via a drive cord, the shutter concealed the image, and at the same moment the pin of the wheel engaged in a slot of the Maltese Cross to rotate it. The shutter then revealed the subject, which remained visible and immobile until the pin engaged the next slot in the Maltese Cross. This highly ingenious system reappeared in 1895–6 in numerous cinematographic cameras and projectors. A good example of a Molteni Choreutoscope Tournant, now extremely rare, survives in the collection of the Eastman House in Rochester, New York.

The 'Giant Choreutoscope' patented by Hughes in 1884 functioned in more or less the same way. Instead of a painted disc, a long rectangular glass plate framed in wood was advanced in a jerky movement by a rack mechanism, driven by a toothed wheel. The shutter was formed by a small piece of ebonite. In this way a small scene consisting of six successive images could be projected. The animation was almost perfect, although its movement was a little jerky and its duration short. However, the handle could be turned in reverse once the glass arrived at the end of its rack. The Giant Choreutoscope (known in France as the

Choreutoscope à bande) was still on sale in Paris in 1911, at the Maison de la Bonne Presse. At that date a lanternist could show this animated slide, which is rare today, for 35 Francs; at the same period the Wheel of Life cost 22.50 Francs. Similar devices which were still available included the Ross chameleon, Newton's disc, and the Benham Teintoscope. Optical illusions did not disappear with the arrival of the cinematograph; if anything the reverse was true.

It is not clear whether the Maison de la Bonne Presse, a religious organization, offered Beale's favourite subject, the 'skeleton dance', which is found in almost all surviving examples of the Choreutoscope. These little hand-painted skeletons fidgeted in all directions, bending femurs and tibias, playing with their skulls, or thumbing their noses. This grotesque and macabre image recalled the first animated slide made by Huygens in 1659, after Holbein's *Dance of Death*: the same themes recur, from century to century, throughout the imagery of the lantern. The Choreutoscope figure, which the audience called the 'Dancing Skeleton', met with great success long before Walt Disney's 1928 animated cartoon *Skeleton Dance* took up the theme once again.

The first photographic animation: the 'Stereoscope'

The appearance of the daguerreotype in 1839, six years after the Phenakistiscope went on sale, did not immediately give rise to the idea of combining the two discoveries, even though they could be found side by side in the shop windows of novelty dealers such as Alphonse Giroux. According to Georges Potonniée, it took the invention of the stereoscope to eventually 'open the eyes of researchers.'[19]

The stereoscope was a peepshow box in the tradition of the eighteenth century, but it gave a partial impression of three-dimensionality, an almost unprecedented effect. Some eighteenth-century peepshows had been fitted with two lenses, but only so that two people could view the show at the same time; on the other hand, as we saw in Chapter 4, some peepshows did create clear effects of perspective and relief. In the stereoscope two flat drawn or photographic images, slightly different from each other, were placed side by side and vertically in the box, opposite a pair of lenses. The viewer looked through both lenses and saw the two images combined as one, superimposed on each other by binocular vision. 'We see objects exactly as they exist in front of us,' stated the scientist Babinet.

The British physicist Charles Wheatstone (1802–75) is generally credited as the inventor of the stereoscope. In 1833, an English writer summarized Wheatstone's as yet unpublished experiments:

> One of the most remarkable results of Mr. Wheatstone's investigations into binocular vision is the following: a solid object, being placed in such a manner as to be seen by both eyes, projects onto each retina a different image; now if these two images are faithfully traced onto paper and presented one to each eye, such that they fall onto the corresponding parts of the two eyes, the original object will appear on the paper, in solid form, and no effort of the imagination can convince one that it is a drawing on a flat surface.[20]

Wheatstone presented his observations at the Royal Society in London on 21 June 1838, and constructed a prototype device with the help of the London optician Murray. This was a mirror stereoscope for viewing three-dimensional geometrical drawings. Another British physicist, David Brewster (1781–1868), invented a prism stereoscope in 1844 using photographic images, whose operation was simpler. Taking stereoscopic photographs was certainly not easy, at least to begin with; the double images had to coincide precisely in their central areas, but vary slightly at their edges. It was initially necessary to use two separate cameras, although cameras with a double lens were very soon manufactured.

David Brewster commissioned an example of his prism stereoscope from the optician George London of Dundee. This was a small wooden box fitted with two eyepieces, each including a prism which produced a refraction of one of the two stereo images. The stereoscopic photographs were inserted into the interior of the box in front of the eyepieces, and illuminated from above through a small mirrored flap. Brewster offered his new device to opticians in London and Birmingham, but without success. In 1850 he travelled to Paris, where he met Abbé François Moigno, an enthusiastic lanternist with connections in British scientific circles, to whom we shall return a little later. Moigno took Brewster to see his friend Duboscq who, with better judgement than his British contemporaries, immediately recognized an excellent business opportunity. In 1851, Duboscq was able to exhibit a binocular stereoscope, constructed along the lines of Brewster's design, at the Great Exhibition in London. Queen Victoria inspected it, and Duboscq appears to have offered her a handsome example of the device. As a result of the excellent publicity arising from the Exhibition, Duboscq soon began to receive numerous orders from Britain. British manufacturers also began to turn their attention to commercial exploitation of the device. Between 1851 and 1857, according to *Le Cosmos*, the magazine edited by Moigno, more than half a million stereoscopes were sold.

Duboscq not only offered excellent and elegant stereoscopes, but also a full catalogue of high-quality views for them, showing the monuments of Paris and the French provinces. According to *Le Cosmos* these pictures, 'double for the stereoscope, single for the magic lantern and the phantasmagoria, are almost entirely masterpieces thanks to the skill and indefatigable enthusiasm of M. Ferrier'.[21] The photographer Ferrier claimed his independence from Duboscq around 1857, to set up his own company in association with Charles Soulier.

On 16 February 1852 Duboscq filed a patent for 'an instrument system known as the Stereoscope', in which no mention was made of Wheatstone, much less Brewster. This blatant injustice was denounced in a trial before the Imperial Court of Paris on 1 April 1859, which brought Duboscq and his former employee Ferrier into opposition. Duboscq always claimed to be the inventor and sole proprietor of the stereoscope, which Ferrier wished to market himself. Ferrier brought to light the British work of the 1830s and 1840s and Duboscq, obviously, lost his case. The argument by Ferrier's defence lawyer, Ernest Pinard (who, in 1857, had the responsibility of summing-up the obscenity case against Charles Baudelaire, author of the infamous *Les Fleurs du Mal*), is particularly interesting. He posed the problem of the concept of an invention and its disclosure to the public, in legal terms:

> Duboscq has been able to popularize the invention of others, to disseminate, by improving it from a commercial point of view, the stereoscopic box . . . If only Duboscq were satisfied with the commercial success which the sale of the stereoscope on a large scale has brought him; *but between that propagation of the discovery and its invention, there is a chasm* which has not been bridged.[22]

This observation could be applied just as well to Daguerre or the Lumière brothers. Duboscq's patent was revoked. However, he had made some very important improvements to Brewster's device, developing several different designs such as the double stereoscope, the binocular or lorgnette stereoscope, and the 'Omnibus', 'Panoramic', 'Pseudoscope', 'Bi-Prism', and even 'Microscope-Stereoscope' models. But these were only improvements. His 'Bioscope' of 1852, on the other hand, was a highly original invention.

The Duboscq Bioscope

On 17 May 1852 Jules Duboscq filed an addition to his patent of 16 February. He described further curious variants of the stereoscope, and noted at the end:

> I claim also the application of the principle of the Stereoscope to M. Plateau's Phenakisticope, in order to show in animation the movement of objects seen with their reliefs and their hollows, whether to a single person in a special apparatus, or to several persons simultaneously by projection onto a screen and with the aid of the Stereoscope.[23]

This ambitious project was suggested to him by Plateau himself, who had devised new combinations for his Phenakistiscope in 1849. By that date the Belgian scientist had reached a state of complete blindness, though even when sightless he never gave up his research. And so in 1849, following a discussion with Charles Wheatstone, he put forward the idea of a new process for obtaining an ideal animated image:

> One could go still further, taking advantage of an idea communicated to me by M. Wheatstone, which consists of combining the principle of the Stereoscope with that of the Phenakistiscope . . . Thus figures simply drawn on paper will be seen indisputably in relief and moving, and in this way will present, in a complete manner, all the appearances of life. This will be the illusion of art brought to its highest degree . . . In order to obtain a pair of drawings suitable to give in the Stereoscope the representation, not just of a simple line perspective, but of an object having a rounded form, such as a statue, and with light and shadow, M. Wheatstone has conceived obtaining, by means of photography on paper, two pictures of an object by placing the daguerreotype in two different positions, such that the two images have the necessary relationship between themselves. One could make in plaster, for example, models of sixteen stages of the regular figure whose image one wishes to produce in the combined apparatus with which we are concerned, then take with the daguerreotype a pair of drawings of each of these sixteen different models, and finally transfer these drawings, with appropriate deformation, onto the two discs. No doubt this would be a long task which demanded the most precise care; but one would simply be rewarded by the marvellous nature of the results.[24]

Wheatstone himself constructed a stereoscope-phenakistiscope around 1868, which was never commercialized. An example survives in the Science Museum in London. In this apparatus, as the viewer looks through the two eyepieces, a handle turns the stereoscopic images inside a round box, with successive pictures presented intermittently and at very close intervals. 'The effect is truly amazing when one sees the image of a completely solid locomotive whose moving parts are all functioning,'[25] said one contemporary observer. But if Wheatstone and Plateau had been the first to dream of animating stereoscopic photography in 1849, it was other researchers who brought this idea into reality. In the forefront, once again, was Duboscq, whose Bioscope gave 'as its name indicates, the impression of relief and movement or the impression of life,'[26] in 1852 (see Fig. 30).

In combining two techniques which they had still barely mastered —those of 'moving photography' and stereoscopy—the researchers had not chosen an easy route. Their ambition was a response to an expectation of the public and a dream of some Utopians: to see the photographic image of a human being, animated in three dimensions on a screen or a stroboscopic disc. These nineteenth-century Prometheans were not, however, chasing an imaginary beast, since three-dimensional cinema is alive and well today—*Dial M for Murder* (Alfred Hitchcock, 1954) is one example. But in spite of successful attempts by Duboscq, the way ahead proved too difficult, and the first 'animators' of photography quickly gave up on stereoscopy in search of a slightly less complicated route.

On 12 November 1852, in a further addition to his patent, Duboscq described his 'Stereoscope-Fantascope or Bioscope', the apparatus which he had promised on 17 May. This never managed to project animated stereoscopic photographs, as he had announced a little rashly:

> To transform the Fantascope [i.e. the Phenakistiscope] to the Stereo-Fantascope or Bioscope all that is required is: 1. to take two stereoscopic images in each of twelve phases of its movement; 2. to place these twelve pairs of images on the rotary disc—the images to be seen through the right eye above, the images to be seen through the left eye below, and vice versa; 3. to place and observe these images by reflection in the mirrors through two slots formed in front of the two eyes; 4. to rotate the disc as in the conventional Fantascope.[27]

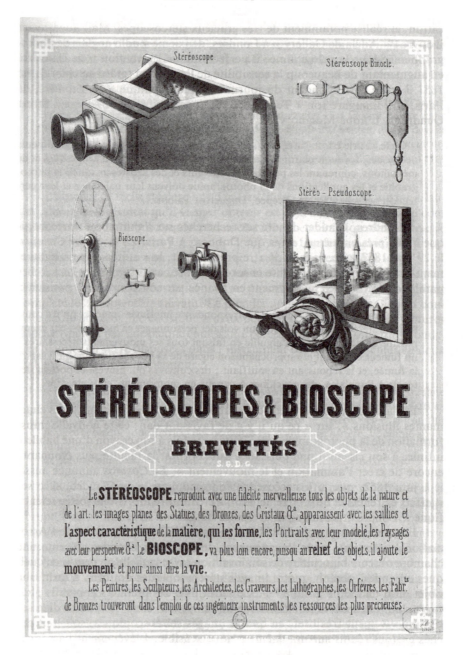

Fig. 30. Advertisement for the Duboscq Bioscope (1853). Collection:
Bibliothèque Nationale.

Duboscq designed three different models of his device, but only the first of these appears to have been sold at his shop at 21 Rue de l'Odéon. This had a disc with twelve slots, mounted on a stand and rotated by a small handle. The viewer would look through this rotating shutter disc to observe a double set of stereo pictures on its other side, reflected towards the viewer by two small mirrors mounted on a shaft. In the second model, the mirrors were viewed through a pair of lenses. For the final model of Bioscope, Duboscq used a toothed cylinder which rotated about its axis, in which each stereoscopic sequence was reflected through the slots between the teeth by small mirrors.

From Duboscq's catalogue we know that the images which could be seen through the 'Bioscopic' disc were photographs, showing for example the illusion of a 'machine' in three dimensions and in full operation. No Bioscope discs have survived to the present day. The same is unfortunately true of the apparatus, which was marketed during 1856 and 1857, apparently without great success. One day an example will be found, and we will be able to appreciate fully the effects of the Bioscope and the quality of stereoscopy and movement Duboscq was able to offer.

Claudet's 'moving photographic pictures'

Antoine François Jean Claudet (1797–1867), the son of a master mariner, was a native of Lyon who emigrated to London in 1829. He worked initially in the optical glass trade, then initiated himself in photography in 1839 in association with Daguerre. Suddenly inspired by this 'Pencil of Nature', to use the apt expression of Claudet's friend Fox Talbot, he purchased a licence to exploit the daguerreotype in Britain. In his London shop in High Holborn, he first offered cameras and images imported from France, such as the collection of *Excursions Daguerriennes* by the photographer Lerebours, and then turned his attentions to production, notably of very graceful stereoscopes. In 1841 he also opened the Adelaide Gallery in London, the second British photographic studio; in the same year he improved Daguerre's 'invention' by greatly increasing the sensitivity of the photosensitive emulsion through the use of chlorine. In 1851 he was a correspondent of the Paris 'heliographic' journal *La Lumière*, and inaugurated his Temple of Photography at 107 Regent Street Quadrant. Abbé Moigno visited him in 1854 and came away filled with wonder:

> This gallery is a long square room, illuminated by a very attractive glazing with octagonal panels forming the ceiling. The upper frieze

consists of arabesques and medallions, containing the portraits of scholars and artists to whom photography and its applications owe their birth and their present perfection: Porta, Niépce, Daguerre, Talbot . . .[28]

Claudet began his research into stereoscopic animation in London at about the same time as Duboscq in Paris. On 29 May 1852 *Le Cosmos* mentioned, without giving a precise description, Duboscq's 'moving stereoscope', which was probably still not completed, but also indicated the parallel research by Claudet, who was clearly ahead of his Parisian competitor:

> M. Claudet, in fact, in a published letter, announces that he has constructed a stereoscope in which one sees persons moving: for example a lady working with a needle and making all the necessary movements; a smoker moving his cigar to and from his mouth as he inhales the smoke, and putting it down as he exhales; some diners drinking and making toasts in English, steam-driven machines in action, etc., etc.[29]

The anonymous author (possibly Moigno) speculated on 'these charming illusions', on

> what is delightful in this new transformation of photography, which now adds to its pencil of infinite skill, to its chisel whose power knows no boundaries, the still more astonishing ability to create animation and movement.[30]

Le Cosmos also announced, on 6 June 1852, that Claudet's 'Fantascopic Stereoscope', with its 'effects of relief and movement', had been shown during a scientific soirée in London, presided over by the Duke of Ross.

On Saturday 4 September 1852, on the occasion of the twenty-second anniversary of the British Association for the Advancement of Science, Claudet presented a binocular camera obscura which he had invented, with which one could 'in a few seconds, obtain four double stereoscopic images, of the same object or the same group.'[31] This would have been one of the first photographic cameras capable of taking the various phases of a brief movement in a very short space of time, in four stereo pairs, giving eight photographs in all on a single plate. The event passed unnoticed. This camera has not been found: did it operate with a shutter disc? In any case it foreshadowed the future science of chronophotography. But in 1853 Claudet, with touching honesty, admitted that 'the nice problem of the stereoscopic phenakistiscope' was not really very easy to solve:

> He [Claudet] is annoyed not to have produced as perfectly as he would wish the simultaneous effects of movement and relief. By passing through the stereoscope eight images of an object in different positions, four in front of each eye, he has succeeded very well in giving the complete impression of movement, as in the conventional phenakistiscope or fantascope of M. Plateau, but without the effect of relief.[32]

The absence of true stereoscopy in his moving pictures concerned Claudet, even though the result he had obtained was in itself spectacular. But he was aware of the work of Duboscq, who in 1852 had succeeded in a quite complicated stereoscopic animation which Claudet later judged, with his characteristic good faith, 'most ingenious' although not 'free of some imperfections'.

On 23 March 1853 Claudet filed a patent for 'Improvements in Stereoscopes' (he was more cautious than Duboscq), which was granted on 23 September the same year. The first device he described consisted of a conventional stereoscope with two eyepieces, which were shuttered alternately by a sliding plate pierced by a small round aperture. The glass slides used with the instrument had to show a movement twice:

> To show a man taking off and putting on his hat, one image must be made with the hat on the man's head, and the other with the hat off and in his hand. If one views the two images together in the stereoscope and moves the plate [the shutter] of the eyepieces forward and back, the man will appear to be taking off his hat. One can also achieve various other illusions of moving figures, dancers, athletes, boxing matches, etc.[33]

Claudet admitted later that this stereoscope was adequate for showing the phenomenon of animation, but 'the illusion of reality suffers in the abrupt passage between the two outer movements and the lack of intermediate phases'. It was therefore necessary to present more images to the viewer. For example, Claudet suggested in his patent, two series of double (stereoscopic) images could be arranged crosswise on a disc, whose axis was connected to the shutter plate of the two eyepieces. By means of a lever, a pin and some toothed wheels, the plate would reveal the crossed double images as it turned in alternate directions. In another version, two series of four pictures passed one after another in front of the lenses of the instrument. This method inspired the French painter Philippe Benoist, whose 'animated-sterioscope' (*sic*) was patented in Britain on 23 August 1856. The efforts of the London engineer Adam Dunin Jundzill should also be mentioned; his 'Kinimoscope' could show 'cartoons in motion', he claimed in his patent of 24 May 1856. Claudet's influence was equally clear in a later patent, filed on 22 August 1873 by the Frenchman André David, for an 'animated stereoscope'.

As for Claudet himself, on 7 September 1865 he read a paper entitled 'Moving Photographic Figures' to a meeting of the British Association in Birmingham, which modestly summarized his research:

> What gives me some hope of success, is the result which I obtained a number of years ago. This was incomplete and imperfect, but if I have not succeeded in obtaining relief with movement, I have managed to make appear moving pictures which retain all the exactitude and perfection of photography.[34]

For want of time, Claudet did not make very much progress with his research between 1853 and 1865. At that latter date, he was still offering his two-image stereoscope, now showing two boxers fighting; he promised himself to turn his efforts again to these animated devices, as soon as he had some spare time. But death intervened on 27 November 1867.

In his 1865 paper, Claudet put forward some new theories on the phenomena of the impressions of light. His very modern explanations emphasized the role played by the brain in analysing the images received by the eyes. He did not specifically mention the brain, but spoke of 'judgement' and 'understanding', which he saw as playing an essential role in the perception and duration of an impression:

> This singular effect is readily apparent in the change between the two images of the boxers. In the one, the arms and fists of one of the two pugilists are close to his body, in an attitude which indicates that he is preparing to strike his adversary; and in the other image, his arms and fists are extended in the position in which he strikes the blow. We have not seen the intermediate positions which the boxer must have taken during the entire combat, but we know that they must have taken place, and our judgement has completed the action. This mental perception is the result of the sensation which through experience our judgement creates upon us, and we experience it as if it had actually taken place.[35]

It was in this paper that Claudet was at his most innovative, as Gérard Turpin has emphasized. In the end his inventions were quite limited: daring for their time, but less so than those of Duboscq. Claudet himself found them a little disappointing, since they did not provide the illusion of three dimensions. On the other hand, his theory of 'mental perception' connected to the phenomenon of the impressions of light was very advanced indeed.

Cook and Bonelli's 'Photobioscope'

In the Photobioscope, whose name specifically referred to the Duboscq Bioscope,[36] the ideas expressed by Plateau and Wheatstone in 1849 were finally brought into reality. This was firstly because this device gave the illusion of movement and three dimensions through a series of stereoscopic photographs, and secondly because the photographs in question represented precisely the subject of which Plateau had dreamed: a plaster model shown successively from all directions. This 'moving sculpture' imagined by Plateau and Claudet (who also filed a patent for a 'Method of Photosculpture' in January 1865) was presented in the form of a small transparent glass disc. Around its circumference, a double row of microscopic circular photographs showed a bust of a man turning about its axis for one whole revolution. In the one surviving disc, a small piece of glass is missing; the remainder carries seventeen tiny stereoscopic views arranged one above the other, making thirty-four photographs in total. There must have been twenty-four pairs, forty-eight images, around the complete disc, allowing a much longer animation than Claudet's eight images or Duboscq's sixteen. The Museum of the CNAM owns what may be the only surviving example of the Photobioscope.

Chevalier Gaetano Bonelli was an Italian, the director of telegraph services in Turin. Henry Cook was an English gentleman from London. It was Bonelli who began the research, on his own in 1862–3, using Duboscq's work as his starting point: 'Mr Bonelli had already made several experiments, but without satisfactory results.'[37] Bonelli described the problems he was having to Cook around the beginning of 1863, and the two men filed a joint patent in Britain on 19 August 1863.

A prototype of the device had certainly been constructed at this time, but like Claudet's devices it did not produce stereoscopy. Nonetheless it was an ancestor of the future Photobioscope. In their patent, Bonelli and Cook explained their method, still rather primitive, for taking a successive series of views:

In carrying out this part of the Invention the figure or body in motion to be represented is photographed in a variety of positions, that is to say, supposing the effect of raising an arm or leg is to be produced the limb must first be represented in its lowest position, then slightly raised, then raised still higher, and so on, until the last figure represents it as raised to its fullest extent.[38]

It was therefore impossible to 'capture' a true movement, and still necessary to simulate it artificially. The photographic plates of the 1860s were still far from instantaneous, using wet collodion (gun-cotton dissolved in alcohol and ether, mixed with potassium iodide) which allowed an exposure time of between three and twelve seconds, still too long for photographing motion.

The pictures Bonelli and Cook produced in August 1863 were microscopic. The two inventors did not explain this choice, but it may have been because the views obtained in this way were sharper and also easier to locate on a small surface. They took their pictures directly onto a glass disc, which they then printed as a positive; the inventors remained very discreet about their method of taking the pictures. The images were spaced around the circumference with mathematical precision. The glass disc carrying the microscopic positive images was then placed in a viewer with a single eyepiece, with a rotating perforated disc which shuttered each image. The images passed in quick succession in front of the observer's eye, which, as in the Phenakistiscope, perceived the effect of a moving picture. This was in itself a very important result, in a device which was much simpler and more advanced than Claudet's. But there was still no stereoscopy.

On 12 June 1865 Bonelli, by now resident in France, was granted another British patent in his own name alone; Bonelli did not mention Cook in this patent, referring only to 'his' invention. The Englishman later took revenge by blowing Bonelli's cover. In this patent Bonelli described a 'Phenakistiscope-Stereoscope' with sixteen images, and a shutter disc incorporating sixteen lenses.[39] Cook condemned this latter development, which was possibly inspired by Uchatius' lantern:

Mr Bonelli believed that in order to achieve the effect it was essential to use for the enlargement as many lenses as there were images; I have always resisted that idea, and in fact, I have proved that by using a perforated black disc and a well-designed arrangement of gear wheels, a single lens gives perfect results.[40]

Henry Cook presented the final stereoscopic form of the apparatus before the Société Française de Photographie on 2 August 1867. Only the viewer known as the Photobioscope was described; the photographic camera 'had not yet arrived from Florence where I had sent it'. The members of the Société moved in single file past the two eyepieces and admired the illusion of three-dimensionality combined with movement. Cook boasted excessively about his research, clearly intending to appropriate practically all the credit for the invention for himself. A poet and visionary, he already imagined a whole range of highly spectacular images:

> I believe that the vital question has been resolved . . . By adding to the photographic machine the combination of a perforated disc and some gear wheels, waterfalls, breaking waves, indeed all movements may be captured . . . Country scenes in which the trees bend in the wind, leaves trembling and shining in the sun, boats, birds gliding on the water whose surface ripples to and fro, the movements of armies and fleets, indeed all imaginable movements, taken in flight, can provide information.[41]

The Photobioscope presented at the Société Française de Photographie and the example preserved in the CNAM (these are probably the same instrument) were constructed by Eugène Deschiens, a precision engineer associated with Duboscq who specialized in electrical and telegraphic instruments, which would perhaps explain how Bonelli came to call on his services. Deschiens worked at 123 Boulevard Saint-Michel, Paris. The instrument is beautifully constructed, with a brass mechanism, wheels and body. Essentially it is of the design described in the patent of 1863, but with the addition of stereoscopy: there were two adjustable lenses and a shutter disc with two slots. An Italian lanternist and photographer, Chevalier V. Alinari, advised Cook and Bonelli on the difficult business of creating the first stereoscopic discs.

Between 1849 and 1867, in eighteen years of research, trial and error, mistakes and successes, the first 'animators' therefore arrived at their goal, which had seemed so Utopian. The previously stiff images of the daguerreotype had taken life and three-dimensional form. The 'vital question' appeared to have been resolved, in Cook's attractive phrase. The snowball of the cinema, set rolling several centuries before, was becoming larger and faster all the time.

10

Great Expectations

'Moving photography' had finally come out of limbo, but in order to
appreciate its beauty it was still necessary, as in the eighteenth century, to
bend over the eyepieces of a peepshow as a solitary viewer. Although
some optician-engineers had taken the direction of individual animated
stereoscopy, others, once again, dreamed of creating a popular spectacle.
The attempts in this direction between 1850 and 1870 were mostly
highly ambitious. Those who wished to *project* animated photographs,
leaving stereoscopy on one side, engaged in some prophetic discussions.
But if imaginations were being fired by the prospect of projected living
images, photography itself lagged some way behind technically, dampen-
ing the excitement. The visionaries made brave predictions (they could
do nothing else, with the wet collodion processes in use from 1851 to
1871) of being able to capture the sixteen or twenty images per second
needed to see the 'leaves trembling and shining in the sun' imagined by
Henry Cook. To the researchers of the middle years of the nineteenth
century, these ideals were little more than fantasies. But far from
admitting defeat, they progressed by trial and error towards viable
technical solutions, and their conclusions gave their contemporaries good
reason for 'great expectations'.

Pierre Séguin's Animated Polyorama

The case of Pierre Séguin is particularly interesting. This professional
lanternist made many attempts to offer his audience animated projection.
As a painter specializing in pictures on glass for the magic lantern,
Séguin made phantasmagoria slides for the magician and lanternist
Henri Robin (real name Dunkel, born Holland *c.*1805, died Paris 1874),
who claimed to be the inventor of a theatrical optical effect known as

apparitions spectrales ('spectral exhibitions'), the method for which had nothing in common with Robertson's Phantasmagoria. In 1863, these 'living impalpable ghosts' met with great success in Paris. Robin exhibited them in a hall at 49 Boulevard du Temple, but it was a rival, the British lanternist John Henry Pepper, who achieved the real triumph with this invention on the stage of the Théâtre Impérial at Le Châtelet. Pepper even had the audacity, much to Robin's displeasure, to patent his 'illusory exhibitions' in France.[1] The perennial projection enthusiast Abbé Moigno went to the Châtelet phantasmagoria and explained the new optical process:

> Three enormous two-way mirrors, about 5 m square, costing almost 4,000 Francs, are arranged vertically below the traps, and may be raised at a given moment to divide the stage into two, parallel to the footlights. These mirrors are sufficiently transparent and colourless for the eye barely to notice their presence. The living person whose image cannot be projected behind the mirror is below the stage; he is given the required pose; he is illuminated by means of two Drummond lights or oxy-hydrogen lamps, and his image, produced by reflection of the rays which it emits at the suitably inclined mirror, will appear at an equal distance behind that mirror, next to the actors who are seen directly.[2]

With this method the audience would see on the stage the diaphanous living image of a real actor, with all his or her natural gestures. In one sense, this transparent moving 'ghost' surpassed all previous attempts at the projection and animation of images. But this was not an easy effect to create, and synchronization between the movements of the 'ghost' in the trap and the flesh-and-blood actor on the stage was very difficult to achieve. However, Robin's living ghosts could be shown with a devilish dexterity, as this account of 20 June 1863 indicates:

> In the first scene M. Robin evokes, to the sound of a drum, his Zouave on the battlefield of Inkermann, who stands before him and shows him his five wounds and his cross. In the second scene, a lady spirit appears to him, a bouquet in her hand, and urges him vigorously to make the table in front of him speak. In the third scene, it is Death, in the form of a skeleton wrapped in white drapery, which she opens little by little to show herself in her hideous nakedness, and who ends by taking away M. Robin himself.[3]

According to his own account, Robin travelled throughout Europe with these 'living impalpable ghosts' from 1847 onwards, before settling permanently in Paris. On 11 December 1862 he founded the 'Salle Robin', one of the great sites of nineteenth-century French projection, and on 1 October 1863 he celebrated the hundredth Paris showing of his optical spectacle. But the competition from Pepper, and the claims of priority by Pepper and another Englishman, Henry Dircks, filled him with bitterness. In 1864 Robin published *L'Almanach Le Cagliostro*, in which he denounced the plagiarism of which he saw himself as the victim. He claimed that the counterfeit had begun at the moment in 1852 when, with his employee Séguin, he attempted to commercialize his 'living ghosts':

> M. Séguin, my painter of phantasmagoria pictures, came to deliver an order and spend several days with me [in London, in 1851]. I showed him the system which I was using for these apparitions: he was amazed by it, and this gave him the idea to construct, with my approval and on the same principles, a toy to which he gave the name *Polyoscope*. He took out a patent for this toy, dated 16 September 1852; but it sold very poorly in France and even less well abroad. Sickened by his lack of success, at the end of two years, he stopped paying the annuities for his patent, which fell into the public domain.[4]

Dircks and Pepper then exhibited the effects of this small Polyoscope on a larger scale, which Robin claimed to have been showing since 1847. This may seem a little strange: Séguin's patent was quite different, concerning a peepshow box very similar to the 1849 'Polyorama Panoptique' of Pierre-Henri-Amand Lefort (see Chapter 7) with dioramic backgrounds showing day–night effects.

Séguin probably made the slides which Robin projected with his 'Agioscope', an improved magic lantern capable of showing large painted scenes, as at the Royal Polytechnic in London. It was also Séguin who painted the phantasmagorias, one of the principal attractions of the Théâtre Robin. So the painter, initiated in all his master's secrets, found himself at the forefront of the techniques of fixed and 'moving' projection. Based on the Polyoscope, an entertaining but not very original toy, he conceived a much more ambitious device, the 'Animated Polyorama'. Séguin filed the patent for this on 20 November 1852, some weeks after that for the Polyoscope:

The Animated Polyorama is an optical instrument of the phantasmagorical type. The effect produced by this instrument is to imitate, in picturesque views, the movements of nature: such as the movements of water, flames, clouds, steam, living persons, in fact all that which has movement in a natural setting.[5]

The novelty of Séguin's idea lay in not using a stroboscopic disc, like his predecessors. As we have seen, the projection of glass discs, while very important from a historical point of view, in actuality proved somewhat disappointing since the very low number of images could give only a limited illusion. Séguin, coming from the 'lanternist' tradition, preferred to use glass slides, which would pass horizontally through the slide carrier of a magic lantern with three lenses.

First of all, he designed a fairly complicated type of animated slide with four sliding glass plates, to which we need not pay very much attention since it does not seem to have been very different from the other effects common at the time. Using this slide and a lantern with three lenses, Séguin succeeded in projecting, for example, the entry of a ship into port. In a first addition to the patent, dated 21 June 1854, he already suggested replacing the painted scenes with photographs. But in the third and last addition, on 26 April 1860, Séguin envisaged the projection of 'pictures perfectly imitating living nature' by a succession of photographic images on glass, representing the different phases of a movement. These slides could be used in the three-lens lantern already used in 1852, but Séguin indicated that it would be possible to use four lenses or even more. If there were only four lenses, one could project, for example:

Soldiers in the process of fighting, or dancers in the process of dancing. On the first [slide] the soldiers have their sabres raised, on the second they are starting to bring them down, on the third a little lower, on the fourth completely.[6]

These views would appear successively on the screen, each replacing the previous one at the very moment when that view disappeared, using the 'dissolving view' technique. Each image was revealed using a metal plate which slid in front of each lens in turn. 'The effect produced will be that the soldiers appear to be striking.' Séguin drew the four soldier figures in the patent specification, and also an attractive little dancer turning around (a typical subject for Phenakistiscope discs):

> By this method one can create all types of moving pictures, by means of paintings or photographic images, by posing living persons and representing them in the various positions necessary to produce the effect described above.[7]

Like Claudet, Séguin was forced to photograph a simulated movement. As already mentioned, these visionaries often came within a whisker of the correct solution, but their hands were tied by a photographic process which was not yet 'sensitive' enough. It is not clear whether Séguin succeeded in projecting with his 'Animated Polyorama'; Robin's programmes make no mention of it. But perhaps Séguin was trying to market his invention on his own account. In 1856 he appeared in *L'Annuaire de Commerce de Paris* ('Paris Business Yearbook'), in the section on optical and scientific manufacturers:

> Séguin the younger, painter, inventor and patentee of an animated polyorama and several other optical instruments; maker of polyoramas and phantasmagoria for drawing rooms and travelling, etc. Orders and exports undertaken. 179, Faubourg Saint-Martin.[8]

Pierre Séguin died around 1884. Part of his stock was sold off on the fairgrounds, advertised at least in part using the curious term 'instantaneous painting'. Possibly this was a reference to retouched photographs.

> BEAUTIFUL PHANTASMAGORIA and its equipment for sale. With a large quantity of single and mechanical pictures, instantaneous painting by the late M. Séguin, the celebrated painter on glass. Enquire of M. Chapellier, proprietor, 1 Rue du Moustier, Vaux-le-Pénil, near Mélun, between 8 o'clock and midday. The lot for cash sale.[9]

This was a sad end for these instruments and slides, which have never resurfaced. But Séguin's idea, which consisted of projecting 'moving' photographic images one after the other, without relying on the stroboscopic disc or stereoscopy, was itself to survive as a feature of all future research.

Du Mont and Ducos du Hauron

The essential principles on which present-day cinematography is based were defined by the Belgian Henry Désiré du Mont in 1861 and, three years later, by the Frenchman Louis-Arthur Ducos du Hauron. Du Mont's research began in 1858–9, when he was a civil engineer at Mons, Belgium. Like Duboscq and Claudet, his first attempts were concerned with stereoscopic animation. On 7 April 1859 he filed a patent in Belgium for a series of devices christened 'Omniscopes', all derivations of the Phenakistiscope: a stroboscopic disc with an independent shutter (inspired by Stampfer); double stroboscopic discs; an ingenious peep-show box, in which several spectators could view animated pictures from a Phenakistiscope disc, by means of a light beam projecting through a lens onto a frosted glass screen; and so on. Altogether nine devices were patented in one go.[10]

In 1861 Du Mont was practising his profession in France, at Villennes on the north-western outskirts of Paris. He had made considerable progress in his research and was able to file a new patent on 2 May of that year. Even if we cannot know the quality of the representations which it claimed to present, this constitutes an important date in the history of the cinema. Du Mont had invented a 'photographic device suitable for reproduction of the successive phases of movement', for example of a dancer, a group of soldiers, or a machine, 'either for the pleasure of the eyes, or for instruction'.[11] Ten or twelve successive pictures would be made in 'several fractions of a second': in 1861 this may have been little more than a pipe-dream. But it would be unfair to write Du Mont off as a simple dreamer, since at this time the idea of 'instantaneous' photographs was very much in fashion. Using various processes, some photographers were beginning to capture movement in full flight. Du Mont claimed to have seen a picture showing a galloping horse, though the quality of the image was not mentioned; the horse may well have been blurred, its shape imprecise. If we look at a seaside photograph of the period, such as one taken in May 1850 by Edmond Bacot by the albumen process, we see immediately that the waves only appear as a confused white mass. In 1855 Auguste Bertsch had proudly presented two instantaneous collodion photographs: a quarter of a second had been sufficient to secure an image of a public square with all the passers-by, but they appeared far from sharp. It was not really until 1871, with the gelatino-bromide 'dry plate' process of Richard Leach Maddox, that 'instantaneous' photography became a reality.

It therefore seems possible that Du Mont's camera was capable of producing a series of successive instantaneous photographs, but that their 'visibility' would have been mediocre. He used three different methods to capture the popular subject of the dancer's movement:

(1) Sensitive glass plates were fixed around a cylindrical or prismatic drum, which turned about its axis inside a camera casing. The movement of the drum brought the plates into the focal plane of the lens, one after another.

(2) The plates were arranged side by side in a long frame which moved intermittently, horizontally or vertically, through the focal plane of the lens (somewhat reminiscent of Séguin's methods).

(3) The plates were placed one behind another in a long box with vertical grooves, which moved stepwise towards the lens. Each time a plate was exposed, it fell down into a second box, moving in the opposite direction to the first. The boxes Du Mont illustrated in his patent contained ten plates, though he later discussed twelve. When the plates had fallen into the lower box, a cover could be slid over the box and the plates could be developed individually in the laboratory.

For each of these methods, the lens was intermittently blocked by a moving black shutter plate, whose movement was synchronized with the mechanism moving the plates. It was all very primitive and jerky, but Du Mont was on the right track. It was another step forward, following Séguin who had also suggested intermittent shuttering of a series of animated pictures, though only for projection.

Unfortunately little evidence of Du Mont's work has been preserved. Not a single photograph has survived, and his 'camera', rediscovered by the historian Georges Potonniée in 1928 in the collections of the Société Française de Photographie, has since completely disappeared. Only a photograph of it remains, as with Robertson's Fantascope. This shows a curious square flat box, resting on a stand. There is a gear mechanism and, above this, a drive motor with a pulley. These do not match the diagrams in the patent, and the device remains very mysterious (Potonniée, unfortunately, did not explain its operation). Du Mont himself presented his 'camera' on 17 January 1862 at the Société Française de Photographie, the same place where Henry Cook had exhibited his Photobioscope. The members of the Société saw a procession of practically all the machines invented for taking and projecting pictures up until 1895. Perhaps, among the audience for Du Mont's paper, whose text was almost identical to his patent, there was a young photographic enthusiast named Louis-Arthur Ducos de Hauron.

The work of Du Mont and Ducos du Hauron seems even more revolutionary when we remember that at the time the majority of photographers were not in the least bit interested in the illusion of movement. Only an elite group of researchers were trying to solve the 'vital question' so important to Henry Cook. In France under the Second Empire the main enthusiasms were for simple stereoscopy and the highly fashionable '*carte de visite*' photographs.

The *carte de visite* idea had been launched by André-Adolphe-Eugène Disdéri (1819–89); it consisted of reproducing a portrait photograph on albumen paper as many times as required, pasting it onto a piece of Bristol board the size of a visiting card, and using it for that purpose among one's acquaintances. The middle classes flocked to Disdéri's Paris shop, at 8 Boulevard des Italiens, to be 'taken' from various angles. Disdéri's camera was actually fitted with four lenses, arranged in two horizontal rows of two, so that on a single plate he could take four identical images with a single release of the shutter. More interestingly, it could also take several different images. A moving frame would gradually reveal the plate, and Disdéri's client could pose as many times as he or she desired. Then he would print each of the views, and the narcissistic middle-class subject would buy a great many copies, perhaps into the hundreds. On these different visiting cards, the subject might appear elegantly dressed (or so he would believe) and casually draped over a wicker chair; daydreaming in front of a open book, which doubtless he had never read; standing upright, nobly gazing into the lens; or in a frock coat and drawn up to his full height, perhaps even with a hand slipped inside his waistcoat like Napoléon.[12]

The desire to produce photographs in series originated from the first double-lens cameras, which were intended for stereoscopy. Instead of a simple binocular camera, Disdéri used four lenses, without stereoscopic effects. Astonishingly, neither Achille Quinet, inventor in 1853 of the 'Quinetoscope' (long before the similar-sounding Edison 'Kinetoscope'), a binocular camera intended to 'reproduce simultaneously two portraits or two monuments',[13] nor Disdéri with his four-lens camera, thought of capturing successive phases of movement, whether simulated or natural. Hundreds of photographers worked on the '*carte de visite*' principle during the Second Empire, but not one appears to have dreamed of using their 'serial' photographs to lead to animation. On 18 March 1865, for example, two photographers named Alexandre Klinsky and Jean-Jacques Maingot patented a photographic camera capable of taking no less than 140 microscopic photographs at the same time. But the idea of gradually uncovering the 140 lenses, to form a series of successive animated pictures, never crossed their minds.

In the 1850s and 1860s, therefore, those who aimed to capture life by photography were very few and far between. Ducos du Hauron

(1837–1920) was certainly the most original and inventive of the few. This curious name concealed a very active researcher, whose theory on three-colour analysis and synthesis, developed in 1868, has formed the basis of all colour photography processes invented since. In February 1920, the three-colour film producer Léon Gaumont, knowing that Ducos du Hauron had fallen on very hard times, sent him 500 Francs 'as a modest homage to the forerunner who showed us the route to follow', meaning the three-colour process rather than the cinematographic technique. We shall see his importance in the latter field shortly. The title of his patent of 23 November 1868, 'Colours in Photography: Solution of the Problem', was not a vain boast: the few surviving examples of his three-colour photographs are quite successful. Curiously, the poet Charles Cros thought of exactly the same process at the same time. Ducos du Hauron was also responsible for some very strange photographic anamorphoses in 1888, and the Anaglyphe, a three-dimensional process which did not need the stereoscope.

His most important patent, as far as we are concerned, was that of 1864. Ducos du Hauron was then resident at 16 Rue Saint-Louis in Agen, in south-western France (he had been born at Langon, in the Gironde). At 2.00 pm on 1 March 1864 he filed an illustrated specification of nineteen pages at the Préfecture of the Département of Lot-et-Garonne. This described the operation of a device intended to 'reproduce photographically any scene with all the transformations which it undergoes during a predetermined time'.[14] Ducos du Hauron devised a whole series of innovative features for this 'cine camera', as it might already be called, which were retained in future designs. Like his predecessors Cook and Du Mont, Ducos du Hauron had a weakness for hyperbole:

> By means of my device, I make myself able particularly to reproduce the passing of a procession, a military review and manoeuvres, the events of a battle, a public festival, a theatrical scene, the movements and dances of one or more persons, the expressions of the physiognomy, and, if one wishes, the grimaces of the human face, etc.; a maritime scene, the movement of the waves (tide), the passage of clouds across a stormy sky, especially in mountainous country, the eruption of a volcano, etc.[15]

He described two separate machines, a 'single' one which would only produce a limited number of images, and a 'double' one with an infinite number of views. The first of these consisted of a camera obscura fitted with a large number of small lenses arranged in rows. The diagram in the patent shows ten rows of fourteen lenses and ten of fifteen lenses, arranged alternately, making a total of 290 lenses. Behind this battery of lenses, an opaque strip of paper or black fabric was wound between a pair of cylinders driven by a handle or motor. Small circular apertures formed in the strip would successively block and reveal each of the 290 lenses.

A sensitized collodion plate, large enough to cover the whole area of the lenses, was placed inside the camera. The cylinders on which the fabric was wound were driven at a constant speed, so that the top row of lenses would be successively uncovered from right to left, then the next row from left to right. At the end of the operation, a series of instantaneous photographs corresponding to the number of lenses would have been exposed onto a single plate:

> These images, when examined one by one, will represent all the successive transformations which take place in the scene represented, from the moment when light penetrates into the first lens to that at which it penetrates the last.[16]

Ducos du Hauron also wanted to project his series of positive images, to pass on his own pleasure to everyone, knowing the illusion would not be complete without the traditional magic lantern. He therefore designed another machine of the same size, but with its lenses arranged to converge towards a screen, so that all the images would appear one after another at a single point, a method already used by Uchatius and Séguin. The light source would be a simple oil lamp with a reflector, or even better, a powerful electric lamp:

> Now if, at a given moment, one concentrates a bright light successively on all the pictures, while making them travel with a certain speed in the same order in which they were taken, their images will be projected one after another at the same point . . . The spectator can only believe that he sees a single image which changes gradually as a result of the effect which operates between one picture and the next . . . This will be in some fashion a living representation of nature.[17]

The double machine operated on the same principle, using two photographic chambers side by side, making a total of 580 lenses. The cylinders carrying the opaque material were much longer and wider. By rapidly replacing an exposed plate with a new unexposed one, while pictures continued to be taken in the other chamber, one could reproduce a scene of a much longer duration. Projection could be achieved in the same manner.

Ducos du Hauron also devised a version for individual viewing, either simple or stereoscopic. Positive prints of the pictures were pasted onto a long strip of paper or fabric, in the order in which they had been taken. In the strip were formed very narrow transverse slots, spaced at regular intervals. The strip was wound over two horizontal cylinders which could be rotated with a handle, so that it passed from one cylinder to the other in front of a concave mirror which reflected each image. The spectator observed the pictures through a black plate pierced with a hole, with the slots in the strip functioning as a shutter. Ducos du Hauron was not satisfied with this individual viewer, and filed an addition to his patent on 3 December 1864 in which he subjected himself to severe criticism. His process, he said, presented five 'inconveniences':

> namely: 1. The necessity for a *considerable* number of images as a result of the *considerable* speed of the strip. 2. The lack of brightness in the images; the light appears all the weaker because the apertures are very narrow. 3. Flickering and inconsistency of the light as a result of the weakening of the perception of light between each passage of an aperture (this cannot be remedied except by an enormous speed). 4. Imperfect clarity. 5. The necessity of having large images to achieve a certain clarity.[18]

He therefore decided to abandon the slots in the strip, and chose instead to fit his machine with movable lenses. In the space between pictures he placed a small rod of boxwood, ivory or metal, which extended below the strip. Each rod would contact and push one of eighteen small metal claws mounted on a strip of fabric wound round two horizontal rollers, slightly spaced from each other. Also on this strip, alternating with the claws, were sewn eight small plates, each carrying a square convex lens in a vertical position. There were therefore eight lenses, which the rod and claw mechanism moved regularly in synchonism with the photographs. All the user had to do was to turn the rollers and watch the images pass through a hole pierced in a plate, as in the previous design. The images and lenses moved past the eye in a straight line, one after the other, with a degree of parallelism which Ducos du Hauron considered 'perfect'. As the next lens replaced the previous one, the next image took up precisely the same position as the preceding one, and so on, until the end of the image strip was reached.

Ducos du Hauron was clearly satisfied with this machine, which he described with precision. On the other hand, he was more circumspect in describing his systems for projecting and taking the pictures. To project the strip of images, he chose to abandon his delicate lantern process with its 290 or 580 lenses. Instead he simply enclosed his new device in a box and illuminated the pictures more strongly. Their image was projected through the mobile lenses, for viewing by the spectators on a screen. The images were printed on opaque paper, so presumably the projecting device used the same principle as the Megascope.

'My lens mechanism manages to give time far swifter wings than those of which the poets speak,' Ducos du Hauron claimed with pleasure. He concluded his patent by setting out some of the 'very curious and entertaining results' which his machine would produce:

> 1. To condense into a few moments a scene which in reality took place over a considerable period of time. Examples: the growth of trees and plants and all the phenomena of vegetation . . . The construction of a building or even a complete town, the succession of the ages of the same individual, the growth of a beard or a head of hair, etc. 2. Equally, to slow down those transformations whose speed sometimes makes them impossible to see. 3. To reverse the order in which a scene or phenomenon takes place; that is to say to start at the end and finish at the beginning. [. . .] N.B.: in a great many cases, one may, instead of photographs, utilize carefully-executed drawings. One may also combine photography and drawing, by drawing an animated subject which changes from one picture to the next onto an unchanging photographic background.[19]

To summarize, Ducos du Hauron's patent of 1 March and its addition of 3 December 1864 envisaged:

(1) A machine with 290 or 580 lenses which allowed taking and subsequent projection of views of successive phases of movement. This mechanism later inspired Louis Le Prince in his sixteen-lens camera of 1888.
(2) A second machine with eight successive moving lenses, allowing taking of views and projection of an extended movement, and incorporating the first attempt to drive a photographic strip at regular speed using a mechanical system.
(3) Anticipation of slow-motion cinematography.
(4) Anticipation of cinematographic animation of drawings.

(5) Anticipation of manual drawn animation, one image at a time (perhaps an inspiration for Émile Reynaud's 'Théâtre Optique' of 1888–92).

(6) Anticipation of showing a scene in reverse (which the Lumières found very amusing in 1895–6).

All this is impressive, but it is also necessary to separate the dreams from the reality. Ducos du Hauron's great handicap, like so many inventors, was that he was not rolling in money. He had his machine constructed by an ordinary locksmith, while he would have done better to employ a precision engineer such as Eugène Deschiens or Antoine Rédier. The locksmith supplied him with an inaccurate machine, and Ducos du Hauron had to admit severe disappointment.

Nothing has survived. Not a scrap of the picture strip, not a single piece of equipment. Nothing remains but the patent, which illustrates a rare imagination. Some historians are suspicious of Ducos du Hauron, claiming that his researches never got beyond the stage of imagination. That is possible. But when he died in 1920, some people remembered that, in the provinces and in the 1860s, this inventor had been able to see 'a beginning of an achievement, like the man who cuts the stones to pave the way'.[20]

Ducos du Hauron was also able to recall his attempts with some pride, when cinematography arrived at its universal triumph in 1896. On 29 August of that year, he filed a new patent for 'novel optical combinations overcoming all intermittence in the illumination of the photographic pictures known as moving pictures (chronophotography)'. He allowed himself a short historical résumé:

> From the year 1864 onwards, and therefore well before the appearance in America of Edison's apparatus known as the Kineto-scope, I invented in France a great variety of devices which themselves gave analysis and synthesis of movement by means of a series of photographs of living beings, taken at very close intervals and then delivered successively in front of the eye by means of rapid substitutions.[21]

Ducos du Hauron claimed that 'circumstances' had prevented him from exploiting his invention. In 1896 he took up his old idea again, always believing that his system of moving lenses was the best. He pronounced himself astonished that Edison had not used it in the Kinetoscope, whose rotating shutter he considered 'primitive'. As for the Cinématographe Lumière, it gave unstable images (a defect which a good many other observers had noted):

> My system based on juxtaposed lenses completely cures this imperfection of Messrs Lumière's device, and similarly cures the shortcomings, which are just as severe, of Edison's device. This system which I created thirty-two years ago has fallen into an undeserved oblivion, as has the whole arrangement of my above-mentioned invention, which however was the earliest in date of all that has been proposed relating to moving photography.[22]

However, the arrangement which he proposed in 1896 was archaic compared to the cameras and projectors of that time. Ducos du Hauron had not kept up with technological evolution. It will be better to remember him instead for his impressive patent of 1864, so important in the history of cinema.

Henry R. Heyl's Phasmatrope

In spite of Ducos du Hauron's fantastic efforts, the various 'cameras' constructed in the 1850s (by Claudet, Cook, Du Mont, and Charles Johnson and Thomas Sutton in Britain) could only photograph about ten successive images, at the most. And most of the time their images showed actors posing to simulate movement. The taking of 'chronophotographic' or 'cinematographic' images therefore already existed in theory (especially after Ducos du Hauron's conception of the sensitive strip of images), but in practice it remained primitive.

Projection of animated photographs, on the other hand, was demonstrated brilliantly in 1870 by the American Henry R. Heyl, in front of an audience of around 1,600 people. It seems very likely that this was the first commercial public exhibition of projected 'moving' photographic images. Heyl's show on 5 February 1870 reactivated research, especially in the United States, and gave some evidence of how profitable 'living' photography would prove to be: the evening's takings came to $850, though Heyl was not the only item on the bill.

Henry Renno Heyl was an engineer, born at Columbus, Ohio, who moved to Philadelphia in 1863. On Saturday 5 February 1870, he took part in an evening organized by O.H. Willard, at the Philadelphia Academy of Music, as part of the 'Ninth Entertainment of the Young Men's Society of St. Mark's Evangelical Lutheran Church'. Heyl brought a projection device, the Phasmatrope, which was described in the programme like this:

> The Phasmatrope.
> This is a recent scientific invention, designed to give various objects and figures upon the screen the most graceful and lifelike movements. The effects are similar to those produced in the familiar toy called the Zoetrope, where men are seen walking, running, and performing various feats in most perfect imitation of real life. This instrument is destined to become a most valuable auxiliary to the appliances for illustration, and we have the pleasure of having the first opportunity of presenting its merits to our audience.[23]

In Willard's studio at 1206 Chestnut Street, Philadelphia, Heyl photographed six successive poses of a couple waltzing, and six others of an acrobat performing a perilous leap. Perhaps Heyl had succeeded in capturing true movement; it cannot have been easy to simulate six different intermediate poses of a perilous leap. The six negatives were then printed as positives onto six lightweight glass plates, each reproduced three times to make a total of eighteen photographs end to end. This therefore represented three repetitions of the same movement, or eighteen successive and continuous phases of movement. The plates were slipped into eighteen vertical carriers arranged around the circumference of a large iron wheel. This was rotated intermittently by a system of ratchet wheels, so that the images were presented one by one to the lens of a magic lantern fitted with a shutter, which was necessary to cut off the light rays during the short interval in which the images moved round. The whole mechanism was operated by a handle. The Phasmatrope, Heyl claimed later, did not cause any flickering of light, with 'the figures appearing to move in most lifelike ways'.[24]

During the show at the Academy of Music on 5 February 1870, the pictures of the dancers were projected while the orchestra played a waltz. This series of images and the Phasmatrope itself have fortunately been preserved[25] at the Franklin Institute, where Heyl gave a second show on 16 March 1870. The magic lantern Phasmatrope could therefore project animated photographs, in front of a large audience. Heyl had combined the ideas suggested by Duboscq, Claudet, Séguin, Du Mont, and Ducos du Hauron, perhaps without being aware of most of their work. After two centuries of research, the beam of the magic lantern had finally recreated the illusion of life, the synthesis of movement.

The antiquated 'lantern of fear' now seemed more than ever to be an indispensable modern invention. To paraphrase Abbé Moigno,[26] one could say that without the magic lantern, drawn or photographed movement 'would have been nothing but a dwarf, a cretin, an idiot', but through projection, it would become 'a giant, an angel with daring wings'.

11

The Magic Lantern
A Sovereign and her Subjects

The Royal Polytechnic Institution

While all these prophets were filing and hammering away at their rudimentary cameras in their laboratories and workshops, the magic lantern continued to fascinate the crowds. The lantern was never so much in demand, so widely sold, so much *à la mode* as in the second half of the nineteenth century.

Magic lantern shows were even more popular in Britain than in the rest of Europe, and British lantern manufacturers and exhibitors were far more numerous than their French counterparts. The Royal Polytechnic Institution in London's Regent Street, founded in 1838 by W.M. Nurse, was the most prestigious nineteenth-century projection venue. Projection has never reached such a highpoint of artistic and technical perfection: the slides shown at the Polytechnic were true works of art, and the greatest lanternists performed there—among others, J.H. Pepper, Henry Langdon Childe, and even Jules Duboscq.

Like the France of Napoléon III, Victorian Britain showed a huge appetite for science and progress and a fascination with scientific instruments and educational spectacle. The Royal Polytechnic Institution was born of this demand, along with other venues dedicated to popular education, such as the Egyptian Hall, the Royal Gallery of Illustration, the Royal Gallery of Practical Science, the Royal Panopticon of Science and Art, and the numerous dioramas and panoramas which sprang up across the whole of Britain. But the Polytechnic was the most celebrated of these 'temples' of projection, and it quickly acquired a symbolic status in the eyes of foreigners, such as Abbé Moigno, who was attempting to import British methods to France (see Fig. 31).

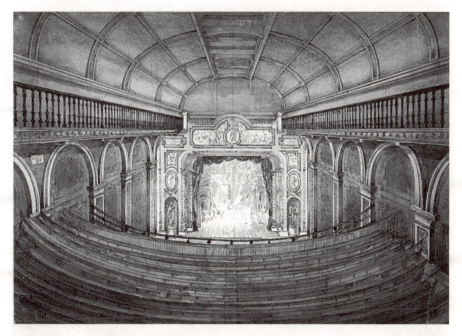

Fig. 31.   Watercolour painting showing the theatre of the Royal Polytechnic Institution in 1882. Collection: Cinémathèque Française, Musée du Cinéma.

The Royal Polytechnic was a gigantic cabinet of curiosities, not dedicated solely to projection. Jumbled in the rooms of its ground and first floors were machines for printing and marbling paper, a lithographic press, an electric steam-generating machine, a machine by Huygens for grinding gold-bearing quartz, samples of iridescent, embossed, and painted paper, a collection of Australian gold and diamonds, electro-magnetic equipment, telegraphs, peep-shows, and so on. In a lecture hall, J.L. King explained the phenomena of physics and James Matthews performed conjuring tricks. The Great Hall was reserved for the magic lantern shows and 'spectre dramas' of Pepper, who was Director of the Polytechnic from July 1854. A hand-painted lantern slide by W.R. Hill[1] shows the Great Hall as a vast splendid room with a coffered ceiling, mainly blue walls decorated with frescoes, and hundreds of the curious promenading on a balcony, the women in crinolines and the men in frock coats and top hats. This hall contained all types of curious scientific instruments, as well as a large tank in which a small sailing boat floated.

Phantasmagoria shows were often presented at the Polytechnic. The projecting microscope, illuminated by oxy-hydrogen gas, was also a great success, and the 'physioscope' (a device derived from the megascope) attracted attention by projecting, as its name suggests, realistic human faces. The most popular attractions, however, remained the magic lantern shows with 'dissolving view' effects. Two, four, and sometimes six lanterns were mounted together for dissolving view shows, using a hand-operated shutter to reveal the four or six objective lenses in sequence. The condenser lenses had to be relatively large, since for most of the time they were projecting slides larger than those generally used in the trade: 17 cm high and 21 cm wide, in the case of the hand-painted slides by W.R. Hill, who worked for Childe.

All the slides shown at the Royal Polytechnic were created by professional slide painters, and must have taken weeks to produce

Fig. 32.   A hand-painted lantern slide from the Royal Polytechnic Institution. Collection: Cinémathèque Française, Musée du Cinéma.

(see Fig. 32). As well as Hill, we should mention Charles Gogin and Fid Page, and Isaac Knott of Liverpool, who created the slides which illustrated Albert Smith's show *The Ascent of Mont Blanc* at the Egyptian Hall in Piccadilly, London. The slides they produced were not items of 'popular' art: the traditional hand-painted lantern slide seemed very primitive in comparision with these magnificent images. As Moigno wrote in 1872, projection had become an art in its own right.

Many of these 'Polytechnic slides', fortunately, have been preserved by British collectors, in the Oxford Museum of the History of Science, and in the Will Day Collection at the Musée du Cinéma in Paris. The Oxford museum has a set of nineteen slides dated 1854 of the Russo-Turkish (Crimean) War; thirteen slides dated 1863 of the Polish Insurrection;[2] some beautiful photographs of Paris, marked 'by Mr England, artist of the London Stereoscopic Company'; and a collection of chromatropes (two hand-painted glass discs, turning in opposite directions to produce a vertiginous effect of intersecting lines and shapes, invented by Childe in about 1843–4). The Paris Musée du Cinéma has some equally splendid sets: a polar expedition (a boat trapped in the ice, the midnight sun, a sailor showing a mirror to an Eskimo); exotic views (the jungle, hunting bison, the fort of Gibraltar, a volcano, the desert); and so on. The British collector Lester Smith owns eight Polytechnic slides (17 by 21.5 cm), possibly painted by Gogin and Page, which illustrate *Aladin, the Wonderful Lamp* and were projected by George Buckland on 26 December 1868 in the Great Hall of the Polytechnic. Finally, the Museum of the Moving Image in London, now sadly closed, formerly displayed some animated slides illustrating Carl Maria von Weber's 1821 opera *Der Freischütz*. Nothing could be more like the phantasmagoria than the finale of Act II: Kaspar, in a fearsome ravine, traces a magic circle and invokes Samiel, a henchman of the Devil. The moon comes out, creatures appear, a storm breaks, midnight chimes and the 'savage huntsman' arrives at a gallop. One of the surviving slides shows Kaspar in the centre of the magic circle. This 'Robertsonian' scene was exquisitely created by Childe in about 1860.

The great beauty of the shows of this time explains part of the confusion and nostalgia among later lanternists as the Cinématographe invaded their screens. The flickering black-and-white (or more often rather grey) photographs of the early cinema seem very sad and lifeless when compared to the dazzling oil colours used on the glass slides of the British, French, and German 'temples': Venetian red, Indian yellow, carmine, Prussian blue, indigo and so on, all transparent and bright as the sun.

The reputation of these slides was so great that, when the Royal Polytechnic Institution closed in 1876 (it reopened in 1882 under the name of the Regent Street Polytechnic), the auction of its equipment raised a fortune, £900 for the slide collection alone. T.C. Hepworth, the noted lanternist and former Polytechnic lecturer, remembered in 1888:

> Those pictures which delighted one or two generations of sightseers at the old Polytechnic, measured about eight inches by five. Some of these pictures were most elaborate works of art; so much so, that at the sale of the belongings of the Polytechnic in 1881, when the Institution as a place of entertainment was broken up, many of these slides realised as much as fifty shillings each.[3]

The Astrometeoroscope constructed by the Hungarian engineer Pichler, already mentioned in Chapter 9 under the subject of the choreutoscope, caused

> some little excitement when . . . [it] was put up for sale. Opticians and others would have been glad to get hold of it, so as to have multiplied it for sale. This led to a brisk competition, ending with Mr. Pichler giving an extravagant price for his own bantling.[4]

This animated slide, which the Polytechnic had kept away from prying eyes in a trunk in order to preserve its secret, produced remarkable results, according to Hepworth: 'The effect upon the screen is most curious, for it seems to be covered with a lacework of geometrical patterns which constantly change their form.'[5]

Abbé Moigno, the 'Apostle of Projection'

'When will Paris have its own Polytechnic Institution?' Abbé Moigno asked impatiently in his magazine *Le Cosmos* in August 1854. He had just returned from England, where he had been dazzled by Pepper's projections. Abbé François Moigno (1804–84) was a true scholar. He entered the Society of Jesus in 1822. In 1840, while he was preparing his *Leçons de Calcul Différential et Intégral* ('Lessons in Differential and Integral Calculus') for publication, Father Boulanger, the Superior of his order, ordered him to interrupt his research and go to teach at Laval in north-western France. Moigno could not abandon the scientific community of the capital, in which he counted Duboscq, Cauchy, Arago, and the great physicist André Ampère (1775–1836) among his friends;

he refused to leave Paris and, in 1844, left the Society. Appointed as chaplain of the Louis-le-Grand high school, he threw his efforts into all sorts of scholarly and popular publications, such as *Le Cosmos* in 1852. This fat, short-sighted, scholarly priest, with a streak of Breton obstinacy, irritated not only the administration of his own order, but also other people in high places. He had many enemies. 'Abbé Moigno is a schemer who only seeks out fools' declared the painter Delacroix in 1847.[6]

In 1852, two years before his visit to the Royal Polytechnic, Moigno had already conceived the idea of using projection to popularize the sciences (a very old idea, as we have already seen from Zahn in the seventeenth century). Only the magic lantern was capable of drawing an audience and capturing their attention: the most difficult explanations would become readily comprehensible when accompanied by a projected picture. This first 'great and courageous enterprise', as he described it, was to come to nothing as a result of the 'Badinguet' government of Napoléon III, as we shall see.

Moigno's patron Bénito de Monfort financed *Le Cosmos*. In 1852 he took a twenty-one year lease on a house at 8 Boulevard des Italiens, at a rent of 18,000 Francs. The public courses planned at the 'Maison du Cosmos' would be given by celebrated scholars, commissioned to speak on the 'spectacle and the study of nature':

> The teaching of the Cosmos is essentially elementary, in order to be understood by all and to enlighten every mind. It proceeds by a series of brilliant and grandiose experiments which reproduce the phenomena in all their splendour and strike the imagination. Each lecture is summarized and illustrated by a greater or lesser number of pictures on transparent glass which are illuminated by electric light and which are hugely magnified on a vast screen.[7]

Education or entertainment? Science or spectacle? Moigno played up this traditional ambiguity by presenting his scientific lectures on the Boulevard des Italiens, among theatres and other popular attractions. To attract more customers, Moigno also planned a 'photographic salon' like Claudet's London establishment, where he would exhibit pictures, equipment, and a collection of stereoscopes belonging to his friend Duboscq. The fee for a course of fifty lectures (from 1 November to 1 May) was 200 Francs, and attendance at a single class cost 5 Francs. Everything was arranged, in Moigno's mind, which was already imagining that the scheme would compete 'we are certain, with the courses of the Polytechnic Institution of London'.[8] But this was to reckon without Napoléon III's Ministry of Public Instruction. Perhaps, like all dictators, the Emperor took a dim view of attempts at popular education. Moigno always remained angry about the decision taken by the Ministry in 1852:

> After objections of every kind, after difficulties without number, after endless steps lasting for more than six months, they replied to us that the instruction which we wished to provide could not be authorized until after the vote and promulgation of the law on higher education. Higher education! This was to do with scientific performances to which we would invite women, young people and children. There were no explanations given. It was an arbitrary and tyrannical decision to endure. We were forced to give up on our plan.[9]

The Abbé was therefore obliged to close the Maison du Cosmos. His patron de Monfort withdrew his support in April 1853. The following year Moigno paid a sad visit to the building at 8 Boulevard des Italiens: the *carte-de-visite* photographer Disdéri was occupying the ground floor, while the former lecture theatre had become the haunt of the magician Hamilton, a pupil of Robert-Houdin. As Moigno put it bitterly, 'there was a place in the sun for conjurors; there was none for a loyal and devout servant of science which was simultaneously progressive and popular'.[10] Much later, the building at 8 Boulevard des Italiens was to accommodate two of the great names of the cinema: Georges Méliès, director of the Théâtre Robert-Houdin, and Clément-Maurice, artistic photographer, friend of the Lumière brothers and one of their camera operators. Certain locations seem to have a special resonance.

Moigno had not had his last word. On 9 June 1864 he launched his 'Public Course in Popular Science' at the Paris premises of the Cercle des Sociétés Savantes (Circle of Learned Societies) at 3 Quai Malaquais. This was far from the great 'temple' he had dreamed of, since the hall was too small. 'Good Providence', in the shape of the council of the Société d'Encouragement pour l'Industrie Nationale (Society for the Encouragement of National Industry), therefore put at Moigno's disposal the large 400-seat hall at 44 Rue Bonaparte (this same society hosted the first showing of the Cinématographe Lumière on 22 March 1895). Moigno held his first session on 14 July 1864, with projected photographs.

It was not until 1872 that Moigno, always true to his 'invincible vocation', finally succeeded in the plan devised in 1852. By then the 'Badinguet' regime had ended in disaster in war and revolution in 1870–1. The new Minister of Public Instruction, Jules Simon, responded favourably to the Abbé's requests. On 1 March 1872 Moigno opened the Salle du Progrès (Hall of Progress) at 24 Rue de Bourgogne, in the centre of the Faubourg Saint-Germain between Rue de Grenelle and Rue Saint-Dominique. This location implied a clientele not at all like that of the *grands boulevards*. But Moigno hauled himself back into the saddle and pronounced himself ready to

> combat vigorously the two inexorable enemies of discovery and invention: the ignorance which kills them as seeds or drowns them at birth, the routine which is put in their way by the unbreakable circle of apathy.[11]

A further challenge was to divert Parisians from 'the foul-smelling atmosphere, stirred up by the winds of all the lowest passions' found in the *cafés-concerts*. For those who preferred not to sit down with an *absinthe* or two, Moigno offered a programme which was both recreational and instructive, at an entrance price ranging from 50 centimes to 2 Francs:

1. *Musical overture* performed on the organ, harmonium and piano . . .
2. *Review of Novelties* . . . Pictures projected with the electric light.
3. *Illustrated Demonstration of Science*, of about one hour in length.
4. *Interval* of a quarter of an hour at most.
5. *Review of History or Geography* . . . Projection of a certain number of pictures . . .
6. *Finale*. We finish with some *optical toys*, the Fantascope, Chromatrope, etc.
7. *Departure*. National tunes and songs of various nations will be played.[12]

A short time later, Moigno found a new patron in the person of Millin de Grand-Maison, who built him a new hall at 30 Rue du Faubourg Saint-Honoré, opened on 1 November 1872. Right up until his death, Moigno remained the 'Apostle of Projection', as he was nicknamed in his lifetime. His excellent book *L'Art des Projections* ('The Art of Projection') of 1872 was the first French technical book devoted entirely to the magic lantern. This work was largely inspired by an anonymous English book (probably by John Martin) entitled *The Magic Lantern: How to Buy and*

How to Use It, published in 1866, from which Moigno reproduced several engravings.

After the opening of the hall at Faubourg Saint-Honoré, the Abbé amassed a vast collection of photographic slides, created by Armand Billon, a professional photographer. Moigno's catalogue of photographic slides, published in 1882, consisted of 4,388 items. All branches of the sciences were represented, even photography, with portraits of Niépce and Daguerre and pictures of the equipment used by Janssen and Marey. The section headed 'Light' included several photographs showing magic lanterns. Of course, the New and Old Testament, the Passion and the Life of Christ occupied several pages, though relatively few (numbers 2,688 to 2,853), considering that Moigno was a man of the church. The majority were scientific pictures: anatomy, botany, chemistry, geology, medicine, zoology, sometimes illustrated with microscopic photographs. In the section headed 'Obstetrics' Moigno was not afraid to include the most graphic photographs (genital organs, for example). The history of France, architecture, fables, and geography were equally well illustrated. Among the portraits were those of Faraday, Tyndall, Edison, Foucault, and Moigno himself.

The 'mechanized pictures' which allowed projection 'of subjects with moving parts' were a 'unique and completely unpublished collection' (catalogue numbers 4,201 to 4,290). For example, there was a slide with a mechanism representing a 'suction pump with movement of the piston, valves and column of water'. This could be the device which Moigno himself described the physicist Bourbouze using at the Sorbonne, around 1870, to show 'the regular action of the pistons and slide valves of steam, gas, or pneumatic engines'. The operation of this slide remains a mystery. Finally, Moigno also offered slides for astronomy, for the Polyorama, 500 'amusing pictures', and some chromatropes and other 'wheels of life'.

In 1882 Moigno had less than two years left to live, but he was still full of energy and enthusiasm:

> We see repeated endlessly that the clergy is not only the enemy, but the extinguisher, the snuffer-out. What a sharp denial our four to six thousand photographs give to this odious slander! It is I, I, a priest of Jesus Christ, who have created teaching through projection in France, and who have introduced it to England, from where it has leapt to America where it gathers momentum. And it is I, a priest, who through my collection available to all, will bring to this eminently popular method of instruction an unforeseen expansion.[13]

Even if Moigno rather exaggerated his influence in the Anglo-Saxon countries, his importance for the development of audio-visual education in France is undeniable. As we shall see, another great cinematic researcher, Émile Reynaud, derived a great deal from the Abbé. Religious and instructive projection was also taken up on a large scale by the Maison de la Bonne Presse, in 1895, in response to the numerous secular popular education societies (Moigno's activities inspired many republican and anti-clerical teachers) which sprang up towards the end of the nineteenth century.

The Salle Robin

There is no need to revisit Robin's 'living impalpable ghosts', already mentioned in Chapter 10 in connection with the painter Séguin. But it is important to return to the great magic lantern projections given at the Salle Robin, at 49 Boulevard du Temple. Henri Robin opened this new hall on 11 December 1862, as a small-scale copy of the Royal Polytechnic Institution:

> The Théâtre Robin is a pleasant little hall situated on the Boulevard du Temple, close to the corner of the Rue du Temple. The entrance hall is vast and spacious, and the arrangement is perfect and worthy of one of our greatest theatres . . . The decor is simple and in good taste: figures of children in porcelain bisque, from the studio of M. Gille, decorate the corridors and attract the admiration of lovers of art, as does the magnificent bust of the Emperor, which is above the booking office. Around the entire cornice of the gallery are painted tablets, also in porcelain bisque from the same studio. These tablets represent the great celebrities of science and magic: Archimedes, Galileo, Palissy, Vaucanson, Franklin, Volta, Newton, Daguerre, Arago, Cuvier, Robertson, Humboldt, Cagliostro, Comte.[14]

Once again the 'fantasmagores' and charlatans found themselves side by side with the great scientists. Robin was not a scholar like Moigno, preferring to style himself as a 'magician'. Even worse, he claimed to be a religious free-thinker.

The price of admission at the Salle Robin ranged between 4 Francs for private boxes and 75 centimes for the gallery. The show began each evening at eight o'clock. As at the Royal Polytechnic, the programme was a cheerful mixture of scientific and entertaining views. Robin borrowed the phantasmagorical techniques of Robertson and Comte, but announced that he had 'the honour to warn the public that the apparitions and ghosts are not frightening; the principal aim of his show is to amuse.' With an improved magic lantern called the 'Agioscope' he projected large hand-painted slides as dissolving views. On 16 January 1863 Robin plagiarized Albert Smith by presenting 'The Ascent of Mont Blanc'; on 18 February 1863 he showed an 'Excursion to the Holy Land, in Syria and Palestine'; on 11 April 'The Earthquake of Lisbon'; on 15 May 'The History of the Formation of the Earth'; on 2 November 1863, 'Natural Phenomena'. An anonymous contemporary reported:

> His Agioscope is just as good as his Fantascope. It is a transparent sheet onto which paint themselves all phases and aspects of the world before the Flood. We see the planet in a flaming gaseous state swirling in space, then cooling gradually, after incalculable centuries and arriving at the fluid state.[15]

On 17 July 1863 Robin asked the famous publisher Louis Hachette for permission to reproduce the magnificent engravings by Gustave Doré illustrating Dante's *Inferno*:

> My intention being to present, in the coming winter, the Phantasmagoria in my theatre, I would like to take several devilish subjects in a work published by yourself, namely Dante illustrated by Gustave Doré. I am therefore asking, Sir, whether you would have any objection to the purpose for which I would use these subjects, and since I would wish to purchase this work, I would request you to be so kind as to indicate to me what would be a reduced price.[16]

Hachette's response is not known, but at the end of the century Alfred Mame authorized the lantern manufacturer Élie Xavier Mazo to produce lantern slides of Doré's illustrations of the Holy Bible (an altogether more respectable subject) which he had published in 1866.

In August 1864 Robin presented another new series on astronomy. This subject excited and amazed the audience, and brought Robin into competition with the astronomer and publisher Camille Flammarion (1842–1925), who was also presenting projections on this topic. The same year, Robin successfully exhibited Ruhmkorff's induction coil, which allowed him 'to throw out sparks which tore the air with a trail of fire 45 cm in length'.[17] Using Duboscq's Lanterne Photogénique, he was also able to present projected microscopic photographs.

Around 1868 Robin was obliged to close his theatre because of a compulsory purchase order. He moved to 36 Avenue Daumesnil, where

Fig. 33. Hand-painted lantern slide: The Fountain of the Innocents, Paris (attributed to Robin and Séguin, *c.*1863–5).

he died in 1874. His equipment has unfortunately never been found. One private collection includes a large lantern, framed in dark wood, 16 cm by 33.5 cm, with an image on glass 12.5 cm square (see Fig. 33) representing the Fontaine des Innocents in Paris in the time of Napoléon III, executed with infinite care and a wealth of detail. The wonderful quality of the painting and the unconventional format recall the slides of the Royal Polytechnic, but it is definitely of French manufacture; this small work of art might tentatively be attributed to Séguin or Robin.

One of the strangest objects in Robin's collection, a stuffed peacock which ate and digested grains of hemp seed, rather like a celebrated mechanical duck constructed by the maker of automata Jacques de Vaucanson (1709–82), was purchased by none other than Georges

Méliès for his collection of 'magic' objects. Méliès also owned various items which had belonged to his idol, Robert-Houdin. But at some point this peacock, mysteriously, vanished into the clouds.

The travelling lanternist's trade

The travelling lanternist's hand-to-mouth trade became obsolete around the middle of the nineteenth century, killed off by the mass production of lantern equipment (see Fig. 34). The lanternists who now offered their services for private performances were professionals with projection equipment of the highest quality, and their shows were far more elaborate than those of the miserable Auvergnats and Savoyards.

Among the great Parisian lanternists offering private shows in the home, Henri Robin features once again. He and his assistant Séguin offered the wonders of the Agioscope and Fantascope to schools and institutions. Further down the scale, one Charles Billy ran a small 'children's theatre' at 39 Rue Marbeuf, then at 14 Rue de la Comète (1878–94) and finally at 96 Rue Saint-Dominique (1895–6). He also organized private shows with the magic lantern. A lanternist named Carré, also known as Adolphon, did the same from the 1880s onwards, based at 120 Boulevard Richard-Lenoir (1886–94), then 70 Rue d'Angoulême (1895–1913), offering the lantern, a puppet theatre, and some magical experiments for shows in private residences. In 1880 Marchal and Buffard, of 1–12 Passage de l'Opéra, offered dissolving view shows to all comers. In 1885 Auguste, at 9 Passage Verdeau, offered 'matinées and soirées of entertaining science and magic lantern shows in the city'. Le Maire, at 2 Rue Chapon, specialized in projection for children, while the lanternist Rodgison preferred to show 'picturesque tours around the globe': a poster from 1881 shows him riding a locomotive transformed into a triunial lantern.

We should also mention Eugène Philipon (?–1874), manager of the *Journal Amusant* and son of Charles Philipon, founder of *Charivari*, the Paris periodical on which the London *Punch* was based. In 1868 Philipon was selling Lampascopes, phantasmagorical shadows, and camera obscuras called 'Miragioscopes', as well as running a service of shows for hire. About twenty lantern slides signed by Philipon have recently been found by a collector, together with a photographic portrait of this lanternist. The slide painting is excellent, and some of the slides have a very original animation mechanism. One of them carries the inscription 'Musée Philipon'.

At the very end of the nineteenth century some new professionals

Fig. 34. A brass and mahogany 'biunial' lantern made by Butcher of London at the end of the nineteenth century. Collection: Laurent Mannoni.

appeared in Paris, for example Louis Morin, of 16 Rue du Havre, and J. Caroly, manager of the monthly *L'Illusioniste*, of 11 Rue du Cardinal-Lemoine and later 20 Boulevard Saint-Germain, at the sign of the Académie de Magie (Academy of Magic). The conjuror Alber (a pupil of Carré-Adolphon), who was employed by the lantern manufacturer Mazo, had 'recommendations of the first order from the Nobility, the Clergy, the Magistrature, Commerce, the Army, Education and Finance'. He gave shows in the French provinces, at châteaux and private homes, and was also responsible for several technical books on projection.[18]

In Germany, Paul Hoffmann (1829–88) is considered to have been the most famous lanternist of this period. This former clock-maker devoted himself completely to projection from 1870 onwards. Assisted by his second wife Mina, he travelled through Germany and the rest of Europe with a magic lantern of his own construction and several series of dazzlingly beautiful slides. These were discovered in 1971 (four large wooden boxes containing 530 slides) and acquired by the Historisches Museum in Frankfurt. Some of them carry the mark of A. Krüss of Hamburg, a company specializing in the manufacture of magic lanterns, camera obscuras, photographic equipment and slides. The subjects Hoffmann presented from 1870 to 1888 were: Dante's *Divine Comedy* (71 slides); the *Odyssey* (76 slides); Richard Wagner's *Nibelungen* (44); Siberia (61); Central Africa (44); Egypt (33); geology (44); the North Pole (32); Pompeii (29); landscapes (35); the Bible, Old and New Testaments (47); astronomy (9); and miscellaneous subjects (17). There is a notable similarity between these subjects and those presented by Robin or at the Royal Polytechnic.[19]

The great lanternists who travelled from town to town in the later nineteenth century had to transport bulky and expensive equipment with them: heavy boxes of slides, a lantern (usually a large instrument with double or triple lenses for dissolving views), illuminant systems, and cylinders of oxygen and hydrogen. Illumination remained a continuous problem, since large-scale shows needed very bright and powerful light, not a simple oil lamp. The arc lamp was ideal, but finding the necessary electricity in the countryside in the nineteenth century was not easy. Lanternists generally used either oxy-hydrogen or oxy-ether light.

Ether illuminants required extreme caution: the devices on the market around 1890 were little more than bombs. A brass reservoir was filled with liquid ether, which was mixed with oxygen gas injected under pressure. A burner nozzle on the top of the reservoir allowed a thin stream of gaseous mixture to escape, which could then be ignited with a match. This small flame was directed against a cylinder of lime, which gave off a very bright light when it reached a state of incandescence. The lantern manufacturer Alfred Molteni put an oxy-ether lamp on the market in 1895 under the name 'Securitas'. It was this device which was being used by the operators of the Joly-Normandin cinematograph on 4 May 1897, at the Paris Bazar de la Charité. The result is well known: when the lamp went out suddenly, the projectionists struck a match to relight it, but meanwhile ether vapour had spread through the projection booth. A terrifying explosion and huge inferno followed. The 'Securitas' bomb caused the death of 143 people, largely from the Parisian aristocracy, much to the delight of the irascible writer Léon Bloy, a bitter opponent of the 'Bazaar' which masqueraded as 'Charity'. Bloy was also the author of a bitter attack on the use of projection by the Catholic Church.[20]

However, long before the disaster at the Bazar de la Charité, projection shows using oxy-hydrogen (a mixture of oxygen and hydrogen gases), oxy-ether (ether and oxygen), oxy-calcium (alcohol and oxygen), and oxy-acetylene (acetylene and oxygen) burners were very common. Rather than pressurized cast iron cylinders, the gas to be mixed was sometimes contained in simple bags, with weights placed on top to create pressure. For a bag of 250 litres of gas, a weight of 60 to 80 kg was needed. The lanternist had to keep an eye on the bags, adjusting the pressure to make sure that the gas lasted until the end of the show, whose end would sometimes arrive rather unexpectedly for lack of fuel. For example on 7 December 1894, in Nantes, the Marquis de la Ferronnays was giving a lecture on Africa in front of an audience of 200. But the lanternist had only been able to obtain a half-full oxygen bag: 'the bag became lower, and the pictures became darker', one sarcastic journalist remarked. The Marquis hurried his delivery, finishing the lecture at full speed: 'it is time, for the bag is empty, absolutely empty and alone, presenting a sad figure . . .'[21] Many lanternists made their own hydrogen and oxygen gases in the hope of avoiding this problem.

Accidents were commonplace. The gas pipes might come unfastened; the cylinder of lime might break, shattering the condenser lens; the gas bags or pipes might explode. Such explosions were usually very violent. In 1891, one English lanternist wrote:

> The most recent explosion took place during a show of one of our principal photographic societies, while a machine with a de Bourdon manometer was in use in highly competent hands. Fortunately nobody was injured. The explosion took place at the moment when the oxygen entered the manometer. The explosion was accompanied by a jet of flame, and a piece of metal flew up to the ceiling where it became deeply embedded.[22]

A lively description of a religious lantern show, given in a convent by travelling lanternists from the Maison de la Bonne Presse, appeared in the monthly magazine *Le Fascinateur* in 1903:

> And finally, behold the operators! Two fine fellows in their Sunday best, one tall and blonde, the other with a bushy beard, carrying what seems to be a 118-kilo high-explosive shell. The Mother Superior hurries up to him—What is that, Monsieur?—It is the oxygen cylinder, Sister!—. . . Is there not any danger, Monsieur? And these rubber tubes, and these great boxes, and this sheet, and this, and that? . . . The immediate, crystal-clear explanations of the two employees of the Bonne Presse do not seem to reassure her completely. She believes she has seen an artillery shell or bomb

entering her house, and her fears are increasing:—Assure me, Monsieur . . . Promise me . . . Are you completely sure that there will be no accident? Think of it! 319 orphans, 28 nuns, 11 servants! . . . However, in the refectory, the operators have arranged the tools of their trade, their weapons of war, on a great table. First of all the projection apparatus with its special cap and slide carrier frame, then the blowtorch which functions as a lamp, the bars of lime, some tongs, connectors, dividing tubes for the gas, a gas cut-off tap, the oxygen cylinder with its key, a hammer, a penknife, a ball of string and a box of matches . . . A turn of the key on the taps, a match and . . . *Fiat Lux!* ['Let there be light!']23

Mass-production of magic lanterns

In the nineteenth century the manufacture of magic lanterns and slides reached vast proportions. The lantern became an inexpensive toy, a child's Christmas present. Every optician sold them, and they found their way into the windows of the department stores and novelty shops. French manufacturers, both individual craftsmen and large firms, flooded the market with glorious polychrome lanterns painted with lacquer in glowing colours. These were wonderful to look at, but their lamp and optical components were often second-rate. Two distinct trades rapidly developed: those who produced *magic lanterns* for children, and those who produced *projection lanterns* for adults (teachers, lecturers, professional projectionists, and so on).

This distinction had been in evidence since the eighteenth century, when some opticians offered cheap 'ordinary' lanterns or 'improved' equipment at significantly higher prices. The first of these were not intended for children, but for amateur projectionists and the fathers of less well-off families. The 'toy lantern' proper did not appear until the nineteenth century, with the rapid development of the novelty industry. The start—faint, but real enough—of the industrialization of the lantern might be taken as Robertson's famous court case, when the methods of his phantasmagoria were revealed to the public gaze. Suddenly everyone wanted to acquire a 'box of ghosts', to use Robertson's description. Opticians and metalworkers set up workshops in response to this new fashion. A new classification of the types of equipment began to establish itself: there was the simple lantern, which was quite cheap; the Megascope or Solar Microscope, which were fairly expensive; and the Fantascope-Megascope, which was very costly. This was made quite clear in the catalogue of the Paris optician Lerebours, whose shop in

Place du Pont-Neuf, on the corner of the Quai de l'Horloge, opened in 1809:

> Ordinary magic lanterns: from 18F to 120F. Phantamascopes, or improved magic lanterns, intended for Phantasmagoria effects, including the Megascopic equipment for opaque objects and pictures: from 250F to 500F. Megascopes, from 150F to 400F.[24]

In France during the First Empire, then, any middle-class gentleman could obtain a lantern for his children for as little as 18 Francs. On the other hand the 'Phantamascope', a copy of Robertson's Fantascope, was a true luxury item (and also a bulky one: the Fantascope-Megascope discovered by Thomas Weynants, described in Chapter 6, is no less than 1.8 m in height). François Molteni, who had made Robertson's equipment, had an even more refined sales policy. At the time of the Empire his shop at 11 Rue du Coq-Saint-Honoré offered small lanterns for as little as 4 *sous*, as well as magnificent wooden fantascopes, mounted on wheels, with 'cat's eye' and rackwork lenses. Between these two extremes he sold small toy fantascopes of plated metal at relatively low cost. Some had brass decorations representing the head of Medusa (an image of which Robertson was fond); children could therefore entertain themselves in the drawing-room by recreating the effects of the Phantasmagoria of the Couvent des Capucines.

Only the names of the most famous French lantern manufacturers are usually mentioned: Duboscq, Molteni, Lapierre, and Aubert. But it only takes a quick look through the Paris *Annuaire du Commerce* yearbook to realize that there were many workshops producing the magic lantern between 1800 and 1900. This flourishing trade is a good indication of the popularity of projection in the home; the list given here is far from complete:

> Blazy-Jallifer, tinsmith, 31 Rue Galande (phantasmagoria and polyorama; operated between 1855 and 1858).
> Bouche, optician, 44 Rue de Bretagne (1851).
> F. Boulanger, 78 Faubourg Saint-Denis, then 44 rue Verbois ('inventor and constructor of the Lampadheroscope'; 1848–85).
> Bourgeois, optician, 32 Rue Saint-Roch (magic lantern and diorama; 1851).
> Buron, optician, 10 Rue des Trois-Pavillons and 9 Rue Charlot (phantasmagoria; 1834–56).

Charles Chevalier, optician, Palais-Royal (phantasmagoria, polyorama, solar microscope; 1840–64).

Colin the elder, turner and finisher, 9 Rue Fontaines-du-Temple ('magic lanterns in brass and gilded tinplate'; 1854–8).

Deffez, 34 Rue Saint-Severin ('phantasmagoria mechanisms and chromatropes'; 1864–85).

Dever, optician, 'À la Bonne Foi', 35 Passage Saint-Roch (1863–77).

Drier, 83 Rue Saint-Martin (phantasmagoria, diorama, polyorama, cosmorama; 1854–67).

Dubray, tinsmith, Rue de Breteuil (1819).

François the elder, fancy goods merchant, 10 Rue Simon-le-Franc ('factory for tinplate toys, such as magic lanterns'; 1843).

Goyon the younger, successor to his grandmother the widow Hénault, 16 Rue Saint-Éloi (1847–9).

Charles Larbaud, fancy goods merchant, 134 Boulevard du Temple (magic lanterns in sheet metal, brass and tinplate; 1852–64).

Désiré Lebrun, optician, 4 Rue Greneta (manufacturer of polyorama, diorama, cosmorama, phantasmagoria; 1843–57).

Jules Louisot, painter on glass, 19 Rue d'Anjou ('large factory for magic lanterns, phantasmagoria, and picture plaques for cemeteries'; 1850–73).

Mercier, father-in-law of Louisot, 21 Rue d'Anjou (1850–64).

P. Ringel, fancy goods merchant, 18 Rue des Trois-Pavillons ('a new style of magic lantern'; 1845–55).

Rocheriou, cabinetmaker, 7 Rue Lesdiguières (polyorama, phantasmagoria; 1853–5).

A. Voisin, 81 Rue Vieille du Temple (lantern, polyorama, shows in town; 1852–1900, amalgamated with De Vere in 1900)

Wallet and Morgan, opticians, 73 Quai de l'Horloge (cosmorama, phantasmagoria, magic lantern, inventors in 1840 of a portable home diorama; 1840–5).

The life of these small workshop businesses was sometimes very short. Only two manufacturers really succeeded in monopolizing the market for toy lanterns: Aubert and Lapierre.

Louis Aubert and the Lapierre family

In 1842 Louis Aubert, a simple metalworker (no relation to the film distributor of the same name who operated in the 1910s, 20s and 30s), bought the Paris business of one Darsac and opened a workshop at 3 Rue Greneta, in an area with many toy dealers, to make magic lanterns in plated sheet metal. In 1844 he designed his own fantascopes for children and also began manufacturing cases for liquid measures, spirit levels, moulds for chocolates and lozenges, and scientific equipment. On 28 October 1854 he filed a patent 'for a system of illumination applicable to magic lanterns, phantasmagorias, polyoramas, etc., known as the Aubert system', in which he boasted the merits of a small constant-level oil lamp and two types of magic lantern. The first design was very simple, square in shape, with four tubular feet and a fluted chimney topped by a ring. The second, illustrated in an addition to the patent on 16 January 1855, was much more elegant: the body of the lantern was cylindrical, with decorative images stamped on its sides, trimmed at top and bottom with finely cut railings painted in red lacquer. The slide carrier was mounted directly to the body of the lantern. In 1855 Aubert was awarded a second-class medal at the Paris Exposition Universelle. During the 1860s he turned to the construction of lampascopes and polyoramas. He moved in 1878 to 25 Rue Pastourelle and sold his business to his main competitor, Lapierre, in 1885.

Aubert's lantern designs were rich in decoration, finished in red, gold, green and blue, and much to the taste of the bourgeoisie of the Second Empire. Aubert knew the secret of a very smooth, bright and pure lacquer, which has never been matched since for quality and appearance. He was certainly the most artistic and imaginative nineteenth-century lantern manufacturer, with no equal in the whole of Europe. He expressed himself not only in colours, but also in numerous strange lantern shapes and thousands of surprising decorations; he was the king of metal-stamping. The chubby bodies of Aubert's lanterns carried reliefs of vases of flowers, figures or allegorical images, all picked out by careful hand-painting. His 'Leçon de Choses' (General Science) lantern, decorated with an image of attentive children in eighteenth-century costume surrounding their teacher, was made in several different colours: gilded all over, with a bright red chimney and lens tube, or in finely detailed multicolours.

Aubert's two masterpieces, now much sought by collectors, were the 'Buddha lantern' (a figure of Buddha, or possibly a smiling mandarin, with a fluted hat which formed the chimney, holding the lens tube on his stomach), which existed in several different sizes and colours, and the 'Eiffel Tower lantern' (see Fig. 35), made for the Exposition Universelle held in Paris in 1889. The Eiffel Tower lantern existed in four sizes, with stamped metal representing the girders and the pinnacle, and the

Fig. 35. Louis Aubert's 'Eiffel Tower' lantern, made for the
Paris Exposition Universelle in 1889.
Collection: Laurent Mannoni.

lens tube fixed to one side of the tower. Perhaps Gustave Eiffel, who
later became one of the principal shareholders of the Gaumont film
company, was aware of this strange object. By that time Aubert was no
longer the proprietor of his own workshop, bought by Lapierre four
years previously; perhaps Lapierre asked his rival to remain in charge of
this shop at 25 Rue Pastourelle. Certainly Aubert's name appeared in the
1889 *Annuaire du Commerce*, with the note 'Lapierre successor'.

Auguste Lapierre, originally from Normandy, also began as a journey-
man metalworker. He set up in 1848 at 1 Rue Saint-Paxent, Paris, close
to the Musée des Arts et Métiers (Museum of Arts and Crafts), and set
about shamelessly copying the work of his rival Aubert. On 29 March
1860, he filed a patent 'for a product of the stamping of metal' which
featured the same square lantern described by Aubert in 1854. This
design proved to be the best-seller for both manufacturers, and can still
be found quite easily in antique shops. The Lapierre patent was rather

foolish, only dealing with the feet of the 'Lanterne Carrée' ('square lantern'), as it was called in Lapierre's catalogues:

> In the shops at present there are many portable tin-plate magic lanterns, which provide a pleasant way of passing some time during long winter evenings. Up to the present time the four feet of these magic lanterns have been completely round and without decoration, that is, small cylinders of tin-plate or truncated cones also of tin-plate, fabricated with a hammer on a rounded last. I have considered that it would be possible to make them differently and more ornately, and to this effect I have created moulds arranged for stamping decorated feet in copper, zinc or tin-plate, by means of a ram or pendulum.[25]

In 1866 Lapierre moved to 21 Rue Michel-le-Comte, in the Beaubourg area of Paris. He sold 'magic lanterns, phantasmagorias, lampascopes, copper and tin-plate levels, spirit levels, and surveyor's squares'—the same specialities as Aubert. In 1875, according to Jac Remise's beautiful book *Magie Lumineuse*, Auguste Lapierre retired and his son Édouard Virgile Lapierre took over the business. Édouard launched some new designs, such as the 'Lampadophore' in nickel-plated copper and the polychrome 'Lampadophore with pictures on circular slides', patented on 6 October 1886, which allowed projection of glass discs printed by chromolithography. The Lampadophore discs showed stories such as *Tom Thumb*, *Little Red Riding Hood*, *Puss in Boots*, and so on, with multiple images though without any attempt to portray movement.

Lapierre's lanterns, always less fanciful than those of Aubert, were nonetheless stunning works of popular art. The 'Lampascope Carré', a sort of baroque biscuit-tin sparkling with red, blue, green and gold arabesques, with a red lens tube and lens cap decorated with a lion's head, was their most beautiful design. There was also the coloured 'Lanterne Riche' ('deluxe lantern'), which was very successful, and the 'Lanterne Salon' ('parlour lantern'), supplied in a box and decorated with two large multi-coloured flowers. These objects, if they have been well preserved, still convey some emotional impact. It is easy to imagine the wonder of a nineteenth-century child opening the cardboard box to discover the Lanterne Riche, for example, which was 55 cm high in its large model and decorated in a riot of colours: a truly luxurious present which deserved its adjective 'magic'.

In 1895 Édouard Lapierre decided to expand, and moved his offices to

38 Quai de Jemmapes. A steam-powered factory was built at Lagny, in the Seine-et-Marne département north of Paris, a far cry from Auguste Lapierre's little metal-beating workshop at Rue Saint-Paxent. In this modern factory, two steam engines drove a forest of shafts, lathes, gears, beaters and hammers, to work glass, metal and wood into the required shapes. In a series of furnaces heated to 1,800 degrees, square blocks of Saint-Gobin crystal glass could be cast to form the lenses, which took three days to cool before they were polished. Further on, workers machine-cut copper, nickel, solid and sheet steel, and tin-plate. Planing machines rotating at 4,800 r.p.m. and saws of every shape and size were used to cut walnut, mahogany, and gum-tree wood. The testing shop alone was 40 m in length.

By that time the polychrome magic lanterns only accounted for a small proportion of production, and the Lapierres concentrated more on large triunial projection lanterns, photographic enlargers, and home cinematographs. On 17 April 1902 Édouard Lapierre, then living in Lagny at 31 Rue Saint-Laurent, made his two sons partners in the business. A company was founded under the name Lapierre Frères et Compagnie. This merged in July 1908 with Jules Demaria's photographic and cinematographic camera manufacturing company: a turning point which symbolized the fact that magic lanterns could no longer compete with the cinema on the *grands boulevards*.

Alfred Molteni

The French market for projection lanterns for professional lanternists was dominated by Jules Duboscq and Alfred Molteni. Both also tried to reach the children's market with small cheap designs, but their influence in that area was small. Duboscq and Molteni maintained that they were 'manufacturers of optical and scientific instruments', not tinkers like Aubert and Lapierre. Duboscq, whose catalogues offered all sorts of scientific lanterns and beautiful astronomical or phantasmagorical moving slides, has already been covered in Chapter 9, but Alfred Molteni (1837–1907) deserves some attention here, in view of his nickname 'La projection faite homme' ('projection made human'). The Molteni name has already been mentioned in connection with Robertson's Fantascope, and the 'Wheel of Life' and Choreutoscope slides. Alfred took over the family firm (founded in 1782) in 1872, and moved it to 44 Rue du Château d'Eau from number 62 of the same street. On 17 February 1873 he filed a patent for a lampascope (a type of parlour lantern which fitted on top of a conventional domestic oil-lamp) and an oil-burning 'Lanterne de Famille' ('family lantern'). All his optical devices were fitted with excellent achromatic lenses, unlike those of the tinsmiths, who neglected the lens in favour of external appearance. Molteni supplied schools, colleges, and universities; he was also always ready to travel to project in person at lectures given by great scholars, such as that given by Jules Janssen on astronomy in September 1878.

Duboscq's design of 'Lanterne Photogénique' was very popular with amateurs; Molteni perfected a rival device which was equally practical and popular. This was a lantern mounted on four brass feet (like Duboscq's), with a mahogany base and brass lens tube, illuminated by oxy-hydrogen light or an arc lamp. Two designs were successfully marketed: one with a conical lens, the other, larger and less common, with a huge brass lens tube 57 cm in length, for a projection 'throw' of 50 or 60 m to the screen. The Lumière Brothers used a Molteni lantern of the first design for their Cinématographe shows of 1895.

Lanternists and fairground entertainers alike found much of use in the shop at 44 Rue du Château d'Eau: double or triple polyoramas, from 350 to 900 Francs (in 1892); oxygen generators; gas bags 'in first quality rubber, able to supply the lamp for between one-and-a-half and two hours'; cast iron weights to pressurize the bags; alcohol and ether lamps; screens; microscopes; and so on. The catalogues of photographic and painted slide sets ran to more than 11,000 items. Alfred Molteni retired in 1903, passing his shops to Radiguet and Massiot. He died in 1907, at Tours.

Several other Parisian concerns tried to compete with the two giants Duboscq and Molteni. Among these were Arthur-Léon Laverne, successor to Albert Gasc and Alphonse Charconnet, two small-scale lantern manufacturers who operated between 1869 and 1877. Laverne took over their business in 1878 and launched some quite elaborate designs of lanterns and megascopes. His shop was at 10 Rue de Malte, from 1869 until the turn of the century; it was taken over in 1890 by Clément and Gilmer. On 14 February 1888, Armand and Alfred Richard founded the Lanternes Magiques Automatiques (Automatic Magic Lantern) company, which aimed to sell coin-operated projection equipment for use at fairgrounds and in public parks. The considerably more dynamic Élie-Xavier Mazo set up in 1892 at 10 Boulevard Magenta, where he rapidly became the main supplier for fairground entertainers, in keen competition with Molteni, and for religious users, which was not at all appreciated by the Maison de la Bonne Presse. In 1896 the Bonne Presse launched a projection service managed by Georges-Michel Coissac, a future historian of the cinema. In the year 1905 alone, the

Bonne Presse sold 462 lanterns and 67,513 slides; in 1908, 1,405 lanterns and 183,646 slides. Operating from 5 Rue Bayard, this powerful Catholic machine launched two specialist magazines for lanternists: *Le Fascinateur* in January 1903 and *Les Conférences* ('Lectures') in 1900. Mazo had already been publishing the monthly *Ombres et Lumière* ('Shadows and Light'), a highly technical magazine, since 1895.

Molteni, Laverne, Mazo, and Gaston Guilbert (who made the lanterns sold by the Bonne Presse), along with many other less well-known craftsmen, found the majority of their customers among lecturers on religious and secular educational subjects. In 1896, there were 1,200 popular education societies in France; by 1905 they numbered 2,772. Some venerable institutions grew out of these, some of which used the lantern for many years to come. In 1893 the Ligue de l'Enseignement (League of Education), founded in 1866 by the teacher Jean Macé, organized a 'projection service for the illustration of popular lectures'. Between August 1895 and August 1896, this service sold 477 lanterns and almost 6,000 slides, and hired out 380 lanterns and 48,000 slides. A proportion of this equipment was supplied by Laverne. Another giant of projection, the Musée Pédagogique (Educational Museum), founded in May 1879, used the lantern from 1896 onwards. In 1896–7, it dispatched 8,859 sets of slides; in 1904–5, 32,060 sets with readings. It is easy to see why the competition between lantern manufacturers was so lively, with such a sizeable market at stake.

In Britain, the magic lantern industry flourished even more widely than in France. John Barnes has compiled a list[26] of nineteenth-century lantern manufacturers and dealers, identifying 112 companies in different sectors of the market. Among the most famous of these were Philip Carpenter, W.C. Hughes, John Millikin, Negretti & Zambra, Newton & Co., Perken & Rayment, J.H. Steward, Walter Tyler, and many others. Steward's triunial lanterns, for example, were magnificent creations: three lanterns arranged vertically, entirely in varnished mahogany, with three large brass lens tubes. There was no polychrome toy lantern manufacture in Britain. The French kept hold of that speciality for a long time; some German manufacturers tried to emulate them, though without the same charm.

Industrialization of lantern slide manufacture

So far as slides were concerned, lanternists at the end of the nineteenth century were spoilt for choice: 11,000 subjects were available from Molteni, over 100,000 from Mazo, 30,000 from Eduard Liesegang of

Fig. 36.   French hand-painted moving lantern slide (*c.*1850).
Collection: Laurent Mannoni.

Düsseldorf, and 8,000 from Krüss, who supplied Paul Hoffmann. In London the choice was even wider: 150,000 subjects in the catalogue of W. & F. Newton, 200,000 in that of E.G. Wood. The majority of these were photographic slides, but there were also plenty of mass-produced printed subjects, chromolithographs, and moving slides.

The mass-production of slides was first perfected by Philip Carpenter (1776–1833). Originally based in Birmingham, he practised his trade as an optician in London at 24 Regent Street between 1810 and 1826. After his death in 1833, the business was taken over by his sister Mary, in partnership with William Westley. Around 1821 Carpenter launched a new design of lantern known as the 'Phantasmagoria', which was highly successful. This was a very solid device in black sheet metal, with a long chimney bent at its midpoint, and achromatic and condensing lenses of the highest quality. Inside was an oil lamp with a reflector. Carpenter also sold a double 'Phantasmagoria' lantern with a rotating cat's-eye shutter for dissolving views. In 1823, another landmark in the world of the lanternist, Carpenter published his book *Elements of Zoology: Being a Concise Account of the Animal Kingdom, According to the System of Linnaeus*.

The book provided explanatory text for a set of fifty-six slides made and sold by Carpenter, showing mammals (twenty-four slides), birds (seven), amphibians (four), fish (five), insects (eight) and worms (eight). The circular glass slides were fixed in holes in a long wooden frame, held in place by a metal ring, with the title 'Copper-Plate Slider' stamped into the wood.

This was the first attempt at mass-production of lantern slides. It was also the first time that a set of slides was put on sale with an accompanying explanatory booklet. To be able to reproduce his zoological series as many times as he wanted, Carpenter engraved all the lines and details of each drawing on a copper printing plate. This was then coated with an ink mixture formed of black paint and varnish. Surplus ink was scraped off to leave it only in the hollows of the engraving, and then a thin adhesive sheet was used to transfer the ink onto a sheet of glass, which was fired at low temperature in a kiln. The outline drawings were then coloured by hand by professional artists, who would also add a black background to highlight the images in the manner of phantasmagoria slides. The result was wonderful, since the outlines of the pictures were extremely thin. The process could not really be considered as true automation, since the painter's hand remained essential for applying the colours, but Carpenter could now produce even the most complicated subjects in any required quantity. The 'Copper-Plate Sliders' sold very well. Carpenter also supplied scientific sets, astronomical views, portraits of the kings and queens of England, 'humorous subjects', scenes from the Bible, and so on. His method of printing was taken up by many European manufacturers, in particular Lapierre.

Auguste Lapierre began producing sets of slides around the 1850s. His painting studio produced rectangular slides bound at the edges with green paper. The drawings were first engraved on copper, following Carpenter's method, and then filled in with colours. From an artistic point of view they do not compare with Carpenter's miniature works of art. But Carpenter's work was often academic (except for his 'humorous subjects', which displayed a savage wit); Lapierre's advantage lay in knowing how to capture everyday life in his slides, which offer an exceptional documentary insight into nineteenth-century life.

Lapierre's output can be divided into three periods. In the first, the printed drawings were quite simple, but full of life and humour. The bright colours were applied with great care, and overall the impression was of a hand-crafted product. Then, probably around 1860, output was increased: the drawings featured more detail, decoration and text, but

Fig. 37. Comic lantern slides by Lapierre, late nineteenth century.
Collection: Cinémathèque Française, Musée du Cinéma.

also began to show the signs of automation. The painter's hand became much more hurried, the colours were less subtle, less bright, and over-lapped the printed outlines. Finally, around 1900, the Lapierre company took the German route and produced chromolithographic slides, which were artistically quite disappointing.

Lapierre slides of the first period offer little scenes taken from life in the streets of Paris: sellers of entertainment, coconuts, vegetables, and plaster figures all appear (see Fig. 37). A huge woman in a red check dress is captioned 'Area of les Halles'; a violin player is chased by an angry dog; a slide entitled 'Paris under water' shows bourgeois citizens wading unhappily through water, beneath large umbrellas. Sometimes subjects are mixed on the same slide without apparent reason: a sorcerer finds himself next to a fat woman frightened by a mouse. But most of the time, the slides present a short narrative in three or four images: horned demons attack young girls in the street; a burglar attempts to break into a building, but the 'noble guard dog' barks and wakes a frightened bourgeois couple; a barber experiences a quite Buñuelesque 'temptation', preparing to shave a client, but finally cutting his head off with his 'sharp razor'.

One slide shows God in the clouds, the sun with a child's face, and the moon surrounded by stars, which are shown with smiling faces (this image, which Méliès would have enjoyed, was published in several different forms). There were also some delightful domestic scenes: a father taking his naked baby in his arms, or a series of family portraits. Sometimes a slide was completely covered in images, leaving scarcely any background space—for example, in a forest thick with well-drawn trees, two robbers await the passage of two fellows. There were also the traditional 'frights' for children: a hideous rascal, a whip in his hand, carrying a weeping child in a basket on his back and wearing a dunce's cap, or an ogre, with red eyes and a large cruel mouth, whipping another child clamped under his arm, while the ogre's wife waits with a large sack. Around the 1850s Lapierre illustrated the fairy tales *Tom Thumb* and *Bluebeard*, in sets of six or twelve slides. He also rapidly established himself as a specialist in the famous children's tales of Charles Perrault (1628–1703).

The slides of Lapierre's second period display some narrative features which suggest the language of the cinema. The Lapierre studio used 'close-ups', 'medium shots', 'establishing shots', and long 'pans'. Framed texts were interspersed between the images, suggesting the explanatory 'intertitles' of the silent cinema. A desire for cutting and *mise-en-scène* seems evident in the way that stories were presented for the screen. The slide painters, it should be remembered, had to construct a narrative in six or twelve slides, often with two images per slide, that is twelve or twenty-four images. To judge from the limited number of such slides which survive, the artists were obliged to use an early form of montage, which was often highly elliptical (this can also be detected in slide sets from other countries). The projection of long stories by the magic lantern certainly influenced—more or less subconsciously—the first cinema practitioners, who were also confronted with a need for conciseness since they had to deliver their scenario in no more than 50 or 100 m of film.

The twelve-slide set *Beauty and the Beast*, produced by Lapierre in the 1870s, took twenty-four images to present a gripping version of the tale written by Jeanne Marie Leprince de Beaumont in 1757. On the first slide the main characters are skilfully introduced: he in all his ugliness, she in all her beauty. On the following slide Beauty has a nightmare, in which the Beast appears to her in a dream-cloud. Dream sequences were very popular with audiences and lanternists, who would sometimes create the dream image with a dissolving view or a superimposition. Numerous early films borrowed this same type of apparition from the projectionists of the nineteenth century. One curious view shows Beauty sitting pensively. Behind her, framed like a painting, is an image of her father in tears. The accompanying text reads 'Beauty sees her father who is sad not to see her any more'. This double representation in the same image was also adopted in numerous early silent films, for instance in *Histoire d'un Crime* ('Story of a Crime') by Ferdinand Zecca, a Pathé film of 1902. The subsequent slides of *Beauty and the Beast* show a dramatic progression, with a rapid appearance of Beauty's family home, the intervention of a fairy, a pathetic and sensitive representation of the Beast, who on the penultimate slide throws himself at the knees of the young woman. Finally there is a happy ending:

No. 23 In the place of the Beast, Beauty sees a handsome prince at her knees.
No. 24 Then they saw at the door of the Palace all their families who had come to their wedding.

One of the most advanced sets produced by Lapierre (some others were far too elliptical in their narration), which can almost be seen as a very well-edited short film, is entitled *La Ferme* ('The Farm'), a set of twelve slides 6 cm by 23 cm, twenty-four images in total, produced during the Second Empire. The first six slides illustrate everyday life in a small provincial village, where 'the air was very good'. A general view of the farm is followed by introduction of the characters: young Julien, his foster brother, the farmer and his workers. Then there are several views of work on the farm: feeding the pigs, chickens and turkeys, the tasks 'performed with much care and activity', milking the cows for 'good warm milk', gathering cherries 'which are so sweet and plentiful this year', making butter, and so on. The twelfth image presents a dramatic break, when Julien, 'the beloved son of the farm', leaves to become a soldier. Life carries on all the same, with the apple harvest, the arrest of 'two terrible robbers', and Sunday Mass. Next we follow the infantryman Julien in Morocco, covering himself in glory by capturing a rebel flag. Image 23 is another dream vision, in which 'brave Julien dreams of his mother, who shows him his grandfather's cross', with the mother appearing in a cloud. Once again, the story ends happily, with the soldier returning to the farm in the final image.

This set is far from primitive in its narration. The 'cutting' is quite subtle, between two overlapping storylines and two different locations. All the same, *La Ferme* is quite exceptional in Lapierre's output. *Little Jacques*, for example, features a quite interesting narrative style, but with some over-long gaps which would require quite a detailed oral explanation of the story from the lanternist: the 'intertitles' alone are not enough to make the story comprehensible. The presence of a narrator, in this particular case, was therefore essential.

Other titles in the Lapierre catalogue included: *The Bluebird*; *The Daughter of Madame Angot*; *Around the World in Eighty Days*; *Mother Michel*; *Riquet à la Houpe* (a fable by Perrault in which a prince learns the relative values of physical beauty and intelligence); *Robinson Crusoe*; *Paul and Virginie*; *The Prodigal Son*; *The Wandering Jew*; *Aladin or the Wonderful Lamp*; *The War of 1870*; *The White Cat*; *Peau d'Âne* (another Perrault fable dealing with princely matrimonial problems); *William Tell*; *Punchinello*; *Little Red Riding Hood*; *Don Quixote*; *Goldilocks*; *Monsieur de la Palisse*; *The Postilion of Longjumeau*; the *Jean* series ('*J'empeste, j'enrage, j'empiffre*'—literally 'I stink, I pester, I stuff myself', with a play on words); biblical, zoological, and historical scenes; landscapes; clever and comical devilish scenes; and so on. *The Temptation of Saint Antony*, which would have fascinated Flaubert or Méliès, was a succession of fantastic phantasmagorical scenes. It included numerous spelling mistakes, and some images which were so devilish that fathers perhaps edited them out of their family shows (the devils were depicted completely naked). There was also a famous set illustrating *Geneviève de Brabant* in six slides of twelve images, produced in several different

Fig. 38. Detail from a Lapierre lantern slide showing the story of Geneviève de Brabant. Collection: Cinémathèque Française, Musée du Cinéma.

formats (see Fig. 38). This beautiful set, which once again included a dream sequence, made a strong impression on the mind of the young Marcel Proust. References to projection are a noticeable motif in Proust's work, for example the well-known description in *Swann's Way* of the images projected by his 'lampascope':

> His horse stepping uncertainly, Golo, filled with a terrible plan, emerged from the small triangular forest which wrapped the slope of a hill in a sombre green, and charged forward towards the castle of poor Geneviève de Brabant.[28]

In France, Lapierre held a virtual monopoly over cheap sets of painted slides, but there were other manufacturers too. Lefranc, of 11 Rue des Batignolles, Paris, produced very attractive scenes, many of which survive in the Bibliothèque Nationale, since he deposited paper prints of all the copper-engraved images there in January 1844. Lefranc illustrated the conquest of Algeria, the fables of La Fontaine, the tales of Perrault, and so on. The slides produced by this artist are very fine, and his devilish scenes very amusing.

Unfortunately very little is known about the makers of moving slides. Molteni, Duboscq, Mazo and many other manufacturers sold high-quality mechanical slides, but the names of the craftsmen who actually made them are unknown. Jac Remise has discovered one very talented slide painter named Desch, who followed Lapierre's method for printing his drawings in quantity, but like Carpenter took enormous care over the painting and the colours used. He began his trade in 1853, to judge from the Paris *Annuaire de Commerce*: 'Desch, artist and painter for the polyorama, phantasmagoria, orders sent to the provinces, 22 Rue Saint-Antoine.' In 1863 he moved his workshop to 69 Rue de la Roquette, and in 1866 to 35 Rue du Chemin-Vert. He seems to have had very itchy feet, and moved on to Avenue Parmentier, then to Rue Sedaine, then Boulevard Richard Lenoir, and on to Rue Saint-Paul. In 1914 he (or more probably his son) was still operating, at 40 Rue de Turenne. Other talented slide painters included Mallet, of 160 and 173 Rue du Faubourg Saint-Martin (1863–7); J. Louisot; Mercier; A. Fillot of 15 Faubourg Saint-Denis (1854–7); Lamiche and Augé of 92 Rue de Bondy (1863-7); and Mesnages of 7 Tour-Passy (1884).

The magic lantern therefore provided a viable living for tinsmiths, opticians, artists, and lanternists: it was a prosperous industry supporting thousands of workers. Innumerable households, in every part of society, had a simple tin-plate lantern or a glorious polychrome lampascope. The Comtesse d'Agoult, better known under her nom-de-plume Daniel Stern, owned one in 1843; the journalist Eugène Chavette, a friend of Henri Rochefort (a journalist and policitician who founded the weekly paper *La Lanterne* in 1868), entertained his friends in 1867 with pornographic shows; Charles Lutwidge Dodgson, better known as Lewis Carroll, gave shows for children in December 1856, with a lantern supplied by Watkin and Hill. At the start of the nineteenth century, the young Honoré de Balzac watched lantern shows, as did the young Charles Dickens. George Sand used one for her marionette shows at Nohant. In 1801, the scientist Ampère showed his son an illuminated *Gargantua*, and much later other scholars such as Louis Pasteur and Marie Curie used the lantern for more serious scientific purposes. No less an institution than the Sorbonne University held regular shows from 1864 onwards. It became a sign of good taste, in aristocratic circles, to offer a magic lantern show. In 1828, the four-year-old Duke of Montpensier, son of King Louis-Philippe, received a lantern for Christmas from the future King Charles X. Even Napoléon III, in spite of his low opinion of Abbé Moigno, gave lantern shows for his son, organized by an officer of engineers. And, if one can believe Luchino Visconti's 1972 film *Ludwig*, even Louis II of Bavaria owned a lantern.

PART FOUR

Inscribing Movement

12

The Passage of Venus and the Galloping Horse

We come now to the last room of a cabinet of curiosities put together over the course of centuries. It is filled with bizarre equipment and the portraits of inventors line the walls in amazing numbers: the years between 1874 and 1895 saw a huge wealth of research. The cinematographic process towards which Ducos du Hauron unconsciously directed his efforts was finally brought into being by Marey and Edison, while the problem of animated projection was magnificently solved by Émile Reynaud, then by the Lumière brothers, among others. The process of invention which had begun such a long time before finally came to a chaotic climax, though in 1895, when the train finally arrived at the station, several drivers were at the controls. This was only natural: there was no single-handed inventor of the technique, spectacle and art of cinematography, but a long chain made up of many generations of researchers, all dependent on each other.

Jules Janssen and the photographic revolver

The final twenty years of this long history began under the sign of Venus—not the Greek goddess Aphrodite, but the planet also known as the 'evening star'. This is more than just a symbolic image for the irresistible attraction of researchers towards the same goal. A French astronomer, Pierre-Jules-César Janssen (1824–1907), succeeded in photographing the different phases of the passage of Venus between the sun and the earth, an extremely rare phenomenon which only occurs twice in a century. The passage of Venus across the solar disc was eagerly awaited by astronomers, since it provided a way of establishing the parallax of the sun and therefore its true distance from earth. The previous observations had been on 5 June 1761 and 3 June 1769. An army of scientists was therefore mobilized across the whole surface of the globe. At the moment of the passage, Venus would pass across the disc of the sun as a perfectly circular small black speck, with a uniform east–west motion.

As early as 1849 a French astronomer, Hervé Faye, had suggested photographing the passage of stars across the meridian. But at that time, the daguerreotype would not allow the taking of successive images of the same movement. In the 1860s, the scientific world prepared feverishly for the next passages of Venus, calculated to take place on 9 December 1874 and 6 December 1882. Britain, the United States, Italy and France decided to mount scientific expeditions to observe and photograph this phenomenon. France alone organized six missions, comprising around 100 scientists in total, to Campbell Island in the Southern Ocean, St Paul Island in the Indian Ocean, Noumea in the southern Pacific, Beijing, Saigon and Yokohama. Jules Janssen, member of the Institut Français, led the expedition to Japan together with Tisserand, director of the observatory at Toulouse, and Picard, a naval lieutenant.

All the French expeditions were equipped with the most precise scientific instruments and photographic cameras with silver plates. But Janssen had also designed a device known as the 'Photographic Revolver' which allowed a series of successive pictures to be taken at regular short intervals. Using this, the whole passage of Venus across the sun could be captured for posterity on a single plate. This method seemed so promising that the British expeditions also adopted Janssen's instrument, and it was used long afterwards for studying eclipses of the sun.

On 17 March 1873, at the Académie des Sciences, Janssen explained the principles of this harmless revolver, based loosely on Plateau's Phenakistiscope. He had designed a system with a rotating disc coated in photosensitive emulsion, whose circumference would be revealed and exposed at successive intervals by an intermittent electrical mechanism. Janssen expected that one sensitive disc could receive 180 microscopic pictures. But the construction of the instrument was not easy, and the final design included a number of modifications.

Janssen went first to Eugène Deschiens, of 123 Boulevard Saint-Germain, Paris, the precision engineer who already constructed Cook and Bonelli's Photobioscope in 1867. Deschiens told Janssen that he would have to give up the electricity and instead built him a prototype with a spring-loaded mechanism, now on display at the Musée du Cinéma in Paris. However, according to Janssen, 'the apparatus was not free of vibrations which were harmful to the clarity of the images'.[1] Dissatisfied, the astronomer then approached the engineer and clock-maker Antoine Rédier (1817–92), of 8 Cour des Petites-Écuries. It was Rédier who constructed the final version, which can now be seen at the museum of the CNAM.

The revolver Janssen used in Japan could capture forty-eight successive images in about seventy-two seconds (the exposure time could be adjusted). Robust in its design, this machine marked the true beginning of chronophotography, already outlined by Du Mont and Ducos du Hauron. At the same time it did not have any significant future, since the sensitive disc (which was 18.5 cm in diameter with a central circular perforation of 9.5 cm) could only record a limited number of images. The Daguerre emulsion could capture the passage of Venus across the sun, but was definitely not sensitive enough to capture successive 'instantaneous' images of humans or animals in motion. Janssen was obliged to use the Daguerre process because of the relatively long image-taking period: a wet collodion plate would have dried quickly and lost its sensitivity.

The instrument was self-contained, and produced the series of images itself without intervention from the operator. The circular plate was inserted in the revolver, and the operator pressed a release pin which activated the clockwork mechanism constructed by Rédier. The mecha-nism drove two metal discs, one carrying the plate and the other having twelve regularly spaced apertures like those of a Phenakistiscope disc. This shutter disc made a complete rotation in eighteen seconds, but the plate disc moved four times more slowly and took seventy-two seconds to complete a rotation. The plate disc was driven by a Maltese Cross gear mechanism, causing it to turn, then stop briefly. The short stoppages were synchronized to occur as one of the apertures passed in front of a small window formed in a fixed plate between the two rotating discs.

The passage of Venus across the sun took place on 9 December 1874, in a year of terrible weather in Japan. Jules Janssen and his wife, on the ship *Ava*, endured a terrible typhoon in the bay of Hong Kong on the night of 22–23 September, which cost thousands of lives in the city. Janssen arrived in Yokohama on 3 October, but the climatic conditions were too poor to allow any observation of the sky. On 24 October, he moved all his equipment (twenty-four crates) to Nagasaki, where an American expedition directed by Davidson had already set up. Around a hundred navvies cleared the ground on a tall hill named Kompira-Yama, and another observation post was established at Kobe. Throughout November the team worked on the instruments. Picard was in charge of the photographic camera, along with Arens, while d'Almeida took charge of the photographic revolver, together with Tisserand and Janssen. Some days before the fateful date of 9 December everything was going very badly, with violent storms and blasts of wind which swept away the equipment. But on 9 December, the weather became 'quite good, although the sky was slightly hazy. . . Providence had allowed, in the middle of this deplorable period, a short respite in our favour',[2] as Janssen put it. The revolver was set up. Its lens was trained on a small mirror fixed to a heliostat (a device following the movement of the sun), which reflected the image of Venus and the sun. A disc was exposed. On 10 December Janssen set a telegram from Nagasaki to Paris.

> Passage observed at Nagasaki and Kobe, interior contacts without ligaments with photographic revolver, some clouds during passage. Venus observed on corona before contact, demonstrating existence of corona.[3]

This photographic proof of the passage of Venus in front of the corona which surrounds the sun, which is only visible during total eclipse, was very important for Janssen, since it proved that the corona was not a refraction effect of the Earth's atmosphere, but a portion of the sun itself. For Janssen, it was a scientific triumph. The revolver had allowed him to prove one of his theories. Before leaving Kobe and Kompira-Yama, he had two small commemorative pyramids built.

Having taken some further successive images of an eclipse of the sun at Singapore on 6 April 1874, Janssen returned to Paris in June. On 13 February 1875 Camille Flammarion published a highly detailed celebratory article on the Janssen expedition in the journal *La Nature*. In August, the machines and pictures were exhibited in Paris at the Société de Géographie, and then in 1876 at the Palais de l'Industrie:

> We saw at the Photographic Exhibition the pictures of the passage of Venus. One can very clearly make out the black spot, the image of Venus projected onto the sun, in all the principal and inter-mediate positions. The clarity and precision of these prints are encouraging for the future.[4]

In fact, the images were not of very high quality. A plate representing an artificial image of the passage of Venus made around July 1874, preserved in the collections of the Société Française de Photographie, is quite foggy. The process was still a long way from Marey's precision chronophotographic images, and a thousand miles from the wonderful *Éclipse de Soleil en Pleine Lune* ('Eclipse of the Sun at Full Moon'), the 1907 Méliès film. But it was Janssen's system which was the most remarkable feature of this attempt. The astronomer was already imagining other uses for his device when he addressed the Société Française de Photographie on 1 April 1876:

> The property of the revolver, to be able to produce automatically a numerous series of closely spaced images as required of a rapidly changing phenomenon, permits us to approach some interesting questions of physiological mechanism relating to the walk, flight and other movements of animals . . . One can imagine, for example, all the interest which it will have for the still obscure question of the mechanism of flight, to obtain a series of photographs reproducing the different aspects of the wing during this action. The principal difficulty at present arises from the slowness of our sensitive materials, in consideration of the very short exposure times which these images demand; but science will certainly overcome these difficulties.[5]

The physiology of movement had concerned scientific and artistic minds for many years. A camera like Janssen's, if it were fast enough, might for example solve the problem of the galloping horse, often represented by painters in a very inaccurate fashion (for example, Géricault's *Epsom Derby* of 1821). As the physiologist Étienne-Jules Marey commented in 1878:

> The gallop is generally the attitude whose representation leaves most to be desired. Leaving aside the present period, I will only refer to the paintings of the last two or three centuries which appear before our eyes all the time. Horses which are supposed to be galloping are represented in a sort of reared-up position, standing on their two hind legs and raising their front legs to equal heights . . . This synchronism of right and left limbs does not exist . . . It is certain, in our own times, that artists make great efforts to represent the horse with accuracy and that many among them succeed. But I cannot allow myself to appreciate the work of my contemporaries.[6]

Janssen's revolver was still too slow and insensitive to capture images of a horse passing at full gallop, as Janssen himself acknowledged. It was the Englishman Eadweard Muybridge and the Frenchman Étienne-Jules Marey who were to succeed in this scientific and technical feat.

Eadweard Muybridge and the photography of motion

The first true photographic analysis of animal movement was achieved by Edward James Muggeridge (1830–1904), known as Eadweard Muybridge, whose work has been studied extensively.[7] Born at Kingston-upon-Thames in England, Muggeridge emigrated to the United States in 1852, where he changed his name to Muggridge, then Muygridge, and finally (around 1869) to Muybridge. He set up business in San Francisco, dealing in the British publications of the London Printing and Publishing Co. Muybridge was initiated in photography by a New York 'Daguerreotypist', Silas Selleck, and in 1867 took a series of beautiful photographs of the Yosemite Valley which made him famous. In August 1870, Muybridge was advertising his services in the press:

> Private Residence [*sic*], Horses, Monuments, Ships. etc., are photographed in the best manner by HELIOS' Flying Studio, Muybridge, 121 Montgomery Street.[8]

It is noticeable that photographs of horses were already one of his specialities.

In 1871 Muybridge married Flora Shallcross Stone, who was then 20 years old and already divorced. In April 1872, at Sacramento, he met Leland Stanford (1824–93), a former Governor of California and President of the Central Pacific Railroad. Stanford was a vastly wealthy man with a passion for horses. He was the proud owner of one of the most famous trotters of the time, a small nervous brown horse named 'Occident', to whom the cinema owes a great deal, as we shall see.

The beginnings of the collaboration between Muybridge and Stanford are quite unclear. The American historian Terry Ramsaye claimed in 1926[9] that a bet between Stanford and a financier named James R. Keene was the origin of the photographic research on Occident. Stanford had claimed that at one point in its gallop, a horse had all its legs clear of the ground, and Keene wagered $25,000 that this theory was false. Muybridge was therefore hired to photograph the galloping horse. This version of events is not based on any document or precise testimony; although it has been repeated many times, several American historians have rejected it.

It has also been suggested that Marey's work on animal motion in France had intrigued Stanford so deeply that he employed Muybridge to verify it. Marey claimed that not only did a galloping quadruped briefly have all four feet off the ground, but also that for a split second it was supported by one front hoof alone. Marey's first observations were made without the aid of photography, with measuring instruments to which we will return later. His fundamental work *La Machine Animale* was published in France in 1873, and in Britain the following year (as *Animal Mechanism*) but the first photographs of Occident had already been taken around April 1872.

In a letter written on 17 February 1879 to Gaston Tissandier, editor of the French journal *La Nature*, Muybridge mentioned the influence which Marey had over the American experiments:

> Please be so kind as to pass on to Professor Marey the assurance of my high regard, and tell him that reading his famous work on animal mechanism inspired in Governor Stanford the initial idea of the possibility of solving the problem of locomotion with the aid of photography. Mr. Stanford consulted me in this regard and, at his request, I resolved to assist him in his quest.[10]

Was Muybridge referring here to his second period of research, which began in 1877 after an interruption of five years? When the first attempts at Stanford's request were made in 1872, all that was required was to capture an 'instantaneous' view of a galloping horse; as we have seen, this was a popular ambition at the time. But the second research period from 1877 was concerned with capturing motion in its entirety. There is no doubt that these new experiments by Muybridge and Stanford on 'animal locomotion' were inspired by the work of Marey.

Stanford's curiosity might also have been fired by certain phenakistiscope discs, for example one published by Delaunnois of Paris around 1833–40. This showed ten successive phases of the gallop of a horse, drawn by hand. Some very fine hand-painted discs also survive which were painted by Lieutenant L. Wachter of the Seventh Regiment of Cuirassiers in the French Army. Wachter had written a book entitled *Aperçus Équestres* ('Equestrian Insights') in 1862, in which he discussed the question of the galloping horse. To illustrate his theory, he created a phenakistiscope disc painted on card, showing the 'Various phases of the gallop in triple time subjected to the test of the Phenakistiscope'.[11] The ten illustrations of the horse in motion were very well executed, and almost identical to the pictures which Muybridge was to produce in 1878.

To judge from an article in the *Daily Alta California* of 7 April 1873, Stanford's enthusiastic interest in horses in general and Occident in particular is enough to explain the wealthy governor's engagement of

Muybridge. Marey, Wachter, and the fanciful story of the bet are not mentioned:

> Quick Work.
> Governor Stanford's fondness for his trotter is well known . . . and he is confident that time will put the brown beauty where he belongs—at the head of the list of trotters. The Governor is a judge of the points of a horse, too, and he appreciated the beauty of movement of 'Occident' as highly as the speed he developed in his trials; and appreciating this beauty of movement, he wanted his friends abroad to participate with him in the contemplation of the trotter 'in action', but did not exactly see how he was to accomplish it until a friend suggested that Mr. E.J. Muybridge be employed to photograph the animal while trotting. No sooner said than done. Mr. Muybridge was sent for and commissioned to execute the task, though the artist said he believed it to be impossible; still he would make the effort. All the sheets in the neighbourhood of the stable were procured to make a white ground to reflect the object, and 'Occident' was after a while trained to go over the white cloth without flinching; then came the question how could an impression be transfixed of a body moving at the rate of thirty-eight feet to the second. The first experiment of opening and closing the camera on the first day left no result; the second day, with increasing velocity on opening and closing, a shadow was caught.[12]

Muybridge finally managed to construct an extremely fast shutter. At the aperture of the camera, which had two lenses, he positioned two vertical plates with a spring release such that they would slide together very rapidly, leaving an aperture of one-eighth of an inch between them for 1/500th of a second. The negative (which has not survived) showed Occident in motion. The likeness was perfect, said the journalist: 'This is considered a great triumph as a curiosity in photography—a horse's picture taken while going thirty-eight feet in a second!'[13]

This was such a novel technical achievement (even though Du Mont had already claimed to have seen a photograph of a galloping horse in 1861) that European photographic circles were at first incredulous. Dr Phipson, the English correspondent of the *Moniteur de la Photographie*, wrote an article entitled 'The Picture of a Galloping Horse' on 1 June 1873. He appeared somewhat sceptical, the more so since the operation of Muybridge's camera seemed incomprehensible to him. On 15 June 1873, Dr Phipson took it all back: without a doubt, photography of movement could not exist:

One of my friends told me yesterday that the editor of the *British Journal* had taken seriously the extract from the San Francisco newspaper referring to the method of photographing a *galloping horse* which I gave in my last letter; according to the *British Journal*, one should not believe that this thing is possible. Bah! No, Mr. Jeremiah Dawson, in reproducing this passage I desired simply to present a specimen of American humour, and it is appropriate to apply a remark of my late lamented friend Babinet, of the Institut: *I am not as stupid as you appear to be.*[14]

It is quite clear that Muybridge was ahead of his contemporaries. Faced with such a wonder, they were astonished, complaining almost of charlatanism. However the photograph of Occident in full gallop was only the beginning of Stanford and Muybridge's work, which soon took an even more spectacular turn. Instead of capturing a single image of movement, they set out to take a whole succession. The horse would be captured in every position of its movement over a given period of time.

The American progress of the invention was interrupted by a violent interlude. On 16 October 1874 Muybridge discovered that his wife had been having an affair with one George Harry Larkyns. Ironically, it was a photograph which revealed the bad news: a portrait of his son Florado, born on 15 April 1874, on which his wife had unwisely inscribed 'Little Harry', indicating that Florado was not his own son. Muybridge took his Smith and Wesson revolver and went to visit Larkyns on 17 October. Like a character in a John Ford or Howard Hawks western, Muybridge aimed his gun at his wife's lover and announced coldly: 'My name is Muybridge and I have a message for you from my wife.' He fired and Larkyns fell mortally wounded.

Muybridge was arrested, but eventually acquitted on 5 February 1875. He returned to photography, making some truly stunning panoramic views of San Francisco. Stanford stood by him, and around the middle of 1877 asked Muybridge to resume work on the studies of Occident. Perhaps excited by Marey's theories on 'animal mechanism', Stanford demanded much higher photographic precision—the instantaneous view of 1872, in spite of all the praise it received, had actually been of quite mediocre quality. On 2 August 1877 Muybridge sent a new photograph to the *Daily Alta California*:

The exposure was made while 'Occident' was trotting past me at the rate of 2:27, accurately timed, or thirty-six feet a second, about forty feet distant, the exposure of the negative being less than the one-thousandth part of a second . . . The picture has been

retouched, as is customary at this time with all first-class photographic work, for the purpose of giving a better effect to the details.
In every other respect, the photograph is exactly as it was made in
the camera.[15]

The method was the same as in 1872, but the speed of the shutter was
greatly increased because it was operated electrically. However the image
did not satisfy the purists: it was said that John Koch, a San Francisco
artist, had retouched it rather too much—was it truly a photograph, or
simply a painting? The 'Automatic Electric Photograph' on albumen
paper was in fact a photographic copy of a painting by Koch, made after
a photograph by Muybridge. There were complaints of trickery, and
Stanford himself was not satisfied with the result. On 11 August 1877,
the *Daily Alta California* explained that Stanford now wanted 'a series of
views taken to show the step at all its stages'.[16]

Muybridge received his patron's instructions and ordered twelve
cameras with Dallmeyer lenses from London. When they arrived, said
the journalist, Occident would pass in front of the twelve lenses, which
would be opened successively by an electrical control system. Everything
was already planned in August 1877, but Stanford and Muybridge had to
wait nearly a year until 11 June 1878 to successfully produce the first set
of 'moving photographs'. A small area of Stanford's ranch at Palo Alto,
California was requisitioned for Muybridge's experiments. On 11 June
1878, Occident remained in his stall. It was another trotter named Abe
Edington, driven by Charles Marvin, who was given the task of running
in front of the array of cameras.

Muybridge explained his process in patents filed in his sole name in
Britain (9 July 1878, 'Apparatus for Taking Instantaneous Photographs
of Objects in Motion'), the United States (27 June and 11 July, 'Improvement in the Method and Apparatus for Photographing Objects in
Motion'), Germany, and France (17 July, 'Improvements in the Taking
of Instantaneous Photographs of Objects in Motion').[17] The British
patent stated the aims of the project clearly:

> The principal object in view is to take photographic views of horses
> that are moving rapidly under speed, in order to determinate the
> posture, position, and relation of their limbs in different portions of
> their step or stride.[18]

It was first necessary to lay out a track for the horse to run on. On one
side of the track, the twelve cameras were arranged in a long shed. On

the other side, facing the cameras, a large white sheet was stretched along a fence about 10 m long, 2.5 m high, and inclined backwards at about 60 degrees.

> It is preferable to paint this background white, so that the horse will stand out in better relief, and his position and posture more distinctly shewn in the photograph.
>
> Near the bottom of this background is painted or otherwise delineated several lines or stripes at different calculated spaces apart, so that the distance of the horse's feet from the ground at the instant the photograph is taken will be shewn upon the picture by the position of the feet with relation to the lines.[19]

Muybridge then stretched threads of cotton or silk across the track, in positions corresponding to the numbers on the screen and connected to the shutter mechanisms of the cameras. The horse's hooves would break the threads one by one, which would release electro-magnets to actuate the two vertical plates of the shutters. As the plates passed each other, they created a small aperture (for 1/2000th of a second, according to Muybridge). In that split second the image of the galloping horse was exposed onto the collodion plate in the camera. And since there were twelve cameras, Muybridge would obtain twelve different sequential pictures of Abe Edington in every phase of his movement.

Muybridge organized press conferences and invited journalists to Palo Alto to watch the 'taking of views' of a mare named Sallie Gardner. The press were highly enthusiastic. On 19 October 1878, the *Scientific American* devoted its cover to the science of 'the horse's motions' and reproduced drawings of six pictures of a horse walking and nine more of another horse trotting. The magazine indicated that the reader could purchase these photographs from Muybridge at Morse's Gallery, 417 Montgomery Street, San Francisco (each print cost $1.50). It also suggested viewing the successive pictures through the slots of a zoetrope. In 1882, Muybridge published zoetrope strips of galloping horses, which were sold in Paris by Alfred Molteni, whose name and address appear in one of Muybridge's notebooks.

In June 1879 W.B. Tegetmeier, editor of the London periodical *The Field*, had the idea of marketing Muybridge's pictures as a strip for the Reynaud Praxinoscope (not for the zoetrope, as Robert Haas states in his book on Muybridge). The strip, measuring 5.5 cm by 65 cm, sold for one shilling, and carried the wording: 'The Gallop, from "Tegetmeier on the Paces of the Horse" arranged by the Author for the Praxinoscope'. The drawings showed twelve silhouettes of a galloping horse, and were finely detailed. Three examples of this remarkable document, which links the American work of Muybridge to that of the Frenchman Reynaud, are known to exist today: one in Muybridge's scrapbook, preserved at Kingston-upon-Thames; another in the splendid collection of David Robinson; and the third in the collection of the author.

In France, Tissandier's weekly *La Nature* was the first to publish several series of photogravure pictures, in its issue of 14 December 1878; *L'Illustration* followed with an article on 25 January 1879. These showed a horse walking in harness (Abe Edington, 106 m per minute, six pictures); at a half-gallop (Mahomet, 200 m/min, six pictures); trotting in harness (Abe Edington, 715 m/min, twelve pictures); the same again (Occident, 727 m/min, twelve pictures); and at full gallop (Sallie Gardner, 1,142m/min, twelve pictures). The original photographs, Tissandier wrote, had been deposited with Muybridge's French representatives, William Morgan-Brown and Brandon, of 1 Rue Lafitte, Paris.[20] Tissandier was fulsome in his praise:

> It only requires a careful examination of the different positions of the horse photographed in each of the accompanying plates, to be aware of the complexity of the movements which it performs, and to recognize that some of these positions appear completely improbable. If an artist had produced this representation by drawing, he would assuredly be accused of indulging in the fantasies of his imagination. But when one knows that these are photographic prints, one admires and puts to good effect the lessons which they reveal.[21]

The publication of Muybridge's pictures had a very important influence on research into photographic animation. Marey, for one, resumed his own work after the article in *La Nature*. Throughout Europe, newspapers gave one or more pages to this Californian event. On 16 April 1879 the Paris magazine *Moniteur de la Photographie* remarked:

> In San Francisco, M. Muybridge has caused quite a sensation with his instantaneous photographs of animals in motion. The science of the zoetrope thus receives a beautiful illustration with the aid of the photographic art; for, in his photographs, it is possible to obtain each phase, however slight it may be, of the movement of a horse, or the flight of a bird, for example. We have here, perhaps, a new application of photography for physiological science.[22]

In May 1879 Muybridge extended his observations to other animals (dogs, cattle, pigs, and so on) and, most importantly, increased the capacity of his image-taking, with twenty-four cameras mounted side by side. Around August 1879 human beings made their way onto the Palo Alto track, perhaps at the suggestion of the painter and photographer Thomas Eakins (1846–1916), who was to become an enthusiastic photographer of motion.

Finally, at the end of 1879, Muybridge too began to wonder about the magic lantern. It was a classic intellectual progression: the inventor perfects a new method of animation, but then needs to exhibit it to everyone 'on the big screen'. But Muybridge could not project his successive photographs, which were too difficult to space around the circumference of a transparent disc. He therefore preferred to paint the different phases of movement onto the surface of a glass disc, with as much accuracy as possible. The images were then placed in a magic lantern with oxy-hydrogen illumination, fitted with a conventional shutter disc rotating in the opposite direction to the continuously revolving image disc (see Fig. 39).

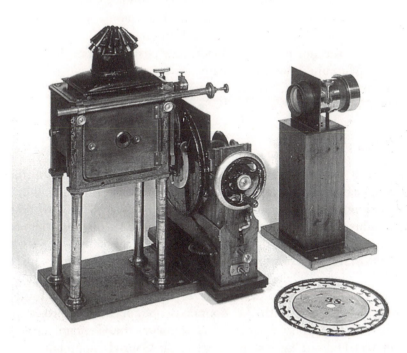

Fig. 39. Muybridge's magic lantern and Zoopraxiscope disc.
Collection: Kingston-upon-Thames Museum and Heritage Centre.

The images Muybridge painted on the glass were very well executed: galloping horses, of course, but also an athlete juggling on horseback, long-distance runners, and flying birds, among others. The figures were slightly stretched so as not to be deformed in projection, since the shutter disc moved very quickly. Muybridge gave his projector several names: 'Zoographiscope', 'Zoogyroscope', 'Zoopraxinoscope', and finally 'Zoopraxiscope'.

It is hardly possible to regard projection with the Zoopraxiscope as a revolutionary new development. We have already seen the previous attempts by Naylor, Uchatius, and Duboscq. If the method was far from new, though, the synthesis of movement was much more precise than in the older systems, since it was based on drawings taken from photographs. But still the projection of hand-painted images could not match the precision of the photographic originals.

The first public projections with the Zoopraxiscope took place on 16 January 1880 before a group of San Francisco worthies. On 4 May Muybridge gave some lectures with his machine (now also christened the 'Magic Lantern Zoetrope' in the press) at the San Francisco Art Association. He also showed numerous slides reproducing old engravings which were inaccurate in their representation of the horse, such as a photograph of a medieval Latin manuscript showing two horsemen with the horses in very inaccurate positions. The Kingston-on-Thames Museum now owns many of these slides, one of which shows Muybridge himself, his face hidden by a large hat, mounted on a fine dappled horse.

Muybridge in Europe

In May 1881 in San Francisco, Stanford and Muybridge published their first collaborative book, *The Attitudes of Animals in Motion*, which collected the photographs made in 1878–9. In August 1881 Muybridge returned to his native country, and then travelled on to Paris, where he was welcomed as a celebrity. On Monday 26 September 1881 the physiologist Marey organized an evening reception for him at his apartment at 11 Boulevard Delessert, near the Trocadéro, where he had been living for some time (he previously lived at 9 Rue Duguay-Trouin). Muybridge gave a show with the Zoopraxiscope, or another projection device, for an élite group of artists and scholars: the German scientist Hermann von Helmholtz; Arsène d'Arsonval; Gabriel Lippmann (later the inventor of a colour photography process); Colonel Émile Duhousset (who had studied the motion of the horse); the photographer Nadar;

Gaston Tissandier of *La Nature*; and Madame Vilbort, wife of the editor of *Le Globe*, among others. As a historical footnote, Madame Vilbort was a long-standing companion of Marey, who sometimes mentioned her in his letters: frail by nature, Madame Vilbort was often unwell. Their liaison produced an illegimate daughter, Francesca, whom Marey loved dearly and passed off as his niece.

An article signed by 'The Devil', possibly written by Madame Vilbort, appeared in *Le Globe* the day after this historic soirée:

> M. Muybridge, an American scholar, gave us the first sight of some experiments which will be the talk of all Paris. On a white sheet he projected some photographs [initially these were simple static slides, without any illusion of movement] showing the horse and other animals in their positions of most rapid movement . . . M. Marey gave his assistance to M. Muybridge and described each picture with charming good humour [Muybridge did not speak French]. We were first shown the marvellous cameras which M. Muybridge uses for his experiments. These differ from conventional cameras . . . in the opening and closing of the lens . . . M. Muybridge then showed us the cameras in position. Twenty-four of them are arranged on a type of stand. Each one captures the image of the animal as it presents itself before it for a short instant, lasting for about two-hundredths of a second . . . There being no animals to photograph in M. Marey's apartment, M. Muybridge contented himself with showing us his results. First, the horse at a trot, then galloping, jumping, refusing and clearing barriers . . . After showing us the twenty-four photographs showing the movements of a horse walking, trotting and galloping, as it passed before the twenty-four lenses, M. Muybridge brought the animal into motion by his *zootropic* process [with the projection lantern]. This was a reproduction—but projected, that is to say enlarged and visible for a greater number—of the curious experiment which the *zootrope* provides on the drawing-room table . . . In this way we saw pass before our very eyes long queues of galloping horses, gathering and stretching themselves with the most amazing fluidity. Then the dogs followed them, running between their legs with their tails in the air. In this devilish procession, this infernal hunt, the stags ran after the hounds, cattle chased the stags, even the very pigs showed delusions of grace and speed as they galloped by. In a similar way photography has captured the flight of birds, in the thousand positions of their wings, as they sometimes hover in front of their bodies, sometimes appear to surround them entirely. But we have not reached the end. The gallery of M. Muybridge knows no boundaries.[23]

Tissandier also printed a short article on Muybridge's projection in *La Nature*: 'We see a clown leap, a horse gallop, a greyhound run, even birds in flight.'[24]

Muybridge and Marey enjoyed an excellent relationship: the Englishman showed visible admiration for the physiologist, who in turn was full of praise for Muybridge's work. A collaborative project between Stanford, Marey, Muybridge, and the French painter Jean-Louis Ernest Meissonier (1815–91), began in 1881. In a letter to Frank Shay on 23 December 1881, Muybridge announced that Meissonier was to publish a book on the horse, with photographs and reproductions of old and modern paintings. Muybridge described the painter as an influential figure in the Paris scene, and indicated that the celebrated Professor Marey would also be involved in the project. He finished by inviting Shay to come 'to my Electro-photo studio in the Bois-de-Boulogne'—Marey's future 'Station Physiologique', then still in an embryonic state. Unfortunately the book never appeared, but the personal and scientific relationship between Muybridge and Marey never cooled.

On 1 October 1881 it was Leland Stanford's turn to visit Paris. He gave a copy of *The Attitudes of Animals in Motion* to Meissonier, and Meissonier painted his portrait. This canvas, 53 cm by 38 cm, is today in the Stanford University Museum of Art in California, and shows Stanford sitting with his elbow resting on an open copy of Muybridge's book. He appears as a strong man, with a short white beard and very bright eyes. Meissonier specialized in equestrian and military scenes. He was a stickler for realism and exactness of detail. Very much in fashion in the France of Napoléon III, when he willingly glorified the great occasions of the First Empire, he became one of the most famous painters in Paris. His well-known painting *1807* (now in the collection of the New York Metropolitan Museum of Art), heavily criticized when it appeared, was described in 1875 by an American tourist in Paris, the novelist Henry James:

> Any new work by M. Meissonier is of course noticeable, but the present one has a special claim to distinction in the fact that it is the largest picture that has ever proceeded from the hand of that prince of miniaturists . . . The work is a yard and a half long and I suppose about three quarters of a yard high . . . The foreground of the picture, to the right, is occupied by a troop of cuirassiers, who are galloping into action . . . They are magnificently painted, and full, I will not say of movement—Meissonier, to my sense, never represents it—but of force and completeness of detail.[25]

Not only was Meissonier not entirely successful at representing movement, but his equestrian figures were mostly inaccurate. Around the middle of October 1881 Muybridge showed his animated photographs to Meissonier, who pronounced himself highly impressed by their exactness. He already imagined being able to revise the positions of the horses in some of his paintings, and in 1887 painted a new 'corrected' version of *1807*.

On 29 October 1881 Meissonier sent out a first series of invitations for an evening of projection in the presence of Muybridge, planned for 3 November in his vast studio-apartment at 131 Boulevard Malesherbes.[26] On Saturday 26 November there was another show, to which Meissonier invited his artistic friends: Jules Claretie, Albert Wolff, Alexandre Dumas the younger, and the painters Eugène Guillaume, Léon Bonnat, Jean-Baptiste Édouard Detaille, Alexandre Cabanel, A.M. de Neuville, and Jean-Léon Gérome. One of Meissonier's letters of invitation has survived:

> My dear friend,
> M. Muybridge from America has showed me a series of photographic projections depicting men and animals in motion. These seemed to me to be of such great interest that I considered that they would be to you as well, and in order that you will be able to enjoy them with some other friends I have requested M. Muybridge to repeat this demonstration.
> Please come next Saturday, the 26th, between eight and nine. You will perhaps derive some pleasure from seeing this thing, and you will bring me a greater pleasure. Come informally, I shall be alone and I have not invited any ladies. With kindest regards, Meissonier.[27]

Alfred Molteni, the famous lantern manufacturer, operated the projector that evening. It has sometimes been claimed that Muybridge used Reynaud's Projection Praxinoscope to show his animated images, but there is no conclusive evidence of this. A journalist from *Le Temps* reported:

> It was a brilliant success and the show was highly curious. The American inventor succeeded, through a series of instantaneous photographs, in capturing the movements of a walking man and a running horse, and with the aid of a rotating mechanism, he projected with electric light the moving image of a man or an animal. It was truly prodigious. The horses galloped; the pedestrians

scurried to and fro; the greyhounds stretched and sprang forward; the clowns leaped on horseback and we saw them, after taking a run-up, drop straight down into the saddle.[28]

After some further shows in Paris, one of which was at the Cercle de l'Union Artistique at Place Vendôme, Muybridge continued his lecture tour in Britain between March and June 1882, assisted by the lanternist Ernest Webster. On 13 March, for example, he was invited to the famous Royal Institution. As in France, British painters showed much interest in the analyses of movement which Muybridge had achieved. However, there was also a curiously hostile reaction. One British magazine published engravings of paintings 'by our greatest artists' showing horses running, and compared them with the Muybridge series photographs (again reproduced as engravings) which had been published in the press, with an indignant commentary:

> The first [the paintings] are all movement, activity and elegance; the second [Muybridge's images] are of an unbelievable rigidity and ugliness! It is evident that instantaneous photography applied to the racehorse, if we are to judge from these photographs, is not as truthful as the artist's pencil. This is, perhaps, the first time that it has been possible to state, with certainty, that the draughtsman's pencil is more true than the photographic camera. Perhaps you ask from where this certainty comes? Why, from common sense: the drawings present us with *movement*, the photographs represent *still* animals, fixed in more or less ghastly positions!—These are curiosities, it is said.—That is the truth.[29]

This reaction contrasted sharply with the general admiration in Paris. It should be said that the engravings presented in the press (for example in *La Nature*) were rather unattractive silhouettes, and that the original images were of better quality. But to deny these pictures any scientific interest, to consider them inaccurate, was a sign of insincerity. In the course of his tour of 1881–2, Muybridge learned about the gelatino-bromide photographic process, which he adopted when he returned to the United States to create better instantaneous images. While in London in 1882, he also had the very unpleasant surprise of the appearance of a book entitled *The Horse in Motion*, published in Boston, written by J.D.B. Stillman, and financed by Leland Stanford. Muybridge's name did not appear on the cover, although his photographs were reproduced inside. As a result a dispute also arose with the Royal Society in London, with whom Muybridge had some serious plans for publication; after the appearance of Stillman's book, the doors of that establishment were closed to him.

'Zoopraxography' in Philadelphia

A furious Muybridge returned to the United States in June 1882 and launched a lawsuit against Stanford. He managed to have the book seized but, contrary to all his rights, finally lost the case: it was impossible to beat the former State Governor and his army of lawyers. Having fallen out with his patron Stanford, Muybridge found new employment in 1884 at the University of Pennsylvania, after a long period of financial difficulty. He began an enormous task, the results of which were eventually published by the University and the J.B. Lippincott Company in 1887 as *Animal Locomotion: An Electro-Photographic Investigation of Consecutive Phases of Animal Movements, 1872–1885*.

This huge work consisted of 781 photogravure plates, totalling about 30,000 images of human or animal movement, divided into eleven 'volumes':[30]

(1). Males (Nude) (65 plates)
(2). Males (Nude); continued (68)
(3). Females (Nude) (89)
(4). Females (Nude); continued (89)
(5). Males (Pelvis Cloth) (72)
(6). Females (Semi-Nude and Transparent Drapery) and Children (79)
(7). Males and Females (Draped) and Miscellaneous Subjects (71)
(8). Abnormal Movements, Males and Females (Nude and Semi-Nude) (29)
(9). Horses (95)
(10). Domestic Animals (40)
(11). Wild Animals and Birds (84)

The edition of 781 plates appeared in several different formats: loose, in pockets of canvas-backed paper, at a cost of $500; bound at a cost of $550; or as a portfolio containing a selection of 100 plates for $100. There was also a complete catalogue of the 781 plates, published separately.

To manage this colossal undertaking, achieved between 1884 and 1887, Muybridge had the benefit of an impressive range of equipment. Sometimes forty-eight cameras were set up at once, and a special

Fig. 40. 'Dancing Girl: A Pirouette', series of successive photographs
from Eadweard Muybridge, *The Human Figure in Motion* (1887).
Collection: Laurent Mannoni.

building was constructed for the project on the campus of the University
at Philadelphia. He was assisted by an expert electrician, L.F.
Rondinella, and a professional photographer, Henry Bell. A scientific
committee including Thomas Eakins, of the Philadelphia Academy of
Fine Arts, was convened to supervise the work. The Philadephia Zoo
was more or less commandeered, along with any passing athlete or
female model. A leading dancer of one of the Philadelphia theatres came
and twirled gracefully in front of the lenses (see Fig. 40).

The photographs of *Animal Locomotion* are amazing. The series of
'Abnormal Movements' is quite uncomfortable: an obese woman, people
with extreme physical disabilities, and so on. The series of photographs
of women is at once marvellously poetic and utterly bizarre, seeming
today to hover between surrealism and eroticism. Visions of female
beauty, completely 'as nature intended' walk on all fours, climb a ladder,
descend a staircase, get dressed, wash, and dry themselves. A naked
woman tips a basin of water over her equally naked colleague. Another,
nude except for a cigarette, sits down with delight on a chair and exhales
a cloud of smoke. Two naked beauties dance a waltz, clasping each other
tightly; two others take tea. A model swings in a hammock, revealing
practically all her charms. This regiment of naked women is stranger
than that of the men, who are mainly confined to exhibiting their
muscles in athletic exercises. All the same there are still some strange
male photographs, such as that of a pair of wrestlers, or an athlete with a
shaved head and an impressive physique. As for the animals, they file
past with greater or lesser degrees of willingness, sometimes with bright

worried eyes turned towards the lenses. The most attractive photographs are those of running cats, and of course those of horses. Elephants are photographed in profile and from behind. Muybridge was always ready to vary the angle from which the pictures were taken, but the depth of field was always restricted by the back wall, which was divided into numbered squares.

Following this immense publication, Muybridge once more undertook lecture tours in Europe. In October 1892, he gave lectures with accompanying projection at the World's Columbian Exposition in Chicago, where a Zoopraxographical Hall had been specially constructed. In 1893 he published a small book entitled *Descriptive Zoopraxography*, with engraved reproductions of the glass discs shown in Chicago. Its frontispiece was a signed portrait of Muybridge, looking somewhat like Moses with his great white beard and severe expression.

The only criticism which can be made of Muybridge, as with other researchers, is that he rigidly adopted a single and unique method of taking pictures. Even though it was improved over the years, a technical solution which involved photographing movement with batteries of twenty-four or even forty cameras in series had no future. If it had appeared to be a revolutionary breakthrough in 1878, by 1890 it seemed completely archaic. It was at this point that Marey succeeded in capturing movement on celluloid film.

13

Marey Releases the Dove

An explorer of movement

In 1890, the physiologist Étienne-Jules Marey pointed the lens of his 'chronophotographic' camera towards an animated scene and obtained a series of successive pictures on celluloid film. At last, life and motion had been captured and secured in all their phases on a flexible, sensitive, transparent base: the film. The cinematographic process had arrived. It certainly still needed improvements, some of which were added later by Edison and the Lumières, among others. Marey himself could never have succeeded without the previous attempts of others, the most important of whom was Muybridge.

Marey was never interested in public or commercial exploitation of his processes. He was not a performing tumbler, he would say, but a physiologist. Like Christiaan Huygens with his magic lantern, he had no desire to become involved in the world of spectacle. But without a technical process, there could be no Seventh Art, no cinema, and Marey was a founding father at the origins of the process. He devoted his entire life to the study of *kinema*, movement, and he developed some remarkable cameras and made some films whose quality is still admired today.

Marey was born at Beaune, in Burgundy, on 5 March 1830. He went to Paris in 1849 and enrolled at the Faculté de Médecine; once he had passed the necessary examinations he entered the service of the surgeon Philippe Ricord (1800–89). A former pupil of the great Guillaume Dupuytren, Ricord specialized in the treatment of venereal diseases. He was impressed by his student Marey and encouraged him along his scientific journey. Other teachers who influenced Marey included Martin Magron, who gave classes in experimental physiology, and the doctor Charles Buisson. He also struck up a friendship with the young Alphonse Milne-Edwards, who took Marey to meet his father Henri, a famous naturalist and one of the founders of French physiology. Marey later recalled:

> I never suspected that the great scholar who was Henri Milne-Edwards would offer the friend of his son, a beginner in physiology, such a simple and warm welcome, that he would encourage his early works and allow them into his *Annales des Sciences Naturelles* ['Natural Science Yearbook']. I retain a deeply grateful memory of that welcome, for it decided for me the career which I must follow.[1]

After a period as an intern in the Cochin hospital in Paris, Marey was awarded his doctorate in 1859, having submitted a thesis on 4 March of that year entitled *Researches on the Circulation of Blood in the Healthy State and in Illnesses*. Like Claude Bernard, his intellectual mentor, Marey then failed his *agrégation* examination (the highest qualification available in France). In 1864 he became, to use his own expression, an 'armchair physiologist' and set himself up at 14 Rue de l'Ancienne-Comédie, on the fourth floor of a house occupied between 1689 and 1770 by the Comédie Française theatre. At the left-hand side of this beautiful building a narrow staircase led up to the attic, which had previously served as a studio for the painters Antoine Gros and Horace Vernet. It was here that Marey decided to set up his laboratory. He had a space 15 m long, 12 m wide, and 8 m in height. The photographer Nadar described this strange location in 1894:

> One had to clamber up to the top of the house to reach this vast loft bathed in light, promoted to the rank of laboratory by the young and already famous professor: but having arrived, one did not regret the ascent, since what was there could not fail to interest. There was a scent of work in the air. A laboratory, yes, but also a menagerie; the place was memorable . . . In impeccable order, among every sort of scientific apparatus and instrument, both the standard ones and the dreams of the past, were cages and aquaria, and the creatures to populate them: pigeons, buzzards, fish, lizards, snakes, frogs . . . A frog escaped from its jar, in a quite exceptional breach of order, and hopped randomly in front of you . . . A tortoise, full of seriousness, progressed without undue haste . . . Under a wire mesh grille, yellow-collared grass snakes nervously stretched their vertebral muscles in delight at the warm temperature . . . Everywhere, in every corner, was Life.[2]

Nadar also noticed some curious graphs:

> These were nothing more than curves, jumps, flurries, capers, spasms . . . They had a fascinating attraction, these sheets on which, in white lines on a funereal black background, the infinite variations on the hymn of life were unfurled.[3]

Marey was happy in his laboratory, a cabinet worthy of Dr Faustus. He was surrounded by numerous students, and lived with his mother, the 'Mother of the Master', as Nadar called her. Marey left the Rue de l'Ancienne-Comédie in 1869, when he succeeded the physiologist Pierre Flourens at the Collège de France. He was then 39 years old, and had already published many remarkable books and articles: *Physiologie Médicale de la Circulation du Sang* (1863; 'Medical Physiology of the Circulation of the Blood') and *Du Mouvement dans les Fonctions de la Vie* (1868; 'On Movement in the Vital Functions'). Marey took as his vocation the study of the movements of the organs, with the aim of understanding their exact functions:

> I have given a greater importance to movement, and I believe with Claude Bernard that movement is the most important action, in that all bodily functions derive their pattern from its accomplishment.[4]

In 1863 he declared that he had lost faith in the methods of observation which physicians had used for many years: 'How can one feel the delicate nuances of the pulse with a finger? How can one keep faithfully the recollection of these fleeting sensations?'[5] And how could the doctor transmit his knowledge to his students? Marey dreamed of scientific instruments capable of recording the 'diverse forms of movement in the vital functions,' since observation of the animal or human 'machine' could not be achieved with the naked eye:

> The best way of rapidly improving this study of the external indications of a function consists of pushing back the limitations of our senses, compensating for their restricted perception, or, by means of certain tricks, making visible or palpable the phenomena which are not naturally so. . .[6]

'It is in search of the laws of life that we must march,' said Marey in concluding his inaugural lecture at the Collège de France. To understand the laws of movement, and of the organs, would make possible a more effective fight against disease and death.

A first range of apparatus, either conceived from scratch or improved from existing designs, allowed Marey to capture images of movement. A graphical plot of the pulse, for example, was obtained in 1863 using the 'Sphygmographe': the artery of the arm was compressed by a flexible spring, which was connected to a lightweight lever whose point inscribed the precise movement of the artery in ink, as it cyclically raised and lowered the spring. To record muscular movement, in 1868 Marey designed the 'Myographe', which precisely transferred each slight jerk of the muscle to the same sensitive lever, whose point then traced onto a rotating cylinder the strange curves which Nadar had admired during his visit to the Rue de l'Ancienne-Comédie.

Marey's recording instruments (Polygraphe, Dromographe, Cardio-graphe, and other thermographs) were constructed and sold by the workshops of Antoine Bréguet, at 39 Quai de l'Horloge.[7] Along with his friend Professor Donders of Utrecht, Marey quickly became the principal specialist in 'chronography' (from the Greek *chronos*, 'time', and *grapho*, 'I write'). At this period the precise measurement of very short intervals of time was a problem still occupying a good number of scholars working in mechanical, physical and physiological research. In 1876 an exhibition of European chronographic equipment took place in London, at the South Kensington Museum, in which Marey played an important part. From chronography to 'chronophotography' was only a short step, but it was not one which Marey took immediately. Ignoring photography, he first pursued his 'graphic process', pushing the capabilities of his recording devices to their limits. For him, the graphic approach was a 'universal language' of science, like Latin for the scholars of old.

One of Marey's most important books, *La Machine Animal* (published in English as *Animal Mechanism*), appeared in 1873. This was the famous book which prompted Stanford and Muybridge to resume their photographic research in 1877–8. In his Introduction, Marey explained the interest of the study of animal and human locomotion, then still very poorly understood:

> If we knew under what conditions the maximum of speed, force, or labour which the living being can furnish, may be obtained, it would put an end to much discussion, and a great deal of conjecture, which is to be regretted. A generation of men would not be condemned to certain military exercises which will be hereafter rejected as useless and ridiculous . . . We should know exactly at what pace an animal

does the best service, whether he be required for speed, or for drawing loads . . .[8]

Concerning the mechanical operations of terrestrial, aquatic or aerial movement, Marey claimed that 'there is nothing that can escape the methods of analysis which are available to us'. With the aid of different 'apparatus for the exploration of movement', he had already succeeded in graphically analysing the walk of humans and horses, and the flight of birds and insects. For the latter, Marey had invented a novel series of highly sensitive sensors. First of all, for measuring the human walk, there was the 'experimental shoe', whose rubber sole contained an air-filled chamber. When the foot contacted the ground, the air was driven out of this cavity through a tube to inscribe on a recording instrument (the rotating cylinder already used in the Myographe) the duration and different phases of pressure of the foot. Marey then analysed the resulting graphs and drew new conclusions, for example on the relationship between body weight and walking action. Using the same method, he studied humans running and jumping. The only problem was that the human 'guinea pig' had to carry the recording equipment with him as he ran or jumped, in order to measure the pressure of the experimental shoes.

Having succeeded in analysis of movement, Marey now wished to achieve its synthesis in order to verify his results. Synthesis would allow him to confirm whether or not the analysis had been made correctly. Marey turned to the zoetrope:

> This instrument, usually constructed for the amusement of children, generally represents grotesque or fantastic figures moving in a riduculous manner. But it has occurred to us that, by depicting on the apparatus figures constructed with care, and representing faithfully the successive attitudes of the body during walking, running, etc., we might reproduce the appearance of the different kinds of progression employed by man.[9]

According to Marey, Mathias Duval, professor of anatomy at the École des Beaux-Arts, had constructed a zoetrope with sixteen images, with each picture drawn from the results of the graphic analysis method. 'When animated at a suitable speed of rotation, the instrument simulates with perfect precision the different movements of walking or running'; if it was turned slowly, one could see the movements at reduced speed, which made it easier to study them. Marey was already interested by stroboscopy, and he later used the 'slow motion' of the zoetrope to observe his chronophotographic strips.

For studying the locomotion of the horse, the experimental shoe was replaced by a rubber ball stuffed with horsehair, attached to the animal's hoof. When the hoof struck the ground, the ball was compressed and forced air into the measuring instrument. When the hoof lifted up, the ball resumed its initial shape and refilled with air. Marey asked a riding stable owner named Pellier to ride the horse and carry in his hand the measuring stylus and cylinder, connected to all four hooves by tubes. As Marey said, it was a good thing that the animal was good-natured.

In this way Marey obtained graphs and general notes on the attitudes of the horse: walking, trotting, galloping, and so on, and his friend Émile Duhousset made some excellent engravings showing the animal in each precise position. Marey showed that the galloping horse was, at a given moment, suspended above the ground, and that then its left hind leg touched ground. Once again, Mathias Duval undertook to draw sixteen successive pictures of the horse and arrange them in the zoetrope. It is perhaps debatable how accurate this synthetic representation, made without any photographic aid, actually was in practice. 'These pictures placed in the instrument give a complete illusion and show a horse which strolls, walks or trots as the case may be,' Marey wrote, but also added: 'These plates [are] still slightly defective.' Duval's zoetrope strips appear not to have survived.

Experiments on the flight of insects, of course, were much more delicate. Marey had to be content with a bee or a wasp simply brushing its wings lightly against the blackened paper of the recording instrument. Finally, Marey's research on the flight of birds revealed so much fundamental information on this virtually untouched subject that he published a large volume on the subject in 1890, after he had started using photography in his investigations. But in 1873, he was still only using his graphic methods. First the Myographe was adapted for a bird, which wore a sort of corset containing the 'experimental apparatus' which captured the contraction of the breast muscles during flight. At the end of each wing, a small device connected or disconnected an electric current linked to a recording stylus, as the wing moved up and down. The bird had to fly wearing this contraption, connected to the recording cylinder by tubes. Marey also installed, in Laboratory Room 7 of the Collège de France, a strange device used only for studying movement. One of his pupils, François-Franck, recalled:

> I still remember a large turntable set up in the centre of the room, which was driven by a steam engine mounted in a wooden shed . . . On this turntable would be harnessed, as the case might be, a subject whose walk was to be studied around a circular track, or a bird flying around the axis of the same turntable.[10]

Marey described his 'turntable' in *La Machine Animale*: it was a complicated and cumbersome assembly, but nonetheless he seemed quite proud of it. However, the pigeon and the buzzard, encumbered by the corset, flew in awkward and unnatural patterns. He had to find, once and for all, a new experimental method.

Chronography assisted by photography

It is not clear what nudged Marey towards photography. Later, when he recounted the story of chronophotography, he freely acknowledged Ducos du Hauron, Janssen, and Muybridge as his predecessors. Going back further in time, he mentioned research by the doctor Ernest-Nicolas-Joseph Onimus, a pupil of Guillaume Duchenne de Boulogne (1806–75), a pioneer of the use of electricity in treating nervous disorders. In a study published in 1865 in the *Journal de l'Anatomie et de la Physiologie* ('Journal of Anatomy and Physiology'), Onimus claimed to be the first person to have used photography for studying the movement of the heart. At this time, photographic plates were sensitized with collodion and were not very fast, but it was precisely this slowness of exposure that Onimus utilized:

> All movement, in order to be fully appreciated, must be fixed on the paper; as is well known, the works of Messrs Chauveau and Marey have made progress in physiological studies in this connection. But one cannot imagine recording with any type of camera the movements of organs as small as the heart of the lower animals. We have had the idea of applying photography to this area of research. We based our approach on the fact that a photographic picture often gives two distinct images of a subject if, during the exposure, the object has not remained completely still. This is known to photographers as blur. The heart, during its contraction and expansion, assumes different positions, and as a consequence photography may manage to reproduce these positions.[11]

Onimus published engravings taken from his photographs (which were actually taken by the photographer Alexandre Martin) in the same journal. He concluded his article by imagining, 'if one could manage to obtain highly sensitive photographic papers', a 'rotating cylinder in the camera chamber to which the photographic paper could be attached'. It would then be possible to record 'the succession of movements of the different portions of the heart'. The idea of a sensitized cylinder was later taken up by Georges Demenÿ and Thomas Edison (not for studying cardiac physiology, but for capturing any type of scene or movement), and it is quite likely that this article by Onimus influenced Marey as well.

Another source of inspiration for Marey appears to have been the research of Dr Charles Ozanam. In 1869 Ozanam was studying the beating of the heart and action of the pulse, with the aid of photography. He presented his equipment (constructed by Bréguet) at the Société Française de Photographie on 2 July 1869:

> A small camera obscura, 35 cm in length by 12 cm in height and 4 cm in width, encloses the whole instrument . . . At about the midpoint of its length, a tubular slider selectively covers or reveals a longitudinal slot, vertical and very narrow, which is the only way in which light may enter. Along the length of this slot is placed the transparent artificial artery, formed by a glass tube whose cavity, about 1 mm in width, is filled with mercury to simulate blood. The lower end of the tube, widened to form a small pyramidal reservoir, is applied directly against the artery or the heart.
>
> A very fine membrane of vulcanized rubber is fixed to the periphery of the reservoir, to retain the mercury and allow it to oscillate freely at each arterial pulse; these oscillations are so sensitive that they reproduce the slightest variations in the undulation of the blood . . . One condition alone is required, which is that the pressure of the artery against the reservoir of mercury causes it to rise to the point at which it shows in the vertical slot formed in the camera obscura.[12]

The artery was therefore recreated artificially by a tube, whose transparent walls allowed the passage of 'light and vision'; the blood was simulated by a column of liquid, whose level was controlled by the pulse of the blood flow. The undulating line represented by the liquid surface was recorded by a cursor device, which carried the photographic plate. The plate, in an innovative development, moved inside the camera obscura at a rate of about 1 cm per second. With the assistance of Edouard Baldus, Ozanam obtained a series of images (or 'photographic sketches') showing the action of the human pulse at all ages from five to sixty-five. The Société Française de Photographie still owns, for example, a trace on albumen paper of 'the pulse of a young lady of eighteen years', showing seventy-four pulses per minute.

Like Onimus, Ozanam referred to Marey's research on the circulation of blood and on physiology in general. However Ozanam made it quite clear that photography allowed progress beyond the graphical methods of observation still advocated by Marey:

> Dicrotism, that is to say a double pulse, has been described by Professor Marey as a normal state of the pulse . . . Our photographic sketch corroborates Doctor Marey's assertion; but at the same time, it resolves the question in a more complete way. It shows, in fact, that the natural pulse is not only dicrotic, but triple and sometimes even quadruple in its development . . .[13]

The year 1873 seems to have marked a watershed in Marey's work. *La Machine Animale* emerged from the presses of the Paris publisher Germer Baillière et Compagnie; on 17 March Jules Janssen revealed the principle of his 'revolver'; and the first rumours of Muybridge's instantaneous photography of the horse Occident appeared in the French press. And finally, Marey certainly studied the abstract of some prophetic remarks made, at a meeting of the Société Française de Navigation Aérienne (French Society for Aerial Navigation), by Alphonse Pénaud and Abel Hureau de Villeneuve, the Secretary-General of the Society. The historian Gérard Turpin has pointed out the importance of this meeting, at which Marey's future chronophotographic research was quite clearly mapped out.[14]

On that day, 24 December 1873, Pénaud read a paper on 'a new method of studying flight'. Pénaud (1850–80) was a close friend of Marey, who gave him a warm tribute at the end of *La Machine Animale*, and was a great pioneer of aviation who patented a type of helicopter in 1876. He took his own life in 1880, having tried in vain to construct it. After referring to 'M. Marey's good works', Pénaud's paper declared:

> M. Hureau de Villeneuve and I have turned our thoughts to light and photography. As a result we propose the study of the theory of the flight of birds with the aid of instantaneous photography. This method is applicable to every possible movement, whether of living beings or inanimate objects . . . Its future is considerable.[15]

Pénaud suggested several methods for photographic recording of movement. He remarked that Marey, possibly following Janssen's paper of 17 March 1873 on his 'revolver',

> has also thought of observing the flight of birds using instantaneous photography. The camera, fitted with a butt, forms a type of photographic rifle which one aims at the bird during its flight, taking the photographic image by pressing on the trigger. This would be a hunt which brought back not the bird but its image. M. Marey was thinking of a single image, but it is clear that if his rifle was converted into a revolver [like Janssen's, but more rapid], one could apply the principle of successive photography to this very innovative device.[16]

Perhaps at Pénaud's suggestion, Marey did create a photographic rifle for taking successive images, as we shall see later. Pénaud then explained the operation of a photographic device which he had designed, but not built, which could produce several successive images separated by a few hundredths of a second. With a rare degree of modesty—'I know practically nothing about photography and what it allows one to do, and I hope that others will complete and bring to fruition the ideas which I am putting forward'—Pénaud described, several years before their time, the processes which Marey would later use for chronophotography:

> It would be best to have no more than one lens, rapidly covered and uncovered by means of a screen moving with a circular or straight motion, pierced by one or more rectangular holes. The plate itself should have a discontinuous, or at least periodic, very variable straight or rotary movement. In the case where one is operating with a black background and the successive images of the bird are separated sufficiently quickly not to overlap each other, the plate could remain stationary.[17]

Discussion followed, and Hureau de Villeneuve pointed out that Janssen already used a screen—that is, a shutter—in his revolver, driven by a rotary mechanism. Jules Armengaud, an engineer who ran a patent agency (he later filed several patents for Demenÿ and Jules Carpentier on chronophotographic subjects), asked whether the lens could be placed in a chamber with a rotating mirror, 'which would transmit the image of the bird onto the plate at regular intervals'. This system was also later used by Marey, in 1888.

'M. Pénaud's paper opens new horizons,' observed Hureau de

Villeneuve in his closing remarks that evening. Ideas had poured out in all directions, some inspired and within a hair's breadth of a correct solution, others utopian or heading in completely the wrong direction. All the participants emerged from the rooms of the Société de Naviga-tion Aérienne on 24 December 1873 fired with enthusiasm, but not one among them ever realized a single part of this ambitious plan. Fortunately, Marey was less disorganized than Pénaud, and set about laying out the ground for chronophotography. It is to him alone that the credit for this should go, even if he was subject to a number of obvious external influences.

The photographic rifle

Pénaud's paper shows that Marey had considered the possibility of capturing the flight of a bird on a photographic plate, using 'a type of photographic rifle', as early as 1873. Pénaud seems to have advised him to fit this rifle with a mechanism similar to Janssen's revolver, in order to capture several successive images. And in April 1876 Janssen himself (as we saw in the previous chapter), announced to the Société Française de Photographie that his revolver could be used for the study of physiology, especially the study of birds. But all of this still did not persuade Marey to take up photography: Janssen's revolver was not rapid enough to capture the flight of a bird. Marey was still reluctant to give up his graphical methods, to which he had devoted a weighty volume.[18] But in the course of 1878 he changed his opinion radically, thanks to the American experiments of Muybridge and Stanford.

Gaston Tissandier's scientific journal *La Nature* once again played an important role in the complicated cross-fertilization of influences. On 28 September and 5 October 1878 it published a study by Marey of 'Moteurs Animés' ('Living Engines'). Fine engravings illustrated the different positions of a horse walking, trotting, and galloping; there were also some reproductions of old engravings, showing horses in 'incorrect' poses (such as the statue of Henri IV on the Pont-Neuf in Paris). Marey concluded with these words: 'In summary, you will observe, the graphical process has numerous applications, highly varied and often of enormous importance.' It seemed to him to have 'a great future'. But on 14 December the same year, *La Nature* published the first successive instan-taneous photographs by Muybridge, showing the horses Occident, Abe Edington, Mahomet, and Sally Gardner in full motion. This was a revelation, a turning point in the history of physiology and photography. Marey wrote to Tissandier on 8 December:

Dear friend, I am in admiration of the instantaneous photographs by M. Muybridge which you published in the last-but-one number of *La Nature*. Could you put me in touch with the author? I would like to ask for his assistance in the solution of some physiological problems which are most difficult to resolve by other methods. On the question of the flight of birds, I have imagined a sort of *photographic rifle* for capturing the bird in one position, or still better in a series of positions indicating the successive phases of movement of its wings . . . It is clear that for M. Muybridge this would be an easy experiment to carry out. And then what beautiful zoetropes he could give us; we would see every conceivable imaginable animal in all its true positions; it would be zoology brought to life. As for the artists, it is a revolution for them, since it will give them the true positions of movement, the positions of the body in unstable equilibrium which cannot be *posed* by a model. You see, my dear friend, that I am overflowing with enthusiasm, reply to me as quickly as possible and believe me ever yours. Marey.[19]

Muybridge himself replied on 17 February 1879 in a very cordial and flattering letter, in which he promised to study the flight of birds. During his visit to Paris in September 1881, Muybridge brought Marey the first sequential photographs of a bird in flight. Marey considered them most disappointing:

The clarity of the images was not sufficient, they lacked what gave such interest to the attitudes of the horse, the arrangement in sequence of the successive positions of the animal. In fact it is not possible to apply to the free flight of a bird the same method used for the horse, which consists of the animal itself breaking electric wires spaced along its path to actuate a series of photographic cameras.[20]

Marey finally decided to construct a prototype of the rifle. Around the end of 1881 he wrote to Janssen to obtain the specifications of the famous 'revolver' which had captured the passage of Venus in 1874. The astronomer replied in January 1882, with a strange letter in which he insisted on the priority of the camera and ideas which he had advocated in 1876, and on the

applications which the instrument could find for the study of the various phases of every phenomenon . . . The study of the movements which take place in walking, running, flight, fall particularly within this context.[21]

Janssen also claimed that his studies for a 'rapid revolver' were already complete, and he intended 'to produce the apparatus' and place it in Marey's hands: 'you will see the advantage which you can take from it.' However Janssen never constructed his 'rapid revolver'. At the start of 1882 an Englishman, William Lawton, asked him for an example of his standard 'slow' revolver of 1874; Janssen referred him to Marey, and from then on left the work of modernizing his invention up to the physiologist.

The photographic rifle, capable of taking an average of twelve pictures per second, was finally completed during the winter of 1881–2. Marey had developed the habit of passing part of the year in Italy, at the Villa Maria Posilippo in Naples. On 4 March 1882 he wrote from there to his collaborator Demenÿ: 'I am sending you some poor examples of photographs of flying birds: nineteen images per second, exposure time 1/700th of a second.'[22] Then on 13 March, Marey informed the Académie des Sciences:

> I have the honour to announce to the Académie that I have recently obtained, by means of instantaneous photography, a complete analysis of the different forms of locomotion, including the flight of birds.[23]

On 27 March 1882, having returned to Paris, Marey presented negative images of birds and bats in free flight at the Académie. On 10 April he explained the operation of his rifle. If Janssen's revolver did not exactly resemble a handgun (it certainly used the Colt mechanism, but in appearance it was closer to a small cannon), Marey's device could well and truly be compared to a rifle. The adjustable lens was located in the 'barrel'. At the rear, mounted on the butt, a large cylindrical breech block contained a clockwork mechanism. The device was aimed through a viewfinder mounted on the butt. When the trigger was pressed, the mechanism began to rotate and drive a central shaft, which made twelve rotations per second and drove all the other moving parts. First there was an opaque disc, with a narrow window which allowed light through for about 1/720th of a second, twelve times per second. Behind this shutter, and on the same shaft, was a second disc pierced by twelve small apertures and with regularly spaced teeth around its circumference. This second disc was rotated intermittently in front of the photographic plate by a reciprocating ratchet which engaged the teeth on the disc's circumference. Finally, a 'changing box' containing twenty-five photographic plates was located on the top of the rifle, to drop the plates one by one into the interior of the device ready to be exposed to light. The series of images obtained could then be rotated in a zoetrope or phenakistiscope to synthesize the movement which had been analysed.

On 10 April 1882 Marey showed his photographs at the Académie once again, particularly those showing a seagull in flight. 'The clarity still leaves something to be desired,' he acknowledged later (on 12 December 1883); he also wrote to Demenÿ that the images were too small. And as with Muybridge's pictures, 'the reproduction of these images by photogravure only produces a black silhouette'. Marey finished this important paper by claiming that he had aimed his rifle at 'horses, donkeys, dogs, and men on foot or on bicycles'.[24] A December 1882 article by Louis Olivier, in Charles Richet's *La Revue Scientifique*, commented: 'We have seen M. Marey photographing from the window of his house people passing at a distance in the road, on foot and in carriages.'[25] A photograph showing a cab drawn by a walking horse, taken from a low angle, accompanied the article.

Marey's rifle was undoubtedly easier to handle, faster and more precise than Janssen's revolver, thanks to the new gelatino-bromide plates, which were much more sensitive than the dageurreotype or collodion. However Marey, having set out on the photographic road, could not be content with his strange hunting expeditions with the rifle which gave him nothing but 'silhouettes' for trophies, and not enough of them at that. He turned his attention to another, even more remarkable, process. The year 1882, which was significant in cinema history for more than one reason, also saw the establishment of the Station Physiologique on the outskirts of Paris, another of Marey's long-standing dreams, and the recruitment of an initially loyal assistant, Georges Demenÿ.

Georges Demenÿ and the Station Physiologique

Demenÿ (1850–1917), 'the constant pillar of the Station Physiologique', as Marey called him, was born at Douai near the Belgian border. He studied unsuccessfully for entry to the École Centrale, moved to Paris in 1874 and followed courses in medicine, biology and physics; he was an attentive student of Marey's lectures at the Collège de France. Demenÿ took up gymnastics enthusiastically, and frequented the Paris gymnasia where he rapidly became strong and fit, though with his short sight and short stature he always remained rather sickly in appearance. In January 1880, with his friend Émile Corra, he founded a Scientific School of Education and a Society for Rational Gymnastics (financed by the city of Paris), which aimed to promote the principles of structured physical education. He became the uncontested leader of French educational progress in this area. He was described as jealous, envious, and very well read in all aspects of the history and theories of gymnastics. From 1880 onwards he wrote numerous manuals, whose contents have not dated. His brother Paul Demenÿ (1844–1918) was a friend of the poet Arthur Rimbaud, one of whose *Lettres du Voyant* ('Letters of a Clairvoyant') of 1871 was addressed to him.

It was Paul Bert, a physiologist and politician, who introduced Demenÿ to Professor Marey in 1880. Demenÿ later recalled:

> The author of *La Machine Animale* and *La Méthode Graphique* attracted us, we had a community of interests with him which created a true sympathy. We received a kind welcome from the master, and we had the pleasure of falling into agreement with him.[26]

The two of them devised a programme of study for the future Station Physiologique which Marey had wanted to establish for a long time. Marey found Demenÿ an 'attentive pupil', an alter ego who was obedient, admiring, zealous, discreet, and highly competent. Their relationship deteriorated later, but for the time being, thanks to Demenÿ, Marey's second 'dream' (the first was the photographic rifle) came into being.

From 1869 until 1881 Marey was restricted by lack of space in the laboratories of the Collège de France. He often moved his equipment into more spacious locations around Paris, at the École de Gymnastique (School of Gymnastics) at Joinville-le-Pont,[27] at the Paris riding stables, or in the Jardin de Luxembourg: 'There I could drive carriages at different speeds, which I would follow carrying the recording apparatus, followed by a tiresome escort of bystanders.'[28] Understandably, Marey dreamed for many years of 'finding a spacious area, in order to combine the workshop, laboratory and experimental grounds'. In 1878 it was suggested that he be allocated the grounds of the Champs-de-Mars (later the site of the Eiffel Tower), but the project came to nothing. Then on 6 August 1881 the President of the Paris Conseil Municipal (City Council), M. de Hérédia, decided to rent a site of 3,500 sq m on Avenue des Princes, close to the Porte d'Auteuil in Bois de Boulogne on the site of the present-day Parc des Princes stadium. On 21 December 1881 the Conseil voted a sum of 22,000 Francs to offer Marey a Station Physiologique, made up of 10,000 Francs for construction of a circular track 500 m in length, plus an annual allowance of 12,000 Francs for running costs.

Marey left Paris in August 1882 for his villa in Naples, leaving Demenÿ in charge of everything: negotiations with the Conseil, preparation of documents, and consulting the architects Ziegler and Sansboeuf over the building plans (a small cottage had to be built to house the equipment). In exchange for this endless dedication Marey helped Demenÿ to obtain his doctorate, thanks to his connections with the Faculté de Médecine, and Demenÿ was appointed as an assistant at the Station Physiologique on 30 October 1882.

Meanwhile, on Thursday 27 July 1882, an interesting debate took place in the Chambre des Députés (Chamber of Deputies, French Parliament) over the allocation of a further allowance of 61,000 Francs to Marey. The transcription of this debate is worth examining since, as Demenÿ put it very aptly, 'it is highly instructive to know the states of mind at this time'. Jules Ferry, the Minister of Public Education and the Arts, had the greatest difficulty in persuading the Deputies—who completely ridiculed Marey's research—to vote through this additional funding. Ferry opened his speech with emotional praise of Marey, who 'over fifteen years has progressed experimental physiology in a truly marvellous fashion'. He explained the physiologist's graphical methods, at which the first cries of incomprehension began to be heard:

> *Jules Ferry*: [. . .] In this manner of thinking, one may study scientifically . . . the question of the best footwear to give to our soldiers. (Noises). The least tiring shoe for the soldier in the field, that which gives the greatest economy of his efforts . . . (Interruptions). By the same procedures, one may determine the best method of harnessing for horses (Interruptions from the right).
>
> *M. Le Provost de Launay*: It is experience which leads to these results!
>
> *Jules Ferry*: I am speaking of work which is known throughout the whole of Europe, and which can hardly be unknown to our honourable colleagues (exclamations and murmurs from the right).
>
> *M. de Brandy-d'Asson*: You demonstrated your understanding of these matters to us during the war, Monsieur Ferry!
>
> *M. Pieyre*: You gave our soldiers shoes made of cardboard![29]

The President of the Chamber, Henri Brisson, had to intervene to re-establish order. Ferry began again, expressing himself astonished 'to see you showing such contempt for matters which interest the scholarly world so greatly'. He returned to his explanation of Marey's work:

> *Jules Ferry*: . . . In this laboratory they study the usage of muscular effort of a horse subjected to different types of diet; these experiments have a direct relevance for the problem of the ration for a military horse . . .

> *M. Haentjens*: We have never seen such a question introduced into the supplementary budget![30]

But Ferry persisted and, in front of a packed Chamber, outlined Marey's 'chronophotographic' ideas (although that term was not to appear until 1885):

> It is necessary to study movements along a track of a given length, to follow them, to photograph them by instantaneous methods which allow the second to be divided into hundredths of a second, and to obtain the facts corresponding to each hundredth.[31]

Ferry requested 61,000 Francs for the construction of a small building, since the Station Physiologique still consisted of nothing more than a 500 m circular track and a shabby hut 'which barely keeps out the rain and sun'. According to Ferry, Marey was photographing 'in conditions which are completely deplorable'. The allowance 'relating to the creation of a Station Physiologique attached to the Department of Natural History' was finally voted through. By March 1883 Marey, like Muybridge in California, at last had his own photographic studio.

The fixed-plate chronophotographic camera

Now everything was in place: the Station Physiologique had been fitted out, and Demenÿ was supervising research there following Marey's instructions. Marey himself spent the winter of 1882–3 in Naples. A talented engineer named Otto Lund was recruited to construct the equipment. He had already assisted in the design of the photographic rifle at the end of 1881. On 24 November 1883 Marey said of Lund:

> We are working continuously with Otto on the photographic equipment, which is coming on well. The artist is putting all his skill

into it. It appears that he prefers working calmly to making improvi-
sations.[32]

On 3 July 1882, Marey presented his new photographic process at the
Académie des Sciences. It was nothing like a rifle or revolver. He had
designed a camera fitted with a large rotating shutter, 1.3 m in diameter,
whose aperture could be widened or narrowed as required to control the
exposure time according to the intensity of the light or in relation to
the shutter's speed of rotation. The shutter made ten rotations per
second, and the length of exposure of the photographic plate was only
about one-thousandth of a second for each image. The shutter was
turned by a gear mechanism mounted on a shaft, driven by gravity with a
150 kg weight located at the rear of the camera. This design of camera
was used at the Station Physiologique in September 1883; there were
other versions, which the historian Michel Frizot has listed.[33]

With this device Marey was able to combine several successive images
on a single photographic plate. To achieve this the subject had to be
white, photographed against a black background. In practice, although
the quantity of light passing through the rotary shutter for each image
was very small, the total amount of light accumulated over a whole
multiple exposure was enough to make the images slightly foggy. The
background therefore had to be made darker. On the advice of the
physicist Eugène Chevreul, Marey constructed a 'black screen', a sort of
shed 3 m deep (by 1886, it was 10 m deep), 15 m long and 4 m high. A
measuring rod was positioned on the ground to estimate the distances
covered, and a chronograph (a dial face of black velvet, against which a
bright needle turned continuously at one revolution per second) was
attached at the upper part of the shed.

The camera was enclosed in a large wooden shed which rolled on
guide rails (another ancestor of the cinematic tracking shot, rather closer
than Robertson's Fantascope), to move towards or away from the screen,
according to the lens being used and the size of images required. An
operator in the shed released the shutter disc as the subject passed in
front of the screen. The subject—a man jumping over an obstacle, for
example—would be shown in all phases of its movement on the same
photographic plate. If the shutter made nine revolutions during the
man's passage across its field of view, he would be shown nine times on
the plate.

Each rotation, bringing the aperture of the disc in front of the lens,
allows the light to pass through for a short moment, which is

sufficient, each time, to create an image. These successive images are produced in different locations on the plate, since the jumper himself occupies different positions in front of the screen when each of the exposures is produced.[34]

The first photographs Marey and Demenÿ produced were published in *La Nature* and the *Comptes-Rendus de l'Académie des Sciences* ('Proceedings of the Académie des Sciences') on 22 July and 2 October 1882. They were somewhat surreal, such as the picture of a man whose image was repeated a dozen times in slightly different positions across a single positive plate. One image showed a horse jumping over a barrier, with a precision never obtained in Muybridge's photographs.

Marey also obtained some very strange geometric images, showing the movement of a human being or an animal with a degree of abstraction worthy of the Futurists. To photograph a human being, Marey dressed his subject (sometimes Demenÿ himself) in a completely black costume, with narrow strips or single points of shiny metal positioned along the outlines and joints of the body, so that the camera would only record the reflections of these strips. For an animal, it was first necessary to cover its body (if it was pale in colour) with lampblack, and glue strips of white or shiny paper along its limbs and joints. This was often quite a difficult preparation, especially when one of the wild residents of the Jardin d'Acclimatation (zoological gardens), for example the elephant, had to be 'chronophotographed'. Marey's geometric pictures had an influence on the modern art of the twentieth century, for example in Marcel Duchamp's famous painting of 1912, *Nu Descendant un Escalier* ('Nude Descending a Staircase').

Marey's process, though still far from perfect, was already infinitely superior to that used by Muybridge, which required twenty or thirty cameras arranged in series in front of the moving subject. 'It is quite clear', wrote Marey in 1889, 'that separate cameras spread over a great length do not record images from the same viewpoint.' Marey's method retained a single point of view: 'There is only one single lens located in a fixed position, like an observer before whom pass the movements to be analysed.'[35] In addition the 'Photochronographe' (the first name Marey used; the word 'chronophotograph' was not officially applied until 1889, at the decision of the Congrès de Photographie) took a series of images at strictly regular intervals. This was not at all the case in Muybridge's system, in which the horses themselves, travelling at varying speeds, released the electric shutters.

In Naples in 1887 Marey made a series of wax models showing eleven

Fig. 41.   Frames from films by Étienne-Jules Marey: a) children playing at the
Station Physiologique (a 90mm film); b) hand movements.
Collection: Cinémathèque Française, Musée du Cinéma.

successive positions of a pigeon. He wrote to Demenÿ, on 19 March of
that year: 'I have finished my first series of birds, it has been cast in
bronze and is quite successful, apart from some details. I am going to
send all this directly to the Institut.' The bronze figures were arranged
one after another to give a clear indication of the progression of wing
movements. At the Académie des Sciences, on 13 June 1887, Marey
showed a large zoetrope in which were arranged a series of bronze
statuettes painted white, representing six successive phases of the flight
of a pigeon (the seagull was also treated in the same way). When
the device was rotated, a view through its slots gave the illusion of
movement: a flying pigeon, with an unprecedented degree of precision
and relief. This synthesis was quite sufficient for Marey, for the time

being. When he needed to illustrate his experiments, he could use a turning zoetrope or project a chronophotographic image with the magic lantern. For example, on 29 June 1883 he reminded Demenÿ: 'Most important: I shall need by Friday some positive photographs for the magic lantern: running, walking, jumping, birds . . . This is for the Société de Physique.'[36]

The photographs taken at the Station Physiologique from 1882 onwards were of wonderful quality. Marta Braun has listed more than 450 such images in her book *Picturing Time: The Work of E.J. Marey*.[37] In this collection, as in the work of Muybridge, a complete carnival of animals troops in front of the 'black screen' of the Bois de Boulogne; there are also some delightful photographs of Marey himself shaking a long pole, to study its vibrations, or bouncing a shiny ball to follow its trajectory.

The paper strip chronophotographe

For many years photographers had complained of the difficulties of handling fragile glass plates. On 7 January 1887 at the Société Française de Photographie, the photographer Paul Nadar (son of Félix) demonstrated the excellent positive and negative paper which had been patented on 27 June 1884 by the Americans George Eastman (1854–1932) and W.H. Walker. Nadar was the representative of the Eastman Dry Plate Film Company for France and its colonies, with a shop at 53 Rue des Mathurins in Paris. It was also Nadar who marketed the famous 'Kodak' camera in France.

Eastman's negative paper, made at Rochester, New York, was evenly coated in a layer of gelatine silver bromide. There were two types of Eastman paper: one had a non-detachable photosensitive layer, the other had a sensitive coating which could be removed from its temporary support paper. Initially Eastman supplied the French trade with rolls of paper on which twenty-four or forty-eight pictures could be taken. The 'Edison–Walker roll carrier frame' could be fitted to all photographic cameras:

> The change from one picture to another may be obtained without any possible error, one is guided by the noise made by a trigger, and on hearing this noise each time one stops; two pins perforate the end of each new surface. This allows the immediate location of the line dividing each picture from the next during development.[38]

Clearly Eastman had already had the idea of perforating the sensitized strip in 1887; not to drive it, but to mark the location of the negatives on the strip. The Kodak, which arrived in France around the end of 1888, was a very light, simple pocket camera. Its paper roll could record 100 different pictures. Thanks to the sensitivity of gelatine silver bromide, instantaneous views of people and animals in motion could be taken in daylight, although not 'successively' in Marey's terms.

For Marey, the invention of the sensitized strip provided an essential new step in his method of taking pictures. Chronophotography on a fixed plate had certain faults which the ever-particular Marey himself criticized. 'If the object is animated with too slow a movement, or if it is performing movements in a single location, the images are imperfectly separated or even completely superimposed.' Some of the Marey pictures taken between 1882 and 1888 are quite difficult to decipher. For example, in the walk of a man who is moving slowly, the images merge together and become confused. To avoid superimposition, it would be necessary to 'move the sensitive surface, such that different points on that surface are presented successively to receive the images of the object'—an idea which had already been proposed by Pénaud in 1873, and even by Ducos du Hauron in 1864. On 15 October 1888, Marey announced at the Académie des Sciences:

> I hope to obtain a series of images on a long strip of sensitized paper, moved with a rapid translatory motion and stopped at the moments of exposure.[39]

On 29 October 1888, a historic day, Marey presented his first 'film' on paper:

> To complete the research which I discussed with the Académie during the first demonstrations, I have the honour to present today a strip of sensitized paper on which a series of images has been obtained, at the rate of twenty images per second.[40]

Less frequent images (ten or twelve per second, for example) and relatively long exposure times would be sufficient to analyse slow movements, but for rapid movements such as the flight of a bird or insect very frequent images (forty to fifty per second) were necessary.

Each time the rotating shutter disc allowed light to pass through, in Marey's revised camera design, it caused an electrical contact during which an electromagnet gripped the sensitized strip and stopped it for a very brief interval. This rather rough arresting of the strip was not entirely satisfactory, although the results obtained at the end of 1888 were already quite remarkable. All cinematographic cameras up to the present day operate on the same principle used by Marey: a sensitized strip must be driven intermittently past the focal point of a lens, with its momentary stoppages corresponding to the opening of the shutter.

The celluloid film chronophotographe

Marey's mind, too, seems to have been in a state of continuous movement, like a recording device, highly sensitive to every scrap of information which might prove useful. Marey had already turned sensitized paper to his advantage by adapting his Chronophotographe in 1888. He did the same with a new support medium, celluloid, which allowed him to make the first 'films' recorded on transparent film.

The invention of celluloid was the work of several individuals. The Englishman Alexander Parkes patented a substance called 'Parkesine' in 1855, and the American brothers Isiah Smith Hyatt and John Wesley Hyatt, of Newark, New Jersey, filed a patent for a similar substance on 15 June 1869. The name 'celluloid' appeared in an American patent of 2 June 1872, filed by the Celluloid Manufacturing Company of Albany. In May 1887 another American, Hannibal Goodwin, filed a patent for a celluloid 'photographic film'; the possibility of using this new support material for photography had already been suggested in France in 1881 by Fortier. Finally, on 9 April 1889, Harry M. Reichenbach and the Eastman Photographic Materials Company filed a new patent in the United States, for a highly transparent celluloid substrate composed of a mixture of methyl alcohol, camphor, nitrocellulose, and acetate. This patent was renewed by Eastman on 22 March 1892, for production of celluloid film such as that used by Edison in 1894.

In 1890, the celluloid substrate went into small-scale production throughout the United States and Europe: in France one factory, the Compagnie Française de Celluloid, was set up at Stains, in the Seine-Saint-Denis département. This new material provoked a great deal of excitement among photographers. In spite of its flammability (cellulose nitrate, mixed with camphor and alcohol, must be handled with great care), once the film had been laminated, compressed, and slowly steamed, it showed many useful qualities, especially elasticity, transparency, and strength.

Marey was supplied with celluloid film by Georges Balagny (1837–1919), a chemist and member of the Société Française de Photographie, and a friend of Albert Londe, the director of the photographic service at the Clinic for Nervous Disorders at the Hospice de la Salpêtrière. This film was 90 mm wide and 1.10 m long; Marey also used Eastman films supplied by his friend Nadar, in January 1891, and Jougla films in April 1891. Balagny had been working on this subject for a long time, and as early as 7 May 1884 had already produced a transparent gelatine silver bromide paper, coated with an adhesive gelatine film before exposure, which was easy to detach afterwards.

On 3 October 1890 Marey filed his first patent on the photography of motion. In it he described his 'photochronographic' film camera:

> This apparatus is arranged to receive successive images on a strip of sensitized film. This film is mounted on enclosed spools; it moves rapidly past the focal point of the lens and stops during the time of exposure.[41]

He designed three different models, driven by electricity, clockwork, and gravity. In each case a roller mechanism pulled the film, which was immobilized by a compressing device for a brief interval at the focal point of the lens. The film path included a spring, which restarted the film once the compression was released: 'Events take place as though the strip had become intermittently extendable, which allows it to progress in short steps under the combined action of a continuous drive and instantaneous stops.'[42] Marey presented his apparatus at the Académie des Sciences on Monday 3 November 1890. He showed a celluloid film, with about thirty images showing the successive positions of a trotting horse, six of which were published in the Proceedings of the Society.

With the assistance of Demenÿ and Lund, Marey now entered the true 'filmic' period of his work. He produced a great many films, which have been relatively well preserved: the Archives du Film at Bois d'Arcy near Paris, the Cinémathèque Française, the Photography Humanities Research Centre of the University of Texas, and other institutions and collectors now own a large number. Marey's film strips are true embryonic stages of the cinema, priceless evidence of the genius of this great researcher, and just as importantly remarkable works of photographic art (see Fig. 41). Their significance in the history of the sciences and arts makes their long-term preservation vital.

Marey explained his intentions in an article published on 25 April 1891 in his friend Nadar's magazine *Paris-Photographe*:

Using this method, one may operate in front of all types of background, illuminated or dark; this allows the study of movements which it is of interest to know in the place where they occur. In this way one will capture the movements of practitioners of different trades in the factory, those of runners and gymnasts on their training grounds, those of all kinds of animals in menageries and zoological gardens.[43]

In fact Marey did not change the location of his camera very much. A few films survive which were shot at Naples or the École de Gymnastique at Joinville, but the majority were made at the Station Physiologique at Bois de Boulogne. The subjects covered were almost the same—perhaps slightly less imaginative, and certainly less ambiguous —as those on the plates Muybridge made in Philadelphia, but Marey and Demenÿ's films, startling in their quality and precision, are all the same sometimes quite odd. There are the conventional subjects: a man walking, both clothed and naked; athletic exercises (Demenÿ and Rousselet often served as models) such as long jumps, high jumps,

Fig. 42. Frames from film by Georges Demenÿ, showing his own hand writing his name. Collection: Cinémathèque Française, Musée du Cinéma.

and dangerous leaps with poles and ropes. In one set of eighteen images, a naked athlete strikes with a stick at empty space—this excellent series was published in 1893 in Marey and Demenÿ's book *Études de Physiologie Artistique* ('Studies in Artistic Physiology'). A man digs with a pick, a blacksmith strikes on his anvil, naked cyclists glide past the camera. Javelin and discus throwers take their turns. Two boxers fight, a man cracks a whip, another climbs a tree. Demenÿ poses smoking a cigarette, playing the violin, or writing his name on a sheet of paper (see Fig. 42). Children play with a ball, soldiers present arms. And there is a whole animated menagerie of dogs, cats, goats, sheep, rabbits, foxes, birds, donkeys, racehorses (Tigris, Bixio, Mistigris, Mireille and others), and even insects and fish.

Other early 'location' films, as they would be called today, captured the movement of waves (one of Marey's first films, *The Wave*, was reproduced in the *Revue Générale des Sciences* on 15 November 1891), or the *Twenty-Four Phases of an Oar-Stroke*, a plate published in Marey's book *Le Movement* in 1894. Some slightly later films (around 1896–7) were made at the Place de la Concorde and other locations in central Paris by Marey's pupils, for example Lucien Bull.

One fascinating series survives which is the work of Demenÿ. In 1893 Alfred Binet, the assistant director of the psychology laboratory at the Sorbonne, made a long study of the 'psychology of conjuring'. Binet went to see the greatest magicians of the time: Méliès, Dickson, Arnould, and Raynaly. He asked the latter two to come to be 'chrono-photographed' at the Station Physiologique, where Demenÿ filmed them one after the other. They performed:

> the *saut de coupe* [a card trick] with one or two hands; the *filage* [a move forming the basis of the 'three card trick']; the disappearing ball; a flourish known as '*rayonnement*'; and so on. The most rapid card trick was the *saut de coupe* with two hands, performed by M. Raynaly in one-tenth of a second.[44]

George Méliès, unfortunately, seems not to have accepted the invitation to 'knock his tricks', in his own phrase, in front of Demenÿ's camera. All the same this episode is notable as the director of the Théâtre Robert-Houdin and future film-maker's first brush with chronophotography.

While Muybridge was creating mildly salacious pictures of women, Marey's work remained curiously modest. There were no naked women at the Station Physiologique. Perhaps Marey was sensitive to judgements on the morality of these films. On 4 August 1892, for example, he wrote to Demenÿ on the subject of some chronophotographs the latter had just sent him: 'You did well to dismiss certain models. The large one with long hair running with a child has the appearance of a pederast capturing his victim.'[45]

Perhaps the most touching film shows Marey chronophotographing himself. In 1954 an article by the historian Jean Vivié reproduced the one film which shows him, apparently making a speech.[46] Wearing a bow tie, with round pleasant face, shining eyes and white beard, Marey conveys an impression of good-natured intelligence. A beautiful portrait of his niece Francesca Noël-Bouton has also survived in the collection of the Cinémathèque Française.

Marey's films were not perforated. This was a major defect, since without perforations the movement of the film throughout the camera was not constant and the pictures were not evenly spaced. On the other hand, the images could occupy the full area of the film, which could be exposed either horizontally or vertically; in the surviving films the images are between 80 and 90 mm wide. The pictures were therefore very clear and easy to study. The number of images varied according to the subject. A strip could contain up to fifty-seven images, if it showed the movement of a small animal, but on average there were between ten and forty images per film.

Chronophotography across Europe

Between 1880 and 1895, in workshops and laboratories throughout Europe, chronophotography came into being in a number of very different forms and systems. Marey's dominance was clear, and he was truly at the forefront of animated photography between 1882 and 1894. The extent of his influence is difficult to trace, but it is certain that from the moment when the basic work by Marey and Muybridge was revealed in the scientific press, it gave rise to many other interesting ideas. Directly in Marey's wake came Albert Londe (1858–1917), who presented a camera obscura with twelve lenses arranged in a ring, operating with a single circular shutter, at the Société Française de Photographie on 3 August 1883.[47]

Léon-Guillaume Bouly (1872–1932) is a much more shadowy figure. On 12 February 1892 he filed a patent for a camera called the 'Cinématographe' (a name which the Lumières later borrowed without fear of legal action, since Bouly did not keep up the annual payments for his patent), whose aim was 'the automatic and uninterrupted achievement of a series of photographs analysing movement'. In Bouly's Cinématographe, the film was driven by a rotating cylinder with a cut-out portion in its surface, and then intermittently stopped by a padded pressure plate. When a handle was turned, the plate lifted, the rotating cylinder moved the film forward and then released it; the plate then lowered to hold the film stationary once again. At that precise moment the shutter uncovered the lens and a picture was exposed:

> This succession of movements is repeated for as long as the handle is rotated, and one can imagine that in this way it is possible for the operator to take, in a very short time, a considerable quantity of photographs in order to make an analysis of the movements of any type of body or animated scene.[48]

At least three Bouly Cinématographes were constructed: the first example is preserved in the Museum of the CNAM and follows the drawings of the 1892 patent, with only slight differences in the shutter. The CNAM also has a second Bouly Cinématographe, donated in 1927 by the Paris precision engineer Gaillard of 104 Boulevard Voltaire, who had made it, probably in 1893. The third Cinématographe can be seen at George Eastman House, in Rochester, New York, and is a reversible camera for films about 48 mm wide.

Bouly actually filed a second patent on 27 December 1893, for a reversible camera—that is, one which could be used not only to take a film, but also to project it once the film had been developed and the lens changed. The Cinématographe Lumière of 1895 was another example of a reversible camera. In his 1893 patent, which did not differ greatly from that of 1892, Bouly explained that all that was necessary was to lift the flap of the pressure plate, so that the light of a magic lantern could shine through the resulting aperature and illuminate the positive film. Bouly's films were not perforated, and the projection speed would probably not have been very constant. But the mysterious Bouly appears, from our viewpoint, to have been one of the most advanced chrono-photographers of his time.

The Englishman William Friese-Greene (1855–1921), together with the lanternist John Arthur Roebuck Rudge and the photographers Frederick Varley and Mortimer Evans, constructed a camera in 1889 which could take between five and ten pictures per second on a roll of bromide paper.[49] Friese-Greene's patent was dated 21 June 1889: already nine months had passed since Marey had achieved chronophotographic pictures on a sensitized strip, and the paper films Friese-Greene obtained were of much higher quality. Rudge's lantern of around 1884 is preserved at the Paris Musée du Cinéma. It allows projection of seven successive pictures to represent a movement: in an echo of Huygens' animated skeleton lantern slide, a man is seen to remove his head from his body (the body is that of Friese-Greene, the face that of Rudge).

Friese-Greene has been glorified to excess by less-than-careful historians, who have elevated his work to the highest level. In 1909, believing in his own importance, Friese-Greene himself wrote stern letters to the whole cinematographic industry to forbid its use of cameras, projectors and transparent films, of which he claimed to be the sole inventor.[50] The British film *The Magic Box*, made in 1950 by the Boulting Brothers and purporting to tell Friese-Greene's story, is a figment of imagination and historical error, inspired by a hagiographic account of Friese-Greene published in 1949. In 1962 the historian Brian

Coe gave a more accurate picture of the inventor, placing him in his contemporary chronophotographic context: Friese-Greene was certainly an adventurous researcher, but his (uncompleted) work was a long way from the same importance as that of Marey, Bouly, or Le Prince, to name only three.

There has been much speculation about the life of Louis Aimé Augustin Le Prince, who was born in 1841 at Metz in north-eastern France. In 1869 Le Prince moved to Leeds, in England, where he married Elisabeth Whitley and joined the Whitley metal-founding and constructional engineering firm. In 1881 he went to the United States, where he created several panoramas on the American Civil War. From 1885, he began to research in animated photography. He designed some multi-lens cameras and on 10 January 1888 filed a patent for a camera and projector with six lenses, capable of producing (he claimed) 960 images per minute.[51] This machine is preserved in the Science Museum in London, and carries the maker's name of H. Mackenstein, who was based between 1884 and 1890 at 23 Rue des Carmes, Paris (then from 1891 at 15 Rue des Carmes). Two sensitized strips, arranged side by side, passed behind the lenses. Eight shutters were released successively, exposing eight photographs on the first strip, eight other shutters were then actuated to expose the second strip, during which time the first strip was moved by a catch, and so on. The mechanism was similar to Ducos du Hauron's, but somewhat simpler. But multiple lenses were not to be of great importance for taking chronophotographic pictures.

Some months later, it appears, Le Prince constructed a new camera, this time with a single lens. In this camera, a strip of sensitized paper, wound onto a reel driven by an intermittent mechanism, moved past the lens and was stopped briefly by a pressure pad actuated by a cam. In October 1888 Le Prince made two films on paper, now preserved at the Science Museum, showing his mother-in-law in John Whitley's garden and a view of the traffic on Leeds Bridge taken through a window of the Hick Brothers hardware shop, a building still standing today. If these films truly date from October 1888 (this information is handwritten on the back of the paper film), Le Prince can be considered on equal terms with Marey, who also made his first films on sensitized paper. Le Prince also had one clear advantage over the physiologist: his films were made in the street, capturing everyday life, not the rather dry scientific study of movement. Marey's camera was much more sophisticated, but Le Prince had a vision which was more artistic, much closer to cinematographic spectacle.

Le Prince was also working hard on the problem of projection of animated photographs. In 1889 he attempted to project successive photographs on glass slides, connected together by a long strip of fabric, with perforations reinforced by metal eyelets (the idea of perforating a strip carrying animated pictures originated with Reynaud in 1888). In 1890 Le Prince succeeded in finding flexible celluloid sheets and adapting them into his perforated strip. To project the celluloid pictures, he constructed a three-lens machine in which three strips were moved at the same time by toothed pulleys, actuated by a Maltese Cross mechanism. We do not know how well this system operated, but the apparatus was demonstrated on 30 March 1890 to Ferdinand Mobisson, secretary of the Paris Opéra Garnier:

> I, the undersigned Ferdinand Mobisson, secretary of the Opéra National in Paris, resident at 38 Rue de Maubeuge, certify by these presents that I have been charged to examine a process of projection of animated images by means of an apparatus which has been demonstrated to me, for which Monsieur Le Prince has taken patent rights in France on 11 January 1888 under the number 188,089, for 'a method and apparatus for the projection of animated images with regard to its adaptation to lyric scenes' and to make a complete study of this system. In witness whereof I have delivered the present certificate to serve for legal purposes. Paris, 30 March 1890, F. Mobisson.
>
> Witnessed by me, Mayor of the 9th Arondissement of Paris, for authentication of the signature of M. Mobisson. Lesage, Paris, 30 June 1890.[52]

This means that it is possible that the first projection of chrono-photographic pictures on celluloid took place on 30 March 1890, but unfortunately Le Prince's projection apparatus has never been found. As for the 'disappearance' of Le Prince, a great deal—perhaps too much—has already been written on that subject, so that the private life of this inventor begins to seem more important than his work. On 13 September 1890, Le Prince was at Bourges in the upper Loire valley. He wrote to his English friend Richard Wilson that he would come to join him in Paris on Monday 16 September, before departing for New York. Le Prince added that he would spend the weekend with his elder brother in Dijon. In front of witnesses, he boarded the train from Dijon to Paris. On 16 September Richard Wilson became worried: Le Prince was not at their meeting-place. He had apparently vanished between Dijon and Paris. Some historians, such as Jacques Deslandes, believe that Le Prince ended his days in the United States, having given up all study of photography, and died in Chicago during the 1910s.

Among other chronophotographers, the German Ottomar Anschütz (1846–1907) of Lissa should be mentioned. In 1887 Anschütz completed a 'Tachyscope' which allowed photographic analysis of movement. This used about ninety pictures on glass, arranged around the periphery of a large vertical steel disc. An electric tube was illuminated thirty times per second to illuminate the passage of each picture of the disc as it was rotated. This was not projection: the analysis was observed directly with the naked eye. Anschütz embarked on his chrono- photographic career in 1885, and even managed to exploit this device commercially; his work is still relatively unknown.[53]

Compared to the 1850s, when researchers were really few and far between, at the end of the nineteenth century there were inventors everywhere. They were all jostling to reach the same 'correct' destination, each of them clutching a different apparatus. Many of them are forgotten today, since their systems did not contain new ideas. Among those who would benefit from serious study are the Englishmen Wordsworth Donisthorpe,[54] William Carr Crofts, and Wallace Goold-Levison; the Germans Kohlrausch and Mach; and the Frenchmen Sébert, Henri Carelles, Alfred Bidal, Georges Lesueur, and Fernand Gossart. All of these invented cameras for taking successive photographs, with greater or lesser degrees of ingenuity. But we will return to Marey, who like the unfortunate Le Prince was turning his attention to animated projection.

Marey's chronophotographic projector

So far Marey had been using the zoetrope to study the synthesis of chronophotographed movement. All the images of the film had to be cut out and glued at regular intervals around the interior of the zoetrope drum. This worked perfectly well, but Marey would have preferred to give lectures illustrated by animated projection, as Muybridge did with his Zoopraxiscope. However, Muybridge's method does not seem to have interested him, because its hand-painted images were relatively imprecise. What Marey wished for, in comments at the Académie des Sciences on 2 May 1892, was:

> to give the eye the sensation of true movement, by projecting the images successively onto a screen, by means of a device which I shall have the honour to present to the Académie in a forthcoming meeting. This apparatus is based on the properties of the

analyser; I call it the *chronophotographic projector*. It allows the showing to a multiple audience of the movements of objects of every kind, successive images of which have been collected by chrono-photography.[55]

However, this presented Marey with a very complex problem. Since the distances between each photograph on the film were not precisely equal, it was impossible to show the film as a whole with a magic lantern fitted with a conventional shutter. Like Le Prince, Marey was therefore obliged to cut out each individual celluloid image and attach it to a long strip of rubber-coated fabric. From his correspondence with Demenÿ, we can follow the work on this new and temperamental machine:

> 4 November 1891: My projection apparatus appears to work, I will make it less noisy . . .
> 21 January 1892: My projection apparatus is proceeding gradually through some appalling difficulties; I remain hopeful . . .
> 26 January 1892: I am waiting for the sun to try out my projection apparatus which works, I hope, although with too much noise and possibly some jumps of the image . . .
> 30 May 1892: I believe I have the solution for a perfect reversible machine giving equidistant images and acting as a projector . . .
> 12 July 1892: I am leaving the pursuit of my studies of the projector until a quieter time. I would hope to transform the chrono-photograph to have perfectly equal intervals between the images, which would make my task much easier, but this equality is still not perfect.[56]

On 16 February 1892, in another letter to Demenÿ (now in a private collection), Marey enquired about a film projector which, according to the American press, Edison had already completed. In fact, as was his habit, Edison had greatly exaggerated the progress of his research, which was still at an early stage. In 1894, in his book *Le Mouvement*, Marey did not seem satisfied with his projector:

> We have therefore constructed a special apparatus, in which an endless length of film containing forty or sixty figures, or even more, is allowed to pass without cessation under the field of an objective.
>
> The illumination, which is from behind, and consists either of the electric light or the sun itself, projects these figures upon a screen. This instrument produces very bright images, but it is noisy, and the projected figures do not appear as absolutely motionless as one could wish.[57]

With his chronophotographic projector, even though its operation was still quite primitive, Marey completed his journey around the cinematographic problem. He had solved the question of taking pictures, by making films on a celluloid base. He had then observed them in the zoetrope, or as projections, although not with the greatest success. But now, at least in the eyes of some of his contemporaries, 'from now on we may consider the problem of projection of movement as having been solved, and on the point of entry into the domain of common practice.'[58]

Those words were pronounced on 10 November 1892 by Mercier, a scientific demonstrator at the Faculté de Médecine, during a lecture on photographic projection. He was quite insistent on this point: 'In making his chronophotographic camera reversible, M. Marey has recently solved the problem of reproducing movement by projection.' Other researchers later found better systems for driving the film regularly and, by perforating the film, succeeded in creating excellent 'apparatus serving for the obtaining and viewing of chrono-photographic pictures', to quote the title of the Lumière patent filed on 13 February 1895 for the reversible camera they called the 'Cinématographe'. Albert Londe, the expert on chronophotography, took up his pen again to explain that, if Marey had not actually solved the problem of projected synthesis of motion,

> from a scientific point of view, it is the photographic analysis of movement which has much greater importance; by this we can discover laws which have been unknown until our times, we enhance our investigative methods; synthesis, on the other hand, if it can serve as a control or verification, if need be, cannot extend the sum of our knowledge.[59]

Marey's projector still exists today, at the Museum of the CNAM. His camera may be seen at the Musée du Cinéma in Paris, the Museum in Beaune, and the Museum of the CNAM. Different designs were used, with technical variations of greater or lesser importance. Marey's assistant Demenÿ also designed some quite ingenious projection systems. He was keen to commercialize his master's techniques; we shall see shortly why and how Demenÿ failed in his attempt to popularize chrono-photography.

Relations between Marey and Demenÿ were always somewhat variable. At the start, Demenÿ put himself completely at his master's disposal, without uttering a word. He asked Marey to correct his scientific papers, and to begin with there was much correcting to do; then little by little

Demenÿ began to express his ideas more clearly, without needing assistance. The young man began to harbour bitter ideas and make sarcastic replies. On 29 March 1889 Marey warned him:

> The community of scientific ideas which we have enjoyed for a certain time is quite certainly altered as a result of the special interests of each of us . . . At a certain age a man who has worked experiences the need to be emancipated and follow his own personal direction. If that moment has arrived for you, I will do all in my power to help create an independent situation for you which meets your tastes.[60]

Their ways did not part in 1889. Demenÿ still needed guidance and Marey's influential protection, and Marey, often in Naples, needed absolutely to be able to rely on his 'Chef de Laboratoire' (Laboratory Head) at the Station Physiologique. Lucid as ever, Marey could see clearly that his pupil was keen to catch up with his master. 'The caterpillar has become a butterfly,' he said of Demenÿ, and from 1890 onwards he allowed the butterfly to fly further and further with his own wings. Demenÿ gave lectures, signed articles, and created his own equipment. Marey would later regret having given the 'butterfly' such freedom.

In 1891, debate at the Station Physiologique had two basic subjects: the projection of films and the commercialization of cameras. At this time, chronophotography was known in international scientific circles, but the public at large knew practically nothing about it, in spite of the numerous popularizing articles in the press. In 1891, the 'chronophotographic spectacle' almost became a reality. On 1 August the administrative board of the Musée Grévin (a landmark of the cinema, as we shall see in connection with Reynaud) decided to sign a contract with Marey for a show based on projection. Unfortunately we do not know the scholar's response, although he was not at all tempted by the idea of a physiological spectacle exhibited on the *grands boulevards*. On 14 October 1891 the Musée Grévin board ordered a device 'to provide photographic projections of the pictures produced by Marey'[61] from a supplier named Guyenet. The plan came to nothing.

The Musée Grévin did, however, manage to present animated chronophotographic projection in July 1891. This was not with Marey's projection device, which did not emerge from Otto Lund's workshop until the following year, but Demenÿ's 'Phonoscope', which was presented at the Académie des Sciences on 27 July 1891 and patented on 3 March 1892.

The Demenÿ 'Phonoscope'

The Phonoscope was given this name because it was intended to 'reproduce the illusion of movement of the words and physiognomy of a person speaking'[62] (see Fig. 43). Demenÿ saw his invention as the starting-point for a new method of educating deaf mutes, who could 'read' the message delivered by watching the lips of the chrono-photographed subject.

First Demenÿ chronophotographed himself in close-up with a Marey camera (see Fig. 44). With his eyes dazzled by the bright mirrors concentrating light onto him, he articulated, with emphasized facial gestures, the short phrases *Je vous aime* ('I love you') and *Vive la France!* The eighteen, twenty, or thirty images obtained were then attached as positives around the circumference of a glass disc (diameters varied between 42 cm and 50 cm, and miniature discs were also made later).

Fig. 43. The Demenÿ Phonoscope, upright model on stand.
Collection: Cinémathèque Française, Musée du Cinéma.

Fig. 44.   Frames from 90 mm film by Georges Demenÿ, showing Demenÿ
himself posing before the Chronophotographe.
Collection: Cinémathèque Française, Musée du Cinéma.

This disc then had to be placed in a projecting lantern—Demenÿ used a
Molteni lantern—fitted with a shutter disc. Another version, intended
for individual viewing, was also constructed.

The Phonoscope belongs to the line of phenakistiscope projectors into
which the works of Naylor, Uchatius, Duboscq, and Muybridge also fit.
There was no real future for this type of disc-based device, which was too
limited in its range of images and too difficult to construct. The true
solution was that which Marey revealed in his film-based projector.
According to a contemporary account, the Phonoscope 'made poor use of
light, with the result that the projections intended to show the phenomenon in front of a large audience were scarcely achievable even with a
great intensity of light'.[63]

However Demenÿ believed that, in spite of its obvious defects, his apparatus was of great interest. For the first time chronophotographic pictures on a disc could be projected in sequence, even if they were a little dark. The press greeted the Phonoscope with great enthusiasm, and it was featured on the cover of *L'Illustration* on 21 November 1891. Demenÿ managed his advertising campaign skilfully, with a press-book including endorsements and articles from Russia, Greece, Egypt, Finland, Sweden, the United States, and elsewhere. He took part triumphantly in the Paris Exposition Internationale de Photographie, organized at the Palais des Beaux-Arts on 20 April 1892. He found himself discussed on equal terms with Janssen, Londe, Lippman, and Marey, and the Phonoscope was exhibited alongside the cameras of the Station Physiologique. According to his own account, Demenÿ could have received 'an avalanche of requests from Barnums and fairgrounds' offering to rent or buy his apparatus. This gave him some pause for thought. For the time being, Marey appeared to take no offence at the gradually increasing fame of his pupil. Instead he made gentle fun of it, as in a letter of 20 April 1892:

> I had already seen your number of *La Nature* [the issue of 16 April]. Thank you for sending it to me. But it scarcely flatters you! It would harm your prospects, if the young women were to see you crying 'Vive la France!' with that pitiful expression.[64]

At the start of 1892 Marey decided to make a few half-hearted attempts at marketing his process. On 30 May he wrote to Demenÿ from Naples: 'If Otto [Lund] can sell cameras, tell the clients to write and sign an order.' He envisaged selling six. On 25 November Marey clarified the position: 'I should be happy to sell a chronophotographic camera, but I am no longer in such a hurry, now that I have paid the constructors.' Very soon he was becoming annoyed: on 24 February 1893 he wrote, 'I have no news of purchasers of the chronophoto; I am waiting'; on 3 April 1893, 'I have undertaken an outlay of 6,000 Francs for the chronophotographic cameras and I have only sold one'.[65] It would be wonderful to know who purchased that one camera.

So between May 1892 and April 1893 Marey only sold a single camera; he was certainly 'waiting' for buyers, since he had not made a single move towards advertising or marketing. The route of commercialization, probably suggested by Demenÿ, no longer seemed the best idea to him. Relations between the two men, already not at their best, rapidly turned sour. Demenÿ saw himself as more commercially minded than his master, and put his cards on the table: he wanted to make money from chronophotography, and had a dream of forming a company to exploit his Phonoscope. From that point, a split became inevitable. Perhaps irritated by his own commercial setback, Marey had no desire to see his methods (the Phonoscope could not have existed without chrono-photography) exploited by a financial company not under his own control, and carrying the name of a lesser machine. Demenÿ was not alone in claiming his independence. The engineer Otto Lund, who had filed a patent for an instantaneous photographic shutter on 23 July 1892, described himself in the 1893 *Annuaire du Commerce* as a supplier of chronophotographic accessories—it is not clear whether this was with or without Marey's permission. Lund continued in this activity until 1911, with a shop at 6 Place de la Sorbonne (1893–1902) and then 11 Rue Gît-le-Coeur. Marey's attitude towards the Société du Phonoscope (Phonoscope Company), the first French attempt to exploit amateur chronophotography on a large scale, rapidly hardened into hostility, much to the detriment of the unfortunate Demenÿ.

The Société du Phonoscope

The Société Générale du Phonoscope, Portraits Vivants et Tableaux Animés (Phonoscope, Living Portrait, and Animated Picture Company) was founded on 20 December 1892 in Paris. The deed of association, consisting of two handwritten pages, has recently been located at the Stollwerck Chocolate Museum in Cologne by Martin Loiperdinger and Roland Cosandey.[66] This remarkable document, strangely, does not appear in the registers of companies in the Archives de Paris. The founders of this 'partnership association' were the German industrialist Ludwig Stollwerck of Cologne; William Gibbs Clarke of Lausanne (represented by François Henry Lavanchy Clarke, 1848–1922, the future Lumière agent in Switzerland); and of course Georges Demenÿ. The registered office was at Demenÿ's home address, 3 Rue Saussier-Leroy in the Seventeenth Arondissement of Paris.

> First Article: The aim of the Company is the industrial and com-mercial exploitation of the apparatus known as the 'Phonoscope', intended to reproduce the illusion of the movements of persons or animated objects, whether by direct viewing or by projection. Its additional aim is the exploitation of all applications and im-provements of the apparatus, among which are: 1. Animated portraits, 2. Moving projections, 3. Application to the Phonograph, 4. Application to automated distributors, 5. Scientific toys.[67]

The capital was 20,000 Francs, with 10,000 each put up by Stollwerck and Gibbs Clarke, to be supplied 'in stages according to requirements'. 'The industrial exploitation will comprise the construction of Phono-scopes and their applications, the fabrication and reproduction of zootropic discs.' Demenÿ brought to the company the 'results of his research, the designs of his invention', and the patents he had already taken out in France and in other countries. He also promised 'his assistance for the organization of the studio and laboratory, and the direction of the technical aspect of the exploitation'. The profits were to be divided in the following way: 5% to the reserve funds, 'a sum sufficient to be determined each year to ensure the depreciation of the equipment over at least ten years',[68] and then one-third each for Demenÿ, Stollwerck, and Gibbs Clarke.

The plan was vast, taking in practically all the possibilities of the future cinematographic industry. Demenÿ believed that thanks to 'amateur chronophotography', everyone would want and could possess a 'living portrait' of a parent or friend: 'How many people would be happy if they could see again in an instant the living features of a lost person!' Once the company had been set up, Demenÿ asked his partners for a little capital to carry out his research. He set himself up (possibly around the end of 1893) in a laboratory at 17 Villa Chaptal, Rue Chaptal, in Levallois-Perret in the northern suburbs of Paris.

However, Demenÿ was still entirely dependent on Marey. Phonoscope discs could only be produced using cameras patented by Marey. 'Chronophotography for all' could only take place with his agreement. And Marey dragged his feet; there was no further cooperation between the two researchers. On 10 April 1893, Demenÿ confided his exasperation to a Paris city councillor named Blondel. This unpublished letter, a rough draft of which has found its way into a private collection in Paris, contains some extremely harsh words about Marey:

> Dear Sir,
> Since 1880, the City of Paris has given me its support in carrying out work on the practical application of physiology to the physical improvement of mankind.
>
> Under a plan of study which I developed with Professor Marey . . . the City of Paris gave the latter an annual allowance of 12,000 Francs with a clearly defined brief.
>
> I have worked almost single-handed for fourteen years to realize this plan, and in spite of M. Marey's continual absences, the

laboratory which I organized has operated extremely well and produced results which are known to everyone.

But little by little, M. Marey changed the direction of the work and I found myself in conflict with him for the sole reason that I remained faithful to my commitments. We were no longer, as at the start, two collaborators in one great cause, but I became a slavish disciple of the master's whims.

Faced with this state of affairs, I could only leave the Station Physiologique, refusing to follow senile and incoherent management which was taking me away from my particular studies.

I did not as a result abandon the work I had started, quite the reverse, in order to continue to perform the programme of studies undertaken for the City of Paris in 1880.

I would ask you to assist me to obtain from the City the pleasure of some premises in which to set up research equipment, the Director of Higher Education having given me reason to hope for the support of the State for the upkeep of this laboratory with one clearly defined goal, that is the application of biology to the physical education of mankind.

Yours etc., G. Demenÿ.

Demenÿ's phrase 'senile and incoherent management' was truly hurtful; even worse, he boasted with some impertinence of his own achievements. We do not know if this letter was ever actually sent, but it does show Demenÿ's state of mind at the time.

Demenÿ sent Marey a contract of partnership, since he could not do without his master's chronophotographic cameras. Marey did not agree at all with its wording, and on 15 July 1893 wrote to Lavanchy-Clarke, then resident at 6 Square du Ranelagh:

Sir, the scheme which you propose lastly of only renting the chronophotographic cameras, is definitely not agreeable to me. I prefer the first [proposal] which consists of selling the cameras to individuals or to scientific institutions with the caveat that industrial exploitation has already been granted. In all cases, it will be necessary to find a form of words which satisfies you without creating too many obstacles for me.[69]

On 16 July Lavanchy-Clarke had a long discussion with Marey, who seems to have been generally suspicious and hesitant. According to Demenÿ, he demanded 40% of the future profits of the company. This figure was considered too high by Stollwerck, who was hoping to profit considerably from the first financial returns of marketing the Phonoscope as a popular slot machine. On 23 July 1893, the three partners met. It was a *coup d'état*: 'The negotiations with M. Marey having not succeeded to date, it is decided to carry on regardless and manage without his cameras.' The next day a furious Marey demanded Demenÿ's resignation as head of his laboratory. On 25 July he repeated his demand in writing:

> I have asked you to send me your resignation without delay, it is a matter of honour for you to withdraw and I do not wish that the Administration should be obliged to intervene. You are well aware that this step is necessary, that you are entirely uninterested in scientific research . . . Requesting you to make haste . . .[70]

This was a real slap in the face for Demenÿ, who had been at the Station Physiologique since its foundation. He was told to pack his bags, like a subordinate employee. Marey had not appreciated his exclusion from the Société du Phonoscope, whose existence in the first place must already have been an irritation.

Mistrusting Demenÿ's behaviour (with some justification), Marey had filed a new patent for his chronophotographic camera on 29 June 1893, in which he desired to

> guarantee the exclusive ownership of a camera allowing the obtaining, on a strip of sensitized film or on a sensitized plate, a series of photographic images corresponding to the successive positions of an animal or object in motion.[71]

However this was to no avail: it is easy to get round a patent by adding a technical detail sufficient to avoid an accusation of plagiarism. On 10 October 1893, Demenÿ filed his own patent for a camera intended 'to take a series of photographic images at equal and very closely-spaced intervals of time on a sensitized film'.[72] The word 'chronophotography', in the interests of discretion, was not mentioned.

The technical detail which Demenÿ devised was very sensible. He himself recalled how the idea came to him for a new film drive system which was more regular and gentle than Marey's pressure plate:

> I was at dinner when someone brought a visiting card to me, and I turned it over and over again in my hand while thinking about the solution to my problem. Then without thinking about it, I wound around this card a length of thread which happened to be to hand, and cried to myself: 'that's it, I have found my thing!' While turning

the card, the thread wound round it in a continuous manner, but its end moved in steps with successive halts.[73]

Demenÿ's patent of 10 October 1893 explained the principle of the new mechanism: a shaft was mounted eccentrically (that is, not coincident with the axis) on a small rotating plate referred to as the 'eccentric reel'. The film passed around the shaft, and as the shaft rotated on its plate it drove the film with alternating stops and forward movements, synchronized with the aperture of the shutter disc. But as the film gradually wound around the shaft, the diameter of the reel increased and the driving speed changed. This was a serious problem, which Demenÿ overcame on 27 July 1894 by the addition of the 'beater cam' to his device. This mechanism was used widely in cinematographic cameras between 1895 and 1910. In a patent addition of 27 July 1894, Demenÿ abandoned his original mechanism and introduced a steel rod into the film path, attached eccentrically to a rotating plate between the two reels which carried the film. As the plate turned, the rod contacted the film to give it an intermittent movement.

Demenÿ took his discovery proudly to the company and asked for a new supply of capital in return. Stollwerck gave this a rather cool reception; he was unimpressed by the beater cam. It was decided to issue some shares: 500 shares in total, 300 for the partners and 200 offered for sale. Several of these share certificates, signed by Demenÿ, Gibbs Clarke, and Stollwerck, are preserved in the archives of the Cinémathèque Française.

Following some further rather confused developments, Demenÿ seized all the shares and demanded the immediate winding-up of the company. According to him, the contracts were finally cancelled on 6 June 1895. In fact, it appears that on that date he actually granted Stollwerck a licence for marketing coin-operated Phonoscopes (which does not rule out the possibility of termination of the original agreements). By this time Demenÿ had already spent 40,000 Francs for equipment and research; he had also been dealing with other partners. We shall return to this subject in Chapter 16, dealing with the events of 1895.

Embroiled as he was in a financial disaster, Demenÿ also had to engage in an unequal contest with Marey. On 23 March 1894 his master once again asked for his resignation, promising to pay him compensation and find him alternative work. On 27 March 1894 Demenÿ replied firmly:

> I cannot voluntarily leave a post which was created for a precise outcome and which I have occupied with the greatest honour for fourteen years, for an allowance of whose provenance and stability I

know nothing. I shall not commit the cowardice of abandoning without a word, almost shamefully, a cause which, being in the general interest, must prevail over personal whim. It is useless to demand my resignation; I am and I remain an employee of the State and representative of physical training in higher education.

In spite of his protests Demenÿ was thrown out: Marey had connections at the Ministry. Demenÿ was given the responsibility of organizing a 'Municipal physical education course', and then in 1902 awarded the chair of applied physiology and the laboratory of the École de Gymnastique. Disillusioned, he later wrote:

> I had obtained results which were too important not to incite jealousy, and the jealousy of the powerful is like the thunderbolts of Jupiter. I could not avoid it, and was struck down.

'Struck down' was an accurate expression: the son had tried to overthrow the father, but had produced the opposite result. Shortly before his death on 15 May 1904, Marey still had the strength to write a vengeful letter, which Demenÿ regarded as 'defamatory'. On several occasions, Marey wrote, 'I was not entirely satisfied with M. Demenÿ's methods':

> However he continued to work closely with me, up until the day when I could no longer accept certain of his methods. I learned that he had found it necessary to modify, in order to make it patentable, and *to exploit in his own name one of my instruments whose description I had already given and which was, as a result, in the public domain.* While legally permissible, this type of action is not among those which, in the scientific world, can be considered acceptable.
>
> *The instrument in question* was none other than *the Chronophotographe of which M. Demenÿ has claimed the authorship.* Today M. Demenÿ believes himself to be free to do anything: he removed a quantity of documents from the laboratory which he is now publishing as his own work . . . The fact of having removed them is the most serious indiscretion which a laboratory employee could commit. M. Demenÿ has written that he parted company with me as a result of differences of opinion; but he appears to have forgotten that a ministerial dismissal hastened his departure.[74]

When this letter was published in the magazine *L'Avion* ('The Aircraft') in 1909, Demenÿ responded aggressively, describing Marey as 'a sick old man, unthinking and full of rancour'. But it would be best to leave this sad quarrel here.

Marey, the Jupiter whom Demenÿ had dared to challenge, had produced an exceptional child, chronophotography or cinematography, which in the years 1893–5 was gathering its strength. Marey left the work of bringing up this new creature to others: Demenÿ (whether he liked it or not), Edison, Lumière, all inventive 'chronophotographists'. And also to Reynaud, an inspired researcher and something of a dreamer, working like Niépce on borrowed money, who was in the end swallowed up by the triumphant cinematographic industry which, in his own way, he inaugurated in 1892.

14

The Big Wheel of Little Mirrors

A disciple of Abbé Moigno

At the end of the nineteenth century, while chronophotography was absorbing the attention of numerous researchers, a lone self-taught independent named Émile Reynaud set out on another road which was just as difficult, but no less rich in potential. Reynaud was deeply rooted in the research tradition of the 'ancients' who, following Huygens, projected brightly coloured animated images through the magic lantern. His mentor, Abbé Moigno, gave him the passion for 'the art of projection': the mechanical slides, dazzling and dizzying chromatropes, bright luminous colours, and moving drawings of the 'wheel of life' and choreutoscope. Reynaud was an artist and a showman, rather than a learned scholar like Marey; he does not seem to have been at all attracted by the 'moderns', the scientific types who were beginning to chronophotograph life itself, albeit in black and white. This relative disinterest in animated photography should not be seen as an error of judgement. It would be hard to criticize Reynaud for his preference for hand-painted images, when we still have the pleasure today of seeing in action some of the wonderful toys he created from 1877 onwards. And his poetic and artistic 'Pantomimes Lumineuses' ('Illuminated Plays') of 1892, a show of 'animated drawings' which attracted about half a million spectators over eight years, was an invention of true inspiration.

Charles-Émile Reynaud, the son of a medal engraver, was born on 8 December 1844 at Montreuil-sous-Bois on the outskirts of Paris. Around the age of fourteen, he was apprenticed to a Paris precision engineer named Gaiffe, with whom he studied optical and scientific instruments. He then moved to Artige et Compagnie, makers of mechanical equipment, where he learned industrial design. Finally he discovered photography, thanks to the expert Adam Salomon. These various skills permitted him to tackle the most difficult optical and mechanical problems with considerable ease.

In 1864 Reynaud met Abbé Moigno. On 9 June of that year, with his customary stubbornness, Moigno had relaunched his 'Public Courses in Popular Science', first at 3 Quai Malaquais, then from 14 July at 44 Rue Bonaparte. It was in this second hall that an excited Reynaud attended one of the Abbé's lectures. With his lantern, Moigno projected his hand-painted or photographic scientific pictures; he explained calmly the antiquity of mankind, the spontaneous generation of living organisms, and the many different worlds. It is not clear whether it was the magic lantern or Moigno's rhetoric which excited the young Reynaud more; in any case he returned several times and finally struck up a friendship with the 'apostle of projection'. Moigno taught him all his methods: dissolving views, phantasmagoria, superimposition, control of optics and oxy-hydrogen gas, handling animated slides, and painting on glass. By way of an encore, he also succeeded in converting him to Catholicism (Reynaud had been raised by parents with secular views, and had never been baptized).

After the death of his father Brutus on 7 December 1865, Reynaud set up home with his mother at Le Puy-en-Velay, his father's family home in the Massif Central. His uncle taught him the sciences and Latin, and Reynaud continued to make projection slides. He subscribed to Moigno's magazine *Les Mondes*, and from 1873 to *La Nature*, having made the acquaintance of its editor Tissandier through Moigno. On 11 January 1873 Reynaud returned to Paris to assist Moigno with his new project: the Salle du Progrès ('Hall of Progress') which he had opened at 24 Rue de Bourgogne. Reynaud took charge of the courses in photography, illustrated by the lantern. The first of these took place on 14 January, but by 3 February the hall had closed for lack of an audience. The young projectionist went back to Le Puy, no doubt somewhat dis-heartened, but definitely infected with the virus of illustrated lecturing. He began to organize public courses in popular science, like those run by Moigno, at the town hall in Le Puy. During the first show, on 9 December 1873,

> the young professor M. Reynaud, for about one hour and a quarter, captured the attention of an audience composed of young students of industry and many of the ladies and young ladies of the town.[1]

In 1874 Reynaud published the first lesson of his course in physical science, which revealed that he was using a projection microscope to show the forms of crystals:

> We place a drop of water on a glass slide and place this slide into our powerful microscope illuminated by oxy-hydrogen light. This is the experiment; you can now notice that after evaporation the drop of water has left a deposit of small geometrically shaped bodies, which resemble small regular cubes. We refer to these as crystals and say that the body has crystallized.[2]

The lantern was also used for spectral analysis and many other experiments. Reynaud had the services of two assistants: his cousin Lucien and the young Pierre Tixier, who was aged nine in 1874. In 1926, the historian Maurice Noverre recorded Tixier's recollections:

> My principal role was the operation of the gas tap. First to make a great light while the professor entered, then almost complete darkness during the projections (sometimes I even extinguished the jets completely, which confused me greatly and led to some disturbance to relight them) . . . Often it was necessary to use two machines, one on the right and one on the left to create dissolves. I remember that in a later lecture [in 1877] we showed the departure of a balloon. We saw its inflation. We saw the aeronauts climb into the basket. Then at the 'all clear' it rose majestically, reached the clouds, passed through them, then returned to its home mooring without accident.[3]

Reynaud had evidently achieved quite a level of proficiency in the processes of projection.

The invention of the Praxinoscope

La Nature, often mentioned in relation to Muybridge and Marey, also played a role in the exploits of Émile Reynaud. On 1 April 1876 this excellent 'review of the sciences and their applications to the arts and to industry' published an article by Charles Bontemps entitled 'Vision and optical illusions'. The Thaumatrope, Phenakistiscope, and Zoetrope were explained, accompanied by engravings. 'One can construct the majority of the instruments which we have listed oneself', the author wrote in conclusion.

This article was not news to Reynaud, who knew quite well what a

MÉD. DE BRONZE EXP^{on} UNIV^{lle} 1889

LE PRAXINOSCOPE
Jouet d'optique produisant l'illusion du mouvement

Basé sur une nouvelle combinaison de l'optique, le PRAXINOSCOPE anime les dessins, leur communique pour ainsi dire la vie, sans perdre de leur finesse et de leur coloris.
Cet instrument fournit une récréation intéressante pour les grandes personnes aussi bien qu'attrayante pour les enfants.

Fig. 45. Advertisement for the Reynaud Praxinoscope.
Collection: Laurent Mannoni.

Phenakistiscope was; but to entertain young Pierre Tixier he decided to make one, showing a man sawing wood. Since the successive images of the Phenakistiscope and Zoetrope were viewed through slots, the images and their colours were dimmed considerably by the rapid passage of the areas of card between the slots. Inspired by previous research (such as the work of Léon Foucault, according to Guy Fihman), Reynaud decided to overcome this defect by using prismatic mirrors. He constructed a much better instrument, the Praxinoscope (from the Greek *praxis*, 'action', and *skopeo*, 'I look'), which he described in a letter to the Académie des Sciences dated 20 July 1877. On 30 August 1877 'M. Reynaud, teacher of sciences of 39 Place du Breuil, Le Puy, Haute-Loire' filed a patent for a still nameless device which gave 'the illusion of movement with the aid of moving mirrors'. The name 'Praxinoscope' first appeared in the British patent of 13 November 1877.

The particular aim of this invention is to produce the illusion of movement by means of drawings representing the successive phases of an action. This aim is the same as that of the instrument by M. Plateau known by the name of Phenakistiscope. But the principle and methods of the current inventor are different from those employed in the latter apparatus.[4]

In the Praxinoscope, the substitution of one image by another was effected by prismatic mirrors so that, since there was no interruption to vision, the brightness and colour of the images was not altered. In its first version, the device consisted of a 'cage of mirrors' (as Reynaud described it), a series of twelve small vertical mirrors, 5.5 cm high and 2.7 cm wide, glued next to each other to form a polygonal prism which was arranged in the centre of a drum whose diameter was twice that of the 'cage'. The drum was supported by a wooden base to rotate about its vertical axis simultaneously with the 'cage' (see Fig. 45). Around the inner surface of the drum was inserted a paper strip, which showed twelve drawings of the same subject in different phases of an action. This strip was arranged so that each picture corresponded to one face of the prism of mirrors. The drum and mirrors were rotated by a simple push of the hand, by turning a handle, or by a small electric motor. The observer looked into the moving mirrors and would see a single moving picture, with quite remarkable clarity and brightness. The Praxinoscope could also be used in darkness: a candle could be placed at the centre of the cage of mirrors, on the fixed pivot axis of the base, with a lampshade concentrating its light onto the drawings. Several viewers, arranged around the circumference of the drum, could watch the animated show at the same time. The patent of 30 August 1877 already mentioned some interesting variations: a stereoscopic version (not actually constructed until 1908) and particularly a Projection Praxinoscope, to which we will return later.

Excited by his invention, Reynaud wanted to market it commercially and to move back to Paris. His mother approved, but his father's family did not. In the end there was a falling-out with his uncle in Le Puy, and in December 1877 Reynaud and his mother Marie-Caroline (née Bellanger, 1808–80) arrived at the Hôtel de la Plata in Paris. The aim was to profit from a particularly special event, the Exposition Universelle which was due to open on 1 May 1878. In February that year they found two apartments at 58 Rue Rodier, a building which still stands today, which served as both a workshop and a home for mother and son. Reynaud agreed a contract with a toy manufacturer, Dubourguet of

Nogent-sur-Marne, who mass-produced the metal drum of the Praxino-scope for him. A mirror cutter supplied the glass for the prismatic cage, and a printer made the lampshade and lithographed picture strips, which Reynaud drew himself.

The Praxinoscope appeared in the novelty goods section of the Exposition Universelle and captured public attention. Alongside it were the polychrome magic lanterns of Lapierre, the Polyorama Panoptique of Lefort, the 'Grimakisticope' of J. Delhomme (a type of stereoscope which deformed photographs into strange anamorphoses, by means of a moving mirror actuated by a clockwork mechanism), the 'Pédémascope' of the Reverend Richard Pilkington (a small variation of the Thauma-trope whose name carries an unfortunate *double-entendre* in French), and so on. But the Praxinoscope was the true 'novelty of the age'. The official report on the novelty goods section, written by Madame Burée, was full of praise:

> The public of the Exposition admired the juggler, the little girl blowing soap bubbles, the two little dogs jumping through a hoop. We will commit the indiscretion of commenting on one drawing which might have been titled 'childish pleasures of winter'. The performers are three little boys who incessantly chase each other. While one of them slides on the ice, with his body thrown back and arms outstretched, the one who has finished his slide jumps over a post as in the game of leapfrog, and the third who has just jumped runs to throw himself back onto the slide in his turn . . . The Praxinoscope appears likely to become a strong rival of the Stereoscope, since it can just as well serve to entertain grown-ups as well as children, and we are certain that it will not take long to enter every drawing-room.[5]

The lithographic strips which Reynaud designed were very graceful indeed. They showed short scenes in twelve images on a pale back-ground, with bright clear colours in the style of the chromolithographs which were so popular in the nineteenth century. For his colours and the subjects Reynaud drew inspiration from the repertoire of the magic lantern slide: a little girl skipping, a watermill, clowns, the *Magic Rose* (imitating the chromatrope), and so on. Some of the strips, such as *The Equilibrist*, recycled the images of a set of zoetrope strips published in Paris in 1867.

Reynaud published three sets of lithographic strips in 1878, measuring 66 cm in length and 5.2 cm in width. Their subjects were:

First series:
1. *The Aquarium*; 2. *The Juggler*; 3. *The Equilibrist* [a boy juggling a cylinder with his feet]; 4. *Feeding the Chickens*; 5. *Soap Bubbles*; 6. *The Spit Roast*; 7. *Dance on the Tightrope*; 8. *The Clever Dogs*; 9. *The Skipping Game*; 10. *Zimm Boum Boum* [a child playing a drum].

Second series:
11. *The Sawyers*; 12. *The Shuttlecock Game*; 13. *The Little Watermill*; 14. *Baby's Dinner*; 15. *The Magic Rose*; 16. *The Butterflies*; 17. *The Trapeze*; 18. *The Swimmer*; 19. *The Musical Monkey*; 20. *The Slide and Leapfrog* [the strip described by Madame Burée].

Third series:
21. *The Charmer* [a small girl feeding birds]; 22. *The Seesaw*; 23. *The Strong Man*; 24. *The Two Rascals* [children tossing a cat in a blanket]; 25. *The Smoker*; 26. *The Game of the Graces* [two girls tossing hoops between sticks]; 27. *The Horsewoman*; 28. *The Steeplechase*; 29. *The Little Waltzers*; 30. *The Clowns*.

Madame Burée was quite correct: the Praxinoscope sold very well. It never quite became the 'strong rival' of the stereoscope (around 1908 Reynaud claimed to have sold 100,000 Praxinoscopes, a small number compared to the 500,000 stereoscopes *Le Cosmos* said were sold between 1851 and 1857), but this charming toy and magnificent present made its entry into a good many better-off homes.

Several versions were already gracing the shelves of the novelty dealers and department stores. There was the standard Praxinoscope, the version operated by a handle, or the version with an electric motor, and several different sizes were produced.[6] They were supplied in a beautiful red cardboard box, decorated with a lithographed label or the simple wording: 'The Praxinoscope—Sujets Animés ['Animated Subjects']—E.R.' The lampshade, in the first version, was blue or green and carried the wording 'The Praxinoscope, animating drawings without reducing their brightness or clarity'. In later versions it was decorated by small drawings taken from Reynaud's repertoire: the two rascals throwing a cat on a blanket, the small girl amusing herself with bubbles, the girl playing with birds, and so on.

Reynaud came away from the 1878 Exposition with an 'honourable mention' and plenty of orders in his pocket. In 1879, he won a silver medal at the Exposition Industrielle de Paris (Paris Industrial

Exposition). In the course of that year he improved the effects of the Praxinoscope immeasurably, making it into a truly marvellous artistic invention.

The Praxinoscope-Théâtre and Toupie-Fantoche

This 'Lilliputian theatre' surpassed all the peepshows invented since the seventeenth century in terms of spectacle. Even in the peepshow boxes of the greatest cabinets of curiosities, it had never been possible to see a scene animated with continuous movement, or with such an effect of life, depth and perspective. Reynaud himself described his new device in his friend Moigno's magazine *Les Mondes* on 5 June 1879:

> By means of a very simple addition to the Praxinoscope, I have succeeded in producing true animated pictures or scenes, with scenery, as if in a Lilliputian theatre. The character in motion appears in the centre of this little stage in startling depth and, in this completely new arrangement, the apparatus itself, the mechanism, disappears to leave visible only the curious illusion produced.[7]

Reynaud filed an addition to his 1877 patent on 7 January 1879, giving an explanation of the Praxinoscope-Théâtre, together with a small descriptive drawing. The device itself was the same as the design of 1877–8, but fixed inside a beautiful mahogany or cardboard box covered in paper (there was also a deluxe version in a thuja-wood box, with ebony inlays). The picture strips of the new Praxinoscope were printed on a black background, making their coloured figures stand out particularly clearly. The figures would appear to spring out of the middle of a background scene, thanks to the new technique:

> This effect is obtained by the addition to the Praxinoscope of a transparent mirror arranged to reflect the image of a scene placed in front of it, while allowing the figure animated by the Praxinoscope to be seen through it. This is a new application of a device already used in theatres to produce *impalpable ghosts*.[8]

But perhaps Reynaud had never liked the phantasmagoria, since he never created any diabolical subjects and did not exploit the ghostly themes so beloved of Pepper and Robin. In the Praxinoscope-Théâtre only the scenery was viewed by reflection: small carefully executed lithographs showing different backgrounds were slipped into the reverse of the box lid, which was held in a vertical position by a hook. A small rectangular opening in the lid allowed the viewer to see, with both eyes, the animated image from the Praxinoscope and the still image of the scenery reflected in the mirror. The mirror was located between the scenery and the animated figures, held in place by a lithographed sheet representing the proscenium of a theatre stage.

Reynaud left the choice of scenery up to the audience: the skipping girl could amuse herself in the interior of a room, but also in the middle of a forest in front of a watching couple as entranced as the audience themselves. The dancers, the smoker (who bore some resemblance to Reynaud, a young man with wavy hair and a black beard) with his attentive dog, the beautiful shuttlecock player, the little farm girl with her chickens, the swimmer, or the strong man easily lifting iron weights, form an amazing series of little sketches, a charming and old-fashioned little world. Reynaud reissued twenty of the strips from his first Praxinoscope with black backgrounds:

First series:
1. *The Juggler*; 2. *The Equilibrist*; 3. *Feeding the Chickens*; 4. *Soap Bubbles*; 5. *The Clever Dogs*; 6. *The Skipping Game*; 7. *The Shuttlecock Game*; 8. *The Swimmer*; 9. *The Horizontal Bar* [new subject]; 10. *Leapfrog* [new subject].

Second series:
11. *The Charmer*; 12. *The Seesaw*; 13. *The Strong Man*; 14. *The Two Rascals*; 15. *The Smoker*; 16. *The Game of the Graces*; 17. *The Horsewoman*; 18. *The Steeplechase*; 19. *The Little Waltzers*; 20. *The Clowns*.

There were twelve lithographed backgrounds, as well as a mirror to go with *The Swimmer*.

The 'Lilliputian theatre' sold just as well as the original Praxinoscope. At the end of the nineteenth century practically all the Paris department stores offered Reynaud's parlour toy over the counter or in their Christmas catalogue. The success of the invention was proved by the fact it was copied both in France and abroad. In Germany, the Bavarian company Ernst Planck offered an imitation Praxinoscope-Théâtre, called the 'Kinematofor or Wheel of Life', in its catalogues up until 1902. It was a poor imitation which did not even use all of Reynaud's methods, with no reflected scenery or transparent mirror. On the other hand, Planck did have the idea of a standard Praxinoscope driven by a small steam engine,

Fig. 46.   Émile Reynaud's Toupie-Fantoche (1879).
Collection: François Binétruy.

a curious device which was still on sale in 1914. But the German picture strips never rivalled the quality of Reynaud's own drawings.

On 26 August 1879, in a third addition to his 1877 patent, Reynaud described the 'Toupie-Fantoche' (literally 'puppet spinning-top'), which was not actually marketed until 1881 (see Fig. 46). This consisted of four triangular mirrors inclined at 45 degrees and joined along their edges to form a truncated pyramid. At the apex of the pyramid a small paper disc was placed, carrying four printed images which represented stages of a movement. When the pyramid was rotated on a wooden handle, the reflections of the four phases of movement became visible in the moving mirrors. This was a simplified Praxinoscope, with a quite limited effect. Reynaud did not sell very many examples of this tiny toy, which as a result is now very rare. He published ten untitled discs, 9.4 cm in diameter, which showed:

1. A small girl playing with a ball; 2. A tightrope dancer; 3. A dancing Chinaman, with a bottle in his hand; 4. A young woman

skipping; 5. A child eating an ice-cream; 6. The face of a cavalier; 7. A frog jumping into water; 8. A gymnast performing on the trapeze; 9. A horse jumping a barrier; [no example of the tenth disc is known to have survived].

All Reynaud's devices rested on the single principle devised in 1877: animation by means of prismatic mirrors. With remarkable imagination and ingenuity, he exploited this catoptric system in every way possible. He was a man who had conceived one single invention, the Praxino-scope, and refined it into variations as the 'theatre', 'spinning top', and 'projection' models.

The Projection Praxinoscope

When Reynaud conceived his Praxinoscope in 1877, he immediately associated it with the magic lantern. For a former lanternist, that was an obvious connection. A first design of Projection Praxinoscope, operating with oxy-hydrogen light, was described in the patent of 30 August 1877. After making several improvements, Reynaud presented his new device at the Société Française de Photographie on 4 June 1880 (see Fig. 47). This was a historic event: Reynaud not only projected his animated drawings onto the screen, but he set the learned assembly to work on an ambitious project:

> M. Reynaud adapted his Praxinoscope to a projection device and projected on a screen all the effects which can be produced by the standard Praxinoscope and the Praxinoscope-Théâtre. After having demonstrated the operation of these different devices to the Société, M. Reynaud commented that the effects would be still more beautiful if, in place of the hand-drawn images representing the different phases of a movement, it were possible to obtain them by means of photography. One would then have a perfection of representation, and exactness of movement which is difficult to obtain by manual drawing. He invited the Société to be pleased to interest itself in this question and attempt to resolve the problem.[9]

If Reynaud did not attempt to approach this 'problem' himself, it was perhaps because it did not truly interest him. We might assume that the artist, the lover of colours, the painter-poet, did not find too much attraction in photographs. But at least he deserves credit for bringing an original idea into the converging flow of research which was moving in

Fig. 47. Émile Reynaud's Projection Praxinoscope (1880).
Collection: François Binétruy.

the direction of projection of animated photography. In 1880 only Muybridge could have supplied successive photographic images for use in the Praxinoscope, since the photographic rifle and Marey's cameras were still no more than ideas.

The Projection Praxinoscope, really an amateur version of the future Théâtre Optique, was first made and sold in 1882. It sold for 60 Francs in 1886, with five subjects on glass and five background scenes. Reynaud sold very few of them, to judge by the rarity of this splendid object today: only four complete examples are known to survive, one at the Frankfurt museum, one in the Eastman House museum, one in Denmark, and one in a private French collection. I have had the opportunity to examine the latter example. There were no paper strips; instead the subjects were lithographed onto small square glass slides, connected to each other by fabric strips to form a flexible strip of twelve images against black backgrounds. These were placed into a modified Praxinoscope, with a flared drum whose walls were partly open. At the centre of the drum, the 'prismatic cage' was also different: the twelve mirrors were inclined at 45 degrees, to form an upside-down truncated pyramid. Adjacent to this Praxinoscope, mounted on a base and driven by a handle, was an oil lamp on top of which a 'Reflectoscope' lantern (capable of showing opaque objects) was placed. This lantern had three functions: it illuminated the glass strips, whose images were reflected strongly from the rotating mirrors; by means of a second lens, the lantern then captured these images and projected them onto a screen; and finally it projected the background scenes which were printed on paper. The result was a superimposition on the screen of the still image of the scenery and moving images from the glass strip.

The Projection Praxinoscope was supplied with an instruction booklet in English and French, and came in two boxes, one blue, the other decorated with an attractive lithographed label. The glass strips were supplied in small cardboard boxes, and the whole apparatus was presented as a luxury item. In the example examined there are five background scenes, identical to those of the Praxinoscope-Théâtre although in a different printing with a white margin containing text. Fifteen glass strips accompany the device, all showing previously published subjects.

Strips:
1. *The Juggler*; 2. *The Equilibrist*; 3. *Feeding the Chickens*; 4. *Soap Bubbles*; 5. *The Clever Dogs*; 6. *The Skipping Game*; 7. *The Shuttlecock Game*; 8. *The Charmer*; 9. *The Seesaw*; 10. *The Strong Man*; 11. *The Two Rascals*; 12. *The Smoker*; 13. *The Game of the Graces*; 14. *The Little Waltzers*; 15. *The Clowns*.

Backgrounds:
1. Interior; 2. Circus; 3. Countryside; 4. Snow Effect; 5. Woodland.

Reynaud did not have time to extend his repertoire. His whole mind was concentrated on another projection device, based on the same principle but much larger and more powerful, which he just about managed to construct in his little workshop at 58 Rue Rodier. This was the large machine known as the 'Théâtre Optique' ('Optical Theatre') which produced wonderful projected scenes. This was the penultimate and most brilliant incarnation of the Praxinoscope, the optical 'toy' invented to relieve the boredom of a child.

The Théâtre Optique

The Théâtre Optique, an enlarged and improved version of the Projection Praxinoscope, was patented by Reynaud on 1 December 1888:

> The aim of the device is to obtain the illusion of movement, no longer limited to the repetition of the same positions at each rotation of the instrument, as necessarily produced by all known apparatus (zoetropes, praxinoscopes, etc.), but having on the contrary an indefinite variety and duration and in this way producing true animated scenes of unlimited development. Hence the name Théâtre Optique given by the inventor of this apparatus.[10]

The patent described the idea of a 'flexible strip, of undetermined length, carrying a series of successive poses, wound and unwound to and from a reel'. This strip was regularly perforated, a method which clearly foreshadowed cinematographic film, the more so since Reynaud once again advocated the use of animated photography:

> This flexible strip may be formed of any opaque or transparent material . . . The positions which are represented there may be drawn by hand, or printed by any reproduction process; in black or in colours, or obtained from nature by means of photography.[11]

In Reynaud's Théâtre Optique the perforated picture strip also drove a large gear wheel which carried the mirrors; in a cinematographic camera the film is driven by a specific mechanism, with the perforations ensuring a regular spacing of the images. This is an important difference, but whatever its function this was the first use of a perforated strip in a machine for projecting animated images.

The Théâtre Optique was offered for sale from 1890 onwards. In *L'Annuaire du Commerce* for 1891, Reynaud appeared in the section on toy manufacturers with the note 'The Praxinoscope, the Théâtre Optique, producing the illusion of movement'. But if the Projection Praxinoscope was not selling very well, the Théâtre Optique was practically unsaleable: it was a complex, fragile, and bulky mechanism which needed animated picture strips to work. Around 1892, Reynaud published a small brochure in which the prices of two different Théâtres Optiques were outlined:

> Théâtre Optique mounted on a metal frame, divisible into two parts, with an oscillating mirror mounted on a detachable wooden

base, electrical contact and striker, accompanied by three scenes [presumably *Un Bon Bock*, *Le Clown et ses Chiens*, and *Pauvre Pierrot!*] with their backgrounds, the whole contained in three wooden chests prepared for transport . . . 2,000 Francs.

Théâtre Optique mounted on a mahogany table, with an oscillating mirror for wall mounting, electrical contact and striker, accompanied by three scenes with their backgrounds . . . 1,750 Francs.

Projection equipment, arranged for the Théâtre Optique, comprising a special inclined condenser lantern and a double lantern, with a stage curtain effect, can also produce conventional projections (polyorama, dissolving views, etc.) . . . 500 Francs.

Each purchaser has the right to three demonstration lessons.[12]

Such a contraption could only be of interest to theatre or fairground operators. How Reynaud could hope to supply three scenes for each order, considering the amount of labour and patience involved, remains a mystery. Between 1888 and 1892 he created three 'animated drawings' on the flexible perforated strip:

A comic scene, with four characters, entitled *Un Bon Bock* ['A Good Beer']. The strip comprises no less than 700 poses and has a length of 50 m; the projection lasts for about twelve to fifteen minutes. An interlude entitled *Le Clown et ses Chiens* ['The Clown and His Dogs'], comprises 300 poses and the strip is 22 m in length, giving a show of six to eight minutes. Finally, the pantomime *Pauvre Pierrot!* ['Poor Pierrot!'], with three characters, comprises 500 poses on a strip of 36 m and lasts from ten to twelve minutes.[13]

The scenarios of these three strips must have appealed to the Parisian mind, demonstrating a light heart and a lively sense of humour. *Un Bon Bock* told the story of a gentleman of leisure courting a pretty waitress in a bistro: while his back is turned, a kitchen boy takes advantage of his preoccupation and drinks his beer. *Pauvre Pierrot!* was a masterpiece of poetry and animation:

Scenery, perspective, characters, costumes, everything is of an astonishing success; everything has its exact depth and correct colouring; it is truly a theatre in action and the illusion is perfect. The scene of poor Pierrot getting thrashed by Harlequin, while he plays his mandolin below the balcony of the deceiver Columbine, is beautifully detailed. We see Harlequin climb the wall and jump into the garden, court the beauty who came at his first call, and hide himself nimbly behind a column on hearing Pierrot opening the door and gallantly presenting a bouquet to Columbine. Then all the intrigue of betrayal unfolds with a truth of movements and appropriate facial expressions which are astounding when one imagines that these actors coming, going, disappearing, weeping and dancing, are nothing more than an optical representation.[14]

The interlude *Le Clown et ses Chiens*, as its title suggests, showed some circus dogs jumping onto a ball and passing through hoops.

The construction of these lengthy dramas was a very delicate task. Over four years from 1888 to 1892, in addition to his usual work managing the Praxinoscope workshop, Reynaud achieved a work of true patience in individually hand-painting some 1,500 images. The little characters were carefully drawn and painted onto gelatine ('crystalloid', as Reynaud described it), a material which was flexible and transparent but quite fragile: it tended to crack under the effect of heat, during the early days of the Théâtre Optique, and Reynaud had to remake several strips. The pictures were on a black background, as in the strips of the Praxinoscope-Théâtre. The small gelatine plates, measuring 6 cm square, were then connected end to end by a double wire, at top and bottom, and separated by small squares of black cardboard of the same size. In each plate was formed a circular perforation.

Reynaud brought the final version of the Théâtre Optique into operation in his workshop at Rue Rodier. He invited his friend Gaston Tissandier, who published a detailed article in the 23 July 1892 issue of *La Nature*. A well-known engraving shows Reynaud at the controls of his new machine, projecting an image from *Pauvre Pierrot!* onto the screen before a (still imaginary) packed audience. Reynaud had given up the idea of trying to market his invention to the fairgrounds and theatre managers. From now on he intended to exploit it himself. The idea of creating a public spectacle with animated photographs arose once more, this time from Tissandier's pen:

> The Théâtre Optique appears at present to comprise the exact equipment for synthesis of series of successive photographs; and it is no doubt in this direction that it will find its principal usage in the future . . .[15]

Pantomimes Lumineuses at the Musée Grévin

Reynaud was therefore on the hunt for a public hall which could accommodate his Théâtre Optique. The matter was settled on 11 October 1892 by a contract between Reynaud and Gabriel Thomas, the director of the Musée Grévin, the famous museum of wax figures founded at 10 Boulevard Montmartre by Arthur Meyer, with the help of the caricaturist Alfred Grévin, on 8 February 1881. In 1892 the museum was managed by the poster artist Jules Chéret, who created a splendid poster for Reynaud:

> We could also describe as radiant this poster, in which the master has shown, slight and trim in her brightly-coloured costume, a well-dressed Columbine with a joyful little face, while in the background a ghostly Pierrot strums the traditional guitar in her honour.[16]

As we have seen, the Musée Grévin had already tried to exploit Marey's photographs in 1891. Reynaud was therefore satisfying an established need. The contract he signed was very restrictive, and with a charming naiveté he delivered himself, bound hand and foot, into the hands of Gabriel Thomas. In effect he committed himself to projecting the three existing strips every day, between three and six o'clock in the afternoon and from eight till eleven o'clock in the evening, with an average of five shows per day and twelve on Sundays and public holidays. He took responsibility for all the costs of the show (staff, furnishings, maintenance of the equipment, and creation of new strips). The museum paid for composition and performance of music, the electrical supply, and the costs and organization of advertising. But the other conditions were quite draconian: Reynaud was obliged to replace part of his show at least once a year, and the new strips had to be submitted to the management for approval. He was not allowed to exhibit the Théâtre Optique on any other stage in France. All the same, he gave a show in Rouen on 3 December 1892: 'The theatre of the *Pantomimes Lumineuses* now only awaits its machinery, which will arrive from Paris this evening with the inventor, M. Reynaud,' reported the *Journal de Rouen*. This must have been the Théâtre Optique from Rue Rodier, not the one installed at the Musée Grévin—Reynaud seems to have constructed three examples in all.

At the Musée Grévin Reynaud received a fixed fee of 500 Francs per month, plus 10% of the takings, after deduction of the public assistance tax. The entrance charge was 50 centimes. The show took place in the Cabinet Fantastique, on the first floor of the museum, which had been occupied by the conjuror Carmelli before Reynaud. In 1892 this room was described like this:

> This hall deserves a visit. Beautiful tapestries in the style of the Italian Renaissance cover beautifully assembled oak and pitch-pine panelling. The ceiling, apparently of coffered and carved woodwork, is supported by stone corbels decorated with grotesque figures. The surround of the stage is in violet Breccia marble set off by brass fittings; in front of this surround is a rich velvet hanging supported by chimeras and cartouches of carved oak. To the left and right of the stage, in stone niches, devilish figures carry the electric light globes.[17]

It was in this truly fantastic room (the decor has not survived, since the room was remodelled in 1900) that Reynaud launched the first public showing of the *Pantomimes Lumineuses* on 28 October 1892. It was an 'absolutely unprecedented spectacle', as the programme claimed with justification, whose 'artistic value is enhanced by the charming melodies of M. Gaston Paulin'. Paulin composed the music for all three scenes, and the sheet music published by Ducrotois was on sale at the Musée Grévin.

The Théâtre Optique was a highly complicated and ingenious machine. No examples survive, although more or less exact reproductions can be seen in several museums in France and other countries. The long picture strip was wound around a first horizontal reel, within reach of the operator. The strip was then driven regularly in front of the condenser lens of a projecting lantern, by means of a large open drum with projecting pins which engaged the perforations of the strip. The strip passed from this drum onto a take-up reel, via three tensioning pulleys arranged along its path. The strip could move forwards or backwards, as required by the projectionist; in *Pauvre Pierrot!* one whole scene depended on the images moving backwards.

The light beam of the lantern passed through each transparent image in turn; the images were then reflected off the usual rotating 'cage of mirrors', which now contained many more prismatic mirrors than the simple Praxinoscope. Another small fixed mirror reflected the animated images from the prisms and directed them through a lens which—in an arrangement worthy of the catoptric combinations of Father Kircher —projected the images onto a large mirror which could oscillate within a wooden frame. This mirror reflected the *Pantomimes Lumineuses* onto a screen of white fabric, and because it was movable it allowed the characters to move around the screen as required for the stories. Finally, as in the Projection Praxinoscope, a magic lantern projected the fixed scenery. A second lantern could also be used, for example for announcing the title, and Reynaud also used the dissolving view effects so beloved by Abbé Moigno. Like Robertson, Reynaud always operated by back-projection, so that his machine remained hidden from the eyes of the audience.

Two acoustic effects were also provided. At the places where the story required sound effects, the picture strip was fitted with small silver strips which actuated an electromagnet. This in turn would operate an electrical noise generator. When it was time for Harlequin to beat Pierrot with his stick, the machine reproduced the sound of the blows with exact synchronism.[18] In technical and artistic quality Reynaud exceeded all his predecessors. Like Robertson before him, but with a great improvement in quality, he offered long projected shows which featured colour, movement and sound.

'The Théâtre Optique is for the time being the highest point of the genre of moving projection,' proclaimed Henri Fourtier, an expert on the subject, in 1893. It was certainly a highly successful show, and the public flocked to the Musée Grévin. In 1894, Julien Lefèvre devoted several pages of his book *L'Électricité au Théâtre* ('Electricity in the Theatre') to the *Pantomimes Lumineuses*. Once again, following Reynaud himself and Tissandier, he commented:

> This machine would present a still greater interest if one could use successive photographs of the same action, such as those obtained by M. Marey.[19]

The idea of projecting chronophotography had by this time been raised several times, and the name of Marey was now specifically mentioned. The Théâtre Optique might effectively solve the old problem of the 'Projecting Chronophotographe' with which the physiologist had been wrestling since 1892. We do not know if Marey went to the Musée Grévin—it seems unlikely that he would have enjoyed that type of establishment. However, in 1894, he mentioned Reynaud's machine in his book *Le Mouvement*:

> Until now, M. Raynaud [*sic*] has only used hand-drawn and painted images; there is no doubt but that with long sequences of chrono-photographic images he would obtain remarkable effects.[20]

And so Marey in his turn was happy to suggest the use of the Théâtre Optique for animated photography, without taking any steps towards action. This is rather disappointing. On the other hand, according to an account by Émile Reynaud's son, around the start of 1894 two visitors by the names of Auguste and Louis Lumière showed a great deal of interest in the methods used at the Musée Grévin.

> At the end of a showing of the *Pantomimes Lumineuses*, two spectators asked the favour of following the operation of the Théâtre Optique from the wings of the Cabinet Fantastique. Reynaud, anticipating, was eager to meet the desire which Messrs Lumière indicated, [and] received them warmly at the little Praxinoscope factory in Rue Rodier . . . Some time later, becoming suspicious on this subject, the scholar remarked to the family one day that 'those gentlemen had come a little too frequently to see his apparatus'.[21]

Of course, having studied the operation not only of the Théâtre Optique, but also Marey's cameras and the Edison Kinetoscope, the Lumières—among other researchers—did eventually manage to combine chronophotography with projection.

This is not the place to retell the whole history of the exploitation of the *Pantomimes Lumineuses* at the Musée Grévin, but we should note its main events. The Board of Management, on 26 April 1893, showed its tyrannical side, noting that Reynaud had not managed to replace his picture strips, and that the original ones were becoming more and more worn. This was inevitable: they passed through the machine sixty times a week, with the pins of the drum tearing at the perforations. And Reynaud had no time to create new scenes, because he performed all the projections himself.

Reynaud was therefore obliged to interrupt the shows at the Musée Grévin between 1 March and 31 December 1894. He used this time to create two new strips, which were projected at the museum at the start of 1895: *Un Rêve au Coin du Feu* ('A Dream by the Fireside'), 29 m in length with 400 hand-painted images; and *Autour d'une Cabine* ('Around a Bathing Hut'), 45 m with 636 pictures. The first strip showed a reveller returning home and falling asleep in his armchair. During a dream sequence, presented (as in magic lantern slides) as a kind of flashback, he sees himself first of all as an infant in the cradle; then older, riding a bicycle; then dancing at a ball, and having his face slapped by a young woman. The dreamer wakes up abruptly. His cat, whom we saw at the start of the scene, comes to rub against him as if in consolation. Curtain. No suggestion of irritating moralizing, just a gentle poetic atmosphere.

The story of *Autour d'une Cabine* is both tender and satirical. This shows the 'misadventures of a Copurchic [a dandy or 'masher'] bathing at the seaside'. The scenery (unfortunately the original slide is lost) showed a beach, with a bathing hut in the foreground and a springboard for diving, and a cliff in the distance. Some seagulls, portrayed exactly in deference to Marey, flap across the screen. A Parisian couple arrive: the pretty woman, her waist tightly corseted, goes into the hut to change, while her husband goes out of picture to do the same. A small dog arrives to play a part in the story. In his turn, a 'masher' or ladies' man arrives; this is the elegant 'Copurchic'. The dog jumps at him, and the masher stumbles and knocks over the Parisian woman. He helps her up. They are both somewhat confused. He immediately declares his passion (in mime), but she cuts him short and locks herself in the beach hut. The masher puts his eye to the keyhole and exhibits his delight at the sight presented to him. But the husband returns, in a bathing costume: he gives the voyeur a kick up the backside and the masher retreats in some embarrassment, but does not give up the pursuit.

While the woman is bathing, the masher conceals himself in the hut. The dog, smelling someone there, begins throwing itself against the wall of the hut. The masher tries unsuccessfully to chase it off, but the dog finally succeeds in capturing his hat and departs in satisfaction. The Parisian couple return. The woman, also now in a bathing costume, opens the door of the hut and immediately closes it again. Her husband realizes the situation, furiously drags the masher from the hut by his ears, shakes him and throws him into the sea. The masher escapes, with the little dog in pursuit. A small boat appears, comes to a halt, and its oarsman unfurls a sail on which appear the words 'La Représentation est Terminée' ('The show is finished').

'La Représentation est Terminée'

Autour d'une Cabine and *Pauvre Pierrot!*, which may be seen in modern reproductions, are small artistic masterpieces which have not aged at all. It took the cinema several years of apprenticeship to begin to approach such a narrative and aesthetic standard. But the Cinématographe took a cruel revenge, as if, being an obsessively precise recreator of life, it could not admit the artistic superiority and fantasy of the Théâtre Optique. Shaky grey images chased away the stunning colours; films shot in the open air or barrack-room comedies replaced the adventures of Pierrot and Columbine, the voyeuristic Copurchic and the pretty Parisienne. The stammerings of the 'new art', at least until the fantasy tales of Méliès, now seem quite drab in comprison to Reynaud's marvellous animated paintings.

In 1895, following the first showings of the Cinématographe Lumière, Gabriel Thomas asked Reynaud to turn his attention to 'animated photography'. Reynaud devised a quite mysterious camera, which has never been found, known as the 'Photo-Scénographe', which could only be used to take pictures. The negative film obtained was cut and enlarged as a positive onto the 6 cm square gelatine sheets always used in the Théâtre Optique, using only three or four selected poses from the sixteen taken each second. Reynaud would then retouch each individual photograph and colour it with stencils. *William Tell*, a 'comic scene' performed by Footit and Chocolat, two clowns from the Nouveau Cirque (New Circus), replaced *Un Bon Bock* at the Musée Grévin from August 1896 and met with some success. After making another film, which took him six months—it was entitled *Le Premier Cigare* ('The First Cigar'), featured the actor Félix Galipaux, and was projected in July 1897— Reynaud gave his last show on 28 February 1900. Before then, he had begun projecting Gaumont actuality films alongside his own show: a cruel mockery, with dull subjects like *The Funeral of Félix Fauré* projected after *Autour d'une Cabine*.

Between 1892 and 1900, more than 500,000 people attended some 12,800 shows of the *Pantomimes Lumineuses*. They were replaced in the Cabinet Fantastique by a second-rate puppet show. During this period, in the face of the enormous market impact made by cinematographic cameras, film projectors, and 'cinematograph lanterns' for children, sales of the Praxinoscope dropped off dramatically. Reynaud constructed one final version, which had been designed in 1877, namely the 'Stéréo-Cinéma', which went on sale in 1908 (Reynaud had filed a patent for a stereoscopic camera on 9 July 1902). An example of this well-constructed device is preserved at the CNAM: it is an individual viewer, in which a quite short series of stereoscopic photographs can be viewed by means of the prismatic mirror drum.

In 1912, aged 68, Reynaud moved to 23 Rue Massé. Disillusioned by the collapse of all his researches, he sold off his magic lanterns, the animated slides which he had used at the town hall in Le Puy, his camera obscuras, and all his tools, to second-hand dealers. A scrap metal dealer bought the Photo-Scénographe and the Stéréo-Cinéma camera by weight. However, as a bulky but very precious relic, Reynaud kept one example of the Théâtre Optique with all its picture strips. His two sons (he had marred Marguerite Remiatte in 1871) were still too young to assist him financially, and in any case he was too proud to ask for their help. The man who had done so much for the cinema found himself, for a short while, as a humble employee in the sound film section of Léon Gaumont's company, and Gaumont tried to help him. In 1911, he took up a post as secretary to an architect.

Reynaud appeared in the *Annuaire Hachette* ('Hachette's Yearbook') until 1914, listed as the manufacturer of the Praxinoscope. Perhaps the publisher forgot to remove him; perhaps he held onto some stock of his parlour toy in case any clients came along. Whatever the case, no clients appeared. Around 1913, in a fit of despair, Reynaud destroyed the only surviving example of the Théâtre Optique with a hammer. His son Paul described the aftermath of this disaster:

> Then came the turn of the scenes themselves. Not knowing how to dismantle them, and reluctant to destroy them by fire for fear of setting light to the house, he decided to drown them. He left in the evening with one or two strips, heading for one of the less busy embankments, on the Tuileries side, and there hurled these small masterpieces into the black waves of the Seine . . . He must have repeated this several times, for five of the seven strips went this way.[22]

The only two Théâtre Optique strips which survive today (along with all the various Praxinoscope strips) are *Pauvre Pierrot!* and *Autour d'une Cabine*. The First World War brought the final blow. Reynaud's two sons left for the front. On 26 March 1917, suffering from a stroke, he was admitted to hospital at Lariboisière, then transferred to the Hospice of Incurables at Ivry. He died on 9 January 1918, at 10.15 a.m.

Between the Théâtre Optique and chronophotographic or cinematographic projection there is no disjuncture, but a continuity, an essential relationship. The 'painted film' has in any case had a brilliant history, for example in the work of Norman MacLaren. Reynaud was therefore not a 'precursor'; what he made was true cinema, both as spectacle and as 'inscription of movement'.

15

Edison and His 'Films Through the Keyhole'

Edison and the 'Optical Phonograph'

The Americans view Thomas Alva Edison (1847–1931) as the inventor of the cinema, in terms of technique, spectacle, and industry. This somewhat xenophobic view needs to be qualified. Not only must earlier work be taken into account, but it is also important to know that the rendezvous between Edison and cinematographic projection—which he had planned from the very start of his research—was in fact a rendezvous well and truly missed. However, Edison's work in the field of 'Moving Pictures' is clearly of the greatest importance, and French cinema history, itself wilfully chauvinist, has often had problems in admitting this.

The Kinetoscope, whose name first appeared from Edison's pen in 1888, was not commercially exploited until 1894. In the tradition of the peepshows of the eighteenth century, it was an individual viewer. But through the eyepiece of the Kinetoscope could be seen a chrono-photographic record—in the same 35 mm format used today, in colour or black and white, silent or with sound—of a short playlet, a sporting event, or an artistic scene, performed by real actors or passers-by. The importance of this event has not been fully understood in France. Marey's chronophotography, in the hands of Edison, ceased to be a purely scientific instrument and became a truly popular spectacle, just as Demenÿ had dreamed. It was a spectacle for the individual viewer, without projection, in the form of a slot machine capable of making large amounts of hard cash. This financial incentive greatly accelerated the progress of the invention of the 35 mm chronophotographic projector.

There is no point in summarizing Edison's biography: this has been retold many times, often in the form of hagiography. In general, he represents the American ideal of the self-taught 'self-made man', who started out as a newspaper seller and finished as the head of a powerful industrial combine. He was flattered by numerous overblown nicknames: 'the greatest inventor of all time', 'the wizard of Menlo Park', 'the universal electrician', 'the electric wizard', and so on. But the invention of the Phonograph was his own achievement, in spite of some previous work by researchers such as Léon Scott de Martainville (1857) and Charles Cros (1877). There was also a mysterious device described by George Sand in February 1870, which could not have been Edison's machine as that was only invented seven years later:

> I have just purchased a musical box . . . It was expensive, but it is worthy of your theatre, it can perform the serious and the light-hearted, sad tunes, dancing tunes, pathetic songs, human voices. In a serious play, it could play the overture; a board to support the instrument and it will go all on its own. One believes one can hear a little orchestra, and the sounds are very beautiful.[1]

We must leave this mystery to historians of sound, and not diminish the credit which is rightfully due to Edison. More importantly for our purposes, the Phonograph formed part of the start of Edison's researches into the animated image. Edison too came under the considerable influence of Muybridge, who gave one of his lectures illustrated by the Zoopraxiscope in West Orange, New Jersey (where the Edison laboratories were located) on 25 February 1888. Two days later, Muybridge visited Edison, and the two of them discussed the possibilities of combining animated photography with the Phonograph. This version of events was later contradicted by Edison: 'No— Muybridge came to Lab to show me picture of a horse in motion —nothing was said about phonogph.'[2] But Edison's recollections are often not to be trusted. An article by a contemporary journalist, published in the *New York World* of 3 June 1888, gives quite clear support of Muybridge:

> Mr. Edison said that Prof. Muybridge, the instantaneous photographer, had visited him lately and had proposed to him a scheme which, if carried to completion, will afford an almost endless field of instruction and amusement. The photographer said that he was conducting a series of experiments recently and had almost perfected a photographic appliance by which he would be enabled to accurately reproduce the gestures and the facial expression of, for instance, Mr. Blaine in the act of making a speech. This was done,

he said, by taking some sixty or seventy instantaneous photographs of each position assumed by the speaker, and then throwing them by means of a magic lantern upon a screen. He proposed to Mr. Edison that the phonograph should be used in connection with his invention, and that photographs of Edwin Booth as Hamlet, Lillian Russell in some of her songs, and other artists of note should be experimented with. Mr. Edison, he said, could produce with his instrument the tones of the voice while he would furnish the gestures and facial expression. The scheme met with the approval of Mr. Edison and he intended to perfect it at his leisure.[3]

Edison, however, seems not to have been very interested in Muybridge's method of taking pictures. What he imagined, straight away, was a type of optical phonograph. He tried to find a name for this device, even before it was constructed: *Motograph* seemed suitable to him, but his patent attorney Eugene A. Lewis, having consulted the learned former governor Daniel H. Chamberlain, advised him to adopt the name *Kinesigraph*. However, this term had already been taken by the Englishman Wordsworth Donisthorpe, whose Kinesigraph of 1878 was a process of taking successive photographs of moving subjects and associating this camera with a Phonograph, with which he claimed to be able to show on screen 'a talking picture of Mr. Gladstone'.[4] It is therefore quite possible that Donisthorpe's device also gave Edison some inspiration. In short, Edison did not dare to 'borrow' the name Kinesigraph, and transformed it instead into *Kinetoscope* (Greek '*kinetos*', movement, and '*skopeo*', I look) to indicate the viewer, and *Kinetograph* for the picture-taking apparatus. On 8 October 1888 Edison filed a caveat (a first draft of a patent, without the same legal status as a full patent):

> I am experimenting upon an instrument which does for the Eye what the phonograph does for the Ear, which is the recording and reproduction of things in motion, and in such a form as to be both Cheap practical and convenient. This apparatus I call a Kinetoscope 'Moving View'.[5]

On 1 October 1888 Marey had announced the principle of his 'photo-chronographic method' at the Académie des Sciences in Paris, and on 29 October of that year he had presented his first films on sensitized strip. The physiologist was therefore some way ahead of Edison, who was nonetheless beginning to show some interest in the photography of movement.

The American historian Gordon Hendricks, in two seminal works published in 1961 and 1966, has retraced the whole history of the invention of the Kinetoscope with great precision. More recently, Charles Musser has conducted a remarkable study of the activities of the Edison Manufacturing Company.[6] The present study draws on these excellent works, and adds the point of view of the French press and some previously unpublished information on the exploitation of the Kinetoscope in France. This was an important historical moment, since this device had a very significant influence on French research on the moving picture.

Development of the Kinetoscope

By 1888, Edison had been made considerably richer by the commercialization of his Phonograph, along with several other successful ventures. At West Orange he had a team of researchers working under his instructions which was without equal: Charles Batchelor, Fred and John Ott, Charles Brown, Eugène Lauste, and William Kennedy-Laurie Dickson, among others.

Dickson (1860–1935), an imaginative young photographer and engineer who had been employed by Edison since 1882, was charged by his boss with construction of the Kinetoscope described in the caveat of 8 October 1888. This was a difficult task: the specifications in the caveat text were precise, but it was not certain that this optical phonograph could function in reality. What was needed, Edison wrote, was to photograph any scene through a microscope lens which was periodically blocked by a shutter. The successive microscopic photographs should then be printed in a spiral around a sensitized rotary cylinder. This, Edison reckoned, could produce 42,000 tiny images spread over the whole surface of the cylinder.[7]

In February 1889 the Edison laboratories opened a budget for financing research into animated photography. In June, with the assistance of Charles A. Brown, Dickson was working on the problem in Laboratory Room Five, pending the construction of a Photographic Building, a small single-storey edifice completed in autumn 1889 and reserved solely for Dickson's work. But the two researchers made hardly any progress, in spite of further caveats from Edison, who at times became impatient and sarcastic. He wrote to Dickson, on 21 February 1889: 'When may I expect to receive the micro photo outfit of Zeiss ordered from you a long time ago?—before 1890?'[8]

Dickson and Brown probably made some attempts at image-taking using a cylinder covered in celluloid around June 1889. Over the course of that year, their research began to bog down. Edison had clearly gone up a blind alley with his 'phonograph' and its microscopic pictures, which never worked satisfactorily for either analysis or synthesis of motion. But in November 1889 there was a complete about-turn: Edison abandoned his optical phonograph to adopt the process of chronophotography on a sensitized strip, as recommended by Marey since 1888. He added one essential element, possibly borrowed from Reynaud: perforation.

Edison was invited to France for the Exposition Universelle which had been inaugurated on 6 May 1889 by the French President. He left the United States on 3 August. During his stay in Paris, where he was unable to avoid some gastric inconveniences due to French cuisine (he later complained of being over-celebrated and overfed), he was invited to visit practically everywhere. On 19 August, he was at the Académie des Sciences in the company of Jules Janssen. Of course he also visited the Exposition and climbed the then new Eiffel Tower.

Accompanied by Marey, who served as his guide to the Exposition, he visited the exhibition of French photography on the first floor of the Palais des Arts Libéraux (Palace of Liberal Arts). More than 300 participants exhibited their works and equipment, among them Eugène Pirou, a future cinema entrepreneur, Nadar with his photographic enlargements on Eastman paper, the Lumière brothers with their gelatino-bromide plates, Janssen with his astronomical photographs, and Londe with his pictures of the Salpêtrière hospital. And, of course, Marey led him to the display on chronophotography, described here by a contemporary:

> M. Marey showed a series of remarkable photographs made at the Institut Physiologique at the Parc des Princes, which allowed him to fix with precision the laws of the flight of birds and the various positions of man and the horse walking at different speeds.[9]

Perhaps Edison also saw, in the novelty goods section, Émile Reynaud's Praxinoscopes and the first version of the Théâtre Optique, assuming that the latter device really was shown. That remains difficult to establish. But the influence of Marey, who showed him his chrono-photographic strips and cameras, seems to be clear enough.

Convinced that the photographic cylinder was a dead end, on his return to West Orange on 6 October Edison composed a new and masterly caveat which clearly reflected the 'French influence', as Hendricks describes it. In this text, dated 2 November 1889, Edison described a sensitized transparent film, perforated on both sides like the strips of the 'automatic Wheatstone telegraph' (no mention was made of Reynaud's French and British patents, filed in December 1888, and Marey was also not cited). This film would pass between two bobbins in front of a lens, with a toothed wheel penetrating the perforations of the strip to drive it constantly. This was a long way from cylinder-based photography, and some distance ahead of Marey's chronophotographic method, which did not use perforated strips and lacked a sufficiently regular drive mechanism.

Around 2 September 1889 Dickson ordered some rolls of Kodak film from George Eastman; he repeated the order in November, presumably at Edison's request. By the end of 1889 everything was in place for the production of chronophotographic moving pictures on perforated film to begin at the Photographic Building in West Orange. And yet research continued to move very slowly, and always in the wrong direction; animated photography was only one of a number of subjects then interesting Edison. In November 1890 Dickson and Brown succeeded in making three series of 'Monkeyshines' (experimental attempts) by wrapping a celluloid film around a cylinder. These 'films' still survive today, showing hundreds of tiny photographs of a man (possibly G. Sacco Albanese, an Edison employee) against a black background, waving his arms as though in an athletic exercise.

The perforated film Kinetoscope

Between November 1890 and the start of 1891 Edison corrected this wrong turning and urged Dickson to follow the instructions of the caveat of 2 November 1889. The optical phonograph was finally abandoned, and the Kinetoscope with a perforated film strip was shown on 20 May 1891, during a visit to the Edison laboratories by the Federation of Women's Clubs:

> They saw, through an aperture in a pine box standing on the floor, the picture of a man. It bowed and smiled, and took off its hat naturally and gracefully. Every motion was perfect, without a hitch or a jerk.[10]

The natural and graceful person the ladies saw in the Kinetoscope was Dickson himself, who was responsible for the construction for this new version of the machine, along with two new collaborators, Charles Kayser and William Heise. However, not everything was yet quite finalized: the Eastman celluloid film used at the start of 1891 was only 19 mm in width, the images were arranged horizontally on the film, and only a single row of perforations was formed at the lower edge of the film.

According to the American magazine *Harper's Weekly*, which reported Edison's ideas, the Kinetograph camera had a horizontal film path and a rotary shutter capable of taking forty-six images per second, that is 2,760 per minute or 165,600 in an hour. These figures, for the time, were quite fictitious, since at the time there was no possibility of producing film stock long enough to take so many images. The press published the ideas with much emphatic and exaggerated praise of Edison, who began to show something of a boastful streak on the subject. On 28 May 1891 he declared, forgetting his predecessors who had discovered the 'base principle' before him:

> Now I've got it. That is, I've got the germ or base principle. When you get your base principle right, then it's only a question of time and a matter of details about completing the machine.[11]

Marey and Reynaud could have told him as much. On 13 June 1891 Edison's ideas had become a little more qualified, but all the same fairly brusque:

> All that I have done is to perfect what has been attempted before, but did not succeed. It's just that one step that I have taken.[12]

It seems quite astonishing that Edison was already making exaggerated claims for the capabilities of his Kinetoscope and Kinetograph, which were still in quite a primitive state:

> With this new device, he says, you will be able to sit in your armchair in your own house, in your drawing room, and see projected onto a screen a whole opera company with the artists acting, gesticulating, speaking and singing.
>
> To achieve this result, Edison places in front of the well-lit stage, for the whole duration of the performance, his Kinetograph in combination with a Phonograph. The orchestra plays, the curtain rises and the opera commences. The two machines work simultaneously; while the Phonograph records the sound, the Kinetograph takes a successive series of instantaneous photographs with a speed of forty-six pictures per second . . .
>
> Having obtained in this way a long strip with an infinite number

of photographic images, one may print positive images onto another strip, and all that is needed is to pass these images through a projection device, taking care to maintain the same speed . . . Add to this the mechanism for driving the Phonograph and you will have the complete description of the equipment.[13]

These claims announced the taking and projection of pictures with sound, but in 1891 everything was still very much at the experimental stage. By making such grandiose boasts about the merits of his imaginary apparatus, Edison created some (understandable) distrust, at least in France:

The information in the above letter appears to us to be more suggestive than actual . . . M. Edison's suggestions could have their time of reality, but at the present moment none of this seems to us to be possible. We shall wait and see![14]

Edison's patents of 1891

On 31 July 1891 Edison composed his patents for the Kinetoscope (see Fig. 48) and Kinetograph. They were filed on 24 August, although not granted by the United States Patent Office until 14 March 1893 (for the Kinetoscope) and 31 August 1897 (for the Kinetograph). The US Patent Office was much more strict than its French counterpart: for each application, a search was carried out to ascertain whether it related to a truly new invention. Strangely, Edison did not take out patents for his two machines in Europe, an omission he would later come to regret.

In the machines described in these patents, the film was always moved horizontally, but was perforated at top and bottom edges, as in the caveat of 2 November 1889. Edison's 'Kinetographic camera' had the advantage, compared to Marey's machine, of driving the film strip much more regularly, as a result of the perforations and a toothed wheel. This wheel turned intermittently, connected to a disc with six teeth which was alternately stopped and rotated by a second notched disc, a system which was finally adopted after some attempts with a Maltese Cross mechanism. The negative film moved stepwise and horizontally through the machine, past the lens. One of the two film bobbins was connected to the central drive shaft of the camera, which was powered by electricity.

The pictures obtained in 1893–5 were made on Eastman or Blair 35 mm film, and measured 25 mm by 19 mm, with four perforations on

Fig. 48. The Edison Kinetoscope, showing films taken with the Kinetograph. The side door is shown open to indicate the internal mechanism; in normal operation the casing was closed. Collection: Laurent Mannoni.

each side of each image. Edison specified that the speed of the film, in both Kinetograph and Kinetoscope, should be forty-six frames per second, which was very rapid. Hendricks has established that the Edison films made in 1894 were in fact shot at between sixteen and forty frames per second, with the speed controlled according to the light levels of the scene to be taken, and with an average speed between thirty and forty frames per second.

The 1891 Kinetoscope was more or less the same as the final version of 1894. It consisted of a wooden casing which (in the production model of 1894) measured 123 cm in height; the sides, sometimes decorated, were 68.5 cm by 45.5 cm; and the machine weighed about 75 kg. An opening in the top of the box allowed the viewer to look into its interior, where a lens magnified the images of the film, which passed continuously at high speed, not intermittently as in the Kinetograph. The film, about 15 m in length and containing around 750 images, was mounted in a loop along a complicated path defined by a series of rollers arranged inside the casing. In the 1891 patent nine rollers were specified; the final design of 1894 had eighteen, not including the two toothed rollers which drove the film.

The images, illuminated by a small electric bulb with a reflector, were interrupted by a rapidly rotating shutter disc 25 cm in diameter, in which was formed a small window 5 mm wide (in the 1894 design). As he or she bent over the eyepiece of the machine, the viewer could not see the rotating disc or the movement of the film. Due to retinal persistence in the eye, there was no impression of interruption of the images, and a continuously animated photographic scene appeared, giving an illusion of movement which was

> almost completely perfect; I say 'almost' since, for some of the very sudden gestures by the figures, for example those of the blacksmiths striking on the anvil, one may still perceive jerks.[15]

The mechanisms of the Kinetoscope and Kinetograph, which were 'of a remarkable delicacy',[16] were also revolutionary in their concept. 35 mm Edison film is still in use today with almost the same frequency of perforation, as are the toothed drive rollers. In Edison's hands chrono-photography acquired a remarkable new precision, as far as analysis and synthesis of motion were concerned, even though as yet there was still no projection. Reynaud, of course, had already supplied an answer to that particular problem.

In October 1892 the American magazine *Phonogram* reproduced the first Edison film in which the images were arranged vertically rather than horizontally. This showed Dickson and his colleague William Heise shaking hands warmly, as if congratulating each other on having launched, along with Edison, the American film production industry.

On 8 May 1893 the Paris newspaper *Le Figaro* devoted its front page to Edison. A French journalist, Octave Uzanne, had visited him in the laboratories at West Orange on Tuesday 26 April. Edison seemed to him to be like an 'old baby, by turns joyful and grumpy', not very concerned with his appearance, 'his back slightly bent, a bowler hat on his head, in a casual jacket with a two-day beard, his shirt cuffs dirty and torn'.[17] The inventor of the Phonograph was hard of hearing, and Uzanne had to shout his congratulations. As the journalist asked to see his latest work, Edison took him into 'a small house' (the Photographic Building) where he encountered 'a worker of intelligent and refined appearance', who presumably was Dickson; Edison did not introduce him to Uzanne, even though this 'worker' had been born, of Scottish parents, in France. Dickson loaded a film into the Kinetoscope, 'a strange box of pale oak, as large as a small sideboard', which Uzanne confused with the Kinetograph camera. While this was happening, Edison strutted about:

> Thanks to this new system, one may see an opera, a play, a person, at the same time as one hears them, and moreover one may capture the gestures of actors and prevent their complete loss to posterity . . . Talma, Rachel, Sarah Bernhardt, Mounet-Sully, all living.[18]

Talma had died in 1826, and Rachel in 1858, but the point was made. Edison admitted, though, that this system would not be perfected 'for two years'. But the 'mysterious box' was ready:

> The worker in charge of it invited me to lean over a glass lens at its upper extremity; I looked: something was released in the mechanism and I saw, dazzled and filled with wonder, a Tyrolean peasant dancing like an epileptic in front of his hut and his mountains (with the wind waving the tops of the trees), lasting for about twenty-five or thirty-five seconds. Nothing was lacking from this crazy apparition; the man thrashed about and turned in all four directions at a speed greater than that of a jig; one could watch the dislocation of his knees, the straightening of his shoes . . . When this frenzied dance came to its end, the little Tyrolean smiled, saluted, and went back into his cottage.[19]

Uzanne straightened up. Edison was looking at him mischievously. He certainly liked to test the reactions of visitors allowed in to gaze upon this new attraction:

> I made a sign to him that I was speechless, with no possible words, almost beyond belief . . . Transported, I cried out:
> —The discovery is complete, when are you going to launch it?
> —I still need eighteen months to two years, this modest and patient worker replied calmly. From now until then, I do not wish for any noise or publicity.[20]

Since the start of 1892 Edison had decided to exploit his Kinetoscope as a slot machine, as Stollwerck and Gibbs Clarke had planned with the Demenÿ Phonoscope. On 26 April 1892 Dickson came up with the term 'Nickel-in-the-Slot Kinetoscope'. There was no question of organizing projection with the magic lantern, which for the time being was a technical impossibility. Edison presumably thought that this would be much less profitable.

Fig. 49. The interior of Edison's 'Black Maria'.
Collection: Laurent Mannoni.

Before supplying these 'mysterious boxes' to the public, they would have to be mass-produced, and the catalogue of 'Edison films' would also have to be increased. So in December 1892, construction started on a photographic studio at West Orange. It was completed in February 1893, although Uzanne did not see it during his visit. This was not quite the first motion picture studio in the world, since Dickson had already made films in the Photographic Building constructed in 1889. Marey's Station Physiologique could also have claimed that title, but the celluloid films made at the Bois de Boulogne in 1890 were purely scientific and not intended for commercial exploitation. However Edison's new studio of 1893 was solely designed and intended for taking pictures: we could therefore consider it as the true ancestor of all the silent and sound stages of the great film studios. This bizarrely shaped, tar-coated building was first pompously christened the Revolving Photograph Building, but the Edison employees soon named it the 'Black Maria', a colloquial expression for the police prison vans of the time (see Fig. 49).

Edison described the strange architecture of this construction in his memoirs:

> Our studio was almost as amazing as the pictures we made in it. We were looking for service, not art. The building itself was about twenty-five by thirty feet in dimensions, and we gave a grotesque effect to the roof by slanting it up in a hunch in the center and arranging shutters that could be opened or closed with a pulley to obtain the greatest benefit from the light.[21]

Inside, the large and heavy Kinetograph camera was supported on a table which could slide on rails, like Marey's Chronophotograph at the Station Physiologique. The actors moved in front of a dark background, lit from the front by the sun through the opening in the roof.

Exploitation of the Kinetoscope in the United States

On the day after Uzanne's article on the Kinetoscope appeared in France, Edison gave the first official demonstration of his machine in more or less its final form. This took place on 9 May 1893 at the annual meeting of the Department of Physics of the Brooklyn Institute of Arts and Sciences. In fact it was George Hopkins who, after projecting some animated Choreutoscope and Wheel of Life slides with a magic lantern, as well as some static slides showing fragments of 35 mm Edison film, invited the audience to view the Kinetoscope which Dickson had brought. The film the audience saw, with great admiration, was entitled *Blacksmithing Scene*.

By 1 April 1894 Edison finally had a first series of twenty-five Kinetoscopes available. A carpenter named James Egan had been hired, on 26 June 1893, to construct the wooden casings. Edison did his accounts:

Kinetoscope experiment	$21,736.25
Labor, etc. on twenty-five kinetoscopes	1,227.48
Photographing building	516.64
Revolving photograph building (Black Maria)	637.67
Total	$24,118.04[22]

It was now becoming urgent to start earning money with this Kinetoscope, which had been occupying Edison's mind since 1888. The Edison Manufacturing Company created a Kinetographic Department in charge of marketing the equipment. Ten Kinetoscopes, each containing a different film, were installed on 6 April 1894 at the Holland Brothers premises at 1155 Broadway, New York. This first Kinetoscope Parlor opened on Saturday 14 April 1894. The films presented were: *Sandow* [a famous strongman], *Horse Shoeing*, *The Barbershop*, *Bertholdi (Mouth Support)* [a contortionist act], *Wrestling Match*, *Bertholdi (Table Contortion)*, *Blacksmithing Scene*, *Highland Dance*, *Trapeze*, and *Roosters*. The machines did not yet work automatically with coin operation. For a 25 cent ticket, the customer had the right to examine a group of five Kinetoscopes; for 50 cents, the films of all ten Kinetoscopes could be viewed. A second Kinetoscope Parlor run by the Hollands opened in Chicago on 18 May 1894, with ten machines, and on 1 June Peter Bacigalupi opened a Phonograph Parlor in San Francisco, with the five remaining Kinetoscopes of the first batch. The machine was an immediate success. From 14 April 1894 to 1 April 1895 the takings of the New York Kinetoscope Parlor were $16,171.56.

Edison ordered a new batch of machines, this time fitted with coin-operated mechanisms, so that an animated scene could be viewed for a 'Nickel-in-the-Slot'. Gordon Hendricks estimates the total number of Kinetoscopes constructed at over 1,000; the Science Museum in London has one which carries the serial number 1,268. To begin with, Edison sold his machines to anyone interested in marketing them. But he quickly changed this view when he realized their success. In August 1894 he entrusted the commercial exploitation in the United States and Canada to the Kinetoscope Company, directed by Norman Raff and Frank Gammon. Edison sold the slot machines for $200 each to this company, which could sell them on at a profit or exploit them itself throughout the two territories. Shortly afterwards two further companies were formed: Otway Latham's Kinetoscope Exhibition Company, and the Continental Commerce Company run by Frank Z. Maguire and Joseph D. Baucus, which had charge of exploitation in Britain.

From 1 April 1894 to 28 February 1895, through these three companies, the Edison Manufacturing Company made $149,548 by sale of Kinetoscopes and $25,882 by sale of films.[23] Having spent $24,118 in creating the machine, Edison could already consider it a fortunate investment. By the end of 1894, thanks to a very efficient network, almost all the large American and Canadian cities had seen the Kinetoscope: Cincinnati on 12 October; Dallas on 2 November; Austin on 10 November; Los Angeles on the same date; Detroit on 11 November (this parlour, at 184 Woodward Avenue, was managed by Charles Urban, who became one of the most important figures in British cinema after 1898); Washington on 12 November; Montreal on 15 November; Minneapolis on 26 November; Davenport on 28 November; Atlanta on 6 December; Memphis on 12 December; New Orleans on 17 December; and so on. Everywhere the reactions were ecstatic:

> It is here! Edison's Kinetoscope!!! Marvelous! Realistic! True to Life! The Most Wonderful and Interesting Invention of This Century of Science. The only actual and literal 'Living Pictures' ever produced. Words fail to describe it—You must see it to Get an Idea of its Remarkable Qualities! Exhibition begins this Evening and Continues Day and Night.[24]

In the United States 'Moving Pictures' were clearly a profitable enterprise. Now industrialists and businessmen, previously inclined to put their money into meat, macaroni, or folding bathtubs, turned an interested eye towards the scholars and technicians who had developed moving picture cameras or new optical boxes of tricks. The scent of money was in the air: in Edison's slot machines, Marey's chronophotography had finally emerged from its scientific cocoon, to become a popular pastime and a profitable industry.

The Edison Kinetoscope films

The visions to be seen in Edison's 'marvellous boxes' were simple fiction films, dramatic or comic sketches, and sporting or aesthetic scenes, either shot inside the Black Maria or in the open air. The attraction Edison offered was:

> for the audience, a true revelation . . . M. Marey only had scientific aims in view; it was to physiological and physical research that he was dedicated . . . The examination in the zoetrope of his film strips is extremely instructive and interesting, but it is not entertaining. M. Edison, on the contrary, has only sought to bring us pleasure, science being not his end but his means. He has succeeded completely.[25]

As these lines by a contemporary French writer make clear, the concept of chronophotographic spectacle was well established in 1894–5. The impatience of Demenÿ, who had already foreseen the commercial value of animated photography in 1892–3, becomes quite understandable. There was a further example in Reynaud, still attracting thousands of spectators to his Théâtre Optique.

The Kinetoscope films were a long way removed from the artistic miracles seen in Reynaud's hand-painted picture strips. They were intended to appeal to the average American, to viewers who were not interested in an edifying work or the reproduction of a work of art for their 5 cents, but wanted a 'film through the keyhole' merging eroticism, violence and action—criteria for success which are still hardly out of fashion. The Edison films of 1894–5 were about 15 m in length. The viewer's 5 cents only bought one showing of the scene: there were no repetitive effects, as has sometimes been claimed.

Cinema histories have often cited the admiring remarks of French journalists on seeing the Lumière films of 1895, for example extolling the total animation of the subjects, such as the moving leaves in the background of the film *Le Déjeuner de Bébé* ('Baby's Dinner'). But similar comments can also be found in contemporary reports of the Edison Kinetoscope, in both French and American publications. We have already seen Uzanne, in 1893, remarking on 'the wind waving the tops of the trees' in an Edison film. Only Jacques Deslandes, during the 1960s, has attempted to redress the general lack of interest in France in the Edison films. A 1991 projection, at the Musée d'Orsay in Paris, of some excellent American copies of the films presented by the American Federation of Arts, provided a genuine revelation, at least for impartial minds.

A couple of examples are *Annabelle Butterfly Dance* and *Annabelle Serpentine Dance*, two beautiful scenes taken at the start of 1895 by Dickson and Heise in the Black Maria, with Annabelle Moore imitating the performance of Loïe Fuller. In France, the public were led to believe that the performer was the great dancer Fuller herself. Illuminated by the sun through the open roof of the Black Maria, seen in full figure, Annabelle dances and waves her long veils. The films are in colour, brightly tinted with stencils. On the floor, a board with the letter 'C' indicates that the film was produced for the Continental Commerce Company of Maguire and Baucus. The letter 'R' which appears in the same way in *Fire Rescue Scene*, made by Dickson and Heise in October or December 1894, indicates that the film belonged to Raff and Gammon. *Fire Rescue Scene* is quite elaborate: firemen with a ladder rescue a young girl from a fire, with smoke effects, actors in costume, and dramatic tension. It is certainly as good a drama as *L'Arroseur Arrosé* (usually known in English as *Watering the Gardener*), the Lumière film of 1895 which is sometimes assumed to have been the first 'fiction film'.

On 9 January 1894 Edison filed the second cinematographic copyright claim; the first Edison Kinetoscopy Record had been deposited at the

Library of Congress in Washington D.C. by Dickson in August 1893, under number 44,732Y, but has not survived. Edison gave the Library of Congress a 'paper print', a strip of paper on which all the images of the negative celluloid film were printed (no public institution at the time would store the highly flammable nitrate film, hence the need to print onto paper). This deposit could be used as legal evidence in case of piracy. The practice of the 'paper print' deposit continued into the 1900s and 1910s, and has allowed the recovery of a large number of early films by rephotographing and reprinting them back onto film stock. The film deposited at the Library of Congress only consisted of forty-five successive images: it was *Fred Ott's Sneeze*, or more precisely *Edison Kinetoscopic Record of a Sneeze, January 7, 1894*. This short experimental film showed one of Edison's employees, Frederick Ott, in the process of sneezing, viewed in 'medium close shot' (or *plan americain*, to use the French term), from the chest upwards.[26]

Dickson and Heise made seventy-five films in 1894. Among the most successful of these, at least in terms of press reaction, was *The Barbershop*, a small sketch of everyday life which the Frenchman Frédéric Dillaye particularly admired:

> A genre painting, the barber's salon, absolutely perfect . . . We find ourselves in the barber's shop. A client arrives, enters, removes his hat and coat which he hangs on a hook, sits down in the chair, lifts his head for the boy to wrap a towel around his neck. The razor goes to work. During this time, other clients come and go, read their newspapers, talk and laugh; and all these events are so clearly reproduced that one could believe them to be performed by living beings.[27]

Quite a picturesque little world, mainly drawn from the music hall and the theatre, began to present itself in West Orange to pose in front of the Kinetograph. It was a truly Barnumesque procession: the strongman Eugene Sandow; the contortionists Edna Bartholdi and George Layman; the animal trainer Harry Welton; and Buffalo Bill's company, filmed in *Bucking Broncho* ('The men and horse of this subject are from Buffalo Bill's Wild West'), *Annie Oakley*, and other subjects, some films from this series being shot in the open air. The Edison catalogue also featured films of grand spectacle (*A Milk White Flag*, with 'thirty-four persons in costume'), an almost 'scientific' film (*In the Dentist's Chair*, in which Dr Colton removes a tooth from an unconscious patient), and 'historical' films such as *Joan of Arc* and *Execution of Mary, Queen of Scots*. In the latter film, made in August 1895, the executioner raises his axe and brings it down brutally to cut off the Queen's head. The trick was a simple one: the camera was stopped at the moment when the Queen placed her head on the block, and she was replaced by a mannequin. The camera was started again, and the headsman could carry out his role with a clear conscience. This type of substitution trick was repeated to excess by the film-makers of 1896–1900, notably Méliès.

Violence formed an integral part of the spectacle: animal fights (*Cockfight*, *The Boxing Cats*), boxing matches (*The Corbett–Courtney Fight*), knife fights (*Mexican Knife Duel*), opium smoking (*Opium Den*), brawls (*Chinese Laundry Scene*[28] or *A Bar Room Scene*, in which the 'cops' arrest a drunk). Sex was also ever-present, much to the anger of the Society for the Suppression of Vice and other moralists. The Gaiety Girls, the belly dances of Dolorita and Fatima, and the underwear of the graceful Carmencita, all satisfied the demands of the 'voyeurs' who frequented the Penny Arcades. These slightly saucy views brought a blush to the cheeks of Senator James Bradley, who visited a Kinetoscope Parlor in July 1894 to judge for himself the morality of the Edison films. Bradley first examined *A Bar Room Scene*, and pronounced himself satisfied: the police were seen to restore order. But the exhibitor then made something of a blunder, as a journalist on the *Newark Evening News* reported with amusement:

> He took a little tin can from a grip that he carried and placed a celluloid roll of pictures in the machine, at the same time remarking to the Senator, who had his eyes glued to the peep-hole: 'Now you will be surprised, Senator. This is one of the best pictures in the collection.'
>
> And the Senator was surprised, but not in the way . . . intended . . . The view was that of Carmencita in her famous butterfly dance, and the Senator watched the graceful gyrations of the lovely Spanish dancer with interest that was ill-concealed. But near the end of the series of pictures the Spanish beauty gives the least little bit of a kick, which raises her silken draperies so that her well-turned ankles peep out and there is a background of white lace.
>
> That kick settled it. The Senator left the peephole with a stern look on his face . . . While he was trying to collect his scattered thoughts sufficiently to give full swing to his wrath Mayor Ten Broeck applied his eye to the peephole . . . The Mayor was also greatly shocked and agreed with the Founder that the picture was not fitted for the entertainment of the average summer boarder, and

the exhibitor was told he would have to send for some new views or shut up shop . . .[29]

The Kinetophone

Edison had been promising the miracle of true projection of animated pictures with accompanying sound since 1888. He achieved part of this ambitious project in 1895 by creating the Kinetophone, a Kinetoscope with a Phonograph located inside its casing. The Phonograph cylinder ran at the same time as the film, giving a musical accompaniment which was heard through rubber tubes connected to the Phonograph and inserted into the user's ears.

Construction of Kinetophones was ordered by Edison around February or March 1895. According to Hendricks, only forty-five Kinetophones were made and sold, and examples of this device are now extremely rare. There are two examples in Europe, at the Science Museum in London and the Musée du Cinéma in Paris. The latter example, miraculously preserved in its original state, carries the serial number 69; it is perhaps an 1894 Kinetoscope which was converted into a Kinetophone in 1895. A metal plate on the front of the casing draws the attention of the passer-by who was perhaps already slightly bored by a year of Moving Pictures: 'Edison's Very Latest'.

Standard Kinetoscopes are also now very rare. Of the thousand or so examples constructed, about ten survive. The Museum of the CNAM in Paris has a very fine example, but it is a British copy manufactured by the great cinema pioneer Robert W. Paul during 1895. On lifting the lid of the casing, Paul's name and address can be seen, engraved on the casting of the mechanism. Edison did not take out patents for the Kinetoscope in Europe, and it was flagrantly copied in Britain and France. The CNAM catalogue attributes this machine to Edison; in terms of conception this is true, but in terms of construction it is not his.

The Kinetophone was first seen in France in May 1895, and was also exhibited in Brussels in August 1895, in the foyer of the Théâtre de l'Alcazar:

> The Kinetoscope is now out of date. Edison has invented the Kinetophone. Not only may one see the Serpentine Dance, but one may hear its accompanying music. One sees the belly dance and hears that entrancing music which pursues one relentlessly at the Exposition d'Anvers. One sees Napoléon parading in front of thirty or so persons, all bustling and struggling about, to the sound of

resounding marches and patriotic songs. The Edison Kinetophone
. . . has achieved a brilliant success as a novelty. And truly the variety
of spectacles which we have seen and heard, and the artistic
perfection with which all this is presented, are well calculated to
create astonishment, admiration and wonder.[30]

The Kinetoscope in Paris

An electrician who has worked for two years in the Edison
laboratory at Orange (New Jersey), M. Georgiadeo, has just brought
a Kinetoscope to Paris; it is reported to be the first one to be seen in
Europe.[31]

The French journalist Henri Flamans wrote these words in July 1894, for
Le Magasin Pittoresque, which published his article in its issue of 1
August. A misprint garbled the name of the demonstrator: this was
not 'M. Georgiadeo', but George Georgiades, a Greek employee of
the Holland brothers, the Edison franchisees in the United States.
Georgiades and his compatriot George Trajedes, who also worked for
the Hollands, went on to exploit several Kinetoscopes without Edison's
authorization in London around the end of 1894, in a shop on Old
Broad Street. Through the inventor Henry W. Short, Georgiades met
Robert Paul at around the same time, and Paul shortly afterwards began
to construct excellent copies of the Edison Kinetoscope for sale in
Britain and France.

The Paris demonstration of July 1894 is therefore important, even if it
did not have a great influence on the exploitation of the Kinetoscope in
Paris. Flamans gave a long description of the machine's mechanism.
Georgiades showed him *The Barbershop*, among other 'American scenes'.
However, Flamans observed, 'There was nothing there, really, which was
a new invention'. He recalled that Marey had been making films on
celluloid strip since 1890. But Edison had 'transformed a scientific
demonstration into a most entertaining spectacle which, in the cities of
the United States, is attracting the crowds today'.[32]

Georgiades was only passing through Paris. It is not clear if he then
went straight to Britain; he arrived there in August or September 1894,
but the first public presentation of the Edison Kinetoscope did not take
place until 17 October, at 70 Oxford Street, London, under the auspices
of Frank Z. Maguire and Joseph D. Baucus of the Continental
Commerce Company. A Kinetoscope probably originating from this
parlour, numbered 141, came up for sale in London in October 1992.

Following the article in the *Magasin Pittoresque*, the arrival of the Kinetoscope in Paris was awaited impatiently. On 19 August 1894, in *Les Annales Politiques et Littéraires*, the famous columnist Henri de Parville complained:

> We shall not have the Kinetoscope in Europe for some time . . . Edison keeps hold of his inventions too much. He does not let them cross the ocean very easily. This is a fault. Good old Europe is absolutely not something to be ignored.[33]

De Parville did not have to wait much longer. In September 1894 (the exact date is unknown) the Kinetoscope returned to Paris, this time as a public attraction on the *grands boulevards*. An example could be seen at 20 Boulevard Montmartre, at the offices of the newspaper *Le Petit Parisien*, where the Edison Phonograph was also exhibited. The appearance of this Kinetoscope is highly mysterious: no documentation of it seems to exist, and there was no advertisement for it in *Le Petit Parisien*.

It was the holders of the French franchise for the Edison Phonograph, the Werner brothers, who were responsible for commercial introduction of the Kinetoscope to Paris. From previously unpublished archive documents it is possible to throw some new light on the commercial exploitation of Edison's Moving Pictures in Paris in 1894–5. There were three Werners: Alexis, the father, who married in Paris on 2 August 1856, when he was a simple mechanic, and his two sons, Michel and Eugène. It was the sons who, on 22 August 1893, founded a company under the name of Werner Frères et Cie. (Werner Brothers & Co.), with a capital of 30,000 Francs, for the purpose of 'the supply and sale of typing machines, copying machines, and all other similar machines'.[34] Edison's name did not appear in the deed of foundation, but in the trade paper *L'Industriel Forain* ('The Fairground Industrialist') of 26 August 1894 the Werners were more precise:

> Edison Phonograph, latest model of April 1894 . . . Our establishment is the only one in France which sells authentic machines provided with documents proving their provenance from M. Edison's factory, which provides a serious guarantee, possessing a vast shop, repair workshop, and large selection of cylinders and spare parts.[35]

The 'vast shop' was located at 85 Rue de Richelieu, Paris. Around the time of founding of the Werner company in 1894–5, a backer named

Fig. 50. Werner Brothers' advertisement for the Edison Kinetoscope, in
L'Industriel Forain 288 (10–16 February 1895).
Collection: Bibliothèque Nationale.

Miss or Mrs Adrienne Charbonnel gave the Werners financial support.
For the sake of gossip, it could be mentioned that Ms Charbonnel and
Michel Werner lived in the same apartment, on the third floor of 9
Rue de Parme, though perhaps no conclusions should be drawn from
this.

As we have seen, a Kinetoscope was operating from September 1894
at 20 Boulevard Montmartre. In October, in a historic moment, the
Werners opened the first Kinetoscope Parlor in France, at 20 Boulevard
Poissonnière. The lease for the shop in Boulevard Poissonnière was
signed before a notary on 4 October 1894, but two different documents
state that the rental took effect from 1 October (the previous tenant had
been a tailor named Franck). This allows more or less exact dating of the
opening of this first Kinetoscope Parlor: either 1 or 4 October 1894.
Henri de Parville rushed over:

> A simple shop completely bathed in electric light . . . What is there?
> What can one see? ask the curious as they draw near. What can one
> see? Look. Inside one can see quite simply some large boxes,
> completely closed and 1.5 metres high; in front of each of them a
> gentleman or lady watches seriously through an eyepiece what is
> going on inside the boxes. Enter, pay your 25 centimes and position
> yourself in front of the first available box.[36]

Inside the boxes could be seen some 'assorted dances', including one of
the Annabelle performances; a cock fight (*The Cock Fight*); a dispute in a
bar (*A Bar Room Scene*); a blacksmith's workshop (*Blacksmith Shop*); and

The Barbershop, greatly admired by Frédéric Dillaye, a future shareholder in the Gaumont company.

On 15 October 1894 the Werners wound up their first company, which had been formed on 22 August 1893. They decided to throw all their efforts into exploitation of the Kinetoscope, possibly as a result of the success it was finding with its first Parisian customers. On 16 October 1894, Alexis Werner, his son Michel and their backer Adrienne Charbonnel founded a new company called Le Kinetoscope Edison, Michel et Alexis Werner, with a capital of 40,000 Francs. Eugène was not a partner (he may have continued running the shop at 85 Rue de Richelieu), but he will return to the story a little later. The purpose of this company was

> the exploitation and sale of 'Kinetoscope' electrical equipment and all other electrical machines and equipment and their accessories . . . The said company will take for its name Le Kinetoscope Edison . . . The registered address is in Paris, at 20 Boulevard Poissonnière.[37]

Once again it was Adrienne Charbonnel who put up the necessary finance: 30,000 Francs, paid in full. Michel Werner supplied the lease for nine years on the shop and its fittings, as well as the sum of 8,000 Francs, and Alexis promised 2,000 Francs.

As specified in the deed of foundation of the second company, the Edison machines went on sale in October 1894 at 20 Boulevard Poissonnière, and presumably also at 85 Rue de Richelieu. 'Everyone will soon be able to install one in his drawing room', said de Parville, but 'it is an extravagance which will cost several thousand Francs.'[38] *Le Moniteur de la Photographie*, on 15 November 1894, could not believe in this enterprise: 'Nobody, for his own private pleasure, will be tempted to lay out the quite considerable sum which this instrument must cost.' In fact, not one single case is known of a purchase by a rich amateur, just as no-one appears to have bought Reynaud's Théâtre Optique when he offered it at 2,000 Francs in 1892. However the Kinetoscope became the object of a quite active trade in France. It was the fairground operators, lured by Werner's advertisements in their trade press (see Fig. 50), who purchased the machine:

> Kinetoscope Edison. Animated scenes. Machine capable of earning its owner 500% on capital by giving public exhibitions. Werner & Co., 20 Bd. Poissonnière.[39]

But as we shall see, the commercialization of the Kinetoscope was to turn out not to be a happy affair for the Werners, as a result of competition.

Antoine Lumière, father of Auguste and Louis, certainly came to see the Werners' 'novelty'; Marcel Proust may also have been entertained by it.[40] Lumière, who was then working at 8 Boulevard des Italiens, might have seen the Kinetoscope at Boulevard Poissonnière, but it also seems possible that there was a second Kinetoscope Parlor in Paris, near the Opéra. In the property register for 20 Boulevard Poissonnière, a tiny handwritten note appears: 'Same establishment at 8 Place de l'Opéra.' Michel Werner rented a shop on 5 December 1894 at 6–8 Place de l'Opéra, a building on the corner of Boulevard des Capucines, to be used as a 'Dealer in games and public amusements'. This may have been a second Kinetoscope Parlor and sales shop, like the business at Boulevard Poissonnière.

In January 1895, Michel Werner presumably reckoned that the Parisian market would prove to be too restricted for the sale and exploitation of slot machines. While retaining control of the Kinetoscope Edison company, he formed another company on 19 January 1895, having decided to 'travel' (to use the fairground expression) ten Kinetoscopes around France himself:

> The object of this company is the exhibition in France and abroad of electrical equipment and especially the earliest possible exhibition in different towns of ten electrical machines, known under the name 'Kinetoscope Edison', and the sale of these machines, with or without their installation.[41]

A certain urgency seems evident; it was necessary to move quickly in this developing market. The new company was financed by a banker named Henry Iselin, who put up 24,000 out of a total capital of 29,000 Francs. The ten Kinetoscopes were costed at 19,000 Francs, or 1,900 Francs each, and were all in 'good condition', Michel Werner claimed.

It is difficult to judge whether Werner really succeeded in travelling his Kinetoscopes in France: fairground operators had already been well involved with exploiting Edison's invention since the start of 1895. The showman Ernest Grenier, for example, exhibited the Kinetoscope (purchased from the Werners or one of their competitors) throughout the provinces. A handbill printed at Saint-Lô, in Normandy, preserved at the Musée des Arts et Traditions Populaires (Museum of Popular Arts and Traditions), reads:

Grenier's. Fairground. Great success!!! Great success!!! Edison Kinetoscope. New animated scene today: The blacksmith's shop. Come and see the Kinetoscope, Edison's latest invention, a truly unbelievable and marvellous spectacle.[42]

Whatever the case, the enterprise founded by Werner and Iselin did not last for long, and it was wound up on 31 July 1895, after an existence of only seven months. The reason for this dissolution is not known. And on 28 September 1895, Alexis Werner withdrew from the company formed in October 1894, for equally unknown reasons. The name of the company, previously Michel and Alexis Werner, became Michel Werner et Cie.

The Werners also had connections with a Belgian company named Société Anonyme l'Edison's Kinetoscope Français (Edison Kinetoscope France Ltd.), founded on 15 January 1895 in Brussels. In spite of its name, this concern did very little business in Paris. The deed of foundation, located in Belgium by Guido Convents, tells us that its founder, Henri Micard de Fleurigny, a (rather mediocre) man of letters living at 33 Rue Marbeuf in Paris, brought to the company 'the rights which he holds from the Continental Commerce Co., 44 Pine Street, New York' (Frank Maguire, Vice-President of the Continental Commerce Co., was one of the first directors of the Belgian company), as well as other more obscure rights which he claimed to hold in France, Monaco and the French colonies. The Werners were not involved directly in this company, but on 1 April 1895 they signed over the lease of the Kinetoscope Parlor at 20 Boulevard Poissonnière to 'M. La Valette, director of the Edison's Kinetoscope Français company'. So Michel and Eugène Werner only retained control of this establishment for seven months. The Belgian company did not hang onto the address for very much longer. By April 1896 it was in liquidation, with the Kinetoscopes sold off to the highest bidder, as *L'Industriel Forain* advertised on 2 August: 'Notice to showmen. Starting 10 August, grand sale of Edison Kinetoscopes and Kinetophones. Very reasonable prices. Apply 20 Boulevard Poissonnière, afternoons.'[43]

But in 1895, in spite of losing their second shop, the Werners had not given up on exploitation of the Kinetoscope. In June 1895 they created a paper company, without legal status, the Compagnie Américaine de Kinetophonographe (American Kinetophonograph Company), with the aim of exploiting the Edison Kinetophone. Perhaps they hoped that this roundabout route would allow them to capture the fairground clientele who seemed not to be beating a path to their door. The legal records of

16 Rue Saint-Marc, where the office of the Compagnie Américaine du Kinetophonographe was located, reveal that this address was rented by one of the Werner brothers, probably Eugène.

Eugène Werner was also responsible for another strange manoeuvre. On 18 June 1895 he filed a patent whose purpose was

> to guarantee for me the exclusive ownership of a new system of equipment by means of which one may view series of photographs reproduced on an endless film, animated with a continuous movement.[44]

The machine which Werner described as 'his' invention was an Edison Kinetoscope, although neither of those names appeared anywhere in the patent. Werner had simply modified the shutter system, using a rotating cylinder pierced by four slots instead of a disc. It is not known if any Kinetoscopes to Werner's design were actually built, but it was a clear act of piracy, all the stranger because it came from Edison's exclusive agent in France.

The abandonment of the Kinetoscope Parlor at 20 Boulevard Poissonnière to the Belgian company, the short life of the firm Michel Werner & Co. from January to July 1895, the withdrawal of Alexis Werner on 1 September 1895, and the dubious activities of Eugène Werner, all tend to suggest that exploitation of the Kinetoscope in Paris, as far as the Werners were concerned, was a long way from being a financial success story. Probably the first months of Kinetoscope exhibition benefited from a novelty or curiosity value, as in the United States, but by 1895 the prospects for the exploitation of this slot machine were certainly dim. As one of the Werner brothers admitted later, in February 1896:

> The Edison Kinetoscope only offered a sufficiently lucrative business by always remaining in the large centres . . . The problem with the Kinetoscope was a large consumption of electrical power which required charging of four batteries every two or three days . . . This was difficult and often almost impossible in the provinces. In addition, [only] a single person could look into the machine and in these circumstances it was necessary to take from the spectator a very high sum of 25 centimes. These were the two reasons (to which one should add the very high cost) which prevented the introduction of the Kinetoscope on the fairgrounds.[45]

And in addition, the Werners' undertaking had been completely undermined by imitators. Since Edison had not taken out a patent for the

Kinetoscope in France, any manufacturer could construct it and exploit it publicly.

In 1894 acquiring an Edison machine from the Werners required an outlay of 'several thousand Francs' (Clément-Maurice later mentioned the figure of 6,000 Francs, which seems high). In January 1895 the Kinetoscope was valued by Michel Werner at 1,900 Francs. But during 1895, in Amsterdam, the World's Phonograph Company distributed an advertising leaflet aimed at the French market, which included the following prices:

> Current prices: complete Kinetoscope (without batteries or photographs): 800 Francs. Four batteries to operate five machines: 310 Francs. Ditto (smaller): 155 Francs. Loop for passage of pictures: 10 Francs. Small spare lamp: 5 Francs. Spare armature for motor: 25 Francs. Brush [electrical conductor for the motor]: 1.50 Francs.[46]

So in the summer of 1895 it was possible to acquire a complete Edison Kinetoscope in Amsterdam for around 1,100 Francs, low enough to tempt some wealthy showmen. The Kinetophone must have been more expensive. On 19 May 1895 two dealers named Gatineau and Viel put the Kinetophone on sale, at 14 Boulevard Poissonnière, a few doors away from the Werners:

> Phonograph-Kinetoscope combined together (new import), certain success, 2,400 Francs. Edison Phonograph, 900 Francs. Kinetoscopes, three views, 1,500 Francs. Cylinders, spare parts. Only serious workshop for repairs. Gatineau and Viel, 14 Bd. Poissonnière, Paris.[47]

On 8 March 1896 Gatineau and Viel were still offering the Kinetoscope, in spite of the explosion of the cinematograph market. They had devised a Kinetophone with three eyepieces, so that 'three persons may see and hear at the same time'.[48] Kinetoscopes were also available from Jacques and Charles Ullmann, at 16 Boulevard Saint-Denis, Paris. It is not clear where these originated: perhaps from the United States; perhaps from London, where the Ullmanns had a shop at 9 Butler Street; or possibly from Switzerland where they had a factory at Saint-Croix. The falling prices in France corresponded to the situation in the United States. According to Hendricks, in June 1895 the cost of the Kinetoscope (when purchased by an Edison concessionary company) went down from $250 to $127.50, and by the end of 1895 it was as low as $70.

But the most dynamic competition for the Werners came from Charles Pathé (1863–1957), the son of a butcher from Alsace. He began exploiting the Edison Phonograph on 9 September 1894, at the fair of Monthéty on the outskirts of Paris. Business was so good that shortly afterwards Pathé travelled to London to acquire Phonographs and cylinders, which he resold at a profit to showmen in France. While in London he bought a Kinetoscope copy from Robert Paul, who by then was constructing them himself. On 19 May 1895, Pathé was able to offer his customers:

> Complete Kinetoscope, 1,700 Francs. Edison Phonograph, 850 Francs with twelve recorded cylinders, four blank cylinders and a battery. Recorded cylinders, 5 Francs. Despatch on receipt of payment, apply to Mr. Pathé, 72 Cours de Vincennes, Paris. Free despatch of Edison catalogue.[49]

1,700 Francs was certainly cheaper than Werner's valuation of the Kinetoscope at 1,900 Francs, and the showmen preferred to buy their equipment from 'Mr Pathé'. On 13 October 1895 he was offering

> Certain fortune to the first exhibitors of our new patented four-viewer Kinetoscope. This device is not very bulky, lightweight and easy to operate, it contains 80 metres of different views. This machine is destined for even greater success than the Phonograph, on its own it can bring in 36 Francs per hour . . .[50]

This machine, known as the 'Photo-Zootrope', was very bulky, in spite of Pathé's claims, and did not sell at all well. Georges Mendel offered it for sale again in the 1900s, but no example is known to survive today. It was the work of Henri Joly, a first-rate engineer, who patented it on 8 November 1895.

Finally, a few obvious facts explain the failure of the Werners' enterprise. In 1895 the fashion was no longer for peepshow boxes restricted to a few individual viewers as in the eighteenth century, but for the complete and popular spectacle of the projected animated picture. All over Europe and the United States work was progressing, not merely to increase the repertoire of the Kinetoscope, but above all to finally bring together chronophotography and the magic lantern. Using the lantern the Moving Pictures on the Kinetoscope films would finally emerge from their box to be shown on the screen, in front of a large audience.

In a symbolic moment in 1899, the Werners' shop at 85 Rue de

Richelieu was taken over by the Compagnie Générale des Cinématographes, Phonographes et Pellicules (General Cinematograph, Phonograph and Film Company). This was a public company with a capital of 2 million Francs, founded by Claude Louis Grivolas and Charles Pathé on 11 December 1897, to replace the small company Pathé Frères founded on 28 September 1896. The unfortunate Werners, after a few attempts at the cinematograph trade, devoted their energies to the construction of motors and bicycles.[51] Charles Pathé, meanwhile, who had started out by selling British copies of the Edison Kinetoscope, must have savoured this moment of conquest of a fiercely contested territory: the embryonic French film industry.

16

The Labourers of the Eleventh Hour

1895 was the year when one of the oldest dreams of humanity was finally realized. The human being and its chronophotographic *alter ego* found themselves face to face, one sitting in a seat in a darkened room, the other moving on a screen, albeit still in silence. It was as though an eye, whose lids had been lifting, slowly, across the centuries, now opened completely on the world. It was a very sharp eye, not only capable of capturing the slightest details of life, which Marey and Edison had known how to do for some time, but above all able to project that life onto a screen.

The idea of using the images of chronophotography to provide the 'visual Repercussions out of Chrystal (*sic*)' for transmission by the 'lantern of fear' was not new. Marey himself had been trying to achieve that difficult transplant since 1892, and Demenÿ and many others had studied this question, without decisive results. Only Reynaud, with his perforated hand-painted strips, had managed to project long animated scenes, with exceptional quality. Edison, for his part, was quite happy to hear the jingling of the nickel entering his (excellent) machine in which regularly perforated 35 mm films passed under the eye of a single spectator. He never attached much importance to the final technical 'addition', which he thought quite likely to 'kill the goose that laid the golden egg', the coin-in-the-slot Kinetoscope.

At the end of 1894 all the elements were in place to bring true chronophotographic spectacle onto the big screen. Fictional films were already being made, the films were already perforated, and various systems of driving the film were working satisfactorily, such as the mechanism of the Edison Kinetograph. Several new researchers, true 'labourers of the eleventh hour' as in the New Testament parable,[1] who would be rewarded with at least as much glory as the inventors of the preceding centuries, were perfecting various more or less successful sorts of film projector, building on previous designs. Marey and Edison had worked for more than ten years on their Chronophotographe and Kinetoscope, but they were not to take the credit for succeeding in the first public showing of animated photographs. The 'newcomers' (as Louis Lumière himself described his position in this business) of the year 1895 carried out a daring raid on the existing techniques, which they set about 'improving' with unstoppable flair. This final chapter covers the years 1895–6 and all these labourers of the eleventh hour: the Lumières, the Lathams, Jenkins, Armat, de Bedts, Joly, Skladanowsky, and others, who between them launched cinematography as both industry and spectacle.

The misfortunes of Georges Demenÿ

We left Demenÿ in a very poor situation: driven from the Station Physiologique by a 'senile and incoherent management', and facing somewhat strained relations with his associates Stollwerck and Gibbs Clark, of the Phonoscope company. Nevertheless Demenÿ, who also had some other financial problems, was not discouraged. He summoned possible sponsors to his laboratory at Levallois-Perret, where his Phonoscope and his Chronophotographe, with its beater cam mechanism (patented on 27 June 1894) which drove the non-perforated film regularly, were on view.

George William de Bedts, the French representative for the films of the European Blair Camera Company, showed great interest in the Phonoscope. De Bedts ran The Anglo-American Photo Import Office, a shop at 368 Rue Saint-Honoré in Paris, which sold all types of photographic cameras, photosensitive papers, and 'new roll films' with fast emulsions. These films, enclosed in an opaque cover to protect them from light, were as transparent as glass, according to an 1894 advertisement.

The first Edison Kinetoscope films, shown in the USA in April 1894, were shot on 35 mm film made by the Blair Camera Company (founded in the US in 1881 by Thomas Henry Blair). In Britain in 1895, Robert Paul and Birt Acres made their first films on material from the European Blair Camera Company, which had been formed in London in 1893. De Bedts, with his stock of Blair films, therefore had a considerable advantage over other pioneers, who were always searching for the ideal film support.

De Bedts and Demenÿ appear to have come to some form of

agreement. In *Le Journal des Débats* of 14 November 1894, Henri de Parville mentioned that the Demenÿ Phonoscope could be obtained at de Bedts' shop, for making 'animated portraits'. In this device, intended to reproduce 'amateur chronophotography' in the drawing room or the fairground, a rotating series of 'living photographs' were viewed through a moving shutter disc. A version with a Molteni lantern, for projecting the image, was also available. A draft contract between de Bedts and Demenÿ exists, but it is from the following year, dated 15 July 1895:

> Mr Demenÿ grants to Mr de Bedts who accepts the following conditions, the exclusive rights for France and her colonies, of patented apparatus and inventions belonging to him relevant to the photography of movement, namely: 1. The series-photography camera, amateur model, 2. The 'Phonoscope' camera for drawing-room use and for animated projections, 3. The positive image discs for Phonoscopes and ordinary zoetropes.[2]

By that date the Lumières had already been projecting films with their 'Cinématographe', in private showings, for nearly four months. Demenÿ retained the exploitation rights for his own Chronophotographe- Projecteur, which was not yet fully perfected:

> Not included in the rights are the cameras intended to project positive images in long strips for theatrical illusions, the series-photography cameras for professionals giving large negative images, and the automatic Phonoscope cameras. The said devices, not being yet constructed, form the object of another branch of exploitation which Mr Demenÿ reserves for himself.[3]

De Bedts accepted responsibility for the laboratory costs, and agreed always to have in his shop 'film of good quality and in quantities sufficient to guarantee delivery'. Demenÿ's new associate had certainly understood that the future did not lie in zoetrope discs or the drawing-room Phonoscope. This contract would have prevented him from directly projecting Demenÿ's chronophotographic films. It was never signed by de Bedts, who emerged a little later, at the end of 1895, as one of the Lumières' principal competitors. And Demenÿ, on 22 August 1895, granted his exploitation licence to Léon Gaumont.

A remarkable fact, overlooked until now, is that it was de Bedts who supplied film to Gaumont and Demenÿ for their first attempts. In a letter of 7 September 1895, Gaumont wrote to Demenÿ:

I was waiting, before despatching the films, to be able to send something of some importance. Apart from the three rolls which you took, Debetz [*sic*] only had three others in the shop. To give us satisfaction, Monsieur Debetz has been happy to cut some 12 cm reels into two, which allows me the pleasure of sending to you today, by parcel post to the address you gave us, fifteen reels of 60 mm width. I hope that you will bring us back some interesting views of your journey.

Monsieur Debetz has told me that he has just obtained the French concession for Edison-type cameras, he showed me some small views in strips of 10 m length which I thought very successful.[4]

This letter indicates de Bedts' dominance of the French market for celluloid. But the last sentence is surprising. We saw in the last chapter that the Werner brothers had exclusive rights for commercial exploitation of the Edison Kinetoscope in France. But, according to Gaumont, in September 1895 de Bedts had 35 mm films for the Kinetoscope and presented himself as Edison's agent. As the exploitation of the American equipment in France had been rather disorderly, and the Werners had shown themselves to be less than brilliant, it is possible that Edison's agents had finally chosen de Bedts to put the situation right. But by September 1895 it was already too late.

For more than a year, from 1894 until August 1895, Demenÿ sought a patron rich enough to launch the Phonoscope properly. Among the individuals of varying wealth who trooped through the laboratory in Levallois-Perret were the still mysterious figures Otto, Kraus, and Prieur, as well as a toy-manufacturer named Abraham Martin. Martin presumably considered commercializing Demenÿ's Phonoscope, but decided not to go ahead, though later, on 25 May 1898, the two men jointly filed a patent for a camera. Another toy-maker, Charles Auguste Watilliaux, of 110 Rue du Temple, asked Demenÿ to make short series of successive photographs for a 'Folioscope' which he patented on 1 May 1896. This was a booklet of chronophotographs printed on paper, which were flicked with the thumb so that the images appeared to come to life (the 'flick book' principle of the Folioscope was invented by an Englishman, John Barnes Linnett, who patented it on 18 March 1868). In 1897, instead of mounting the images in a booklet, Watilliaux arranged a series of Demenÿ photographs around a shaft, mounted horizontally in a small box of cardboard or metal and fitted with a handle. An example of the Demenÿ–Watilliaux Folioscope, now very rare, is preserved in the Musée du Cinéma in Paris.

But Demenÿ must have known that he should not rely on manufacturers of fancy goods to assure the mass manufacture and sale of his costly and delicate pieces of apparatus. He decided instead to turn to the large industrial companies: first of all, the Lumière brothers.

The company Antoine Lumière et ses Fils (Antoine Lumière and Sons) was founded on 5 January 1884 in Lyon, based at 15 Rue de la Barre. Its object was stated as 'the exploitation of photography of all types and the sale of gelatino-silver-bromide photographic plates'. The three partners were Claude Antoine Lumière (1840–1911), a merchant resident at 16 Rue de la Barre, Lyon, and his two sons Auguste Marie Nicolas Lumière (1862–1954) and Louis Jean Lumière (1864–1948), the latter aged only 19 but emancipated by a declaration made by his father.[5]

Through the enormous success of its instantaneous photographic plates, sold under the brand name 'Étiquette Bleue' ('Blue Label'), the company transformed itself into a public company with a capital of 3 million francs, in documents deposited at Lyon on 2 May 1892. By 1894, it was producing some 15 million photographic plates per year and employed 300 workers. The steam-powered factories at Rue Saint-Victor and Cours Gambetta, in the Monplaisir suburb of Lyon, were among the most important photographic industries in the world.

The Lumières became rich and well known in scientific and photographic circles, and published regularly in scholarly journals. On 25 July 1891, for example, Auguste and Louis Lumière contributed an article on a 'new process of photography' to *Paris-Photographe*, the beautiful journal run by Nadar. Another article in the same issue gave a precise explanation of Marey's chronophotographic methods, with an engraving showing the physiologist's camera, already using 90 mm celluloid film. Louis Lumière's later claim that '[in 1894] I knew nothing of the work of Marey'[6] is scarcely credible.

On 6 October 1894 Demenÿ, on the hunt for money as ever, wrote to 'Messieurs Lumière sons':

> I have already had the occasion to correspond with you on the subject of the industrial preparation of perforated glass discs used for zoetropic negatives for illuminated projection. I know, on the other hand, the interest which you maintain in all the popularizations of scientific progress in photography. I have constructed some models of simplified equipment whose operation is simple and reliable enough to be placed in the hands of the amateur, that is to say to come out of the laboratory . . . I had, to assist me in my attempts, two partners, but the business is significant enough to be put onto a

larger footing and I am on the point of expanding our little research company. I would be most pleased if you were to take part and, to enlighten you on the state of our business, I am sending you a prospectus as well as a small note on the amateur equipment.[7]

The Lumières' reply, dated 9 October, survives in Demenÿ's scrapbook. He underlined one phrase of the letter bitterly:

the business which you have mentioned to us appears to us to be *genuinely interesting*, and we will not fail to come to see you during our next visit to Paris. . .[8]

In November or December 1894 Louis Lumière took his turn to visit Demenÿ's laboratory in Levallois-Perret. 'We did not discuss anything technical, I did not see any equipment,' he stated later. It is quite possible that Demenÿ showed him nothing: unlike Reynaud, he avoided revealing his methods to any 'newcomer'. But these two experimental technicians must have talked of mechanisms, or at least discussed chronophotography and its results; in any case, Demenÿ wrote to Lumière again on 28 December 1894 concerning some 'proofs' which he wished to send him. In this letter Demenÿ also informed Lumière that Lavanchy-Clarke, the representative of his partner Gibbs Clarke, was leaving for the South of France and wished to meet him. Some time later Lumière managed to poach Lavanchy-Clarke, who became one of the agents of the Cinématographe Lumière in Switzerland.

It is difficult to state for certain that Demenÿ had a great influence on Louis Lumière's researches. At the very least, he perhaps served as a 'stimulant' for the industrialist, who hurried to work on his own chronophotographic apparatus as soon as he returned to Lyon.

The Lumière 'Domitor'

The name 'Cinématographe' which Léon-Guillaume Bouly had coined on 12 February 1892 appeared from Louis Lumière's pen in 1895, but not on the patent of 13 February 1895, nor even on its subsequent Certificates of Addition, contrary to what has often been maintained. Antoine Lumière initially proposed to christen the apparatus the 'Domitor' (from 'dominator'), as if to indicate that it would be superior to all others.[9] In the end 'Cinématographe' appeared to be both more exact and more scientific, and the mysterious Bouly could not protest: his second patent of 27 December 1893 had lapsed, since the annual fee had only been paid once. At the end of 1894, the name 'Cinématographe' was therefore in the public domain.

There is great confusion over the conception of the Cinématographe Lumière. The two brothers told so many different versions in later life—mixing different accounts at different times, each promoting his own claim to attribute the merit to himself—that the truth became completely obscured, a nice irony for inventors whose very name translates as 'light'. Most of the pioneers of cinematography displayed faulty memories, with a tendency to exaggerate and predate their work: this was certainly the case for Edison, the Lumières, Méliès, Raoul Grimoin-Sanson, and others. To add to the difficulty, the Lumière archives have disappeared; there will never be an opportunity like the one Gordon Hendricks had in combing the archives of West Orange to re-establish the truth of the invention of the Edison Kinetoscope.

There is a mass of work on the Lumières:[10] hagiographic texts, studies of greater or lesser seriousness, even an anti-Lumière pamphlet[11] which echoes the polemical research of Maurice Noverre and Merritt Crawford. Existing biographies have the disadvantage of being chauvinist and partial, and many current French researchers have the unfortunate tendency to isolate Louis Lumière, as if he were the *only* person working on a chronophotographic projector in 1895. There were some extremely interesting pioneers contemporary with the Lumières; researchers of the greatest importance, who often had a more correct vision of the cinematographic spectacle, and whose achievements are never studied.

There is nothing to be gained by citing all the contradictory versions and dubious theories about the development of the Cinématographe Lumière at the start of 1895. The only plausible testimony appears to be that of Charles Moisson, chief engineer at the Lumière factory, who declared in 1930:

> During the summer of 1894 [more probably about October–November 1894], the father Lumière arrived in my office, where I was with Louis, and took out of his pocket a piece of a Kinetoscope film which he had acquired from the Edison agents, and said word for word to Louis: 'Here is what you have to do because Edison is selling this at crazy prices, and the agents want to make these films in France, to have them better marketed' . . . This piece of film, which I still have in front of my eyes, and which was about 30 cm long, was exactly the same pattern as current film stock: four perforations per image, the same width and same spacing. It showed

a scene at the barber's [i.e. *The Barbershop*]. After that, we began some apparatus research, first of all with Auguste Lumière, simply with the aim of perfecting chronophotography.[12]

According to some sources, it was Clément-Maurice, the photographer based at 8 Boulevard des Italiens, who dragged his friend Antoine Lumière to the Werner Brothers' shop at 20 Boulevard Poissonnière. During the 1950s, after Louis Lumière had died, his brother Auguste presented another version of the facts: it had been he who had seen the Kinetoscope, 'at the start of 1895, in Rue de la République in Lyon'; a little later he changed his mind and recalled that 'it was one evening in March 1894'.[13] But the Edison Kinetoscope did not arrive in Paris until September 1894, and in Lyon not until 16 June 1895. Auguste Lumière added, in his *Mémoires*, that it was he who had thought of projecting the Edison films using a magic lantern. The only certainty is the great influence of the Kinetoscope on the conception of the Cinématographe Lumière. The two brothers used the same film format, 35 mm; only the perforations were changed, with one round hole on each side of the image instead of the four rectangular perforations on each side of the Edison film.

So at the end of 1894 research was in progress at Lyon-Monplaisir on the construction of a chronophotographic camera and projector. But at present there is no evidence that the Lumière brothers made films, either on paper or celluloid, in 1894. To quote Vincent Pinel on this subject, 'we do not believe that the Cinématographe was in working order before January 1895'.[14]

It was definitely the Lumières who found the complete solution to the problem of projection of chronophotographic films. Nobody in Europe or the United States had managed this with sufficient efficiency before the historic showing of 22 March 1895; that is enough to allow the Lumières the great and true merit which is theirs alone.[15] However this should not be exaggerated: the cinematographic industry would have come about without the Lumières; other apparatus was being perfected very quickly during the first months of 1895; and the influence of the Lumières on development of the film projector in the United States was approximately zero.

On Wednesday 13 February 1895, at 12.00 noon, a patent was filed at the Lyon offices of the Préfecture du Rhône (local government) by two engineers named Lépinette and Rabilloud, on behalf of Auguste and Louis Lumière. It concerned an apparatus 'serving for taking and viewing chrono-photographic pictures'; it is noticeable that Louis Lumière made no attempt to conceal the derivation of the idea in his choice of terminology. The two brothers were in the habit of taking out their patents jointly, but it was Louis who had designed the clever mechanism of the Cinématographe. As with the Edison Kinetoscope in 1894, the mechanism of the Lumière apparatus:

> is characterized by operating in intermittence on a regularly perforated strip, so as to impart successive displacements separated by periods of rest, during which the printing of pictures is carried out.[16]

The Lumières did not only borrow the name 'Cinématographe' from Bouly. Like the apparatus he had described in 1893, their camera was also 'reversible': it could also be used as a projector, and also as a film printer, a point which Bouly had not considered. Marey and Edison had opted for two completely separate instruments, one for taking the pictures, and the other for projection, and in the longer term they were right. The years 1895–1900 saw the appearance of hundreds of different 'reversible' cameras, but then there was a rapid return to the previous method of separating the two mechanisms.

The reversible chronophotographic device described in the Lumière patent of 13 February 1895 was modified on 30 March and 6 May 1895, and again on 28 March and 18 November 1896. A prototype was hand-crafted by Charles Moisson; this machine is now in the museum of the CNAM in Paris. The later examples were mass-produced by the engineer Jules Carpentier. The complete mechanism was driven by a handle connected to a central shaft, on which was mounted an eccentric cam; in the first design this cam was rounded, but in the Certificate of Addition of 30 March 1895 it became triangular. As the triangular cam turned it imparted a reciprocating movement to a vertical frame, causing it to slide up and down in a pair of grooves. A horizontal blade mounted on the vertical frame carried two small claws at one end.

On the opposite side of this mechanism was a vertical channel, through which the perforated film descended from a small wooden magazine on top of the camera casing. The film was pulled downwards by the two claws as they penetrated each perforation and descended on the sliding frame, then released when the claws retracted during their ascending movement. The claws then came back to pull the film down again, and so on. This movement was synchronized with a rotating shutter, a disc with a large cut-out section which uncovered a small window between the lens and the film, so that the window was uncovered during the moments when the claws withdrew from the film and caused it to stop. The exposure time was estimated at 1/50th of a second, and it was possible to take about sixteen images a second.

A number of problems were immediately obvious. The shutter was too far open, or the speed not fast enough. The projected images flickered and brought tears to the eyes of many viewers. The claw mechanism, though it was excellent for taking images, was a little too brutal for projection, and the images shook and jumped around. Louis Lumière tried to correct these defects throughout 1895 and 1896, but these always remained the weak points of the Cinématographe. But in spite of everything, the machine was far superior to the majority of the 1895 projectors, whatever their origin.

The first showing of the Lumière 'projection Kinetoscope' took place on 22 March 1895 at the Société d'Encouragement pour l'Industrie Nationale, at 44 Rue de Rennes (now 4 Place Saint-Germain-des-Prés) in Paris, a beautiful building which still exists today. At the invitation of Mascart, the President of the Société, Louis Lumière came to lecture on the cinematographic industry, 'and more particularly on the workshops and industrial products of the Lumière plate company, whose head office is in Lyon'.[17] Lumière showed positive photographic slides, slides coloured by the Lippmann method, and his reversible chronophotographic camera, at the time still without an official name. The audience was limited, only a few tens of invited guests:

> With the aid of a kinetoscope of his own invention, he projected a most curious scene: factory workers leaving at dinner time. This animated view, showing in complete motion all these people hurrying into the street, produced the most striking effect, and a repeat of the projection was demanded by the whole audience, filled with wonder. This scene, which lasted for only about a minute, consisted of no less than 800 successive pictures; everything was there: a dog coming and going, cyclists, horses, a cart at full trot, and so on.[18]

This first film Louis made, *La Sortie des Usines Lumière* ('Leaving the Lumière Factory'), immediately aroused lively interest. This slice of everyday life, a 'representation of the real' so full of animation, was shown again and again. Lumière had been expecting his coloured slides to be the success of the evening; in spite of the enthusiastic praise for his film, it was only afterwards that he realized the commercial and artistic importance of the animated photographs.

In the hall of the Société d'Encouragement was the engineer Jules Carpentier (1851–1921). A former pupil of the Paris Polytechnique, Carpentier had bought the Ruhmkorff workshops at 20 Rue Delambre in 1878. He specialized in the fabrication of precision optical and electrical instruments: metronomes, melographs, melotropes, the Photo-Jumelle (a stereo device), and so on. He was also a talented technician. Barely eight days after Lumière's projection at the Société d'Encouragement, Carpentier filed his own patent for an apparatus for 'projection of instantaneous photographs of animated scenes on a film strip', which he christened the 'Cynégraphe'.[19] This consisted of a reversible camera which had some great qualities (an intermittently rotating toothed wheel which drove the perforated film regularly) and some defects (a double film strip and double lens). In a Certificate of Addition of 27 April 1895 Carpentier described the film, which had triangular perforations like Edison's, but only one hole on each side of the image like Lumière's. The Lumière influence on the Cynégraphe was clear. The showing of 22 March, and the further private views which followed (17 April at the Sorbonne, 10 June in Lyon, and others), together with articles in the press, released a new wave of chronophotographic research in France and the rest of Europe, directed this time towards reversibility and the spectacle of the projection of movement.

The Latham Panoptikon and Eidoloscope

The same period saw the first chronophotographic projections in America, completely independent of the research being carried out by the Lumières or Carpentier. The Kinetoscope Exhibition Company, one of three companies responsible for exploiting Edison's 1894 invention, was directed by two brothers, Otway and Gray Latham. Their father, Woodville Latham, was a chemistry teacher. The Lathams spent much time seeking to improve the capabilities of the Edison Kinetoscope. They specialized in films of boxing matches, which were much appreciated by the American public. But a whole match could not be represented on only 15 m of film. Otway Latham, or perhaps an associate named Enoch J. Rector, had the idea of increasing the length of the Edison film strips and reducing the running speed to thirty images per second instead of the normal forty.

On 15 June 1894 the Lathams and Rector commissioned Dickson to film a fight of six rounds, between Michael Leonard and Jack Cushing, in the Black Maria. In July the Kinetoscope Exhibition Company ordered twelve modified Kinetoscopes from Edison, each capable of containing 150 ft (about 48 m) of film. *The Leonard–Cushing Fight* was exhibited with great success at the Latham brothers' Kinetoscope parlour at 83 Nassau Street, New York, in August 1894. The spectator put a nickel in a first machine, to see one round (slightly curtailed) of about a minute, then moved to a second Kinetoscope to view, for another nickel, the second round, and so on up to the end of the sixth round. Naturally, some thrifty people went straight to the sixth Kinetoscope, to see only the end of the fight, and so the film in the last machine suffered the greatest wear. With this formula the Latham brothers rapidly filled their cash register. They repeated the experiment with another long 'sensational' film shot in September 1894, which received an enthusiastic press reaction: *The Corbett–Courtney Fight*, between the boxers Peter Courtney and James Corbett. This was shown in the Kinetoscope parlour in New York, then in Boston, Chicago, San Francisco, and elsewhere.

This series of boxing films, very popular as they were, perhaps gave the Lathams the original idea for the 'Magic Lantern Kinetoscope' which saw the light of day in 1895. Instead of presenting the rounds through the eyepiece of a series of cumbersome boxes of limited capacity, why not project the films directly onto a screen with a magic lantern, in a room in front of a paying audience? It is not known exactly which of the three Lathams had the idea of dragging the films out of Edison's 'goose with golden eggs' to show them to everyone: Woodville stated that it was one of his sons, but they, having been well brought up, declared that the idea came from their father.

To make their film projector, the Lathams had the benefit of exceptional technical support. William Kennedy-Laurie Dickson, who had constructed the Kinetoscope for his employer Edison, was kind enough to come to their aid. He did this secretly, behind Edison's back; Dickson no longer saw eye to eye with 'the wizard', and left West Orange on 2 April 1895. Dickson persuaded the Lathams to take on one of his friends, the Frenchman Eugène Lauste (1856–1935), who had also worked for Edison between 1886 and April 1892. Lauste, one of the future inventors of the sound film, was like Dickson an inspired technician.[20]

Around December 1894, after several months of research aided by Dickson, Lauste perfected a projection apparatus which moved the film without an intermittent mechanism. The perforated film was wider than in the Kinetoscope, presumably to avoid legal problems with Edison. Lauste and Dickson also constructed a camera with intermittent movement capable of taking forty images per second, like the Kinetograph at West Orange. A first film was shot in February 1895, featuring

Woodville Latham. It was shown in New York on 21 April 1895, a month after Lumière's showing in Paris, in front of guests and journalists in a shop-cum-workshop belonging to the Lathams at 35 Frankfort Street. The projection device was first christened 'Panoptikon', but it soon became the 'Eidoloscope'. This first American showing of films projected by magic lantern was described by the *New York Sun* on 22 April 1895:

> MAGIC LANTERN KINETOSCOPE.
>
> [. . .] The continuous film of photographic pictures with slots cut in the edges to catch the teeth of a sprocket that keeps it from slipping is reeled in front of the electric light of a sort of magic lantern, and so the pictures are thrown successively on the screen with sufficient rapidity to produce the well-known kinetoscope or zoetrope effect of animated pictures [the pictures were shuttered by a rotating slotted disc].
>
> The pictures shown yesterday portrayed the antics of some boys at play in a park. They wrestled, jumped, fought, and tumbled over one another. Near where the boys were romping a man [played by Woodville Latham] sat reading a paper and smoking a pipe. Even the puffs of smoke could be plainly seen, as could also the man's movements when he took a handkerchief from his pocket. The whole picture on the screen yesterday was about the size of a standard window sash, but the size is a matter of expense and adjustment.[21]

This projector, lacking intermittent stoppage of the film, was certainly not superior to the Lumière machine, but there is no doubt that it worked. Edison reacted furiously, the same day. He threatened the Lathams with a lawsuit, since their perforated film was very similar to that of the Kinetoscope. 'That's a fraud,' declared Edison. And once again he promised, as in 1892:

> In two or three months . . . we will have the kinetophone perfected, and then we will show you screen pictures. The figures will be life size, and the sound of the voice can be heard as the movements of the figures are seen.[22]

Disregarding Edison's threats, at the end of 1894 the Lathams formed the Lambda Company to exploit their projector and films; this later became the Eidoloscope Company in 1896. After the showing of 21 April 1895, the Lathams began mass-production of films. On 4 May, the boxing match between Young Griffo and Charles Barnett was filmed on the roof of Madison Square Garden. The 'Eidolograph' camera, lighter in weight than the Edison Kinetograph, ran for eight minutes without interruption. By this time it is likely that Lauste and Dickson had made an important modification to this intermittent-drive camera: in two places the film path formed a loop, so that the force of the drive mechanism on the film would not be too violent. This 'Latham Loop' was later used in the majority of projectors, and the same idea was patented in France by Henri Joly on 26 August 1895.

On 20 May 1895, at 156 Broadway, New York, the Lathams opened a public exhibition of the Eidoloscope and its 'Living Moving Pictures'. For a few cents New Yorkers could watch the boxing match between Griffo and Barnett, but also admire other curious subjects:

> You'll sit comfortably and see fighters hammering each other, circuses, suicides, hangings, electrocutions, shipwrecks, scenes on the exchanges, street scenes, horse-races, football games, almost anything, in fact, in which there is action, just as if you were on the spot during the actual events. And you won't see marionettes. You'll see people and things as they are.[23]

The poster for 'Latham's Eidoloscope' announced proudly: 'This is the first practical exhibition of subjects showing Actual Life Movements on a screen ever made in the world.'[24] This was not really correct, since the Lumières had succeeded before them; but leaving that detail aside this was certainly the first *commercial* projection of films in the whole world. The machine was presented in many cities in the United States in the course of 1895, but it was not the expected triumph. Possibly the images were of poor quality. The Eidoloscope, with its continuous film drive mechanism, did not have a great future, and like the Lumières in France, the Lathams had to face competition from some very active rivals.

Jenkins and Armat's 'marvellous electric Phantoscope'

Thomas Armat (1866–1948) was a real-estate agent who had been interested in Moving Pictures for some time. At the 1893 Chicago World's Fair he had taken a close and admiring look at the Anschütz Tachyscope.[25] The following year he discovered Edison's Kinetoscope films. And at the Bliss School of Electricity he met Charles Francis Jenkins (1867–1934) of Richmond, Indiana, then a stenographer working for the Treasury Department. Jenkins became one of the Edison counterfeiters: on 24 November 1894 he patented the 'Phantoscope', a modified Kinetoscope in which the film, with round perforations, followed a very simple path, driven by a wheel with four teeth and illuminated by two rotating electric lamps. But to avoid openly pirating Edison, Jenkins was obliged to make his films himself. On 12 December 1894 he filed a patent for a 'Kinetographic camera' with four rotating lenses. It is not known what results he obtained with this machine.[26]

On 25 March 1895 Armat and Jenkins formed a partnership for constructing a film projector. They were aided by Edward F. Murphy, who worked at the Columbia Phonograph Company, which had opened a number of Phonograph Parlors in 1894, some of which contained Kinetoscopes. By the end of August 1895 the projector was almost complete. On 7 September, Jenkins announced to Edward Murphy:

> The lantern is simplicity itself, Ed, and I know you'll be pleased with it. It is the grandest success you could imagine. I am blessed glad it's finished, too, for I'm dreadfully tired living with it day and night.[27]

Jenkins and Armat took out a patent describing their Phantoscope projector on 28 August 1895. The film was driven by a mechanism in which a small wheel with a single tooth was periodically engaged by another larger wheel with fourteen notches, giving the perforated film an intermittent forward motion. Armat and Jenkins had also experimented with a Maltese Cross intermittent drive, and declared themselves the inventors of the 'loop' already advocated by Latham. But in 1896 they reverted to another process, which was simpler if also rather noisy. In January 1896 the American journal *The Photographic Times* published an article on Demenÿ's beater-cam Chronophotographe, patented in France on 27 July 1894 as a Certificate of Addition. The two Americans had no hesitation in taking up this excellent drive mechanism for their projector. Demenÿ had no chance: misunderstood in his own country, and pirated by the Americans.

Armat and Jenkins had three examples of the Phantoscope constructed in the workshop of John Schultzbach in Washington. Two of these were installed in separate halls at the Cotton States Exposition in Atlanta, at the end of September 1895, while the third machine was kept as a spare in case of breakdown. On 21 October 1895, the *Atlanta Journal* was full of praise:

THE MARVELLOUS ELECTRIC PHANTOSCOPE.
This is unquestionably the most wonderful electric invention of the
age. It is the first public exhibition and nothing like it has ever been
seen before, consequently it is difficult to describe.

By means of this wonderful invention you see a perfect reproduction, full life size, of the living originals, every act and motion
absolutely perfect, even to the wink of an eye.

Repertoire includes two acts from *Trilby*; one act from *1492*;
Carmencita, Sousa's Band; dances, fist fight; Annabelle in the Sun
and Serpentine dances; a cock fight and numerous other interesting
subjects.[28]

These were all Edison films, some of which had been hand-coloured at
the request of Armat and Jenkins. The showings of the Phantoscope did
not meet with great success, and to make matters worse, on 15 October
1895 the two halls of the Exposition were destroyed in a fire. We might
also doubt the quality of the showings: Kinetoscope films, intended to be
lit from behind by an eight-volt bulb, were shot on slightly opaque
celluloid, and the projected images must have been dark and tiring to
watch.

In spite of all that, the Atlanta projections represent a very important
event. In his book *The Emergence of Cinema*, the historian Charles
Musser accords more importance to these first showings than to those by
the Latham brothers. According to Musser, Armat and Jenkins' show
constituted the first true example 'of *modern commercial cinema* in the
United States'[29] (and, one might add, in the whole world), because
unlike the Lathams' device it used an intermittent film drive mechanism,
the basis of all modern projection.

The showings in Atlanta greatly accelerated American research. At the
same Exposition were Gray Latham, with the Eidoloscope, and Frank
Harrison with the slot machines of Raff and Gammon's Kinetoscope
Company. The whole of the small American moving picture world met,
spied on each other, and cast curious eyes over the different mechanisms.
After watching the Eidoloscope and Phantoscope shows, Harrison
judged the latter to be particularly impressive, and alerted Raff and
Gammon. At the end of December 1895, while Jenkins was showing
one of the Phantoscope machines at Richmond, Indiana (it had opened
to the public on 29 October), Thomas Armat received a visit in
Washington from Frank R. Gammon. Armat gave him a private projection with the Phantoscope, and the co-director of the Kinetoscope
Company declared himself 'surprised'. He had not believed, Armat later

said, that someone had finally managed to make a machine to project animated photographs.

Armat came to an agreement with the Raff and Gammon company. They would exploit the Phantoscope, but would carefully erase the names of its two true inventors: Armat, who fully agreed in exchange for some large monetary compensation, and Jenkins, who protested in vain against this coup. The Phantoscope, now known as the 'Vitascope', was marketed under the sole name of Edison. 'The Latest Marvel' of the 'inspired inventor' was presented to the public on 23 April 1896 at Koster and Bial's Music Hall, 34th Street and Broadway, New York. 'Edison's new wonder' had arrived, the press proclaimed.

So Edison achieved—though only just—the rendezvous with projection which he had missed several times since 1888. He now believed that he held the new 'goose with golden eggs', even though he had acquired it thanks to a quite shameful trick. However, in 1896 and subsequent years the animated photograph industry was to become an immense phenomenon, and the competition from the 'labourers of the eleventh hour' would be tough for Edison. Without repeating the history of the birth of the American cinematographic market in 1896—for more on this subject see the works of Charles Musser—it is necessary all the same to say a few words about the Edison company's principal competitor.

The American Mutoscope Company

Dickson had helped the Lathams and Lauste to construct their Panoptikon. He had also given considerable assistance to one of his engineer friends, Harry Norton Marvin, and another former Edison employee, Herman Casler, whom he had met during 1892. In 1894, Dickson had the idea of another type of Kinetoscope, the 'Mutoscope'. This was derived from the 'flick-book' or Folioscope, already mentioned in connection with Demenÿ, which worked by manually flicking through a booklet of photographs or drawings showing the different phases of a movement, giving a simple and effective animation.

The principle of the Mutoscope was very simple. Dickson proposed to mount a whole series of photographic views, representing the successive positions of a moving subject, onto a wheel. The wheel was turned by a handle, and the paper pictures were stopped for a brief moment, one by one, by a small bracket, which gave the spectator the impression of an animated scene. As in the Kinetoscope, this view was enlarged by a lens, and as in the Kinetoscope there was also a coin-operated system to release the mechanism for use. The nickel fell into a small cast-iron cash box at the bottom of the device, in the models marketed in 1897. A small bulb was all that was required to illuminate the passage of the pictures, so its electrical system was very limited, unlike the Edison Kinetoscope. The viewer, leaning over the eyepiece, controlled the speed of the images him or herself by turning the handle. It could be stopped at a particularly interesting moment; many Mutoscopes showed slightly racy scenes (in Britain the machine became known as 'What the Butler Saw' as a result of its typical subject matter).

On 21 November 1894 Casler, now living in Syracuse, New York, filed a patent for the Mutoscope in his own name only. A prototype appears to have been working since 10 November. With the Mutoscope, Casler and Dickson had simplified the principle of the Kinetoscope, and Edison could not protest. But the two technicians still needed to produce some films. Once again, they got round the Edison patents by devising a different drive system, using unperforated film, although this was still not enough to prevent a bitter 'patent war'. In December 1894 Casler constructed a prototype camera called the Mutograph, with the collaboration of Harry Marvin, John Pross, and Dickson. This was completed in March 1895, and Casler showed it to Elias Bernard Koopman, a businessman who had also decided to take the plunge into the moving image industry. Dickson, meanwhile, left Edison on 2 April 1895 and rejoined his friends Casler and Marvin at Canastota, New York, where he helped them to make their first films (for example, a boxing match between Al Leonard and Bert Hosley).

The Mutograph camera was operated by electricity, like the Edison Kinetograph. The film was very wide: 70 mm, unperforated, and with an image area four times larger than that of Edison film. The film was intermittently driven by an eccentric beater cam, and it was perforated by the camera at the moment when it stopped in front of the lens and the image was taken. Two claws pierced holes in the edges of the film, and then withdrew. The film could then be printed onto paper (the perforations allowed exact spacing of the images) and the images selected were attached to the Mutoscope wheel. All that remained was to place a nickel in the slot and turn the handle.

On 27 December 1895 (the day before the Lumières' first public show at the Grand Café in Paris), the American Mutoscope Company was founded in Jersey City. The founders and shareholders were Casler, Dickson, Koopman, and Marvin. The capital amounted to 2 million dollars. But from November 1895 onwards, the principals of the American Mutoscope Company had also been trying to project films. Dickson, who was in constant contact with the cutting edge of international chronophotography, had realized that the future lay in projection onto the big screen. He gave up work on the Mutoscope—which was highly successful in 1897, and in the end effectively banished the Kinetoscope from the fairgrounds—and with the help of Casler perfected the 'Biograph', a projector for wide non-perforated film. The film was driven by friction, with a pressure plate to stop the film in front of the lens. The first showing of the Biograph took place at Pittsburgh, on 14 September 1896, and this projector then rapidly overtook the Edison Vitascope and Cinématographe Lumière, among other machines being exploited across the United States.

Joly and Pathé in France

Charles Pathé had set out to import the coin-operated Kinetoscopes made by Robert Paul, of 44 Hatton Garden, London, into French fairgrounds. The exact date when Paul started mass-production of Kinetoscopes is not known, but it was probably at the start of 1895.[30] In collaboration with the photographer Birt Acres, Paul had also designed a camera for increasing the film repertoire of the Kinetoscope. The Acres camera was patented in Britain on 27 May 1895, but the two colleagues had been successfully taking films on perforated 35 mm stock since 29 March. Paul had the audacity to send a sample to Edison and propose a partnership.

Pathé followed a similar path, but he had neither the technical knowledge of Paul, a professional scientific instrument maker, nor the photographic skill of Acres. He certainly noticed that the fairground clientele were becoming bored of always seeing the same worn-out, broken, reglued, scratched Edison films. If the trade paper *L'Industriel Forain* can be believed, Pathé did not begin exploiting the Paul Kinetoscope until May 1895. It was probably about this time (not in December 1894 or January 1895 as Maurice Noverre claimed in 1930[31]) that he received the help of Henri Joly, a photographic engineer, who was certainly familiar with Marey and Demeny's chronophotographic methods, since he had attended the École de Gymnastique at Joinville, where the two physiologists often went to take their pictures.

Joly offered to make a camera for Pathé, in order to shoot new films for the Kinetoscope. A legal agreement was concluded between them on 13 June or 13 August 1895. Pathé advanced the necessary funds, and Joly set to work. By 26 August 1895 Joly had succeeded, as his patent filed on that date demonstrates. As in the Lumière patent of 13 February 1895, there were explicit references to Marey (and to Edison): the device was a 'new chronophotographic camera' which could also function as a Kineto-scope.

The Joly camera could have seriously rivalled the Lumière machine. The perforated film was driven by two toothed rollers—the Edison system, later taken up universally but not used by the Lumières—and by a small metal pin which pushed the film and then released it. This was a variation of the Demenÿ beater cam movement, and Joly later had some problems on this score with Léon Gaumont, Demenÿ's last partner. Joly also had the idea of incorporating the film loop, already used in the United States. The Joly machine was reversible, and could also function for 'moving projection':

> By placing behind the apparatus a sufficient source of light equipped with a reflector and a condenser, one can obtain on a screen the image which is found on the film.[32]

In October 1895 Henri Joly made some slightly saucy films such as *Le Bain d'une Mondaine* ('Bath of a Lady of Society'). Pathé was completely happy with the results, and asked *L'Annuaire du Commerce* to publish the following advertisement in their 1896 edition. To be included in the 1896 edition the text had to be submitted before 1 October 1895:

> (Projection equipment). Pathé, *animated equipment*, 72 Cours de Vincennes.

> (Kinetoscope). Improved Edison system Kinetoscope or Kinetograph and Phonokinetoscope. Projection equipment. *Sole manufacturer of films in Europe*, sole agent for multi-lens Kineto-scopes and improved Phonographs. Pathé and Co., 72 Cours de Vincennes.[33]

So by about October 1895 Pathé, like Paul in Britain, was in a position to supply new 35 mm films to the fairgrounds. But Paul had not yet succeeded in projecting his films, while Pathé, thanks to Joly, had a genuine 'moving projection' machine. However, no public showing was organized. There were two reasons for this: firstly, like Edison, Pathé and Joly were convinced that the future lay in coin-operated Kine-toscopes. Joly designed a 'Photo-Zoetrope' on 8 November 1895, a multi-viewer Kinetoscope which was not a success (Pathé confirmed in his memoirs that he only sold 'two or three'). And secondly, according to

Pathé, the perforations of Joly's 35 mm films were not regular, which prevented good projection. This seems strange, and it is hard to understand why Joly, who had overcome more difficult problems, did not achieve regular perforation of the film. In fact, Pathé's later explanations on this subject are coloured by embarrassment; he behaved badly towards Joly who, for his part, committed a number of indiscretions. The cinematographic industry, as Demenÿ, the Lathams, and Armat and Jenkins were already aware, did not come into being without a number of acts of betrayal, dubious compromises, and knives in the back.

By the end of 1895, Pathé could no longer finance Joly's research. Bizarrely, he suggested to Joly that he and his young wife should move into his premises at 72 Cours de Vincennes; perhaps he also wanted to keep an eye on what Joly was doing. Joly began to lose patience, becoming 'nervous, irritable . . . He overworked himself, not leaving the workshop until late in the night. In addition, he became suspicious, like the majority of inventors.'[34] Pathé described Joly as half-crazy, a very irritable person, whom his wife tried vainly to calm down. On the other hand Maurice Noverre, in his biography of Joly, depicts Pathé as a crook, a real swindler who profited from the 'genius' of the unfortunate 'inventor'. Presumably the truth is located somewhere between these two versions and would be very hard to disentangle. The cause of the courageous Noverre's anger in 1930 was the fact that Pathé was then the head of one of the largest film companies in the world, while Joly, its 'initiator', was trying to scrape a living as a night watchman.

In October or November 1895 Pathé's financial situation improved slightly as a result of selling Joly's films to a mysterious person whom Pathé, later, preferred not to name: 'a gentleman whom I shall call Delman.'[35] If we turn that name around we read 'Mandel'. This seems very likely to have been Georges Mendel, a dealer in photographic equipment of 22 Boulevard Saint-Denis. Mendel became a pioneer of the cinema (he filed a patent on 1 December 1896) and, during the 1900s, of the sound film, in association with none other than Joly. Pathé sold him the films Joly had made for between 500 and 600 Francs. These films, according to Pathé, were also poorly perforated. Shortly afterwards Mendel returned, gave him back the films and demanded an immediate refund. But Pathé refused (regretfully, as he recalled later) and kept the money. Following this dubious incident, Pathé noticed that his collaborator had developed a strange attitude:

> I noticed that for several days M. Joly went out every afternoon without reason. Each time, he returned in a state of increasing

feverishness. What could these mysterious comings and goings conceal? I searched hard, I came to no discovery.[36]

Pathé became a kind of doorkeeper, spying (with a feverishness equal to Joly's own) on his inventor's excursions 'without reason'. The explanation soon became clear: Joly had met George William de Bedts, the former partner of Demenÿ. Joly saw de Bedts as the ideal promoter for his 'moving projection' equipment, and a contract between them appears to have been signed in about December 1895. But in the end Joly associated himself with the engineer Ernest Normandin, who bought all his early patent rights and marketed Joly's 'improved Cinématographe' throughout France.

Faced with the popular success of the Cinématographe Lumière, Pathé at last understood the importance of the machines Joly had constructed. The result was quite unpleasant. Pathé brusquely gave his associate and his wife notice to leave the apartment at 72 Cours de Vincennes. Worse still, Pathé had hidden the Joly camera away. After initiating the butcher's son into chronophotography, the technician found himself out in the street, without any compensation and without any of his equipment. Thus relieved of his 'irritable' associate, Pathé decided to waste no time in setting out on the route the Lumières had inaugurated in France: public exploitation of projected 35 mm films. By 3 May 1896 he was in a position to offer his fairground clientele a film projector—whether this was a Joly machine or a copy of the Cinématographe Lumière is a complete mystery:

> Continental Kinetoscope Phonographe. Eknétographe Pathé. Cinématographe type. Moving projection equipment. Ch. Pathé, Paris, 72 Cours de Vincennes. A certain fortune within months of exploitation. The equipment is working in the main establishments in Paris.[37]

On 10 May Pathé placed a second advertisement, in which the projector was called the 'Kinétographe'—the word 'Eknétographe' was perhaps a mistake by the printers of *L'Industriel Forain*.

On 9 June 1896, Pathé filed a patent for a film projector in Paris. It was certainly not a machine of his own invention; even though he had been 'initiated' by Joly, he remained practically useless at precision engineering. Pathé's patent contained nothing original, amongst the flood of hundreds of machines invented in France during 1896. It is revealing to note that, on that day in June 1896 when Pathé's agent

Armengaud visited the Paris Patent Office at 2.00pm, he was followed at 3.00pm by the Benoist and Berthiot company, filing for a 'projection device called Héliorama'; at 3.20pm by the pioneer Ambroise François Parnaland, future founder of the Éclair company, filing for a good quality reversible camera; and at 3.40pm by Adolphe Kohn with another film projector. A kind of cinematographic frenzy took over many minds in 1896.

But in that same year Pathé (like Gaumont) had to face a lawsuit which could ruin him, or at least seriously hold up his development. Pathé himself described this lawsuit, in his 1926 memoirs *Souvenirs et Conseils d'un Parvenu*:

> I received a visit from one M. Giraud, a justices' clerk, with whom I agreed the sale of a cinematograph and a series of twelve or fifteen films, each about 15 m in length, for an inclusive sum of 12,000 or 15,000 Francs [in another version of his memoirs, Pathé remembered 18,000 or 20,000 Francs]. I overestimated my abilities, and the extended stay which I made in the darkroom, from which I only emerged for meals, had the effect of making me ill, and this caused a delay of six weeks before I delivered the films, of which my client then refused to take delivery. He sued me for a refund of the deposit he had paid me, and a payment of 20,000 Francs in damages, representing the wasted expenses he had incurred in Moscow, where he had intended to set up a cinematograph operation. By default, I was fined the full amount of his demand. It was complete ruin at the moment when I was certain of a definite success.[38]

The records of this lawsuit are in the Villemoisson section of the Archives de Paris. On Tuesday 23 June 1896 Pathé, 'dealer, of 72 Cours de Vincennes', was summoned before the Tribunal de Commerce (Business Court) of Paris. The plaintiff was Charles Girod (not Giraud), who described himself as a teacher from Nice, not a clerk of the court as Pathé recalled. Girod lived in Paris, at 2 Rue de la Tour d'Auvergne. He claimed 20,000 Francs from Pathé in damages, plus 5,000 Francs for costs. The Tribunal de Commerce declared that the case was beyond its competence, and asked the professional photographic trade association to settle the case. This association, some time later, gave judgement in favour of Girod.

Fortunately Pathé, now on the verge of ruin, managed to persuade his brother Émile to sell his wine business in order to launch him in the phonograph and cinematograph trade. On 28 September 1896 Charles

438

Pathé, 'electrician, resident in Paris at 72 Cours de Vincennes' and his brother Émile, 'electrician, resident at Saint-Mandé, 22 Avenue de la Tourelle', founded a company in their joint names

> having for its object the manufacture and sale of electrical equipment, notably of Fluoroscopes [X-Ray apparatus commercialized by Edison] and of Kinetographs, etc., as well as the exploitation of all patents relating to this type of manufacture. This company will exist under the corporate name Pathé Frères.[39]

The office of the new company, which was capitalized at 40,000 Francs, was established at 98 Rue de Richelieu, very close to the shop run by the Werner brothers. This was only the beginning of Pathé's adventure. Having started from nothing, he founded with Louis Grivolas a gigantic cinematographic empire which dominated worldwide for many years. Along with Gaumont and some other more modest newcomers, Pathé created the French cinema industry, whose economic history still awaits proper study.

Léon Gaumont

The career of Léon Gaumont is also highly fascinating. He was another 'labourer of the eleventh hour' who, like Pathé, was to succeed to a quite amazing extent in the commercial exploitation of chronophotography. Unlike Pathé, Gaumont possessed great technical knowledge, having trained as an engineer in the workshops of Jules Carpentier. Gaumont had become interested in animated photography in 1881, when he was aged 17 and employed by Carpentier. In a small notebook —a quite astonishing document—he recorded some very informed reflections on pre-cinematographic research. He dreamed it would be possible

> to photograph a play, with a crowd of pictures each second. One would therefore have a whole series of the movements of the actors which one could view at home in the same length of time as the photography or the telephone reproducing the voice, and also have the whole play by seeing the actors in steady movement, that is to say to see the legs and arms, by projection on a large screen . . .[40]

This was accompanied by a sketch in the margin, showing a horizontal strip of photographs passing the focal point of a lens. The intermittent shuttering, Gaumont wrote, was produced by a mirror which replaced each image with the next, a system perhaps inspired by Reynaud.

In 1893 Gaumont joined the staff of the Comptoir Général de Photographie (Photographic General Store) at 57 Rue Saint-Roch in Paris, which was then managed by Félix Richard. The brothers Jules and Félix Richard had founded a precision instrument manufacturing company on 24 July 1882. On 29 November 1891 Félix Richard left that business and took over the Comptoir de Photographie, which had also been founded in 1882 by the Picard brothers and one Perrichont. In June 1895, Félix Richard offered to sell his business to Gaumont for 50,000 Francs. Gaumont hesitated, remarking that the business was not worth that much. However, the shop had done good business selling Carpentier's 'Photo-Jumelle', and Richard assured the young Gaumont that Carpentier would continue to supply the Comptoir Général with his photographic equipment. Reassured by this verbal promise, Gaumont agreed to take over the store, and the deal was completed on 7 July 1895. But on 28 May 1895 Félix Richard had lost the right to sell the Photo-Jumelle or to claim any exclusive arrangement with Carpentier; his own brother Jules had taken him to court in 1893, after Félix unwisely declared himself to be the 'general agent for the firm of Carpentier'. Possibly Gaumont was unaware of this, or possibly he believed that the dispute had been resolved. In any case, on 12 January 1896 he wrote to Félix Richard to reproach him for bad faith:

> When you offered me last June the chance to acquire the Comptoir Général de Photographie, I remarked to you that the business of that establishment was of little value and a long way from the value of 50,000 Francs, if the exclusive rights to the Photo-Jumelle were not maintained.
>
> Although Mr J. Carpentier did not give me personally any precise agreement, you had no hesitation in confirming to me that Mr J. Carpentier had formally promised to continue for your successor all the advantages which he had afforded you . . . I was therefore inclined to believe you, since I had never doubted your word and you repeated very formally and on several occasions the same promises to my partners. But, after nearly seven months, not only have the rights to the Photo-Jumelle not been afforded us, but quite to the contrary I have been given to understand categorically at Rue Delambre [the Carpentier workshop] that it was completely futile to insist or to think of this.
>
> This state of affairs naturally translates itself into a considerable fall in turnover, and also in the loss of influence of the Comptoir in

the photographic market, not to mention the fact that this situation is getting worse every day.

In the name of my partners and myself, I am asking you in what way you propose to compensate us for the very serious wrong which has caused us to be in this situation.[41]

In spite of this dispute, Félix Richard later (in 1907) became one of the shareholders of the Gaumont company. Meanwhile Richard had to make another appearance before the Tribunal de Commerce on 13 June 1896, in the interminable lawsuit his brother had brought against him in 1893. This letter from Gaumont shows clearly that the business affairs of the Comptoir Général, in 1895 and 1896, were problematic. We shall see shortly that the marketing of chronophotography would be no picnic either.

On 10 August 1895, in Paris, Gaumont founded a joint stock company with benefit to himself, with the aim of exploiting the Comptoir Général de la Photographie. The partners were prestigious: Gustave Eiffel, creator of the tower; Joseph Vallot, director of the Mont Blanc observatory; and a less famous figure, the stockbroker Alfred Besnier. The capital was 200,000 Francs, of which Eiffel put up 50,000, Vallot 75,000, and Besnier 25,000. The remaining 50,000 Francs were supplied by Gaumont, who had sole management and control of the company, which was named L. Gaumont et Cie. The deed of foundation, signed by Eiffel, Vallot (at Chamonix), Besnier, and Gaumont, also includes a brief inventory of the stock held at 57 Rue Saint-Roch. Apart from an 'Anschütz machine' valued at 190 Francs, there was still nothing to do with chronophotography. Gaumont also sold projecting lanterns, and filed several patents for this type of equipment during 1895. Gaumont had bought the Comptoir Général on 7 July 1895; in August, *La Revue Trimestrielle*, a quarterly periodical published by the shop, announced the transfer of control:

> I have the honour to inform you that I have disposed of my business of equipment construction and general photographic supplies to Messrs L. Gaumont et Cie. M. Gaumont has already been my collaborator for the past two years, and under his direction, the Comptoir Général de Photographie will continue the traditions which have ensured it the support of its numerous clientele. F.M. Richard.[42]

It is difficult to put a precise date on the association between Georges Demenÿ and the Comptoir Général de Photographie. It seems to have taken place in two stages. Around September 1894, Demenÿ signed a 'very advantageous contract' with Félix Richard, but the latter 'had to abandon the undertaking because of court proceedings'.[43] According to his own account, Demenÿ therefore turned to the Lumières, which suggests the dating of September 1894 for his contract with Richard, since his letter to the Lumières was written in October.

Demenÿ's tracks are quite complicated. At the end of 1894, and again on 15 July 1895, he had also negotiated with de Bedts, although without reaching any conclusion. On 6 June 1895 Demenÿ awarded Ludwig Stollwerck, his former partner from Cologne, a licence giving him the rights to make and market chronophotographic cameras and Phonoscopes with a coin-operated mechanism. But by this date the Phonoscope company was already dying. Around February 1895 Demenÿ once more offered his equipment to Félix Richard; but from July of that year it was with Gaumont that he would do business.[44]

On 25 May 1895, following the example of the Lumière brothers, Demenÿ converted his Chronophotographe into a reversible machine, or at least filed a Certificate of Addition to his patent of 10 October 1893 to that effect. But like his former master Marey, he still did not use perforated film, and so his projector could not function correctly. In any event Gaumont decided, as a first step, to market the beater-cam Chronophotographe for taking pictures, and the Phonoscope for projection or individual viewing.

The Demenÿ-Gaumont 'Biographe' and 'Bioscope'

Georges Demenÿ and Léon Gaumont signed a contract in Paris on 22 August 1895, and it was registered before a notary four days later. At Demenÿ's suggestion, Gaumont would have the exclusive rights to market Demenÿ's inventions, namely his patents of 3 March 1892 (for the Phonoscope), 30 June 1893 (picture discs for the Phonoscope), and 10 October 1893 (chronophotographic camera):

> Mr Gaumont will be free to exploit these machines as he sees fit, to sell them at whatever prices he wishes, to make all publicity which he judges useful, without Mr Demenÿ being able to intervene in the commercial part of the exploitation. Mr Gaumont will pay to Mr Demenÿ, by way of a licence fee: 1. 75 Francs for each photographic camera sold, whatever its sale price, for images of a format smaller than 60 mm by 90 mm. Above that format the licence fee will be fixed at 150 Francs. 2. 25 Francs for each Phonoscope sold. 3. 2

Francs per Phonoscopic disc produced without the assistance of Mr Demenÿ. 4. 5 Francs per disc reproduced from original negatives which may be supplied by Mr Demenÿ, up to a total of twenty copies, above which figure the licence fee shall also be 2 Francs. The original negatives will become the property of Mr Gaumont.[45]

Gaumont paid Demenÿ an advance of 6,000 Francs against future licence fees due to him. The marketing of the reversible Chronophotographe, which was still not complete, was the subject of an individual clause:

The large theatrical projection machines, that is to say the reversible cameras able to use films containing at least two hundred images, are not included in the present licence under the same conditions as the other models, that is to say Mr Gaumont may not sell them, but he must construct them following the instructions of Mr Demenÿ, on behalf of and at the expense of the latter, Mr Gaumont refraining from making similar equipment for other persons, with the exception of a machine for the purpose of advertising his business. For his part Mr Demenÿ will refrain from constructing such machines elsewhere than through the establishment of Mr Gaumont.[46]

In 1896, when the cinematographic spectacle took off in a big way, it would be necessary to make hasty changes to this contract and to modify that last clause, as we shall see a little later.

On 17 October 1895 Gaumont registered the two trademarks which were to designate the Demenÿ–Gaumont machines: *Bioscope* to indicate the former Phonoscope, and *Biographe* to replace the word 'Chronophotographe'. Two advertising leaflets, also serving as operator's instructions, were published at the end of 1895, one describing each device.

This commercialization was an important event: thanks to Gaumont and Demenÿ, any moderately well-off amateur could own a 'cinema' in 1895, even if the films were not perforated and the Phonoscope (or Bioscope) remained barely workable as a projector. With the Biographe camera, according to the author of the leaflet,

the movements of water and air, swirls of dust, smoke, waterfalls, the waves of the sea, the movements of swimming and flying, the most infinitely small movements can now be photographed . . . Normal human activities, walking, running and jumping may be analysed with greater ease . . .[47]

This was still the route planned by Marey, study of the movements of the human being and animals; Demenÿ, who probably wrote this text, preferred his machine to remain scientific. But if he did not imagine 'fiction films' like those of the Edison Kinetoscope, he nonetheless stated that the Biographe could be useful to artists 'keen to research into nature, by all methods, the true characters of expression and of life'. The portrait artist, he claimed, 'will abandon the posed portrait for the living portrait', and 'the simple bystander could commit a series of titillating indiscretions'—it is not clear what this was intended to indicate. In short, 'sportsmen, artists, scholars, photographers, lecturers, reporters, advertisers, and doctors will all find use for the Demenÿ machine'.[48]

The Biographe was a beautiful camera of varnished wood, of very high quality in spite of the lack of film perforations. It allowed a series of eighty successive images, on average, to be taken on a film 60 mm wide at a speed of between eight and twenty pictures per second. A surviving example can be seen in the collection of the Société Française de Photographie. If Demenÿ had only had the good idea of copying Edison, as the Lumières did, by perforating the film strip, he would have taken the credit for putting the first truly workable camera on the market, well before the Lumières (who did not decide to sell their cameras until 1897) and ahead of the many pioneers of 1896. Unfortunately for Demenÿ and Gaumont, although the Biographe remained an excellent chronophotographic camera, the films taken with it could only be projected using the heavy Phonoscope or Bioscope discs, the capacity of which was limited, on average, to thirty images.

The glass Bioscope disc measured 42 cm in diameter (a miniature version, 10 cm in diameter, was also marketed at the start of 1896). The thirty chronophotographic images, each measuring 3 cm by 4.5 cm, were arranged in series around its circumference. The amateur could make his or her own Bioscope discs, since the Comptoir Général sold the necessary glass discs and masks. But construction of the disc was very delicate: each image had to be very precisely located on the glass, or the projection would fail. The Comptoir Général invited its clientele to send their negatives to 57 Rue Saint-Roch, where a special studio would take care of the composition and assembly of the discs.

The Bioscope existed in two versions: one for individual viewing (Demenÿ sketched this model, mounted on a wooden base, on one of the letters he received from Marey, dated 10 June 1893); the other supplied with a Molteni lantern and intended for projection. With this machine it was possible:

in families, to keep living records of the ancestors, only a turn of the handle is needed to show the children their living grandparents and see again their own baby faces, an idea original enough to attract the amateurs . . . As well as these recreations, the Bioscope can also teach the movements of man and the animals, its place is just as much in the school as in the living room.[49]

The advertisement published by the Comptoir Général made the daring claim that the Bioscope would replace the printed book. However, very few examples of either machine were sold, and the prices remained relatively high:

Demenÿ Chronophotographe, with anastigmatic, iris diaphragm, screw mount Zeiss lens, double action movable viewfinder, six reels, twenty-four black paper strips: 750 Francs. Negative film, 3 m long: 4 Francs 50. Negative film, 5 m long: 7 Francs 50.

Demenÿ Bioscope permitting viewing in motion of scenes and animated subjects taken with the chronophotographic camera, together with two pierced glass discs for mounting films and a turned wooden base, 250 Francs. Without base: 225 Francs. Demenÿ disc, [from the] Comptoir collection, each 15 Francs, six for 75 Francs.

Large printing frame for contact printing Bioscope positives onto film or glass, 50 Francs. Paper discs with thirty apertures for composition of positive discs, 0 Francs 50. Pierced glass Bioscope discs, with gelatino-chloride emulsion, per half-dozen, 36 Francs. PROJECTION. Special support with lantern and condenser, oxygen-ether burner, 175 Francs.[50]

The Biographe and Bioscope without any accessories (discs, masks, films, screen, developing tank, etc.) would set the amateur back more than 1,100 Francs. This was certainly less than the Cinématographe Lumière (offered for 1,650 Francs in May 1897 with all its numerous accessories for taking and projecting pictures included), but the technical results were not the same.

When the Cinématographe Lumière illuminated the screen of the Grand Café in Paris on 28 December 1895, Gaumont finally understood that the Biographe had to be reversible and had to use perforated film. He abruptly abandoned the Bioscope, for which there was no demand in any case. With the assistance of Léopold René Decaux, who would later become the director of the Gaumont company's technical workshops, he and Demenÿ tried to convert the Biographe into a hybrid machine, simultaneously a camera and projector. Demenÿ told Gaumont, on 8 March 1896, that he had obtained 'satisfactory results'. However nothing was possible without perforation of the films, and this modification was made on 11 April 1896. The film was perforated regularly on both sides, still driven by the beater cam and by two toothed wheels. On 27 April 1896 a projection show with the new machine was given at the Comptoir Général.

The contract which Demenÿ and Gaumont had signed on 22 August 1895 was modified on 6 May 1896. Gaumont abandoned the marketing of the miniature Phonoscope with its 10 cm diameter discs, and of the large Phonoscope with coin-operated mechanism, to Demenÿ. However Gaumont also undertook—Lumière permitting—to mass-produce and to market a camera which could also project the film:

> The licence covers the exploitation in France and abroad, as well as the fabrication and sale, of 1. the machines called Phonoscopes, for domestic and projection use, 2. discs for the Phonoscopes, 3. reversible and non-reversible chronophotographic cameras of the Demenÿ system, 4. film pictures intended for animated projection, 5. the exploitation by commercial showings and by renting of equipment and pictures.[51]

There was even the suggestion of opening a showing venue, with 'ten theatrical projection machines':

> The revenues of this exploitation will be controlled by turnstiles, the indications of which will be read each day and communicated to Mr Demenÿ by a form signed by the managers of each location and countersigned by Mr Gaumont et Cie. Of this gross revenue, Mr Gaumont will pay 20% to Mr Demenÿ.[52]

As far as is known, Gaumont did not open any sort of 'cinema' in 1896. There was certainly a presentation at Châtelet by Jacques Ducom, on 14 November 1896, of *La Biche au Bois* ('The Doe'), a 60 mm hand-coloured film made by Demenÿ, but this used only one single projection machine. It was not until 1900, for the Paris Exposition Universelle, that Gaumont organized a cinematographic spectacle with six 35 mm projectors, arranged next to one another on the first floor of the Paris City Pavilion.

Shortly after this revised contract was agreed, relations between the two collaborators began to turn sour, mainly as a result of an unexpected lawsuit which brought Gaumont into opposition with another great pioneer, who has already been mentioned: Henri Joly. While Decaux and Demenÿ were working on the new reversible Chronophotographe in 1896, Gaumont had to wrestle with a truly absurd piece of business. On 27 February 1896, he received a registered letter sent by a lawyer, Charles Thirion:

> Our client M. Joly, who, on 26 August 1895, took out a patent in France for a chronophotographic camera, has learned that you are manufacturing cameras similar to that which forms the object of his patent.
>
> M. Joly is aware that his camera consists of an improvement on that patented by M. Demenÿ, and as a result he does not have the rights to exploit it commercially under pain of an infringement suit which could be taken out against him by M. Demenÿ under the provisions of Article 19 of the Law of 5 July 1844. But under the terms of the same Article, M. Joly intends to prevent you manufacturing his camera which you know to be patented.
>
> M. Joly hopes that this warning will be sufficient for you to cease your manufacture. If this is not the case, he will be obliged to apply to the courts to oblige you to respect the rights conferred to him by his patent . . .[53]

This was a strange complaint. The patent for the beater cam, invented by Demenÿ, had been filed on 27 July 1894, as an addition to the patent of 10 October 1893; therefore it was Joly, in his patent of 26 August 1895 describing a reversible camera whose system was similar to Demenÿ's, who was the plagiarist. Even the lawyer Thirion's letter had given that impression, not without a degree of cynicism.

In the opinion of one of Gaumont's lawyers, it appeared that Joly (by then financed by Normandin) was trying to extract a sum of money in exchange for withdrawing his complaint: 'M Joly is infringing us but we cannot proceed without coming to agreement [with him].' Joly even visited Demenÿ in an attempt to extract a licence fee from him. Gaumont reacted vigorously, forbidding Joly from using the Demenÿ system. Joly ignored him, and counter-attacked: on 26 November 1896 he sent the bailiffs in to Gaumont's premises, and all the Demenÿ cameras were seized. This was a severe blow for the young manufacturer, for the Comptoir Général de Photographie, and for the launch of the reversible Chronophotographe. The bad news travelled fast, and some uneasy buyers wrote to Gaumont:

Dear Sirs, very desirous to acquire a camera for animated photography, and having heard much good of yours (the Demenÿ camera),
I would be most grateful if you could send me its description as soon
as possible. There is a further matter on which I would like to be
reassured. I have heard that Normandin [Joly's partner] has caused a
number of seizures of cameras similar to his. I have even heard that
the Demenÿ camera itself has been seized. You will understand,
gentlemen, that unless I can be enlightened on this point I shall find
it difficult to decide, being reluctant to see a seizure take place of a
camera which I have acquired.[54]

The case came before the courts shortly after, and naturally Gaumont
won. But time and money had been lost. As the lawyer of the Comptoir
Général wrote, this dubious suit resembled a genuine attempt at
sabotage:

> We can assume that those who attack us and who present no
> sufficient financial standing to compensate us, are not acting on
> their own behalf, but for the benefit of interests who conceal their
> own identity and wish to destroy the original works which they are
> plagiarizing without risk to themselves. Justice must be done to
> similar actions!

In the course of 1896, in this unpleasant atmosphere, Gaumont received
two further letters in the following style:

> Sir, being an inventor and proprietor of several trademarks, I do not
> like counterfeiters . . . I have seen on sale at a certain shop here a
> camera whose principle appears to me to be the exactly the same as
> that which you have patented . . . When I asked the vendor directly
> if it was not the Demenÿ patent mechanism, he told me several times
> 'Oh no!' . . .
>   I inform you that henceforward my information (shameful if you
> want, it is all the same to me) must be paid for, money being rather
> short for me at the moment . . . For payment for my information, it
> is up to you to make me an offer. Regards. A. Rateau, 25 Margaret
> Street, Regent Street, London W.[55]

The name of Auguste Rateau was mentioned by Henry Hopwood, in
1899, in his book *Living Pictures*. By that time Rateau had himself filed a
patent in London, on 24 February 1897, for a reversible camera called
the 'Rateaugraph'.
    Exasperated by Demenÿ's slowness, the slump in sales of reversible

cameras, and the 'Joly case', Gaumont decided abruptly to end his association with the unfortunate Demenÿ. He wrote to him on 6 October 1896:

> In spite of the strong complaint which we made to you, and in spite of the discount to which we have just agreed, we are not receiving new orders for Chronos, all our clients being taken from us by the competition. Under these conditions, we have to inform you that as a result of the numerous costs which we have incurred in marketing your Chronophotographe, we prefer to place you completely at your liberty.[56]

This move, resembling Pathé's decision concerning Joly, was quite unjust. The films had been perforated since 11 April 1896; since 18 October Gaumont had been boasting in the foreign press of the merits of the Demenÿ 'Chrono' and its 60 mm perforated films, which an advertisement of 13 December 1896 announced as 'the only one which allows coverage of 40 square metres'. The machine was working well. It was one of the best of 1896, and it eventually sold reasonably well, especially in its 35 mm version of 1897 (see Fig. 51).

On 16 July 1901 Demenÿ, then living at Issy-les-Moulineaux and wearied by successive setbacks, sold the rights of his 1893 patent and its seven Certificates of Addition to the Gaumont company, for the miserable sum of 500 Francs. The 35 mm Demenÿ–Gaumont 'Chronos' were appreciated by operators all over the world up until 1914, among them 'Mademoiselle Alice Guy, cinématographiste', Gaumont's secretary who became better known as the first female film director. Meanwhile Gaumont displayed increasing prosperity: on 3 December 1906 Léon Gaumont et Cie. transformed itself into the Société des Établissements Gaumont, with a capital of 2.5 million Francs.

Demenÿ died on 26 December 1917, after a long illness, at 7 Rue Tourlaque in Paris; he was buried at the Montmartre cemetery on Saturday 29 December 1917, during a period of Arctic weather. He had never ceased to claim, with equal measures of tactlessness and truth, his part in the invention of the cinema. Rejected by the friends of Marey and by Gaumont, he is viewed with a certain contempt by the 'Lumiéristes' of yesterday and today. The tragedy of Demenÿ was to have had to carve his trail between two symbolic figures: Marey, who would always remain his teacher and the true creator of chronophotography; and Lumière, one of the most celebrated disseminators of chronophotographic projection in Europe. Demenÿ was of the same mind as Marey, in spite of their

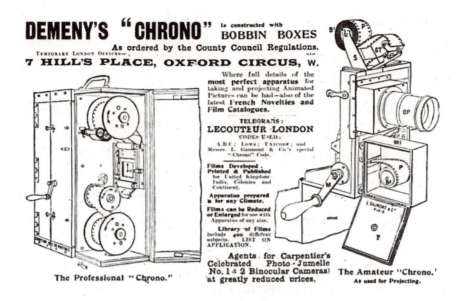

DEMENY'S "CHRONO" is constructed with **BOBBIN BOXES**

As ordered by the County Council Regulations.

TEMPORARY LONDON OFFICES—

7 HILL'S PLACE, OXFORD CIRCUS, W.

Where full details of the most perfect apparatus for taking and projecting Animated Pictures can be had—also of the latest French Novelties and Film Catalogues.

TELEGRAMS:
LECOUTEUR LONDON
CODES USED:
A.B.C.; Lows; Unicode; and Messrs. L. Gaumont & Co.'s special "Chrono" Code.

Films Developed, Printed & Published for United Kingdom, India, Colonies and Continent.

Apparatus prepared for any Climate.

Films can be Reduced or Enlarged for use with Apparatus of any size.

Library of Films include 400 different subjects. LIST ON APPLICATION.

Agents for Carpentier's Celebrated Photo-Jumelle No. 1 & 2 Binocular Cameras) at greatly reduced prices.

The Professional "Chrono."

The Amateur "Chrono."
As used for Projecting.

Fig. 51. British advertisement for the 60 mm and 35 mm Demenÿ–Gaumont 'Chrono', in *The Photographic Dealer* 27 (August 1898). Collection: Bibliothèque Nationale.

differences, and he remained a man of the laboratory, not a tradesman or businessman. As one of the old school, unlike the newcomers of 1895–6, he never knew how to turn animated photography into nickels or banknotes.

The first Cinématographe Lumière

For all this time, even if he still did not have a clear idea about how to exploit it, Louis Lumière had been working to perfect his new machine. The Cinématographe shows given before invited audiences in Lyon and Paris had all been very well received. Should he put his reversible camera on open sale, or would he finally decide to exploit moving images on the *grands boulevards*? In truth, for the time being Lumière could not see any precise future for his Cinématographe. He did not imagine that chrono-photography would give birth to a 'seventh art', a giant industry, and in 1895 nobody else would have dreamed of such a possibility either. All the same, Lumière was remarkably slow. In this respect he resembled Edison, who had designed his Kinetoscope in 1891 but did not present it before the public until 1894.

After the showing at the Société d'Encouragement on 22 March 1895, Jules Carpentier offered to undertake commercial manufacture of the Cinématographe for Lumière. Lumière hesitated. Finally, eight months after meeting Carpentier, he made his mind up at last: twenty-five examples of the Cinématographe were to be constructed at Rue Delambre. From the correspondence exchanged between Lumière and Carpentier, we can follow the difficult development of a final design quite closely. These two engineering fanatics exchanged ideas on the most precise technical details almost like lovers. They understood each other completely, and their collaboration was harmonious. Their letters clearly show the anxiety of the manufacturer faced with competition: Lumière was now eager to see the first twenty-five examples emerge from the Carpentier workshops, to wipe out the threatening rivals.

Carpentier himself could easily have been one of the Lumières' most serious competitors. As already mentioned, on 30 March 1895 he had patented a 'Cynégraphe' using perforated film. He did not give up work on improving his process for taking pictures (he took out patents on 18 and 30 March 1896 for different intermittent drive mechanisms), but he put his own interests aside to give priority to Lumière. Carpentier wrote to him on that subject on 22 December 1895:

> I have done everything and will do everything to assist you with devotion. Although this meant putting off the creation of my own system, which I have established in principle, I applied myself first of all to constructing and perfecting your machines. I wished to show you by this how I understand friendship and hospitality. At this price, I believe, I have captured your affection; I am satisfied and convinced that it will only bring me happiness in the future.[57]

In October 1895 Carpentier finished 'machine no. 1', the first Cinématographe, which was to serve as a prototype for the twenty-five others. For several months this machine shuttled between the workshops in Paris and the Lumière offices in Lyon-Monplaisir to receive successive improvements. On 14 October, Louis Lumière declared his satisfaction:

> We send you today the machine which I have shown to my brother on his return here, the fine construction of which he, like myself, appreciates . . . I hasten to add that we will be very happy to entrust the construction of the machine to you. We would wish to stress our interest in speeding up the construction of the first twenty-five machines as much as possible, and rely on your kind cooperation on this subject.[58]

Suddenly, Lumière seemed impatient. But he was also a real perfectionist, which delayed the completion of the final design. The growing competition disturbed him greatly. In a letter to Carpentier on 2 November 1895 he maintained:

> We shall be very happy to receive some news on the construction of the first twenty. They are hot on our heels from all sides, and my father in particular would like this to be ready by now, because he wishes to involve himself in this business . . . De Bedts (the Anglo-American Import Office) continues to make the greatest possible noise about his Chronos, and it would be most regrettable if he were to show something before us.[59]

De Bedts had been selling Demenÿ machines from his shop in Paris as early as November 1894. At the end of 1895 he was in discussions with Joly, who was trying to find a partner other than Pathé. De Bedts, at least for a while, was therefore *au fait* with the work of both. It is not clear what the 'Chronos' which Lumière mentioned in November 1895 actually were—possibly Demenÿ or Joly cameras? Around that time, it appears, de Bedts had either a workable reversible camera or a 35 mm film projector. Carpentier's reply on that subject, on 4 November 1895, was formal:

> I know that Mr de Bedts is very active: his trial machine exists; he has made some films and has projected them. Their dimensions are exactly the same as those of the Edison Kinetoscope. But he is not yet ready, I believe, to deliver these machines. For our part we are not losing a minute.[60]

De Bedts filed the first cinematographic patents of 1896: on 10 January for a 'punching machine for perforating films', and then on 14 January for an 'intermittent motion mechanism applicable to chrono-photographic cameras and equipment for animated projection'. This reversible camera, named 'Kinétographe' in an explicit reference to Edison, was of excellent construction. There are four surviving examples: at the Science Museum in London; at Eastman House in Rochester, New York; at the Société Française de Photographie in Paris; and at the Cinemateca Portuguesa in Lisbon.

The Kinétographe camera was compact (23.5 cm high, 16.5 cm wide and 20.5 cm long) and weighed no more than 5 kg. The drive mechanism was inspired by Edison's, with two toothed wheels arranged vertically, one above the other. The higher wheel, which was smaller, had only three teeth around its circumference, which was thus divided into three equal sections. One by one these teeth engaged in each of ten groups of teeth arranged around the circumference of the larger second wheel. The second wheel was therefore driven intermittently, with equal periods of movement and rest as a result of the different arc lengths of the sections of the two wheels. This mechanism was connected to a toothed feed device which pulled the film through, and also to the shutter, which had two apertures.

The perforated 35 mm film, 30 m in length and arranged on an upper bobbin, passed over a first smooth roller, to which was attached a small guide roller. Here the film formed a loop—the same loop claimed simultaneously by the Lathams, Armat and Jenkins, and Joly. It then passed the focal point of the lens, met a further guide roller, then the toothed wheel, and finally the second wheel, which was driven by a belt with a metal spring connected to the central drive shaft of the camera. To convert the camera to a projector, all that was needed was to change the lens, thread in the positive film, open the rear door of the machine and place a light source behind it.

De Bedts, a pioneer of whom cinema historians have (unjustly) taken little notice, perhaps because it was not he who presented himself before the public at the end of 1895, was therefore a very serious competitor for the Lumières. And he did not make the same mistake as they did: his Kinétographes went on open sale from the start of 1896. Because of this, de Bedts was very probably the first manufacturer to offer a reversible 35 mm camera on the French market, followed by a camera for amateurs which was patented on 29 October 1896. He was also the founder of the first French cinematographic company, an event which took place on 15 January 1896, in Paris, when de Bedts formed the Société G. de Bedts et Cie. with a capital of 15,000 Francs. His partners were André Castelni, an advertising agent, and Guillaume Sabatier, who since December 1894 had been running the daily illustrated paper Le Quotidien Illustré. The company's office was at 368 Rue Saint-Honoré, the same address as de Bedts' shop:

> This company has the object of the exploitation and sale of various machines used for the preparation of strips or films for the repro-duction of moving images, and machines for the photography and reproduction of moving images (chronophotographic machines).[61]

This involved exploiting the two de Bedts patents (the perforator and the reversible camera), and continuing to market the films made by the

Blair Camera Company of Boston, New York and Chicago and the European Blair Camera Company of London. De Bedts was already considering an innovative use of the cinematographic process for commercial advertising: 'The company has as a further object advertising which could be carried out with the aid of these machines.'[62] The journalist Sabatier wanted to project animated advertisements, using the de Bedts Kinétographe, onto the roof and shopfront of *Le Quotidien Illustré* at 4 Rue du Faubourg Montmartre. It is not known whether or not these projections were carried out successfully.

The capital of the company was not great. Sabatier and Castelni put up a sum of 10,000 Francs, and opened an account of 15,000 Francs at the Crédit Lyonnais bank in the name of de Bedts. But he would not get very far with a company whose financial foundations were so shaky: it is almost impossible to launch a machine and process with access to so little capital. The principal partner Sabatier also had other worries; *Le Quotidien Illustré* closed around the middle of 1896, which certainly put an end to the plans for cinematographic advertising. Sabatier took over control of the much more important daily *L'Éclair*.

The fall of de Bedts was rapid and his company was wound up on 15 July 1898. He tried to continue selling photographic materials from his shop in Rue Saint-Honoré, but soon had to close that as well. In 1902 he could be found living in the suburbs of Paris, at 6 Rue de Progrès, Asnières. He joined a man named Henri Léonardon in founding a small shop for import and export of miscellaneous goods (it is not clear quite what), at 5 Rue de Stockholm, in Paris. Then—when or to where is now unknown—he disappeared. The technicians and workers of the first wave, like Reynaud, de Bedts, Parnaland, Joly, and even Méliès, none of whom were able to transform themselves into financiers, were all sooner or later swept away by the industrialists and businessmen: Pathé, Claude Grivolas, Gaumont, and others of their kind.

The Cinématographe: final modifications

On 4 November 1895 Carpentier once again sent off 'machine no. 1' after some further modifications, notably to the shutter. Carpentier wrote: 'this device [the shutter] will not be very convenient for the layman.'[63] Perhaps Louis Lumière was intending to sell the Cinématographe to any passing amateur, but that appears still to have been undecided. He naturally wished that the machine should be easy to use, whether for exploitation by the Lumière representatives or for lesser mortals.

Carpentier was himself rather impatient, and worried by Lumière's 'perfectionism': 'Our machines are under construction and we must not delay them by last-minute modifications.' The question of celluloid was also pressing. 'As for the film strips, are you now making them without difficulty?'[64] Lumière, unlike de Bedts, had great difficulty in finding a supply of celluloid. He dealt with the New York Celluloid Company, who sent him complete sheets. These then had to be cut, perforated, and coated with photographic emulsion. He also tried the services of Victor Planchon, but confided to Carpentier on 11 November that 'nothing useful has yet been produced by him',[65] although Planchon did deliver satisfactory results in January 1896.

On 25 November 1895 Lumière appeared to be leaning towards open sale of the Cinématographe, rather than reserving it for agents or franchise holders: 'When we launch this business commercially, we will wish to be ready for as large an expansion as possible.'[66] On 28 November Carpentier warned that the shutters for the production machines would be made of ebonite, a fragile but lightweight material. Louis made some more small technical comments on machine no. 1, and regretted being a nuisance. Carpentier replied on 2 December:

> I completely forbid you to say that you are being tiresome, a bore, or a nit-picker, when you indicate to me defects to be corrected or improvements to make to the machines which we are making for you.[67]

Machine no. 1 was back at Lyon-Monplaisir again. On 4 December Louis turned his attention to the maker's plate which would be attached to the front of the machine, below the lens. He asked Carpentier to engrave, in white letters on a black background:

CINÉMATOGRAPHE
Auguste et Louis Lumière
Breveté S.G.D.G.
J. Carpentier, Ingénieur-Constructeur
Paris

The finishing touches to the Cinématographe were very delicate. Lumière and Carpentier noticed a small amount of play in the main shaft of the mechanism, the result of an error by a machinist. It would be rectified, Carpentier promised, by 9 December, but the delay was getting worse. Should the film take-up box be nickel plated? Would the velvet pads around the aperture get in the way of the film? Should the velvet pads be singed at the edges? Carpentier was becoming impatient:

> In two days' time you will receive machine no. 2, with the altera-tions perfected. But you must understand that the modifications, which I agree are inevitable, which we are going to introduce, hamper our progress and stop our production . . . How much I wish that we had a definite design and that we could begin to attack the order for 200![68]

So the plan was now to construct, as well as the first series of twenty-five, a further batch of 200 Cinématographes. This was a large number: perhaps Lumière had finally decided to market them by open sale, or perhaps the 200 machines were reserved for franchise agents. The Lumière brothers definitely discussed this question at Lyon-Monplaisir. Their father Antoine, meanwhile, was more than keen to organize a commercial public showing on the *grands boulevards*. He believed in the 'cinematographic spectacle', while his two sons, who were less artistic and less bohemian, did not take such a favourable view of public exploitation aimed at the 'common herd'.

On 14 December 1895 Antoine went to take a close look at the Cinématographe in the Carpentier workshops at Rue Delambre. The idea of opening a showing venue in Paris began to take shape. But on 15 December Louis was worried once again. A 'certain Monsieur Terme' had come to see him and, it seemed to him, boasted that he had succeeded in constructing a film projector. Lumière was afraid that this new inventor would go to Carpentier and give him an order for construc-tion of his machine. The engineer reassured Lumière:

> I will never undertake the construction of a Cinématographe for anyone, without first having spoken to you about it . . . Nobody has come to me who wants this. Mr Terme has not even knocked at my door yet.[69]

This mysterious new rival may have been either Jules Terme, who filed a patent for a reversible camera on 9 March 1896, or perhaps Joseph Marie Terme, constructor of the 'Cinématoterme' of 15 July 1896. On 22 December 1895 another threat appeared, this time from Germany. Carpentier wrote to Lumière:

> I learned recently that M. Marchand, director of the Folies-Bergère, is preparing to show a Cinématographe on his stage. He has even let

me know that he would be very pleased to see the machines which I am constructing. I went to see him, as if to prevent him going to wasted effort, but mainly to find out the news. I will say nothing about the way in which one is received in that world: the most elementary manners and politeness are completely unknown. However I learned that the . . . *turn* which will be presented to the public at the start of January comes from Cologne, that it really does consist of cinematographic projections, and that the artist exhibiting them across Europe claims to represent people in motion . . . life-size. M. Marchand would like to see our own *turn*, in order to judge whether it is as amazing as that which he is awaiting.[70]

Carpentier's distaste for 'that world', the *demi-monde* of actors and footlights, is readily apparent. In November he had also received similar offers from the Musée Grévin, already anxious to rid itself of Reynaud. As for the German from Cologne, this must have been another great cinema pioneer, Max Skladanowsky (1863–1939).

The Skladanowsky Bioskop

Whether the Lumières liked it or not, it was Skladanowsky who organized the first public commercial showing of films in Europe. This took place in Berlin, on 1 November 1895. Through researchers like Paul Hoffmann and Ottomar Anschütz, Germany had strong traditions of the magic lantern and chronophotography. At Cologne on 25 August 1895 one Paul Müller had already filed a patent for a machine for both taking and projecting pictures. The drive system was a type of pressure frame, like Marey's mechanism, but the film was perforated.[71]

Max Skladanowsky was the son of a professional projectionist, Carl Skladanowsky, who was himself an experimenter with the lantern. From 1879 onwards, Carl and his sons Max and Emil presented magic lantern shows across the whole of Germany. In 1892 Max constructed his first chronophotographic camera, and on 20 August of that year filmed his brother Emil in forty-eight successive images. During the summer of 1895 Max invented a better camera, using a helical wheel drive, and designed a projector called the 'Bioskope' which he patented on 1 November 1895; the contemporary German press sometimes referred to it as 'Bioscop' or 'Bioskop'. The films he projected were perforated and reinforced with metal eyelets. On the same day they filed their patent, the Skladanowsky brothers exhibited 'Das Bioskop' at the Berlin Wintergarten, where it ran from 1 to 30 November 1895. An entrance fee was charged, the show lasted fifteen minutes, and anyone could watch this 'turn', as Carpentier would have scornfully described it. Nine films were projected:

1. *Italienischer Bauerntanz* ['Italian Peasant Dance'], performed by two children.
2. *Komisches Reck* ['Comical Horizontal Bar'] with the Milton Brothers.
3. *Das Boxende Känguruh* ['The Boxing Kangaroo'] with Mr Delaware.
4. *Jongleur* ['Juggler'] with Petras.
5. *Acrobatisches Potpourri* ['Acrobatic Medley'] with eight performers.
6. *Kammarintzky* [Russian national dance] with the three Tscherpanoff Brothers.
7. *Serpentintanz* ['Serpentine Dance'] with Mlle Ancion.
8. *Ringkampf* ['Fight in the Ring'] with Greiner and Sandow.
9. *Apotheose* ['Apotheosis'] with the Skladanowsky Brothers.

A complete variety bill in fifteen minutes. The life-size representations of the Bioskop were obtained by projecting an original series of moving pictures. By means of electricity, the Bioskop restored life precisely in all its natural detail, so that one might believe one was looking at reality.[72]

The German press reacted with enthusiasm—much more so than the French press after the first showings of the Cinématographe Lumière, as Jacques Deslandes has noted. All the same, the Skladanowsky machine was not superior to those invented in France at the same time. Skladanowsky used a complicated double-strip film system, in which images from each strip were alternately blocked by a rotating shutter. This historic projector still exists, at the Deutsches Filmmuseum in Babelsberg, and the films have also survived. Much to the chagrin of the Lumières, this heavy and barely workable machine marked the true birth of public commercial exploitation of chronophotographic films in Europe.

The Lumière show of 28 December 1895

Skladanowsky never made it to the Folies-Bergère. But the Lumières now realized that it had become urgent to offer the public one of the 'turns' so despised by Carpentier. Antoine Lumière was very anxious to present the Cinématographe in Paris; he, at least, believed in the connection between the world of spectacle and chronophotography.

Antoine Lumière was an endearing personality. An artist in paint and photography, he was capricious, extravagant, and much more extrovert than his two sons, who next to him presented rather sad, bourgeois, serious figures. Auguste and Louis were forced to adopt this severe economic attitude, since Antoine had already very nearly destroyed their business. In 1893 Antoine sold his shares in the company Antoine Lumière and Sons to outside interests, in order to pay for the construction of several luxurious villas at La Ciotat, Évian, La Turbie, and Monplaisir. His bank account was soon empty, and he eventually ran up a debt of a million and a half Francs. In a state of panic the two sons watched their father's shares captured by financiers who disrupted the board of directors, which had until then been very family-based. Fortunately, a friend intervened: Victor Vermorel of Villefranche (whose descendant M. Auboin-Vermorel owns a wonderful collection of cinematographic machines), advanced the money needed to pay off the creditors. The outside interests were driven off the board of directors. Vermorel, 'industrialist, officer of the Légion d'Honneur, and Senator', was quickly reimbursed and joined the board of the company.

Antoine was full of admiration for the Cinématographe Lumière–Carpentier. Presumably, as a habitué of Parisian *café-concerts*, he saw this machine as a new type of magic lantern with tenfold possibilities, a new 'sensational attraction'. It was he who managed the show of 28 December 1895. Louis confirmed this in a letter of 31 December: 'My father plagued us to let him organize the showings in Paris and we have tried not to involve ourselves in them at all.'[73] With the help of the photographer Clément-Maurice (under his real name, Clément Maurice Gratioulet), Antoine Lumière sought out an ideal venue for exploiting the Cinématographe. This proved to be the Salon Indien of the Grand Café, at 14 Boulevard des Capucines. Clément-Maurice recalled later:

> M. Volpini, owner of the Grand Café, with whom we had taken a one-year lease for his basement, preferred to take 30 Francs per day for the rent rather than the 20% of receipts which we had offered him. He had practically no confidence in the success of the undertaking![74]

The historians Martin Loiperdinger and Roland Cosandey have discovered a letter dated 16 April 1896 from Ludwig Stollwerck, Demenÿ's former partner, in which he described a visit to the Grand Café:

M. Lumière has rented an underground billiard room at the Grand Café, which is reached by a steep unpleasant staircase. In this space of 12 m by 8, they project ten different views every quarter of an hour, each lasting between fifty and sixty seconds, onto a wall 280 cm wide by 2 m high. He is asking 1 Franc for entrance: there are 180 seats and standing room for about thirty or forty.[75]

The Cinématographe projector was mounted on a wooden trestle, illuminated by a Molteni lantern and carefully hidden behind a screen of black cloth. On Saturday 28 December 1895 the decor was completed by two turnstiles controlling the entrance to the Salon, more than a hundred café chairs, and a ventilation fan. Antoine sent invitations to his friends. Jules Carpentier received this hasty note:

> Dear Monsieur Carpentier, I will see to it that by six o'clock all will be ready. Therefore be at the Grand Café at that time with the people you wish to bring. Handshake. A. Lumière.[76]

But curiously Carpentier missed the first showing. On 30 December 1895 he wrote to Louis:

> My dear friend,
> Here your Cinématographe has entered a new phase of its life, and the première which it gave on Saturday evening was a great success; I send you my warm congratulations. I was unfortunately not at the celebration; notified the day before by a simple printed handbill [perhaps Carpentier did not receive the invitation], I was not able to free myself from previous engagements for that evening; but I asked at the last moment for invitations for my brother-in-law M. Violet and for M. Cartier, and these two friends reported to me the impression shared by all the audience, that it was excellent. The audience was very numerous. That was inevitable.[77]

Louis made his apologies to Carpentier on 31 December:

> We have been very annoyed, my brother and I, by what we have learned from you concerning the showing last Saturday . . . It is probable that it was Ducom who supplied the famous Maison Richard with admission cards, because Ducom is a friend of Maurice and my father attaches great importance to collaboration with the latter. Please accept all my apologies for this absurdity.[78]

This correspondence gives a little further information on the guest list for this historic evening—later on a great many contemporaries claimed to have been present at this première. Jacques Ducom, a professional photographer, and future author of technical books on the cinema, was operating the Molteni lantern; his job was to supervise the electric arc lamp. Charles Moisson, who had created the first version of the Cinématographe at the start of 1895, was delegated to turn the handle. Clément-Maurice was in charge of the cash desk and Antoine Lumière strutted proudly about receiving the guests; among them, perhaps, was Georges Méliès, as well as a number of journalists. According to Clément-Maurice thirty-three curious people paid to get in at the price of 1 Franc.

The projection started with a stationary image, with no explanatory title—Reynaud at the Musée Grévin and Skladanowsky in Berlin had taken care to project the title of the film with a magic lantern before running their film strip. One spectator, it was reported, showed his dissatisfaction: 'The magic lantern again!' But then Moisson began to turn the handle. The image began to move,

> becoming alive. It was a factory gate which opened and allowed a stream of male and female workers to flow out, with bicycles, dogs running, carts; all of these bustling and swarming around. It was life itself, it was movement captured in real life.[79]

Ten films appear to have been projected on that first Saturday. The programme, a small handbill given out to passers-by on the following days, listed the titles and gave a short explanation:

> The Cinématographe. Salon Indien, Grand Café. 14 Boulevard des Capucines, Paris. This machine, invented by Messrs Auguste and Louis Lumière, allows the capture in a series of instantaneous pictures of all the movements which pass in front of the lens in a given period of time, and then reproduces these movements by projecting them life-size on a screen in front of a whole room of people. Current subjects: 1. Workers leaving the Lumière factory in Lyon. 2. Trick riding. 3. Fishing for Goldfish. 4. Disembarkation of the Congrès de Photographie at Lyon. 5. Blacksmiths. 6. The Gardener. 7. The Meal. 8. Jumping into the Blanket. 9. The Place des Cordeliers in Lyon. 10. The Sea.

The photographic quality of these films was surprisingly clear. At the end of the projection Antoine Lumière was triumphant. Everyone

Fig. 52.   Chromolithographic print, showing the Cinématographe Lumière projecting a stylised version of *L'arrivée d'un train en gare de La Ciotat* (*c.*1896). Collection: Laurent Mannoni.

surrounded and congratulated him. He may have spoken with Méliès (although a degree of caution is advisable about the claims of that great pioneer, who had the tendency to modify his recollections), who offered to buy the Cinématographe. Lumière brushed him off:

> Young man, my invention [*sic*] is not for sale . . . For you, it would be ruinous. It may be exploited for a while as a scientific curiosity; beyond that it has no commercial future.[80]

Even if he did not actually make quite such a sweeping statement, it appears that the Lumières were mistaken about the commercial tactics to follow concerning the Cinématographe.

The Gold Rush

In January 1896 the Salon Indien at the Grand Café was never empty. Showings began at 10.00am and went on until 11.00pm; a police officer had to direct the crowd outside 14 Boulevard des Capucines. As Stollwerck said, in his letter of 16 April 1896:

> The room is full almost all day. At the start, he [Lumière] was taking 600 Francs per day, which went up to 800 Francs and then 1,000 Francs, and three weeks later, while I was in Paris, he was taking each day between 2,500 and 3,000 Francs; now with the good weather and the great flood of tourists the daily receipts have gone as high as 4,000 Francs.[81]

In spite of this triumph Louis Lumière had finally chosen, after all his hesitations, to keep the exclusive rights to his reversible camera. It would not be put on sale. Lumière entrusted his operator-projectionists with the work of assembling the 'Catalogue of Views for the Cinématographe' and showing it around the world. Félix Mesguich, Francis Doublier, Alexandre Promio, Gabriel Veyre, Marius and Pierre Chapuis, Matt Raymond, and others undertook the conquest of territories until then untouched by animated projection in the name of Lumière.[82] However they also ran into strong opposition in some countries, such as the United States where the history of Moving Pictures was already highly charged. In any case, with or without Lumière, the cinema was expanding everywhere, circling the globe with great speed, much like the magic lantern in the seventeenth century.

By adopting the commercial strategy of franchising semi-independent operators, the Lumières very quickly lost their technical monopoly and were marginalized by the cinematographic industry, which came into being behind their backs in 1896–1900. It made no difference that the Cinématographe Lumière was not on sale, when hundreds of engineers, photographers and amateurs were bypassing the Lumière patent and making their own machines. Louis quickly realized his mistake: in April 1896 the ubiquitous de Bedts had the cheek to install his projecting Kinétographe in the Isola Brothers' premises, right opposite the Salon Indien. Meanwhile, two doors away at 12 Boulevard des Capucines, Eugène Pirou successfully presented his 'Cinématographe' (actually a Joly projector) at the Café de la Paix.

Very few of the pioneers used Lumière film, in which each frame carried a circular perforation on each side. Almost all preferred the Edison perforations, with four holes per frame, although some, such as Parnaland, planned to perforate the film laterally and centrally. By 1897 the Lumières were forced to construct a modified Cinématographe projector using 'American perforations'. Louis specified to Carpentier:

> It would be most kind of you to let us know the current state of affairs—as quickly as possible because the competitors are gaining

ground—and it will be advantageous to be able to launch it in two months' time if possible.[83]

In 1897, therefore, the Lumières performed a U-turn, and placed the Cinématographe on open sale. An advertisement in *La Nature* for 27 February 1897 announced:

> Cinématographe Lumière now on sale. Agent: Office Central de Photographie, 47 Rue de Rennes, Paris. Price: 1,500F. Complete outfit, with all accessories and six films: 2,500F. Picture strips fitting all current machines, without equal for quality: 50F.[84]

A leaflet published later by the Lumière company stated that the Cinématographe had been on sale 'since 1 May 1897' and that it 'should not be confused with its more or less imperfect imitators, sold at much lower prices . . . The price of the complete outfit, delivered in Lyon, with all its accessories is 1,650 F.' Since the reversible camera was still quite expensive, in 1897 the Lumières also offered two designs of a simple projector, sold at 300 Francs, with a claw mechanism which could handle both Lumière and Edison films.

This complete commercial *volte-face* by the Lumières is curious. The gross receipts from the Cinématographe, up to 30 June 1896, amounted to the fantastic figure of 1,060,805 Francs.[85] Perhaps the Lumières noticed a drop in receipts at the end of 1896; perhaps they were alarmed by the flood of rival machines cluttering the market. When they finally decided to put their camera on sale, it was too late. Everywhere there were little boxes with handles; the situation was similar to the occasion, nearly a century earlier, when Robertson noted with amusement the presence of 'ghost machines' at every street corner.

Among the hundred or so machines launched in 1896 was one produced by the Werner brothers, first named the 'Cinétographe' and then the 'Phantographe'. It was patented on 4 February 1896, but its mechanism had perhaps been completed by one of Edison's rivals, Charles E. Chinnock. 'Fortune is assured for those exhibiting with this machine,' claimed the Werners, who supplied their fairground clientele with 'sensational' films from February 1896 onwards:

> Execution scene, Indian wars on the prairies; political discussion at a meeting; lynch law; frontier scene, etc. All these scenes are of great dramatic interest and of real artistic value. With the first rays of

spring sunshine, one can make new views of the actuality of Parisian life.[86]

Other competitors included the Clément and Gilmer 'Vitagraph',[87] in which the image (according to their advertisements) would not shake, and the 'Héliocinégraphe' of Perret and Lacroix, from Agen, which was a 'robust, small, compact machine, of high precision, eliminating flicker and shaking of the picture'. The American company Sartony had a studio at 12 and 16 Rue Duphot in Paris, where, using their 'Photobioscope' (which retailed at 1,000 Francs in August 1896), one could take films of 'prepared scenes, groups, harnessed horses, cyclists, water scenes, and all special scenes'. In September 1896 Henri Joly, still in association with Normandin, offered the 'true improved Cinématographe', which

> does not damage films; its operation is faultless, without shaking or flicker. Beware of worthless copies . . . One can make a fortune with a good machine, one will be ruined with a bad one![88]

Evidently Joly was not concerned about 'borrowing' the name 'Ciné-matographe'. After all, the Lumières would not dare to protest, remembering the shade of Léon Bouly. All the manufacturers insisted on the quality of *their* projector, as would be expected in normal competition. In practice, some of these machines worked very well, while others were ten times worse than the Lumière machine, which did have a tendency to shake the image. For many years, film projectors continued to make spectators weep; there was even talk, later, of 'cinematophthalmia' or 'cinema blindness'.[89]

At the French Patent Office, throughout 1896, it was a free-for-all. More or less everyone came to file the description of their camera, accompanied by a drawing sometimes cobbled together in a great hurry. There were all sorts of contrived variations on the Demenÿ beater cam, the Lumière claw mechanism, the Marey pressure frame, the Edison sprocket wheel, the Maltese Cross, and even Reynaud's prismatic mirrors. Name after name was coined, usually ending in 'graphe' or 'scope': the 'Photothéagraphe' of Ambroise-François Parnaland was filed on 25 February 1896;[90] the 'Aléthoscope' of Paul Mortier on 17 February; the 'Cinémagraphe' of the widow Labarthe on 26 February; the 'Cinographoscope' of the Pipon brothers on 2 March; the 'Photo-tachygraphe' of Raoul Grimoin-Sanson on 5 March; the 'Viroscope' of Louis-Claude Brun on 27 March; the 'Photocinématographe' of Jean Anatole Jost on 31 March; the 'Zographe' of Paul Gauthier on 22

Fig. 53.   Georges Méliès' Kinétographe Robert-Houdin (1896).
Collection: Cinémathèque Française, Musée du Cinéma.

April; the 'Luminographe' of Émile Chasseraux on 27 April; the 'Mouvementoscope' of Joseph Zion on 1 May; and various others such as the 'Pantobiographe', 'Badizographe', 'Chronovivographe', 'Lapiposcope' (by Alban Lapipe), and 'Biographe' (by Albert Kirchner, known as Léar).

Paul Armand Tournachon, son of the famous photographer Nadar, did not escape the virus, but his reversible camera, patented on 24 June 1896, was hampered by making an infernal noise (two examples are preserved in the collection of the Paris Musée du Cinéma). De Bedts sold examples of his excellent 'Kinétographe'. Gaumont attempted to overcome his legal headaches by finally launching the Demenÿ 'Chrono'; Georges Méliès and his associates Eugène Lucien Reulos and Lucien Korsten marketed their 'Kinétographe Robert-Houdin' (patented on 4 September 1896) which projected 'without deformations, vibrations, or displacements' (see Fig. 53). Meanwhile in the United States, the situation was just as anarchic: not even Edison had managed to protect his monopoly over animated pictures. In his 1898 book *Animated Pictures*, Charles Francis Jenkins gave a list of 109 different machines,

Fig. 54. The magic lantern meets the cinematograph: a hybrid projector, made in 1902 by Raoul Grimoin-Sanson and Jules Demaria, capable of projecting fixed slides as well as moving pictures.
Collection: Laurent Mannoni.

ranging from the 'Muscularscope' to the 'Klondikoscope' via the 'Sygmographoscope' and 'Mimimoscope'.

In this way the cinema, like the magic lantern in the seventeenth century, took wings from the laboratories and engineers' workshops without the authorization of its first 'inventors'. It was the showmen—a race regarded with contempt by Carpentier, just as they had been by Huygens—who revealed to the public the marvels and unexpected artistic possibilities of animated projection. Louis Lumière was only one of the links in the long cinematographic chain, which included many other researchers. It would be wrong to leave in the shadows, after more than a century of projection of the chronophotographic spectacle, some of the other vital links in this chain: Huygens, Robertson, Plateau, Muybridge, Marey, Reynaud, Edison, and many others. Over several centuries, it was they who brought the 'good old magic lantern' to this apotheosis.

Appendix A

Museums displaying interesting items relating to the history of 'pre-cinema' media

Belgium
Musée du Cinéma, 9 Rue Baron Horta, Brussels.

Canada
Cinémathèque Québecoise, 335 Boulevard de Maisonneuve, Montréal, Québec.

France
Musée du Cinéma Henri Langlois, Palais de Chaillot, Paris.
Musée National des Techniques, Conservatoire National des Arts et Métiers (CNAM), 292 Rue Saint-Martin, Paris.
Musée Marey, Rue de l'Hôtel de Ville, Beaune.
Musée Français de la Photographie, 78 Rue de Paris, Bièvres.
Institut Lumière, 25 Rue du Premier-Film, Lyon.
Musée Nicéphore Niépce, 28 Quai des Messageries, Chalon-sur-Saône.

Germany
Deutsches Filmmuseum, Schamainkai 41, Frankfurt-am-Main.
Deutsches Museum, Museumsinsel 1, Munich.
Hessisches Landesmuseum, Gebrüder Grimm-Platz 5, Kassel.

Italy
Museo Nazionale del Cinema, Palazzo Chiablese, Piazza S. Giovanni 2, Turin.
Minici Zotti Collection, Prato della Valle 1, Padova.

United Kingdom
Science Museum, Exhibition Road, South Kensington, London.
National Museum of Photography, Film and Television, Bradford, West Yorkshire.
Kingston upon Thames Museum and Heritage Centre, Fairfield West, Kingston, Surrey.
British Photographic Museum, Bowden House, Totnes, Devon.

United States
International Museum of Photography, George Eastman House, 900 East Avenue, Rochester, NY.

Appendix B

Report of the Scientists Jamin and Richer on the Phantasmagorie of Robertson and the Phantasmaparastasie of Clisorius (17 July–2 August 1800).

[*Translator's note*: A previous English translation of this document by Mike Bartley appeared in the *New Magic Lantern Journal*, Vol. 7, No. 3 (November 1995). I am grateful to Mike Bartley and David Robinson for permission to refer to this translation in making my own. Any errors in the present translation are, of course, my own. R.C.]

On 28 Messidor, in Year VIII of the French Republic [i.e. 17 July 1800], at eight o'clock in the evening, we, Pierre Noël Jamin, Professor of Physics not subject to licence, resident at the Palais du Tribunat, Paris, an expert nominated by Citizen Léonard André Clisorius, sole proprietor of the establishment known in Paris under the name of Phantasmaparastasie, resident at No. 400 Rue Coquillère, Paris, and of [*sic*] Citizen Martin Aubé [Aubée], painter and artist not subject to licence, and Albert Aubé his son resident at Rue du Temple, opposite Rue Portefoin, Paris, and Citizen Jean-François Richer, mechanical engineer to the government not subject to licence, resident at Rue and Enclos des Capucines, Paris, an expert nominated by Citizen Gaspart Robert known as Robertson, Professor of Physics not subject to licence, resident at Rue and Enclos des Capucines, Division of Place Vendôme, Paris, at the request of the said Robert visited the buildings of the former [Hôtel des] Fermes on Rue de Grenelle [Saint] Honoré, the premises of the Phantasmaparastasie, where arriving in the room preceding that occupied by the audience we witnessed the removal of the seals placed on the door of the said audience hall which was opened in our presence, after entering which Citizen Robert showed us the judgement given by the Tribunal de Paix of the Division of La Halle au Bled on 14 Prairial last [3 June 1800], duly signed and registered, which in order to do justice to the parties orders that there shall be a process of verification of the instruments, tools, and methods, by two expert scientists who will be respectively nominated, one by Citizens Aubé and Clisorius, and the other by the said Citizen Robert, or appointed, which experts will compare the machine of the defendants and of the petitioner, will establish the difference, if any, and will prepare a report in which the parties or their representatives may assist and enact depositions and observations which they consider appropriate for the report made and added thereto by the parties.

And subsequent to the summons made at the request of Citizen Robert by legal document through Citizen Thiebaut, bailiff, dated 22 Messidor of the present month [11 July 1800], duly signed and delivered to Citizens Clisorius and Aubé father and son, to present themselves at the location where we are on the twenty-fourth of the said present month, in order to be present if required at the operation and verification by us the experts directed by the said judgement, with the declaration that for lack of comparison or finding someone to stand in for them, we would begin the process whether they were absent or present, and on the twenty-fourth the seals could not be removed as a result of difficulties raised by the parties, the session was postponed until yesterday and then today and, in accordance with the said judgement, we were required to proceed to the operations stated under the respective rights of the parties. [Signed], *Robertson.* Approved with twenty-three words deleted.

This being complied with, we were proceeding with the said operations when, wishing to enter the hall, we became aware that it was almost night, that it was impossible to continue with the operations entrusted to us by the said judgement, for which reason, by agreement with the parties present and their counsel, we postponed the session until 1 Thermidor next [20 July 1800] at four o'clock p.m. precisely, at which day and time all the parties present promised to attend without summons and signed with us while reserving all their rights, approved with eleven words deleted,

[signed] *P.N. Jamin, Richer, Clisorius, Martin Aubée, Guiffrou.*

And on the said day, 1 Thermidor Year VIII of the Republic [20 July 1800], at four o'clock p.m., in accordance with the above-mentioned postponement, we, Jamin and Richer, the expert scientists named, described, and resident as above, visited the said Fermes buildings, location of the Phantasmaparastasie, where we met Citizen Robert who requested us, in accordance with the afore-mentioned judgement, to proceed with the operations decreed by it, as a consequence of which, after the seals applied to the entrance door of the hall intended for spectators of the Phantasmaparastasie show had been removed, we entered into the said hall and proceeded as follows.

We noted in the said hall a lamp suspended from the floor [the floor above, i.e. the ceiling] by three chains, whose wick appears to be moved by an upper wire arranged horizontally and originating in the rear of [the room] where we are.

Further towards the back of the said hall, a curtain is raised as required, on which is painted a tomb supported by caryatids, which curtain descends directly in front of the length of a sheet stretched vertically, at a distance of about two-thirds of a metre from the partition behind, and situated between the sheet and the partition is a small side door leading into the second room.

Finding nothing further to note in the said audience room, we entered the second room wherein we noted a wooden structure fitted with four cross-members, the last of which is covered by a cushion which appears to be intended to prevent the impact of the box against the end of a frame which we found running in the direction of the sheet, which appears to have been attached to the tiles of the floor by spiked feet, the said structure being approximately three and two-thirds metres long and two-thirds of a metre wide, which structure Citizen Clisorius told us had been left standing vertically against the wall before his departure for Switzerland and belongs to Citizen Baclau [the name is unclear], a scientist.

A further square box of two-thirds of a metre in length at one end and three-quarters of a metre at the other. At the back of this box a door which could be closed as required, and at the front a long square tube projected from the front of the apparatus by about half a metre in length and a quarter of a metre in width, in which is a lens glass mounted on a frame which is movable by hand in a slide, the said box is carried on a table with four legs joined together by crossbars at their lower part, the two side ones [bars] are fitted with two wheels which appear, according to our experiment, intended to roll along the frame.

Two plates, one of copper and the other of tin-plate, intended for the imitation of thunder.

A cardboard tube intended for the imitation of hail. A further tube one-third of a metre square and a quarter of a metre high on the wall which separates the second [room] from the third, appearing to be intended to receive a lens glass. This box appears to be closed by a cover suspended at its upper part, this tube is precisely in the direction of the sheet.

Having found nothing further to note in the said room, we passed into the third, wherein we noted in relation to the tube to which we just referred an oil lamp with four burners [here there is a deleted phrase: 'five oil lamps of which four have glass covers without reflectors'] directed obliquely in the direction of the tube, two reflectors to the left and three below, and finally we noted that the three rooms are aligned in the same direction and the back wall of the room in which we were is painted black.

After which, having attended until nine o'clock and finding nothing further to report, before departing we declared an adjournment until the fifth of the present month at midday, at the premises of Citizen Robertson, Enclos de la Rue des Capucines, where the parties and their counsel have promised to attend to support our operations, the said parties and counsel having signed with us, approved with thirty-nine words deleted,

[signed] *P.N. Jamin, Richer, Robertson, Clisorius, Martin Aubée, Guiffrou.*

5 Thermidor [24 July 1800]. And on the said day 5 Thermidor at midday, we repaired according to the above declaration to the residence of Citizen Robert,

located in Paris at the Rue et Enclos des Capucines, where we met the said Citizen Robert who requested us, in the presence of Citizens Clisorius and Aubé, to proceed with our operations in accordance with the judgement set forth elsewhere, in compliance with which request we [deleted: 'proceeded as it may be'] were going to proceed, when Citizen Clisorius remarked to us that in order to proceed properly and to avoid describing all the machines at Robertson's premises which might be irrelevant to the dispute, we had three operations to carry out, the first to consider the patent which Citizen Robert has, to examine the machines contained in the said patent. The second, to observe the machines set out in the said patent which are located in the premises of the said citizen, and to describe them. The third, to compare the machines of Citizen Robertson with those of Citizen Clisorius, and he requested us that in order to follow this natural order, Citizen Robertson should be obliged to present his patent to us immediately.

At that time Citizen Robert presented his patent to us, and then conducted us into the audience hall, wherein we saw in the centre of the room a lamp suspended by three connected chains, joined at their upper part; in addition a controlling cord partly of string, partly of metal wire, connected to the wick to cause it to move into the body of the lamp and leading behind the sheet.

Citizen Clisorius observed that Robert's lamp differed from that of Clisorius in that the junction of the three branches is further from the ceiling here than at the premises of Citizen Clisorius and that the controlling cord is of metal and string.

We observed a curtain on which is painted a tomb, supported by a wire, which curtain is raised perpendicularly. Clisorius observed to us, when at the far end of the room, that it differs in that it is completely covered in black cloth. Behind is a transparent sheet, which is spaced from the wall by approximately half a metre, which separation allows communication from the first to the second room.

Finding nothing further to report in the first room, we passed into the second. Therein, we first observed a wooden frame secured to the floorboards by spiked feet, which has the following dimensions: four and two-thirds metres in length, two-thirds of a metre in width, connected by three lower cross-members and a fourth upper member covered with a small cushion to prevent the impact of the machine which moved over it; the description of which we shall now give.

This machine is a rectangular box of two-thirds of a metre in one dimension and a little more than half a metre in the other, the height is three-quarters of a metre. On the front is a square wooden tube of a little more than one-sixth of a metre square, extending into the box by one-ninth of a metre and with a little less than one-third of a metre extending out. In the tube is a lens glass in its frame, which is moved by hand by means of a lateral slide. It [the machine] is carried by a table one metre in height whose four legs are fitted with cross-members at their lower part. To each of the four is attached a wheel which allows movement of the box along the frame in the direction of the sheet.

Having attended for an hour and a quarter, we adjourned our session until tomorrow, 6 Thermidor Year VIII [25 July 1800] on which day the parties, [and] their authorized agents, have promised to attend without summons, and have signed,

[signed] *Clisorius, Martin Aubée, Guiffrou, Robertson, P.N. Jamin, Richer.*

On the said day 6 Thermidor, as a result of the meeting yesterday, we repaired to the establishment of Citizen Robert where, at his request, we proceeded with the operations prescribed by the judgement.

On this occasion Citizen Albert Aubé the son attended, who stated that he approved of all that which had taken place here in his absence, and for the defence of all his rights, he does not object to whatever process may take place in the operations prescribed by the said judgement and signed,

[signed] *Albert Aubée.*

Also in attendance were Citizens Clisorius and Martin Aubé above named, who observed jointly with Citizen Albert Aubée the son, that concerning the frame it differed from that of Clisorius, in that it was not joined by cross-members, that the holes present at this time are only from cross-members added afterwards to give the apparatus of Citizen Robert a resemblance to the apparatus of Citizen Clisorius, which is proved by their mobility.

Secondly, that the main members of the frame are different, in spite of the description of them given by Citizen Robert, by a groove which extends along the length of each part of the frame, that each of the said parts is lined by an iron plate, that the said frame here extended to the two side walls and at the premises of Citizen Clisorius, it did not do so.

Turning then to the rectangular casing, they observed that the said apparatus had been made after the event, as indeed appears from what follows. That the legs of the table which supports the said box, the sides of the said table, [and] the box itself are new, that the interior if it had been used would be blackened by the smoke of the oil lamps more heavily than it is at the present time, that the wheels are not impregnated by the large amounts of oil which cover each side of the frame [the track on the floor], that the box which had been used for the four years in which Citizen Robertson has performed the Phantasmagorie should display some traces of handling, that however it is neither worn nor rubbed, that when it is moved the said box produces a noise which has not been heard by any member of the audience, that the roughness of the wheels also proves what they suggest, that they maintain that this machine is cleverly copied from that of Citizen Clisorius and that it does not even conform to that of his [Robertson's] claimed patent, in view of the fact that that of his patent is not fitted with pulleys nor with the brackets to support them, that Citizen Robert in wishing to imitate Citizen Clisorius has copied him very poorly, in that the wheels of the said Clisorius are set into the lateral members at a certain distance from the legs, raised or lowered according to the retraction or extension of a rod connected to the lateral members.

They added that the internal slider of the tube is at the side and makes a great deal of noise when operated, that the said slider is not present at all on the apparatus of Clisorius, that in his tube the glass is moved by means of a cord. That a further proof of the newness of the tube was the lack of a closure, that he had not yet had time to attach a door to the side to close the opening which he has formed, that there is no projecting chimney. That they could describe an infinite number of further differences, in which he had not had the skill to copy Citizen Clisorius; but to cut matters short they turned to examination of the support which was genuinely used to carry the box, which when placed on the frame and compared in its movement was found to be infinitely smoother, sliding more easily and without noise, that the oil with which the legs were impregnated indicated that it [the box] was previously used [with] the support described above, that they claimed that the machine which Citizen Robert presented as the object for comparison is incapable of producing the effects which he produces daily before the public with his other machine which he has concealed from our view, in proof of which they demanded that the said Citizen Robert operate in front of us with the machine just as it is and without any accessories, demanded that the focal length of the lens be measured, in addition reserving [the right] to make in future any other observations to which the objects presented might give rise.

Following the above observations, to which Citizen Robert stated that he did not wish to reply, we, Citizens Richer and Jamin, continued with our operations.

We began by measuring the focal length of the above-mentioned lens, which we found to be approximately one metre.

We then found two other lenses encased like the first, which Citizen Robert told us were intended for the same use.

At the end wall of the second room and directed towards the sheet, we noted a square wooden tube, three decimetres [30 cm] in width and three-and-a-half decimetres in height, projecting out of the wall by one decimetre, this tube carries a mounted lens glass, eleven centimetres in diameter and secured in position. We noted at the upper part of this tube a cover or hinged door held by a cord which appeared to lead into the third room adjacent to the one where we are.

In addition a table of tin-plate used to imitate thunder, and a roll of cardboard used to imitate hail. Finding nothing further to observe in the second room we passed into the third one.

There we observed, in the wall which separates it from the second [room], the continuation of the wooden tube fitted therein, projecting by about one-fifth of a metre on our side. We saw on each side of this tube a lamp with four burners arranged in a direction oblique to that of the tube. We also observed that these oil lamps were each carried by a wooden stand. The back wall of this third room was covered in black cloth.

Having nothing further to report in the three above-mentioned rooms, we brought the present statements of the days and year stated above to a close, postponing the verification of the methods; which will commence at the establishment of Citizen Clisorius on 9 Thermidor [28 July 1800] at precisely five o'clock in the afternoon. Approved with sixty-one words deleted,

[signed] *P.N. Jamin, Richer, Robertson, Guiffrou, Clisorius, Martin Aubée, Albert Aubée.*

And on the said day, 9 Thermidor Year VIII, at [five] o'clock in the afternoon, in front of us the above-mentioned and undersigned experts, after having invited Citizen the Commissioner of Police to be present for the observance of the removal of the seals, with which he complied, there appeared before us the above-mentioned Citizen Robertson, assisted by Citizen LeBon, and the also above-mentioned Citizens Clisorius and Aubée the father and Albert Aubée the son, described and resident as above, [and] signed with us the said Citizens Clisorius and Aubé father and son assisted by Citizen Delahaye who signed with them,

[signed] *Clisorius, Jamin, Robertson, LeBon, Richer, Martin Aubée, Albert Aubée.*

And in fact Citizens Clisorius and Aubée remarked to us that they were astonished to see the door of the room where the seals were open without their participation, and even that persons were in the said room without them.

That they were essentially ready to carry out what appeared to be required [by] our operations at the last session, but that having a concern that Citizen Robertson should not know his method so that he could imitate it, he [Clisorius] would not proceed to the demonstration of his methods until Citizen Robertson and he recorded by writing on a paper, which would be sealed with two seals, their two methods of operating, which paper shall be delivered to the arbitrators. That until then, he will give no idea of demonstrations, so that Citizen Robertson could not say that his method is recorded in his patent, since they maintained that their process was not that which he had described in his patent, and we signed with their counsels,

[signed] *Clisorius, Delahaye, Martin Aubé.*

[Here are twenty-six lines which are barely legible. The sense is that Robertson 'did not justify the removal of the seals which had taken place', that there was 'abuse' by Clisorius and Aubée, and that he 'will not respond any further' to questions about the processes. Robertson signed along with his counsel LeBon.]

At this we the above-named and undersigned arbiters, considering that there was a means of bringing the parties together, and of avoiding the disadvantage which one of them appears to fear, with the agreement of all parties present, adjourned the session until the eleventh of the present month at precisely nine o'clock in the morning at the establishment of Citizen Clisorius where we are at present, to proceed to the verification of the methods which he uses, and then immediately and without interruption proceed to the premises of Citizen Robert-son for the verification of the methods of Citizen Robert-son, at which day and time the parties have promised to attend without need of summons, and all the parties have signed with us in this place,

[signed] *Robertson, LeBon, Jamin, Richer, Clisorius, Martin Aubée, Albert Aubée, Guiffrou, Delahaye.*

With the arrival of this day, 11 Thermidor Year VIII [30 July 1800], we, Jean-François Richer and Pierre Noël [Jamin] the above-mentioned and under-signed experts, in performance of our postponement of the ninth of this month went at nine o'clock in the morning to the Hôtel des Fermes on Rue Grenelle [Saint] Honoré, where the spectacle of the Phantasmaparastasie was established, to proceed with the continuation of our operations, and where we met Citizen the Superintendent who, after having verified the seals in our presence and that of the porter, removed them and allowed us entry into the said show where we proceeded as follows.

And immediately we requested Citizens Clisorius and Aubé to demonstrate successively to us their processes and the use of the instruments relevant to the Phantasmaparastasie as described above. First operation.

Citizen Aubée the younger drew a figure which he then cut out, he suspended it upside-down in an upper opening closed by a slider which he told us was used to move the figure forwards and backwards. In the said box were two oil lamps with reflectors to the right and left of the said box next to the lens glass, serving to illuminate the said figure. At the back of the box and at the sides of the oil lamps are placed sheets of tin-plate forming shades to prevent the light of the oil lamps from throwing its rays onto the lens glass. When they lit the two oil lamps, the inverted figure appeared portrayed the right way up on the transparent sheet, and by moving the box forwards or backwards along the above-described frame, the figure became larger or smaller on the transparent sheet, and they offered to perform the same effects with the same box without making use of the frame, which we arbiters having accepted, the said citizens removed the lower support of the table which directs the said table and the box along the above-mentioned frame with pincers and a hammer. When the wheels rested on the ground, they moved the machine forwards and backwards until it was stopped in its movement at a distance of two-thirds of a metre from the transparent sheet by one of the spiked feet driven into the tiles, and presumed to be the connectors of the frame to the said tiles. We also noted that the said box directed in this way had a bouncing motion which it did not have on the frame. Then Citizen Clisorius informed us that the said box was only used for opaque objects, and could give no other result, [and] he offered to demonstrate his other methods for transparent bodies, to which Citizen Robert replied that he opposed the introduction into the said location of any other machine not included in the statements, that the operation of the experts had the sole purpose of recording the objects which had been under seals and comparing them with his own, and that he will demonstrate that the present apparatus can be used just as well for transparent bodies, and signed,

[signed] *Robertson, Clisorius.*

In the light of this observation by Citizen Robert we concluded our experiments on this item and requested Citizens Clisorius and Aubé to operate the square tube fitted into the wall which separates the second room from the third. Citizens Clisorius and Aubé replied that since this square tube gives the same results for opaque bodies as the box whose use they have demonstrated, they no longer use the said tube in which they pointed out to us that there is no longer a lens; that if however we require it, they offered to show their method at the present time, and signed,

[signed] *Clisorius, Martin Aubée.*

To which Citizen Robert replied that since they were offering to show their methods at the present time, and the experts were only present to know them, he required that their offer be accepted, since the judgement ordered it. And he signed,

[signed] *Robertson.*

Considering that it is agreed between the parties that the said tube in the wall can perform the same effects and other larger ones, we believed that it was pointless to proceed to the verification of the effects of the said tube, moreover Citizen Clisorius did not have the lens necessary to be fitted into it.

And considering that there was nothing further to observe in the place where we were, we decided with the consent of all the parties present to repair to the premises of Citizen Robertson, in order to continue our operations there, and we have signed with all the parties, approved with six words deleted,

[signed] *Jamin, Richer, Albert Aubée, Martin Aubée, Robertson.*

Arriving at the premises of Citizen Robertson with the parties appearing in the case, we requested Citizen Robertson to demonstrate to us his methods and the operation of the instruments relevant to the Phantasmagorie described previously.

First operation.

Citizen Robertson drew a figure which he then cut out, he held it first in his hand, then suspended it in the interior of the box in an upside-down position, the figure was portrayed on the transparent sheet in an upright position. Inside the box was an oil lamp with four burners placed at the side of the tube to illuminate the said figure. Then the figure increased or diminished in proportion on the transparent sheet according to whether the said box was moved backwards or forwards on its frame.

Citizen Clisorius pointed out that when the figure was reduced on the transparent sheet to the natural size of the paper, the rays of light from the box spilled out around the object, which had not taken place at his establishment and is an imperfection, that in addition there are two flat pieces of cardboard at the base which were not present at the first examination, and that furthermore a curtain had been added to the opening of the door, and he requested us to check the focus of the lens and signed,

[signed] *Clisorius, Martin Aubée.*

Citizen Robert replied to this that he invited Citizens the experts to note whether the box has the same door which it carried at the first examination. As for the small rays of light of which Citizen Clisorius had complained, they were caused by the fuss he had made over the greater or lesser size of the object, whose relative sizes had not even been verified. As for the focus of the lens, it is absurd to wish to measure the focus of the lens at ten o'clock in the evening, as he had asked. In addition he maintained that in the examination made at his, Robertson's, premises, the experts had found three lenses, and that he could operate with the one which suited him. In addition to give greater perfection to the object he most regularly used a second lens glass, which prevents spherical aberration.

[signed] *Robertson.*

Second operation.

To operate with the tube fitted into the wall which separates the second room from the third, and which is fitted with a lens glass, Citizen Robertson, after lighting his two oil lamps with four burners, made appear on the trans- parent sheet an opaque figure which was reproduced there at natural size, although it was only approximately one-fifth of a metre [in size]. Then he made appear on the same transparent sheet his own face enlarged to the same proportions.

Citizen Robertson confined himself to these two operations, [but] Citizen Clisorius after the said operations requested that he should proceed to a third, which is that of transparent bodies, as this is the most essential component of the phantasmagorie, and signed,

[signed] *Clisorius.*

Citizen Robertson replied that the operations described above appeared to him more than sufficient to establish the similarity of the implements, instruments and methods of Citizen Clisorius with his own; he did not believe it necessary for that, with the experts, to consent to the operations asked by Citizen Clisorius which could have no other purpose than to set a trap for either the experts or for justice, since that operation cannot be performed with only the instruments found behind the seals, that he is certain that he [Clisorius] had brought something in a handkerchief, which the citizen does not know and does not wish to accept, finally that since the judgement given between the parties orders the verification solely of the objects found behind the seals, it was not necessary to attend to foreign objects prepared or brought in after the event. In consequence and by means of this our operations are at an end and nothing further remains for us except to present the result according to our knowledge and our conscience, he requested that it would please him to close our report and signed with reservation of all his rights,

[signed] *Robertson, LeBon.*

And Citizen Clisorius replied that the judgement of which Citizen Robertson requested the execution orders the verification of all the methods which the plaintiff and defendants employ, that it was for the execution of this judgement that he had brought from his establishment in a handkerchief a magic lantern to show the transparent bodies, the principal object of the Phantasmaparastasie, not in the least to set a trap for us, but on the contrary to enlighten us; that the judgement does not specify solely the objects behind the seals, that therefore it is wrong that Citizen Robertson does not wish to present the methods of transparent bodies, and signed with reservation of all his rights,

[signed] *Clisorius.*

Having nothing further to note, we closed and terminated the present proceedings, reserving the completion of our report to follow, and signed with all the parties on the above-mentioned days and year. Approved with one word deleted,

[signed] *P.N. Jamin, Richer, Robertson, Clisorius, Martin Aubée, Guiffrou, Albert Aubée, LeBon.*

Opinion of the Experts.

On 14 Thermidor Year VIII [2 August 1800] of the French Republic, we, Citizens Richer and Jamin, met in the scientific laboratory of the said Citizen Jamin, in agreement to write our opinion arising from the present proceedings, and having previously compared them with each other, we found such slight differences, that we believed it more appropriate to recast them into a single [report], after clarifying to each other and agreeing on the draft which follows.

A dispute has arisen between two operators of optical illusions concerning the instruments and methods which they use to produce these illusions of pure charlatanism. We apply this name to effects which, without advancing by a single step or making any progress in the pursuit of the sciences, serve only to capture the admiration and above all the money of the Public, to whom they are careful not to explain the causes.

These two operators are on one hand Citizen Robertson the Phantasmagorician, and on the other Citizens Clisorius and Aubé father and son the Phantasmaparastasians. I, Jamin, have never known the latter before being nominated as their arbiter. As for Citizen Robertson I knew him nine years ago. He then called himself Robert, and attended my free course in Physics with a young man entrusted to his care. I have not seen him since.

The question to decide between Citizen Robert the plaintiff and Citizens Clisorius and Aubé the defendants is this. Did Clisorius and Aubé imitate the instruments of which Robert claims the sole right of usage by virtue of a patent granted to him. We will not enter here into the question of knowing whether by virtue of this accusation Citizen Robert had the power and right without any preliminary examination to place seals on the property of Clisorius and his associates while the latter was travelling in Switzerland. This fact is not within our jurisdiction, and we only mention it by way of explanation of what will follow.

We consider, among the instruments to be compared between the parties, four quite distinct objects. 1. An optical box positioned on a table. 2. A wooden frame formed of two rails upon which this table slides. 3. A tube fitted with a lens glass attached to a wall, fitted in the rear with oil lamps to illuminate opaque objects. 4. A magic lantern used for transparent bodies.

In addition to these instruments there are two further objects to consider. 1. A lamp in the room for the spectators. 2. A curtain raised and lowered in front of a frame or transparent sheet of gummed or pasted cloth on which are presented the objects offered to the curiosity of the spectators. We begin with these two.

Lamp. Clisorius' lamp appears to us with certain small differences constructed on the same principles as that of Robert. But both of them, to our eyes, are absolutely similar to the one which was seen in Paris several years ago in the experiments in flammable air of the Dutchman Mr Diller, and which suddenly illuminated or plunged into darkness the spectators of these experiments.

Curtain and transparent sheet. Clisorius' curtain and transparent sheet appear to us equally similar to those of Robert. If there is a slight difference between the distance of the two of them, if the transparent sheet is pasted or gummed, if one of the curtains is painted in one fashion and the other in another, this does not seem to us to be important enough to note. We pass on to the instruments proper.

Box and table supporting it. Clisorius' optical box and the table which supports it appear to us to have much in common with those of Robert. There are certain differences. Clisorius' box has a chimney on top exceeding the height of the box. Robert's does not have one. The first has a door at the rear. The second has a lateral opening where on our first visit was a rough door held by a simple nail, and on our second visit a curtain.

Clisorius' box and the slider which causes the lens glass to move forwards and backwards perform their motion without any noise which can be heard by the spectators. Robert's box and slider cause a very distinct noise to be heard, as was noted in the examination. The first is marked by smoke inside as a result of the oil lamps; Robert's is not so. Moreover it does not have a lateral rack, although that illustrated in the patent carries one. We therefore conclude that Clisorius could not have copied a new box later than his own, of which Robert's appears instead to be the imitation. We therefore conclude also that Robert's box has never been used in the experiments previously conducted, as we said to him in person in the presence of the parties and their defenders, during the verification of the methods.

Wooden frame. The wooden frame on which Clisorius' box slides appears to us to be approximately the same as Robert's. That the latter may be longer than the former and does not have upper cross-members, does not seem of great importance to us. Clisorius claims that this frame does not belong to him, and that he operates without its assistance by placing the wheels of his table on the floor. This is true; but it operates more imperfectly and with a rocking motion because of the unevenness of the floor and was not even able to reach more than two-thirds of a metre from the transparent sheet as a result of the spiked plates which remained fixed to the floor.

Tube fitted into the wall. The tube fitted into the wall which separates the second room from the third is approximately the same in the establishment of Clisorius as in that of Robert. The differences comprise: 1. In a greater or lesser extension from the wall. 2. In the arrangement or the number of oil lamps behind. 3. In that there was a lens glass in Robert's, and there was not one in Clisorius', and that the latter attributed this to the fact that he no longer makes use of it. We shall not dwell on this tube, since it is known to all Scientists under the name of *Megascope*, and that it is used to cause opaque bodies to appear on the transparent sheet at an enlarged size.

Magic lantern. This is specifically the instrument which Clisorius and Robert use for transparent bodies and for almost all the experiments of the Phantasmagorie and Phantasmaparastasie. All that is required to perform them is to move the magic lantern closer to or further from the transparent sheet while extending, in the first case, and retracting in the second, the tube at the front of the box. It was impossible for us to compare the two magic lanterns of Clisorius and Robert, the latter not wishing to allow Clisorius to make use of it, because he did not believe it necessary to permit the introduction of a device which was not behind the seals, and consequently he did not himself make any use of his own [lantern]. We add in conclusion that it appeared to us that for the operations of the Phantasmagorie and the Phantasmaparastasie, three rooms are required adjacent to one another, and that their arrangements and uses were the same in the two shows. Such is the opinion which we, Richer and Jamin, hold in common agreement on the instruments and methods verified by us, as much at the establishment of Citizen Clisorius and his associates as at the establishment of Citizen Robert known as Robertson. In witness of which we have signed the present deed jointly, on the above-mentioned days and year,

[signed] *P.N. Jamin, J.F. Richer.*

Registered at Paris, 17 Thermidor Year VIII [8 August 1800], folio 150.

Notes

Chapter One: Dark Rooms and Magic Mirrors, p. 3

1. Francesco Maurolico, *Photismi de Lumine et Umbra* (Naples, 1611), and *Theoremata de Lumine et Umbra* (Lyon, 1613).
2. Roger Bacon, 'De Multiplicatione Specerium', in *Opus Majus* (London, 1733), 358.
3. Cited in Pierre Duhem, *Le Système du Monde* (Paris, Hermann, 1915), Vol. III, 505.
4. Cited in Georges Potonniée, *Histoire de la Découverte de la Photographie* (reprinted Paris: J-M. Place, 1989), 28.
5. Cited in Potonniée, op. cit., 20, and in Helmut Gernsheim, *The Origins of Photography* (London: Thames & Hudson, 1982), 10.
6. Leonardo da Vinci, *The Notebooks of Leonardo da Vinci*, Vol. I, trans. Edward MacCurdy (London: Jonathan Cape, 1938, new ed. 1956), 216.
7. Cited in Potonniée, op. cit., 20, and in Gernsheim, op. cit., 10.
8. John Baptista Porta (Giovanni Battista della Porta), *Natural Magick* (London: Thomas Young and Samuel Speed, 1658), 363.
9. Porta, op. cit., 364–5.
10. François d'Aguillon, *Opticorum Libri VI* (Anvers, 1613), 47.
11. L-V. Thiéry, *Guide des Amateurs et des Étrangers Voyageurs à Paris (Paris, 1787), Vol. I, 687.*
12. Jean-François Nicéron, *La Perspective Curieuse* (Paris, 1652), 21–2.
13. Jean Leurechon, *Récréation Mathématique* (Pont-à-Mousson, 1621), 98–9, 103.
14. Nicéron, op. cit., 21–2.
15. Pierre Le Lorrain, Abbé de Valmont, *La Physique Occulte ou Traité de la Baguette Divinatoire* (Amsterdam, 1693), 302.
16. Mario Bettini, *Apiaria Universae Philosophiae Mathematicae*, Vol. I (Bologna, 1642), 38–43.
17. Cited in Potonniée, op. cit., 31.
18. Vincent Chevalier, French Patent of 10 June 1823.
19. Nicéron, op. cit., 21–2.
20. Camera obscuras of this type are discussed in John H. Hammond, *The Camera Obscura* (Bristol: Adam Hilger, 1981), and Michel Auer, *150 Ans d'Appareils Photographiques* (Hermance, Switzerland, 1989).
21. Chérubin d'Orléans, *La Dioptrique Oculaire* (Paris, 1671), 285–8. 'L'oeil artificiel' was also used as a generic term for the camera obscura in the eighteenth century; see P. Ango, *L'Optique* (Paris, 1682), 199.
22. Athanasius Kircher, *Ars Magna Lucis et Umbrae* (Rome, 1646), 811–12.
23. Johann Christoph Sturm, *Collegium Experimentale Sive Curiosum* (Nuremberg, 1676), 161–2.

24. Jurgis Baltrušaitis, *Le Miroir* (Paris: Elmayan-Seuil, 1978).

25. Roger Bacon, *De Mirabili Potestate Artis et Naturae* (Paris, 1893), 14.

26. Della Porta, op. cit., 365–6.

27. Giorgio di Sepi, *Romani Collegii Societatis Iesu Musaeum Celeberrimum* (Amsterdam, 1678).

28. Sophie de Hanovre, *Mémoires et Lettres de Voyages* (Paris: Fayard, 1990), 227.

29. Kircher, op. cit., 799. For more on Kircher, see: *Athanasius Kircher: Jesuit Scholar* (Provo, Utah: Friends of Brigham Young University, 1989); J. Fletcher, *Athanasius Kircher und Seine Beziehungen zum Gelehrten Europa Seiner Zeit* (Wiesbaden, 1988); Valerio Rivosecchi, *Esotismo in Roma Barocca* (Rome, 1982); *Enciclopedismo in Roma Barocca* (Venice, 1986); Joscelyn Godwin, *Athanase Kircher* (Paris, 1980); Catherine Chevalley, '*L'Ars Magna Lucis et Umbrae* d'Athanase Kircher', *Baroque* (proceedings of the 10e Session d'Étude du Baroque, Montauban, 1987); and *Dictionary of Scientific Biography*, Vol. VII (Princeton University, 1973).

30. Kircher, op. cit., 818.

31. Jacques Ozanam, *Récréations Mathématiques et Physiques*, Vol. I (Paris, 1694), 252. Ozanam restates the process of using the 'artificial lantern'.

32. Kircher, op. cit., 887.

33. Kircher, op. cit., 892.

34. Nicéron, op. cit. (1638 edition), 77.

35. Kircher, op. cit., 901.

36. Kircher, op. cit., 907–14.

37. Daniel Schwendter, *Deliciae Physico-Mathematicae et Physicae* (Nuremberg, 1638), 287.

38. Gaspar Schott, *Magia Universalis Naturae et Artis*, Part I (Würzburg, 1657), 425–6.

39. Bettini, op. cit., Book IV, 27.

40. Schott, op. cit., 426. With the exception of this somewhat enigmatic reference, there is not the slightest mention of a projection lantern in Schott's *Magia Universalis*.

Chapter Two: Light in the Darkness, p. 28

1. Mathurin Régnier, *Oeuvres Complètes*, Satire XI (Paris, 1911), 124.

2. Jean Prevost, *La Première Partie des Subtiles et Plaisantes Inventions* (Lyon, 1584), 54–5.

3. Prevost, op. cit., 54–5.

4. 'No. 525. A *lanterne tournante*, decorated with various well-painted grotesque figures': E.F. Gersaint, *Catalogue Raisonné d'une Collection Considérable de Diverses Curiosités en Tous Genres Contenues dans les Cabinets de Feu Monsieur Bonnier de la Mosson* (Paris, 1744), 130.

5. Henri Langlois, *300 Années de Cinématographie*, leaflet produced by Glenn Myrent (Paris, Musée du Cinéma, 1984), 19.

6. Omar Khayyám, *The Rubáiyát of Omar Khayyám*, trans. Edward Fitzgerald (London, 1859). The 'Magic Shadow-show' comparison appears in verse XLVI.

7. 'Luminarium nocturnum, quo nemo in Anglia uti potest propter mala quae com illo faciunt latrones.'

8. *Journal d'un Bourgeois de Paris sous le Règne de François Ier.* (Paris, L. Lalanne, 1854), 13–14.

9. Johann Wolfgang van Goethe, *The Sorrows of Werter*, trans. Daniel Malthus (1789; repr. Oxford and New York: Woodstock Books, 1991), 63.

10. Pierre Le Lorrain, Abbé de Valmont, *La Physique Occulte ou Traité de la Baguette Divinatoire* (Amsterdam, 1693), 301.
11. Balthazar de Monconys, *Voyages*, Vol. I (Paris, 1695), 73.
12. J.A. Worp, *De Briefwisseling van Constantin Huygens*, Vol. I (1911), 88.
13. Worp, op. cit., 94.
14. Christiaan Huygens, *Correspondance*, Vol. I (The Hague: Société Hollandaise des Sciences, 1888), 357.
15. For more on this subject see the fascinating book by David S. Landes, *L'Heure qu'il est* (Paris: Gallimard, 1987).
16. Marin Mersenne, *Correspondance*, Vol. XII (Paris: C. de Waard and B. Rochot/Éditions du CNRS, 1972), 10, 29.
17. Mersenne, op. cit., Vol. XIV (1980), 534.
18. Huygens, *Correspondance*, Vol. 2, Supplement 18a.
19. *Catalogus Variorum* [. . .] (The Hague, 1695). Five of Kircher's books could be found in Huygens' library: *Magnes, Sive de Arte Magnetica* (1641), *Musurgia Universalis* (1650), *Obeliscus Pamphilius* (1650), *Iter Extaticum II* (1660), and *Sphynx Mystagoga* (1676), as well as a compilation by Johann Kestler, *Physiologia Kircheriana Experimentalis* (1680). Of course Huygens also owned all the classic texts of optics, by Al-Hazen, della Porta, d'Aguillon, Hooke, Tacquet, Nicéron, Dechales, Grimaldi, Schott, Molyneux, Ango, and others.
20. Huygens, *Oeuvres Complètes*, Vol. XXII, 197. The original drawing is preserved at the Library of the University of Leiden (ms. Hug. 10, f.76v.).
21. Huygens, *Correspondance*, Vol. I (1888), 16–17.
22. Huygens, *Correspondance*, Vol. III (1890), 47.
23. H.L. Brugmans, *Le Séjour de Christiaan Huygens à Paris, Suivi de son Journal de Voyage à Paris et à Londres* (Paris, 1935). See also *Huygens et la France*, colloquium of the CNRS (Paris: Vrin, 1982).
24. Huygens, *Correspondance*, Vol. IV, 102.
25. Huygens, *Correspondance*, Vol. IV, 109.
26. Huygens, *Correspondance*, Vol. IV, 111. The identity of 'cousin Micheli' and the nature of his service for the Duc d'Aumale are unknown.
27. Huygens, *Correspondance*, Vol. XXII, 82.
28. Huygens, *Correspondance*, Vol. IV, 197.
29. Huygens, *Correspondance*, Vol. IV, 125.

Chapter Three: The 'Lantern of Fear' Tours the World, p. 46

1. Balthazar de Monconys, *Voyages*, Vol. IV (Paris, 1695), 437 and 460.
2. Samuel Pepys, *The Illustrated Pepys: Extracts from the Diary*. Selected and edited by Robert Latham (London: George Rainbird, 1979), 161.
3. de Monconys, op. cit., 458.
4. Huygens, *Correspondance*, Vol. IV, 266.
5. Huygens, *Correspondance*, Vol. V, 161.
6. Claude-François Milliet Dechales, *Cursus seu Mundus Mathematicus*, Vol. II (Lyon, 1674), 665.
7. Kircher, *Ars Magna Lucis et Umbrae* (Amsterdam, 1671), 768.
8. Oligerus Jacobacus, *Musaeum Regium, seu Catalogus Rerum*, 2nd ed. (Copenhagen, 1710), A II 2.
9. Robert Hooke, 'A contrivance to make the Picture of any thing appear on a Wall, Cub-board, or within a Picture-frame, &c. [. . .]', *Philosophical Transactions*, 38 (17

August 1668), 741–4. Robert Hooke was also the author of *A Description of Helioscopes* (an instrument for safe observation of the sun), published in London in 1676.

10. Landes, *L'Heure qu'il est* (Paris: Gallimard, 1987), 190.
11. Hooke, op. cit.
12. ibid.
13. ibid.
14. William Molyneux, *Dioptrica Nova, A Treatise of Dioptricks*, 2nd ed. (London, 1709), 183–4.
15. ibid.
16. Francesco Eschinardi, *Centuria Opticae Pars Altera* (Rome, 1668), 133–6, 221.
17. Kircher, *Ars Magna Lucis et Umbrae* (Amsterdam, 1671), 768.
18. ibid., 769.
19. ibid., 769–70.
20. ibid., 770.
21. ibid., 770.
22. Johann Gabriel Doppelmayr, *Historische Nachricht von den Nürnbergischen Mathematicis und Kunstlern* (Nuremburg, 1730), 111.
23. Charles Patin, *Travels thro' Germany, Swisserland, Bohemia, Holland, and Other Parts of Europe [. . .]* (London: 1696), 232–6.
24. Doppelmayr, op. cit., 113.
25. Johann Christoph Sturm, *Collegium Experimentale sive Curiosum* (Nuremburg, 1676), 163.
26. Sturm, *Collegii Experimentalis sive Curiosi* (Nuremberg, 1685), 236–41.
27. Johannes Zahn, *Oculus Artificialis Teledioptricus sive Telescopium* (Würzburg, 1685), 256–7; (2nd ed. 1702), 731–3.
28. See J.B. Wiederburg, *Einleitung zu den Mathematischen Wissenschaften* (Jena, 1735), 736.
29. See for example the French Patents of 9 September and 27 December 1828, issued to Louis Marie Rehaist, a bronze caster of 29 Rue des Gravilliers, Paris, for a 'lamp of constant level with device which shows the time in the night'. See also *La Nature*, 1112 (1 December 1894), 12–14.
30. Zahn, op. cit., 1st ed. 258–9; 2nd ed. 734–5.
31. Zahn, op. cit., 2nd ed., 551.
32. Zahn, op. cit., 1st ed. 255–6; 2nd ed. 730–1.
33. Zahn, op. cit., 1st ed. 255–6; 2nd ed. 730–1.
34. 'C.L.G.', *Les Projections Vivantes* (Paris, *c*. 1900), 29.
35. See for example Sturm, *Mathesis Juvenilis*, 2 vols. (Nuremburg, 1699–1701).
36. Abraham du Pradel (Nicolas de Blegny), *Livre Commode des Adresses de Paris pour 1692* (repr. Paris: Paul Daffis, 1878), 241.
37. Antoine Furetière, *Dictionnaire Universel Contenant Généralement tous les Mots Français*, Vol. II (The Hague and Rotterdam, 1690). Pierre Richelet published his *Dictionnaire François* in 1679–80, but did not offer a definition of 'magic lantern' in that edition.
38. Pierre Le Lorrain, Abbé de Vallemont, *La Physique Occulte ou Traité de la Baguette Divinatoire* (Amsterdam, 1693), 420–1.
39. Le Lorrain, op. cit. A translation and discussion of this reference is given in Ron Morris, 'The Magic Lantern in 1693', *New Magic Lantern Journal*, Vol. 1, No. 1 (April 1978), 3.
40. See I Samuel, xxviii, 11.

41. Huygens, *Traité sur la Lumière* (Paris: Gauthier-Villars, 1920).
42. Huygens, *Opuscula Posthuma quae Continent Dioptricam* (Lyon, 1703).
43. Huygens, *Oeuvres Complètes*, Vol. 13 (1916), 770, 786, 820. For further reading on the life of Huygens, see: Christiaan Huygens, *Oeuvres Complètes*, Vol. 22 (The Hague, 1950); H.J.M. Bos, 'C. Huygens' in *Dictionary of Scientific Biography*, Vol. VI (New York, 1972); and *C. Huygens: le Temps en Question* (Institut Néerlandais, 1979).
44. See for example Jacques Ozanam, *Récréations Mathématiques et Physiques*, Vol. I (Paris, 1694), 252–3.
45. Cited in Isabelle and Jean-Louis Vissière, *Lettres Édifiantes et Curieuses de Chine* (Paris: Garnier-Flammarion, 1979), 13.
46. See J. Dehergne, *Répertoire des Jésuites de Chine de 1552 à 1800* (Rome and Paris: Letouzy et Ané, 1973), 391; and C. Sommervogel, *Bibliothèque de la Compagnie de Jésus*, Vol. III (Brussels, 1892).
47. Jean-Baptiste du Halde, *Description Géographique, Historique, Chronologique, Politique et Physique de l'Empire de la Chine*, Vol. III (Paris, 1735), 268–9.
48. ibid.
49. ibid.
50. ibid.
51. ibid.

Chapter Four: *Magic Lumineuse* in the Country and the City, p. 75

1. T. de Banville, *La Lanterne Magique* (1883; Paris, 1921), 9.
2. *Lanterne Magique of Toverlantaern* (Amsterdam[?], n.d.). Fourteen plays dated from September 1782 to March 1783, including: *Le Nouveaux Lanterne Magique ou Comique Toverlantaern d'Ollande*, December 1782; *De Vrolyke Walon met de Rarekiek-Kas*, September 1782; *De Goudasche en Utrechtsche Optica*, 1783; *Het Lanterne Magique der Stad Gend* ('The Magic Lantern of the Town of Ghent'), n.d.
3. ibid.
4. Massin, *Les Cris de la Ville* (Paris: Albin-Michel, 1985), 55.
5. Marc-Mitouflet Thomin, *Traité d'Optique Méchanique* (Paris, 1749), 183.
6. *La Lanterne Magique ou le Mississippi du Diable* (The Hague, n.d.).
7. ibid.
8. *La Lanterne Magique aux Champs-Élysées* (n.p., n.d.).
9. ibid.
10. ibid.
11. *Les Affiches du Poitou*, 21 March 1776.
12. Bernard-Valville, *La Lanterne Magique ou le Retour des Époux* (Paris, 1801). A critical account of this play appears in *Affiches, Annonces et Avis Divers*, 182 (2 Germinal, Year VIII [22 March 1800]).
13. ibid.
14. J-A. Nollet, *Leçons de Physique Expérimentale*, Vol. 5 (7th ed., Paris, 1783), 567.
15. Comte de Paroy, *Mémoires* (Paris, 1895), 278. This book is mentioned in E. Roux-Parassac, *Et l'Image s'Anima* (Paris, 1930), 29.
16. ibid.
17. ibid.
18. ibid.
19. ibid.
20. ibid.

21. Edme-Gilles Guyot, *Nouvelles Récréations Physiques et Mathématiques*, Vol. II (Paris, 1799), 152–6.

22. M. Préaud, P. Casselle, M. Grivel, and C. Le Bitouzé, *Dictionnaire des Éditeurs d'Estampes à Paris sous l'Ancien Régime* (Paris: Promodis, 1987), 246.

23. Ed. de Keyser, 'Les Vues d'Optique', *Bulletin de la Société Archéologique, Historique et Artisque Le Vieux Papier*, 198 (January 1962), 246.

24. Jean-Jacques Rousseau, *Correspondance Générale*, Vol. 12 (Paris, 1929), 151–3.

25. See Maria Adriana Prolo and Luigi Carluccio, *Il Museo Nazionale del Cinema Torino* (Turin: Museo Nazionale del Cinema, 1978), and Carlo Alberto Zotti Minici, *Il Mondo Nuovo: Le Meraviglie della Visione* (Milan: Mazzotta, 1988).

26. This print, preserved in the Bibliothèque Nationale, was printed by André Basset the younger, publisher of *vues d'optique*.

27. Guyot, op. cit.

28. Émile Campardon, *Les Spectacles de la Foire*, Vol. 2 (repr. Geneva: Slatkine, 1970), 203.

29. Grollier de Servière, *Recueil d'Ouvrages Curieux de Mathématique et de Mécanique ou Description du Cabinet de Monsieur Grollier de Servière* (Lyon, 1738), 28.

30. ibid.

31. Edme-François Gersaint, *Catalogue Raisonné d'une Collection Considérable de Diverses Curiosités en tous Genres Contenus dans les Cabinets de Feu M. Bonnier de la Mosson* (Paris, 1744), 145. See also *Le Faubourg Saint-Germain, la Rue Saint-Dominique, Hôtels et Amateurs* (Paris, 1984), 150–63.

32. ibid.

33. ibid.

34. Johann Konrad Gütle, *Zaubermechanick oder Beschreibung Mechanischer Zauberbelustigungen* (Nuremburg and Altdorf, 1794), 180.

35. *La Lanterne Magique de la France, Nouveau Spectacle de la Foire Saint-Germain* (n.p., 1789), 1–3.

36. Vicomte de Mirabeau, *La Lanterne Magique Nationale*, three issues of 38, 30 and 21 pages.

37. *La Lanterne Magique ou Fléaux des Aristocrates* (Berne, 1790). Other similar texts are *La Lanterne Magique ou les Grands Conseillers de Joseph de Bon* (Paris, 1787), and *La Lanterne Magique, Spectacle National pour les Aristocrates* (n.p., n.d.).

38. ibid.

39. [Antoine Caillot], *La Lanterne Magique de la Rue Impériale* (Paris, n.d.), 8.

40. Jean-Pierre Claris de Florian, *Le Singe qui Montre la Lanterne Magique* (numerous French editions, illustrated by V. Adam in 1838, by Grandville, by B. Rabier, and others).

41. Frédéric Dillaye, *Les Jeux de la Jeunesse* (Paris, 1885), 359.

42. Pierre-Jakez Hélias, *Le Cheval d'Orgueil* (Paris: Plon, 1982), 234; Jeanne Nabert, *Les Termagics* (Paris: Plon, 1936). The Irish film *Knocknagow*, made in 1917 by Fred O'Donovan, features a peepshow box. More recently, Ettore Scola used a reproduction peepshow in his film *La Nuit de Varennes* (1982), and Bill Douglas employed a similar fairground device in his 1987 film *Comrades*.

Chapter Five: 'Life and Motion': The Eighteenth-Century Lantern Slide, p. 104

1. Christian Gottlieb Hertel, *Anweisung zum Glasschleifen* (Halle, 1716), 121.

2. ibid.
3. J-A. Nollet, *L'Art des Expériences*, Vol. III (Paris, 1770), 335–336.
4. Johann Bernhard Wiedeburg, *Einleitung zu den Mathematischen Wissenschaften* (Jena, 1735), 761.
5. [C.L. Deneke], *Volständiges Lehrgebäude der Ganzen Optik* (Altona, 1754), 747.
6. ibid.
7. *Vie Privée du Maréchal de Richelieu* (Paris: Éditions Desjonquères, 1993), 177.
8. Mme de Graffigny, letter to M Devaux, 11 December 1738, in *Choix de Lettres du XVIIIe Siècle* (Paris, 1946), 191.
9. Voltaire, *Correspondance*, Vol. XI (Paris: Gallimard, 1987), 902.
10. See John Jones, 'Trying to Date some Long Slides' in *The Ten Year Book* (London: Magic Lantern Society, 1986), 74–9.
11. Benjamin Martin, *The Young Gentleman and Lady's Philosophy, in a Continued Survey of the Works of Nature and Art by Way of Dialogue*, Vol. II (London, 1772), 288–9.
12. E. Riccomini, 'Diapositives de Maître', *FMR* 28 (1990), 127–42.
13. Christoff Weigel, *Künstler und Handwerker in Nürnberg* (Nuremburg, 1698), 218.
14. Zacharias von Uffenbach, *Merkwürdige Reisen durch Niedersachsen Holland und Engelland*, Vol. II (Ulm, 1753), 50, 62.
15. Samuel Johannes Rhanaeus, *Novum et Curiosum Laternae Augmentum* (Jena, 1713), 3.
16. Nollet, *Leçons de Physique Expérimentale*, Vol. V, 7th ed. (Paris, 1783), 572.
17. Petrus van Musschenbroek, *Essai de Physique*, Vol. II (Leyden, 1751), 608–9.
18. ibid.
19. ibid.
20. Nollet, *L'Art des Expériences*, 338.
21. van Musschenbroek, op. cit.
22. E-G. Guyot, *Nouvelles Récréations Physiques et Mathématiques*, Vol. II (Paris, 1799), 250.
23. William Hooper, *Rational Recreations*, Vol. II (London, 1774), 40–1.
24. Johann Christian Wiegleb, *Die Natürliche Magie* (Berlin, 1779), 152. See also the same author's *Magie oder die Zauberkräfte der Natur* (Berlin, 1784), 256–7.
25. Jonathan Swift, *Journal to Stella*, Vol. II, ed. Harold Williams (Oxford: Basil Blackwell, 1974), 647. Harold Williams suggests that the 'moving Picture' referred to here could have been a clockwork machine rather than a projection. See also the remarks of André Gide on this passage, in his *Journal* (Paris, 1951), 976.
26. Johann Michael Conradi, *Der Dreifach Geartete Sehe-Strahl* (Coburg, 1710), 115.
27. Hertel, op. cit., 118.
28. Willem Jacob Storm van s'Gravesande, *Éléments de Physique*, Vol. II (Paris, 1747), 220–5. The engraving appears in the English translation *Mathematical Elements of Natural Philosophy*, Vol. II (London, 1737), 104.
29. Heinrich Johannes Bytemeister, *Catalogus Apparatus Curiosum*, 2nd ed. (Helmstedt, 1735), 13.
30. Nollet, *L'Art des Expériences*, 331.
31. ibid.
32. Deneke, op. cit., 747ff.
33. Auguste and Louis Lumière, French Patent 266,870 of 10 May 1897.
34. Guyot, op. cit., 249.
35. Balthazar de Monconys, *Voyages*, Vol. IV (Paris, 1695), 437 and 460.
36. J-F. Montcula, *Histoire des Mathématiques*, Vol. III (Paris, 1802), 449; M. Daumas, *Les Instruments Scientifiques* (Paris, 1953), 204–5.
37. Henry Baker, *Le Microscope à la Portée de Tout le Monde* (Paris, 1744), 12. The text

here is retranslated from the French edition, rather than taken from the English original, *The Microscope Made Easy* (London, 1743).

38. Martin, op. cit., 186.
39. Baker, op. cit., 27.
40. Henry Baker, 'An Account of Mr Lecuwenhoek's Microscopes', *Philosophical Transactions*, Vol. XLI no. 458, 503–18.
41. M.F. Ledermuller, *Amusements Microscopiques*, Vol. III (Nuremburg, 1768), 9.
42. ibid.
43. Reproduced in Marat, *Découvertes de M. Marat sur le Feu, l'Électricité et la Lumière* (Paris, 1779).
44. ibid.
45. Leonhard Euler, *Lettres à une Princesse d'Allemagne sur Quelques Sujets de Physique et de Philosophie*, Vol. I (Paris, 1842), 355.
46. Cited in R. Smith, *Cours Complète d'Optique*, Vol. II (Avignon, 1767), 510.
47. Étienne Gaspard Robertson, *Mémoires Récréatifs*, Vol. I (Paris, 1831), 80.
48. Charles continued his work under the Revolution: 'On 1 December at the Louvre, J.A.C. Charles will commence his course on experimental physics, which will take place on Tuesdays, Thursdays and Saturdays at 11 o'clock in the morning and 6 o'clock in the evening'. (*Affiches, Annonces et Avis Divers*, 133, 29 November 1792).
49. Funck-Brentano, *Marat* (Paris, 1941), 62; J. Massin, *Marat* (Paris, 1988), 58–60.
50. Marc-Mitouflet Thomin, *Instruction sur l'usage des lunettes ou conserves pour toutes sortes de vues* (Paris: Claude Lamesle, 1746), 125–7.

Chapter Six: The Phantasmagoria, p. 136

1. Henri Decremps, *La Magie Blanche Devoilée* (Paris, 1784), 105–7.
2. ibid.
3. Edme-Gilles Guyot, *Nouvelles Récréations Physiques et Mathématiques*, Vol. 2 (Paris, 1799), 254.
4. Christlieb Benedikt Funk, *Natürliche Magie, oder Erklärung Verschiedner Wahrsager- und Natürliche Zauberkünste* (Berlin, 1783), 152.
5. Johann Samuel Halle, *Magie oder die Zauberkräfte der Natur* (Berlin, 1784), 232–3.
6. *Affiches, Annonces et Avis Divers*, 350 (16 December 1792), 5189.
7. *Affiches, Annonces et Avis Divers*, 357 (23 December 1792), 5282.
8. *Affiches, Annonces et Avis Divers*, 73 (14 March 1793), 1083.
9. M. Breton, *Les Savants de Quinze Ans*, Vol. II (Paris, 1811), 331.
10. 'La Phantasmagorie', *La Feuille Villageoise* 22 (28 February 1793), 508. This text was pointed out by Jérôme Prieur, whose essay *Séance de Lanterne Magique* (Paris, 1985) gives a fine study of the occurrences of projection in literature.
11. ibid, 506. See also *La Feuille Villageoise* 34 (23 May 1793), 170, for an article on magicians in which the 'phantasmagore of Paris' is mentioned once again.
12. Breton, op. cit., and *La Feuille Villageoise*, op. cit.
13. *La Feuille Villageoise* 22, 506–7.
14. ibid.
15. ibid.
16. Anonymous article dated Paris, 22 March 1793, in *Journal des Luxus und der Moden*, April 1793, 230.
17. J.B. Montucla, *Histoire des Mathématiques*, new edition ed. Jérôme de Lalande, Vol. III (Paris, 1802), 551.

18. For example, *Les Fureurs de l'Amour* (Paris, 1799), or *Pelisson c'est le Diable* (Paris, 1807).

19. Hermann Hecht, 'The History of Projecting Phantoms', *New Magic Lantern Journal*, Vol. 3, No. 2 (December 1984), 2–6.

20. Pierre Delrée, 'Robertson, Physicien et Aéronaute Liégois', *La Vie Wallonne*, Vol. XXVIII (Liège, 1954); Françoise Levie, *Étienne-Gaspard Robertson* (Quebec: La Préambule, 1990). See also the entry in the Belgian *Biographie Nationale*, Vol. XIX (Brussels, 1906), 496–507. The first volume of Robertson's *Mémoires* was republished in 1985 (Langres: Café-Climat Éditeur). The original edition is now very rare: *Mémoires Récréatifs Scientifiques et Anecdotiques du Physicien-Aéronaute E.G. Robertson*, Paris, 1831 and 1833 (2 vols, advertised in *Bibliographie de la France* on 29 January 1831 and 1 March 1834).

21. Cited in Delrée, op. cit., 19.

22. Comte de Paroy, *Mémoires* (Paris, 1895), 282.

23. ibid.

24. *Les Mondes*, 23 (16 July 1863).

25. ibid.

26. *Affiches, Annonces et Avis Divers*, 121 (20 January 1798), 2224.

27. Chanoine Lecnau, *Histoire de Satan* (Paris, 1861), 438.

28. *Affiches, Annonces et Avis Divers*, 126 (25 January 1798), 2364.

29. *Affiches, Annonces et Avis Divers*, 137 (5 February 1798), 2495–6.

30. *Journal de Paris*, 124 (23 January 1798), 536–7.

31. *L'Ami des Lois*, 955 (28 March 1798), 1.

32. *Affiches, Annonces et Avis Divers*, 288 (16 July 1798), 5847.

33. Honoré de Balzac, *Les Illusions Perdues* (Paris: Gallimard, 1952), 944. Balzac also describes a phantasmagoria show (without naming it as such) in *La Peau de Chagrin*.

34. Étienne-Gaspard Robertson, French Patent 109 of 17 March 1799 (expired 17 March 1804).

35. Archives de Paris, D31 U3 C13, no. 91.

36. The reserve collection of the CNAM includes a square optical tube from a Fantascope, which is quite large and fitted with a 'cat's eye' diaphragm.

37. See Thomas Weynants, 'The Moisse-Weynants Fantascope', *New Magic Lantern Journal* Vol. 7, No. 2 (September 1994), 10–11.

38. Reports by Aubert, 10 June 1800 and 7 October 1800. Archives de Paris, DQ 10 256 and DQ 10 258.

39. *Affiches, Annonces et Avis Divers*, 109 (8 January 1799), 1891.

40. Undated eight-page programme (after Year IX [1800–1]) preserved at the Bibliothèque Nationale.

41. ibid.

42. E.J. Ingannato, *La Femme Invisible et son Secret Dévoilé* (Paris, n.d. [1800]); see also *Le Courrier des Spectacles*, starting 12 Pluviose Year VIII (31 January 1800).

43. ibid.

44. Robertson, *Mémoires*, Vol. I, 278.

45. *Courrier des Spectacles*, 1086 (23 February 1800), 4.

46. *Courrier des Spectacles*, 1092 (7 March 1800), 3.

47. Robertson, *Mémoires*, Vol. I, 297.

48. ibid.

49. Archives de Paris, report of 3 June 1800, D4 U1 21.

50. *Affiches, Annonces et Avis Divers*, 112 (11 January 1799), 1940.

51. *Affiches, Annonces et Avis Divers*, 149 (17 February 1799), 2572.

52. *Affiches, Annonces et Avis Divers*, 135 (3 February 1799), 2316.

53. *Affiches, Annonces et Avis Divers*, 180 (20 March 1799), 3179; 195 (4 April 1799), 3475.

54. *Affiches, Annonces et Avis Divers*, 170 (11 March 1800), 2719.

55. *Courrier des Spectacles*, 1189 (6 June 1800), 4.

56. Archives de Paris, report of 14 April 1800, D4 U1 21.

57. *L'Ami des Lois*, 1721 (26 May 1800), 3.

58. *Courrier des Spectacles*, 1189 (6 June 1800), 4.

59. Archives de Paris, report of 3 June 1800, D4 U1 21.

60. Archives de Paris, report by Jamin and Richer, 17 July 1800, D4 U1 21. Jamin noted that he had known Robertson for nine years, that is since 1791: 'He then called himself Robert, and attended my free course in physics.'

61. ibid.

62. ibid.

63. ibid.

64. ibid.

65. Archives de Paris, D4 U1 22.

66. Archives de Paris, D1 U1 C53, 22 April 1801 and 19 August 1802; D1 U1 C52, 9 September 1802; D1 U1 C57, 12 July 1803.

67. Robertson, *Mémoires*, Vol. I, 320–1.

68. For an excellent article on this subject see X. Theodore Barber, 'Phantasmagorical Wonders: The Magic Lantern ghost show in nineteenth-century America', *Film History* Vol. 3 (1989), 73–86.

69. For a fuller account of Philipstahl, see Mervyn Heard, 'Paul de Philipstahl and the Phantasmagoria in England, Scotland and Ireland', *New Magic Lantern Journal* Vol. 8, No. 1 (October 1996), 2–7; Vol. 8, No. 2 (October 1997), 11–16; and Vol. 8, No. 4 (December 1999), 6–13).

70. Paul de Philipstahl, British Patent 2,575 of 26 January 1802, 'Apparatus for Reflecting Objects'.

71. William Nicholson, 'Narrative and explanation of the appearance of phantoms and other figures in the exhibition of the Phantasmagoria', *Journal of Natural Philosophy*, February 1802, 147–50.

Chapter Seven: From Panorama to Daguerreotye, p. 176

1. Ralph Hyde, *Panoramania! The Art and Entertainment of the 'All-Embracing' View* (London: Trefoil/Barbican Centre, 1988).

2. Robert Barker, British Patent 1,612 of 19 June 1787, 'Apparatus for Exhibiting Pictures'. The full text of this patent is reprinted in Laurent Mannoni, Donata Pesenti Campagnoni, and David Robinson (eds), *Light and Movement: Incunabula of the Motion Picture 1420–1896* (Gemona: Cineteca del Friuli/Le Giornate del Cinema Muto, 1995), 157–8.

3. ibid.

4. *The Times*, 10 January 1792. A fuller text of this advertisement is given in Hecht, op. cit., item 99A.

5. *The Times*, 5 September 1793. See Hecht, op. cit., item 100A.

6. *Journal des Luxus und der Moden*, December 1800, 642–9.

7. *Journal des Luxus und der Moden*, June 1800, 290–2.

8. Robert Fulton, French Patent 46 of 25 February 1799. The document totals approximately 120 pages, including all the administrative matter.

9. ibid.
10. Robertson, *Mémoires*, Vol. I.
11. *Journal des Luxus und der Moden*, June 1800, 298.
12. *Courrier des Spectacles*, 1092 (1 March 1800), 3.
13. Archives de Paris, DQ 10 257 and 1367.
14. James Thayer, extension to Fulton, op. cit.
15. Pierre Prévost, French Patent of 15 April 1816.
16. *Journal d'Indications*, 2 January 1810.
17. *Gazette de France*, 26 June 1810.
18. Charles-François-Paul Delanglard, French Patents 1,779 of 25 March 1822 and 2,555 of 3 February 1825.
19. Charles Ogé Barbaroux, French Patent 3,540 of 4 February 1828.
20. Gué, French Patent 3,888 of 2 February 1829.
21. Georges Potonniée, *Daguerre Peintre et Décorateur* (Paris: repr. J.M. Place, 1989).
22. *Observations Critiques sue Quelques-uns des Tableaux les plus Remarquables de l'Exposition* (Paris, 1812), 7.
23. Alfred de Vigny, *Journal d'un Poète* (Paris, 1949), 13.
24. Archives de Paris, D31 U3 C20, no. 15.
25. *Journal des Théâtres*, 1318 (11 July 1822), 3.
26. Honoré de Balzac, letter to Laure Surville of Bayeux, 20 August 1822, in *Lettres à sa Famille* (Paris, 1950), 77–8.
27. *Journal des Théâtres*, 1321, (14 July 1822), 3.
28. Augustin Haton, French Patent of 21 March 1823.
29. Pierre Henri Amand Lefort, French Patents 7,974 of 21 February 1849 and 14,365 of 25 August 1852.
30. Undated programme (*c.*1834–7) in a private collection.
31. *Courrier des Théâtres*, 9 March 1839; cited in Potonniée, op. cit., 67.
32. *Le Moniteur de la Photographie*, 20 (15 October 1874), 156.
33. Thomas Wedgwood and Humphry Davy, 'An Account of a Method of Copying Paintings upon Glass and of Making Profiles, by the Agency of the Light upon Nitrate of Silver', *Journal of the Royal Institution*, Vol. 1, No. 9 (22 June 1802), 170–4.
34. Joseph-Nicéphore Niépce, *Lettres 1816–1817* (Rouen: Pavillon de la Photographie, 1973), 23.
35. Cited in Paul Jay, *Niépce: Genèse d'une Invention* (Chalon-sur-Saône, 1988), 106.
36. Niépce's paper was published in Daguerre's book *Historique et Description des Procédés du Daguerréotype et du Diorama* (Paris, 1839), 39–46.

Chapter Eight: The Pirouette of the Dancer, p. 201

1. For more discussion of this subject see Jacques Aumont, *L'Image* (Paris: Nathan, 1991).
2. Lucretius, *De Rerum Natura*, Book IV, 768–74, trans. R.C. Trevelyan (Cambridge: Cambridge University Press, 1937). In 1852, a German named Sinsteden noted this passage as an anticipation of Plateau's Phenakistiscope. He gave a dubious translation of Lucretius' verse; by way of reply Plateau published an interesting correction in *Le Cosmos*, 13 (25 July 1852), 308.
3. Leonardo da Vinci, *The Notebooks of Leonardo da Vinci*, Vol. I, trans. Edward MacCurdy (London: Jonathan Cape, 1938; new ed. 1956), 230.
4. Johannes Segner, *De Raritate Luminis* (Göttingen, 1740), 5–8.

5. Patrice d'Arcy, 'Mémoire sur la Durée de la Sensation de la Vue', *Histoire de l'Académie Royale des Sciences, Année 1765* (Paris, 1768), 439–51.

6. J.M., 'An Account of an Optical Deception', *Quarterly Journal of Science*, Vol. X (January 1821), 281–3.

7. Peter Mark Roget, 'Explanation of an Optical Deception in the Appearance of the Spokes of a Wheel seen Through Vertical Apertures', *Philosophical Transactions of the Royal Society of London*, 1825, Part I, 131–40.

8. For a fuller account of the thaumatrope, see John Barnes, *Dr Paris's Thaumatrope or Wonder-Turner* (London: The Projection Box, 1995).

9. Charles Babbage, *Passages from the Life of a Philosopher* (London, 1864). Cited in Henry Hopwood, *Living Pictures* (London, 1899), 5–6, and in Hecht, op. cit., item 237D.

10. Eugène Julia de Fontenelle, *Manuel de Physique Amusante* (Paris, 1826), 327.

11. Joseph Plateau, 'Sur la Durée des Sensations que les Couleurs Produisent dans l'Oeil', *Correspondence Mathématique et Physique*, Vol. III (Brussels, 1827), 27.

12. Plateau's thesis was reprinted in January 1930, in Maurice Noverre, *Le Nouvel Art Cinématographique* (Brest: Noverre, 1930).

13. Augustin Charpentier, *La Lumière et les Couleurs au Point de Vue Physiologique* (Paris, 1888); and A. and L. Lumière, *Cinématographe-Type*, undated 36-page pamphlet (*c.*1897) printed at Lyon. The German Max Skladanowsky projected at 16 images per second with his 'Bioskop' of 1895.

14. Plateau, 'Sur les Apparences que Présentent Deux Lignes qui Tournent Autour d'un Point, avec un Mouvement Angulaire Uniforme', letter dated 20 November 1828, published in *Correspondance Mathématique et Physique*, Vol. IV, 393.

15. Plateau, letter of 12 March 1829, in *Briefwisseling met A. Quetelet* (Brussels, 1948).

16. *Bulletin de l'Académie Royal des Sciences et Belles-Lettres de Bruxelles*, Vol. II (Brussels, 1836), 7.

17. Instruction leaflet for Plateau Anorthoscope (Paris, 1836).

18. Plateau, 'Lettre Adressée à MM. Les Rédacteurs des Annales de Physique et de Chimie sur une Illusion d'Optique', *Annales de Physique et de Chimie*, Vol. 48, No. 17 (1831), 281.

19. Michael Faraday, 'On a Peculiar Class of Optical Deceptions', *Journal of the Royal Institution*, Vol. I (1831), 205–23.

20. Plateau, 'Sur un Nouveau Genre d'Illusions d'Optique', *Correspondance Mathématique et Physique*, 6 (Brussels), 365–8. The title page of this volume is dated 1832, but Plateau's article must have appeared in February 1833.

21. ibid.

22. J.C. Poggendorff, 'Stroboskopische Scheiben, Phänakistikop, Phantasmaskop', *Annalen der Physik und Chemie*, Vol. XXXII, No. 40, 646–8.

23. Simon Stampfer and Mathias Trentsensky, Austrian Patent 1,920 of 7 May 1833, published in *Beschreibung der Erfindungen und Verbesserungen* (Vienna, 1843), 303. This translation is from Hecht, *Pre-Cinema History*, item 146C.

24. Poggendorff, op. cit.,, 647.

25. Plateau, *Bulletin de l'Académie Royale des Sciences et Belles-Lettres*, Vol. III, No. 1 (Brussels, 1836), 10.

26. W.G. Horner, 'On the Properties of the Daedaleum, a New Instrument of Optical Illusion', *The London and Edinburgh Philosophical Magazine and Journal of Sciences*, January 1834, 36–40.

27. Plateau, in J.F.W. Herschel, *Traité de la Lumière*, Vol. II (Paris, 1833), 489.

28. For a remarkable catalogue of stroboscopic discs see David Robinson, 'Masterpieces of Animation 1833–1908', *Griffithiana* 43 (December 1991).
29. Plateau, *Briefwisseling met A. Quetelet*.
30. Alphonse Giroux, French Patents 5,361 of 29 May 1833 (granted 5 August 1833), and 5,489 of 22 August 1833 (granted 16 November 1833).

Chapter Nine: The 'Vital Question' Resolved, p. 223

1. T.W. Naylor, letter in *The Mechanic's Magazine*, 1027 (15 April 1843), 319. This item is reproduced in full in Mannoni, Pesenti Campagnoni, and Robinson (eds), *Light and Movement: Incunabula of the Motion Picture 1420–1896*, 328.
2. Franz von Uchatius, 'Apparat zur Darstellung beweglicher Bilder an der Wand', *Sitzungsberichte der Mathematisch-naturwissenschaftlichen Klasse der Kaiserlichen Akademie der Wissenschaften*, 1853, 482–5.
3. ibid.
4. ibid.
5. Étienne-Jules Marey, letter to Georges Demenÿ, 24 January 1892.
6. Police file on Jules Duboscq, preserved at the CNAM (20 330/1); history of the Duboscq business in *Historique et Catalogue de Tous les Instruments d'Optique* (Paris, 1885). There is also an excellent study of the 'Duboscq years' by Gérard Turpin in *La Cinémathèque Française*, 19 (March 1987).
7. *Le Cosmos*, 17 (26 October 1855), 493.
8. I am grateful to Gérard Turpin for drawing this source to my attention.
9. This catalogue is in the collection of the CNAM.
10. J.H. Pepper, *Cyclopaedic Science Simplified* (London, 1869), 74, and *The Boy's Playbook of Science* (London, n.d. [*c*.1881]), 313.
11. Catalogue, *Instruments d'Optique et de Précision Ph. Pellin*, n.d. (after 1900); acquired by the CNAM in September 1903.
12. Augustin Gomez Santa Maria, French Patent 80,397 of 7 March 1868.
13. ibid.
14. Brown's device is described in Hopwood, *Living Pictures* (London, 1899), 46.
15. Thomas Ross, British Patents 681 of 6 March 1869 and 2,685 of 10 October 1871.
16. *La Nature*, 473 (24 June 1882), 64.
17. T.C. Hepworth, *The Book of the Lantern: Being a Practical Guide to the Working of the Optical (or Magic) Lantern* (London: Wyman & Sons, 1888), 97.
18. W.C. Hughes, British Patent 13,373 of 9 October 1884.
19. Potonniée, *Les Origins du Cinématographe* (Paris: Paul Montel, 1928), 20–1.
20. *Le Cosmos*, 9 (28 August 1857), 549.
21. *Le Cosmos*, 4 (23 May 1852), 79. Ferrier published numerous catalogues of stereoscopic and lantern pictures between 1857 and 1870. His business was then taken over by Léon and J. Lévy.
22. *Le Moniteur de la Photographie*, 6 (1 June 1861).
23. Jules Duboscq, French Patent 13,069, addition of 17 May 1852.
24. Plateau, 'Troisième Note sur de Nouvelles Applications Curieuses de la Persistance des Impressions de la Retine', *Bulletin de l'Académie Royale des Sciences de Bruxelles*, Vol. XVI, No. 7 (1849), 38–9.
25. *Le Moniteur de la Photographie*, 23 (1 December 1873), 180.
26. Duboscq, French Patent 13,069, addition of 12 November 1852.
27. ibid.
28. *Le Cosmos*, 6 (11 August 1854), 155.

29. *Le Cosmos*, 5 (29 May 1852), 103.
30. ibid.
31. *Le Cosmos*, 23 (3 October 1852), 541.
32. *Le Cosmos*, 2 (June 1853), 40.
33. Antoine Claudet, British Patent 711 of 23 March 1853.
34. Claudet's paper was published in French in *Le Moniteur de la Photographie* 15 (15 October 1865), 114–16, and reprinted (with commentary by Gérard Turpin) in *Antéciné* 1 (January 1990).
35. ibid.
36. As we shall see later, Georges Demenÿ borrowed the name 'Bioscope' for one of his cameras in 1895. The year after, throughout the world, numerous cinematographic dealers and manufacturers made free with it in their turn, to identify their film cameras and projectors. The term 'Photobioscope' was not destined for the same posterity, though there was one camera-projector of this name, marketed by the Paris company Sartony in 1896.
37. Henry Cook, paper presented on 2 August 1867, *Bulletin de la Société Française de Photographie*, Vol. XIII, No. 15 (August 1867), 201–2.
38. Gaetano Bonelli and Henry Cook, British Patent 2,063 of 19 August 1863.
39. Bonelli, British Patent 1,588 of 12 June 1865. Bonelli's French Patent 67,635 of 9 June 1865 made no reference to stereoscopy.
40. Cook, paper of 2 August 1867.
41. ibid.

Chapter Ten: Great Expectations, p. 248

1. J.H. Pepper and H. Dircks, French Patent 58,286 of 11 April 1863; J.H. Pepper and T.W. Tobin, French Patents 67,596 of 30 May 1865 and 79,230 of 18 January 1868. The equivalent British Patents are listed in the Bibliography.
2. *Les Mondes*, Vol. I, No. 21 (2 July 1863), 577–8.
3. ibid.
4. Henri Robin, *L'Almanach Le Cagliostro* (Paris, 1864), 19–20.
5. Pierre Séguin, French Patent 14,977 of 20 November 1852 for the Animated Polyorama. The French patent for the Polyoscope was number 14,510 of 16 September 1852.
6. Séguin, French Patent 14,977, addition of 26 April 1860.
7. ibid.
8. *L'Annuaire de Commerce de Paris*, 1856. Another dealer named Séguin appeared in *L'Annuaire de Commerce*, between 1887 and 1896, at 14 Boulevard Saint-Michel.
9. *Le Voyageur Forain*, 13 (1–30 September 1884).
10. Henry Désiré du Mont, French Patent 42,843 of 17 November 1859.
11. Du Mont, French Patent 49,520 of 2 May 1861.
12. For more on '*cartes de visite*' and French photography in general, see the excellent account given in André Rouillé, *La Photographie en France* (Paris: Macula, 1989).
13. *Le Moniteur de la Photographie*, 2 (15 January 1862), 168.
14. Louis Ducos du Hauron, French Patent 61,976 of 1 March 1864.
15. ibid.
16. ibid.
17. ibid.
18. Ducos du Hauron, French Patent 61,976, addition of 3 December 1864.

19. ibid.
20. *Le Petit Bleu du Lot-et-Garonne*, 2 September 1920.
21. Ducos du Hauron, French Patent 259,399 of 2 August 1896.
22. ibid.
23. Programme, *Ninth Entertainment of the Young Men's Society of St. Mark's Evangelical Lutheran Church, Philadelphia, to be given at the Academy of Music by O.H. Willard, Esq., on Saturday Evening, February 5th, 1870. In aid of the library fund.* See Hecht, *Pre-Cinema History*, item 257A.
24. H.R. Heyl, 'A Contribution to the History of the Art of Photographing Living Subjects in Motion, and Reproducing the Natural Movements by the Lantern', *Journal of the Franklin Institute*, 4 (April 1898), 310–1.
25. Four images of the dancers are reproduced in Frederick A. Talbot, *Moving Pictures* (Philadelphia, n.d. [1923]), 12.
26. Moigno used this phrase to describe the stereoscope and the importance of photography for its effectiveness. See *Le Cosmos*, 1 (May 1852), 9.

Chapter Eleven: The Magic Lantern: A Sovereign and her Subjects, p. 264

1. This image is reproduced in W.F. Ryan, 'Limelight on Eastern Europe: the Great Dissolving Views at the Royal Polytechnic', in *The Ten Year Book* (London: Magic Lantern Society of Great Britain, 1986), 48–55. For more on the Poly- technic see Abbé Moigno, 'Nouvelles d'Angleterre', *Le Cosmos*, 4 (28 July 1854), 85–7.
2. These images are reproduced in Ryan, op. cit. See also 'Lantern Slides in the Oxford Museum', in Dennis Crompton, David Henry, and Stephen Herbert (eds), *Magic Images* (London: Magic Lantern Society, 1990), 71–4.
3. T.C. Hepworth, *The Book of the Lantern: Being a Practical Guide to the Working of the Optical (or Magic) Lantern* (London: Wyman & Sons, 1888), 97.
4. Hepworth, op. cit., 181.
5. Hepworth, op. cit., 182.
6. Eugène Delacroix, *Journal*, Vol. I (Paris: Plon, 1932), 215.
7. *Annuaire du Commerce de Paris* (Paris, 1853), 'Revue Industrielle' section, 2248.
8. *Le Cosmos*, 16 (15 August 1852).
9. Abbé Moigno, *L'Art des Projections* (Paris, 1872), I–II.
10. ibid.
11. *Les Mondes*, Vol. XXVII, No. 5 (1 February 1872), 177.
12. Moigno, op. cit., IX–X.
13. Moigno, *Enseignement de tous par les Projections . . . Catalogue des Tableaux et Appareils* (Paris, n.d. [1882]), V.I.
14. Henri Robin, *L'Almanach Le Cagliostro* (Paris, 1864), 9.
15. *Secrets et Mystères de la Sorcellerie* (Paris, 1865), 308.
16. J. Mistler, *La Librairie Hachette* (Paris, 1964), 154.
17. *L'Illustration*, 23 July 1864, 63.
18. See Alber, *La Projection au XXe Siècle* (Paris: Mazo, n.d. [1904], among other titles.
19. D. Hoffmann and A. Junker, *Laterna Magica* (Berlin, 1982). This very fine album contains reproductions of most of Hoffmann's slides.
20. Léon Bloy, *Journal*, May 1897 (Paris, 1963), 222–3.
21. *Photo-Journal*, 62 (February 1895), 39.
22. *Paris-Photographe*, 9 (30 December 1891).

23. *Le Fascinateur*, 2 (1 February 1903), 37.

24. Lerebours, *Notice d'Instruments de Physique, d'Optique et de Mathématique* (Paris, 1809), 7–8.

25. Auguste Lapierre, French Patent 44,516 of 29 March 1860.

26. John Barnes, 'A List of Magic Lantern Manufacturers and Dealers Active During the Nineteenth Century' in Crompton, Henry and Herbert (eds), *Magic Images*, 19–30. This excellent list covers all the major participants, but its 112 entries are by no means a complete survey of the nineteenth-century British lantern trade and much work remains to be done on this subject.

27. See John Barnes, 'Philip Carpenter', *New Magic Lantern Journal*, Vol. 3, No. 2 (December 1984), 8–9.

28. Marcel Proust, *À la Recherche du Temps Perdu* (Paris: Gallimard/Pléiade, 1978), 9. The story of Geneviève de Brabant was also later adapted for the cinema by the Pathé company in 1907.

Chapter Twelve: The Passge of Venus and the Galloping Horse, p. 299

1. Jules Janssen, *Oeuvres Scientifiques*, Vol. I (Paris, 1929), 304.

2. ibid., 312–13.

3. ibid., 308; *La Nature*, 99 (24 April 1875), 335.

4. *Année Scientifique et Industrielle*, 1876 (Paris, 1877), 528.

5. Janssen, op. cit., 339.

6. Étienne-Jules Marey, 'Moteurs Animés, Expériences de Physiologie Graphique', *La Nature* 279 (5 October 1878), 295. See also Solange Vernois, 'L'Esthétique de Mouvement et ses Polémiques au XIXe Siècle', *Hommage à E.J. Marey* (Beaune: Musée Marey, 1991), 15–36.

7. See for example Gordon Hendricks, *Eadweard Muybridge: The Father of the Motion Picture* (London: Secker & Warburg, 1975); Robert B. Haas, *Muybridge: Man in Motion* (Los Angeles and London, 1976); *Eadweard Muybridge*, catalogue of German exhibition, 1976.

8. Hendricks, op. cit., 29.

9. Terry Ramsaye, *A Million and One Nights* (London, 1964), 23.

10. *La Nature*, 303 (22 March 1879), 246.

11. This beautiful disc is reproduced in Marshall Deutelbaum, *'Image' on the Art and Evolution of the Film* (Rochester, New York, 1979), 3.

12. *Daily Alta California*, 7 April 1873, cited in Hendricks, op. cit., 47.

13. ibid.

14. *Le Moniteur de la Photographie*, 12 (15 June 1873), 94.

15. Cited in Hendricks, op. cit., 99.

16. *Daily Alta California*, 11 August 1877, cited in Hendricks, op. cit., 101.

17. Eadweard Muybridge, British Patent 2,746 of 9 July 1878; US Patents 212,864 of 11 July 1878 and 212,865 of 27 June 1878; French Patent 125,692 of 17 July 1878. Muybridge also filed a patent in France, on 21 December 1877, for a 'mechanism for distributing the time accurately to a series of dials spaced from each other'.

18. Muybridge, British Patent 2,746 of 9 July 1878. The full text is reprinted in Mannoni, Pesenti Campagnoni, and Robinson (eds), *Light and Movement: Incunabula of the Motion Picture 1420–1896*, 270–7.

19. ibid.

20. The company Brandon & Sons was founded in Paris on 29 May 1889 by David,

Raphaël, and Douglas Brandon, along with Mary Nelson Bartlett, to operate an engineering research bureau. The Brandons acted as Muybridge's patent agents in France.

21. *La Nature*, 289 (14 December 1878), 23–6.
22. *Le Moniteur de la Photographie*, 16 April 1879.
23. *Le Globe*, 27 September 1881, 2.
24. *La Nature*, 436 (8 October 1881), 303.
25. Henry James, *Parisian Sketches: Letters to the* New York Tribune *1875–1876*. Ed. Leon Edel and Ilse Dusoir Lind (London: Hart-Davis, 1958), 33–7.
26. Jacques Deslandes, *Histoire Comparée du Cinéma*, Vol. I (Tournai, 1966), 101.
27. Jean-Louis Meissonnier, letter preserved in a private collection.
28. *Le Temps*, 29 November 1881, 3.
29. Reprinted in *Le Moniteur de la Photographie*, 21 (1 November 1882), 167.
30. The list here is compiled from Eadweard Muybridge, *Muybridge's Complete Human and Animal Locomotion: all 781 Plates from the 1887 Animal Locomotion*. 3 vols. (New York: Dover Publications, 1979).

Chapter Thirteen: Marey Releases the Dove, p. 320

1. Cited in Charles A. François-Franck, *L'Oeuvre de E.-J. Marey* (Paris, 1905), 8.
2. *Paris-Photographe*, 1894, 3–4.
3. ibid.
4. Étienne-Jules Marey, *Du Mouvement dans les Fonctions de la Vie* (Paris, 1868), 6.
5. Marey, *Physiologie Médicale de la Circulation du Sang* (Paris, 1863), 4.
6. ibid., 9 and 47.
7. Bréguet catalogue, *Instruments de Physiologie de E.-J. Marey* (Paris, 1884). The Sphygmographe cost 120 Francs, the Myographe 100 Francs, and the Polygraphe 450 Francs.
8. Marey, *Animal Mechanism: A Treatise on Terrestrial and Aerial Locomotion* (2nd ed. London: Henry S. King & Co., 1874), 2–3.
9. ibid., 137.
10. François-Franck, op. cit., 11.
11. Ernest Onimus, 'Applications de la Photographie à l'étude des mouvements du coeur chez les animaux inférieurs', *Journal de l'Anatomie et de la Physiologie*, Vol. II, No. 22, 337–40.
12. *Bulletin de la Société Française de Photographie*, July 1869, 172–7.
13. ibid.
14. Gérard Turpin, 'Aux sources de la chronophotographie', *La Cinémathèque Française*, April 1987.
15. *L'Aéronaute*, 3 (March 1874), 90–100.
16. ibid.
17. ibid.
18. Marey, *La Méthode Graphique dans les Sciences Expérimentales et Principalement en Physiologie et en Médecine* (Paris, 1878).
19. *La Nature*, 291 (28 December 1878), 54.
20. Marey, *La Méthode Graphique*, 2nd ed. (Paris, 1885), 12.
21. Cited in R. Buhot, *La Voix de Marey* (Boulogne, 1939), 45.
22. Étienne-Jules Marey, letter to Georges Demenÿ, 4 March 1882. The Marey-Demenÿ correspondence cited in this chapter is preserved at the Cinémathèque Française and is to be published in Thierry Lefebvre, Jacques Malthête, and Laurent Mannoni

(eds), *Correspondance Marey-Demenÿ* (Paris: AFRHC-BiFi, 2000). Other letters by Marey and Demenÿ in private collections have also been consulted.

23. *Comptes-Rendus de l'Académie des Sciences*, Vol. 94 (1882), No. 11, 683–4.
24. *Comptes-Rendus de l'Académie des Sciences*, Vol. 94, No. 15, 1013–20.
25. Louis Olivier, 'La Photographie du Mouvement', *La Revue Scientifique*, 26 (23 December 1882), 802–11.
26. Georges Demenÿ, *Les Bases Scientifiques de l'Éducation Physique* (Paris, 1902), 7.
27. Henry Joly, who was to become one of the main rivals of Louis Lumière in 1895, also worked at the École de Gymnastique.
28. Marey, *La Revue Scientifique (Revue Rose)*, Vol. II, No. 26 (29 December 1894).
29. *Journal Officiel*, Parliamentary Debates, sitting of 27 July 1882, 1460.
30. ibid.
31. ibid.
32. Marey, letter to Georges Demenÿ, 24 November 1883.
33. See Michel Frizot, *La Chronophotographie* (Beaune: Association des Amis de Marey, 1984).
34. Marey, 'La Station Physiologique de Paris', *La Nature*, 539 (29 September 1883), 275–9.
35. Marey, 'La Photochronographie', *Archives de Physiologie Normale et Pathologique*, 5th series, Vol. I, No. 29, 508–17.
36. Marey, letter to Georges Demenÿ, 29 June 1883.
37. Marta Braun, *Picturing Time: The Work of E.J. Marey* (Chicago, 1992). Michel Frizot includes some fine Marey images in *La Chronophotographie*, op. cit., and *E.J. Marey* (Paris: Photo-Poche, 1984).
38. *Le Moniteur de la Photographie*, 3 (1 February 1887), 21.
39. *Comptes-Rendus de l'Académie des Sciences*, Vol. 107, No. 16, 607.
40. *Comptes-Rendus de l'Académie des Sciences*, Vol. 107, No. 18, 677.
41. Marey, French Patent 208,617 of 3 October 1890, 'for a photochronographic device'.
42. *Comptes-Rendus de l'Académie des Sciences*, Vol. 111, No. 18, 627.
43. *Paris-Photographe*, 1 (25 April 1891), 7–8.
44. *Le Temps*, 12 October 1893.
45. Marey, letter to Georges Demenÿ, 4 August 1892.
46. *Bulletin de l'AFITEC*, special issue on Marey, 1954, 4–5.
47. Londe was the author of *La Photographie Moderne* (Paris, 1896) and *La Photographie Instantanée* (Paris, 1897), in which he described his research. For a very good study of Londe see Denis Bernard and André Gunthert, *L'Instant Rêvé Albert Londe* (Nîmes-Laval: Jacqueline Chambon-Trois, 1993).
48. Léon-Guillaume Bouly, French Patents 219,350 of 12 February 1892, for 'a photographic device for the automatic and uninterrupted achievement of a series of photographs analysing movement known as the Cinématographe'; 235,100 of 27 December 1893, for the 'Cinématographe Léon Bouly'; and 419,771 of 22 August 1910 (granted to Léon Bouly and Abel Chollet), for a 'flexible strip phonograph'.
49. See Brian Coe, 'W. Friese-Greene and the Origins of Kinematography', *Photographic Journal* Vol. 102, Nos 3 and 4 (March and April 1962).
50. *Ciné-Journal*, 11–17 July 1909.
51. Louis Aimé Augustin Le Prince, US Patent 376,247 of 10 January 1888; British Patent 423 of 10 January 1888; French Patent 188,089 of 11 January 1888. For more on Le Prince, see G. Potonniée, 'La Vie et les Travaux de Le Prince', *Bulletin de la SFP*, 5 (May 1931); E. Kilburn Scott, 'Career of Le Prince', *Journal of the*

SMPE, 17 (July 1931); J. Vivié, 'Le Prince, son Oeuvre et son Destin', *Bulletin de l'AFITEC*, 29 (1969); and Christopher Rawlence, *The Missing Reel* (London: Collins, 1990).

52. Cited in Jean Vivié, 'Un précurseur oublié: L.A. Augustin Le Prince, son oeuvre et son destin', *Bulletin de l'AFITEC*, 29 (1969), 9.

53. See Deac Rossell, *Ottomar Anschütz and his Electrical Wonder* (London: The Projection Box, 1997) for a good account of Anschütz's chronophotographic work.

54. An excellent account of Donisthorpe and Crofts is given by Stephen Herbert and Mo Heard, *Industry, Liberty and a Vision: Wordsworth Donisthorpe's Kinesigraph* (London: The Projection Box, 1998).

55. *Comptes-Rendus de l'Académie des Sciences*, Vol. 94, 989.

56. Marey, letters to Georges Demenÿ, dates as cited.

57. Marey, *Movement*, trans. Eric Pritchard (London: William Heinemann, 1895), 318.

58. *La Photographie*, 10 (December 1892).

59. Albert Londe, 'La Reproduction du Mouvement par la Photographie', *Le Chasseur Français*, 133 (15 June 1896), 16.

60. Marey, letter to Georges Demenÿ, 29 March 1889.

61. J.J. Meusy and V. Schwartz, 'Le Musée Grévin et le Cinématographe: l'Histoire d'une Rencontre', *1895*, 11, 26.

62. Demenÿ, French Patent 219,830 of 3 March 1892.

63. *La Photographie*, 10 (December 1892).

64. Marey, letter to Georges Demenÿ, 20 April 1892.

65. Marey, letters to Georges Demenÿ, dates as cited.

66. Martin Loiperdinger and Roland Cosandey, *Des Sous Comme s'il en Pleuvait: Quatre Documents pour Servir à l'Histoire du Cinématographe* (Lausanne: Université de Lausanne, 1992); and 'L'Introduction du Cinématographe en Allemagne', *Archives* 51 (November 1992).

67. ibid.

68. ibid.

69. Marey, letter to François Lavanchy-Clarke, 15 July 1893.

70. Marey, letter to Georges Demenÿ, 25 July 1893.

71. Marey, French Patent 231,209 of 29 June 1893.

72. Demenÿ, French Patent 233,337 of 10 October 1893.

73. Demenÿ, *Les Origines du Cinématographe* (Paris: Henry Paulin, 1909), 25.

74. This document was kindly drawn to my attention by Mme Marion Leuba, curator of the Musée Marey at Beaune.

Chapter Fourteen: The Big Wheel of Little Mirrors, p. 364

1. Article in *La Haute-Loire*, cited in Maurice Noverre, *Émile Reynaud: Sa Vie et ses Travaux* (Brest, 1926), 23. Noverre's book, the work of a passionate and courageous historian, remains indispensable.

2. Émile Reynaud, *Cours Publics de Sciences Physiques: Première Leçon* (Le Puy, 1874), 22.

3. Noverre, op. cit.

4. Reynaud, French Patent 120,484 of 30 August 1877 and British Patent 4,244 of 13 November 1877.

5. Mme Burée, 'La Bimbeloterie', *Études sur l'Exposition de 1878*, Vol. VII (Paris, 1879), 114–15.

6. The various different designs of Praxinoscope, its strips, discs and publicity

materials, were listed in Laurent Mannoni, 'Inventaire du Matériel Commercialisé d'Émile Reynaud', paper given at the International Conference on Émile Reynaud held at the Cinémathèque Française on 31 October 1992.

7. *Les Mondes*, Vol. 49, No. 6 (5 June 1879), 229.
8. Reynaud, French Patent 120,484, addition of 7 January 1879.
9. *Bulletin de la Société Française de Photographie*, Vol. 26, No. 6 (June 1880), 153–4.
10. Reynaud, French Patent 194,482 of 1 December 1888.
11. ibid.
12. This document is preserved at the Cinémathèque Française.
13. H. Fourtier, *Les Tableaux de Projections Mouvementées* (Paris, 1893), 2.
14. *Journal de Rouen*, 339 (4 December 1892), 2.
15. *La Nature*, Vol. 20 (23 July 1892), 127.
16. *Journal de Rouen*, 338 (3 December 1892).
17. Illustrated brochure of the Musée Grévin, n.d. (1892).
18. According to Julien Pappé, one small section of the original picture strip for *Autour d'une Cabine* survives.
19. Julien Lefèvre, *L'Électricité au Théâtre*, (Paris, n.d.[1894]), 228.
20. Marey, *Le Mouvement* (Paris, 1894), 306.
21. Noverre, op. cit., 46. The Lumières referred to the Reynaud Praxinoscope in their French Patent 243,543 of 14 December 1894, filed shortly before their patent for the Cinématographe. This related to a method for synthesizing colours from a succession of monochrome images, using a device related to the zoetrope or Praxinoscope modified for that purpose.
22. Noverre, op. cit., 65.

Chapter Fifteen: Edison and his 'Films Through the Keyhole', p. 387

1. George Sand, letter to her son dated 3 February 1870, in *Correspondance*, Vol. XXI (Paris, Garnier, 1986), 811.
2. Cited in Gordon Hendricks, *The Edison Motion Picture Myth* (Berkeley and Los Angeles: University of California Press, 1961), 12.
3. *New York World*, 3 June 1888, cited in Charles Musser, *The Emergence of Cinema: The American Screen to 1907* (New York: Charles Scribner's Sons, 1990), 62.
4. *Nature*, Vol. XVII, No. 430 (24 January 1878), 242. See also Wordsworth Donisthorpe, British Patents 4,344 of 9 November 1876 and 12,921 of 15 August 1889, and Herbert and Heard, *Industry, Liberty and a Vision*, 30ff.
5. Cited in Hendricks, *The Edison Motion Picture Myth*, 158.
6. See Hendricks, *The Edison Motion Picture Myth*, and *The Kinetoscope: America's First Commercially Successful Motion Picture Exhibitor* (New York: Beginnings of the American Film, 1966); Musser, *The Emergence of Cinema*, and *Before the Nickelodeon: Edwin S. Porter and the Edison Manufacturing Company* (Berkeley and Los Angeles: University of California Press, 1991).
7. In France, somewhat later, Georges Demenÿ was also the inventor of an optical phonograph, patented as an addition dated 25 August 1892.
8. Cited in Hendricks, *The Edison Motion Picture Myth*, 24.
9. Henri Fourtier, *La Photographie et ses Applications*, extract from technical review of the Exposition Universelle (Paris, 1891), 253.
10. *Phonogram*, May 1891, 122–3, cited in Musser, *The Emergence of Cinema*, 68.
11. 'The Kinetograph', *New York Sun* 28 May 1891, 2, cited in Musser, *The Emergence of Cinema*, 71.

12. *Harper's Weekly*, 13 June 1891, cited in Martin Quigley, Jr., *Magic Shadows: The Story of the Origin of Motion Pictures* (Washington, D.C.: Georgetown University Press, 1948), 135.

13. Léo Backelant, 'Le Kinétographe', letter dated 28 May 1891 to the Belgian periodical *Hélios*, reproduced in *Le Moniteur de la Photographie*, 13 (1 July 1891), 98–9. See also *Le Cosmos*, 339 (25 July 1891).

14. *Le Moniteur de la Photographie*, 13 (1 July 1891), 99.

15. *Annuaire Général et International de la Photographie* (Paris, 1895), 15.

16. *La Nature*, 1116 (2 October 1894), 323–6.

17. *Le Figaro*, 8 May 1893, 1.

18. ibid.

19. ibid.

20. ibid.

21. Thomas Edison, *The Diary and Sundry Observations of Thomas Alva Edison*, ed. Dagobert D. Runes (New York: Philosophical Library, 1948), 69.

22. Cited in Musser, *The Emergence of Cinema*, 75.

23. ibid, 84. The films were sold for between $10 and $15.

24. *Washington Evening Star*, 8 October 1894, cited in Hendricks, *The Kinetoscope*, 63.

25. *Annuaire Général et International de la Photographie* (Paris, 1895), 16.

26. Kemp R. Niver, *Early Motion Pictures: The Paper Print Collection in the Library of Congress* (Washington D.C., 1985), 86–7.

27. Frédéric Dillaye, *Les Nouveautés Photographiques* (Paris, 1895), 158–9.

28. Some frame reproductions from this film appear in Dickson's own book on the Kinetoscope: W.K.-L. Dickson and Antonia Dickson, *History of the Kinetograph, Kinetoscope and Kinetophonograph* (New York, Albert Bunn, 1895).

29. *Newark Evening News*, 17 July 1894, cited in Hendricks, *The Kinetoscope*, 77–8.

30. *Hélios Illustré*, 128 (15 August 1895), 127.

31. *Le Magasin Pittoresque*, 1 August 1894.

32. ibid.

33. *Les Annales Politiques et Littéraires*, 19 August 1894.

34. Archives de Paris, D31U3 C247, no. 1846.

35. *L'Industriel Forain*, 264 (26 August–2 September 1894).

36. Henri de Parville, *Le Journal des Débats*, 14 November 1894, 1. The article was reprinted in *Les Annales Politiques et Littéraires*, 13 January 1895.

37. Archives de Paris, D31U3 C270, no. 2249.

38. De Parville, *Le Journal des Débats*, 14 November 1894.

39. *L'Industriel Forain*, 288 (10–16 February 1895).

40. See Marcel Proust, *À la Recherche du Temps Perdu*, Vol. 1 (Paris: Pléiade, 1978), 7. Proust makes this passing metaphorical reference to the Kinetoscope in the early pages of *Swann's Way*; the classic English translation by C.K. Scott Moncrieff, *Remembrance of Things Past*, (mis)renders this as 'Bioscope'.

41. Archives de Paris, D31U3 C276, no. 233.

42. Cited in Jacques Deslandes and Jacques Richard, *Histoire comparée du cinéma*, Vol. 2 (Tournai: Casterman, 1968), 115.

43. *L'Industriel Forain*, 2 August 1896.

44. Eugène Werner, French Patent 248,254 of 18 June 1895.

45. *L'Industriel Forain*, 342 (23–29 February 1896).

46. Cited in F.V. Zglinicki, *Der Weg des Films* (Berlin, 1956).

47. *L'Industriel Forain*, 302 (19–25 May 1895).

48. *L'Industriel Forain*, 344 (8–14 March 1896).

49. *L'Industriel Forain*, 302 (19–25 May 1895).
50. *L'Industriel Forain*, 323 (13–19 October 1895).
51. For more details see Laurent Mannoni, '1894–1895: Les Années Parisiennes du Kinetoscope Edison', *Cinémathèque*, Spring–Summer 1993, 47–57.

Chapter Sixteen: The Labourers of the Eleventh Hour, p. 416

1. See Matthew, xx, 1–16.
2. This contract is preserved in the Archives Marcel Demenÿ, Paris.
3. ibid.
4. Léon Gaumont, letter to Georges Demenÿ, 7 September 1895.
5. The deed of foundation of the company is preserved in the Archives of the Département of Rhône.
6. Cited in Jacques Deslandes, *Histoire Comparée du Cinéma* (Tournai, 1966), 213.
7. G. Michel Coissac, *Histoire du Cinématographe* (Paris, 1925), 243–6; *Ciné-Tribune*, 6 (8 July 1920), 63–4.
8. Louis Lumière, letter to Georges Demenÿ, 9 October 1894.
9. In recent years the name 'Domitor' has been revived as the name of the International Association to Promote the Study of Early Cinema. For more information see the Domitor web site, http://cri.histart.umontreal.ca/domitor
10. See, among other recent publications: Bernard Chardère, Guy and Marjorie Borgé *Les Lumière* (Lausanne: Payot, 1985); Jacques Rittaud-Hutinet, *Les Frères Lumière et Leurs Opérateurs* (Seyssel: Champ Vallon, 1985); and Vincent Pinel, *Lumière* (Paris: Anthologie du Cinéma, 1974).
11. Léo Sauvage, *L'Affaire Lumière* (Paris, Lherminier, 1985).
12. Cited in Georges Sadoul, *Lumière et Méliès* (Paris: Lherminier, 1985), 12.
13. Interview with Auguste Lumière, *Paris-Match*, 260 (20–7 March 1954).
14. Pinel, op. cit.
15. This is to leave aside the story of Jean Acme Le Roy, a pioneer who may have projected films in 1894. Some American historians have thrown strong doubt on Le Roy's claims; his projector, photographed by Merritt Crawford, bears a strong resemblance to devices made after 1896.
16. Auguste and Louis Lumière, French Patent 242,032 of 13 February 1895.
17. *Bulletin du Photo-Club de Paris*, April 1895, 125.
18. ibid. On the various different versions of the film mentioned here, *La Sortie des Usines Lumière*, see Pinel, op. cit.
19. Jules Carpentier, French Patent 246,246 of 30 March 1895.
20. Eugène Lauste had founded a company in Paris on 1 October 1878, along with Léon Wyder, to deal in electrical signal bells and other electrical equipment, based at 193 Rue du Faubourg Poissonnière. Lauste went to work for Edison at the New York electrical supply company in 1887, and moved to West Orange in the following year.
21. *New York Sun*, 22 April 1895, reproduced in Terry Ramsaye, *A Million and One Nights: A History of the Motion Picture* (London: Frank Cass & Co., 1964), facing 137.
22. ibid.
23. *New York World*, 28 May 1895, 30, cited in Charles Musser, *The Emergence of Cinema: The American Screen to 1907* (New York: Charles Scribner's Sons, 1990), 96.
24. Poster for Latham Eidoloscope, reproduced in Musser, *The Emergence of Cinema*, 98.

25. Thomas Armat, 'My Part in the Development of the Motion Picture Projector', *Journal of the SMPE*, Vol. 24, March 1935; biographical note, *Journal of the SMPE*, Vol. 25, December 1935.
26. C. Francis Jenkins, 'The Phantoscope', *Journal of the Franklin Institute*, Vol. 145, No. 1 (January 1898), 79; and *Animated Pictures* (Washington, D.C., 1898).
27. Cited in Musser, *The Emergence of Cinema*, 103.
28. *Atlanta Journal*, 21 October 1895, cited in Musser, *The Emergence of Cinema*, 104.
29. ibid.
30. For more on Paul's early activities, see John Barnes, *The Beginnings of the Cinema in England 1894–1901*, Vol. 1 (Exeter: University of Exeter Press, 1998).
31. Maurice Noverre, *Le Nouvel Art Cinématographique*, 5 (January 1930), 65.
32. Henri Joly, French Patent 249,875 of 26 August 1895.
33. *Annuaire du Commerce de Paris*, 1896 edition, 1720 and 2104.
34. Charles Pathé, *De Pathé Frères à Pathé Cinéma* (Lyon: Premier Plan, 1970), 29.
35. Pathé, *Souvenirs et Conseils d'un Parvenu* (Nice, 1922), 78. For more on Mendel, see Laurent Mannoni, 'Du Cinématographe Parisien au Cinémato-Gramo-Théâtre: Georges Mendel, Pionnier du Cinéma 'Muet' et Sonore', *Archives* 53 (April 1993).
36. ibid.
37. *L'Industriel Forain*, 352 (3–9 May 1896).
38. Pathé, *Souvenirs et Conseils d'un Parvenu*.
39. Archives de Paris, D31U3 C311, no. 2066. Charles Pathé had already founded a joint stock company on 20 March 1896, in partnership with the Widow Fourel of Neuilly-Plaisance, for 'the exploitation of a café-restaurant establishment known by the name of the Café de la Finance'. In the deed of foundation of that company, Pathé gave his address as 1 Rue Monsieur le Prince, Paris; the company was based at 66 Rue de Provence, and capitalized at 50,000 Francs.
40. Cited in *Bulletin de l'AFITEC*, special issue 1952, 7.
41. Léon Gaumont, letter to Félix Richard, 12 January 1896.
42. *La Revue Trimestrielle*, August 1895.
43. Georges Demenÿ, *Les Origines du Cinématographe* (Paris, 1909).
44. The Cinémathèque Française has a letter from Richard to Demenÿ, dated 25 February 1895. A second letter, dated 3 April 1895, is signed by Gaumont, 'pp. F-M. Richard', and was probably dictated by Richard. In a third letter of 25 July 1895, Gaumont signed on his own behalf, and it was he alone whe took on the project for commercializing the Demenÿ equipment.
45. Contract between Georges Demenÿ and Léon Gaumont, 22 August 1895, reproduced in Marie-Sophie Corcy, Jacques Malthête, Laurent Mannoni and Jean-Jacques Meusy (eds), *Les Premières Années de la Société L. Gaumont et Cie.: Correspondance Commerciale de Léon Gaumont 1895–1899* (Paris: AFRHC, 1998), 452–5.
46. ibid.
47. Anon (probably Demenÿ), *Chronophotographie Pour Tous* (Paris, n.d.), 3.
48. ibid.
49. Anon, *Notice sur le Bioscope* (Paris, n.d.), 4.
50. ibid.
51. Contract between Demenÿ and Gaumont, 6 May 1896. Reprinted in Corcy et al., op. cit., 455–61.
52. ibid.
53. Charles Thirion, letter to Léon Gaumont, 27 February 1896. Reprinted in Corcy et al., op. cit., 429.

54. E. Lousteau of Le Blenil, Dordogne, letter to Léon Gaumont, 12 December 1896; a photographer named E. Galinou from Montauban wrote on the same subject on the same date. Reprinted in Corcy et al., op. cit., 431–2.

55. Alphonse Rateau, undated letter to Georges Demenÿ [late 1896?]. Reprinted in Corcy et al., op. cit., 432–4.

56. Cited in *Le Cinéopse*, 16 (December 1920), 534.

57. Jules Carpentier, letter to Louis Lumière, 22 December 1895. The Lumière correspondence cited in this chapter was previously published in Jacques Rittaud-Hutinet (ed.), *Auguste et Louis Lumière: Correspondances 1890–1953* (Paris: Cahiers du Cinéma, 1994), and in English (in a different translation) as Auguste and Louis Lumière, *Letters*, trans. Pierre Hodgson (London: Faber & Faber, 1995).

58. Louis Lumière, letter to Jules Carpentier, 14 October 1895.

59. Louis Lumière, letter to Jules Carpentier, 2 November 1895.

60. Carpentier, letter to Louis Lumière, 4 November 1895.

61. See Laurent Mannoni, 'George William de Bedts et la Commercialisation de la Chronophotographie' in *Les vingt premières années du cinéma français: actes du colloque international de la Sorbonne Nouvelle* (Paris: PSN/AFRHC, 1995).

62. ibid.

63. Carpentier, letter to Louis Lumière, 4 November 1895.

64. ibid.

65. Louis Lumière, letter to Jules Carpentier, 11 November 1895.

66. Louis Lumière, letter to Jules Carpentier, 25 November 1895.

67. Carpentier, letter to Louis Lumière, 2 December 1895.

68. Carpentier, letter to Louis Lumière, 9 December 1895.

69. Carpentier, letter to Louis Lumière, 22 December 1895.

70. ibid.

71. Paul Müller, German Patent 92,247 of 25 August 1895.

72. F. von Zglinicki, *Der Weg des Films* (Berlin, 1956), 241. See also M. Lichtenstein, 'The Brothers Skladanowsky', in Paolo Cherchi Usai and L. Codelli (eds), *Prima di Caligari* (Pordenone, 1990), 312–5; and Joachim Castan, *Max Skladanowsky: oder der Beginn einer deutschen Filmgeschichte* (Stuttgart: Füsslin Verlag, 1995).

73. Louis Lumière, letter to Jules Carpentier, 31 December 1895.

74. V. Perrot, *Une Grande Première Historique* (Paris, 1939), 10.

75. Cited in Martin Loiperdinger and Roland Cosandey, 'L'Introduction du Cinématographe en Allemagne', *Archives* 51 (November 1992), 9.

76. Antoine Lumière, letter to Jules Carpentier, 28 December 1895.

77. Carpentier, letter to Louis Lumière, 30 December 1895.

78. Louis Lumière, letter to Jules Carpentier, 31 December 1895.

79. *La Poste*, 30 December 1895.

80. Cited in Maurice Bessy and Lo Duca, *Georges Méliès: Mage* (Paris: Prisma, 1945), 43.

81. Cited in Loiperdinger and Cosandey, op. cit., 9.

82. On this subject see Jacques Rittaud-Hutinet, op. cit. However Rittaud-Hutinet's 'Lumiériste' outlook, which tends to minimize the importance of the Lumières' competitors in 1895–6 in order to enhance the reputation of his heroes, gives an oversimplified view of the picture.

83. Louis Lumière, undated letter to Jules Carpentier, preserved in a private collection.

84. *La Nature*, 27 February 1897.

85. Bernard Chardère, *Lumières sur Lumière* (Lyon, 1987), 185. Chardère's opinions, unfortunately, are also quite chauvinistically 'Lumiériste'.

86. *L'Industriel Forain*, 342 (23–29 February 1896).
87. An example of the Clément and Gilmer Vitagraph has been identified by the author in the collection of the Société Française de Photographie. The shutter of this high-quality machine is formed by a rotating cylindrical tube, into which a pair of diametrically opposite openings have been cut.
88. *L'Industriel Forain*, 372 (20–26 September 1896).
89. See Thierry Lefebvre, 'Une "Maladie" au Tournant du Siècle: La "Cinématophthalmie"', *Revue d'Histoire de la Pharmacie*, 297 (1993), 225–30.
90. For more on Parnaland, see Laurent Mannoni, 'Ambroise-François Parnaland: Pioniere del Cinema e Cofondatore della Società Éclair', *Griffithiana*, May 1993, 10–30.

Select Bibliography

Books

Aguillon, Francois d'. *Opticorum Libri VI*. Anvers: Moreti, 1613.

Alber. *La Projection au XXe Siècle*. Paris: Mazo, n.d. [1904].

Alber. *Trente Années d'un Art Mystérieux*. Saint-Amand: A. Clerc, 1924.

Alhazen [Ibn Al-Haytham]. *Opticae Thesaurus Alhazeni Arabis Libri VII*. Basle: F. Risner, 1572.

Allen, John. *The Magic Lantern: its Invention and History*. London: Dean and Son, 1873.

Altick, Richard D. *The Shows of London: a Panoramic History of Exhibitions*. Cambridge, Massachusetts, and London: Belknap Press of Harvard University Press, 1978.

Ango, Pierre. *L'Optique*. Paris: Estienne Michallet, 1682.

Annuaire du Commerce et de l'Industrie Photographiques. Paris: Charles Mendel, 1902, 1911, 1914.

Anon. *Fantasmagoriana, ou Recueil d'Histoires d'Apparitions de Spectres*. Paris: F. Schoell, 1812.

——*La Lanterne Magique aux Champs-Élysées*. n.p., n.d. [Paris, 1775].

——*La Lanterne Magique de la France*. n.p. [Paris], 1789.

——*La Lanterne Magique de la Rue Impériale*. n.p. [Paris]: Cellot, 1815.

——*La Lanterne Magique de l'Île d'Elbe*. Paris: Setier Fils, 1815.

——[Mme de Courval?]. *La Lanterne Magique Morale et Instructive*. Paris: E. Pochard, 1827.

——*La Lanterne Magique: ou Fléaux des Aristocrates*. Berne [Paris]: Dubois, 1790.

——*La Lanterne Magique: ou le Mississippi du Diable*. The Hague: Mathieu, n.d. [late seventeenth century].

——*Lantern Readings: Miscellaneous Tales No. 1*. n.p., n.d. [London: York & Son, *c*.1890].

——*Lantern Readings: The Stately Homes of England*. n.p., n.d.

——[James Martin?] *The Magic Lantern: How to Buy and How to Use It*. London: Houlston & Wright, 1866.

——*Secrets et Mystères de la Sorcellerie*. Paris: Lebrigre-Duquesne, 1865.

——*Spectres, Fantômes, Apparitions*. Paris: Vallée, 1863.

Aumont, Jacques. *L'Image*. Paris: Nathan, 1990.

——*L'Oeil Interminable*. Paris: Séguier, 1989.

Aumont, Jacques, André Gaudreault and Michel Marie (eds). *L'Histoire du Cinéma: Nouvelles Approches*. Paris: Publications de la Sorbonne, Colloque de Cerisy, 1989.

Bacon, Roger. *Opus Majus*. London: Samuel Jebb, 1733.

Baker, Henry. *Le Microscope à la Portée de Tout le Monde*. Paris: Jombert, 1754.

Baltrušaitis, Jurgis. *Aberrations*. Paris, Flammarion, 1983.

——*Anamorphoses*. Paris, Flammarion, 1984.

——*Le Miroir*. Paris: Elmayan-Le Seuil, 1978.

Balzer, Richard. *Optical Amusements: Magic Lanterns*. Lexington, Massachusetts: published by the author, 1987.

Bapst, Germain. *Essais sur L'Histoire des Panoramas et des Dioramas*. Paris: Imprimerie Nationale, Masson, 1891.

Barnes, John. *Catalogue of the Barnes Museum of Cinematography: Part II*. St Ives, Cornwall: Barnes, 1970.

——*Dr Paris's Thaumatrope or Wonder-Turner*. London: The Projection Box, 1995.

——*The Beginnings of the Cinema in England 1894–1901. Vol. 1: 1894–96*. Exeter: University of Exeter Press, 1998.

——*The Beginnings of the Cinema in England 1894–1901. Vol. 2: 1897*. Exeter: University of Exeter Press, 1996.

——*The Beginnings of the Cinema in England 1894–1901. Vol. 3: 1898*. Exeter: University of Exeter Press, 1996.

——*The Beginnings of the Cinema in England 1894–1901. Vol. 4: 1899*. Exeter: University of Exeter Press, 1996.

——*The Beginnings of the Cinema in England 1894–1901. Vol. 5: 1900*. Exeter: University of Exeter Press, 1997.

Barnouw, Erik. *The Magician and the Cinema*. New York and Oxford: Oxford University Press, 1981.

Bellet, Daniel. *Les Dernières Merveilles de la Science*. Paris: Garnier, n.d. [1899].

Bennett, Colin N. *The Handbook of Kinematography*. London: Kinematograph Weekly, 1913.

Bergeret, A., and F. Drouin. *Les Récréations Photographiques*. Paris: Charles Mendel, 1891.

Bernard, Denis, and André Gunthert. *L'Instant Rêvé Albert Londe*. Nîmes-Laval: Jacqueline Chambon-Trois, 1993.

Bernard-Valville. *La Lanterne Magique ou le Retour des Époux*. Paris: Fages, 1801.

Beroville, H. de. *Peinture des Vues sur Verre et des Tableaux Mécanisés*. Paris: Mazo, 1896.

Bertin, Théodore Pierre. *La Lanterne Magique ou Spectacle Amusant*. Paris: H. Vauquelin, 1815.

Bettini, Mario. *Apiaria Universae Philosophiae Mathematicae*. Bologna: B. Ferroni, 1642.

Blanchère, H. de la. *Monographie du Stéréoscope*. Paris: Amyot, n.d. [1861].

Bonanni, Philippo. *Musaeum Kircherianum sive Musaeum A.P. Athanasio Kirchero [. . .]*. Rome: 1709.

Braun, Marta. *Picturing Time: the Work of Étienne-Jules Marey*. Chicago and London: University of Chicago Press, 1992.

Breton, J.L. 'La Chronophotographie', *Revue Scientifique et Industrielle de l'Année*. Paris: E. Bernard, 1897.

Breton, M. *Les Savants de Quinze Ans*. Paris: Lepetit, 1811.

Brewster, David. *Letters on Natural Magic*. London: John Murray, 1833.

Brisson, Jacques Mathurin. *Dictionnaire Raisonné de Physique*. Paris: Hotel de Thou, 1781.

Brownlow, Kevin. *Hollywood: the Pioneers*. London: Collins, 1979.

Brunel, Georges. *Le Chronophotographe Demenÿ*. Paris: Comptoir Général de Photographie, 1897.

——*Le Cinématographe Joly-Normandin*. Paris: Normandin, 1897.

——*L'Héliocinégraphe Perret et Lacroix*. Agen: Perret et Lacroix, 1897.

——*Le Kinétographe Méliès et Reulos*. Paris: Méliès et Reulos, 1897.

Buhot, René. *La Voix de Marey*. Boulogne: R. Buhot, 1937.

Burch, Noël. *La Lucarne de l'Infini*. Paris: Nathan, 1991.

Bytemeister, Heinrich Johannes. *Bytemeister Bibliothecae Appendix Sive Catalogues Apparatus Curiosum Artificialum et Naturalium . . .* Helmstedt: Bytemeister, 1735.

Campardon, Émile. *Les Spectacles de la Foire*. Geneva: Slatkine Reprints, 1970.

Carpenter, Philip. *A Companion to the Magic Lantern*. London: Carpenter, 1823.

Castan, Joachim. *Max Skladanowsky: oder der Beginn einer deutschen Filmgeschichte*. Stuttgart: Füsslin Verlag, 1995.

Chadwick, William Isaac. *The Magic Lantern Manual*. London: Frederick Warne, n.d. [1878].

Chardère, Bernard, Guy Borge and Marjorie Borge. *Les Lumière*. Lausanne and Paris: Payot/Bibliothèque des Arts, 1985.

Charles, Émile. *Roger Bacon*. Paris: Hachette, 1861.

Cherchi Usai, Paolo. *A Trip to the Movies: Georges Méliès, Filmmaker and Magician*. Pordenone: Biblioteca dell'Immagine/Giornate del Cinema Muto, 1990.

Cherchi Usai, Paolo, and Lorenzo Codelli (eds). *Prima di Caligari: Cinema Tedesco 1895–1920*. Pordenone: Biblioteca dell'Immagine, 1990.

Chérubin d'Orléans. *La Dioptrique Oculaire*. Paris: T. Jolly and S. Bernard, 1671.

Chevalier, Arthur. *Étude sur la Vie et les Travaux Scientifiques de Charles Chevalier*. Paris: Bonaventure et Ducessois, 1862.

Chevallier, H. [Paul Gavarni]. *Étrennes de 1825: Récréations Diabolicofantasmagoriques*. Paris: Blaisot, Giroux, Gide, 1825.

Claudet, Antoine. *Sur les Figures Photographiques Mouvantes*. Republication ed. Gérard Turpin. Paris: Antéciné, 1990.

Coe, Brian. *The History of Movie Photography*. Westfield: Eastview Editions, 1981.

Coissac, G. Michel. *Histoire du Cinématographe*. Paris: Gauthier-Villars, 1925.

——*La Théorie et la Pratique des Projections*. Paris: Maison de la Bonne Presse, n.d. [1906].

Cook, Olive. *Movement in Two Dimensions*. London: Hutchinson, 1963.

Corcy, Marie-Sophie, Jacques Malthête, Laurent Mannoni and Jean-Jacques Meusy (eds). *Les Premières Années de la Société L. Gaumont et Cie.: Correspondance Commerciale de Léon Gaumont 1895-1899*. Paris: AFRHC, 1998.

Cosandey, Roland, André Gaudreault and Tom Gunning (eds). *Une Invention du Diable? Cinéma des Premiers Temps et Religion*. Sainte-Foy and Lausanne: Presses de l'Université Laval/Payot, 1992.

Crompton, Dennis, David Henry and Stephen Herbert (eds). *Magic Images*. London: Magic Lantern Society, 1990.

Dagognet, François. *Étienne-Jules Marey*. Paris: Hazan, 1987.

Dagron, Prudent René. *La Poste par Pigeons Voyageurs*. Tours and Bordeaux, 1871.

Daguerre, Louis Jacques Mandé. *Historique et Description des Procédés du Daguerréotype*. Paris: Giroux, 1839.

Daumas, Maurice. *Les Instruments Scientifiques aux XVIIe et XVIIIe Siècles*. Paris: Presses Universitaires de France, 1953.

Dechales, Claude François Milliet. *Cursus seu Mundus Mathematicus*. Lyon, 1674.

Decremps, Henri. *La Magie Blanche Dévoilée*. Paris: Langlois, Tiger et Decremps, 1784.

Delree, Pierre. 'Étienne-Gaspard Robertson' in *La Vie Wallonne*. Liège, 1954.

Demenÿ, Georges. Collection of press cuttings edited by Marcel Demenÿ, *c.*1950.

——*Études sur les Appareils Chronophotographiques*. Evreux: Herissey, n.d.

——*Le Portrait Vivant*. Douai: Dechristé, n.d.

——*Les Bases Scientifiques de l'Éducation Physique*. Paris: Félix Alcan, 1902.

——*Les Origines du Cinématographe*. Paris: Henry Paulin, n.d. [1909].

——*Mécanisme et Éducation des Mouvements*. Paris: Félix Alcan, 1904.

——*Sur la Chronophotographie*. Paris: Gauthier-Villars, 1892.

[Demenÿ-Gaumont]. *Chronophotographie Pour Tous*. Paris: Comptoir Général de Photographie, n.d. [1895].

Deslandes, Jacques. *Histoire Comparée du Cinéma*, Vol. I. Tournai: Casterman, 1966.

Deslandes, Jacques, and Jacques Richard. *Histoire Comparée du Cinéma*, Vol. II. Tournai: Casterman, 1968.

Deutelbaum, Marshall. *'Image' on the Art and Evolution of the Film*. New York: Dover, 1979.

Dickson, William Kennedy-Laurie, and Antonia Dickson. *History of the Kinetograph, Kinetoscope and Kinetophonograph*. New York: Albert Bunn, 1895 (reprinted Ayer Company, 1984).

Dillaye, Frédéric. *L'Art dans les Projections*. Paris: Comptoir Général de Photographie, n.d. [1896].

Dolbear, Amos Emerson. *The Art of Projecting*. Boston and New York, 1877.

Donnadieu, A.L. *La Photographie Animée: Ses Origines, son Exploitation, ses Dangers*. Lyon: E. Vitte, 1897.

Doppelmayr, Johann Gabriel. *Historische Nachricht von den Nürnbergischen Mathematicis und Künstlern*. Nuremberg: Peter Conrad Monath, 1730.

——*Visionis Sensum Nobilissimum ex Obscurae Camerae Tenebris . . .* Nuremberg: Meyer, 1699.

[Dreux du Radier]. *Essai Historique sur les Lanternes*. n.p., n.d. [Dôle, 1755].

Ducom, Jacques. *Le Cinématographe Scientifique et Industriel*. Paris: L. Geisler, 1911.

Duhem, Pierre. *Le Système du Monde*, Vol. III. Paris: A. Hermann et Fils, 1915.

Eder, Josef Maria. *Geschichte der Photographie*. Halle: Wilhem Knapp, 1905.

——*La Photographie Instantanée*. Paris: Gauthier-Villars, 1888.

Edison, Thomas A. *The Diary and Sundry Observations of Thomas Alva Edison*. New York: Philosophical Library, 1948.

Eisner, Lotte H. *The Haunted Screen*. Berkeley: University of California Press, 1969.

Eschinardi, Francesco. *Centuria Problematum Opticorum*. Rome: H. Corbelletti, 1666–8.

Euler, Leonhard. *Lettres de L. Euler à une Princesse d'Allemagne*. Paris: Hachette, 1842.

Faideau, F. *Les Amusements Scientifiques*. Paris: Librairie Illustrée, n.d. [c.1895].

Fau, Docteur, and Charles Chevalier. *Nouveau Manuel Complet de Physicien-Préparateur*. Paris: Roret, 1853.

Ferrier et Soulier. *Catalogue Général des Épreuves Stéréoscopiques sur Verre et Lanternes Magiques*. Paris: Léon et J. Lévy, 1870.

Fielding, Raymond. *A Technological History of Motion Pictures and Television*. Berkeley, Los Angeles and London: University of California Press, 1983.

Figuier, Louis. *L'Année Scientifique et Industrielle*. Paris: Hachette, 1857–1914.

Fleury, Marianne de, Dominique Lebrun, and Olivier Meston. *Musée du Cinéma Henri Langlois*. Paris: Maeght, 1991.

Fouque, Victor. See Niépce, below.

Fourtier, Henri. *La Pratique des Projections*. Paris: Gauthier-Villars, 1892–3.

——*Les Tableaux de Projections Mouvementées*. Paris: Gauthier-Villars, 1893.

——*Manuel Pratique de la Lanterne de Projection*. Paris: A. Laverne, 1889.

Francis, David. *The Origins of the Cinema*. Dynevor Castle, 1968.

François-Franck, Charles A. *L'Oeuvre de E.J. Marey*. Paris: Octave Douin, 1905.

Franklin, Alfred. *Dictionnaire Historique des Arts, Métiers et Professions*. Marseille: Laffitte Reprints, 1987.

Frippet, E. *La Pratique de la Photographie Instantanée*. Paris: J. Fritsch, 1899.

Frizot, Michel. *E.J. Marey: La Photographie du Mouvement*. Paris: Centre Georges Pompidou, 1977.

——*La Chronophotographie*. Beaune: Association des Amis de Marey/Ministère de la Culture, 1984.

Frizot, Michel, and Dominique Païni (eds). *Sculpter-Photographier, Photographie-Sculpture*. Paris: Louvre Marval, 1993.

Füsslin, Georg. *Optisches Spielzeug*. Stuttgart: Verlag G. Füsslin, 1993.

Gastine, Louis. *La Chronophotographie sur Plaque Fixe et sur Pellicule Mobile*. Paris: Gauthier-Villars, n.d. [1897].

Gaudreault, André (ed.). *Ce que Je Vois de Mon Ciné . . .* Paris: Méridiens Klincksieck, 1988.

——*Pathé 1900: Fragments d'une Filmographie Analytique du Cinéma des Premiers Temps*. Sainte-Foy and Paris: Presses de l'Université Laval/Presses de la Sorbonne Nouvelle, 1993.

Gernsheim, Helmut. *L.J.M. Daguerre: The History of the Diorama and the Daguerreotype*. London: Secker & Warburg, 1968.

——*The Origins of Photography*. London: Thames & Hudson, 1982.

Gersaint, Edme François. *Catalogue Raisonné d'une Collection Considérable de Diverses Curiosités*. Paris: Barois et Simon, 1744.

Giard, Émile. *Le Livre d'Or de la Photographie*. Paris: Charles Mendel, n.d.

Girard, Jules. *La Chambre Noire et le Microscope*. Paris: F. Savy, 1870.

Grandpré, Jules de. *Le Magicien Moderne*. Paris: Fayard, n.d. [1878].

Grollier de Servière. *Recueil d'Ouvrages Curieux de Mathématique et de Mécanique . . .* Second edition. Lyon: David Frey, 1738.

Gunning, Tom. *D.W. Griffith and the Origins of American Narrative Film*. Urbana and Chicago: University of Illinois Press, 1993.

Gutle, Johann Konrad. *Zaubermechanik: oder Beschreibung Mechanischer Zauberbelustigungen*. Nuremberg and Altdorf, 1794.

Guyot, Gilles E. *Nouvelles Récréations Physiques et Mathématiques*. Paris: Gueffier, 1769–70; new edition 1799.

Haas, Robert Bartlett. *Muybridge: Man in Motion*. Berkeley, Los Angeles and London: University of California Press, 1976.

Halde, Jean-Baptiste du. *Description Géographique, Historique, Chronologique, Politique et Physique de l'Empire de la Chine*. Paris: Le Mercier, 1735.

Halle, Johann Samuel. *Magie: Oder die Zauberkräfte der Natur*. Berlin: J. Pauli, 1783–86.

Hammond, John H. *The Camera Obscura*. Bristol: Adam Hilger, 1981.

Hammond, John H., and Jill Austin. *The Camera Lucida in Art and Science*. Bristol: Adam Hilger, 1987.

Hauy, René Just. *Traité Élémentaire de Physique*. Paris: Veuve Courcier, 1821.

Hecht, Hermann. *Pre-Cinema History*. Ed. Ann Hecht. London: Bowker Saur/British Film Institute, 1993.

Hendricks, Gordon. *Beginnings of the Biograph*. New York: Theodore Gaus' Sons, 1964.

——*Eadweard Muybridge*. London: Secker & Warburg, 1975.

——*The Edison Motion Picture Myth*. Berkeley and Los Angeles: University of California Press, 1961.

——*The Kinetoscope*. New York: Theodore Gaus' Sons, 1966.

Hepworth, Cecil M. *Animated Photography: the ABC of the Cinematograph*. London: Hazell, Watson & Viney, 1897; second edition 1900.

Hepworth, Thomas Cradock. *Manuel Pratique des Projections Lumineuses (Le Livre de la Lanterne de Projections)*. Paris: Société d'Éditions Scientifiques, 1892 (translation of 1888 first edition of *The Book of the Lantern*).

——*The Book of the Lantern*. Sixth edition. London: Hazell, Watson & Viney, 1899.

Herbert, Stephen, and Mo Heard. *Industry, Liberty, and a Vision: Wordsworth Donisthorpe's Kinesigraph*. London: The Projection Box, 1998.

Herigone, Pierre. *Le Supplément du Cours Mathématique*. Paris: published by the author, 1642.

Herschel, John. *Traité de la Lumière*. Paris: Malher et Cie., 1829.

Hodges, John Alfred. *The Lantern-Slide Manual*. London: Hazell, Watson & Viney, 1892.

Hoffmann, Detlev, and Almut Junker. *Laterna Magica*. Berlin: Frölich und Kaufmann, 1982.

Hooper, William. *Rational Recreations*. London: Davis, Robson, Law, Robinson, 1774.

Hopkins, Albert A. *Magic: Stage Illusions and Scientific Diversions, Including Trick Photography*. New York: Munn & Co., 1898. Reprinted New York: Dover Publications, 1976.

Hopwood, Henry V. *Living Pictures*. London: Optician and Photographic Trades Review, 1899. Reprinted New York: Arno Press, 1970.

Household, G.A., and L.M.H. Smith. *To Catch a Sunbeam: Victorian Reality Through the Magic Lantern*. London: Michael Joseph, 1979.

Hrabalek, Ernst. *Laterna Magica*. Munich: Keyser, 1985.

Hulfish, David S. *Motion-Picture Work*. Chicago: American Technical Society, 1915.

Humphries, Steve. *Victorian Britain Through the Magic Lantern*. London: Sidgwick & Jackson, 1989.

Huret, Jules. *La Catastrophe du Bazar de la Charité*. Paris: F. Juven, 1897.

Hutchison, G.A. *Indoor Games and Recreations: A Popular Encyclopaedia for Boys*. London: Religious Tract Society, 1891.

Huygens, Christiaan. *Oeuvres Complètes*. The Hague: Société Hollandaise des Sciences, 1888–1950.

——*Opuscula Postuma, Quae Continent Dioptricam*. Lyon: C. Boutesteyn, 1703.

——*Traité de la Lumière*. Paris: Gauthier-Villars, 1920.

Huygens, Constantin. *De Briefwisseling van Constantijn Huygens*. 's Gravenhage: Martinus Nijhoff, 1911.

Hyde, Ralph. *Panoramania! The Art and Entertainment of the 'All-Embracing' View*. London: Trefoil Publications and Barbican Art Gallery, 1988.

Jacobaeus, Oligerus. *Museum Regium . . .* Copenhagen, 1710.

Janssen, Jules. *Oeuvres Scientifiques*. Paris: Société d'Éditions Géographiques, Maritimes et Coloniales, 1929.

Jay, Paul. *Niépce: Génèse d'une Invention*. Chalon-sur-Saône: Société des Amis du Musée Nicéphore Niépce, 1988.

Jenkins, Charles Francis. *Animated Pictures*. Washington: Jenkins, 1898. Reprinted New York: Arno Press, 1970.

Jombert, Charles Antoine. *Méthode pour Apprendre le Dessin*. Paris: Jombert, 1755.

Jones, Bernard E. *The Cinematograph Book*. London: Cassell & Co., 1921.

Joseph-Renaud, J. *Le Cinématographe de Mariage*. Paris: Flammarion, n.d. [1898].

Julia de Fontenelle, Jean-Sébastien Eugène. *Manuel de Physique Amusante*. Paris: Roret, 1826.

——*Nouveau Manuel Complet de Physique*. Paris: Roret, 1850.

——*Nouveau Manuel Complet des Sorciers*. Paris: Roret, 1841.

Kestler, Johann Stephan. *Physiologia Kircheriana Experimentalis*. Amsterdam: Janssonio-Wesbergiana, 1680.

Kircher, Athanasius. *Ars Magna Lucis et Umbrae in Decem Libros*. Rome: Hermanni Scheus, 1645, 1646; second edition Amsterdam: Joannem Janssoniu, 1671.

Kress, E. *Historique de Cinématographe*. Paris: Cinéma-Revue, n.d. [1912].

Krunitz, Johann Georg. *Oekonomisch-Technologische Encyclopädie*. Berlin, 1794 (Vol. 65) and 1825 (Vol. 140).

Lagny, Michèle. *De l'Histoire du Cinéma: Méthode Historique et Histoire du Cinéma*. Paris: Armand Colin, 1992.

Landes, David. *L'Heure qu'il est*. Paris: Gallimard, 1987.

Ledermuller, Martin Frobene. *Amusements Microscopiques*. Nuremberg: Delanoy, 1764–8.

Lefebvre, Thierry, and Laurent Mannoni (eds). 'L'Année 1913 en France'. *1895*. Paris and Pordenone: A.F.R.H.C., 1993.

Lefèvre, Julien. *L'Électricité au Théâtre*. Paris: A. Grelot, n.d. [1894].

——*La Photographie et ses Applications aux Sciences, aux Arts et à l'Industrie*. Paris: J.B. Baillière, 1888.

Leonardo da Vinci. *Léonard de Vinci et l'Expérience Scientifique au XVIe Siècle*. Colloques Internationaux du CNRS. Paris: CNRS/Presses Universitaires de France, 1953.

——*The Notebooks of Leonardo da Vinci*. Trans. Edward MacCurdy. London: Jonathan Cape, 1956.

Lerebours, Noël Marie Paymal. *Notice d'Instruments de Physique, d'Optique et de Mathématiques*. Paris: Lerebours, 1809.

Lescaboura, Austin C. *Behind the Motion-Picture Screen*. New York, 1919. Reprinted New York: New York Times, 1980.

Leurechon, J. *Récréation Mathématique*. Pont-à-Mousson: Jean Appier Hanzelet, 1626.

Levie, Françoise. *Étienne-Gaspard Robertson*. Québec: Le Préambule, 1990.

Liesegang, Eduard. *Die Projections-Kunst für Schulen, Familien . . .* Düsseldorf: Liesegang, 1882.

Liesegang, Franz Paul. *Dates and Sources*. Ed. and trans. Hermann Hecht. London: Magic Lantern Society, 1986.

——*Zahlen und Quellen: zur Geschichte der Projektions-Kunst und Kinematographie*. Düsseldorf, 1926.

Löbel, Léopold. *La Technique Cinématographique*. Paris: Dunod et Pinat, 1912.

Londe, Albert. *La Photographie Instantanée*. Paris: Gauthier-Villars, 1886.

——*La Photographie Moderne*. Paris: G. Masson, 1888 and 1896.

Lumière, Auguste, and Louis Lumière. *Catalogue des Vues pour Cinématographe*. Monplaisir-Lyon, n.d. [1905].

——*Cinématographe-Type*. Lyon, n.d.

——*Cinématographes A. et L. Lumière et Materiel pour Projections Animées*. Lyon, n.d. [*c*.1903].

——*Notice sur le Cinématographe Auguste et Louis Lumière*. Lyon: L. Decléris et Fils, 1897.

——*Resumé des Travaux Scientifiques*. Lyon and Paris: Union Photographique Industrielle, 1914.

McLuhan, T.C. *Voyage en Terre Indienne*. Paris: Filipacchi, 1985.

Maison de la Bonne Presse. *Catalogue A: Projections Lumineuses, Appareils et Accessoires*. Paris: Maison de la Bonne Presse, 1909.

——*Catalogue B: Projections Lumineuses, Séries de Vues*. Paris: Maison de la Bonne Presse, 1909.

——*Projections Lumineuses, Cinématographes, Catalogue Spécial des Appareils.* Paris: Maison de la Bonne Presse, 1911.

Mannoni, Laurent. *Demenÿ: Pionnier du Cinéma.* Douai: Pagine, 1997.

——*E.J. Marey.* Milan and Paris: Mazzotta/Cinémathèque Française, 1999.

——*Le Mouvement Continué: Catalogue Illustré de la Collection d'Appareils de la Cinémathèque Française.* Milan and Paris: Mazzotta/Cinémathèque Française, 1996.

——*Trois Siècles de Cinéma.* Paris: Réunion des Musées Nationaux, 1995.

Mannoni, Laurent, Donata Pesenti Campagnoni, and David Robinson (eds). *Light and Movement: Incunabula of the Motion Picture 1420–1896.* Gemona: Cineteca del Friuli/Le Giornate del Cinema Muto, 1995.

Marcy, Lorenzo J. *The Sciopticon Manual.* Philadelphia: Sherman & Co., 1871.

Marey, Étienne-Jules. *Développement de la Méthode Graphique par l'Emploi de la Photographie.* Paris: Masson, n.d. [1884].

——*Du Mouvement dans les Fonctions de la Vie.* Paris: Germer Baillière, 1868.

——*La Machine Animale.* Paris: Germer Baillière, 1873.

——*La Méthode Graphique.* Paris: Masson, 1878.

——*Le Mouvement.* Paris: Masson, 1894.

——*Physiologie du Mouvement: Le Vol des Oiseaux.* Paris: Masson, 1890.

Marey, Étienne-Jules, and Georges Demenÿ. *Études de Physiologie Artistique Faite au Moyen de la Chronophotographie.* Paris: Société d'Éditions Scientifiques, 1893.

Marion, Fulgence. *L'Optique.* Paris: Hachette, 1874.

Martin, Benjamin. *The Young Gentleman and Lady's Philosophy.* Second edition. London: W. Owen, 1772.

Matuszewski, Boleslav. *Une Nouvelle Source de l'Histoire (Création d'un Depot de Cinématographie Historique).* Paris: Impr. de Noizette, 1898.

Mazo, Elie Xavier. *Catalogue No. 50 E. Mazo.* Paris: Mazo, 1913.

——*Manuel Mazo de Projections.* Paris: Mazo, n.d. [*c.*1910].

Merrill, Brian L. *Athanasius Kircher.* Provo, Utah: Friends of the Brigham Young University, 1989.

Meunier, Stanislas. *Les Glaciers: Rédaction Sténographique d'une Conférence.* Paris: Molteni, 1876.

——*Les Projections Lumineuses et l'Enseignement Primaire.* Paris: Molteni, n.d. [1885].

Milano, Alberto. *Viaggio in Europa Attraverso de Vues d'Optique.* Milan: Mazzota, 1990.

Minici Zotti, Carlo Alberto. *Il Mondo Nuovo: Le Meraviglie della Visione.* Milan: Mazzotta, 1988.

Minici Zotti, Laura. *Le Lanterne Magiche.* Padova, 1988.

Moigno, Abbé. *Enseignement de Tous par les Projections: Catalogue des Tableaux et Appareils.* Paris: Le Cosmos-Les Mondes/Gauthier-Villars, n.d. [1882].

——*L'Art des Projections.* Paris: Les Mondes/Gauthier-Villars, 1872.

——*Le Stéréoscope, Ses Effets Merveilleux. Pseudoscope, Ses Effects Étranges.* Paris: A. Franck, 1852.

——*Répertoire d'Optique Moderne.* Paris: A. Franck, 1847.

Molteni, Alfred. *Catalogue des Lanternes Magiques, Fantasmagories, Polyoramas, Tableaux et Accessoires No. 47.* Paris: Molteni, n.d.

——*Instructions Pratiques sur l'Emploi des Appareils de Projection.* Paris: Molteni, 1878.

Molyneux, William. *Dioptrica Nova: A Treatise of Dioptricks.* Second edition. London: B. Tooke, 1709.

Monconys, Balthasar de. *Voyages.* Paris: P. Delaulne, 1695.

Montucla, Jean-François. *Histoire des Mathématiques.* Paris: H. Agasse, 1802.

Morrison-Low, A.D., and J.R.R. Christie. *Martyr of Science: Sir David Brewster*. Edinburgh: Royal Scottish Museum Studies, 1984.

Musschenbroek, Pierre van. *Essai de Physique*. Leyden: Samuel Luchtmans, 1751.

Musser, Charles. *Before the Nickelodeon: Edwin S. Porter and the Edison Manufacturing Company*. Berkeley: University of California Press, 1991.

——*The Emergence of Cinema: The American Screen to 1907*. New York: Charles Scribner's Sons, 1990.

Musser, Charles, and Carol Nelson. *High-Class Moving Pictures*. Princeton: Princeton University Press, 1991.

Muybridge, Eadweard. *Animal Locomotion: An Electro-Photographic Investigation of Consecutive Phases of Animal Movements*. 11 vols; 781 plates 48.5 x 62 cm. Philadelphia: University of Pennsylvania, 1887.

——*Animal Locomotion: The Muybridge Work at the University of Pennsylvania*. Philadelphia, n.d. [1888].

——*Animals in Motion*. London: Chapman and Hall, 1907.

——*Descriptive Zoopraxography*. Philadelphia: University of Pennsylvania, 1893.

——*The Human Figure in Motion*. London: Chapman and Hall, 1901.

Newton, Isaac. *Opticks: or a Treatise of the Reflexions, Refractions, Inflexions and Colours of Light*. London: Sam. Smith & Benj. Walford, 1704.

Nicéron, Jean-François. *La Perspective Curieuse*. Paris: Pierre Billaine, 1638; Paris: F. Langlois, 1652.

Niépce, Isidore, and Victor Fouque. *Historique de la Découverte Improprement Nommée Daguerréotype* and *La Vérité sur l'Invention de la Photographie*. Reprinted Paris: Jean-Michel Place, 1987.

Niépce, Joseph Nicéphore. *Lettres*. Rouen: Pavillon de la Photographie, 1973.

Niewenglowski, G.H. *Traité Pratique des Projections Lumineuses*. Paris: Garnier, 1910.

Niver, Kemp R. *The Paper Print Collection in the Library of Congress*. Washington: Library of Congress, 1985.

Nollet, Abbé. *L'Art des Expériences*. Second edition. Paris: Durand-Neveu, 1770.

——*Leçons de Physique Expérimentale*. Seventh edition. Paris: Durand-Neveu, 1779.

North, Joseph H. *The Early Development of the Motion Picture 1887–1909*. New York: Arno Press, 1973.

Noverre, Maurice. *Le Nouvel Art Cinématographique*. Brest: Noverre, 1925–30. [15 pamphlets, including *Émile Reynaud: Sa Vie et ses Travaux*, No. 4, 1926].

Oettermann, Stephan. *Das Panorama: Die Geschichte eines Massenmediums*. Frankfurt-am-Main: Syndikat, 1980.

Ogonowski, E. and Violette. *La Photographie Amusante*. Paris: Société Générale d'Éditions, n.d. [1894].

Ozanam, Jacques. *Récréations Mathématiques et Physiques*. Paris: Jean Jombert, 1694. New edition Paris: Claude A. Jombert, 1778.

Païni, Dominique. *Conserver, Montrer: Où l'On ne Craint pas d'Édifier un Musée pour le Cinéma*. Crisnée: Yellow Now, 1992.

[Paris, John Ayrton]. *Philosophy in Sport Made Science in Earnest*. London: Longman, Rees, Dome, Browne & Green, 1827.

Paroy, Comte de. *Mémoires*. Paris: Plon, 1895.

Pathé, Charles. *Souvenirs et Conseils d'un Parvenu*. Paris, 1926.

Patin, Charles. *Travels Thro' Germany, Swisserland, Bohemia, Holland, and Other Parts of Europe*. London, 1696.

Pepper, John Henry. *The Boy's Playbook of Science*. London: Routledge and Warne, 1860.

Perriault, Jacques. *Mémoires de l'Ombre et du Son*. Paris: Flammarion, 1981.

Pinel, Vincent. *Lumière*. Paris: Anthologie du Cinéma, 1974.

Plateau, Joseph. *Bibliographie Analytique des Principaux Phénomènes Subjectifs de la Vision*. Brussels: F. Hayez, 1878.

Plessen, Marie-Louise von (ed.). *Sehsucht: Das Panorama als Massenunterhaltung des 19. Jahrhunderts*. Bonn: Stroemfeld, Roter Stern, 1993.

Pomian, Krzysztof. *Collectionneurs, Amateurs et Curieux*. Paris: Gallimard, 1987.

Porta, Giovanni Battista della. *Magiae Naturalis: Sive de Miraculis Rerum Naturalium*. Naples: Matthiam Cancer, 1558. New edition in 20 vols., Naples: H. Salvianum, 1588.

——*Natural Magick*. London, 1658.

Potoniée, Georges. *Histoire de la Découverte de la Photographie* and *Daguerre: Peintre et Décorateur*. Reprinted Paris: Jean-Michel Place, 1989.

——*Les Origines du Cinématographe*. Paris: Paul Montel, 1928.

Prevost, J. *La Première Partie des Subtiles et Plaisantes Inventions*. Lyon: Antoine Bastide, 1584.

Prieur, Jérome. *Séance de Lanterne Magique*. Paris: Gallimard, 1985.

Pringle, Andrew. *The Optical Lantern for Instruction and Amusement*. London: Hampton, Judd & Co., 1890.

Prolo, Maria Adriana, and Luigi Carluccio. *Il Museo Nazionale del Cinema Torino*. Turin, 1978.

Ramsaye, Terry. *A Million and One Nights*. London: Frank Cass, 1964.

Rawlence, Christopher. *The Missing Reel*. London: Collins, 1990.

Remise, Jac, Pascale Remise and Regis van de Walle. *Magie Lumineuse*. Paris: Balland, 1979.

Reynaud, Émile. *Cours Public de Sciences Physiques Fait à l'Hôtel de Ville*. Le Puy: Veuve Peyron, 1874.

Rhanaeus, Samuel Johann. *Novum et Curiosum Laternae Magicae Augmentum* . . . Jena: Prelo Nisiano, 1713.

Ristow, Jurgen. *Vom Geisterbild zum Breitwandfilm*. Leipzig, 1989.

Rittaud-Hutinet, Jacques. *Les Frères Lumière et Leurs Opérateurs*. Seyssel: Champ Vallon, 1985.

——*Les 1,000 Premiers Films*. Paris: Philippe Sers, 1990.

Robertson, Étienne-Gaspard. *La Minerve: Vaisseau Aérien Destiné aux Découvertes*. Vienna: Degen, 1820.

——*Mémoires Récréatifs Scientifiques et Anecdotiques*. Paris: published by the author and by Librairie de Wurtz, 1831–3.

——*Noticias Curiosas, Sobre el Espectaculo de Mr. Robertson*. Madrid: S. Imprenta del Censor, Carrera de S. Francisco, 1821.

Robin, Henri. *Le Cagliostro: Histoire des Spectres Vivants et Impalpables*. Paris: Dépôt Central des Almanachs, Pagnerre, 1864–5.

Robinson, David. 'Masterpieces of Animation 1833–1908'. *Griffithiana* 43, December 1991.

——*Origins of the Cinema: Catalogue of an Exhibition*. London: Cumberland Antiques, 1964.

——*The Lantern Image: Iconography of the Magic Lantern*. London: Magic Lantern Society, 1993.

Roch, Eugène. *Essai sur les Voyages Aériens d'Eugène Robertson*. Paris: Landois et Bigot, 1831.

Rosen, J. *L'Histoire d'une Industrie: Le Cinématographe*. Paris: Société d'Éditions Techniques, n.d. [1912].

Rossell, Deac. *Ottomar Anschütz and his Electrical Wonder*. London: The Projection Box, 1997.

Rouille, André. *La Photographie en France*. Paris: Macula, 1989.

Ruggieri, Claude. *Précis Historique sur les Fêtes, les Spectacles*. Paris: Bachelier-Delaunay-Barba, 1830.

Sadoul, Georges. *Histoire Générale du Cinéma, Vol. 1: L'Invention du Cinéma 1832–97*. Paris: Denoël, 1948, 1977.

——*Lumière et Méliès*. Paris: Lherminier, 1985.

Salt, Barry. *Film Style and Technology: History and Analysis*. London: Starword, 1992.

Sauvage, Léo. *L'Affaire Lumière*. Paris: Pierre Lherminier, 1985.

Schott, Gaspar. *Magia Universalis Naturae et Artis*. Bamberg: J. Martin Schonwetter, 1677.

——*Technica Curiosa sive Mirabilia Artis*. Nuremberg, 1664.

Schwendter, Daniel. *Deliciae Physico-Mathematicae*. Nuremberg: J. Dumsers, 1636.

See, Armand. *Reproduction Analytique and Synthétique des Scènes Animées par la Photographie: Le Cinématographe de MM. A. et L. Lumière*. Lille: Le Bigot, 1896.

Seeber, Guido. *Der Praktische Kameramann*. Berlin: Lichtbildbühne, 1927.

Sepi, Giorgio di. *Romani Collegi Societatis Jesu Musaeum Celeberrimum*. Amsterdam: Jansson-Weisberg, 1678.

[Séraphin]. *Feu Séraphin: Histoire de ce Spectacle*. Lyon: N. Scheuring, 1875.

s'Gravesande, Guillaume Jacob van. *Mathematical Elements of Natural Philosophy*. London: J. Senex, W. Innys, R. Manby, and T. Longman, 1737. (French edition, *Éléments de Physique*, Paris: Jombert, 1747).

Smith, Albert E. *Two Reels and a Crank*. New York: Doubleday, 1952.

Smith, Robert. *Cours Complet d'Optique*. Avignon: Veuve Girard et F. Seguin, 1767.

Spehr, Paul C. *The Movies Begin: Making Movies in New Jersey 1887–1920*. Newark: Newark Museum, Morgan and Morgan, 1977.

Stetten, Paul von. *Kunst—Gewerb—Handwerksgeschichte der Reichs-Stadt Augsburg*. Augsburg, 1779.

Stillman, J.D.B. *The Horse in Motion*. Boston: James R. Osgood & Co., 1882.

Sturm, Johann Christoph. *Collegii Experimentalis sive Curiosi*. Nuremberg, 1685.

——*Collegium Experimentale sive Curiosum*. Nuremberg: W. and J.A. Endteri, 1767.

Talbot, Frederick A. *Moving Pictures*. London: Heinemann, 1912; and Philadelphia: J.B. Lippincott, n.d. [1923].

Temple, Louis du. *Introduction à l'Étude de la Physique*. Paris: J. Hetzel, n.d. [c.1870].

Thomin, Marc Mitouflet. *Traité d'Optique Méchanique*. Paris: J.B. Coignard, A. Boudet, 1749.

Tissandier, Gaston. *Les Récréations Scientifiques*. Paris: Masson, 1881.

Toulet, Emmanuelle. *Cinématographe: Invention du Siècle*. Paris: Découvertes Gallimard, 1988.

Trutat, Eugène. *La Photographie Animée*. Paris: Gauthier-Villars, 1899.

——*Traité Général des Projections*. Paris: Ch. Mendel, 1897–1902.

Turpain, A. *La Lumière*. Paris: Delagrave, 1913.

Uffenbach, Zacharias Conrad von. *Merkwürdige Reisen . . .* Frankfurt and Leipzig: J.F. Gaum, 1753.

Vallemont, Pierre Le Lorrain, Abbé de. *La Physique Occulte ou Traité de la Baguette Divinatoire*. Amsterdam: Adrian Braakman, 1693; new edition 1696.

Vitoux, Georges. *La Photographie du Mouvement*. Paris: Chamuel, 1896.

Vivie, Jean. *Traité Général de Technique du Cinéma: Historique et Développement de la Technique Cinématographique*. Paris: BPI, 1946.

Wiegleb, Johann Christian. *Die Natürliche Magie*. Berlin: Friedrich Nicolai, 1782–86.

Wolff, Christian. *Cours de Mathématique*. Paris: Jombert, 1747.

Woodbury, Walter B. *Science at Home: A Series of Experiments*. London: English Mechanic, n.d. [*c*.1870].

——*The Sciopticon Manual*. London: W. Woodbury, n.d. [*c*.1875].

Wright, Lewis. *Optical Projection*. London: Longmans, Green & Co., 1891.

Zahn, Johannes. *Oculus Artificialis Teledioptricus sive Telescopium*. Wurzburg, 1685–6; second edition 1702.

Zglinicki, Friedrich von. *Der Weg des Films*. Berlin: Rembrandt Verlag, 1956.

Periodicals

1895. Paris: Association Française de Recherche sur l'Histoire du Cinéma, 1986–94.

Affiches, Annonces et Avis Divers. Paris, 1798–1800.

AFITEC. Paris: Association Française des Ingénieurs et Techniciens du Cinema, 1947–73.

Après l'École. Paris, 1895–7.

Archives. Toulouse: Institut Jean Vigo, 1987–94.

Avenir Forain, L'. Bordeaux and Paris, 1904–14.

Bulletin de la Société Française de Photographie. Paris, 1855–96.

Bulletin Phonographique et Cinématographique: Les Inventions et les Industries Nouvelles. Paris, 1899–1900.

Ciné-Journal. Paris, 1908–20.

Cinémathèque. Paris: Cinémathèque Française, 1992–4.

Cinéopse. Paris, 1919–25.

Comptes Rendus Hebdomadaires des Séances de l'Académie des Sciences. Paris, 1839–1900.

Conférences, Les. Paris, 1900–7.

Cosmos, Le. Paris, 1852–96.

Courrier des Spectacles, Le. Paris, 1799–1801.

Fascinateur, Le. Paris, 1903–14.

Film History. London, 1987–94.

Griffithiana. Gemona: Cineteca del Friuli, 1978–94.

Illusioniste, L'. Paris, 1903–10.

Immagine. Rome: Associazione Italiana per le Ricerche di Storia del Cinema, 1986–94.

Industriel Forain, L'. Paris, 1883–1910.

Journal of the Society of Motion Picture and Television Engineers. Washington, D.C., 1916–93.

Lumière, La. Paris, 1851–67.

Mise au Point, La. Paris, 1897–1904.

Mondes, Les. Paris, 1863–73.

Moniteur de la Photographie, Le. Paris, 1861–96.

Nature, La. Paris, 1873–1900.

New Magic Lantern Journal. London: Magic Lantern Society, 1978–98.

Ombres et Lumière. Paris, 1895–1914.

Optical Magic Lantern Journal and Photographic Enlarger. London, 1889–96.

Paris-Photographe. Paris, 1891–4.

Phono-Ciné-Gazette. Paris, 1905–9.

Photogramme, Le. Paris, 1897–1901.

Photographic Dealer and Optical and Scientific Apparatus Trades Journal. London, 1896–7.

Photographie, La. Paris, 1892–7.
Photo-Revue. Paris, 1889–1900.
Projection, La. Paris, 1897–9.
Revue de Photographie. Paris: Photo-Club de Paris, 1903–8.
Science et Industries Photographiques. Paris, 1920–9.
Vie Scientifique, La. Paris, 1895–6.

Patents

Abbreviations: AT—Austrian Patent; CH—Swiss Patent; DE—German Patent; FR—French Patent; GB—UK Patent; US—United States Patent

Acres, Birt. GB 10,474 of 27 May 1895. *Improved apparatus for enabling photographic images to be taken, projected, or viewed in rapid succession.*
——GB 10,603 of 28 April 1897. *Improvements in apparatus for taking, viewing, and projecting photographs of moving objects.*
——GB 12,939 of 9 June 1898. *Improvements in cinematographic apparatus.*
Adams, Walter Poynter. GB 16,785 of 19 November 1888. *Improvements in magic lantern slides and apparatus in connection therewith.*
Aivas, Albert, and F.G. Hoffman. FR 255,116 of 28 March 1896. *Nouveau système de projecteur dit Projecteur Animé.*
Alberini, Filoteo, Anchise Cappelletti, and Lionello Ganucci-Cancellieri. FR 291,835 of 18 August 1899. *Cynésigraphe à séries.*
Alexandre, Joseph. FR 258,692 of 6 August 1896. *Perfectionnements aux appareils pour la photographie et la projection du mouvement.*
Allen, Samuel Wesley. GB 7,656 of 16 April 1895. *Improvements in optical lanterns.*
Anderton, John, and Alfred Lomax. GB 25,100 of 27 December 1894. *Improvements in Kinetoscopes.*
Anschütz, Ottomar. GB 23,042 of 14 December 1892. *Improvements in coin freed apparatus for exhibiting optical illusions.*
——FR 242,886 of 15 November 1894. *Procédé de projection d'images à mouvement stroboscopique.*
Argand, Aimé. FR 486 of 17 July 1802. *Lampe à miroir semi-parabolique.*
Armand, Louis. FR 262,120 of 1 December 1896. *Substitution du verre au celluloïd dont on se sert actuellement pour les bandes photographiques dans les projections du cinématographe.*
Armat, Thomas. GB 359 of 6 January 1896. *Improvements in the method of and apparatus of objects in motion.*
——US 673,992 of 19 February 1896. *Vitascope.*
——US 578,185 of 26 September 1896. *Vitascope.*
——FR 301,167 of 12 June 1900. *Perfectionnements dans les appareils pour la projection d'images animées.*
Arrowsmith, John. GB 4,899 of 18 February 1824. *An improved mode of publicly exhibiting pictures of painted scenery of every description [. . .] which I denominate a Diorama.*
Aubert, Louis. FR 21,204 of 28 October 1854. *Système d'éclairage applicable aux lanternes magiques, fantasmagories, polyoramas, etc., dit système Aubert.*
Bagrachow, Grégoire. FR 274,957 of 12 February 1898. *Biographoscope populaire Bagrachow.*

——FR 281,418 of 16 September 1898. *Appareil cinématographique à vision triple dit Trioscope familial.*

——FR 309,353 of 25 March 1901. *Appareil pour la prise et la projection des vues animées.*

Barbaroux, Charles Ogé. FR 3,540 of 4 February 1828. *Panorama voyageur.*

Bargigli, Anatole Simon Gaëtan. FR 262,507 of 21 August 1896. *Appareil dit Era pour la prise et la projection des photographies dites animées.*

Barker, Robert. GB 1,612 of 19 June 1797. *An entire new contrivance or apparatus, which I call* La Nature à coup d'oeil, *for the purpose of displaying views of nature at large by oil painting, fresco, water colours, crayons, or any other mode of painting or drawing.*

Baron, Auguste. FR 261,650 of 26 November 1896. *Système d'appareil pour projections circulaires animées, dit Cinématorama.*

——FR 276,628 of 4 April 1898. *Système d'appareil perfectionné pour enregistrer et reproduire simultanément les scènes animées et les sons qui les accompagnent.*

——FR 294,384 of 16 November 1899. *Système d'appareil pour projections panoramiques circulaires animées, en couleurs et parlantes, dit Cinématorama parlant.*

Baron, Auguste, and Frédéric Bureau. FR 255,317 of 3 April 1896. *Système d'appareil servant à enregistrer et à reproduire simultanément les scènes animées et les sons.*

——FR 256,926 of 3 June 1896. *Système de machine à perforer les pellicules photographiques et autres matières sous forme de rubans.*

Baronnet, Paul. FR 256,485 of 20 May 1896. *Modèle de lanterne magique à bandes de sujets déroulants.*

Bazin, Charles, and Lucien Leroy. FR 256,684 of 26 May 1896. *Mécanisme applicable aux appareils chronophotographiques et aux cinématographes.*

Bedford, Robert, and Auguste Nicolas Nepveu. FR 6,350 of 7 January 1835. *Optique d'un nouveau genre qu'ils nomment Diorama de salon.*

Benoist, F., and L. Berthiot. FR 257,084 of 9 June 1896. *Appareil de projection dit Héliorama.*

Benoist, Philippe. FR 16,055 of 5 April 1853. *Instrument d'optique dit Images animées.*

——GB 1,965 of 23 August 1856. *An improvement in the construction of sterioscopes* [*sic*].

Berjonneau, Pascal Hilaire Julien, Louis Marcel Rambaud, and Alexandre Menard. FR 255,988 of 30 April 1896. *Appareil à prendre et projeter des photographies en série pour donner l'illusion du mouvement et dénommé le Cinématoscope Ramberné.*

Berry, Miles. GB 8,194 of 14 August 1839. *A new or improved method of obtaining the spontaneous reproduction of all the images received in the focus of the camera obscura.*

Berthier, Poulenc Frères. FR 253,453 of 25 January 1896. *Appareil chronophotographique système Berthier.*

Berthon, Louis Alfred, Charles François Dussaud, and Georges François Jaubert. FR 268,369 of 1 July 1897. *Système combinant le microphonographe avec le cinématographe en vue de la reproduction simultanée des scènes de la vie animées et de la parole, du chant et des sons qui les accompagnent.*

Berville, Jean-Charles-Jules. FR 77,421 of 8 August 1867. *Instrument dit Diomanorama.*

Bickle, Thomas Edwin. GB 20,281 of 10 November 1892. *An improved mechanical toy.*

Binet, Roger. FR 256,284 of 12 May 1896. *Appareil chronophotographique.*

Blair, Thomas Henry. GB 12,458 of 27 June 1895. *Improvements in or relating to photographic cameras.*

Blair Camera Company. US 512,655 of 24 June 1889. *Photographic camera-shutter.*

Block, Adolphe. FR 281,247 of 9 September 1898. *Stéréoscope automatique à déclenchement monétaire.*

Bonelli, Gaetano. GB 1,588 of 12 June 1865. *A new or improved method of obtaining or producing optical illusions.*

——FR 67,635 of 9 June 1865. *Application de la photographie microscopique aux effets des images animées, dite Biophotographie.*

Bonelli, Gaetano, and Henry Cook. GB 2,063 of 19 August 1863. *An improved mode of and apparatus for producing by the aid of photography optical illusions of moving animals and bodies.*

Bonn, Jacob. GB 8,418 of 21 April 1896. *Improvements in connection with the projection of photographs of animated subjects.*

Borie, Augustin-Eugène. FR 258,755 of 8 August 1896. *Appareil appelé le Photo-optique Borie.*

Borie, Eugène. FR 75,548 of 18 March 1867. *Microscope solaire portatif et photographique.*

Bouchard, Désiré. FR 210,569 of 5 January 1891. *Relief des projections à obturation alternatives combinées.*

Bouillonne, Albert de. FR 257,002 of 6 June 1896. *Nouvel appareil photochronographique.*

Bouly, Léon Guillaume. FR 219,350 of 12 February 1892. *Appareil photographique instantané pour l'obtention automatique et sans interruption d'une série de clichés analytiques du mouvement ou autres dit le Cinématographe.*

——FR 235,100 of 27 December 1893. *Appareil réversible de photographie et d'optique pour l'analyse et la synthèse des mouvements dit le Cinématographe Léon Bouly.*

Bouly, Léon, and Abel Chollet. FR 419,771 of 22 August 1910. *Phonographe à bande flexible.*

Bourraux Frères. FR 296,566 of 26 January 1900. *Appareil pour observer directement les images cinématographiques à déroulement continu, dit le Mimoscope système Chasseraux.*

Brennan, Louis. GB 2,623 of 18 February 1890. *A method of and apparatus for producing pictures or designs appearing to move and change.*

Brodbeck, Charles, and Juan Ferrer y Girbeau. FR 257,321 of 17 June 1896. *Appareil pour l'obtention et la projection des épreuves photographiques donnant l'image des objets en mouvement.*

Brun, Louis Claude. FR 255,107 of 27 March 1896. *Appareil à photographier les corps en mouvement dit le Viroscope.*

Bull, Lucien, and Miltiade Kossonis. FR 283,645 of 2 December 1898. *Appareil pour la vision des images cinématographiques dit l'Iconoscope.*

Bünzli, René. FR 296,332 of 20 January 1900. *Stéréoscope animé dit Animateur stéréoscopique.*

Bünzli, René, and Victor Continsouza. FR 261,292 of 14 November 1896. *Nouvel appareil pour l'obtention et la projection de la photographie animée.*

——FR 294,549 of 21 November 1899. *Animateur stéréoscopique.*

Büttner. FR 270,692 of 23 September 1897. *Kinématoscope composé d'un cylindre ou rouleaux pourvu de plaquettes flexibles et d'une baguette de retenue.*

Campbell, Charles Milton. FR 267,257 of 25 May 1897. *Kinetoscope.*

Canellas, Joseph Marie. FR 256,834 of 1 June 1896. *Nouveau système de commande pour la production des photographies animées.*

Carelles, Henri, and Alfred Bidal. FR 228,524 of 10 March 1893. *Obturateur chronophotographique dit le Vaucanson.*

Carpentier, Jules. FR 236,035 of 3 February 1894. *Châssis à circulation pour projections.*

——FR 246,246 of 30 March 1895. *Appareil pour projections de photographies instantanées de scènes animées sur bandes pelliculaires dénommé Cynégraphe.*

——FR 254,883 of 18 March 1896. *Mécanisme de traction intermittente pour l'entraînement des bandes chronophotographiques, pour la photographie et les projections.*

——FR 255,164 of 30 March 1896. *Appareil pour photographier des scènes animées avec bandes pelliculaires dit Phototrope.*

Casler, Herman. US 549,309 of 21 November 1894. *Mutoscope.*
——FR 249,286 of 30 July 1895. *Mutoscopes, montrant les changements de position d'un ou plusieurs corps en mouvement.*
——GB 16,388 of 10 July 1897 (filed in US on 10 December 1896). *Improvements in Cinematographs and like Machines.*
——FR 267,037 of 18 May 1897. *Perfectionnements aux appareils à vues consécutives.*
——FR 269,294 of 3 August 1897. *Mécanisme d'amenée et de manipulation de tissus pour appareils à vues consécutives; machines à projections et autres appareils.*
Cauche, François. FR 10,025 of 8 November 1839. *Nouveau moyen de redresser les images photogéniques sans affaiblissement de lumière et par une combinaison de courbes achromatiques.*
Charles, Louis Henri. FR 255,702 of 20 April 1896. *Nouveau mode de commande de la pellicule dans la photographie animée.*
Chassereaux, Émile. FR 214,891 of 16 July 1891. *Nouvel appareil automatique d'annonces réclames dénommé Phare mécanique pour annonces.*
——FR 228,466 of 7 March 1893. *Système d'appareil de projection pour annonces-réclames dit Multiplicateur angulaire.*
——FR 255,887 of 27 April 1896. *Appareil dit Luminographe fonctionnant comme appareil chronophotographique et de projection.*
Chauvin, Robert Jean. FR 264,678 of 5 March 1897. *Cinématographe Chauvin.*
——FR 267,593 of 5 June 1897. *Cinématographe Chauvin second modèle.*
Cherrier, Jules. FR 158,389 of 6 November 1883. *Impression sur verre appliquée aux projections lumineuses en usage dans l'enseignement en général, sous la dénomination la Vitrographie.*
Chevalier, Louis-Arthur. FR 49,326 of 20 April 1861. *Perfectionnements au mégascope réfracteur achromatique de Charles Chevalier.*
Chevalier, Vincent. FR [number unknown] of 10 June 1823. *Chambre obscure à prisme dite Chambre obscure universelle.*
Chicago Recording Scale Company. FR 272,458 of 23 November 1897. *Appareil perfectionné pour prendre, agrandir et projeter des images successives d'objets animées.*
Ckiandi, Alexandre Henri. FR 150,708 of 19 August 1882. *Système d'inscription avec projection lumineuse.*
Claparède, Siméon, and Société Léon Gaumont. FR 276,554 of 31 March 1898. *Système de reproduction des scènes animées par vision directe ou par projection.*
Claudet, Antoine François Jean. GB 711 of 23 March 1853. *Improvements in stereoscopes.*
——FR 65,834 of 13 January 1865. *Procédé de photosculpture.*
Collings, John Hillery. GB 6,780 of 5 April 1894. *Improvements in optical advertising appliances.*
Compagnie Générale de Phonographes, Cinématographes et Appareils de Précision. FR 328,321 of 7 January 1903. *Production mécanique de sujets coloriés pour rubans ou films de cinématographes.*
——FR 380,889 of 22 October 1906. *Machine à colorier mécaniquement les films.*
——FR 381,485 of 9 November 1906. *Appareil de projections cinématographiques.*
Continsouza, Pierre Victor. FR 255,937 of 28 April 1896. *Appareil photographique à bande sensible continue pour la fixation et la reproduction des scènes animées.*
Copp, Charles Percy. GB 2,204 of 27 January 1897. *Apparatus for projecting living pictures.*
Corthesy, Jules Hippolythe. FR 273,806 of 5 January 1898. *Perfectionnements apportés aux moyens d'obtenir des effets d'optique tels que ceux appelés 'tableaux vivants' ou cinématographiques.*

Coudray, Marie Auguste. FR 256,159 of 11 May 1896. *Le Kinéstéréographe, ou appareil destiné à obtenir et à projeter sur un écran alternativement avec deux objectifs des vues de scènes animées.*

Coulon, Henri-François. FR 152,222 of 21 November 1882. *Appareil à projection ou lanterne magique dite la Petite Parisienne.*

Coulon, Henri, and Clément et Gilmer. FR 258,080 of 15 July 1896. *Perfectionnements aux appareils à projection.*

Coynart, Charles Marie. FR 255,608 of 16 April 1896. *Nouveau mode de projection pour vues animées.*

Dagron, Prudent René. FR 41,361 of 21 June 1859. *Microscope bijou à effets stéréoscopiques.*

Dalphin, E., and C. Sivan. CH 11,755 of 28 May 1896 (also FR 262,244 of 15 December 1896). *Appareil perfectionné pour l'exposition à la lumière de rubans pelliculaires sensibilisés et pour la projection de séries d'images photographiques tirées sur rubans pelliculaires.*

Damoizeau, Jules. FR 258,538 of 1 August 1896. *Appareil chronophotographique pour la photographie et la projection de scènes animées.*

Darling, Alfred, and Alfred Wrench. GB 17,248 of 21 July 1897. *Improvements in Cinematographic apparatus.*

——GB 23,591 of 9 November 1898. *An improved camera and apparatus for producing cinematograph and other pictures and for exhibiting cinematographic pictures.*

Darras, Alphonse. FR 257,131 of 10 June 1896. *Perfectionnements apportés à la cinématographie.*

D'Arthois, Étienne, Louis Passot, and Albert Renaut. FR 12,422 of 1 October 1851. *Application de l'électricité aux jeux d'optique.*

David, André. FR 100,076 of 22 August 1873. *Appareil binoculaire dit stéréoscope animé.*

De Bedts, George William. FR 253,103 of 10 January 1896. *Poinçonneuse destinée au perforage des films ou pellicules utilisées pour la photographie et la reproduction des images mouvementées.*

——FR 253,195 of 14 January 1896. *Système de mécanisme à mouvement intermittent applicable aux appareils chronophotographiques et aux appareils pour projections animées.*

——GB 6,503 of 24 March 1896. *Improvements in the mechanism of chrono-photographic, kinetoscopic, and lantern-projection apparatus.*

——FR 260,841 of 29 October 1896. *Système d'appareil chronophotographique et de projection pour vues animées.*

Delanglard, Charles François Paul. FR 1,779 of 25 March 1822. *Le Géorama.*

——FR 2,555 of 3 February 1825. *Machine dite Géorama, propre à l'étude de la géographie.*

Demenÿ, Georges. FR 219,830 of 3 March 1892. *Appareil dit Phonoscope reproduisant l'illusion des mouvements de la parole et de la physionomie par vision directe ou par projection au moyen d'une lumière.*

——FR 231,232 of 30 June 1893. *Disques à images positives pour phonoscopes et leur mode de préparation.*

——FR 233,337 of 10 October 1893. *Appareil destiné à prendre des séries d'images photographiques à des intervalles de temps égaux et très rapprochés sur une pellicule sensible.*

——FR 257,257 of 15 June 1896. *Appareil chronophotographique réversible à images continues.*

——FR 262,017 of 9 December 1896. *Appareil chronophotographique.*

——FR 278,285 of 25 May 1898. *Système d'appareil destiné à prendre des séries d'images photographiques et pouvant servir aussi à la vision ou à la projection de ces images.*

Desflaches, Jean Louis Antoine. FR 257,819 of 4 July 1896. *Appareil photographique à projections mouvementées dit le Différentiel.*

Desmarets, Albert, Henri Demeyer and Albert Auguin. FR 254,502 of 4 March 1896. *Appareil chronophotographique.*

——FR 254,869 of 18 March 1896. *Perfectionnements aux appareils chronophoto-graphiques.*

——FR 254,870 of 18 March 1896. *Perfectionnements apportés aux appareils chronophoto-graphiques.*

Desvignes, Peter Hubert. GB 537 of 27 February 1860. *Improvements in apparatuses for exhibiting photographic, stereoscopic, and other pictures, models, figures and designs.*

Deverdun, Paul Nicolas. FR 66,896 of 5 April 1865. *Système de tableaux dioramiques dit tableaux fondants, réunissant plusieurs tableaux et effets dans un seul.*

Dickson, William Kennedy Laurie. US 636,500 and 636,642 of 27 September 1897. *Consecutive view-apparatus.*

——US 695,916 of 22 October 1898. *Consecutive view-apparatus.*

Disclyn, Léon. FR 262,730 of 31 December 1896. *Appareil pour reconstituer l'action de sujets animés par un mouvement continu dit Chronoscope Parisien.*

Dolne, Lambert. FR 123,875 of 15 April 1878. *Lanterne magique microphotographique.*

Dom, Auguste Charles. FR 263,487 of 27 January 1897. *Appareil chronophotographique dit Cinéma Dom.*

Donisthorpe, Wordsworth. GB 4,344 of 9 November 1876. *Improvements in apparatus for taking a succession of photographic pictures and for exhibiting such pictures.*

Donisthorpe, Wordsworth, and William Carr Crofts. GB 12,921 of 15 August 1889. *Improvements in the production and representation of instantaneous photographic pictures.*

——FR 209,174 of 28 October 1890. *Perfectionnements dans la production et la représentation des images photographiques instantanées.*

Doyen, Eugène Louis. FR 296,635 of 29 January 1900. *Appareil pour la reproduction photographique et pour la projection lumineuse de scènes animées.*

Duboscq, Louis Jules. FR 13,069 of 16 February 1852. *Système d'instrument dit stéréoscope, faisant paraître en relief des images photographiques faites sur des surfaces planes, même sur des matières transparentes, du verre, etc., et pouvant projeter les images agrandies sur des écrans.*

Dubouloz, Joseph, and Demaria Frères. FR 279,149 of 29 June 1898. *Appareil perfectionné dit Zoographe pour la photographie, l'observation et la projection de scènes animées.*

Ducos du Hauron, Louis Arthur. FR 61,976 of 1 March 1864. *Appareil destiné à reproduire photographiquement une scène quelconque, avec toutes les transformations qu'elle a subies, pendant un temps déterminé.*

——FR 83,061 of 23 November 1868. *Les couleurs en photographie: solution du problème.*

——FR 250,862 of 17 September 1895. *Polyfolium dialytique, tirages photographiques en trois couleurs.*

——FR 259,399 of 29 August 1896. *Nouvelles combinaisons d'optique supprimant toute intermittance dans l'éclairement des tableaux photographiques dits mouvementés (chronophotographies) et permettant de réduire considérablement le nombre des épreuves positives.*

Du Mont, Henry-Désiré. FR 42,843 of 17 November 1859. *Appareils dits Omniscopes.*

——FR 49,520 of 2 May 1861. *Appareil photographique propre à reproduire les phases successives d'un mouvement.*

——GB 1,457 of 8 June 1861. *A photographic apparatus, having for object to reproduce the successive phases and shiftings of a motion.*

Duncan, William Henry. GB 934 of 7 January 1884. *Improvements in apparatus for changing dissolving views.*

Dupuis, Léon, and Ernest Forestier. FR 267,471 of 1 June 1897. *Kinetoscope-cinématographe dit le Dupfor's.*

Durand, Charles Amand, and John Clayton. FR 153,054 of 11 January 1883. *Genre de papiers transparents dits Papyrodiaphanie pour les projections scientifiques et récréatives.*

Dusaulchoix. FR 2,087 of 29 January 1816. *Galerie historique, pittoresque et amusante, ou cours d'histoire générale par tableaux.*

Eastman Photographic Materials Company Ltd. FR 202,496 of 10 December 1889. *Procédé et appareil pour la fabrication des pellicules photographiques ou autres.*

Edison, Thomas A. US 403,536 of 24 August 1891. *Apparatus for exhibiting photographs of moving objects.*

——US 589,168 of 24 August 1891. *Kinetographic Camera.*

Edwards, Benjamin Joseph. GB 10,226 of 16 July 1884. *Changing the slides or pictures in the magic lantern and for exhibiting dissolving views with a single lantern.*

Edwards, Ernest. GB 849 of 23 March 1867. *Improvements in photographic pictures, and in apparatus for producing them.*

Ehrlich, Richard. FR 256,402 of 16 May 1896. *Lanterne magique à boîte cylindrique pouvant être posée sur le corps d'une lampe quelconque.*

Electrical Wonder Company Ltd. FR 228,129 of 22 February 1893. *Perfectionnements dans les appareils ou moyens pour montrer les illusions d'optique.*

Elkan, Albert, and Jacques Sternberg. FR 270,883 of 10 September 1897. *Nouvel appareil photographique servant à la prise et à la projection d'épreuves chronophotographiques.*

Evans, Mortimer. GB 3,730 of 8 March 1890. *Improvements in or applicable to photographic cameras.*

Fabregue, Félix, and Jean Godefroy. FR 86,949 of 25 August 1869. *Système de publicité dite fantasmagorie, publicité par l'application de la photographie transparente sur verre avec ou sans coloris.*

Fahrni, Ernest. FR 266,991 of 17 May 1897. *Livret cinématographique.*

Farnum, William Carlton. FR 250,987 of 15 October 1895. *Perfectionnements aux kinetoscopes pour annonces et exhibitions.*

Fechter, Charles. FR 59,212 of 25 June 1863. *Perfectionnements dans les moyens de produire sur la scène des effets dits Illusions spectrales.*

Fenaut, Jacques Désiré. FR 120,935 of 30 October 1877. *Appareil solaire destiné spécialement à l'agrandissement et à la projection des objets opaques.*

Fescourt, Félix. FR 313,153 of 1 August 1901. *Cinématographe simplifié dit Zoescope.*

Fleury, Jules. FR 119,858 of 11 August 1877. *Dispositions apportées dans la construction des appareils à projections lumineuses.*

Foesterling, H.O. FR 282,666 of 3 November 1898. *Appareil à projection.*

Fontenoy, Eugène. FR 268,100 of 22 June 1897. *Appareil pour photographie et projections animées.*

Fouche, Edmond. FR 252,603 of 19 December 1895. *Perfectionnements dans l'application des miroirs tournants à la mise en évidence des images successives représentant un sujet animé.*

——FR 255,269 of 2 April 1896. *Cinématoscope applicable à la photographie, à la vision directe, à la projection, en vues simples ou stéréoscopiques.*

Fournet, Auguste, and Octave Nadaud. GB 3,116 of 27 November 1866. *A magic camera.*

Frey, Hugues Eugène. FR 315,957 of 15 November 1901. *Appareil à projections spécialement destiné aux grandes projections et à l'obtention de décors de théâtre par projections.*

——FR 316,157 of 22 November 1901. *Procédé de projections par l'emploi simultané et combiné d'un appareil à projections, projetant un paysage ou un décor en couleurs avec ou sans changement d'effets, et d'un cinématographe ou autre appareil similaire projetant des personnages animés dans ledit paysage ou décor.*

Friese-Greene, William. GB 22,954 of 29 November 1893. *Improvements in apparatus for exhibiting panoramic, dissolving, or changing views, and in the manufacturing of slides for use therewith.*

——GB 17,930 of 25 September 1895. *Improvements in photographic cameras and magic lanterns.*

——US 563,853 of 20 January 1896. *Photographic-printing apparatus.*

——GB 22,928 of 15 October 1896. *Improvements in apparatus for taking photographs, or for exhibiting photographic and other transparencies.*

——GB 21,649 of 14 October 1898. *Improvements in taking and in projecting photographic images, in means therefor, and in photographic negatives.*

——FR 304,308 of 5 October 1900. *Perfectionnements apportés aux appareils kinetoscopiques et cinématographiques.*

Friese-Greene, William, and Mortimer Evans. GB 10,131 of 21 June 1889. *Improved apparatus for taking photographs in rapid series.*

Friese-Greene, William, and John Alfred Prestwich. GB 17,224 of 4 August 1896. *Means for taking and reproducing kinetoscopic pictures.*

Fulton, Robert. FR 150 of 25 February 1799. *Panorama, ou tableau circulaire sans bornes, ou manière de dessiner, peindre et exhiber un tableau circulaire . . .*

Galy Cazalat, Antoine. FR 5,299 of 23 March 1833. *Microscope à gaz.*

Garchey, Louis Antoine, and Antoine Regny. FR 257,317 of 17 June 1896. *Figures animées pour la projection de l'ombre de certaines de leurs parties au moyen d'une lumière mobile sur l'écran.*

Garcin, Henri, and Alexandre Salle. FR 240,790 of 21 August 1894. *Nouveau système de panorama optique par projections mouvantes et animées.*

Gasc, Albert, and Alphonse Charconnet. FR 84,887 of 20 March 1869. *Perfectionnements apportés aux instruments d'optique.*

Gaudin, Pierre Ignace Alexis. FR 13,398 of 8 April 1852. *Système pour prendre des épreuves simultanées ou successives à l'usage du stéréoscope.*

Gaumont, Léon. FR 250,459 of 21 September 1895. *Perfectionnements dans la lanterne pour projection.*

——FR 293,329 of 13 October 1899. *Système mécanique de commande des cinématographes permettant de produire à volonté une marche continue ou intermittente.*

——FR 296,016 of 9 January 1900. *Système de production de bandes cinématographiques reproduisant des événements, actualités ou autres, par la représentation de déplacements simulés d'objets . . .*

——FR 298,764 of 30 March 1900. *Lanterne double à projections.*

——FR 312,613 of 11 July 1901. *Dispositif de commande électrique synchrone d'un phonographe et d'un cinématographe.*

——FR 328,145 of 18 November 1902. *Système de réglage de la concordance du synchronisme dans les appareils comportant la combinaison d'un phonographe et d'un cinématographe.*

Gauthier, Paul. FR 261,327 of 16 November 1896. *Mécanismes servant à prendre et à reproduire des photographies animées.*

——FR 255,773 of 22 April 1896. *Appareil d'enregistrement et de reproduction d'images animées par la photographie dit le Zographe.*

Gavioli, Claude. FR 92,201 of 11 July 1871. *Genre de jouet dit Troposcope.*

——FR 130,531 of 7 May 1879. *Chromatrope à musique.*

Gilles et Fils. FR 223,821 of 20 August 1892. *Appareil multiplicateur pour la production de photographies successives sur une même plaque.*

Giroux, Alphonse. FR [number unknown] of 29 May 1818. *Mécanisme ajouté à l'instrument d'optique nommé Transfigurateur ou Kaleïdoscope, pour lequel il sollicite un brevet de perfectionnement.*

——FR 5,361 of 29 May 1833. *Brevet d'importation pour un objet d'optique nommé Phenakisticope.*

Gomez Santa Maria, Augustin. FR 80,397 of 7 March 1868. *Application à la lanterne magique du phénisticope [sic], cette application produisant l'animation des images et constituant le Dinascope.*

Gonord, François. FR 1,379 of 10 July 1818. *Procédés à l'aide desquels il imprime, par aspiration, sur porcelaine et sur toute espèce de matières.*

Gossart, Fernand. FR 238,308 of 5 May 1894. *Système d'appareil chronophotographique pour obtenir une succession très rapide de clichés instantanés.*

Goudeau, Auguste-Jacques, and Jules Richard. FR 337,169 of 28 November 1903. *Système d'appareil cinématographique.*

Grenier-Villerd, Prosper, and Victor Bestion de Camboulas. FR 256,753 of 29 May 1896. *Perfectionnements aux appareils de projection des épreuves photographiques.*

Grimoin-Sanson, Raoul. FR 254,515 of 5 March 1896. *Appareil appelé le Phototachygraphe Sanson.*

——FR 261,244 of 13 November 1896. *Projecteur multiplex dit Projection Sanson.*

——FR 272,517 of 25 November 1897. *Nouvel appareil permettant de photographier et de projeter sur un écran circulaire des vues animées panoramiques en couleur par le Cinécosmorama Sanson.*

Grivolas fils, Claude. FR 263,574 of 2 February 1897. *Appareil pour projections chronophotographiques sans scintillements.*

——FR 266,131 of 20 April 1897. *Appareil pour obtenir et projeter des images chronophotographiques.*

Gué. FR 3,888 of 2 February 1829. *Un bateau qu'il appelle Hydrorama, ou spectacle géographique et historique.*

Guyot de Lisle, Auguste Charles, and Louis Jules Maréchal. FR 74,075 of 10 December 1866. *Système de réclames et d'annonces mobiles à l'aide d'appareils d'optique, de la lumière électrique, et d'images photographiques.*

Hallett, Henry Watson. GB 629 of 6 March 1867. *An improved mode of and means for producing optical illusions.*

Hangard, Georges Paul. FR 197,474 of 15 April 1889. *Procédé de production d'un nouveau genre d'images photographiques dit Portraits Vivants.*

Hartley, Frederick William. GB 46 of 7 January 1868. *Improvements in optical illusions used in conjunction with the magic lantern.*

Haton, Augustin. FR [number unknown] of 21 March 1823. *Nouveau système de tableaux mécaniques pour l'exécution de Cosmorama, Panorama et Diorama, qui donnera le moyen de déplacer à volonté les corps inanimés, de faire mouvoir ceux organisés, et de représenter les incendies, les volcans et les irruptions.*

Hazan, Nissim. FR 259,524 of 8 September 1896. *Système perfectionné d'appareil à produire la photographie des scènes animées et à en faire la projection.*

Henckel, Paul. FR 263,636 of 1 February 1897. *Projections de scènes animées par lanterne magique, lampascope ou autres appareils du même genre et dispositif réalisant les dites projections.*

Hepworth, Cecil Milton. GB 11,923 of 13 May 1897. *Improvements in or relating to apparatus for exhibiting photographic pictures.*

Holst, Johann Wilhelm. FR 261,859 of 3 December 1896. *Perfectionnements aux chambres cinématographiques.*

Hough, James Edward. GB 9,881 of 18 May 1895. *Improvements in means for viewing a series of pictures for the purpose of obtaining from same an appearance of movement.*

Hughes, William Charles. GB 13,371 of 9 October 1884. *An improved form of lantern front for magic lanterns.*

——GB 13,372 of 9 October 1884. *An improved frame for rapidly changing the pictures in a magic lantern.*

Hunebelle, Edouard. FR 260,513 of 17 October 1896. *Système d'appareil pour la photographie et la projection des vues animées.*

Jenkins, Charles Francis. US 536,569 of 24 November 1894. *Phantoscope.*

——US 560,800 of 12 December 1894. *Kinetographic camera.*

Jenkins, Charles Francis, and Thomas Armat. US 586,953 of 28 August 1895. *Phantoscope.*

Joly, Henri. FR 249,875 of 26 August 1895 (addition of 23 July 1896). *Nouvel appareil chronophotographique.*

——FR 251,549 of 8 November 1895. *Photozootrope à un ou plusiers oculaires.*

——FR 254,836 of 17 March 1896 (addition of 17 April 1896). *Appareil chronophotographique pouvant également servir à la projection des positifs.*

——FR 256,388 of 15 May 1896. *Dispositif permettant d'éviter le scintillement dans la projection des vues obtenues par la chronophotographie.*

——FR 256,389 of 15 May 1896. *Procédé de préparation des pellicules à projection reproduisant le mouvement en vue de donner du relief aux images projetées.*

——FR 296,067 of 11 January 1900. *Mouvement synchronique de rotation de deux mobiles, applicable aux appareils cinématographiques et phonographiques combinés.*

Jost, Jean Anatole. FR 255,176 of 31 March 1896. *Système d'appareil double à photographies multiples et à projections dit Photocinématographe.*

Joux, Lucien. FR 261,296 of 14 November 1896. *Nouvel instrument produisant l'illusion du mouvement au moyen de bandes chronophotographiques opaques.*

Jundzill, Adam Dunin. GB 1,245 of 24 May 1856. *An instrument for animating stereoscopic figures.*

Keevil, Henry. GB 2,241 of 8 June 1877. *Producing the optical effects known and called the dissolving scenes by means of a new optical adaptation for that purpose.*

Key, John Thomas. GB 6,431 of 13 May 1886. *Improvements in apparatus for holding and exhibiting views and the like in magic lanterns.*

Kirchner, Albert (a.k.a. Léar). FR 270,671 of 22 September 1897. *Biographe perfectionné dit Biographe français.*

——FR 274,531 of 31 January 1898. *Appareil chronophotographique dit Biographe français Léar.*

Kirchner, Albert (a.k.a. Léar), and Paul Antelme. FR 262,913 of 9 January 1897. *Appareil chronophotographique perfectionné.*

Klinsky, Alexandre, and Jean-Jacques Maingot. FR 66,641 of 18 March 1865. *Instrument microscopique à foyer immobile produisant 140 épreuves à la fois.*

Kohn, Adolphe. FR 257,092 of 9 June 1896. *Appareil pour la photographie et la projection des vues animées.*

Koopman, Elias B. FR 275,567 of 3 March 1898. *Perfectionnements dans les appareils permettant de voir des images successives, dits Mutoscopes.*

Kronke, Émile. FR 270,480 of 14 September 1897. *Chambre photographique portative pour la production rapide d'épreuves successives.*

Krüss, Société A. FR 78,989 of 28 December 1867. *Instrument d'optique appelé A. Krüss Wunder-Camera ou chambre noire.*

Labarthe, Veuve. FR 254,071 of 18 February 1896. *Appareil pour reproduire le mouvement de déplacement d'une bande pelliculaire sur laquelle ont été faites préalablement des photographies par la chronophotographie.*

——FR 254,298 of 26 February 1896. *Appareil donnant l'illusion du mouvement au moyen de photographies dit Cinémagraphe automatique.*

Lacomme, Jean Marie Auguste. GB 2,202 of 8 August 1870. *Improved means of exhibiting in the open air advertisements, photographic views, portraits, or pictures, and also for decorating the fronts of theatres and other buildings.*

Lacroix, Théophile Eugène. FR 298,328 of 17 March 1900. *Système d'appareil pour vues animées.*

——FR 301,765 of 30 June 1900. *Système d'appareil perfectionné pour vues animées.*

Lafon, Elie-Jules. FR 44,711 of 24 April 1860. *Procédé d'impression chromolithographique sur verre.*

Landais, Paul François. FR 311,843 of 17 June 1901. *Appareil à vues animées dit Vivoscope ou cinématographe à main.*

——FR 311,844 of 17 June 1901. *Appareil à vues animées dit Théascope.*

Lapierre, Auguste. FR 44,516 of 29 March 1860. *Application d'estampage des métaux.*

Lapierre, Édouard. FR 178,392 of 6 October 1886. *Nouveau système de lanterne magique dite Lampadophore à vues sur verres circulaires.*

Lapipe, Alban. FR 255,095 of 26 March 1896. *Machine à perforer les matières flexibles avec amenage automatique.*

——FR 259,549 of 8 September 1896. *Nouveau système d'appareil pour la prise et la projection de vues photographiques animées dit le Lapiposcope.*

Laporte, Pierre de. FR 273,605 of 27 December 1897. *Cinématographe des Salons.*

Larranaga y Loyola, Luis. FR 158,356 of 3 November 1883. *Publicité diurne et nocturne à projections lumineuses multiples.*

Lartigue, Laurent. FR 254,399 of 2 March 1896. *Appareil dénommé Photopolygraphe Lartigue.*

Latham, Woodville. GB 4,841 of 3 March 1896. *Improvements in means of apparatus for exhibiting pictures of moving objects by projecting them into a screen or other surface.*

——US 707,934 of 1 June 1896. *Projecting-kinetoscope.*

——US 600,113 of 26 December 1896. *Apparatus for photographing objects in motion and for projecting pictures.*

Laverne, Arthur Léon. FR 126,247 of 26 August 1878. *Perfectionnements apportés aux lampes universelles pour projections.*

Lebrun, Léon. FR 233,836 of 4 November 1893. *Appareil de photographie appelé le Photo-disque polygraphe.*

Lee, Frederick Marshall, and Edward Raymond Turner. GB 6,202 of 22 March 1899. *Means for taking and exhibiting cinematographic pictures.*

Lefebvre-Durufle, Léon. FR 80,372 of 7 April 1868. *Application de la lanterne magique à la publicité au moyen d'un foyer lumineux.*

Lefevre, Henri-Alexandre. FR 48,965 of 19 March 1861. *Instrument d'optique dit Lampadoscope.*

——FR 115,429 of 9 November 1876. *Lampadorama ou lampascope bilampadaire servant de chambre noire et de lanterne magique.*

Lefevre, Henri. FR 124,047 of 24 April 1878. *Mégascope Lefevre, pour projections scéniques d'objets opaques.*

Lefort, Pierre-Henri-Amand. FR 7,974 of 21 February 1849. *Perfectionnements apportés dans la construction des appareils d'optique dits Polyorama panoptique.*

——FR 14,365 of 25 August 1852. *Instrument d'optique dit Eidoscope.*

Lépine, Charles. FR 293,075 of 9 October 1899. *Appareil cinématographique de salon.*

Le Prince, Louis Augustin. US 376,247 of 10 January 1888. *Method of and apparatus for producing animated pictures of natural scenery and life.*

——GB 423 of 10 January 1888. *Improvements in the method of and apparatus for producing animated photographic pictures.*

——FR 188,089 of 11 January 1888. *Méthode et appareil pour la projection des tableaux animés.*

Leroy, Maurice. FR 257,965 of 10 July 1896. *Nouvel appareil chronophotographique.*

——FR 261,976 of 8 December 1896. *Nouvel appareil chronophotographique.*

Lesueur, Georges. FR 233,316 of 10 October 1893. *Appareil projecteur de précision à changement d'image instantané.*

Levy et ses Fils, Société. FR 260,870 of 30 October 1896. *Nouveau dispositif de mécanisme moteur de la pellicule pour appareils de photographie et de projection de scènes animées.*

Levy, Société. FR 271,768 of 29 October 1897. *Appareil genre kinétoscope destiné à des vues animées sur papier, dit Motoscope.*

Linnett, John Barnes. GB 925 of 18 March 1868. *Improvements in the means of producing optical illusions.*

Lumière, Auguste, and Louis Lumière. FR 243,543 of 14 December 1894. *Procédé de synthèse des couleurs par succession rapide d'images monochromes.*

——FR 245,032 of 13 February 1895 (additions of 30 March 1895, 6 May 1895, 28 March 1896, and 18 November 1896). *Appareil servant à l'obtention et à la vision des épreuves chronophotographiques.*

——FR 259,045 of 20 August 1896. *Reproduction simultanée des mouvements et des sons dans les projections de scènes animées.*

——FR 259,515 of 10 September 1896. *Appareil de vision directe des épreuves chronophoto-raphigues, dit Kinora.*

——FR 261,204 of 11 November 1896. *Appareil permettant la vision de photographies en couleurs.*

——FR 266,870 of 10 May 1897. *Perfectionnements aux appareils de projection pour cinématographes.*

——FR 269,741 of 21 August 1897. *Appareil dit le Biora destiné à la vision des images chronophotographiques.*

——FR 278,347 of 31 May 1898. *Perfectionnements à l'obtention et à la projection des images chronophotographiques.*

——FR 305,092 of 3 November 1900. *Appareil destiné à recevoir et à montrer les images stéréoscopiques d'objets en mouvements.*

——FR 306,772 of 29 December 1900. *Appareil photographique panoramique réversible.*

Lumière, Louis. FR 205,106 of 21 April 1890. *Système de chambre noire avec succession mécanique des glaces.*

——FR 208,980 of 17 October 1890. *Obturateur instantané pour appareils de photographie.*

Lund, Otto. FR 223,195 of 23 July 1892. *Obturateur photographique.*

Lutticke, George-Frederick. FR 222,697 of 29 June 1892. *Perfectionnements dans les coulisses des lanternes magiques.*

Maiche, Louis, and Charles Maiche. FR 256,600 of 22 May 1896. *Appareil permettant de voir des images en mouvement et en relief.*

Marcy, Lemuel James. GB 1,563 of 22 May 1872. *Improvements in magic lanterns.*

Marey, Étienne-Jules. FR 208,617 of 3 October 1890. *Appareil photochronographique.*

——FR 231,209 of 29 June 1893. *Appareil chronophotographique applicable à l'analyse de toutes sortes de mouvements.*

——FR 257,177 of 12 June 1896 (additions of 5 February 1897 and 11 June 1898). *Chronophotographe perfectionné réversible projecteur.*

——FR 289,167 of 24 May 1899. *Dispositif de réglage du mouvement de la pellicule positive dans le chronophotographe projecteur en marche.*

Maskelyne, John Neville. GB 11,639 of 28 May 1896. *An improved apparatus for securing, or exhibiting in series, records of successive phases of movement.*

Masson, Jules, and Ernest Marabelle. FR 254,072 of 18 February 1896. *Appareil servant à l'obtention et à la vision des épreuves chronophotographiques.*

Maurice, Joseph. GB 1,049 of 27 March 1868. *Improvements in the means or method of producing optical illusions.*

Mauvillin, Pierre. FR 76,590 of 25 May 1867. *Appareil d'optique produisant l'animation des figures en leur donnant différentes apparences.*

May, Charles W. FR 76,420 of 14 May 1867. *Instrument d'optique dit Zoetrope, propre à produire des illusions agréables et amusantes.*

Mazo, Élie Xavier, and Alexandre Salle. FR 255,383 of 7 April 1896. *Nouveau système d'appareil optique destiné au tirage photographique et à la projection des objets animés.*

Méliès, Georges, Lucien Korsten and Lucien Reulos. FR 259,444 of 4 September 1896. *Appareil destiné à prendre et à projeter les photographies animées.*

Ménage, Thomas Martin, and Lambert Cherpitel. FR 13,839 of 12 June 1852. *Genre de diorama à effets animés.*

Mendel, Georges. FR 261,771 of 1 December 1896. *Appareil pour la photographie et la projection des scènes animées dit le Cinématographe Parisien.*

Mersanne, Ernest de. FR 89,332 of 26 February 1870. *Application d'un effet dit effet de fantasmagorie à divers jouets tels que toupies, tourniquets, etc., et en général à un axe quelconque animé d'un mouvement rapide de rotation.*

Messager, Georges. FR 257,730 of 30 June 1896. *Appareil pour photographier et projeter des scènes animées, dénommé Pantomimographe.*

Moklin, Alexandre. FR 268,798 of 17 July 1897. *Bande pour cinématographes.*

Molteni, Jules, and Alfred Molteni. FR 98,169 of 17 February 1873. *Perfectionnements dans les appareils d'optique tels que fantasmagories, lanternes magiques, lampascopes, etc.*

Mortier, Paul. FR 254,090 of 17 February 1896. *Appareil dénommé Aléthoscope, destiné à enregistrer photographiquement les scènes animées et à les reproduire soit par projection, soit par vision directe avec ou sans illusion du relief.*

——FR 254,697 of 12 March 1896. *Appareil servant à photographier des scènes quelconques et à les reproduire par projection sur un écran.*

Mortier, Paul, Gaston Rousseau and Charles Rousseau. FR 268,145 of 25 June 1897. *Appareil pour la reproduction de scènes animées dit le Moto-Simplex.*

Motte, Henri. FR 205,310 of 26 April 1890 (addition of 26 July 1890). *Panorama-illusion à images distancées et mobiles.*

Moussaye, Marquise de la. FR 114,500 of 14 September 1876. *Aléthoscope.*

Müller, Paul. DE 92,247 of 25 August 1895. *Vorrichtung zur Aufnahme und Projektion von Reihenbildern.*

Murer, Théodore. FR 80,545 of 18 April 1868. *Application du thaumatrope aux bijoux et aux objets usuels.*

Muybridge, Eadweard. FR 121,743 of 21 December 1877. *Mécanisme et transmission servant à distribuer avec précision l'heure à plusieurs cadrans éloignés les uns des autres.*

——GB 2,746 of 9 July 1878. *Apparatus for taking instantaneous photographs of objects in motion.*

——US 212,864 of 11 July 1878. *Improvement in the method and apparatus for photographing objects in motion.*

——FR 125,692 of 17 July 1878. *Perfectionnements dans la prise des photographies instantanées d'objets en mouvement.*

Nepveu, Auguste Nicolas. FR 4,300 of 21 November 1829. *Panorama d'un genre nouveau qu'il nomme Panorama de salon.*

Oller, Joseph, and Amédée Pierre Varlet. FR 255,857 of 25 April 1896. *Système d'appareil pour projections animées.*

Optique, Société l'. FR 259,599 of 11 September 1896. *Appareil à mouvements alternatifs pour la photographie instantanée et la projection de ces photographies—système P. Gautier.*

Oulton, Joseph, William Shaw, and Reginald Adams. GB 7,817 of 14 April 1896. *Improvements in apparatus for taking and exhibiting series of photographs.*

Palias, Casimir. FR 282,804 of 8 November 1898. *Cinémascope.*

Parnaland, Ambroise-François. FR 254,249 of 25 February 1896. *Nouvel appareil photographique pouvant également être employé comme appareil cronophotographique [sic] dit Photothéagraphe.*

——FR 254,540 of 5 March 1896. *Appareil de reproduction de scènes animées d'après des vues enregistrées chronophotographiquement, dit le Kinébléposcope.*

——FR 256,140 of 6 May 1896. *Appareil pour la reproduction chronophotographique de la projection de scènes animées.*

——FR 257,089 of 9 June 1896 (additions of 6 August 1896, 7 November 1896, 6 March 1897 and 28 February 1899). *Appareil pour la reproduction chronophotographique et la projection de scènes animées.*

Pascual, Miguel. FR 257,926 of 11 July 1896. *Appareil photographique automatique.*

Pathé Frères. FR 257,067 of 9 June 1896. *Mécanisme à périodes de marche et d'arrêt applicable aux appareils photographiques, projecteurs et à tous autres appareils.*

Paul, Robert William. GB 4,686 of 2 March 1896. *Improvements in apparatus for projecting kinetoscope pictures on the screen.*

——DE 93,120 of 18 April 1896. *Serien-Apparat.*

Péan, Laurent René Marie. FR 102,339 of 26 February 1874. *Instrument d'optique dit l'Animateur.*

Pepper, John Henry. GB 498 of 29 February 1864. *Improvements in arranging apparatus for representing spectral and other images on a stage.*

Pepper, John Henry, and Henry Dircks. GB 326 of 5 February 1863. *Improvements in apparatus to be used in the exhibition of dramatic and other like performances.*

——FR 58,286 of 11 April 1863. *Perfectionnements dans les appareils employés pour les représentations dramatiques et autres.*

Pepper, John Henry, and Thomas William Tobin. GB 222 of 26 January 1865. *A new or improved apparatus for illusory exhibitions.*

——FR 67,596 of 30 May 1865. *Appareil produisant des apparitions illusoires.*

——GB 3,139 of 6 December 1865. *Improvements in apparatus for illusory exhibitions.*

——FR 79,230 of 18 January 1868. *Perfectionnements dans les appareils employés pour produire des illusions sur les théâtres.*

Perret et Lacroix, Société. FR 257,582 of 29 June 1896. *Appareil destiné aux photographies animées, dénommé l'Héliocinégraphe.*

——FR 262,946 of 9 January 1897. *Appareil pour la photographie et la projection de scènes animées.*

Person, Jean-Baptiste Vivant. FR 102,605 of 11 March 1874. *Appareil d'optique à deux fins dit Stéréo-Mégascope.*

Person, Jean-Baptiste Vivant, and Alphonse Dupré. FR 68,915 of 30 September 1865. *Stéréoscope polyorama.*

Petit, Ademor N. US 560,367 of 7 December 1895. *Apparatus for exhibiting successive photographs.*

Petrzywalski, Jean. FR 77,641 of 28 August 1867. *Photomégascope.*

Pettenkofer, Adolph. US 571,496 of 17 November 1896. *Kinetoscope.*

Philipstahl, Paul de. GB 2,575 of 26 January 1802. *Apparatus for reflecting objects.*

Phillips, Edwin Burbage, and Henry Courteen. GB 4,978 of 31 March 1890. *Improvements in toys, shades, and advertising devices, and in methods of actuating the same.*

Pipon, A., and J. Pipon. FR 254,394 of 2 March 1896. *Cinographoscope Pipon Frères.*

Planchon, Victor. FR 206,878 of 8 July 1890. *Perfectionnements dans les procédés photographiques dits pelliculaires.*

Ponti, Carlo, and Joseph Ponti. GB 1,988 of 10 July 1862. *An improved apparatus for viewing photographic pictures and the preparation of photographic pictures to be used in such apparatus.*

Poplawski, Victorin Jean. FR 266,472 of 29 April 1897. *Appareil pour la reproduction par vision directe des scènes animées dit Zooscope universel.*

Potter, Edward Tuckerman. GB 14,171 of 2 October 1888. *Improvements in magic lanterns.*

Poupinet, Jeanne. FR 257,938 of 9 July 1896. *Perfectionnement aux appareils pour la production de la chronophotographie.*

——FR 258,596 of 3 August 1896. *Nouvelle disposition d'un mécanisme appliqué à faire avancer une bande celluloïde automatiquement pour les épreuves chronophoto-graphiques . . .*

Prépognot, Albert. FR 272,140 of 12 November 1897. *Perfectionnements dans les appareils cinématographiques.*

——FR 272,141 of 12 November 1897. *Appareil permettant de prendre des vues animées et de les reproduire avec l'illusion du relief.*

Prestwich, John Alfred. FR 266,632 of 4 May 1897. *Perfectionnements dans les moyens pour prendre et reproduire des images kinetoscopiques.*

——GB 17,831 of 18 August 1898. *Improvements in apparatus for animated photography and optical projection.*

——FR 285,358 of 27 January 1899. *Nouveau mécanisme d'entraînement des pellicules ou films pour cinématographes.*

Prévost, Pierre. FR [number unknown] of 15 April 1816. *Pour l'art de peindre les panoramas.*

Raleigh, Charles. FR 289,996 of 16 June 1899. *Perfectionnements dans les appareils pour prendre des séries de vues photographiques se succédant rapidement, et les présenter de même.*

Régnier, Auguste Louis. FR 7,800 of 15 December 1848. *Diorama miniature.*

Rehaist, Louis Marie. FR 3,678 of 4 August 1828. *Lampe à niveau constant avec appareil qui donne l'heure la nuit.*

Reich, Theodore. GB 12,128 of 3 June 1896. *Improvements in apparatus for making or exhibiting zoëtropic and similar pictures.*

Reignier, Jean-Claude, and François Morand. FR 258,956 of 21 August 1896. *Mécanisme applicable à faire avancer automatiquement une bande photographique dans les appareils chronophotographiques.*

Reulos, Lucien. FR 282,546 of 29 October 1898. *Appareil cinématographique.*

Reynaud, Émile. FR 120,484 of 30 August 1877. *Appareil pour obtenir l'illusion du mouvement à l'aide de glaces mobiles.*

——GB 4,244 of 13 November 1877. *An improved apparatus for the production of optical illusions called the Praxinoscope.*

——FR 194,482 of 1 December 1888. *Appareil dit Théâtre Optique.*

——FR 322,825 of 9 July 1902. *Appareil stéréocinématographique.*

Ricardet-Seaver, Francis, and Léon Pernot. FR 258,934 of 17 August 1896. *Appareil photographique dénommé Chromo-Vivographe.*

Rigg, John Henry, and Ernest Othor Kumberg. FR 255,467 of 11 April 1896. *Perfectionnements apportés à la construction des kinématographes, kinétographes . . .*

Robertson, Étienne-Gaspard. FR 109 of 7 Pluviose Year VII [26 January 1799]. *Pour un appareil qu'il nomme fantascope et qu'il annonce être le perfectionnement de la Machine de Kircher.*

Robinot, Alexandre Camille. FR 37,985 of 6 September 1858. *Tableaux mouvants représentant des figures, objets et sujets de marine, genre mécanique produisant divers effets, pour jouets d'enfants et amusements.*

Rose, William W. GB 3,156 of 8 November 1867. *A revolving apparatus for exhibiting figures and other objects in apparent motion.*

Roslin d'Ivry, Jean Baptiste. FR 257,551 of 24 June 1896. *Système d'appareil perfectionné pour la projection des photographies animées dit le Badizographe.*

Ross, Thomas. GB 681 of 6 March 1869. *Improvements in slides for magic lanterns.*

——GB 2,685 of 10 October 1871. *Improvements in instruments or apparatus for producing pictures of bodies apparently in motion or of changing colours, which pictures may either be viewed by direct vision or be exhibited by the magic lantern.*

Rous, Joseph. FR 256,124 of 6 May 1896. *Le Motographe.*

Routledge, William, Augustus Rosemberg, and William MacDonald. GB 16,080 of 21 July 1896. *Improvements in or relating to apparatus for taking, viewing, or projecting photographic images in rapid succession.*

Sandow, Eugen. GB 17,565 of 27 July 1897. *Improvements in or relating to the production and exhibition of the pictures of moving objects.*

Sappey, Marcel. FR 257,268 of 16 June 1896. *Photoscope, nouvel appareil pour photographies successives.*

Sarrault, Jean-Joseph. FR 14,414 of 30 August 1852. *Substitution d'épreuves photographiques positives sur verre aux gravures décalquées employées jusqu'à ce jour dans la peinture sur verre.*

Sauvage, Frédéric. FR 5,870 of 2 June 1834. *Instrument qu'il nomme Physionotype, propre à prendre l'empreinte des figures humaines.*

Schelheimer, Michel. FR 1,895 of 11 July 1922. *Procédé pour les peintures sur glace, optique, miroir multipliant et verre.*

Schmidt, C.W., and André Christophe. FR 257,231 of 13 June 1896. *Appareil enregistreur photographique du mouvement.*

——FR 258,662 of 4 August 1896. *Procédé d'appareil photographique enregistreur du mouvement.*

Schoeller, Alfred. FR 289,701 of 8 June 1899. *Perfectionnements aux mutoscopes.*

Schonner, Jean. FR 196,168 of 19 February 1889. *Perfectionnements apportés aux images pour les lanternes magiques.*

Séguin, Pierre. FR 14,150 of 16 September 1852. *Appareil d'optique dit Polyoscope.*

——FR 14,977 of 20 November 1852 (additions of 21 June 1854, 14 April 1855, and 26 April 1860). *Polyorama animé.*

Shaw, William Thomas. GB 1,260 of 22 May 1860. *Improvements in thaumatropes or phenakistiscopes.*

Short, Henry William. FR 255,292 of 3 April 1896. *Nouveau genre de Kinétoscope.*

——FR 268,047 of 21 June 1897. *Nouvel appareil kinétoscopique sans mécanisme dit Filoscope.*

Simpson, Henry. GB 8,185 of 30 April 1892. *Improvements in and relating to magic lanterns and to the manipulation of the same.*

Skladanowsky, Max. DE 88,599 of 1 November 1895. *Vorrichtung zum intermittirenden Vorwärtsbewegen des Bildbandes für Photographische Serien-Apparate und Bioskope.*

Smith, George. FR 134,056 of 21 November 1879. *Perfectionnnements dans la construction des lampes destinées aux lanternes magiques et d'autres usages.*

Smith, George Albert. GB 26,671 of 24 November 1906. *Improvements in and relating to kinematograph apparatus for the production of coloured pictures.*

Soleil, Jean-Baptiste. FR 769 of 29 September 1812. *Nouvelle chambre obscure perfectionnée dite Pronopiographe.*

Solomons, Samuel. FR 70,338 of 8 February 1866. *Perfectionnements apportés aux transparents pour lanternes magiques.*

Stampfer, Simon, and Mathias Trentsensky. AT [number unknown] of 7 May 1833. *Auf die Erfindung der Stroboskopischen Scheiben.*

Storer, William. GB 1,183 of 29 June 1778. *An optical instrument called an Accurate Delineator . . .*

Symons, Walter. GB 5,759 of 14 March 1896. *Improved movable devices for producing optical illusion changes.*

Talbot, William Henry Fox. GB 13,664 of 12 June 1851. *Improvements in photography.*

Tavan, Gustave. FR 257,117 of 13 June 1896. *Appareil de chronophotographie appelé le Pantobiographe.*

Taylor, John Edward. FR 196,521 of 6 March 1889. *Nouvelle méthode pour disposer des glaces dans une construction quelconque de manière à obtenir une illusion d'optique.*

Terme, Joseph Marie. FR 258,071 of 15 July 1896. *Nouveau système d'appareil pour la photographie animée dit le Cinématoterme.*

Terme, Jules, and Arsène Maroussem. FR 254,625 of 9 March 1896. *Mécanisme permettant d'obtenir sur pellicules photographiques des séries d'images pouvant être vues directement ou projetées.*

Tournachon, Paul Armand (a.k.a. Nadar), and Eugène Defez. FR 257,550 of 24 June 1896. *Appareil pour photographier et projeter des images animées.*

Trevor, David. GB 2,193 of 20 July 1869. *New or improved apparatus for facilitating the production of photographic pictures . . .*

Urban, Charles. FR 450,413 of 11 November 1912. *Perfectionnements aux appareils photographiques employés dans la cinématographie en couleurs.*

Van Tenac, Charles Louis. FR 97,177 of 14 November 1872. *Instrument d'optique destiné à la projection agrandie des objets plans, dit lanterne populaire de projections instructives.*

Varley, Frederick Henry. GB 4,704 of 26 March 1890. *Improvements in cameras for photographing objects in motion.*

Vidocq, Eugène François. FR 5,654 of 26 March 1834. *Perfectionnements apportés à la fabrication d'un papier dit sensitif.*

Viney, Hippolyte. FR 275,160 of 19 February 1898. *Bioscope, appareil destiné à obtenir par la photographie la projection du mouvement sans scintillement.*

Viton de Saint-Allais, Comte. FR 53,239 of 24 February 1862. *Lanterne dite dioramique stéréoscopique.*

Walbourg de Bray. FR 100,154 of 26 August 1873. *Réclames, adresses de nuit projetées sur la voie publique ou contre les murs et écrans, par la lanterne à projection.*

Wallet, Jean Baptiste, and Charles Alexandre Morgand. FR 11,972 of 23 October 1840. *Nouvelle optique avec modification de lumière appelée par les inventeurs Diorama portatif des salons.*

Watilliaux, Charles Auguste, and Siméon Claparede. FR 256,039 of 1 May 1896. *Appareil donnant l'illusion du mouvement par la succession rapide de photographies ou dessins.*

Wegener, Arnold. FR 256,363 of 13 May 1896. *Appareil produisant le mouvement pour la photographie.*

Werner, Eugène. FR 248,254 of 18 June 1895. *Appareil permettant de voir les photographies animées.*

Werner, Eugène, and Michel Werner. FR 253,708 of 4 February 1896. *Appareil chronophotographique pouvant également être employé comme appareil de projection.*

——FR 260,768 of 27 October 1896. *Appareil chronophotographique pour prendre et projeter les photographies animées.*

Werner, Eugène, Michel Werner, and Georges Monier. FR 254,908 of 19 March 1896. *Appareil chronophotographique pouvant également être employé comme appareil de projection.*

Wier, Marshall Arthur. FR 207,505 of 8 August 1890. *Moyens nouveaux pour exposer une succession de pellicules photographiques.*

Winsor. FR 604 of 27 April 1818. *Instrument d'optique qu'il nomme Kaléidoscope.*

Witklin, Ilia. FR 254,862 of 18 March 1896. *Appareil dénommé le Kinétographe Witlin.*

Wolff, Philipp. FR 274,692 of 4 February 1898. *Kinétoscope.*

Wollaston, William Hyde. GB 2,993 of 3 January 1806. *An instrument whereby any person may draw in perspective, or may copy or reduce any print or drawing.*

Wray, Cecil. GB 182 of 3 January 1895. *Improvements in or relating to the kinetoscope.*

——GB 19,181 of 31 August 1896. *Improvements in apparatus for exhibiting kinetoscopic or zoetropic pictures.*

——FR 260,923 of 2 November 1896. *Appareil facilitant la projection d'images chronophotographiques ou kinetoscopiques au moyen d'une lanterne de projection.*

——FR 270,003 of 28 August 1897. *Perfectionnements aux appareils chronophotographiques.*

Wrench, Alfred. GB 13,674 of 20 June 1896. *Improvements in or connected with cameras and optical lanterns.*

——GB 17,881 of 12 August 1896. *Improvements in cinematographs.*

——FR 263,996 of 12 February 1897. *Perfectionnements aux cinématographes et aux chambres noires pour prendre des vues cinématographiques.*

Zion, Joseph. FR 256,036 of 1 May 1896. *Appareil photographique dit Mouvementoscope.*

Zion, Joseph, and Eugène Gautier. FR 258,523 of 31 July 1896. *Appareil pour tirer et projeter des photographies de scènes animées.*

Index of Names